LEARNING AND EDUCATION: PSYCHOANALYTIC PERSPECTIVES

EMOTIONS AND BEHAVIOR MONOGRAPHS
MONOGRAPHS
Monograph No. 6

edited by
George H. Pollock, M.D., Ph.D.

LEARNING AND EDUCATION: PSYCHOANALYTIC PERSPECTIVES

edited by

KAY FIELD, M.A.
BERTRAM J. COHLER, Ph.D., AND
GLORYE WOOL, M.D.

INTERNATIONAL UNIVERSITIES PRESS, INC.

Madison   Connecticut

Copyright © 1989, George H. Pollock

All rights reserved. No part of this book may be reproduced by any means, nor translated into a machine language, without the written permission of the publisher.

Library of Congress Cataloging-in-Publication Data

Learning and education : psychoanalytic perspectives / edited by Kay
  Field, Bertram J. Cohler, and Glorye Wool.
    p. cm.—(Emotions and behavior monographs; monograph no.
6)
  Bibliography: p.
  Includes index.
  ISBN 0-8236-2954-6
  1. Learning, Psychology of. 2. Psychoanalysis. 3. Educational
psychology. I. Field, Kay. II. Cohler, Bertram J. III. Wool,
Glorye. IV. Series: Emotions and behavior monographs; no. 6.
LB1060.L414 1989
370.15'23—dc20
                                                         89-35513
                                                            CIP

Manufactured in the United States of America

This volume is dedicated, with gratitude, to our predecessors in the field of psychoanalysis and education:

Miss Anna Freud
Miss Helen Ross
Mrs. Sadie Nesbitt
Dr. Joan Fleming

Contents

Contributors

E. JAMES ANTHONY, M.D.   Professor, Department of Psychiatry, Washington University, St. Louis, Missouri

MICHAEL FRANZ BASCH, M.D.   Faculty, Institute for Psychoanalysis, Chicago

H. E. BERNSTEIN, M.D.   Faculty, Institute for Psychoanalysis, Chicago

GASTON E. BLOM, M.D.   Professor of Psychiatry, Department of Child Psychiatry and Child Development, Boston University School of Medicine

BERTRAM J. COHLER, Ph.D.—William Rainey Harper Professor of Social Sciences, The College; Professor in the Departments of Behavioral Sciences, Education, and Psychiatry, University of Chicago

LINDA A. COZZARELLI, M.A.   Ann Martin Children's Center, Piedmont, California

KERSTIN Ek, Ph.D.   Physical Therapist, Solna, Sweden

RUDOLPH EKSTEIN, Ph.D.   Clincial Professor, University of California, Los Angeles; Faculty, Los Angeles and Southern California Psychoanalytic Institutes

MIRIAM ELSON, M.A.   Lecturer, School of Social Service Administration, University of Chicago

KAY FIELD, M.A.   Director, Teacher Education Program, Institute for Psychoanalysis, Chicago

BENJAMIN GARBER, M.D.   Training and Supervising Analyst, Institute for Psychoanalysis, Chicago; Attending Psychiatrist, Michael Reese Hospital; Clinical Assistant Professor, University of Chicago

STANLEY I. GREENSPAN, M.D.   Chief, Infant and Child Development Services Program, Division of Maternal and Child Health, HRSA, DHHS; Clinical Pro-

fessor of Psychiatry and Behavioral Science and
Child Health and Development, George Washington
University Medical School

ANN FLECK HENDERSON, M.S.W.   Clinical Developmental Institute, Simmons College School of Social
Work

RICHARD KAUFMAN, M.D.   Professorial Lecturer, University of Chicago Department of Psychiatry, Division
of Child Psychiatry; Faculty, Institute for Psychoanalysis, Chicago

ROBERT KEGAN, Ph.D.   Clinical Developmental Institute, Harvard School of Education

MADHAV KULKARNI, Ph.D.   Rehabilitation Specialist,
Division of Rehabilitation Medicine, College of Os-
teopathic Medicine, Michigan State University

BONNIE E. LITOWITZ, Ph.D.   Associate Professor, Department of Linguistics, Northwestern University, Ev-
anston, Illinois

NER LITTNER, M.D.   Faculty, Institute for Psychoanalysis, Chicago

HYMAN L. MUSLIN, M.D.   Professor of Psychiatry, University of Illinois Medical School; Faculty, Continuing Education Division, Institute for Psychoanalysis,
Chicago

GIL G. NOAM, Ed.D., Dipl. Psych.   Director, Evaluative
Services, Hall-Mercer Children's Center, McLean
Hospital, Belmont, Massachusetts

GERHART PIERS, M.D.   Former Director, Institute for
Psychoanalysis, Chicago

MARIA W. PIERS, Ph.D.   Founding Dean, Erikson Institute, Chicago

SALLY PROVENCE, M.D.   Senior Research Scientist, Yale
University Child Study Center; Professor Emeritus,
Child Development and Pediatrics, Yale University
Child Study Center

BARBARA ROCAH, M.D.   Faculty, Institute for Psychoanalysis, Chicago

DONALD D. SCHWARTZ, M.D.   Faculty, Institute for Psychoanalysis, Chicago

MARILYN SILIN, M.A.   Faculty, Teacher Education Program, Institute for Psychoanalysis, Chicago

MARTIN A. SILVERMAN, M.D.   Clinical Professor of Psychiatry, Training and Supervising Analyst, and Chairman of the Child Analysis Training Program of the Psychoanalytic Institute, New York University Medical Center

IRENE P. STIVER, Ph.D.   Director, Psychology Department, McLean Hospital, Harvard Medical School, Belmont, Massachusetts

FRANCES M. STOTT, Ph.D.   Professor, Erikson Institute, Chicago

RITA SUSSMAN, Ph.D.   Scientific Staff, Michael Reese Hospital, Chicago

RALPH W. TYLER, Ph.D.   Director Emeritus, Center for Advanced Study in Behavioral Sciences

EDUARDO VAL, M.D.   Professor of Clinical Psychiatry, University of Illinois; Faculty, Institute for Psychoanalysis, Chicago

ERNEST S. WOLF, M.D.   Faculty, Institute for Psychoanalysis, Chicago

GLORYE WOOL, M.D.   Faculty, Teacher Education Program, Institute for Psychoanalysis, Chicago

Acknowledgments

A volume such as this owes its existence to our experiences with our own parents, children, teachers, students, psychotherapists, and colleagues, all of whom taught us what it means to learn how to learn, and whose imprint on our own learning provided the anlage for our compelling interest in exploring the linkages between learning and becoming in these different life contexts. The diverse meanings and vicissitudes of learning across the life course—in the family, the classroom, and the treatment situation—is demonstrated as we consider the wealth of new knowledge from developmental studies, clinical material, and research findings, all of which create a new vision and a challenge to us to begin the difficult process of collating all of this to bring us closer to seeing the whole person. Therefore, to all of our teachers from all the contexts of our lives we express our gratitude.

The present volume was first inspired by a conference, The World of Learning: From Motive to Meaning, held in April 1982, sponsored by the Teacher Education Program of the Institute for Psychoanalysis in Chicago, as part of its fiftieth anniversary celebration. The success of this effort led us to plan this volume. Dr. George H. Pollock, former President of the Institute for Psychoanalysis, who first encouraged us to undertake this volume, and who generously supported its preparation and gave of his counsel and guidance in our work, was both our "teacher" and our friend. We are particularly thankful to Ernest Wolf, M.D., who collaborated with us in a variety of ways, in the choice of contributors and in his incisive editorial comments and suggestions. Additionally, we very much appreciate the invaluable editorial assistance contributed by Marilyn W. Silin (co-author of chapter 28) and Miriam Elson (author of chapter 27). We also want to thank the many other people, too numerous to mention here by name, who helped make the conference successful and thereby motivated our current volume. Special thanks are also due to the faculty and students of the Teacher Education Program, and to the late Dr. Joan Fleming, who helped us see, conceptualize, and explore the interface of education and psychoanalysis. These colleagues, Richard Herbig, Ner Littner, Harold Balikov, and Nancy Marks, deserve great credit for the many ways their ideas and insights have contributed to our thinking. Christine Susman's exceptional patience, dedication, and tact helped us every step of the way in bringing this volume into being. Her high skill and commitment to the administrative and clerical tasks involved, together with her editorial comments on the content, were much appreciated.

Finally, we want to thank the people in our personal lives, who, through their patience, support, devotion, and deep understanding of the demanding nature of this undertaking, made it possible for us to complete our work. We are deeply grateful to Anne Cohler and Edmund Field for all the ways they gave of themselves.

KAY FIELD, BERTRAM COHLER, GLORYE WOOL

Foreword

GEORGE H. POLLOCK, M.D., Ph.D.

"To enter the world of learning a child must be motivated. To embrace the world of learning, to make it his own, a child must make it one of personal meaning. How we make sense of our encounters with the people and things in our environment—what impels or impedes our lifelong urge to learn and transform ourselves—are central questions occupying professionals in all the human sciences and mental health professions." With these words, the Teacher Education Program of the Institute for Psychoanalysis introduced the theme of a conference on "The World of Learning: From Motive to Meaning," held in 1982 as part of a year-long celebration of fifty years of psychoanalysis in Chicago. The interest stimulated by this conference encouraged the editors to undertake this work. While the major papers presented appear here, albeit in expanded and updated versions, the editors sought to broaden the scope of professional inquiry initiated in this conference by inviting scholars and practitioners representing an even wider range of disciplines and theoretical points of view, to examine the diverse meanings and vicissitudes of learning across the life course—in the family, the classroom, and the treatment situation. The aim of this volume, like that of the conference that inspired it, is to examine the processes of learning and the different developmental pathways leading from motive to meaning. The focus and unifying theme of this excellent book is centered on how, when, and why some chil-

dren and adults become passionate about learning while
others avoid and resist it.

Despite the burgeoning interest in learning among
scholars and practitioners in the fields of education, psychoanalysis, mental health, linguistics, sociology, and
developmental psychology, our knowledge and understanding of the vicissitudes of the learning process remains fragmented, conflicting, and confusing. There is
no unified theory about the etiology of learning disorders,
let alone agreement on issues of diagnosis and treatment.
Psychoanalysts point to the powerful influence of developmental factors; neurologists emphasize organicity; so-
ciologists focus on environmental variables; and educators
and learning specialists in the schools emphasize techniques and methodology. Clearly, progress toward an integrated, holistic understanding of the learning process
hinges upon the recognition of the enormous complexity
and pressing need for interdisciplinary discourse and collaboration.

It is in this spirit, and in the hope of promoting the
cross fertilization of ideas that such interdisciplinary inquiry engenders, that the editors, in cooperation with the
Institute for Psychoanalysis, present this work. While
psychoanalytic theories comprise the dominant frame of
reference in this collection, other perspectives are represented as well. Instead of being antagonistic to other
theoretical and clinical orientations to learning, psychoanalysis illuminates areas of complementarity between
them. A psychodynamic developmental exploration of the
learning process across the life course opens an expanded
vista on the complex and interrelated mental processes
that form the very wellsprings of our humanness. The
focus on motive and meaning in learning provided the
unifying theme and the means for encompassing the myriad contextual and situational variables that influence
the learning process.

We are honored to have this opportunity to present

in this volume original contributions by eminent authorities.

Learning and Education: Psychoanalytic Perspectives will be an invaluable resource and reference work that should be of interest to sophisticated, psychoanalytically oriented readers and to professionals in many other schools of thought and practice. Several chapters in this volume (Field, Cohler, Littner, Stott, Elson, Cozzarelli and Silin, Basch) open a window on the vicissitudes of the learning process in the context and conditions of school and classroom. Over two decades of experience in the Institute's pioneering Teacher Education Program, and, more recently, the Clinical School Services Program (an outgrowth of TEP) have served as a laboratory in vivo for the data and conceptualizations presented in those chapters. The Institute for Psychoanalysis in presenting this volume wishes to honor Kay Field, through whose efforts, along with those of her dedicated colleagues, conceived and developed the TEP in such fashion that it is, and has become, a model for other such programs elsewhere.

We hope that the reader will share our enthusiasm for this extraordinarily rich and wide-ranging collection of articles on the learning process. It is our hope that its emphasis on the seamlessness of human learning will encourage further interdisciplinary collaboration.

Part I

Psychoanalysis and Education:
Theoretical and Historical

Introduction: Part I

Study of the place of psychoanalysis in education, understood as formal instruction, parallels that of psychoanalysis itself. Discussing the relevance of psychoanalysis in the study of education, Freud (1925) observed that:

> None of the applications of psychoanalysis has excited so much interest and aroused so many hopes, and none, consequently, has attracted so many capable workers as its use in the theory and practice of education. It is easy to understand why, for children have become the main subject of psychoanalytic research, and have replaced in importance the neurotics on whom its studies began. Analysis has shown how the child lives on, almost unchanged, in the sick man as well as in the dreamer and the artist; it has thrown light upon the motive forces and impulses which set its characteristic stamp upon the childish nature; and it has traced the stages through which a child grows to maturity. It is not surprising, therefore, that an expectation should have arisen that psychoanalytic work with children would benefit the work of education, whose aim it is to guide and assist children upon their forward path and to shield them from going astray [p. 273].

3

Indeed, from the outset, both the nursery and the classroom have served as an arena for testing psychoanalytic
concepts regarding learning and development. The series
on the Psychoanalytic Study of the Child began in Europe
as one devoted to the study of education and development
(Kris, 1948). Anna Freud and D. Burlingham's Montes-
sori school in Vienna provided some of the first detailed
observations regarding emotional factors interfering in
development (A. Freud, 1979).

Just as the classroom has been a significant source of
observational data relevant to understanding developmental processes, applications of psychoanalysis to the
study of educational and developmental processes has
closely paralleled advances within psychoanalysis itself.
Freud's (1900, 1911, 1915) initial topographic, economic,
and dynamic approaches to the study of learning and
development has long provided the basis for study both
of learning and emotional factors said to interfere in prof-
iting from instruction. Particularly as derived from
Freud's discussion of primary and secondary process, or
the means by which ideas become thoughts, much early
discussion focused on motives and thoughts, and the extent to which learning was bound in conflict as yet another compromise formation (Cohler, 1972a, b). From this
perspective, learning was viewed as problematic (Bernfeld, 1925; Ekstein, 1966): effort expended in fostering
the child's development of reality testing was likely to
insure more effective learning in the classroom. This perspective has been cogently reviewed in chapter 8 by Gerhart Piers and Maria Piers.

With Hartmann's (1939) formulation of the adaptational point of view, and White's (1959, 1963) extension
of this perspective in discussion of the development of
competence, the relative autonomy of learning was recognized. It became possible to consider learning as a process enjoyable for its own sake, beyond its role as a
disguised means for the satisfaction of wishes based on

the nuclear neurosis. At the same time, much of the application of psychoanalytic approaches to the study of motivation continued to emphasize problems in learning, rather than intrinsic satisfaction derived from increased mastery (Murphy, 1962; Murphy and Moriarty, 1976). The contributions of this approach are summarized by Anthony in chapter 5, which also emphasizes the important contributions of Piaget's work to psychoanalytic understanding of learning and development, a perspective also elaborated by Greenspan in chapter 9. These two chapters show the importance of this emphasis upon mastery as essential in appreciating the psychoanalytic perspective to the study of education.

Earlier applications of psychoanalysis to education are reviewed in the now classic volume, edited by Ekstein and Motto, *From Learning to Love to Love of Learning* (New York: Brunner/Mazel, 1969). Perhaps the most synthetic review to that date, papers in that volume show both the significance of early childhood experience in the later capacity to learn, and also the role of conflict as a major problem interfering in learning. In the brief reprinted chapter from that volume, as well as in the chapter prepared especially for the present volume, Ekstein reviews the major conclusions from this earlier volume.

Implicit in many of these papers is the assumption that the classroom is a major resource for insuring mental hygiene during the years of childhood and adolescence, and the need for teachers to be mental health professionals as well as classroom instructors. Indeed, since Freud's discussions of psychoanalysis and education, it had been believed to be desirable for all classroom teachers to be conversant with psychoanalysis and to have undergone personal analysis (Fenichel, 1945; Peller, 1946). Indeed, as the quote from Freud (1925) suggests, study of the classroom was relevant not only as a laboratory for the study of developmental processes, but also as an opportunity for intervention in order to foster mental health.

However, unmet expectations regarding the classroom as an intervention setting, and the teacher as a psychotherapist, may have compromised the larger contribution of psychoanalysis as a means for understanding and enhancing learning in school.

Over the course of the past two decades, there have been dramatic advances in our earlier views regarding both the relevance of psychoanalysis for classroom mental health and the very nature of learning and development. Studies of the school as a small-scale society have pointed to the need for understanding the classroom from both an organizational and developmental perspective. In particular, the variety of constraints imposed upon public school teachers may interfere in realization of curricular goals. Further, changes within psychoanalysis have affected the manner in which learning is viewed. Most important in this regard has been increased attention to issues of the self of the student and to the complex interaction between learning and self esteem.

Psychoanalytic theorists of development from perspectives as diverse as those of G. Klein (1976) and Stechler and Kaplan (1980), to that of Kohut and his colleagues (Goldberg, 1982; Basch, 1983) have stressed the significance of self regard and tension regulation for the ability to succeed in the classroom. Perhaps the most explicit effort to relate self regulation to learning has been expressed by H. E. Bernstein in chapter 6. Writing from a point of view more explicitly influenced by the writings of Heinz Kohut, Muslin and Val's paper in this section focuses on factors fostering the student's capacity to use the help and information provided by the instructor. While their chapter focuses on issues in supervision of psychiatric residents, their discussion points the way to a self psychology perspective on factors likely to foster learning in the classroom.

In part, this increased concern with the place of self

regulation for the capacity to profit from instruction re-flects the larger concern within psychoanalysis with the study of personality development and developmental psychopathology during the earliest years of life, prior to resolution of the nuclear neurosis, as an influence upon later adjustment. In part, this increased concern with issues of self reflects an increased personological focus (Murray and associates, 1937) within psychoanalysis. As a result both of Bernfeld's earlier (1944, 1951) review of Freud's pre-psychoanalytic histologic research and Sulloway's (1979) encyclopedic review of the impact of this formative study upon Freud's goals in psychoanalytic study, together with critiques by Gill (1976) and G. Klein (1976) regarding the role of metapsychology as a statement of Freud's world view not directly relevant for emergence of clinical psychoanalytic theory, and G. Klein (1976) and Schafer's (1976, 1983) clarification of the contributions of the clinical theory as the basis of psychoanalytic inquiry, increased attention has been paid to the emergence of this clinical theory.

Central to the concept of clinical theory is focus upon the experienced or subjective world, rather than the time/space world. Just as there has been a shift from metapsychology to psychology in the renewed appreciation of the clinical theory, there has been a shift in emphasis from motive, understood as an abstract force represented by the metapsychological points of view of psychoanalysis, to an emphasis upon meaning, or the student's subjective experience of what takes place in school. Implications of what takes place in the classroom for the student's own emerging sense of talents and skills, including self as learner, is of critical importance for understanding subsequent response to curriculum and teachers. For example, instructors frequently encounter students whose academic records reflect distinction in studies, and yet who are unable to attain any pleasure from success. This response suggests the significance of

understanding the manner in which students experience
the process of learning and in being able to help students
whose problems in regulating ambitions lead them to
sacrifice achievement for maintenance of sense of personal integration.

To date, although Jones's (1968) concept of the "subjective curriculum" is implicitly relevant, there has been
little explicit effort to apply the clinical theory in an effort
to reformulate the relevance of psychoanalysis for study
of education; Tyler's chapter in this section, reviewing
the place of schooling in contemporary society, is consistent with much of Jones's earlier formulation. Cohler's
chapter in the present section represents one such effort.
Other papers in this section reflect the traditional view
of the implication of psychoanalysis for the study of education. This chapter attempts to bridge more traditional
and contemporary psychoanalytic developmental perspectives in reviewing the contributions of the clinical
theory in psychoanalysis to enhancing instruction in
school.

REFERENCES

Basch, M. (1983), The concept of "self": An operational definition. In:
     Developmental Approaches to the Self, ed. B. Lee & G. Noam.
     New York: Plenum Press, pp. 7–58.
Bernfeld, S. (1925), Sisyphus, or the Limits of Education, trans. F.
     Lilge. Berkeley: University of California Press, 1973.
———— (1941), Freud's earliest theories on the school of Helmholtz.
     Psychoanal. Quart., 13:341–362.
———— (1944), Freud's scientific beginnings. Imago, 6:163–196.
———— (1951), Sigmund Freud, M.D., 1882–1885. Internat. J. Psycho-
     Anal., 32:204–217.
Bettelheim, B. (1969), Psychoanalysis and education. The School Re-
   · view, 77:73–86.
Cohler, B. (1972a), Psychoanalysis, adaptation, and education: I. Real-
     ity and its appraisal. Psychol. Rep., 30:695–718.
———— (1972b), Psychoanalysis, adaptation, and education: II. Devel-
     opment of thinking. Psychol. Rep., 30:719–740.
Ekstein, R. (1966), Pleasure and reality, play and work, thought and
     action. In: Children of Time and Space, of Action and Impulse.

New York: Appleton-Century-Crofts, pp. 285–297.
―――― (1969), The learning process: From learning to love to love of learning. In: *From Learning to Love to Love of Learning*, ed. R. Ekstein & R. Motto. New York: Brunner/Mazel, pp. 95–98.
Fenichel, O. (1945), The means of education. *The Psychoanalytic Study of the Child*, 1:281–292. New York: International Universities Press.
Freud, A. (1979), The principal task of child analysis. *Bull. Hampstead Clinic*, 1:11–16.
Freud, S. (1900), The Interpretation of Dreams. *Standard Edition*, 4&5. London: Hogarth Press, 1953.
―――― (1911), Formulations on the two principles of mental functioning. *Standard Edition*, 12:218–226. London: Hogarth Press, 1958.
―――― (1915), The unconscious. *Standard Edition*, 14:166–215. London: Hogarth Press, 1957.
―――― (1925), Forward to August Aichorn's *Wayward Youth*. *Standard Edition*, 19:273–275. London: Hogarth Press, 1967.
Gill, M. (1976), Metapsychology is not psychology. In: *Psychology vs. Metapsychology: Psychoanalytic Essays in Memory of George S. Klein*, ed. M. Gill & P. Holzman. *Psychological Issues* Monograph 36. New York: International Universities Press, pp. 71–105.
Goldberg, A. (1982), The self of psychoanalysis. In: *Psychosocial Theories of the Self*, ed. B. Lee (with assistance of K. Smith). New York: Plenum Press, pp. 3–22.
Hartmann, H. (1939), *Ego-Psychology and the Problem of Adaptation*, trans. D. Rapaport. New York: International Universities Press.
Jones, R. (1968), *Fantasy and Feeling in Education*. New York: New York University Press.
Klein, G. (1976), *Psychoanalytic Theory: An Exploration of Essentials*. New York: International Universities Press.
Kris, E. (1948), Psychoanalysis and education. *Amer. J. Orthopsychiat.*, 28:622–634.
Murphy, L. (1962), *The Widening World of Childhood*. New York: Basic Books.
―――― Moriarty, A. (1976), *Vulnerability, Coping and Growth*. New Haven, CT: Yale University Press.
Murray, H., & Associates (1937), *Explorations in Personality*. New York: Oxford University Press.
Peller, L. (1946), Incentives to development and means of early education. *The Psychoanalytic Study of the Child*, 2:397–415. New York: International Universities Press.
Rapaport, D., & Gill, M. (1959), The points of view and assumptions of metapsychology. In: *The Collected Papers of David Rapaport*, ed. M. Gill. New York: Basic Books, 1967, pp. 795–811.
Schafer, R. (1976), *A New Language for Psychoanalysis*. New York: Basic Books.

———— (1983), *The Analytic Attitude.* New York: Basic Books.

Stechler, G., & Kaplan, S. (1980), The development of the self: A psychoanalytic perspective. *The Psychoanalytic Study of the Child,* 35:85–105. New Haven, CT: Yale University Press.

Sulloway, F. (1979), *Freud: Biologist of the Mind.* New York: Basic Books.

White, R. W. (1959), Motivation reconsidered: The concept of competence. *Psychol. Rev.,* 66:297–333.

———— (1963), *Ego and Reality in Psychoanalytic Theory. Psychological Issues* Monograph 11. New York: International Universities Press.

Chapter 1

Psychoanalysis and Education: Motive, Meaning, and Self

BERTRAM J. COHLER, Ph.D.

The alliance between psychoanalysis and education has a long and complex history. Since Freud's initial contributions to the study of learning and development, there has been great interest in the application of his theory of mental conflict to the study of learning and education. Further, psychoanalysis and education share a common interest in factors associated with effective intervention in order to enhance development. Many of the pioneers in psychoanalysis, including Anna Freud, Dorothy Burlingham, Ernst Kris, August Aichorn, Erik Erikson, Sigfried Bernfeld, Melanie Klein, and Susan Isaacs, had been trained both as educators and as analysts, further enhancing the relationship between these two disciplines.

In spite of initial efforts at uniting these two disciplines, it has been difficult to realize this goal. First problems resulted from a somewhat naive assumption regarding the comparability of the classroom and the psychoanalytic interview, leading to the belief that analysis of teachers, together with a curriculum emphasizing such

Thanks are extended to Dr. Frances Stott for a careful reading and critique of a previous version of this chapter.

developmentally relevant concerns as sexual enlightenment, would foster mental health (Hug-Hellmuth, 1919;
A. Freud, 1927; Peller, 1946; Pearson, 1954). The effect
of this misguided zeal was to discourage educators from
serious consideration of the contributions of psychoanalytic perspectives to the study of education (Zachry,
1941; Kris, 1948).

More recent problems in the alliance between psychoanalysis and education have resulted from the manner in which psychoanalytic concepts of the mental
apparatus have been applied to the study of learning. In
particular, there has been confusion between Freud's philosophy of science and contributions which are more distinctively psychoanalytic in the study of mental
development and learning in school.

The present chapter focuses primarily on students and
learning. A major problem with discussion of psychoanalysis and education is the extent to which teachers
feel burdened and overwhelmed by the demands and expectations of a society which values product more than
process. Recent comments in the media, noting the extent
to which elementary- and secondary-school teachers have
been recruited from the ranks of less-able students further contributes to the lowered morale of the teaching
profession. The meaning of teaching for teachers, factors
determining selection of teaching as a career, and issues
in career development clearly demands a separate and
detailed discussion. In the present instance, it is assumed
that teachers are in schools where they will be able to
realize their own career goals.

This chapter considers the relationship between education and developmental perspectives in psychoanalysis and suggests some ways in which a more effective
alliance between these two disciplines might be realized,
based on significant changes within psychoanalysis itself.
These changes have led to a shift from concern with
psychoanalysis as a model of psychic functioning, based

on metapsychological points of view (Freud, 1900, 1901, 1909b, 1911, 1915; Rapaport and Gill, 1959), to renewed concern with the clinical theory in psychoanalysis as a means for understanding the subjective world. The clinical theory is particularly concerned with those wishes and intents which lead persons to experience self and others, and such phenomena as learning, in particular ways, based on present constructions of the course of life as a whole (Novey, 1968; G. Klein, 1976; Schafer, 1980–1981; Cohler, 1982). Accompanying this shift from the mechanistic metapsychology to increased concern with clinical perspectives, there has been renewed concern with such issues as self or person, which might enhance the capacity to learn in school and to see oneself as a competent student, able to learn and to feel satisfied with scholarly accomplishments, not just during the years of elementary and secondary school, but also across the years of college and graduate or professional education.

METAPSYCHOLOGY, MENTAL DEVELOPMENT, AND LEARNING

Most often, psychoanalytic consideration of education has stressed the significance of past experience, understood in terms of the genetic point of view, as a primary determinant of the child's problems in learning and going to school. This genetic point of view, emphasizing retrospective or reconstructive study of the manner in which the past influences the present, may be contrasted with a prospective developmental approach, less often employed in psychoanalytic study of the past, but perhaps more useful than the genetic point of view in understanding both the origins of problems in learning as well as the ability to learn in spite of personal conflicts.

CONTRASTING PSYCHOANALYTIC
PERSPECTIVES ON DEVELOPMENT

The genetic approach is often regarded as the defining characteristic of psychoanalytic study (Freud, 1913; H. Hartmann and Kris, 1945; Rapaport and Gill, 1959; Zetzel and Meissner, 1973; Solnit, 1982). This approach is based on reconstruction of events early in the analysand's life which determine present actions, based on interpretation of transference and transferencelike phenomena in the psychoanalytic interview (Freud, 1896b, 1914a, 1937b). As Freud (1913) observed:

> Not every analysis of psychological phenomena deserves the name of psychoanalysis. The latter implies more than the mere analysis of composite phenomena into simpler ones. It consists of tracing back one psychical structure to another which preceded it in time and out of which it developed. . . . [F]rom the very first psychoanalysis was directed towards tracing developmental processes. It began by discovering the *genesis* of neurotic symptoms, and was led, as time went on, to . . . construct a genetic psychology [pp. 182–183].

Consistent with Breuer and Freud's (1895) initial communication on the psychopathology of hysteria, Zetzel and Meissner (1973) have noted that psychoanalysis seeks more than a demonstration that past memories and associated feelings may be recalled in the present, in circumstances which are experienced as historically similar to those of the past. Rather, the past is viewed as coactive, together with the present, as an epigenetic organization, in determining present experience. This genetic approach has best been summarized by H. Hartmann and Kris (1945) who observed that:

> The genetic approach in psychoanalysis does not only deal with anamnestic data, nor does it intend to show

> only "how the past is contained in the present." Genetic propositions describe why, in past situations of conflict, a specific solution was adopted; why the one was retained and the other dropped, and what causal relation exists between these solutions and later development. Genetic propositions refer to the fact that in an adult's behavior, anxiety may be induced by outdated conditions, and they explain why these conditions may still exercise influence [p. 14].

This genetic point of view (H. Hartmann and Kris, 1945; Rapaport and Gill, 1959) is not limited to anamnestic connections, in the sense that, following Freud's initial understanding of this term (Breuer and Freud, 1895), past memories and associated feelings are recalled in the present, in circumstances experienced as historically similar. Rather, it is epigenetic, in the terms first used by Freud in letters to his early collaborator Fliess (especially letter 52, Freud [1896b]), regarding the implications of early experiences with erotogenic zones for later development, and most explicitly stated in letters 59 and 72 (Freud, 1897b, 1897c), the three essays (Freud, 1905a), the introductory lectures (1915–1917a), the case study of Da Vinci (1910b), the case study of the "Wolf-Man" (1914–1918), and the later cultural work *Moses and Monotheism* (1939).

The genetic approach, which is necessarily reconstructive and inferential, may be contrasted with the prospective or developmental approach employed in much social science inquiry, founded on direct observation, concerned with issues of stability and change in the life history. This approach has generally been rejected within psychoanalysis on the grounds that it is inconsistent with empathic observation based on transference, or transferencelike reenactments observed within the clinical interview.

If the defining characteristic of psychoanalysis is understood as the study of the subjective world of wishes and intents, using an empathic and experience-near mode of observation, rather than an experience-distant form of social psychological study (Fliess, 1942; Kohut, 1959, 1982), then, as Freud (1909a, 1920a,b) recognized, it may be possible to observe the prospective course of development from within the psychoanalytic framework. Freud was clearly aware of the limitations and advantages of each approach when he wrote (1905a) that:

> Psychoanalytic investigation, reaching back into child-hood from a later time, and contemporary observation of children, combine to indicate to us still other regu-larly active sources of sexual excitation. The direct ob-servation of children has the disadvantage of working upon data which are easily misunderstandable; psy-choanalysis is made difficult by the fact that it can only reach its data, as well as its conclusions, after long detours. But by cooperation, the two methods can attain a satisfactory degree of certainty in their findings [p. 201].

In this comparison of retrospective or genetic and pro-spective, or truly developmental approaches to the study of lives, Freud explicitly acknowledged the advantage of each approach. While committed primarily to the genetic approach, Freud did attempt prospective study (1897a, p. 192; 1909a; 1920b, pp. 14–16), and viewed this ap-proach as complementary to reconstruction of develop-ment based on the genetic approach. Important findings consistent with this developmental approach have been reported more recently by such distinguished psychoan-alytic investigators as K. Wolf (1953), Erikson (1950), Spitz (1965), Murphy (1962, 1972), and Sander (1962, 1976).

DEVELOPMENT AND FREUD'S THEORY OF MIND

Freud's interest in the retrospective study of develop-ment, leading to the formulation of the genetic point of view, may be traced to his concern with the field of developmental neurobiology, beginning with his first research during his medical school years (Bernfeld, 1941, 1949, 1951; Holt, 1965; Eissler, 1978; Sulloway, 1979). Later study during the years between 1882 and 1891 continued this earlier interest. Inspired, in part, by the work of Darwin, Haeckel (1868), and J. H. Jackson, Freud sought to demonstrate that phylogenetically, the earliest structures persist over time; they may become more complex but they are never replaced (Bernfeld, 1951). The connection between careful microscopic studies and his subsequent approach to the study of the past in particular lives is dramatically illustrated in Freud's comment in lecture 22 of the introductory series that:

> [A]s a young student, I was engaged under von Brucke's direction on my first piece of scientific work, [and] I was concerned with the origins of the posterior nerve-roots in the spinal cord of a small fish of very archaic structure (the larval form of the brook lampry), I found that the nerve-fibres of these roots have their origin in large cells of the posterior horn of grey matter, which is no longer the case in other vertebrates. But I also discovered soon afterwards that nerve cells of this kind are present outside the grey matter the whole way to what is known as the spinal ganglion of the posterior root; and from this I inferred that the cells of these masses of ganglia had migrated from the spinal cord along the roots of the nerves. This is also shown by their evolutionary history. But in this small fish the whole path of their migration was demonstrated by the cells that had remained behind . . . [1915–1917a, p. 340].

The genetic point of view, derived from this early neurobiological study, may be much more significant as a statement of Freud's philosophy of science, based on his earliest work as a brain scientist, across the last quarter

of the nineteenth century, than as a defining characteristic of the psychoanalytic approach to the study of development (Freud, 1905a). Perhaps nowhere else in
Freud's work, as in these comments in *The Introductory
Lectures on Psychoanalysis,* does he so directly relate his
earliest laboratory studies in developmental neurobiology to his later psychoanalytic study of the psychic apparatus.

Subsequent psychoanalytic study of development has
maintained this earlier assumption of an equivalence
between development and genesis (Zetzel and Meissner,
1973). Abraham's epigenetic formulation (1924) systematized much of Freud's earlier, often implicit, discussions of genesis. This epigenetic approach was later
elaborated by Glover (1930, 1932a), H. Hartmann and
Kris (1945), Spitz (1959), and Erikson (1950). Significantly, little of this more recent discussion of the genetic
principle in psychoanalysis has been based on clinical
observation. While Spitz's observational studies are among
the most important in the history of child development,
and while Erikson's own early work was founded on detailed clinical study, in the case of each theorist, epigenetic formulations have been presented separately from
the consideration of clinical-observational findings.

Confusion remains within psychoanalysis regarding
the importance of the genetic point of view for the study
of lives, as contrasted with developmental perspectives
based on prospective observation. Freud viewed the study
of child development primarily as a means for validating
assumptions derived from his earlier comparative neurobiological studies, providing the intellectual foundations for the genetic point of view. As he notes (1905b),
in discussing the place of child psychology within psychoanalysis: "Child psychology, in my opinion, is destined
to perform the same useful services for adult psychology
that the investigation of the structure or development of
the lower animals has performed for research into the

structure of the higher classes of animals. Few deliberate efforts have hitherto been made to make use of child psychology for this purpose" (p. 127).

Too often, following Freud's 1913 comment regarding the importance of the genetic point of view within metapsychology, together with H. Hartmann and Kris's (1945) and Rapaport and Gill's (1959) restatements of this genetic point of view, it is assumed that this retrospective focus must be an essential element of the psychoanalytic approach to the study of lives over time. It is less often realized that this genetic point of view, as with other aspects of Freud's metapsychology, is much more a reflection of his particular philosophy of science than an essential component of the psychoanalytic approach to the study of persons (G. Klein, 1976; Gill, 1976, 1983; Warme, 1982).

METAPSYCHOLOGY, MENTAL FUNCTIONS, AND LEARNING

Largely as a result of Freud's own training in developmental neurobiology, and his acceptance of a philosophy of science based on work by Helmholtz and, in particular, his own teacher, Brucke, Freud formulated an intellectual viewpoint emphasizing a comparative method in which present structures were seen in terms of earlier structures. Later, when he began the study of mind, Freud (1895) relied upon this same developmental neurobiological model as a means of explaining the role of the past in determining present experience (Stengel, 1963). From the time of Freud's first efforts to study mental life in terms acceptable to late nineteenth-century brain science, much of psychoanalytic scholarship has been devoted to the extension of this basic model, which was most completely described in chapter 7 of *The Interpretation of Dreams* (1900), the essay on "The Unconscious" (1915), and *The Introductory Lectures* (1915–1917a).

The model which emerged from Freud's efforts to extend his understanding of brain processes into psychological functions extended a mechanistic and biologically
based approach to the study of wishes and intents which
has continued up to the present time (Solomon, 1974;
Holt, 1965, 1976; McCarley and Hobson, 1977; Hobson
and McCarley, 1977; E. Hartmann, 1983; Kandel, 1983;
J. G. Jacobson, 1983; Basch, 1984a; Kohut, 1984). As
ultimately summarized in H. Hartmann's (1939) discussion of adaptation and formalized in Rapaport and Gill's
(1959) portrayal of the metapsychological points of view,
the need for survival ultimately becomes the essential
motive for attending to reality (Gill and Klein, 1964).

In the years after 1895, and the first systematic presentation of the model of the psychic apparatus in the
Project and, in less physiological terms, chapter 7 of *The
Interpretation of Dreams* (1900), Freud was especially
concerned with the means by which particular aspects of
need and reality were acknowledged, appearing in consciousness. At least to some extent, he was principally
concerned with the study of attention, understood as the
basis for the appearance of particular contents in consciousness. The topographic and economic points of view
were proposed as a means of explaining the differential
selection of perceptions from the body and the external
world as factors entering into awareness. Resolution of
this problem was necessary as a first step in the creation
of a more effective model of the mind than that posed by
the experimental psychology of his time. Explicating the
three systems of the psychic topography, first in the *Project* (1895), and then restated in chapter 7 of *The Interpretation of Dreams* (1900), Freud concluded, in the essay
on the two principles of mental functioning (1911), that:

> The increased significance of external reality height-
> ened the importance, too, of the sense organs that are
> directed toward the external world, and of the *con-*

sciousness attached to them too. Consciousness now learned to comprehend sensory qualities in addition to the qualities of pleasure and pain which hitherto had alone been of interest to it. A special function was instituted which had periodically to search the external world, in order that its data might be familiar already if an urgent need should arise—the function of attention. Its activity meets the sense impressions half way, instead of awaiting their appearance [p. 220].

From this perspective, attention represents a developmental achievement, providing greater satisfaction in the external world than is possible as a consequence of remembered past satisfactions alone. Deploying attention enhances adaptation, including both awareness of needs or wishes, and also determining satisfaction of these wishes. Learning depends upon the capacity for attention, as well as the related function of concentration, in order to attain those reality adaptive skills which ultimately provide more effective forms of satisfaction (Erikson, 1950; Rapaport, 1951a,b). Over time, practice in deploying these cognitive skills enhances their effectiveness in providing for adaptation. As Holt (1962) and Schwartz and Schiller (1970) both have emphasized, the repetitive process of deploying a quantum of energy to some aspect of consciousness (hypercathexis) fosters development of a stable structure.

Psychoanalytic formulations of the mental apparatus have stressed the interrelated attributes of attention or concentration, reality testing and sense of reality, judgment, capacity for secondary process mental activity, or true logical thought, and relative autonomy of these and other ego functions, freed from immediate drive demands, as the outcome of a developmental process, beginning in earliest infancy and leading to increased discrimination between need and reality (Ferenczi, 1913; H. Hartmann, 1950, 1952, 1956; Rapaport, 1960; Frosch, 1962; Noy, 1979). Earlier, less complete and satisfying forms of satisfaction are replaced by those which are more satisfying and reality adaptive.

Regulation and control of impulses, together with postponement of present gratification in favor of more satisfying and adaptive forms of future satisfaction, increase the child's capacity to learn in school. However, as Bettelheim (1969a) has noted, the degree of renunciation of formal pleasure required by schooling, over the course of many years, may be difficult for the child to accept. Indeed, while the child may sometimes derive a sense of pleasure from learning (Buhler, 1954; R. W. White, 1963; Ekstein, 1969b), difficulties posed by the task of instruction and learning sometimes appear to be more salient for children than sources of satisfaction (Bernfeld, 1925; A. Freud, 1927, 1954; Bettelheim, 1969a,b).

Consideration of attention, together with the related ego functions of concentration, reality testing, sense of reality, judgment, and, ultimately, the integrative or synthetic capacity of the ego (H. Hartmann, 1939, 1950, 1951, 1953), may be relevant for the study of education, including factors facilitating learning in school (Cohler, 1972a,b) as, indeed, for the larger field of experimental and educational psychology (Rapaport, 1942, 1951a,b). For example, a panel discussion on learning and psychoanalytic theory (Aronson, 1972) maintains that psychic conflict may be understood in terms of a learning theory perspective. Greenspan (1975) attempts a similar effort, showing that concepts of reality and adaptation are important not just within psychoanalysis but, more generally, in the study of learning.

Greenspan maintains that rapprochement between the disparate perspectives of psychoanalysis and learning theory in psychology is possible, once psychoanalysis is able to recognize the extent to which reality can influence actions outside of the subjective realm. Considering each of the metapsychological points of view, Greenspan shows that concepts of drive, structure, and adaptation all focus on issues of stimulus and response, and that difference in perspective is accounted for largely by difference in views of behavior, concluding that "for a complete behavioral analysis, the variables considered by both psychoanalytic and operant learning theories should be combined" (1979, p. 59). Anthony (see chapter 4), adopts a similar perspective, suggesting that Freud's effort in the project, as later enlarged by Rapaport and his colleagues, represented an important first step in the formulation of a psychoanalytic theory of learning.

A major problem with efforts at reconciling the disparate perspectives of experimental psychology and psychoanalysis is that, most often, these efforts yield little more than the translation of concepts from psychoanalysis into those of operant approaches to learning (Sherwood, 1969). However, demonstrating that such translations from one theoretical system to another are possible is not equivalent to providing an explanation, even in those instances, such as the repetition compulsion, where such translations may be clinically useful. Of even greater concern is the assumption that interest in subjective understandings of self and others, long regarded as a defining characteristic of psychoanalysis, could be discarded in an effort to create a unifying theory of learning. It is an irony that these approaches to the integration of psychoanalysis and learning theory continue precisely the same functional, mechanistic concept of psychological activity that Freud sought to dispel with the creation of a psychology based on conflict (G. Klein, 1976).

RESEARCH FINDINGS AND THE REVISION OF METAPSYCHOLOGY

Much of more recent study of the application of psychoanalysis to education has continued Freud's initial emphasis upon a biologically based mechanistic philosophy of science (Chatthah, 1981), based on evolutionary study of the psychic apparatus, rather than a theory of meaning, based on the manner in which persons experience their lives (Home, 1966; G. Klein, 1976; Warme, 1982). It may be for this reason that Piaget's work has been so attractive for psychoanalysis. Significantly, Piaget shared Freud's comparative evolutionary perspective on the origin and development of actions (see chapter 12), considering acquisition of knowledge as a part of the process of adaptation to the environment. This biologically determined perspective on adaptation is consistent with H. Hartmann's (1939) views on adaptation, as well as with the later definition of the adaptive point of view in psychoanalytic metapsychology (Rapaport and Gill, 1959). As Piaget has observed: "Adaptation of the subject to the objects of its knowledge does exist and is merely a particular example of the organism's adaptation to its environment . . . the criterion of adaptation is success of this adaptation, whether it be a matter of survival or of comprehension" (1967, p. 180).

Systematic presentations of Piaget's work, portraying the relevance of this work to psychoanalysis, have been provided by a number of developmentally oriented investigators. Overall, discussion of the relevance of Piaget's work for psychoanalysis has focused primarily on infancy, and the relevance of Piaget's discussion of the sensorimotor phase, across the first year-and-a-half to two years of life, in understanding the basis for stable relationships with others (Wolff, 1960, 1966; Spitz, 1965; Decarie, 1965; Jackson, Campos, and Fischer, 1978; Greenspan, 1979). First contributions by Wolff (1960) and Cobliner (1965) emphasized the continuing interplay between intrinsic, maturational factors and subsequent experience as determinants of adaptation which is increasingly reality adaptive. Cobliner, in particular, notes the similarity between the perspectives of Piaget and Freud in explaining the development and functioning of the mental apparatus. Greenspan (1979) has provided a detailed comparison of the similarities and differences in the views of these two theorists, and views Piaget's contributions as essential for the formulation of a general psychology of development. A similar integrative effort has been provided by Basch (1977).

An exception to this use of Piaget in the application of psychoanalysis to the study of education is to be found in Anthony's (1976) discussion of conflicts involved in acquisition of knowledge. While Anthony's discussion of problems interfering with the child's ability to learn, as in the drive to acquire knowledge, is a masterful portrayal of the struggles by preschool and school-aged children to learn, it is less clear that use of Piaget's genetic epistemology clarifies this discussion of problems in learning in school, except by analogy. Indeed, Anthony (1976, p. 255) appears to recognize the problems involved in the use of Piaget's concepts, noting the many revisions required in order to integrate Piaget's formulation of the acquisition of knowledge with the focus on personal meaning and conflict so essential for the creation of a psychoanalytic theory of learning (Anthony, 1961).

Even the most casual reading of Piaget's work shows that he had an incomplete understanding of psychoanalysis. Although he was very critical of Freud's work, Piaget could not resist discussion of such concepts as affect and the unconscious (Piaget, 1954, 1967). Within Piaget's cognitive epistemology, issues of affect and consciousness are understood principally in terms of a socially shared understanding of actions and intents, the realm of morality, rather than in terms of subjective worlds of particular persons. There is also a difference in the timing of developmental processes portrayed by these two theorists; Piaget maintains that evocative memory or stable representations of the external world may not be possible before eighteen to twenty-four months of age.

However, beyond this difference in the understanding of some particular concepts, Freud and Piaget shared a view of development rooted in biology (Piaget's first research concerned the functions of a species of mollusk, and was not unlike Freud's own first biological studies of the brook lamprey in Brucke's laboratory). Further, each theorist endorses the basic premise that individual development is a recapitulation of development of the species, although Piaget (1976), following Waddington's (1957, 1966) discussion, is much more explicit than Freud regarding particular mechanisms of heredity which are related to this recapitulation. For each theorist, the goal of the study of individual development concerns larger intellectual issues. Piaget was concerned with understanding the origins of knowledge, and viewed the stages he outlined as a means for describing the means by which knowledge is acquired. Subsequent use of Piaget's outline of development as a guide to curriculum formation largely diminishes the significance of this contribution, just as the use of Freud's outline of libidinal development in teaching diagnosis and treatment has so often tended to reduce the complexity of psychoanalytic thought to a formula.

Similar problems are to be found with the mechanistic developmental formulations provided by each theorist. Increasing differentiation and integration of the psychic apparatus may be realized across the course of development from earliest childhood, in a manner consistent with much of contemporary developmental theory (Werner, 1927, 1957; Broughton, 1978, 1981; Feffer, 1982). Piaget's most complete statement of the mechanics of development (1975) encounters difficulty similar to that of Freud in explaining transition from one stage to another (Jackson, Campos, and Fischer, 1978; Haroutunian, 1983). Essential to Piaget's developmental formulation is the assumption that, with maturation of the nervous system, previous explanations of cause and effect are no longer sufficient and satisfying. This imbalance (Piaget, 1975) spurs efforts at new and, it is assumed, more complete and reality adaptive explanations, leading to reequilibration in terms which provide more logically correct explanations of the external world, increasing human understanding and fostering increased reality adaptation (Gelman and Baillargeon, 1983).

At each stage of development, reequilibration at a higher level of functioning is achieved through related functions of assimilation, providing an explanation in ways which transform and enhance present understandings, and accommodation, which organizes this explanation in terms of external phenomena. Assimilation and accommodation always work in tandem in fostering reequilibration, with accommodation insuring better adaptation and assimilation functioning to provide continuing integration of experience. As Piaget notes, in commenting upon the transition from sensorimotor to preoperational schemata:

> [T]he scheme of the permanence of objects, constructed by the sensorimotor intelligence, marks the starting point for operational conservation schemata in thought . . . it is impossible, if one recognizes the existence of more or less generalized schemata on the behavioral level, from reflexes and habit formation up to the many constructions set up by the sensorimotor intelligence, not to consider imagination and thought schemata as adaptive schemata in the biological sense of the word. . . . [A]t every level these schemata are constantly differentiated by continuous accommodation to new conditions, an adaptation resulting from the equilibrium between the accommodation and the assimilation [1967, p. 182].

Considering the extent to which Freud and Piaget shared a common philosophy of science, it is hardly surprising that their accounts of development would be

viewed as consistent (Basch, 1977), or that effort would
be made to integrate their theories of the course of the
developmental process (Wolff, 1960; Cobliner, 1965;
Greenspan, 1979; Kegan, 1982, 1983). Central to these
integrative efforts is the belief that substitution of Piaget's genetic epistemology for Freud's mechanistic genetic point of view might resolve those problems in
Freud's own formulation of development which stem from
his adherence to the experimental science of his time, or
correct inaccuracies resulting from his more limited understanding of the course of cognitive development in
early childhood. Based on these assumptions, efforts have
been made to update Freud's genetic point of view using
Piaget's concepts, together with those of information science (Basch, 1977; Rosenblatt and Thickstun, 1977a,b;
Peterfreund, 1971, 1978; Greenspan, 1979).

However, serious problems arise in trying to "correct"
Freud's experience-distant metapsychology in terms of
the particular concepts important to the experimental
science of a different time, such as is provided in the use
of findings from cognitive science in contemporary efforts
to rescue metapsychology. In the first place, these efforts
only continue Freud's initial confusion regarding the
place of a particular philosophy of science in understanding the course of lives over time. If the unique contribution of psychoanalytic perspectives is in providing a
means for understanding the significance of wishes, intents, and the way in which the realm of private experience influences actions, then problems arise in the use
of an approach based on functions, mechanisms, and
models of a psychic apparatus in the effort to study meanings and intents.

In the second place, the particular philosophy of science perceived as relevant in making sense of Freud's
metapsychology changes over time, with successive generations rewriting metapsychology in terms most relevant for that time. While these intellectual efforts may

be useful in clarifying the nature of Freud's own contributions as a pioneering cognitive scientist (Pribram and Gill, 1976), it is less certain that these efforts increase an understanding of origins and later transformations of that subjective world of experience which is of particular concern to psychoanalysis.

In the third place, the use of findings from allied fields in a continuing effort to revise the inherently mechanistic qualities of metapsychology in terms of contemporary philosophy of science subjects these findings to the same reification as in Freud's own use of the findings of his time in his initial formulation of metapsychology. Changing understanding of cognitive and affective development requires continuing efforts to rewrite metapsychology, incorporating the most recent findings from the fields of developmental psychology and the brain sciences in order that metapsychology might be most relevant to contemporary findings in these allied fields.

Clearly, Freud's appeal to experimental findings of his day in support of the assumptions of metapsychology presents problems for contemporary study of brain and behavior, including the experimental psychology of learning. However, continuing efforts to revise Freud's metapsychology in terms acceptable to each generation within the psychoanalytic community both continues Freud's own lack of clarity between philosophy of science and the study of meanings and intents, and also detracts from advances in those areas of psychoanalysis where it is more suited to make contributions to knowledge. In particular, psychoanalysis may be less relevant in understanding the development of mechanisms of learning than in understanding the child's particular experience of going to school, including sense of self-esteem and capacity to participate with zest in learning.

Findings from developmental research are clearly of some relevance to the clinical perspective in psychoanalysis, pointing to additional issues for study, such as factors contributing to the child's ability to learn in school, and to remain resilient to problems at home, such as among some children of psychiatrically ill parents (Anthony and Cohler, 1987), or factors leading to self-righting tendencies in development (Emde, 1981, 1985). Use of a developmental rather than a genetic approach to the psychoanalytic study of education emphasizes the complex interplay of present experience of learning and going to school viewed in terms of the course of development from earliest childhood. This developmental approach also emphasizes the significance for understanding the child's experience of learning and going to school which results both from ever changing transactions with the social world (Berger and Luckmann, 1966; Cole and Scribner, 1974; Vygotsky, 1978; Riegel, 1979), and from increased appreciation of the changing meaning for the child of going to school, particularly during the adolescent years, when there is an increased sense of the future as related to present and past, and renewed efforts to maintain the sense of continuity of self and experience (Cohler, 1982).

MEANING AND SELF IN THE PSYCHOANALYTIC STUDY OF EDUCATION

Study of education from a metapsychological perspective continues Freud's own experience-distant, biologically based model of mental development which was founded upon early work by Helmholtz, Brucke, and functionalist European psychology in the last half of the nineteenth century (Bernfeld, 1941). Efforts at portraying the process of learning and education in terms of ego functions (Freud, 1911; Rapaport, 1951a), reviewed by Cohler (1972a, b), appears to achieve little more than translation of complex experiences and personal meanings shaped by experiences over a lifetime into mechanistic forces. Use of other, biologically based formulations of development, such as those of Piaget, information processing, or artificial intelligence, continue an emphasis upon function and mechanism rather than more experience-near concerns with the meaning for the child of going to school (and for the teacher, of teaching).

As Klein (1976) has noted, it is an irony that focus upon metapsychology perpetuated the same mechanistic approach which Freud had sought to change with the introduction of the study of wish, intent, and meaning in the clinical theory. An alternative to an approach focused on function and mechanism, the clinical theory leads to the study of learning and going to school in terms of the student, founded upon the child's experience of self and social context.

Experiential approaches to the study of education have been made possible largely as a result of dramatic changes, across the past two decades, in clarifying the distinctive contributions of psychoanalysis. Beginning with the *Festschrift* for Rapaport (Holt, 1967), reconsidering the twin concepts of primary and secondary process, and continuing with Klein's (1976) posthumous reconsideration of psychoanalytic theory, the collection of essays in memory of Klein, edited by Gill and Holtzman (1976), and Schafer's (1972, 1978) reconsideration of the nature of motivation in psychoanalysis, increased clarity has been realized regarding Freud's goals in the construction of metapsychology (Abrams, 1971).

This intensive reconsideration of the place of metapsychology within psychoanalysis has led to a particularly critical review of the contribution of the economic point of view (Rosenblatt and Thickstun, 1970, 1977a,b; Applegarth, 1977; Gill, 1977; Swanson, 1977; Wallerstein, 1977). However, there has been less agreement regarding the contribution of the genetic point of view. Some discussion (Sherwood, 1969; Schimek, 1975; Klein, 1976; Cohler, 1980a, 1984; Schafer, 1980–1981; Spence, 1982; Anthony and Cohler, 1987) has questioned the assumptions underlying this approach to the study of lives over time. Consistent with this critique of the genetic point of view, other discussion of the genetic point of view has noted the problems arising from the assumption that wishes and intents can be understood in terms of biological mechanisms and functions (Kohut, 1959, 1977; Home, 1966; Gill, 1976, 1983; Muslin, 1981; Warme, 1982; Goldberg, 1982, 1983). Other theorists, maintaining a natural science orientation to the study of lives have been less willing to reconsider the assumptions of this genetic point of view (Wallerstein, 1976; Modell, 1978; Brenner, 1980; Frank, 1979; Holt, 1981; Shevrin, 1981; E. Hartmann, 1983; Richards, 1982).

A third group of theorists (Rubenstein, 1976; Eagle, 1980; Meissner, 1980) has attempted to rescue metapsychology by preserving the so-called scientific emphasis of the philosophy of science, while rejecting specific assumptions regarding the metapsychological points of view (Freud, 1915; Rapaport and Gill, 1959). These theorists have expressed particular concern regarding increased emphasis upon issues of interpretation and meaning in the clinical theory, which would appear to transform psychoanalysis from a scientific into a humanistic discipline. These theorists are concerned that, if the psychoanalytic study of lives is viewed merely as another form of discourse or narrative, based on the study of the collaboration of analyst and analysand in an effort to make sense of the analysand's life history, as observed through interpretation of transference or transference-like reenactments (Cohler, 1980a; Schafer, 1980b, 1981; Spence, 1982), then it may be impossible to break the "hermeneutic circle" (Hirsch, 1967, 1976; Hoy, 1978) or to provide external validity for interpretations.

MEANING, INTERPRETATION, AND SELF-INTEGRATION

Freud's epochal volume on dreams (1900) has most often been viewed as an effort to translate the metapsychology, previously portrayed in the *Project* (1895), into psychological terms (Basch, 1976). Freud (1913) believed that it was his mechanistic model of the mind which represented the most significant contribution of psychoanalysis to other scholarly disciplines. Indeed, *The Interpretation of Dreams* is noted more for the major metapsychological statement in chapter 7, than for the discussion of distortion in dreams, as portrayed in chapter 4, or the dreamwork, as portrayed in chapter 6. This discussion of the means by which the meaning of dreams may be understood provides the foundation for an alternative clinical approach in psychoanalytic study concerned with meaning rather than with study of mechanisms and functions. Throughout the book, Freud goes to great lengths to show that dreams represent the fulfillment of a wish, using a variety of means of censorship.

Understanding the meaning of the analysand's communications and presentations of self through study of the transference, essential to the clinical theory, reflects Freud's incredible powers of observation. It may well be that years of detailed microscopic study led not just to preoccupation with philosophy of science but, of even greater significance for the subsequent history of psychoanalysis, the capacity to notice apparently inconsequential aspects of actions and utterances and to make sense of apparently randomly connected thoughts.

Reconsideration of metapsychology as little more than Freud's expression of his philosophy of science (Gill, 1976; G. Klein, 1976) suggests that it is actually his method of observation, using "evenly-suspended" attention (1912, p. 111) and relying upon empathic understanding of the analysand's communications, so well shown in Freud's (1905a, 1909b) presentation of his own clinical work, and his discussion of the analysis of the transference neurosis (Freud, 1914a), which may be the most distinctive contribution of psychoanalysis to other scholarly disciplines in the humanities and social sciences, including the field of education.

Unlike the philosophy of science, which provided the basis of his metapsychology, and which Freud believed could be verified in terms of an emerging positive method, the only means available for evaluating the accuracy of these interpretations of meaning was the increased sense of conviction on the part of both analyst and analysand that the interpretation made apparently irrelevant and confusing phenomena more sensible and less difficult to understand (Freud, 1937b; Cohler, 1980a; Schafer, 1980b, 1982; Cohler and Grunebaum, 1981). As G. Klein (1976) has noted, much of Freud's genius was in creating "a psychology of the meanings and syntheses arising out of crises in an individual's life time" (p. 54).

Study of Freud's description of the psychoanalytic treatment of Dora and of Paul Lorenz (the Rat-man) clearly shows the nature of this collaborative effort at understanding meaning, including vivid examples of the interpretation of transference, so important in the construction of a followable narrative of the life history, based on the history of the analysis itself. Indeed, as Schafer (1979, 1980b, 1981) has noted, the only history with which analyst and analysand are concerned is the life history constructed on the basis of their analytic relationship. That interpretation of the transference is most complete which leads to the most mutually understandable or followable narrative of that relationship (Cohler, 1980a).

Consistent with Schafer's (1979, 1980b, 1982) formulation, the clinical interview may be viewed as an encounter between two persons. Empathically informed, experience-near, detailed observation of lives over time is clearly central to that interpretive activity which is the basis of psychoanalytic inquiry concerned with issues of self and meaning (Fliess, 1942; Kohut, 1959, 1982; Warme, 1982). The narrative created as a result of this collaborative activity becomes like a text to be understood, with the only possible interpretive activity that which is based on the shared activity of these two participants. Schafer (1980b, 1980–1981, 1981) has suggested that a major contribution of the clinical psychoanalytic method may be the creation of a narrative shared by analyst and analysand, based on a history of reenactments observed and interpreted by the analyst, which permits the analysand to regain a sense of personal coherence and the capacity to respond more effectively to subsequent life changes.

This approach to the study of meaning contained within a narrative, pioneered by Freud in his clinical studies and papers on technique, representing the clinical theory in psychoanalysis (G. Klein, 1976; Warme, 1982) is consistent with the continuing effort within the social sciences away from a mechanistic study of lives. This approach, formulated by Habermas (1967, 1983), Ricoeur (1970, 1977, 1983), H. White (1973, 1978), Geertz (1972, 1974), and others, has been termed *interpretive social science* by Rabinow and Sullivan (1979). As Habermas (1983) has emphasized, the distinction between interpretive and normative social science should be based on the domain studied. Together with such fields as anthropology and history, psychoanalysis relies upon what is said, together with the manner in which it is said, or the formal characteristics of communication, as the phenomenon which is to be studied. Habermas observes that:

> [E]very science that admits meaningful expressions as part of its object domain has to cope with the methodological consequences of the participatory role of an interpreter, who does not "give" meaning to things observed, but instead explicates the given meaning of expressions that can be understood only from within processes of communication . . . [1983, p. 256].

While this view of psychoanalysis as a discipline concerned with the study of meaning and intents raises questions regarding accepted modes of explanation, the interpretive approach may resolve many of the problems posed by psychoanalysis understood as metapsychology, emphasizing the study of functions and mechanisms. As Gill (1983) has observed:

> [A]s presently constituted, metapsychology is in a different universe of discourse from that of meaning —namely, the natural science universe of force, energy, and space. As such it is incompatible with a hermeneutic science. . . . [T]he energy discharge point of view is conceptually parallel to the generally accepted psychoanalytic metapsychology and the conception of psychoanalysis as a natural science. . . . [P]sychoanalysis can and should be a hermeneutic science which obeys all the canons of science but deals in the dimensions of human meanings, not in the dimensions of natural science [p. 534].

Viewed as an interpretive social science, the task of psychoanalysis, including application to such areas of study as education, is to understand the manner in which persons make sense of experience including the meaning of such life changes as going to school, and the use of schooling, from elementary school through college and beyond, in the struggle to maintain a coherent sense of self, leading to the creation of a followable narrative of the life history, and to reconcile hopes and aspirations with the reality of what can be learned, and with the limits of what can be taught. As a result of areas of study which are particularly liked and disliked, and teachers particularly liked and admired, students continue to revise their own presently understood plans for the future changing their relationship to what they are learning in school.

It should be noted that emphasis upon issues of meaning and interpretation within psychoanalysis does not replace the need for continuing concern with issues of theory construction and validation. In response to renewed interest in the clinical theory in psychoanalysis, and interpretive social science more generally, emphasizing communication and meaning, a number of psychoanalytic scholars have expressed concern that this approach might require psychoanalysis to renounce any claims to being a science, or to providing objective explanations of human behavior (Frank, 1979; Modell, 1978, 1981; Holt, 1981; Edelson, 1984). For these critics of the interpretive perspective, the romanticism apparently contained in a theory which permits little external validation contrasts directly with the rational-explanatory mode developed by Freud. While recognizing the problems inherent in a positivistic approach, these critics of the interpretive approach follow Polanyi (1974), who has suggested that the concept of scientific models may be useful in the social sciences, as long as it is understood that social science theory is not falsifiable in the manner earlier proposed by Popper (1959).

For example, these critics of a clinical-interpretive social science maintain that the clinician's empathic responses must be validated against external criteria (Holt, 1961). The problem with this approach, as Gadamer (1970) has demonstrated in his critique of Dilthey's historicism, is that the social scientist cannot remain "value free" in the process of inquiry, or stand outside of the subject matter addressed: psychoanalytic study is based on a relationship or narrative uniquely shaped by the dialogue between participants in the clinical interview in a manner analogous to the interpreter's study of a text. The very involvement of the interpreter in the dialogue means that it is impossible to see the world through the eyes of another without ourselves becoming a constituent element of that interpretive activity.

PSYCHOANALYSIS AND THE CONCEPT OF SELF

The concept of self is one which has been difficult to understand within psychoanalysis (Meissner, 1983). Following Freud's initial comment, in "Civilization and its Discontents" (1930), where he states that "there is nothing of which we are more certain than the feeling of our self, of our own ego" (p. 65), H. Hartmann (1950), Laplanche and Pontalis (1967), and Kernberg (1982) all maintain that Freud never intended a sharp distinction between the terms *ego* and *self*. These commentators note that the translation of the term *Ich* from German into the English term *ego* preserves the sense of this term as a system. The editors of the *Standard Edition* note (Strachey, 1961, p. 8) that, in a few places, they have translated the term *ego* as *self*, and confirm the observation that it is difficult to make clear distinctions between these two terms. Bettelheim (1983) suggests that the inflected meaning of the term *ego*, in German, is a reflective or introspective "I" or "me," supporting Schafer's emphasis upon an active self as central to the psychoanalytic study of lives (1972, 1980a, 1980–1981).

Contemporary discussion of the term *self* in the psychoanalytic literature may be traced to H. Hartmann, Kris, and Lowenstein's (1946) paper on the theory of psychic structure, and H. Hartmann's (1950) paper on the theory of the ego, advocating that the term *ego* be replaced by the term *self*, since this latter term is most congruent with observed clinical phenomena. Hartmann (1950) suggests that the term *self* be understood as equivalent to the term *person*, as contrasted both with the *objects* (including other persons), and the *ego*, as terms used in connection with Freud's theory of the mental apparatus. Reconsidering this earlier view, Goldberg (1982, 1983) notes that this concept must include both a sense of continuity of experience, and also of the body and bodily functioning, and affirms the importance, within psychoanalytic study, of retaining an intrapsychological perspective, focused on the experience of others, rather than an interpersonal concept of self. It is this concern with the subjectively construed or intrapersonal experience of regulation and confidence in the capacity to realize important goals (Basch, 1983a) which differentiates psychoanalytic perspectives on the self from those of interpersonal approaches, such as that provided by Kegan (1982) and extended and elaborated by Noam, Kohlberg, and Snarey (1983) and Noam (see chapter 23).

Initial work was followed by E. Jacobson's (1964) definitive discussion of the self. Concerned essentially with representations of self, and with factors contributing to the capacity to maintain a sense of coherence in the midst of life changes, Jacobson's description of the self emphasizes those emotionally laden images of experience, which remain the realm of subjective experience. However, Jacobson maintains a distinction between this subjective world and both ego processes, referring to structures such as identifications, which foster regulation of drives, and identity, referring more directly to a sense of differentiation from others. Development (and learning) consists of increasing stabilization of structures which foster increased (secondary) autonomy from drives, enhancing a sense of continuity and coherence and insuring realization of ambitions according to standards early learned within the family.

The contributions of ego psychology to the study of psychic autonomy point to the problems encountered in the equation of self and ego (Blum, 1982). While virtually all theorists working within this tradition are agreed that the self is the realm of subjective experience, this experience-near understanding of persons and lives over time, so well portrayed in Jacobson's discussion of coherence, is then discarded in favor of the experience-distant, metapsychological concept of the ego (Rangell, 1982). Supporting Jacobson's conclusions, both Moore and Fine

(1968) and Kernberg (1982) deplore the inclusion of the concept of self as a distinctive psychoanalytic concept. Ego psychology maintains that terms such as *self* or *person* are too closely tied to commonsense psychology and to psychosocial rather than distinctively psychoanalytic approaches to be useful as psychoanalytic constructs. Schafer (1980–1981), and particularly Gill (1983), prefer the term *person* as being more suitable within psychoanalytic inquiry for many of the same reasons that it is rejected within the tradition of ego psychology.

However, in his far-ranging review of the contemporary status of psychoanalysis, Gill notes (1983, p. 526) that the term *person* is to be preferred both because it is not encumbered by metapsychology and because it is anchored in the interpersonal situation. This latter justification poses problems for psychoanalysis as an intrapersonal psychology. Indeed, the unique significance of the psychoanalytic approach is that it focuses upon the subjective world and upon the manner in which interpersonal relations are experienced. Viewed in the context of the present discussion, the advantage of the psychoanalytic approach to the study of learning and going to school is the extent to which it fosters concern with the student's experience of schooling, and with the ways in which problems in learning, such as in reading, writing, and calculation, enhance or threaten the sense of self coherence. In this sense, the concept of person, while initially culturally constructed (Parsons, 1952, 1955, 1958; Geertz, 1972, 1974), refers to sense of coherence of the present, viewed in terms both of a presently remembered past and an anticipated future.

As this chapter suggests, it may be the clinical rather than the metapsychological perspective which represents the most enduring psychoanalytic contribution to the study of education. Concern with the intrapsychic *experience* of the social surroundings (the life space, as portrayed both by Lewin [1949] and Redl and Wineman

[1951]) is of central importance in understanding the contribution of psychoanalysis to the study of lives. While there are serious problems in Erikson's psychosocial theory (1950), these problems arise less from the fact that Erikson is concerned with the relation of person and surround than with the fact that he had continued a tradition in which biological postulates, together with a mechanistic portrayal of development, in a manner most consistent with Abraham's (1921, 1924) formulation, rather than leading to increased understanding of the manner in which relations with others are experienced at successive points across the course of life including possible discontinuities perceived in development over time. Erikson's portrayal of so-called psychosocial development, as much as other psychoanalytic discussion of development, tends to reify rather than clarify the developmental processes, providing mechanistic descriptions of modes, zones, and stages which may not be consonant with the course of life (Neugarten, 1969; Gergen, 1977, 1982; Kagan, 1980; Emde, 1981).

EMPATHY AND THE ORIGINS OF THE SELF

In adulthood, as across the course of life, the experience of being understood, or of empathy, leads both to attainment of an increased sense of coherence or a meaning of life (Weber, 1905–1906), as well as to feelings of renewed self-integration and well-being (Lecky, 1945). In clinical psychoanalysis, the analyst's ability to experience reciprocally the analysand's own private experience (Fliess, 1942; Goldberg, 1983), particularly reenactments of earlier life experiences with the analyst, in the creation of a jointly constructed narrative or life history of this relationship (Schafer, 1980–1981; Cohler, 1982; Spence, 1982; Freeman, 1984) fosters the analysand's increased sense of personal integration. The analyst's effort to understand the analysand's own life, using the empathic method, leads the analysand to feel increased self-coherence or congruence (Kohut, 1974, 1977, 1984; Kohut and Wolf, 1978).

Within psychoanalysis, following Fliess's initial formulation of the process of "tasting" the analysand's experience (1942), a process still portrayed in the rather wooden, positivistic mode of ego psychology, other than Schafer's (1959) discussion of generative empathy in the therapeutic situation, and Greenson's (1960, 1967) discussion of empathy and psychoanalytic technique, there has been little explicit consideration of this mode of observation, with the exception of Kohut's (1959) seminal contribution clarifying the nature of vicarious introspection, noting that: "We designate phenomena as mental, psychic, or psychological if our mode of observation includes introspection and empathy *as an essential constituent*. The term 'essential' in this context expresses (a) the fact that introspection or empathy can never be absent from psychological observation, and (b) that it may be present alone" (p. 462). Kohut differentiates this introspective activity both from intuition, which implies a mystical and undisciplined use of the "hunch," as well as from natural science modes of observation, including that employed by Mahler and her colleagues in developing the stages of separation-individuation (Mahler, Pine, and Bergman, 1975). Twenty-five years later, in his last published works, Kohut (1982, 1984) returned to this subject of empathic observation which, in the meantime, had received much additional study (Schafer, 1980–1981; Bornstein and Silver, 1981; Buie, 1981; Schwaber, 1981; Basch, 1983b, Lichtenberg, Bornstein, and Silver, 1984). Once again, Kohut emphasized the significance of this mode of observation of the subjective realm, the unique contribution of psychoanalysis as a method of scholarly study, detailing the significance of this point of view for clinical study: "Empathy is the operation that defines the field of psychoanalysis. No psychology of complex mental states is conceivable without the employment of empathy. . . . [W]e define it as 'vicarious introspection' or, more simply, as one person's [attempt to] experience the inner life of another while simultaneously retaining the stance of an objective observer" (1984, p. 175).

Discussing the significance of empathy for maintaining the capacity for the sense of self-integration or cohesion resulting from the experience of having been understood, Stechler and Kaplan (1980) observe that:

Crucial to Freud's model of development was the notion of the transformation of early conflicts into later ones. . . . [A]s we understand psychoanalytic developmental theory, intrapsychic order and motivations arise from experienced discontinuity. The capacity to function in accordance with an internal self-regulating organization is a developmental acquisition originating in innumerable attempts to resolve experienced breaches of expectancy. That is the external facet of the experience. Internally it may be viewed as an experienced breach of integration. The growing child's manifest behavior, viewed from within this perspective, can thus be understood as reflecting efforts to deal with incompatible tendencies that result in crises of integration [pp. 86–87].

Following a position proposed most explicitly in G. Klein's (1976) posthumous volume, Stechler and Kaplan (1980) suggest that "structures which are available to the person to guide his actions originate in these ongoing efforts to resolve the inevitable breaches in integration" (p. 87). A similar perspective may also be found in the work of Kohut (1982, 1984) who notes the therapeutic benefit derived from the feeling of being understood, expressed by the term *self-selfobject,* by Lichtenberg (1980, 1981; Lichtenberg, Bornstein, and Silver, 1984) stressing the importance of feelings of self-cohesion for successful adjustment, and perhaps best summarized by Basch (1983a) in his definition of the self as:

> [A] symbolic abstraction from the developmental process. The self refers to the uniqueness that separates the experiences of an individual from all others while at the same time conferring a sense of cohesion and continuity on the disparate experiences of that individual throughout life. The self is the symbolic transformation of experience into an overall goal directed construct [p. 53].

From this perspective, the self is an expression of feelings of coherence and integration; this sense of personal integration, in turn, is shaped from earliest childhood, with attainment of a sense that tension states can be modulated. Initially, caretaker efforts are experienced as a part of self, more or less capable of such efforts at regulation (Cohler, 1980a). Only later in infancy is there realization that the caretaker exists separately. To the extent that early caretaker efforts, experienced as a function of self, are experienced as successful in resolving tension states, there is increased conviction of self as a source of personal integration or identity, and competence (Huizenga, 1983). Even in the absence of a sense of self as viewed as fully capable of modulating tensions, where there is some capacity for the experience of another as a possible source of help, both the act of being understood, and the consequence of this understanding, represented by a revised and more coherent personal narrative, is of value in the construction of a more stable sense of self.

Much of Winnicott's (1953) discussion of the transitional object, as well as more recent discussion of transmuting internalization, following experienced breaches of empathy, including implications for the maintenance of self-selfobject ties, discussed by Kohut and his associates (Kohut, 1971, 1977; Wolf, 1980; Tolpin and Kohut,

1980; Basch, 1984a,b,c) or "evoked companions" (Stern, 1985) are consistent with this view of self and factors influencing development and later psychopathology of the self. Just as persons feeling depleted and fragile are not able to learn new ideas which threaten a tenuous adjustment, even though there is a capacity for such learning, problems children have in learning in school may be much more the consequence of problems in self-integration, including both problems in their sense of inner coherence, and in the experience of themselves as competent learners, than of a curriculum demanding cognitive competence not yet developmentally relevant, as previously suggested by educators adopting Piaget's genetic epistemology as the basis for the curriculum (Kamaii, 1968).

THE ORIGIN OF PROBLEMS IN LEARNING: THE CONTRIBUTION OF SELF PSYCHOLOGY

Psychoanalytically informed discussion of problems in learning in school generally have emphasized the extent to which these problems reflect the reenactment of conflict associated with the nuclear or "oedipal" or structural neurosis (Freud, 1900, 1909a,b, 1910a, 1914–1918, 1915–1917a, 1923, 1932–1933; Koff, 1960). Inclusion of envy, guilt, and reparation, as in the work of Melanie Klein (1923, 1931), continues this emphasis on feelings of exclusion and rivalry with parents, as the basis for structural conflicts, reflected in problems in learning in school, although phrased in terms most relevant for the postulated earlier appearance of the nuclear neurosis. Most recently, formulations of psychology of the self have called into question the importance of the nuclear conflict as the basis for problems such as those of school learning.

Redefining the concept of structure to refer to the regulation of tension, based on the experience of early optimal frustration in development, Kohut (1977, 1982, 1984) suggests that adverse outcomes of the child's increased awareness of the family romance appear only when there is already a deficit in self-esteem. The problem with the Oedipus story, as Kohut suggests (1982, p. 404), is that Oedipus was a rejected child, abandoned to die in the wilderness. Consistent with R. W. White's (1959) concept of competence as an intrinsic developmental force, Kohut protests the necessarily adverse outcome expected for the oedipal conflict, noting the joy which children feel in expressing their assertiveness and in showing a sense of competence.

At least to some extent, it may be possible to reconcile Kohut's reformulation of the nuclear neurosis with the more traditional psychoanalytic approach to the study of development. Kohut's critique of the nuclear neurosis is founded on a concern with the effect of this developmental event upon the child's experience of self-esteem. Starting from the experience-near perspective of the child's view of self, rather than from the mechanistic and experience-distant perspective of Freud's biological model, Kohut's formulation focuses on the child's resolution of the family romance in terms consistent more generally with problems shown by students in school. Problems in learning, and in demonstrating this learning in papers and in examinations and, more generally, in performing in terms of talents and ideals, do reflect lowered self-esteem. A boy unable to resolve feelings of constant rivalry with his father may rebel against what he feels to be authoritarian teachers. Psychoanalytic study of students unable to produce written work shows that many such students either feel inadequate and unable to attain the success of their fathers, or fear that their own success will actually exceed that of their fathers, leading to feelings of guilt at succeeding in the family romance, together with possible concern regarding possible retaliation for their success.

Kohut's discussion of the impact of personality development during childhood is particularly important for the study of psychoanalysis and education. Focusing upon the child's experience of the so-called nuclear conflict, rather than upon the impact of this conflict for development of psychic structure, Kohut's observation that the outcome of this conflict can lead to enhanced sense of efficacy is important in the study of self-esteem and learning. From the perspective of psychoanalysis and education, study of the manner in which the child experiences the family romance, just as the manner in which the child experiences earlier caretaking, is important in appreciating the variety of factors contributing to enhanced sense of self as learner.

The problems presented by this reformulation of nuclear conflict are to be found both in the replacement of one sovereign explanation by another, as well as by continued reliance not just upon the child's experience of caretaking, but the actuality of the time-space context in which this caretaking takes place. As Winnicott (1960b), Gedo (1979), and Gedo and Goldberg (1973) have emphasized, construction of the self must be viewed in terms of the totality of development. As Gedo (1979) notes: "[T]o put the matter into a truly epigenetic context, the conflicts of relatively later phases of development, such as the Oedipus complex in its entire configuration, actually consist of mental attributes maintained as a consequence of other ongoing conflicts that are legacies of earlier phases of development" (p. 33). Kohut's contribution is important in stressing factors codetermining the child's experience of the family romance. However, the child's place in the course of development during the third to fifth years of life also plays an important role. At least in our own culture, fantasies related to the issue of rivalry and retaliation, and attendant fears, appear during these years in all children (Shapiro, 1977), and must be resolved in some way. It is in the resolution of this issue that the child's experience of the course of development as a whole is so important.

Problems are also presented in Kohut's formulation as a result of his continued concern not just with the child's experience of caretaking, but with the time-space context of this care. Frequent reference is made to supposed real aspects of the child care context of analysand's reports, with deficits in self-regard attributed to relevant parental deficits. It may be that this concern with the actuality of caretaking is merely a reflection of Kohut's capacity to enter empathically into the analysand's experience of childhood. However, as Schafer (1981, 1982) has emphasized, portrayals of parents at any one phase of the analysis are most relevant to the shared construction of analysand and analyst, rather than to the time-space world. As Kohut has emphasized, the unique contribution of the psychoanalytic method is concern with the experience-near rather than social psychological realm of development. Central to this psychoanalytic perspective is concern with the extent to which wishes and intents, rather than situation and context, is the important arena of study. Attributing the child's capacity to resolve tensions in terms of the time-space characteristics of parents, rather than in terms of the child's construction of the experience of caretaking (Winnicott, 1953) focuses concern with the time-space rather than the experiential arena of development.

This discussion suggests that diverse psychoanalytic perspectives on the course of development are important in understanding determinants of self-esteem, including the capacity to transform inner tensions in such a manner that effective learning in school may be realized. While earlier discussions of the origins of learning difficulties may have placed too much emphasis upon the experience of issues of rivalry and competition associated with the nuclear conflict of the oedipal phase of development, clearly these issues are critical in understanding the origins of problems in going to school. It is also important to view such issues as rivalry in terms of self-esteem as a whole, including the significance for the resolution of these concerns of the capacity for self-soothing and for being able to use others in appropriate ways in confirmation of self integrity (Horton, 1981).

Students with a positive sense of self may feel able to tackle complex mathematical operations, and even take a chance on initial failure, while those with greater uncertainty regarding their own competence may view initial failures as confirmation of the inability to succeed, even though both children may have attained the same level of cognitive development. Murphy (1962, 1972), R. W. White (1963), and Bernstein (see chapter 6) all note that learning can be a source of satisfaction. Satisfaction with success in school may help to overcome feelings based on early childhood of having to be dependent upon others in realizing satisfaction of needs. As Bernstein notes, the courage to take chances and to try to solve new and challenging problems, in turn, must be based on the assumption that mastery is possible, stemming from an enhanced sense of self.

Emergence of the courage to try, as both Bernstein and also Wolf (chapter 15) note, is based not just on the child's experience of good enough caretaking, understood as a function of oneself, but also on continuing, empathically expressed respect of caretakers and, later, teachers. As Kohut (1971, 1977) and Wolf (1977) have suggested, feelings of well-being, including sense of confidence in tackling cognitive challenges, are based on a sense of cohesive self, particularly that aspect of the cohesive self emphasizing successful resolution of challenges. As Wolf (1977) notes:

> Kohut postulates that a calm but energetic feeling of well-being requires psychologically an enduringly balanced pattern of relationships polarized between a per-

son's largely unconscious ambitions on the one hand, and his similarly unconscious ideals on the other, with native talents serving as mediating structures between these two poles. This total configuration is experienced as a healthy sense of self, it evokes a strong subjective conviction of selfhood and has therefore been termed a "cohesive self" [p. 210].

To the extent that the caretaking which is provided across the first years of life, and initially experienced by the child as a function performed by the self, is experienced by the child as a failure to effectively resolve tensions inevitable across the course of development, this early experienced failure becomes the basis for later experience of the self as deficient and unable to attain feelings of coherence and integration, including modulation of ambitions and talents, leading to feelings of inner depletion often masked by grandiose achievements. This distortion of self corresponds to Winnicott's (1960b) description of the false self, or deficits in self-regard as portrayed by Kohut (1971, 1977) and associates (Tolpin, 1971) and it represents a collapse of feelings of cohesion and increased doubts that challenges can be mastered, or that trying to learn new material will be successful, and it presents particular difficulties in learning and in being able to succeed in school (Shane, 1984).

THE PLACE OF EMPATHY IN TEACHING AND LEARNING

Both as a method of observation, concerned with study of the impact of classroom and curriculum, and as a means for fostering the effectiveness of the teacher to teach and of the student to learn, the empathic method represents a cardinal contribution of psychoanalysis to the study of education. As a consequence of feeling understood and, as a result, feeling more integrated and able to learn, the empathic approach is central in fostering mastery of the curriculum. Indeed, it is through the use of this empathic method that the contribution of the psychoanalytic approach to the study of education may be transformed from the approach of cognitive psychology, as valuable as that approach is for the problems it seeks to study (Glaser, 1984), to an approach which is truly distinctive of clinical psychoanalytic inquiry. Many of these issues have been discussed in Bettelheim's (1950, 1955) classic volumes on teaching disturbed children, in Ekstein's (1969a) discussion of the curriculum, and in Jones's (1968) volume reporting on work with junior high school students who were participating in the experimental social studies program "Man, A Course of Study."

Jones was called in as a consultant when the junior high school social science curriculum, using films and other ethnographic materials, appeared not to be well accepted by students in one school, and he observed the children's reactions to the curriculum. For example, one film portrayed an Eskimo family leaving an older family member to die on the ice-pack. Jones noted that children seemed to have a difficult time discussing the meaning for them of what they saw in the film. Many of these children lived in homes shared with grandparents, and they were terrified by the consequences of deserting these grandparents. Working with these children in groups, based on his own empathic observation of their response to the film, Jones was able to foster discussion of students' own feelings and to use this discussion in order to help them master the curriculum. It is important to note that Jones was less concerned with the implications for mental health in the classroom than with the use of this empathic approach to the curriculum as a way of realizing the effectiveness of a course designed largely in terms of the principles of cognitive development. Learning was facilitated by recognizing the meaning of the curriculum for these children, and using this recognition as a part of the process of teaching.

This subjective dimension of learning, contained in the subjective meaning for the children of the Eskimo film, or subjective curriculum, the nature of which is appreciated using the empathic clinical method, together with the transferencelike response to the teacher, is a part of the process by which what the child learns in school becomes an enduring part of his or her own personal world. Educational experiences which foster the subjective curriculum are likely to be most effective in promoting learning (Schwab, 1954; Katz and Sanford, 1962; Jones, 1968). Just as contemporary education maintains that the curriculum must be relevant to the child's developing capacity for abstract or propositional knowledge, in a similar manner, appreciation of the child's unique experience of what takes place in school adds to the success of education in realizing its goals, from the preschool years to higher education. Without considering the child's own understanding of the experience of schooling, through empathic observation of the child's response to the curriculum, so well shown in Jones's study of the impact of "Man, A Course of Study," the curriculum remains two-dimensional and fails to become a part of the child's own world of experience.

In addition to the significance of the empathic method as a means for studying the impact of the curriculum, shown so well in Jones's study of the impact of "Man, A Course of Study," the very effort to understand the significance of the curriculum for these students enhanced their feelings of personal integration or self cohesion, leading to increased receptivity to new learning. Consistent with this view, Wolf (1982, 1983; see chapter 15) notes the value of this empathic mode of observation as a means of understanding the manner in which the analyst is used by the analysand as a selfobject or source of understanding during periods of personal crisis.

The ambiance of both the analytic and educational setting is enhanced as both analyst and teacher acknowledge the analysand or student's concerns and accept the need to be admired and to serve as a source of inspiration for continued efforts. Both Wolf (see chapter 15) and Bernstein (see chapter 6) suggest, in somewhat different terms, that classroom teachers, in the course of their everyday activities as teachers, perform many of the same functions for students in fostering learning, which are performed by the analyst within the psychoanalytic interview. Although the mutative interpretation (Strachey, 1934) is an indispensable element of the psychoanalyst's role, just as clear and organized presentation of the curriculum is indispensable for the teacher's role, in each instance, unless the analysand or student feels understood and supported through the analytic or learning alliance (Zetzel, 1958; Greenson, 1967), it is difficult for the analysand to have the courage to examine previously unacknowledged or disavowed wishes, or for the student to maintain the courage necessary to learn new and difficult material (Bernstein, chapter 6).

Idealization of favorite teachers who become not just models for students' own future hopes, but who also assist students to modify these hopes in terms of what may actually be attained, tempering grandiose expectations with realistic support and approval for new learning, in terms of goals which may more appropriately be realized (Schafer, n.d.) contributes to students' continuing efforts to attempt even more complex learning (Schafer, n.d.; Shane, 1984; Bernstein, chapter 6; Wolf, chapter 15). As Shane (1984) observes:

[A] child with unrealistically high ideals may unconsciously set standards for himself so unreasonable that he experiences a chronic sense of failure. Such children are often precocious. Their skills and talents may be above average, but their standards and ideals always

exceed them. They worry a great deal and are nagged
with doubts and fears of failure [p. 195].

Further, because of these unrealistic ideals, such accomplishments as a superbly written essay or a high test
score fail to provide a sense of satisfaction. Each new
attainment leads to increased depreciation and dispar-
agement of self, since these "real world" attainments pale
in comparison with the self's expectations.

One of the most difficult aspects of teaching involves
helping these talented young people to understand this
gulf between aspirations and actual attainment. While
in no way advocating that teachers should assume a therapeutic role, consistent with the psychoanalytic contribution to understanding the problems of learning and
going to school, use of the empathic method permits
teachers to recognize this dilemma so often faced by very
gifted students, and help these students to see this dilemma for themselves. The teacher's capacity to be of
help in resolving this dilemma is fostered by the student's
idealization of the teacher. Admiring a favorite teacher,
the student uses the teacher's more moderate goals as a
function of the self, permitting some reconciliation of this
disparity between ideals and attainments. In contrast
with psychoanalytic intervention, this use of the teacher
as part of the self development is not interpreted. Based
on empathic understanding of the student's dilemma, the
teacher is able to accept the student's use of the teacher
as an ideal in the continuing development of self.

Teachers often find it difficult to accept students'
needs to idealize them. Feeling concerns about their own
intellectual attainments which parallel those of students,
teachers may disparage these efforts by their students to
idealize them. In one prestigious college, a program was
developed in which faculty would serve as advisors for
first- and second-year students. The program foundered
when, after some months, faculty began to complain that

students "put them on a pedestal" and didn't sufficiently recognize their failings. Although distinguished in their own scholarly fields, many faculty felt vulnerable to the same concerns as their students, and were unable to accept students' needs to idealize them, and to use them in their own efforts to resolve the paradox between aspiration and attainment.

A number of studies, particularly those of personal development across the college years, have shown the significance for students' learning of the faculty's capacity to accept idealizations (Katz, 1962). For example, in a study of undergraduates in an elite men's college, Heath (1968) has shown that faculty most able to let themselves be admired and looked up to by students were also felt to be the most important when students were interviewed some years after completion of collegiate studies (Adelson, 1962). Further, Thistlewaite (1959) has shown that even at the most advanced level of doctoral education, such tempering of lofty goals is essential if students are to complete their dissertation research. The capacity of faculty to relate warmly with students was a more powerful predictor of later capacity for independent research than any other single attribute of graduate study.

Where faulty integration of the self has taken place, schooling itself may be arduous. Learning threatens a precarious integration of the self, challenging the student's tenuous esteem. In a residential treatment center for very bright but troubled children and adolescents, a number of innovations were created to teach these troubled children. Access to snacks was of some assistance in helping these children, at least for the moment, provide comfort for themselves even as they learned material which they believed to be beyond their ability. Scheduled work breaks, study in small groups, and a curriculum designed in terms of the interests of particular children, all were employed in teaching these children, along with continuity in classroom teachers over a number of years

(Hall, 1971), enhancing the teachers' capacity to assist students in the development of a stable self-structure. Particular effort was devoted to creation of a curriculum consonant with the child's fragile sense of self.

For example, one adolescent boy, feeling particularly vulnerable, was preoccupied with knighthood and King Arthur. Sexually assaulted and physically abused as a youngster, he believed that armor offered the only certain protection. As knowledgeable as any university-trained historian in styles of armor, he worked for a time as an apprentice at a well-known local museum specializing in the Middle Ages. At the same time, this adolescent boy read at the third-grade level, and was at about the second-grade level in his mathematical skills. A series of graded readings was designed concerning tales of King Arthur and his knights, as well as other myths of the same period. An arithmetic curriculum was designed using story problems based on alchemy! Even the spelling list was built around words relevant to that historical period.

After three years of a curriculum tailored to the needs of this gifted but troubled adolescent, he had gained six years of school achievement and was nearly up to grade. At the same time, while appreciating this student's talents, great effort was devoted to helping him realize the connection between preoccupation with chivalry and knighthood and feelings of particular vulnerability which were disguised as arrogance to such an extent that some faculty found it painful to work in the classroom with this young man.

Efforts at understanding, together with a shared concern to understand the meaning of the particular narrative of self and others constructed by this adolescent boy in a desperate search for wholeness, led to a marked decrease in arrogance, increased sense of self, and increased personal and academic competence. Indeed, efforts to understand the meaning of chivalry in this boy's life may have been as significant as the curriculum constructed on the basis of this understanding, in fostering academic progress. Feeling understood, it became possible for this adolescent to have the courage to overcome earlier deficits in learning which were so personally painful and so difficult to realize.

Recognition of the existence of personal meanings associated with the curriculum need not be viewed as compromising the function of the school in preparing the child for effective instrumental activity in the larger community, portrayed so well in Erikson's (1950) discussion of the tension between industry and inferiority in middle childhood. Clinical psychoanalytic perspectives should facilitate rather than interfere with learning in school. Learning is enhanced by an appreciation of such factors as the child's relationship with both teachers and fellow classmates, the personal significance of the curriculum, and the importance of a sense of self as a requisite for taking on the challenge of new learning.

It should be noted that this chapter has focused primarily on the significance of psychoanalytic perspectives for study of the student's participation in schooling. Parallel study is required of the teacher's participation in education. Prior formulations of psychoanalysis and education often have stressed the significance of the teacher for the child's learning. As a result of such expectations, increased strain is placed on the already overburdened teacher's role. Particularly in contemporary society, where public education has become so politicized, caution must be exercised in expecting overburdened classroom teachers to be both teachers and counselors. The hope that teachers may allow themselves to be idealized by their students does not imply that teachers must necessarily discuss this idealization with their students, but only that they understand the basis for this need for idealization.

FROM EXPERIENCE-DISTANT TO EXPERIENCE-NEAR PERSPECTIVES IN THE PSYCHOANALYTIC STUDY OF EDUCATION

Application of the concepts and methods of psychoanalysis to the study of learning and going to school was among the first areas of collaboration among psychoanalysis and other disciplines. Education and psychoanalysis both share common interests in the process of development and concern with the most effective form of intervention or remediation (E. Klein, 1945, 1949; Hoffer, 1945; Peller, 1946, 1956; Pearson, 1954). This collaboration has been particularly significant in the field of child analysis, where many of the first child analysts were also trained as educators. Indeed, some of the most enduring contributions to the study of problems in learning resulted from the unique educational and clinical perspectives of Anna Freud (1927), Dorothy Burlingham, Melanie Klein, August Aichorn (1925), Sigfried Bernfeld (1925), Richard Sterba, Willi Hoffer, and others. These pioneering contributions have been reviewed by Ekstein and Motto (1969), and reveal the scope and breadth of understanding of childhood made possible by psychoanalytically informed pedagogy.

At the same time, even in these early contributions, problems have continued in this alliance between the two disciplines. Earliest efforts at applying psychoanalytic concepts in the classroom stressed implications for mental hygiene and emphasized the importance of the classroom as the area in which retrospective-genetic propositions could be tested. Although some psychoanalytic educators had believed that psychoanalysis could become the dominant theory of pedagogy, it was clear that not all teachers could be analyzed, or that psychoanalysis could provide a complete theory of learning and development.

Freud's initial training in neurobiology had led him to accept the new positivism as the mode of investigation in psychoanalysis; application of this approach to the study of development had suggested both that psychological development could be understood in a manner analogous to the development of the nervous system in the primitive species which had been the subject of investigation during his years as an experimental scientist. This approach to processes such as fixation and regression, initially formulated in Freud's prepsychoanalytic study of developmental neurobiology, had inspired him to seek analogous phenomena, both in the clinical setting, which was necessarily retrospective, and the classroom, which provided an opportunity for prospective study. However, the very assumptions underlying Freud's earliest investigations were not derived from psychoanalysis itself but were based on continuing interest in validation of a biologically based theory of development.

Since this biologically formulated theory of function and mechanism was incompatible with psychoanalytic concern with issues of meaning and intent, it became clear that child study and treatment, in the classroom and the consulting room, could not provide observations which were required in order to provide validation for a biologically determined, epigenetic theory of psychological development (Cohler, 1972a,b). Since this view of development was founded outside the realm of experience, it was virtually impossible either to prove or disprove the assumptions regarding development which were postulated. Efforts to resolve this paradox through revision of the genetic point of view in terms of Piaget's genetic epistemology (Basch, 1977; Greenspan, 1979), another functional, biologically based formulation, appears not to have resolved fundamental problems in the creation of a psychoanalytic developmental psychology, a psychology of learning.

Initial disappointment in the use of psychoanalytically informed education and child study as a means of primary prevention, and as a source of observations for

the validation of the genetic point of view in metapsychology, led to problems in the continuing alliance between these two approaches to the study of development,
learning, and remediation. The tradition of ego psychology, which continued emphasis upon a nonexperiential
realm of observation in an effort to transform psychoanalysis into an experimental psychology, further increased the gulf between these two disciplines concerned
with development and change, and child study more generally. Experience-distant formulations of function and
mechanism characteristic of ego psychology were in striking contrast with the experience-near, empathically derived observations of the consulting room and the
classroom.

More recently, as a result both of the careful study of
the origins of psychoanalysis (Sulloway, 1979; Basch,
1984a), and also increased scrutiny of the philosophy of
science, both within psychoanalysis and the social sciences, there has been dramatic reconsideration of psychoanalytic contributions, and also reevaluation of
metapsychology, generally assumed to be the essential
contribution of psychoanalysis as a theory of mental functioning (Meissner, 1976, 1980). In part, this critical reevaluation has been inspired by a consensus that the
experimental approach of ego psychology led away from
what has been agreed as the basis of psychoanalytic contributions to the arts and letters and the social sciences.

G. Klein's (1976) critical review of ego psychology as
little more than a translation of psychoanalytic concepts
into terms more generally considered as a part of experimental psychology served as the impetus for the reevaluation of the essential contributions of psychoanalysis.
Klein's important statement, together with Gill's (1976)
efforts at clarifying the distinctive contributions of the
clinical theory of psychoanalysis, as contrasted with the
general theory, or metapsychology, which was seen as
little more than Freud's own statement of his philosophy

of science, together with Schafer's (1972, 1978, 1980–1981) discussion of the significance of meaning and action within psychoanalysis, clarified long-standing misunderstandings regarding the place of the general and clinical theories within psychoanalysis.

Reconsideration of the contribution of the place of metapsychology within psychoanalysis was also assisted by efforts at understanding the nature of psychoanalysis as a science, including such issues as proof and validity. While disagreeing in fundamental respects regarding the significance of validity as a test of psychoanalytic propositions, contributions of Polanyi (1974), Kohut (1959, 1971), and both Sherwood (1969) and Ricoeur (1970, 1977) have called attention to the disparity between the approach of psychoanalysis as a human science and empirical approaches which cannot accommodate the validity of empathy or disciplined clinical judgment as methods of study. Considered together with contributions of Geertz (1972, 1974), Habermas (1967, 1983), Rabinow and Sullivan (1979), and others, the emerging tradition of interpretive social science offers new promise for the creation of a means of disciplined, systematic study of wishes and intents, based on the study of meaning, which is most consonant with the subject matter of psychoanalysis.

Finally, recent interest in the study of self or person, as contrasted with hypothesized functions or mechanisms characteristic of ego psychology, has had important implications both for psychoanalysis as a discipline within the human sciences and for education itself. As a result of prospective investigations of development by psychoanalytically informed investigators such as Sander, Stechler, and Emde, from quite disparate points of view within psychoanalysis, concepts such as self coherence or personal integration have largely replaced the earlier, more mechanistic concept of the synthetic function of the ego as a means for describing the major integrative concept in the psychoanalytic study of the life cycle. Renewed interest in the self has led to increased concern with the meaning of learning for students, and increased appreciation of the role of the subjective curriculum, or the new educational psychology (Jones, 1966) for increasing the impact of schooling for students from preschool through high school and college.

Concern with the intrapersonal world, and with the manner in which teacher and curriculum are experienced by students, builds on pioneering psychoanalytic contributions in this area, as enhanced through increased appreciation of the importance of the teacher in helping students to modulate ambitions and attain appropriate goals. This emphasis upon the use of the empathic method of clinical psychoanalysis does not require that the teacher adopt a mental hygiene perspective, or that the teacher must be burdened with obligations to provide a corrective experience in the manner discussed in earlier psychoanalytic contributions to the study of education. Rather, it assumes that the empathic mode of understanding the student's experience of the curriculum is central to the task of teaching, as in clinical psychoanalysis. Efforts such as that described by Jones (1968) are focused on learning and curriculum, and not on remediation. Use of the empathic approach, and concern with the subjective curriculum, is essential to effective teaching, just as this empathic mode is essential to effective psychotherapy.

In this renewed study of the student's private world as a determinant of response to learning, it is important to include both traditional understandings of learning problems, including fear of competition with the experienced parents of early childhood, the focus of the nuclear conflict traditionally discussed in clinical psychoanalytic study of problems in learning, and more recent consideration of problems in modulating inner tensions and living up to hoped for goals and ideals, as factors relevant to problems in learning and going to school. Just as both sectors of personality are important in understanding clinical problems, each sector is important in understanding problems of learning in school. Concern with competition with classmates, and with possible retaliation of classmates envious of attainments, together with fears either of exceeding parental attainments, or of disappointing parental aspirations, all are relevant in understanding the basis of problems in going to school.

Indeed, the first specifically psychoanalytic contribution to education (M. Klein, 1923) portrayed a thirteen-year-old boy who disliked attending school because of his fear of standing up for recitation. This fear, in turn, was related to the child's concern with issues of competition, including concerns that schoolmates would taunt him if he were to be more successful in class exercises than they were. In each of the four cases discussed in this early contribution, Klein stresses the impact of the child's subjectively experienced concerns as the basis of the dislike of school. In each instance, the child felt particular concern regarding possible retaliation by envious classmates in response to the child's successful performance. Klein also relates the particular meaning attributed by children to particular letters and numbers as obstacles to learning. For example, the number 3 was particularly significant for one six-year-old boy learning to count because of feelings of exclusion from the close relationship between his parents.

Klein (1931) further demonstrated the impact of feelings of envy and alternating feelings of destructive rage and self-directed aggression in the case of a seven-year-old boy with a learning inhibition. Issues of guilt over expression of angry and destructive feelings, particularly as expressed in terms of sexual feelings toward his mother, created such anxiety that the child was unable to learn in school. Cohler (1972a) describes an overweight, emotionally empty girl unable to learn the 8's in the multiplication tables because of the meaning of "eight" and "ate," reflecting her wish to devour others in order to have them inside her and replace these feelings of loneliness. This same meaning of the number 8 is reflected more generally in contemporary education: Sesame Street, the popular children's television learning program, teaching the quantity of eight, shows a number of successively larger eight-legged creatures, each devouring smaller eight-legged creatures.

Blanchard (1946) describes the problems of two children with reading disabilities unable to learn the letter "c" because of its association with an open mouth, ready to bite. Each child had a baby sister, and each expressed rage at the baby, as well as fear of retaliation for such feelings. Many of the same issues are portrayed dramatically in Sendak's (1963) children's book *Where the Wild Things Are.* Koff (1960) further elaborates the power of Klein's position for understanding the basis of problems in both letter and number forms, noting the manner in which such forms become a part of censorship of unacceptable wishes, appearing particularly in connection with visual learning and remaining active in the realm of fantasy.

These earlier psychoanalytic contributions, focused largely on meaning rather than structure of thought as the basis of psychoanalytic contributions to the study of learning and going to school, clearly recognized the importance of understanding the meaning for the child of particular aspects of the curriculum (Fenichel, 1945; Sterba, 1945; Kris, 1948, 1950). For example, Strachey (1930), discussing problems of learning to read, notes the extent to which some students seem to be "omnivorous" readers, devouring as much material as possible. Reading is often facilitated by eating at the same time: Bettelheim (1969a), discussing the education of culturally disadvantaged youngsters, notes the many problems these children encounter in having to learn on an empty stomach, feeling hungry and depleted at a time when they are expected to learn new material. Ekstein (1969a) has noted that learning in school is parallel in many ways to learning the capacity to take in nourishment during earliest infancy. As the child receives essential nutriments through the process of learning he also learns to love and to be loved, suggesting not only that the curriculum provides intellectual sustenance, but also plays an important role in the student's development of a sense of self.

There is much discussion today within psychoanalysis of the psychology of the self, and somewhat contradictory formulations of self development and psychopathology. Much of this controversy has focused on the nature and content of interpretations in the evolving psychoanalytic process as the most appropriate and mutative forms of clinical intervention (Strachey, 1934; Fenichel, 1938–1939; Loewald, 1960; Schafer, 1978; Gill, 1982; Kohut, 1984). While there are many ways in which this controversy may be understood, viewed from a historical perspective, this controversy illustrates a shift from psychoanalysis as a means for explaining mechanisms to concern with meanings and intents of the analysand's communications and presently maintained life story. From the perspective of psychoanalytic contributions to the study of learning and going to school, more recent discussion of the mutative quality of the interpretation, across theoretical perspectives, has emphasized the importance of concern with issues of self and meaning.

Over the past several years there has been marked controversy regarding the role of metapsychology and the natural science perspective within psychoanalysis (Holzman, 1985; Wallerstein, 1986; Anthony and Cohler, 1987). Study of the early history of psychoanalysis has suggested that this natural science perspective was principally an expression of Freud's world view rather than an essential contribution of psychoanalysis toward the study of developmental processes. The significant contribution of psychoanalysis to the study of developmental processes is to be found in the clinical theory rather than in the metapsychology. Application of the clinical theory to the study of education has resulted in increased concern with the meaning of the schooling experience for students, including maintenance of feelings of self-worth and confidence. This increased focus on the experience-near or subjective world of the student marks a return to the tradition which marked initial contributions of psychoanalysis to education, but with a significant addition. While, as in these initial contributions of M. Klein, Strachey, Blanchard, Ekstein, and Motto, there is concern with the personal significance of the curriculum, more recent study does not attempt the theoretical reification which marked initial contributions.

Psychoanalytic inquiry regarding education should focus both on factors interfering with learning, but also those contributing to enhanced learning. A psychoanalytically informed study of the intrapersonal world of the classroom, using the empathic method so central to psychoanalysis, focusing on the meaning for students of both classroom and curriculum, offers renewed promise for understanding the role of earlier experiences in determining students' response to the classroom, as well as for enhancing the learning process itself.

REFERENCES

Abraham, K. (1921), Contribution to a discussion on tic. In: *Selected Papers on Psychoanalysis*. New York: Basic Books, 1953, pp. 323–325.

———— (1924), A short study on the development of the libido. In: *Selected Papers on Psychoanalysis*. New York: Basic Books, 1953, pp. 418–501.

Abrams, S., reporter (1971), Models of the psychic apparatus. *J. Amer. Psychoanal. Assn.*, 18:131–142.

Adelson, J. (1962), The teacher as a model. In: *The American College: A Psychological and Social Interpretation of Higher Learning*. New York: John Wiley, pp. 396–417.

Aichorn, A. (1925), *Wayward Youth*. New York: Viking Press, 1953.

Alexander, J., & Friedman, J. (1980), The question of the self and self esteem. *Internat. Rev. Psychoanal.*, 7:365–374.

Anthony, E. J., reporter (1961), Learning difficulties in childhood. *J. Amer. Psychoanal. Assn.*, 9:124–134.

—— (1976), Freud, Piaget, and human knowledge: Some comparisons and contrasts. *The Annual of Psychoanalysis*, 4:253–280. New York: International Universities Press.

—— Cohler, B. (1987), eds., *The Invulnerable Child.* New York: Guilford Press.

Applegarth, A. (1977), Psychic energy reconsidered: A critique. *J. Amer. Psychoanal. Assn.*, 25:599–602.

Aronson, G., reporter (1972), Learning theory and psychoanalytic theory. *J. Amer. Psychoanal. Assn.*, 20:622–637.

Basch, M. (1976), Theory formation in chapter VII: A critique. *J. Amer. Psychoanal. Assn.*, 24:62–100.

—— (1977), Developmental psychology and explanatory theory in psychoanalysis. *The Annual of Psychoanalysis*, 5:229–263. New York: International Universities Press.

—— (1983a), The concept of the self: An operational definition. In: *Developmental Approaches to the Self,* ed. B. Lee & G. G. Noam. New York: Plenum Press, pp. 7–58.

—— (1983b), Empathic understanding: A review of the concept and some theoretical considerations. *J. Amer. Psychoanal. Assn.*, 31:101–126.

—— (1983c), Some theoretical and methodological implications of self psychology. In: *The Future of Psychoanalysis,* ed. A. Goldberg. New York: International Universities Press, pp. 431–442.

—— (1984a), The selfobject theory of motivation and the history of psychoanalysis. In: *Kohut's Legacy: Contributions to Self Psychology,* ed. P. Stepansky & A. Goldberg. Hillsdale, NJ: Analytic Press, pp. 3–20.

—— (1984b), Selfobjects and selfobject transference: Theoretical implications. In: *Kohut's Legacy: Contributions to Self Psychology,* ed. P. Stepansky & A. Goldberg. Hillsdale, NJ: Analytic Press, pp. 21–42.

—— (1984c), Selfobjects, development, and psychotherapy. In: *Kohut's Legacy: Contributions to Self Psychology,* ed. P. Stepansky & A. Goldberg. Hillsdale, NJ: Analytic Press, pp. 157–171.

Berger, P., & Luckmann, T. (1966), *The Social Construction of Reality.* Garden City, NY: Doubleday/Anchor Books, 1967.

Bernfeld, S. (1925), *Sisyphus, or the Limits of Education,* trans. F. Lilge. Berkeley: University of California Press, 1973.

—— (1941), Freud's earliest theories on the school of Helmholtz. *Psychoanal. Quart.*, 13:341–362.

—— (1949), Freud's scientific beginnings. *Imago*, 6:163–196.

—— (1951), Sigmund Freud, M.D., 1882–1885. *Internat. J. Psycho-Anal.*, 32:204–217.

Bettelheim, B. (1950), *Love Is Not Enough*. New York: Free Press/Macmillan.
―――― (1955), *Truants from Life*. New York: Free Press/Macmillan.
―――― (1969a), Psychoanalysis and education. *School Rev.*, 77:73–86.
―――― (1969b), The education of emotionally and culturally deprived children. In: *From Learning to Love to Love of Learning*, ed. R. Ekstein & R. Motto. New York: Brunner/Mazel, pp. 235–244.
―――― (1983), *Freud and Man's Soul*. New York: Alfred A. Knopf.
Blanchard, P. (1946), Psychoanalytic contributions to the problem of reading disabilities. *The Psychoanalytic Study of the Child*, 2:163–187. New York: International Universities Press.
Blum, H. (1982), Theories of the self and psychoanalytic concepts: Discussion. *J. Amer. Psychoanal. Assn.*, 30:959–978.
Bornstein, M., & Silver, D., eds. (1981), On empathy (special issue). *Psychoanal. Inq.*, 1/3:322–489.
Brenner, C., (1980), Metapsychology and psychoanalytic theory. *Psychoanal. Quart.*, 59:189–214.
Breuer, J., & Freud, S. (1895), Studies on Hysteria. *Standard Edition*, 2. London: Hogarth Press, 1955.
Broughton, J. (1978), The development of concepts of self, mind, reality, and knowledge. In: *New Directions for Child Development: Social Cognition*, ed. W. Damon. San Francisco: Jossey-Bass, pp. 75–100.
―――― (1981), Piaget's structural developmental psychology, IV: Knowledge without a self and without history. *Hum. Develop.*, 24:525–550.
Buhler, C. (1954), The reality principle. *Amer. J. Psychother.*, 8:626–647.
Buie, D. (1981), Empathy: Its nature and limitations. *J. Amer. Psychoanal. Assn.*, 29:281–307.
Chattah, L., reporter (1981), Metapsychology: Its cultural and scientific roots. *J. Amer. Psychoanal. Assn.*, 29:689–698.
Cobliner, W. G. (1965), The Geneva school of genetic psychology and psychoanalysis. In: *The First Year of Life*, ed. R. Spitz. New York: International Universities Press, pp. 301–356.
Cohler, B. (1972a), Psychoanalysis, adaptation and education: I. Reality and its appraisal. *Psycholog. Rep.*, 30:695–718.
―――― (1972b), Psychoanalysis, adaptation, and education: II. The development of thinking. *Psycholog. Rep.*, 30:719–740.
―――― (1980a), Developmental perspectives on the psychology of the self in childhood. In: *Advances in Self Psychology*, ed. A. Goldberg. New York: International Universities Press, pp. 69–116.
―――― (1980b), Adult developmental psychology and reconstruction in psychoanalysis. In: *The Course of Life*, Vol. 3, ed. S. Greenspan & G. Pollock. Washington, DC: U.S. Government Printing Office, pp. 149–201.
―――― (1982), Personal narrative and life-course. In: *Life-Span Behavior and Development*, Vol. 4, ed. P. Bottes & O. G. Brim, Jr. New York: Academic Press, pp. 206–243.

—— (1984), Approaches to the study of development in psychiatric education. In: *The Role of Psychoanalysis in Psychiatric Education*, ed. S. Weissman & R. Thurnblad. New York: International Universities Press, 1987.

—— Grunebaum, H. (1981), *Mothers, Grandmothers, and Daughters*. New York: John Wiley.

Cole, M., & Scribner, S. (1974), *Culture and Thought*. New York: John Wiley.

Decarie, T. G. (1965), *Intelligence and Affectivity in Early Childhood*. New York: International Universities Press.

Eagle, M. (1980), George Klein's *Psychoanalytic Theory* in perspective. *Psychoanal. Rev.*, 67:179–195.

Edelson, M. (1984), *Hypothesis and Evidence in Psychoanalysis*. Chicago: University of Chicago Press.

Eissler, K. (1978), Biographical sketch, Sigmund Freud. In: *Sigmund Freud*, ed. E. Freud, L. Freud, & I. Grubrich-Simitis. New York: Harcourt, Brace & Jovanovich/Helen and Kurt Wolff, pp. 10–39.

Ekstein, R. (1969a), Psychoanalytic notes on the function of the curriculum. In: *From Learning to Love to Love of Learning*, ed. R. Ekstein & R. Motto. New York: Brunner/Mazel, pp. 47–57.

—— (1969b), The child, the teacher, and learning. In: *From Learning to Love to Love of Learning*, ed. R. Ekstein & R. Motto. New York: Brunner/Mazel, pp. 65–76.

—— Motto, R. (1969), Psychoanalysis and education—an historical account. In: *From Learning to Love to Love of Learning*, ed. R. Ekstein & R. Motto. New York: Brunner/Mazel, pp. 3–27.

Emde, R. (1980), Ways of thinking about new knowledge and further research from a developmental orientation. *Psychoanal. & Contemp. Thought*, 3:213–235.

—— (1981), Changing models of infancy and the nature of early development: Remodeling the foundation. *J. Amer. Psychoanal. Assn.*, 29:179–219.

—— (1985), From adolescence to midlife: Remodeling the structure of adult development. *J. Amer. Psychoanal. Assn.*, 33 (Supplement):59–111.

Erikson, E. H. (1950), *Childhood and Society*. New York: W. W. Norton, 1964.

Feffer, M. (1982), *The Structure of Freudian Thought*. New York: International Universities Press.

Fenichel, O. (1938–1939), *Problems of Psychoanalytic Technique*. Albany, NY: Psychoanalytic Quarterly Press, 1941.

—— (1945), The means of education. *The Psychoanalytic Study of the Child*, 1:281–292. New York: International Universities Press.

Ferenczi, S. (1913), Stages in the development of a sense of reality. In: *First Contributions to Psychoanalysis*. New York: Brunner/Mazel, 1980, pp. 213–239.

Fliess, R. (1942), The metapsychology of the analyst. *Psychoanal. Quart.,* 11:211–227.

Fraiberg, S. (1969), Libidinal object constancy and mental representation. *The Psychoanalytic Study of the Child,* 24:9–47. New York: International Universities Press.

Frank, A. (1979), Two theories or one? or none? *J. Amer. Psychoanal. Assn.,* 27:169–207.

Freeman, M. (1984), History, narrative, and life-span developmental knowledge. *Hum. Develop.,* 27:1–19.

Freud, A. (1927), The relation between psychoanalysis and pedagogy. In: *Psychoanalysis for Teachers and Parents,* trans. B. Low. New York: Emerson Books, 1954, pp. 92–114.

―――― (1954), Psychoanalysis and education. *The Psychoanalytic Study of the Child,* 9:9–15. New York: International Universities Press.

―――― (1976), Dynamic psychology and education. In: *Collected Papers,* Vol. 8. New York: International Universities Press, 1981, pp. 307–314.

Freud S. (1895), Project for a scientific psychology. *Standard Edition,* 1:295–387. London: Hogarth Press, 1966.

―――― (1896a), Letter 41. In: *The Origins of Psychoanalysis: Letters to Wilhelm Fliess, Drafts, Notes: 1887–1902* ed. M. Bonaparte, A. Freud, & E. Kris. New York: Basic Books, 1954, pp. 156–157.

―――― (1896b), Letter 52. In: *The Origins of Psychoanalysis: Letters to Wilhelm Fliess, Drafts, Notes: 1887–1902,* ed. M. Bonaparte, A. Freud, & E. Kris. New York: Basic Books, 1954, pp. 173–181.

―――― (1896c), Further remarks on the neuropsychoses of defense. *Standard Edition,* 3:159–185. London: Hogarth Press, 1962.

―――― (1897a), Letter 58. In: *The Origins of Psychoanalysis: Letters to Wilhelm Fliess, Drafts, Notes: 1887–1902,* ed. M. Bonaparte, A. Freud, & E. Kris. New York: Basic Books, 1954, pp. 191–192.

―――― (1897b), Letter 59. In: *The Origins of Psychoanalysis: Letters to Wilhelm Fliess, Drafts, Notes: 1887–1902,* ed. M. Bonaparte, A. Freud, & E. Kris. New York: Basic Books, 1954, p. 193.

―――― (1897c), Letter 72. In: *The Origins of Psychoanalysis: Letters to Wilhelm Fliess, Drafts, Notes: 1887–1902,* ed. M. Bonaparte, A. Freud, & E. Kris. New York: Basic Books, 1954, pp. 225–227.

―――― (1898), Letter 84. In: *The Origin of Psychoanalysis: Letters to Wilhelm Fliess, Drafts, Notes: 1887–1902,* ed. M. Bonaparte, A. Freud, & E. Kris. New York: Basic Books, 1954, pp. 246–247.

―――― (1900), The Interpretation of Dreams. *Standard Edition,* 4&5. London: Hogarth Press, 1958.

―――― (1901), The psychopathology of everyday life. *Standard Edition,* 6. London: Hogarth Press, 1960.

―――― (1905a), Three essays on the theory of sexuality. *Standard Edition,* 7:135–243. London: Hogarth Press, 1953.

―――― (1905b), Fragment of an analysis of a case of hysteria. *Standard Edition,* 7:3–124. London: Hogarth Press, 1953.

—— (1909a), Analysis of a phobia in a five year old boy. *Standard Edition*, 1:5–152. London: Hogarth Press, 1955.

—— (1909b), Notes upon a case of obsessional neurosis. *Standard Edition*, 11:153–318. London: Hogarth Press, 1955.

—— (1910a), Five lectures on psychoanalysis. *Standard Edition*, 11:9–58. London: Hogarth Press, 1957.

—— (1910b), Leonardo Da Vinci and a memory of his childhood. *Standard Edition*, 11:63–138. London: Hogarth Press, 1957.

—— (1911), Formulations on the two principles of mental functioning. *Standard Edition*, 12:218–226. London: Hogarth Press, 1958.

—— (1912), Recommendations to physicians practising psychoanalysis. *Standard Edition*, 12:109–121. London: Hogarth Press, 1958.

—— (1913), The claims of psychoanalysis to scientific interest. *Standard Edition*, 13:165–192. London: Hogarth Press, 1955.

—— (1914a), Remembering, repeating, and working through. *Standard Edition*, 12:147–156. London: Hogarth Press, 1958.

—— (1914b), On narcissism: An introduction. *Standard Edition*, 14:73–104. London: Hogarth Press, 1957.

—— (1914–1918), From the history of an infantile neurosis. *Standard Edition*, 17:1–122. London: Hogarth Press, 1955.

—— (1915), The unconscious. *Standard Edition*, 14:166–216. London: Hogarth Press, 1957.

—— (1915–1917a), The Introductory Lectures on Psychoanalysis. *Standard Edition*, 15/16. London: Hogarth Press, 1961–1963.

—— (1915–1917b), Mourning and melancholia. *Standard Edition*, 14:239–258. London: Hogarth Press, 1957.

—— (1917), A metapsychological supplement to the theory of dreams. *Standard Edition*, 14:222–236. London: Hogarth Press, 1951.

—— (1920a), The psychogenesis of a case of homosexuality in a woman. *Standard Edition*, 18:145–172. London: Hogarth Press, 1955.

—— (1920b), Beyond the pleasure principle. *Standard Edition*, 18:7–66. London: Hogarth Press, 1955.

—— (1920c), Group psychology and the analysis of the ego. *Standard Edition*, 18:65–144. London: Hogarth Press, 1955.

—— (1923), The ego and the id. *Standard Edition*, 9:12–59. London: Hogarth Press, 1961.

—— (1925a), An autobiographical study. *Standard Edition*, 20:7–76. London: Hogarth Press, 1959.

—— (1925b), Preface to Aichorn's *Wayward Youth*. *Standard Edition*, 9:273–275. London: Hogarth Press, 1961.

—— (1930), Civilization and Its Discontents. *Standard Edition*, 21:64–148. London: Hogarth Press, 1961.

—— (1932–1933), New Introductory Lectures on Psychoanalysis. *Standard Edition*, 22:5–184. London: Hogarth Press, 1964.

—— (1937a), Analysis terminable and interminable. *Standard Edition*, 23:209–254. London: Hogarth Press, 1964.

—— (1937b), Constructions in analysis. *Standard Edition*, 23:144–208. London: Hogarth Press, 1964.

—— (1939), Moses and Monotheism. *Standard Edition*, 23:1–208. London: Hogarth Press, 1964.

Frosch, J. (1962), A note on reality constancy. In: *Psychoanalysis—A General Psychology: Essays in Honor of Heinz Hartmann*, ed. R. Lowenstein, L. Newman, M. Schur, & A. Solnit. New York: International Universities Press, pp. 349–376.

Furer, M., reporter (1962), Psychic development and the prevention of mental illness. *J. Amer. Psychoanal. Assn.*, 10:606–616.

Gadamer, H. G. (1970), *Harmeneutik und Ideologikritik*. Frankfurt: Suhrkamp.

Gedo, J. (1979), *Beyond Interpretation: Toward a Revised Theory of Psychoanalysis*. New York: International Universities Press.

—— Goldberg, A. (1973), *Models of the Mind: A Psychoanalytic Theory*. Chicago: University of Chicago Press.

Geertz, C. (1972), Deep play: Notes on the Balinese cockfight. *Daedalus*, 11:1–37.

—— (1974), From the native's point of view: On the nature of anthropological understanding. In: *Local Knowledge: Further Essays in Interpretive Anthropology*, ed. C. Geertz. New York: Basic Books, 1983, pp. 55–72.

Gelman, R., & Baillargeon, R. (1983), A review of some Piagetian concepts. In: *Handbook of Child Psychology*, Vol. 3, ed. J. Flavell & E. Markman. (P. H. Mussen, General Editor). New York: John Wiley, pp. 167–230.

Gergen, K. (1977), Stability, change, and chance in understanding human development. In: *Life-Span Developmental Psychology: Dialectical Perspectives*, ed. N. Daton & H. Reese. New York: Academic Press, pp. 136–158.

—— (1982), *Toward Transformation in Social Knowledge*. New York: Springer.

Gill, M. M. (1976), Metapsychology is not psychology. In: Psychology versus Metapsychology: Psychoanalytic Essays in Memory of George S. Klein, ed. M. M. Gill & P. Holzman. *Psychological Issues*, Monograph 36, 1/9:71–105. New York: International Universities Press.

—— (1977), Psychic energy reconsidered: Discussion. *J. Amer. Psychoanal. Assn.*, 25:581–598.

—— (1982), *Analysis of Transference*, Vol. 1. New York: International Universities Press.

—— (1983), The point of view of psychoanalysis: Energy discharge or person? *Psychoanal. & Contemp. Thought*, 6:523–552.

—— Klein, G. (1964), The structuring of drive and reality: David Rapaport's contributions to psychoanalysis and psychology. *Internat. J. Psycho-Anal.*, 45:483–498.

Glaser, R., (1984), Education and thinking: The role of knowledge. *Amer. Psycholog.*, 39:93–104.

Glover, E. (1930), Grades of ego-differentiation. In: *On the Early Development of Mind.* New York: International Universities Press, 1956, pp. 112–122.

—— (1932a), A psychoanalytic approach to the classification of mental disorders. In: *On the Early Development of Mind.* New York: International Universities Press, 1956, pp. 161–186.

—— (1932b), On the etiology of drug addiction. In: *On the Early Development of Mind.* New York: International Universities Press, 1956, pp. 187–215.

Goldberg, A. (1982), The self of psychoanalysis. In: *Psychosocial Theories of the Self,* ed. B. Lee. New York: Plenum Press, pp. 3–22.

—— (1983), Self psychology and alternative perspectives on internalization. In: *Reflections on Self Psychology,* ed. J. Lichtenberg & S. Kaplan. Hillsdale, NJ: Analytic Press, pp. 297–312.

Greenson, R. (1960), Empathy and its vicissitudes. *Internat. J. Psycho-Anal.,* 41:418–424.

—— (1967), *The Technique and Practice of Psychoanalysis,* Vol 1. New York: International Universities Press.

Greenspan, S. (1975), A Consideration of Some Learning Variables in the Context of Psychoanalytic Theory: Toward a Psychoanalytic Learning Perspective. *Psychological Issues,* Monograph 33, 1/9. New York: International Universities Press.

—— (1979), Intelligence and Adaptation: An Integration of Psychoanalytic and Piagetian Developmental Psychology. *Psychological Issues,* Monograph 47/48, 3&4/12. New York: International Universities Press.

Guntrip, H. (1961), *Personality Structure and Human Interaction.* New York: International Universities Press.

Habermas, J. (1967), *Knowledge and Human Interests.* Boston: Beacon Press, 1971.

—— (1983), Interpretive social science vs. hermeneuticism. In: *Social Science as Moral Inquiry,* ed. N. Haan, R. Bellah, P. Rabinow, & W. Sullivan. New York: Columbia University Press, pp. 251–269.

Haeckel, E. (1868), *Natural History of Creation. (Naturaliche Schopfungsgesichte).* Berlin: Georg Reimer, 1968.

Hall, D. (1971), A case for teacher continuity. *School Rev.,* 80:27–49.

Haroutunian, S. (1983), *Equilibrium in the Balance: A Study of Psychological Explanation.* New York: Springer-Verlag.

Hartmann, E. (1983), From the biology of dreaming to the biology of the mind. *The Psychoanalytic Study of the Child,* 37:303–335. New Haven, CT: Yale University Press.

Hartmann, H. (1939), *Ego Psychology and the Problem of Adaptation.* New York: International Universities Press.

—— (1950), Comments on the psychoanalytic theory of the ego. In:

Essays on Ego Psychology. New York: International Universities Press, 1964, pp. 113–141.

—— (1951), Technical implications of ego psychology. In: *Essays on Ego Psychology.* New York: International Universities Press, 1964, pp. 142–154.

—— (1952), The mutual influences in the development of ego and id. In: *Essays on Ego Psychology.* New York: International Universities Press, 1964, pp. 155–182.

—— (1953), Contribution to the metapsychology of schizophrenia. In: *Essays on Ego Psychology.* New York: International Universities Press, 1964, pp. 241–267.

—— (1956), Notes on the reality principle. In: *Essays on Ego Psychology.* New York: International Universities Press, 1964, pp. 241–267.

—— Kris, E. (1945), The genetic approach in psychoanalysis. *The Psychoanalytic Study of the Child,* 1:11–30. New York: International Universities Press.

—— —— Lowenstein, R. (1946), Comments on the formation of psychic structure. *The Psychoanalytic Study of the Child,* 2:11–38. New York: International Universities Press.

Heath, D. (1968), *Growing Up in College: Liberal Education and Maturity.* San Francisco: Jossey-Bass.

Hirsch, E. D. (1967), *Validity in Interpretation.* New Haven, CT: Yale University Press.

—— (1976), *The Aims of Interpretation.* Chicago: University of Chicago Press.

Hobson, J. A., & McCarley, R. (1977), The brain as dream state generator: An activation-synthesis hypothesis of the dream process. *Amer. J. Psychiat.,* 34:1335–1348.

Hoffer, W. (1945), Psychoanalytic education. *The Psychoanalytic Study of the Child,* 1:293–307. New York: International Universities Press.

Holt, R. R. (1961), Clinical judgement as a disciplined inquiry. *J. Nerv. & Ment. Dis.,* 133:369–382.

—— (1962), A critical examination of Freud's concept of bound vs. free cathexis. *J. Amer. Psychoanal. Assn.,* 10:475–525.

—— (1965), A review of some of Freud's biological assumptions and their influence on his theories. In: *Psychoanalysis and Current Biological Thought,* ed. N. S. Greenfield & W. C. Lewis. Madison: University of Wisconsin Press, pp. 93–124.

—— ed. (1967), Motives and Thought: Psychoanalytic Essays in Honor of David Rapaport, *Psychological Issues,* Monograph 18/19, 2&3/5. New York: International Universities Press.

—— (1976), Drive or wish? A reconsideration of the psychoanalytic theory of motivation. In: Psychology versus Metapsychology: Essays in Memory of George S. Klein, ed. M.M. Gill & P. Holzman. *Psychological Issues,* Monograph 36, 1/9:158–197. New York: International Universities Press.

————— (1981), The death and transfiguration of metapsychology. *Internat. J. Psycho-Anal.*, 8:129–143.

Holzman, P. (1985), Psychoanalysis: Is the therapy destroying the science? *J. Amer. Psychoanal. Assn.*, 33:725–770.

Home, H. J. (1966), The concept of mind. *Internat. J. Psycho-Anal.*, 47:42–49.

Horton, P. (1981), *Soothing: The Missing Dimension in Psychiatry.* Chicago: University of Chicago Press.

Hoy, D. (1978), *The Critical Circle: Literature, History, and Philosophical Hermeneutics.* Berkeley: University of California Press.

Hug-Hellmuth, H. (1919), *A Study of the Mental Life of the Child.* Washington, DC: Nervous and Mental Diseases Publishing Company.

Huizenga, J. (1983), The relationship of self-esteem and narcissism. In: *The Development and Sustaining of Self-Esteem in Childhood,* ed. J. Mack & S. Ablon. New York: International Universities Press, pp. 151–162.

Jackson, E., Campos, J., & Fischer, K. (1978), The question of decalage between object permanence and person permanence. *Develop. Psychol.*, 14:1–10.

Jacobson, E. (1964), *The Self and the Object World.* New York: International Universities Press.

Jacobson, J. G. (1983), The structural theory and the representational world: Developmental and biological considerations. *Psychoanal. Quart.*, 52:543–563.

Jones, E. (1953), *The Life and Work of Sigmund Freud,* Vol. 1. New York: Basic Books.

————— (1966), Education in depth and the new curricula. In: *Contemporary Educational Psychology,* ed. R. Jones. New York: Harper Torchbooks, pp. 1–16.

————— (1968), *Fantasy and Feeling in Education.* New York: New York University Press.

Kagan, J. (1980), Perspectives on continuity. In: *Constancy and Change in Human Development,* ed. O. G. Brim, Jr., & J. Kagan. Cambridge, MA: Harvard University Press, pp. 26–74.

Kandel, E. (1983), From metapsychology to molecular biology: Explorations into the nature of anxiety. *Amer. J. Psychiat.*, 140:1277–1293.

Katz, J. (1962), Personality and interpersonal relations in the college classroom. In: *The American College,* ed. N. Sanford. New York: John Wiley, pp. 365–395.

————— Sanford, N., (1962), The curriculum in the perspective of the theory of personality development. In: *The American College,* ed. N. Sanford. New York: John Wiley, pp. 418–444.

Kegan, R. (1982), *The Evolving Self.* Cambridge, MA: Harvard University Press.

————— (1983), A neo-Piagetian approach to object relations. In: *De-*

velopmental Approaches to the Self, ed. B. Lee & G. G. Noam.
New York: Plenum Press, pp. 267–307.

Kernberg, O. (1982), Self, ego, affects, and drives. *J. Amer. Psychoanal. Assn.,* 30:893–917.

Klein, E. (1945), The reluctance to go to school. *The Psychoanalytic Study of the Child,* 1:263–279. New York: International Universities Press.

———— (1949), Psychoanalytic aspects of school problems. *The Psychoanalytic Study of the Child,* 3/4:369–390. New York: International Universities Press.

Klein, G. (1976), *Psychoanalytic Theory: An Exploration of Essentials.* New York: International Universities Press.

Klein, M. (1923), The role of the school in the libidinal development of the child. In: *Contributions to Psychoanalysis: 1921–1945.* London: Hogarth Press, 1955, pp. 68–86.

———— (1931), A contribution to the theory of intellectual inhibition. *Internat. J. Psycho-Anal.,* 12:206–218.

Koff, R. (1960), A summarization of the literature on learning difficulties. Paper presented at Mid-winter meetings, American Psychoanalytic Association, New York.

Kohut, H. (1959), Introspection, empathy, and psychoanalysis: An examination of the relationship between mode of observation and theory. *J. Amer. Psychoanal. Assn.,* 7:459–483.

———— (1971), *The Analysis of the Self.* New York: International Universities Press.

———— (1974), Remarks about the formation of the self. In: *The Search for the Self: Selected Writings of Heinz Kohut, 1950–1978,* Vol. 2, ed. P. Ornstein. New York: International Universities Press, pp. 737–770.

———— (1977), *The Restoration of the Self.* New York: International Universities Press.

———— (1982), Introspection, empathy and the semi-circle of mental health. *Internat. J. Psycho-Anal.,* 63:395–407.

———— (1984), *How Does Analysis Cure?* ed. A. Goldberg & P. Stepansky. Chicago: University of Chicago Press.

———— Wolf, E. (1978), The disorders of the self and their treatment: An outline. *Internat. J. Psycho-Anal.,* 59:413–425.

Kris, E. (1948), On psychoanalysis and education. *Amer. J. Orthopsychiat.,* 28:622–634.

———— (1950), On preconscious mental processes. *Psychoanal. Quart.,* 19:540–560.

LaPlanche, J., & Pontalis, J. B. (1967), *The Language of Psychoanalysis,* trans. D. Nicholson-Smith. New York: W. W. Norton, 1973.

Lecky, P. (1945), *Self-consistency: A Theory of Personality.* Garden City, NY: Doubleday/Anchor Books, 1961.

Lee, B., Wertsch, J., & Stone, A. (1983), Towards a Vygotskian theory of the self. In: *Developmental Approaches to the Self*, ed. B. Lee & G. Noam. New York: Plenum Press, pp. 309–342.

Lewin, K. (1949), *Field Theory in Social Science*. New York: Harper & Row.

Lichtenberg, J. (1975), The development of the sense of self. *J. Amer. Psychoanal. Assn.*, 23:453–484.

——— (1980), Clinical application of the concept of a cohesive sense of self. *Internat. J. Psychoanal. Psychother.*, 8:85–114.

——— (1981), The empathic mode of perception and alternative vantage points for psychoanalytic work. In: On Empathy, ed. M. Bornstein & D. Silver. *Psychological Inquiry Monograph*, 1/3. New York: International Universities Press.

——— Bornstein, M., & Silver, D. (1984), *Empathy*. Hillsdale, NJ: Analytic Press.

Litowitz, B., & Litowitz, N. (1983), Development of verbal self expression. In: *The Future of Psychoanalysis*, ed. A. Goldberg. New York: International Universities Press, pp. 397–427.

Loewald, H. (1960), On the therapeutic action of psychoanalysis. *Internat. J. Psycho-Anal.*, 41:16–33.

McCarley, R., & Hobson, J. A. (1977), The neurobiological origins of psychoanalytic dream theory. *Amer. J. Psychiat.*, 134:1211–1221.

Mahler, M., & McDevitt, J. (1982), Thoughts on the emergence of the sense of self, with particular emphasis on the body self. *J. Amer. Psychoanal. Assn.*, 30:827–848.

——— Pine, F., & Bergman, A. (1975), *The Psychological Birth of the Human Infant*. New York: Basic Books.

Meissner, W. W., reporter (1976), New horizons in metapsychology: View and review. *J. Amer. Psychoanal. Assn.*, 24:161–180.

——— (1980), Metapsychology—Who needs it? *J. Amer. Psychoanal. Assn.*, 28:921–938.

——— (1983), Phenomenology of the self. In: *The Future of Psychoanalysis*, ed. A. Goldberg. New York: International Universities Press, pp. 65–96.

Modell, A. (1978), The nature of psychoanalytic knowledge. *J. Amer. Psychoanal. Assn.*, 26:641–658.

——— (1981), Does metapsychology still exist? *Internat. J. Psycho-Anal.*, 62:391–402.

Moore, B., & Fine, B. (1968), *A Glossary of Psychoanalytic Terms and Concepts*. New York: American Psychoanalytic Association.

Murphy, L. (1962), *The Widening World of Childhood*. New York: Basic Books.

——— (1972), Some mutual contributions of psychoanalysis and child development. *Psychoanal. & Contemp. Thought*, 2:99–123.

Neugarten, B. (1969), Continuities and discontinuities of psychological issues into adult life. *Hum. Develop.*, 12:121–130.

——— (1979), Time, age and the life-cycle. *Amer. J. Psychiat.*, 136:887–894.

Noam, G. G., Kohlberg, L., & Snarey, J. (1983), Steps toward a model of the self. In: *Developmental Approaches to the Self*, ed. B. Lee & G. G. Noam. New York: Plenum Press, pp. 59–142.

Novey, S. (1968), *The Second Look: The Reconstruction of Personal History in Psychiatry and Psychoanalysis*. Baltimore, MD: Johns Hopkins University Press.

Noy, P. (1979), The psychoanalytic theory of cognitive development. *The Psychoanalytic Study of the Child*, 34:169–216. New Haven, CT: Yale University Press.

Parsons, T. (1952), The superego and the theory of social systems. In: *Social Structure and Personality*. New York: Free Press, 1964, pp. 17–33.

———— (1955), Family structure and the socialization of the child. In: *Family, Socialization and Interaction Process*, ed. T. Parsons & F. Bales. New York: Free Press, pp. 35–131.

———— (1958), Social structure and the development of personality: Freud's contribution to the integration of psychology and sociology. In: *Social Structure and Personality*. New York: Free Press, pp. 78–111.

Pearson, G. (1954), *Psychoanalysis and the Education of the Child*. New York: W. W. Norton.

Peller, L. (1946), Incentives to development and means of early education. *The Psychoanalytic Study of the Child*, 2:397–415. New York: International Universities Press.

———— (1956), The school's role in promoting sublimation. *The Psychoanalytic Study of the Child*, 11:437–449. New York: International Universities Press.

Peterfreund, E. (1971), Information, Systems and Psychoanalysis. *Psychological Issues*, Monograph 25/26, 1&2/7. New York: International Universities Press.

———— (1978), Some critical comments on psychoanalytic conceptualizations of infancy, *Internat. J. Psycho-Anal.*, 59:427–441.

Piaget, J. (1940), The mental development of the child. In: *Six Psychological Studies*. New York: Random House/Vintage, 1967, pp. 1–70.

———— (1954), *Intelligence and Affectivity: Their Relationship during Child Development*, trans. T. Brown & C. E. Kaegi. Palo Alto, CA: Annual Reviews, 1954.

———— (1967), *Biology and Knowledge*. Chicago: University of Chicago Press, 1971.

———— (1975), *The Development of Thought: Equilibration of Cognitive Structures*. New York: Viking Press, 1977.

———— (1976), *Behavior and Evolution*, trans. D. Nicholson-Smith. New York: Pantheon Books, 1978.

Polanyi, M. (1974), Scientific Thought: Essays by Michael Polanyi, ed. F. Schwartz. *Psychological Issues*, Monograph 32, 4/8. New York: International Universities Press.

Popper, K. (1959), *The Logic of Scientific Discovery*, rev. ed. New York: Harper & Row, 1968.

Pribram, K., & Gill, M. (1976), *Freud's Project Reassessed*. New York: Basic Books.

Rabinow, P., & Sullivan, W. (1979), The interpretive turn: Emergence of an approach. In: *Interpretive Social Science: A Reader*. Berkeley, CA: University of California Press, pp. 1–21.

Rangell, L. (1982), The self in psychoanalytic theory. *J. Amer. Psychoanal. Assn.*, 30:863–891.

Rapaport, D. (1942), *Emotions and Memory*. New York: International Universities Press.

—— (1951a), Toward a theory of thinking. In: *The Organization and Pathology of Thought*. New York: Columbia University Press, pp. 698–730.

—— (1951b), The conceptual model of psychoanalysis. In: *The Collected Papers of David Rapaport*, ed. M. M. Gill. New York: Basic Books, 1967, pp. 405–431.

—— (1960), On the psychoanalytic theory of motivation. In: *The Collected Papers of David Rapaport*, ed. M. M. Gill. New York: Basic Books, 1967, pp. 853–915.

—— Gill, M. M. (1959), The points of view and assumptions of metapsychology. In: *The Collected Papers of David Rapaport*, ed. M. M. Gill. New York: Basic Books, 1967, pp. 795–811.

Redl, F., & Wineman, D. (1951), *Children Who Hate*. New York: Free Press.

Richards, A. (1982), The superordinate self in psychoanalytic theory and in the self psychologies. *J. Amer. Psychoanal. Assn.*, 30:939–957.

Ricoeur, P. (1970), *Freud and Philosophy*. New Haven, CT: Yale University Press.

—— (1977), The question of proof in Freud's psychoanalytic writings. *J. Amer. Psychoanal. Assn.*, 25:835–872.

—— (1983), *Time and Narrative*, Vol. 1, trans. K. McLaughlin & D. Pellauer. Chicago: University of Chicago Press.

Riegel, K. (1979), *Foundations of Dialectical Psychology*. New York: Academic Press.

Rosenblatt, A., & Thickstun, J. (1970), A study of the concept of psychic energy. *Internat. J. Psycho-Anal.*, 51:265–278.

—— —— (1977a), Energy, information, and motivation: A revision of psychoanalytic theory. *J. Amer. Psychoanal. Assn.*, 25:537–558.

—— —— (1977b), Modern Psychoanalytic Concepts in a General Psychology. *Psychological Issues*, Monograph 42/43, 2&3/11. New York: International Universities Press.

Rubenstein, B. (1976), On the possibility of a strictly clinical psychoanalytic theory: An essay in the philosophy of psychoanalysis. In: Psychology versus Metapsychology: Essays in Memory of George S. Klein, ed. M. Gill & P. Holzman. *Psychological Issues*, Monograph 36, 1/9:229–264. New York: International Universities Press.

Sander, L. (1962), Issues in early mother-child interaction. *J. Amer. Acad. Child Psychiat.*, 1:141–166.

—— (1976), Infant and caretaking environment: Investigation and conceptualization of adaptive behavior in a system of increasing complexity. In: *Explorations in Child Psychiatry,* ed. E. J. Anthony. New York: Plenum Press, pp. 129–166.

Schafer, R., (1959), Generative empathy in the treatment situation. *Psychoanal. Quart.,* 28:342–373.

—— (1972), Internalization: Process or fantasy. In: *A New Language for Psychoanalysis.* New Haven, CT: Yale University Press, 1976, pp. 155–178.

—— (1978), *Language and Insight.* The Sigmund Freud Memorial Lectures, 1975–1976, University College London. New Haven, CT: Yale University Press.

—— (1979), The appreciative analytic attitude and the construction of multiple histories. *Psychoanal. & Contemp. Thought,* 2:3–24.

—— (1980a), Action language and the psychology of the self. *The Annual of Psychoanalysis,* 8:83–92. New York: International Universities Press.

—— (1980b), Narration in the psychoanalytic dialogue. *Crit. Inq.,* 7:29–53.

—— (1980–1981), Action and narration in psychoanalysis. In: *The Analytic Attitude.* New York: Basic Books, 1983, pp. 240–256.

—— (1981), *Narrative Actions in Psychoanalysis.* Worcester, MA: Clark University Press.

—— (1982), The relevance of the "here and now" transference interpretation to the reconstruction of early development. *Internat. J. Psycho-Anal.,* 63:77–82.

—— (n.d.). Talent as danger: Psychoanalytic observations on academic difficulty. New Haven, CT: Yale University Health Service.

Schimek, J. (1975), The interpretation of the past : Childhood trauma, psychical reality, and historical truth. *J. Amer. Psychoanal. Assn.,* 23:845–865.

Schur, M., & Ritvo, L. (1970), The concept of development and evolution in psychoanalysis. In: *Development and Evolution of Behavior: Essays in Memory of T. C. Schneirla,* ed. L. Aronson. San Francisco: Freeman, pp. 600–619.

Schwab, J. (1954), Eros and education. *J. Gen. Ed.,* 8:54–71.

Schwaber, E. (1981), Empathy: A mode of analytic listening. In: On Empathy, *Psychological Inquiry,* 3/1:357–392, ed. M. Bornstein & D. Silver. New York: International Universities Press.

Schwartz, F., & Schiller, P. (1970), A Psychoanalytic Model of Attention and Learning. *Psychological Issues,* Monograph 23, 3/6. New York: International Universities Press.

Sendak, M. (1963), *Where the Wild Things Are.* New York: Harper & Row.

Shane, E. (1984), Self psychology: A new conceptualization for the understanding of learning-disabled children. In: *Kohut's Legacy: Contributions to Self Psychology*, ed. P. Stepansky & A. Goldberg. Hillsdale, NJ: Analytic Press, pp. 191–203.

Shapiro, T. (1977), Oedipal distortions in severe character pathologies: Developmental and theoretical considerations. *Psychoanal. Quart.*, 46:559–579.

Sherwood, M. (1969), *The Logic of Explanation in Psychoanalysis*. New York: Academic Press.

Solnit, A. (1982), Early development as reflected in the psychoanalytic process. *Internat. J. Psycho-Anal.*, 63:23–38.

Solomon, R. (1974), Freud's theory of mind. In: *Freud: A Collection of Critical Essays,* ed. R. Wollheim. Garden City, NY: Doubleday/Anchor Books, pp. 25–52.

Spence, D. (1982), *Narrative Truth and Historical Truth*. New York: W. W. Norton.

Spitz, R. (1959), *A Genetic Field Theory of Ego Organization*. New York: International Universities Press.

────── (1965), *The First Year of Life*. New York: International Universities Press.

Stechler, G., & Kaplan, S., (1980), The development of the self: A psychoanalytic perspective. *The Psychoanalytic Study of the Child,* 35:85–105. New Haven, CT: Yale University Press.

Stengel, E. (1963), Hughlings Jackson's influence in psychiatry. *Brit. J. Psychiat.,* 109:348–355.

Sterba, E. (1945), Interpretation and education. *The Psychoanalytic Study of the Child,* 1:309–317. New York: International Universities Press.

Stern, D. (1985), *The Interpersonal World of the Infant*. New York: Basic Books.

Strachey, J. (1930), Some unconscious factors in reading. *Internat. J. Psycho-Anal.,* 1:322–331.

────── (1934), The nature of the therapeutic action of psychoanalysis. *Internat. J. Psycho-Anal.,* 15:127–159.

────── (1961), Editorial note. *Standard Edition,* 19:8. London: Hogarth Press.

Sulloway, F. (1979), *Freud, Biologist of the Mind: Beyond the Psychoanalytic Legend*. New York: Basic Books.

Swanson, D. (1977), A critique of psychic energy as an explanatory concept. *J. Amer. Psychoanal. Assn.,* 25:603–634.

Thistlewaite, D. (1959), College environments and the development of talent. *Science,* 130/3367:71–76.

Tolpin, M. (1971), On the beginnings of a cohesive self. *The Psychoanalytic Study of the Child,* 26:316–352. New Haven, CT: Yale University Press.

────── Kohut, H. (1980), The disorders of the self: The psychopathology of the first years of life. In: *The Course of Life: Psychoanalytic Contributions Toward Understanding Personality*

Development, Vol. 1, ed. S. Greenspan & G. Pollock. Washington, DC: U.S. Government Printing Office, pp. 425–442.

Vygotsky, L. (1978), *Mind in Society: The Development of Higher Psychological Processes*, trans. & ed. M. Cole, V. John-Steiner, S. Scribner, & E. Souberman. Cambridge, MA: Harvard University Press.

Waddington, C. (1957), *The Strategy of the Genes*. London: Allen & Unwin.

——— (1966), *Principles of Development and Differentiation*. New York: Macmillan.

Wallerstein, R. (1976), Psychoanalysis as a science: Its present status and its future tasks. In: Psychology versus Metapsychology: Essays in Memory of George S. Klein, ed. M. M. Gill & P. Holzman. *Psychological Issues*, Monograph 36, 4/9. New York: International Universities Press.

——— (1977), Psychic energy reconsidered—introduction. *J. Amer. Psychoanal. Assn.*, 25:529–536.

——— (1986), Psychoanalysis as a science: A response to the new challenges. *Psychoanal. Quart.*, 40:414–451.

Warme, G. E. (1982), The methodology of psychoanalytic theorizing: A natural science or personal agency model. *Internat. Rev. Psychoanal.*, 9:343–354.

Weber, M. (1905–1906), *The Protestant Ethic and the Spirit of Capitalism*, trans. T. Parsons. New York: Scribners, 1958.

Werner, H. (1927), *The Comparative Psychology of Mental Development*. New York: Harper & Row, 1940.

——— (1957), The concept of development from a comparative and organismic point of view. In: *The Concept of Development*, ed. D. Harris. Minneapolis: University of Minnesota Press, pp. 125–148.

White, H. (1973), *Metahistory: The Historical Imagination in Nineteenth Century Europe*. Baltimore, MD: Johns Hopkins University Press.

——— (1978), Interpretation in history (1972–73). In: *Tropics of Discourse*. Baltimore, MD: Johns Hopkins University Press, pp. 51–80.

White, R. W. (1959), Motivation reconsidered: The concept of competence. *Psycholog. Rev.*, 66:297–333.

——— (1963), Ego and Reality in Psychoanalytic Theory. *Psychological Issues*, Monograph 11, 3/3. New York: International Universities Press.

Winnicott, D. W. (1953), Transitional objects and transitional phenomena. In: *Collected Papers*. New York: Basic Books, 1958, pp. 229–242.

——— (1960a), The theory of the parent-infant relationship. *Internat. J. Psycho-Anal.*, 41:585–595.

——— (1960b), Ego distortion in terms of true and false self. In: *The*

Maturational Process and the Facilitating Environment. New York: International Universities Press, pp. 140–152.

Wolf, E. (1977), "Irrationality" in a psychoanalytic psychology of the self. In: *The Self: Psychological and Philosophical Issues,* ed. T. Mischel. Oxford: Basil Blackwell, pp. 203–223.

—— (1980), On the developmental line of selfobject relations. In: *Advances in Self Psychology,* ed. A. Goldberg. New York: International Universities Press, pp. 117–130.

—— (1982), Comments on Heinz Kohut's conceptualization of a bipolar self. In: *Psychosocial Theories of the Self,* ed. B. Lee. New York: Plenum Press, pp. 23–42.

—— (1983), Empathy and countertransference. Paper presented at the meetings of the Chicago Psychoanalytic Society, March.

Wolf, K. (1953), Observation of individual tendencies in the first year of life. In: *Problems of Infancy and Childhood: Transactions of the Sixth Conference,* ed. M. Senn. New York: Josiah Macy Foundation.

Wolff, P. (1960), The Developmental Psychologies of Jean Piaget and Psychoanalysis. *Psychological Issues,* Monograph 17. New York: International Universities Press.

—— (1966), The Causes, Controls and Organization of Behavior in the Young Infant. *Psychological Issues,* Monograph 17, 1/5. New York: International Universities Press.

Zachry, C. (1941), The influence of psychoanalysis in education. *Psychoanal. Quart.,* 10:431–444.

Zetzel, E. (1958), The therapeutic alliance in the analysis of hysteria. In: *The Capacity for Emotional Growth.* New York: International Universities Press, 1970, pp. 182–196.

—— Meissner, W. W. (1973), *Basic Concepts of Psychoanalytic Psychiatry.* New York: Basic Books.

Chapter 2

From Learning for Love to Love of Learning

RUDOLF EKSTEIN, Ph.D.

Recent developments in the field of psychoanalysis permit us to envision a new relationship between education and psychoanalysis. In this relationship the teaching profession will gain not only mental health principles, diagnostic understanding, and information about the application of psychotherapy in the case of the emotionally labile child, but will benefit from analytic insights to improve the processes of teaching and learning. It seems to me that a new kind of collaboration between the fields of psychoanalysis and education is developing. If this is indeed the case, it may be based in part on the acceptance of a simple definition Freud once gave us of the nature of mental health, which he saw as "the capacity to love and to work."

At the age of five or six, the child becomes a part of the formal school system. The teachers meet a condition in the child of this age, prepared by his growth process in the family situation. This condition is characterized through his current capacity "to love and to work," which

---

This chapter was first published in *From Learning to Love to Love of Learning* (1969), New York: Brunner/Mazel.

is a function of his state of development and maturation. The success of the teacher depends largely on the child's capacity for love and work.

We speak, of course, about age-appropriate capacities. We must constantly keep in mind what is meant in each phase of development of the child when we speak of his capacity or his lack of capacity to love and to work. What the child brings to the nursery school and to kindergarten frequently looks more like a capacity to play. We must always be aware, however, that the play of the small child is his way of working.

To the extent that the child brings these capacities into the schoolroom, the teacher is in a position to initiate a new process of learning. This new process goes through a demonstrable pattern, and repeats itself year after year, in class after class, and at different age levels. The repetition of this process will not, of course, be unvaried repetition. Its variations will depend on the child's states of maturity and development, and also on the teacher's capacity to provide for the process itself. As a matter of fact, one must keep in mind that the capacity to teach—as well as the capacity to learn—is a function of the readiness "to love and to work."

As teacher and children meet in the beginning of the school year, they size each other up and attempt to establish a relationship. The teacher-student relationship establishes the requirements for a mutually satisfying work experience. The relationship is based on love in the broadest sense of the word, which includes natural antagonism and aspects of anger when the relationship proves unrewarding. The children quickly realize they must earn the love, the praise, and the rewards of the teacher. It is because of this desire of the child to be accepted, to be recognized, to be rewarded, to be marked as a good student that he is willing to work.

Work at this stage, then, is usually based on the need for love. Of course, the teacher, too, needs to be basically accepted by the child. It is the teacher who must prepare the way for a relationship based on respect and affection, which will establish the conditions of the work situation. The child can then identify with the teacher, with his goals and needs; and in like manner, the teacher needs to identify with the child and his task. As this occurs, both teacher and child somehow participate in a process, the initial feature of which is that one must work in order to get the respect and the affection of the other.

For many people, this first phase of the process never stops. One may well say of such people, be they teachers or children, that they have not gone beyond the first step of a process which must be distinguished by additional characteristics, if it is to be a truly fruitful and positive one.

The problem of the teacher is to develop the process in such a way that he can reverse the phrase "work for love," and help the child toward that stage at which he will primarily learn because of "love of work."

I suggest that the new collaboration between psycho-analysis and education, now pushing beyond the field of mental health, must be concerned with further investigations of the learning process to tell us how one can slowly change the psychological attitudes and capacities of the child from the stage of "work for love" to that of "love of work."

The nature of learning has been investigated by learning theorists and educational psychologists. Academic psychology has given us a great deal of valuable experimentation as well as models for learning. I borrow from the paper by Gerhart and Maria Piers in which reference is made to three aspects of learning considered by the learning theorists (see chapter 8). The first, as described, for example, by conditioning and reinforcement theories, sees in learning an accomplishment which is based on constant and endless repetition. This form of learning has always been underestimated by progressive education, since the progressive educator usually stresses aspects of learning which place a premium on curiosity, insight, and discovery. However, even within a milieu which strongly relies on insight learning, there is the necessity to insure the development of skills and knowledge acquired through procedures based on repetition and conditioning.

The second model for learning is one which stresses the relationship between the teacher and the child. Love and hate, the positive and the negative features in this relationship, can be utilized for learning. Up to now, psychoanalysis has paid more attention to this model of learning than to the first mentioned, yet psychoanalytic theory and knowledge about personality organization provide ample opportunity for the study of the significance of repetitive processes, as in "working through."

We have already mentioned the learning theorists' third mode of learning, insight learning. The model for this type of learning is based on our knowledge of the nature of creativeness and inventiveness.

The learning theories have never fully succeeded in integrating these different aspects of learning. It seems to me that the present contribution of psychoanalysis to the field of education might be one in which we study the process of learning as it develops from one stage to the other. I suggest that we shall find that all three of these aspects of learning have their place in the total process, but each differs in importance in the various stages in which a child finds himself.

I suggested earlier that the first phase in the process of learning is that in which one works in order to get love. In this phase, much of learning might be mastery through repetition. During this repetition, identification with the teacher slowly grows. As identification develops, learning based upon the relationship becomes more and more dominant. With this identification with the teacher's ways of working and thinking, with his interests and curiosities,

with his attitudes toward knowledge and skill, the identificatory processes themselves may lead to the third
phase. Here, the reward and the punishment, the good
and the bad mark, the love or the rejection of a teacher
will not be the dominant feature, or the primary motivation for the child. These factors may give way to the
child's learning to love the work itself, with its progress,
discovery, and mastery of skill and knowledge. Motivation for reward, for love, will be replaced by inner motivation, and the outer-directed child will have become
an inner-directed one. If this is the sequence of learning
events, we can see how deeply the modes of learning must
influence the modes of character.

It is apparent that each change in the school situation—change of teacher or of subject—will shift the nature of the process. It is easy to prove that a child who
has this capacity for inner direction with one specific
teacher, this true and genuine interest in work and learning, might come to another teacher and have to start the
whole process all over again. Acquired functions can be
lost temporarily. In fact, to some extent the fluidity of
this process will always exist.

I must also reemphasize, of course, that these different
phases of learning are not exclusive, but are, rather, different dominant phases. In each learning process, the
others will be alive as well.

The best teacher would be one who is capable of integrating the principles of all the learning modes and
using them in accordance with his understanding of
where a child or a group of children may be at any given
moment. Such a teacher is not committed to one specific
tool of teaching but can shift these tools in accordance
with the needs of the child. Indeed, the best teacher needs
to have a mature capacity for love. If he has a primitive
capacity, his teaching is a function only of his own need
to be loved and admired by the child. Instead of developing a teaching process by which the child can use him

for reaching the goal of learning, he brings about an aborted process.

The work of teachers and analysts together should be the investigation of this teaching process. We must see how we can free forces in the child to help him go through these three positions and thus make him truly capable of learning. The nature of work—learning—so frequently has stressed the pain and the repetition and the threats of a demanding society. Consequently, too often, there has been the tendency to overlook the pleasure in the acquisition of knowledge; the joy of discovery, the satisfaction from natural and worthwhile curiosity; the gratitude for skills and knowledge; the opening of new worlds. Perhaps this has occurred because our school systems so often seem to have been dominated by learning motivations based on acquiring good grades; on competing for a place in the sun; on going to a famous college. Such goals, however, are only characteristic of the initial phase of the process which leads us to greater rewards of joy and pleasure, of an expanding world, of a wish to contribute. And, for teachers, there is the additional reward that our own development can reach that phase which enables us successfully to permeate the teaching process with the love for work, the love of learning.

Chapter 3

From the Love of Learning to the Love of Teaching

RUDOLF EKSTEIN, Ph.D.

More then a decade ago my coauthor and I selected as the title for a volume of essays *From Learning for Love to Love of Learning* (Ekstein and Motto, 1969). We meant to describe the changing ways and motives of the learning child and tie these ways to the ever changing developmental task of the growing young person. The focus then was the child and the task of the book was to inform teachers about the child as a learner. This task was inspired by the late Anna Freud's work, *Psychoanalysis for Teachers and Parents* (1930).

In about 1935, I joined the Lehrgang für Pädagogen, in Vienna, Austria, a course for psychoanalytic pedagogues. Very soon I became aware that I was learning not only about the child and insight into the child's way of relating to the teacher, the classroom situation, other children, and curriculum, but I was discovering myself as a student of teaching. It became clear to me that the teacher himself, if he is to be successful, will have to go through the kind of development that will move him from an appreciation of the personal self to a deeper understanding of the professional self. This indeed was a new developmental task.

In later years, when I became a teacher of teachers,
I soon realized that the training of teachers, and I would
prefer to say the education of teachers, the second education, is a truly psychological task both for him who
helps teachers develop as well as for the teachers who,
during their days at teachers' colleges, and later during
in-service training, must go through complex phases of
development.

During the first stage at a teacher's college, at first
without direct contact with children, the teacher once
more becomes a student, a child, often in opposition to
the college, the administration, or the college professors.
He often develops transferences to teachers and the institution which unless they are resolved and understood
may lead to disaster. And not all students at a teacher's
college will be capable of reaching the desired goals even
if they know the material and pass the examinations.
They will find it difficult to move on to the second or third
childhood; that is, the final individuation which leads to
the establishment of a professional self. This identification once more with the student, with the role of the
learner, may turn into an obstacle that cannot be overcome. The young student who is to become a teacher
might overidentify so much with the learning child that
he will not be able to make his peace with the institution,
the community, the parents, the principal, and his supervisor. He may see himself as a victim and may be
unable to move out of that position.

As he or she still identifies with the child, the struggle
may be continued and the student teacher will resist
identification with the adult world, the professors, and
the school; and often that struggle may be so drawn out
that the individual will not find his own identity. This
struggle against identification during the different phases
of learning is a necessary one. Erikson (1968), in his contribution concerning identity formation, has made it
abundantly clear that only he who has struggled against

identification will finally identify. Passive acceptance of the things that we are taught will not allow us to create a positive identification because it can only be accomplished through inner struggle.

When the student teacher finally arrives at the school and can move away from passive observation to active work in the classroom, he has entered the second stage of teacher training. At this point the intellectual knowledge has to be translated into teaching activity. One might say that the teacher now passes through phases of development which are similar to those discussed in earlier communications concerning the child's moving from learning for love to the love of learning (Ekstein and Motto, 1969). The teacher will at first teach in order to get love. He wants to be loved by the children, the master teachers and supervisors, by the principal, the parents, and by his peer group. And there are rewards to be earned. There are the first evaluation periods which will decide whether one can go on with training or not. One may finally get one's first real job and struggle to achieve permanent status in the school. Evaluations by the school, the threat of complaining parents, the first visit by the principal in the classroom, the meetings with the master teacher, will be a continuing challenge for the teacher-to-be.

The teacher may look forward to the point of permanent employment, and there may be many good teachers who, by that time, have given up striving and are satisfied to have made it, to have a secure salary that will increase year by year. In short, such teachers will permit their professional occupation to turn into a routine. This will be particularly true if they are employed in a large school in the insecure atmosphere of today's school system and are constantly transferred from one school to another. They will have reached a no-man's land, a blind alley, and often one has the impression when looking at school organization throughout the country that all too many teachers require no more than a vague identity, enough to tolerate themselves but without inspiration, without any desire to work on their own personality, on their own professional skill. Such teachers do not undertake the constant search to keep becoming but rather are satisfied with merely being.

What are the sources, the emotional and social forces which would help a teacher to move beyond that deadlocked position in order to teach for love and the admiration of the children; the positive response of parents or supervisor, or principal; the remuneration and increased salary? How can they become people who love teaching to such a degree that they must strive continually for self-development and learning? In other words, how can they become people who will teach well because they themselves have not given up learning?

We live in a social world which is in a state of constant crisis. Usually the institutions that deal with the education and development of the next generation are the ones that are the most embattled. Insecurity keeps school systems in a state of constant upheaval. As the political moods change, school systems, from kindergarten to university, are constantly threatened by budget cuts, administrative changes, uncertainty, and a lack of appreciation of the value of continuity. We live through periods where children and teachers move constantly from school to school and are not allowed to experience continuity. I recall the experience of one teacher who was transferred three times during one year in order to allow, statistically, the correct distribution of different groups of children and teachers. She had just been able to turn the mass of children in her classroom into a functioning group who had developed a positive relationship with her that made learning possible. She was told by the administration to tell the children only on the very last day of the term that she was leaving. The children, who were to lose their teacher, cried and expressed great distress, were full of anger, and did not want to go to school any longer. She was also left feeling very angry, having to move to another, distant community where she was to continue her employment.

We have learned from psychology that continuity in the upbringing and education of children is essential for positive emotional development, for the capacity to love, and to learn and work.

The mature teacher might often be able to meet obstacles of this sort but it will not be easy. Can one work under any conditions?

I have described the first few steps in the development of a teacher, but I think it should be clear that the anxieties and formidable tasks of the first few years of teaching are by no means all that is involved in the steady development of the professional self, the movement toward the love of teaching.

One might think that the different tasks that the teacher has to meet, developmental tasks which include the problem of discipline in the classroom and the capacity to form groups. The teacher must teach the group without ever losing touch with the individual, and slowly be able to grow beyond the classroom, to relate to his fellow teachers, and be able to collaborate with them. He also must slowly develop responsibilities in the whole school community of parents, teachers, and children, and the capacity to assume administrative responsibilities which are concerned not merely with the classroom but with the school system itself.

New teaching methods, tried in one's own classroom, may have to be conveyed to other teachers. In time, one will also want to become a master teacher, a supervisor of teachers, and perhaps also develop administrative responsibilities.

I do not know whether that will be what every teacher should aspire to. For some teachers, the work in the classroom will be life's work in itself, but one that can be improved continually even though the teacher may choose not to step out of the classroom situation.

As a matter of fact, one may hope that even those who become guidance counselors and deal more directly with parents, who become assistant principals or principals, should have an opportunity to return to the classroom with the children again, and perhaps also be student teachers and once more learn.

During my own professional development, a personal analysis for teachers was made available and inspired many. This cannot be a universal requirement but should be more widely available. The best the community of a psychoanalytic institute can do is to put its strength into its teachers of teachers and to create scholarships for such programs of further self-improvement.

In the past, it seemed that Americans felt they should do everything to give their children a better opportunity in life. But in recent years, during the never ending crisis situations in education, the child has become a football in the power struggle. Can one hope that Americans will once more provide the best for their children? In such an atmosphere the love of teaching and the love of learning will be but two sides of the teacher's multifaceted professional self.

My old teacher, Siegfried Bernfeld, who wrote about *Sisyphus, or the Boundaries of Education* (1925), saw the teacher as a Sisyphus who must try and try again, in a never ending struggle. I have often wondered, in less pessimistic moments, whether the teacher might not one day choose as his hero Prometheus, who stole the fire from the gods and brought it to man. Prometheus was at first punished by the gods, but under Pallas Athena, the Greek goddess, and the most powerful deity in the days of Pericles, the days of freedom in Athens, Prometheus was honored. Our teachers will be as good as our communities allow them to be. The love of teaching then depends on our capacity to love the teachers to whom we entrust our children in that loving circle of trust and understanding.

REFERENCES

Bernfeld, S. (1925), *Sisyphus, or the Boundaries of Education.* Berkeley: University of California Press, 1973.

Ekstein, R., & Motto, R. (1969), *From Learning for Love to Love of Learning.* New York: Brunner/Mazel.

Erikson, E. (1968), *Identity, Youth and Crisis.* New York: W. W. Norton.

Freud, A. (1930), *Psychoanalysis for Teachers.* London: Allen & Unwin, 1931.

Chapter 4

The Psychoanalytic Approach to Learning Theory (With More Than a Passing Reference to Piaget)

E. JAMES ANTHONY, M.D.

Although dealing mainly with the psychoanalytic approach to learning, this chapter will also refer to Piaget's theories since they offer the only adequate alternative to the psychodynamic viewpoint. Like psychoanalysis, Piaget makes use of a developmental framework with an orderly succession of stages, and with the formation of elaborate mental structures through the functioning of various mental mechanisms. The ego that gradually emerges in both systems has an autonomous capacity to learn about the external environment, even though this is not singled out for special consideration. A learning ego is an essential requirement for any psychological thesis claiming to relate the human organism to its environment. An acceptable theory of learning must therefore explain the working of this learning ego as the intermediary between the mind and its ambience. It presupposes the operation of a reality principle that regularly overrides the pleasure principle, the capacity for close and sustained attention that fixes itself to an external area of interest, the unimpeded reception of the external stimuli by appropriate and intact organs of perception, the long-circuiting of excitations through cognitive structures that involve thinking, reasoning, and judging, the arrangements for long-term storage within specialized memory systems, and, finally, the discharge of such excitations on demand, indicating that successful learning has occurred within varying degrees of competence. In human learning, there is a further mysterious phenomenon or epiphenomenon which is "lit up" during the course of the perceptual impingements and generates a sense of awareness or consciousness. The ego not only learns but learns consciously. Without this, learning would be blind, but psychoanalysis, from early on, anticipated its absence by postulating unconscious learning; that is, learning that seeps through to the inner mental structures without prior illumination by consciousness.

The learning ego does something more than just assimilate from the outside environment: it differentiates what is actually there on the external side from what is imagined, wished for, or even hallucinated.

It will be noted that a general theory of learning subsumes a number of related constructs dealing with reality testing, attention, cathexis, memory, and consciousness (with perhaps another world of learning linked to unconsciousness). The general theory would also assume a concept of adaptation between organism and environment.

SOME SPECIFICS OF LEARNING WITH RESPECT TO A GENERAL LEARNING THEORY

There are two ways of looking at the environment "out there": actively or passively. Does the individual reach out to the external situation and explore it for himself, or is he simply the passive recipient of experience? Does he learn by himself and for himself or is he taught by others whose job is to infiltrate his mind and establish a body of knowledge predetermined by them? There also are two polarized theories that have been put forward (Popper, 1972): the "bucket" theory envisions the mind as a container into which perceptions are poured with little effort on the part of the individual except to experience them and reproduce them on demand. In contrast, the "searchlight" theory has the mind actively engaged in searching, scanning, and selecting from the buzzing sensory confusion around. Thus appropriate parts of the environment are incorporated into the mind for purposes that are already set up within the individual. During his development, the child becomes an increasingly sophisticated observer and his learning ego is actively engaged in planning and preparation. He does not "have" an observation: he "makes" it. Every observation is triggered by a question pertaining to something that interests the child, stirs his curiosity, and arouses his exploratory activity. To paraphrase Aristotle, all the child's learning begins in wonder. In this context, one is reminded of Goethe's comment that every time one looks at something, in essence one makes a theory. It is this perpetual theory making that stimulates the spirit of learning. The child "learns from experience" only if he pursues experience, and only in response to the changing quality of his mind and the changing state of the environment.

Learning, therefore, supposes the existence of some system of expectations that can be reformulated by a series of questions. In this sense, the child hovers in the epicenter of a "horizon of expectations" (Popper, 1972) that is made up of the sum total of conscious, preconscious, and unconscious expectations. As development occurs, the level of consciousness broadens and becomes more inclusive and more exactly articulated, and the "horizon of expectations" constitutes an internal frame of reference that is constantly being altered by continued learning experiences. Once this inner model has been erected, anticipation becomes possible along with the capacity to make elementary predictions and test them by experience. If these are falsified or confirmed, notions of explanation are developed that lead to assumptions about the world that are constantly revised during the course of development. This is what is meant by active learning and is reflected in Piaget's comment that whenever you teach a child something, you prevent him from inventing it (Bringuier, 1980).

There is a difference, with degrees of overlap, between the child who wants to learn and the child who wants to be taught; that is, between the active and passive stance. Many different motivations have been ascribed to the former type of child. Differences in exploratory zeal have been noted in infancy, as if what Karl Bluhler (1930) referred to as *Funktionslust* (functional pleasure) was inherent even in the immature human organism. This almost immediate engagement with the environment takes place in such disposed infants before any degree of separation, individuation, and autonomy has emerged. This is not to gainsay the importance of the facilitating environment that imposes no inhibiting prohibitions on inquisitive, reaching out activity. The psychoanalytic viewpoint would point to the absence of significant repressing forces on the epistemophilic drives so that the acquisition of knowledge is not confused with primal interests, forbidden sexual curiosity, illicit, sadistic, and destructive wishes, and the erotic and aggressive unconscious interpretation of signs and symbols utilized in the three Rs. In children who want to learn, the autonomous learning ego is relatively immune to conflict. The child who wants to be taught has different motives for learning: the wish to remain in close dependency with the teaching parent or parent surrogate; the desire to please his teacher; an eagerness to feed passively on the omniscience of the adult; and the symbolic enjoyment of the learning environment as a bountiful breast. Learning inhibitions would relate to a fantasied conception of knowledge as a danger to symbiotic embeddedness and the threat of growing away from the teacher.

The level of cognition is related to the ability to learn, but the interaction is not a simple one. The overall competence in learning has to do not only with cognitive power but also the individual's capacity to exchange effectively with the learning environment and thus adapt himself to it with increasing success. In rote learning, knowledge may be assimilated, stored, and retrieved without much thought or understanding, and the same is true of motor learning, conditioned learning, and habit formation which is automatized after repeated associations. Meaningful learning, on the other hand, involves a considerable exercise of such cognitive processes as judgment and understanding. Some theorists have even concluded that thinking or reasoning is different from learning, requiring a withdrawal from the commonsense world, metaphorical rather than practical language, and a disinterest in translating knowledge into action. It has been described, perhaps a little too fancifully, as the soundless dialogue that the person carries on within himself in comparative solitude, and the learning environment, such as the classroom, is not felt to be the best setting for its operation.

More recently, different ego styles of learning have been differentiated. Some minds, for example, may approach the learning situation openly and flexibly and make use of it as an opportunity for wide-ranging divergent activities. In contrast, the converging style reduces the problem to be learned and limits the scope of inquiry to the area under consideration. The learning ego functions less diffusely with this focused approach that also stresses exactitude and coherence. (There was some slight evidence earlier on to suggest that these learning differences may be related to differences in right and left brain functioning, but this has lost support in recent years.)

There is also evidence indicating that some individuals learn more efficiently through one sensory modality (vision, for instance) than another (hearing) because of increased sensitivity in the dominant modality.

AN EARLIER PSYCHOANALYTIC APPROACH TO LEARNING

In 1895, at the age of thirty-nine, Freud produced a "Project for a Scientific Psychology" in three weeks of intensive work. He had not started on a grand scale but soon found himself touching on phenomena from the very "center of nature" and with a topic that covered "the whole of psychology." He had doubts about the Project from its inception, and even greater doubts when he was shown his manuscript in old age and wanted immediately to destroy it. Although he shared all his ideas at this time with his friend Fliess, he held this particular product back because, he said, it was rather like "sending a girl's six-month's fetus to a Ball!" However, he felt more confident when it was done, announcing that the barriers had been raised, the veils had fallen away, and that it was possible to see through the details of the neuroses to the determinants of consciousness. Everything, at this moment of completion, seemed to fit together: the gears were in mesh and the model gave the impression of being a machine that could really run by itself, and was therefore self-regulating. He could scarcely contain himself with delight. Later, he apologized to Fliess: "I can no longer understand the state of mind in which I hatched out the psychology; I cannot make out how I came to inflict it on you" (p. 285).

The Project is important for two reasons: within it, there is the nucleus of a large part of Freud's later theories, and also the germ of a learning theory. Freud ultimately disowned it and wanted it eradicated from his bibliography because the Project is completely outer-directed, with all the emphasis being placed upon the environment's impact upon the organism and the organism's reaction to it. The inner events—the excitations, the "instincts," the "defensive" operations—are scarcely shadows of what was still to come. Yet, the material is surprisingly up to date with the latest developments in information theory and cybernetics. It was a brain model equipped with memory and feedback mechanisms for correcting errors in the machine's negotiations with the environment. Another reason for Freud's disavowal was that the neuronal framework had no way of accounting for consciousness which for him was the "one beacon light in the darkness of depth-psychology." Curiously, the varying factors in this early theory that later felt so alien to him were the ones necessary for a theory of learning—an active interchange with the environment, a memory system, procedures for reality testing and attention cathexes, and the presence of a range of cognitions such as judgment and reproductive, practical, observant, and theoretical thought.

The crucial learning in the Project has to do with the distinction between a perception and a memory that is similar to it and with the same amount of cathexis. A coincidence between the two cathexes is a biological signal for ending the thinking process and initiating action. If there is noncoincidence, thought continues. How does this look within the neuronal machinery?

> If neurone a coincides but neurone c is perceived instead of neurone b, then the activity of the ego follows the connections of this neurone c and, by means of a current of Qn along these connections, causes new cathexes to emerge until access is found to the missing neurone b. The image of a movement arises which is interpolated between neurone c and neurone b; and, when this image is freshly activated through a movement carried out in reality, the perception of neurone

b, and at the same time the identity that is being
sought, are established [Freud, 1895, p. 328].

One can see how unlike Freud this passage sounds, and
how like later Piaget it reads. Whereas Freud seemed to
start with what sounds suspiciously like cybernetics and
information theory, Piaget ended with this. However,
Freud, like Piaget, had vivid pictures in his mind as a
background to these abstractions. To illustrate the passage above, he uses a favorite analogy of the hungry baby.

> Let us suppose, for instance, that the memory image
> wished for [by the baby] is the image of the mother's
> breast and a frontal view of its nipple, and that the
> first perception is a side view of the same object, with-
> out the nipple. In the baby's memory there is an ex-
> perience, made by chance in the course of sucking, that
> with a particular head movement the front image turns
> into the side image. The side image which is now seen
> leads to the [image of the] head movement; an exper-
> iment shows that its counterpart must be carried out,
> and the perception of the front view is achieved [Freud,
> 1895, pp. 328–329].

When Freud's attention turned intrapsychically, the
possibility of any further development in this highly sophisticated learning theory was lost.

LATER PSYCHOANALYTIC THEORIES OF LEARNING

The next step to Freud's theory came very much later
and Rapaport, trained in both cognitive psychology and
psychoanalysis, recognized both the need for a learning
theory in psychoanalysis as well as the learning theory
already implicit in the Project. Rapaport (1950) returned
to the relationship between organism and environment
that had disappeared from the psychoanalytic scene and

insisted on a theory of adaptation in which both drive and environment were codeterminants. This was the basis for the construction of an adequate learning theory, but there were other requisites such as an understanding of consciousness, a recognition of external reality representing the "book" from which the organism learned, a need for internal mental not neuronal structures that made the retention of impressions from the outside world possible, and attention cathexes that raised the level of excitations above a threshold. Rapaport postulated that since the quantity of attention cathexis was limited, excitations would be in competition for it. When an excitation (internal or external) attracted cathexis in a sufficient amount, for a sufficient length of time, and with sufficient frequency a structure was formed that could take the form of a memory trace, an idea, a relationship between ideas, or a defense. A great deal of cathexis attention went into the building of such structures, but once erected the cathexes were released except for a small portion retained in the structure, and this surplus cathexis became available again for attention and further structure formation. Rapaport added another degree of freedom for his learning theory: whereas Hartmann had felt the need for a learning ego relatively autonomous from internal drives, Rapaport felt that there were good theoretical reasons to have it relatively autonomous from the outer environment. Although able to maintain these independencies when thinking was in progress, at all other times it required excitations from both sources as essential nutriment. Because the internal mental structures persist and remain effective when when deprived of stimulus nutriment, the organism continued to stay receptive to stimulation.

For Rapaport, learning was an "abiding change wrought by experience" and the change necessitated the formation of structure. It was attention that became the center of his approach to a learning, and, as attention increased, to a certain point consciousness developed and the individual became aware of his learning environment. But attention cathexis was central. One is reminded here of the old story of the mule whose owner sold it to a customer with the promise that the mule could be taught to do anything. In fact, the mule, in very mulish fashion, refused to do anything at all and the customer accordingly complained to the previous owner. The latter took a stick and hit the mule strenuously on the head after which the mule performed perfectly well. "You see," he said, "he is very able to learn, but first you have to gain his attention!" Rapaport was convinced that psychoanalysis needed a learning theory and that Freud's theory of consciousness and structure formation represented a good beginning.

> If and when a learning theory is developed which can account for such consequences of those processes of learning and unlearning which are observed clinically, psychoanalysis as a theory will change in character. From a theory built to account for the general characteristics of observed processes, and based only on the requirement that its propositions be consistent with each other and with the empirical data it accounts for, it will change into a theory whose propositions will be, translatable into terms of the "microanatomy" of processes of change wrought by experience (learning) and thus into a theory whose propositions will be amenable to independent tests [Rapaport, 1952, p. 138].

It was not until Hartmann's expansion of the ego concept to include certain autonomous developments many years later that psychoanalysis moved closer to a learning theory. Coupled with this came his concept of the neutralization of the drive that freed the ego to become an organ of learning. The autonomous attributes of the ego developed in part from experiential learning and in part from maturation, but the latter did not in any way undermine the specific importance of learning processes for ego development. The learning ego could progress as long as the sphere of conflict did not interfere with it, but when neurosis was rampant learning could rapidly become conflictual.

According to Hartmann a large number of primary processes were gradually transformed into secondary processes. However, certain primary process activities did represent a kind of "primordial learning" in as much as they helped the child to differentiate his inner and outer worlds. As a consequence, his sense of reality was enhanced until fully consonant with what was taking place in the external environment. It almost looked, according to him, as if the child was prepared from before birth for his encounter with the world in which he was about to live, and preadapted to exigencies. "The apparatus of perception, memory, motility, etcetera, which help us to deal with reality are, in a primitive form, already present at birth; later they will mature and develop in constant interaction, of course, with experience; the varying system to which we attribute these functions, the ego, is also *our organ of learning*" (Hartmann, 1964, p. 246).

The ego, in this complex perspective, is the adapter, the integrater, and the mediator between external reality and the other internal psychic systems. The optimal functioning of the organism as a learner requires ego autonomy from the demands of the id and ego autonomy from the demands of the environment. The young child must take the giant step from the pleasure principle to self-preservation and self-regulation and in the process develop a "knowledge of reality" that is at first fragmentary and vulnerable to distortion but later is able to hold up for most of the time even under stressing circumstances.

The main early sources of learning about the real environment are derived from the child's own body in relation to the people around him, and it is his dependence upon his environment that provides the "essential factor" in this primary learning. Primary learning is the *necessary antecedent to all secondary learning.* As the ego becomes more mature, more resilient, better adapted, more controlled, and more integrated, the more able it is to function as "the organ of learning." However, one must keep in mind that it is the protracted helplessness and dependence of the human infant that promotes the influence of environmental factors and increases the capacity for learning.

With Erikson (1957) the outer environment had become all important, providing a rich field for learning in continuous psychosocial interchanges. As the child reached latency, when his more pressing drives were detoxified, formal learning became more dominantly a part of everyday life, and allowed him to function as an industrious and competent learner.

In general, it was along with the development of psychoanalytic ego psychology, the direct observation of early development from a psychoanalytic perspective, and child analysis, all conducive to a renewed interest in the environment as a dynamic psychosocial milieu (Anthony, 1981), that a psychoanalytic learning theory became not only feasible but practical.

Another interesting departure in the direction of learning is its application to the process of psychoanalysis and the psychoanalytic situation. The assumption was that, during the course of treatment, a substantial amount of unlearning, learning, and relearning took place, and that this learning in its various forms led to improvement or cure.

How did this therapeutic learning take place? More recent psychoanalytic work has tended to discuss the process involved while overlooking the structural requirements outlined by Rapaport and Hartmann. A number of technical aspects have been touched upon: that learning changed qualitatively during the course of psychoanalytic treatment; that learning deepened as treatment progressed; and that later learning, unlike earlier learning, was incorporated permanently into the mode of thinking and judging. It was postulated that at the beginning of treatment, learning took place mainly by association, and that as therapy continued, insightful learning began to take place more frequently. In the final stage, learning took place through identification with the therapist, incorporating his mode of handling the anxiety-laden material that emerged in the analysis (Piers and Piers, chapter 8). Szasz (1963) described three stages of sophistication with regard to therapeutic learning, each of which can be illustrated in a simple analogy. A stranger comes to a town and wants to find a particular landmark. The first person that he asks gives him explicit directions; the second person presents him with a map; and the third with paper to make a map based on a grid system. Protolearning is a feature of every beginning treatment, but it is also an example of the didactic approach. Ortholearning includes understanding of the situation and insightful discoveries about oneself; metalearning is learning about learning and represents the metapsychology of the learning process in the course of which one becomes self-analytic.

One does not see each of these steps in all psychotherapy, nor do they always appear in such regular sequence, but they do suggest that therapeutic learning is a complex process and involves different layers of the psyche. A psychotherapist like Winnicott tended to lay less emphasis on learning per se, and more on the creative, self-regulatory and self-generative process in both psychological treatment and psychological development. The child or the child patient is not learning, nor is he being taught by his parents or his therapist; he is discovering or inventing solutions or mastering problems imposed by development or developmental conflict. Clearly this viewpoint does not contradict the occurrence of learning as an integral part of psychotherapy. This learning includes learning about oneself at the different levels of access; learning about therapy and the therapeutic process; learning, even in rudimentary fashion, about the theory of therapy; learning about the therapeutic situation and its potentials and limits; learning about the therapist and his therapeutic style; and learning about one's psychopathology and why it came into being at a particular moment in time. There is a "book" of learning involved in every case to which must be added the therapist's learning about his patient, and about himself in the process of therapy. To what extent learning is connected with getting better is still a moot point; as is well known, the therapeutic relationship can effect cures without any apparent learning having taken place, and insight in itself is no guarantee of improvement.

A THEORY OF LEARNING DERIVED FROM PIAGET'S WORK

As with Freud, the complete works of Piaget have only a sparse reference to learning, and similarly there is no specific Piagetian learning theory as such, although it is possible to construct one from his work. Like Freud, Piaget was a structuralist in that he postulated the formation of certain mental structures that were crucial for learning about external reality. The process of intake or assimilation resulted in the formation of structures (or schemata) that gradually built up into a system, each part of which was related to the others. Because of this reciprocity, none of the parts could undergo change without affecting changes in all the other parts. Structures altered over time by a process of transformation. With a knowledge of the environmental excitation and the response to it of the organism, it was theoretically possible to predict how the organism would react if the situation was submitted to certain modifications. In accordance with all other structural theories, including Freud's, structures could exist in manifest and latent forms.

Piaget explicitly restricted the notion of learning to an acquisition of new knowledge that derived primarily from contact with the environment. He contrasted it on the one hand with maturation, as did psychoanalysis, and on the other, with an ever-changing interaction between organism and environment over the course of development. Knowledge was not something that could be obtained passively from the outside but had to be *actively constructed* by the child in accordance with the "searchlight" theory of the mind.

At least on paper (since formulating a learning theory was not his goal), Piaget could be expected to have the same problems as psychoanalytic theorists in putting together a comprehensive learning theory, because he too sought to base his psychology on biology, and to bring constitution, maturation, and environment together. The growth of knowing structures (epistemology) could be called learning, but for Piaget this was learning of a different kind to what was commonly meant by the term. He contrasted rote learning with meaningful learning in which comprehension was an indispensable prerequisite.

The next question had to do with the relationship of intelligence to learning, and of both to the process of mental equilibration that underlay the development of operational intelligence. Piaget found that intelligence had its own laws of internal growth and that its successive acquisitions were not merely drawn accumulatively from the environment. Sensorimotor behavior, symbolic functioning, representations, concrete and formal operations were but different names for the continuous, functionally identical nature of intelligence.

No special experience was needed to acquire the concept of conservation and no special experience could teach it before there was maturational readiness, or so Piaget thought and theorized to the objection of most learning theorists. In contrast, special teaching was necessary to learn that Washington, DC, was the capital city of the United States, and this learning experience was as necessary for the twelve-year-old as for the three-year-old, and worked in both cases if the children were sufficiently motivated. The first acquisition (of conservation) was due to the process of equilibration depending on no *particular* bit of environmental information but simply on normal living and biological time, whereas the second acquisition was due to learning and depended on a particular bit of knowledge that had to be provided by the environment. In this respect, Piaget was not an empiricist or an idealist. He was a "constructive interactionist" for whom knowledge grew through an active exchange between child and his environment that allowed the child gradually to construct a world model as the outcome of his experience at any given stage of his development.

All this meant that in every learning situation, according to Piaget, one could distinguish the maturational aspect involving a set of operations peculiar to the developmental stage and an environmental aspect concerned with learning a particular bit of knowledge. Learning an identical external task therefore differed according to the inner structures available. Because of this biological basis, it made no sense to Piaget to speak of an environmental event unless there was an organism capable of responding to it. Like Rapaport, he was against having theories that focused on the need for externally imported motivations that served to connect the organism and the environmental event. For him, the internal nature of the organism corresponded to the aspect of the environment toward which the organism reacted or adapted in a meaningful manner, and this structuring includes both an aspect of knowing and an aspect of affect.

We now see how much closer Piaget's framework is to psychoanalysis than to stimulus-response (S-R) learning theories, since both are concerned with a dynamic mode of learning in its broadest sense, which includes:

1. An ongoing interaction between organism and environment for the purpose of adaptation.
2. The formation of structure as an integral part of that interaction.
3. An attention that selects certain portions of the environment for special treatment.
4. A growth of knowledge in which cognition and affect both play a part.
5. A resulting grasp of consciousness *(prise de conscience)*.

The twin mechanisms of assimilation (taking in) and accommodation (adjusting to change) achieve a balance in the process of equilibration. Structures (or schemata) multiply by differentiation and prepare the organism for relation to new environmental experiences and further assimilation. As the structure develops, the interest in the environment and attention to particular parts of it grows. Piaget speaks of an "optimal zone of interest" surrounding the organism. For him, then every kind of learning in the strict sense implies the functioning of assimilating schemata and the developing network of schemata has no absolute beginning: for every schema there is a previous schema and a subsequent one. If the acquisition of new knowledge is the law of development, and if all learning in the strict sense is conditioned by logical or prelogical structuring, the basic mechanisms of learning are not different from the equilibration process of the whole developing intelligence. Even rote learning is never a mere copy or association caused by external factors. The structuring contribution of the assimilating organism enters as a necessary component into every learning situation and explains why no result of learning can be merely a function of factors external to the learning process itself.

To put it simply, Piaget limits the meaning of learning in the strict sense to the acquisition of knowledge that derives essentially from a particular external contribution and differentiates this from the process of equilibration that regulates the growth of operational schemata according to contributions *internal* to the organism. The problem of learning, therefore, implies a delicate balance between internal and external contributions. The *content* of a schema is linked to learning while its *form* is related to equilibration. *Accommodation is more closely related to learning, assimilation to equilibration.* Although, one should keep in mind that the overall equilibration relates to both assimilation and accommodation.

Although all this is not too dissimilar from the psychoanalytic framework constructed by Rapaport (1959) (and we have to remember that Rapaport is indebted to Piaget for his concept of stimulus-nutriment provided by the environment), the process of equilibration is a difficult one to comprehend, to apply to particular cases, or to relate meaningfully to psychoanalysis. It is never quite clear whether equilibration and learning are distinctly different; whether learning is precondition to equilibration; whether equilibration is a precondition to learning; and whether the two are mutually, reciprocally interactive. The last is probably nearest the truth. Although Piaget says that all theories of learning must implicitly or explicitly take account of equilibration, he is not too informative about how the two processes relate although he hints at the notion that all learning must move toward some sort of stability. However, he would agree with Rapaport that the proper function of learning is to derive knowledge of the object, and this would be true from both a cognitive and affective point of view. For example, a child develops, during the first eighteen months of life, a concept of the object as permanent and localizable in space and time, and subject to the laws of causality; at the next stage, the object becomes a plaything that can be symbolized so that it can stand for other objects and substitute for them; later, the object is endowed with animistic properties so that it is dynamically alive; at the same time it acquires a name that is eternally fixed and cannot be altered for the child at this stage; still later the object is recognized as answering to the laws of conservation, starting with matter and proceeding to weight and volume. As mentioned earlier, the object in psychoanalytic theory also undergoes various vicissitudes of change during the course of development.

In speaking of learning in relation to cognitive development, Piaget (1974) refers to it as "a topic so near to my heart." In Geneva (Inhelder, Sinclair, and Bovet, 1974) special learning experiments were designed to examine the acquisition of knowledge, and the "cognitive conflicts" that are generated and resolved in such learning situations. This recent approach follows on Piaget's earlier work on the cognitive unconscious (1946), in which he begins his argument with Binet's notion (1894) of "thought as an unconscious activity of the mind." Piaget (1973) also felt that the day would come when "the psychology of cognitive functions and psychoanalysis will have to fuse in a general theory which will improve both, through mutual correction."

Piaget contended that the cognitive system was remarkably comparable in every way to Freud's affective system in that both included partially or completely unconscious innermost mechanisms, and both made use of resistances that walled off "complexes." If an appreciable number of such cognitive "complexes" was established, the individual would find it difficult to learn. The transitions from preoperational thinking to concrete operational thinking and to abstract operational thinking all represent hazards in the course of cognitive development and hold-ups at any of these mode changes could also interfere with learning that was appropriate to the developmental stage.

In 1974 Piaget asked himself what learning was in fact and came up with an interesting debate within himself. He did not agree with the school of Hull that learning was the *only* source of development; nor did he agree with others for whom it constituted a modification of development. In his opinion, "Development cannot be reduced to a series of bits of learning and the notion of competence has to be introduced as a precondition for any learning to take place" (p. xiii). What was observable in any learning experiment was the fact that, with a strange confrontation, habitual thinking modes underwent a conflict with momentary regression followed by an acceleration that then resulted in a stable acquisition.

Piaget felt that in the area of learning and teaching, three important questions remained to be answered: whether what was learned through teaching remained stable or whether in large part it disappeared with time; second, whether observed accelerations in the acquisition of knowledge were accompanied in any general developmental deviations; and finally, whether the child who passively received information from the teacher would be unable to learn anything without such help in the future, an effect that would undermine a child's creative capacities.

Today, one thinks of learning within an epigenetic framework according to which there is a constant interaction between environmental and maturational influences. A child learns when his curiosity is awakened about something new, and when he experiences a feeling of conflict because the situation does not correspond with his preconceptions. The child learns when he becomes surprised, astonished, and intrigued. But the "surprise" element has no effect if the child does not yet possess the cognitive equipment which enables him to fit the unforeseen phenomena into a deductive or inferential

framework. The developmental level is what both Piaget
and psychoanalysis emphasize. The child takes in according to what Piaget has called his "assimilation
norms" (by analogy with the reaction norms of the ge-
nome). The competence for learning is closely related to
the level of sensitivity to information from the external
environment and this learning competence is not limited
to isolated responses but to a general system of approach
through the "book" of the environment. The learning ego
becomes increasingly responsive to the wealth of environmental knowledge confronting it, because of the fa-
cilitations provided by nonobtrusive personnel and the
development of self-regulatory learning propensities. Inhelder et al. (1974) in their study in Geneva of the relationship of learning to cognitive development make two
important comments: Regulatory mechanisms play an
essential part both in cognitive development and in organic life, since they participate in two processes fundamental to all living activity, which also constitute the
two poles of learning: the preservation of existing structures, on the one hand, and their modification or enrichment in response to the needs of adaptation, on the other
(1974, p. 271); and in the same context, "learning is a
constantly renewed process of synthesis between continuity and novelty" (p. 272).

CLINICAL ILLUSTRATION

Jamie came into analysis because of underachievement
in the fifth grade of his elementary school. He was recognized as "obviously a bright boy" but his attention in
the classroom had been sporadic. His teachers felt sure
that he had good potential borne out by his IQ test, but
he did not seem to have a basis for better learning. In the
treatment situation, he behaved with extreme passivity
and would treat an interpretation as if it was a seductive
overture to which he needed to surrender without ques-

tion. He was not a boy who wanted to learn; nor was he a boy who wanted to be taught; what he wanted, in fact, was not at all clear in the early part of the treatment, when his habitual response was to assimilate uncritically whatever was offered by the therapist. However, the assimilation seemed disconnected with any structure, so that nothing seemed to be retained or used further in the service of working through. He said that whenever he tried to think, a cloud appeared to descend on his thoughts and everything became fuzzy. This was likely to happen when the teacher talked about "stuff" that had no existence, and insisted that you had to follow all the steps in your mind. It was very different from fitting things together in the carpentry class when you could measure the different pieces of wood and cut them down accordingly. His teacher wrote to me to say that Jamie was "perilously close to failing" and did not seem to realize the seriousness of the situation. He looked as if he was paying attention in class but it was obviously into one ear and out the other. He did not seem to know how to learn and there was no way of teaching him. Yet, one was "struck by his obvious brightness." His attention cathexes were obviously weak and there was a striking apathy and lack of curiosity in his approach to classroom material and tasks. The teacher complained that he was often deaf to what was going on in class as if he was locked into his own private world. "He does not have a responsive mind and I keep thinking that his mind is just fluid with nothing there to grab at what I am trying to get through to him. At times I feel almost like shaking him out of his stupor." Here the teacher is apparently talking about apparent structures and the level of awareness to outside excitations. If there was any learning ego, it was functioning very weakly.

What can one say about Jamie's drive and environment, since one or the other or both had to be held responsible for his defective learning behavior? In the treatment situation it became clear that his mind was largely preoccupied with sexual matters and that his pre-consciousness was habitually loaded with erotic day-dreams. He enjoyed telling his therapist dirty jokes that implied a marked degree of sexual knowledge and inter-est. When he spoke about sexual matters, he did so with an adultomorphic precocity. It became apparent that his autonomous ego was flooded with libidinal excitations and that any curiosity he had was predominantly voyeur-istic. Every part of the learning ego had been affected: he was imperceptive to anything but the erotic; he forgot everything except erotic content, such as his jokes, and seemed oblivious to any demands of educational reality. He did not seem to know or to care about the learning milieu.

Jamie's environment had been disturbed from the age of four onward. His parents had undergone an acrimon-ious divorce, and the hostilities did not subside with the break-up of the marriage. The two children, Jamie and his sister (who also had a learning disability, although not so extreme as Jamie's), were used as weapons in the endless battle between the parents. When Jamie went to visit his father in another city, he reported back to his therapist that he had "investigated" his father's sexual secrets and had made some exciting discoveries. He had always felt that his father was a jerk, but he was now convinced about it. He brought to the session several piec-es of evidence to indicate that his father was a "sexual maniac." He had found a contraceptive in one of the draw-ers, a *Playboy* magazine under the bed; a pornographic movie cassette hidden behind the television set; a pair of female underpants in his father's cupboard. He presented all these to his therapist in a manner of a successful prosecuting attorney and wanted the father condemned as an unfit parent. In contrast, he said, his mother lived an exemplary life. She was a teacher who took her teach-ing very seriously and came down heavily on poorer scholarship. After an explosive confrontation with Jamie, his mother would retire to her bedroom in tears, complaining of a severe headache. After a while, Jamie would creep into bed with her, hold her tightly, and comfort her. He told his mother that she was fortunate to be rid of the "jerk" and that they could be happy together without him.

In the early phase of therapy, Jamie said that he wanted to learn but that he was "dumb" and he wondered whether the therapist could cure his dumbness and make it easy for him to absorb his schoolwork. He started to bring his homework into the sessions and to do it while attending to the therapist. Eventually, he admitted that he was not doing either successfully: he was not learning any better and he was not feeling any better.

He next focused on his jealousy of his sister and felt that the mother often preferred her "just because she was a girl." He too could easily become a girl: it just meant wearing girl's clothes and letting his hair grow. When this material was pursued further in the direction of his castration anxiety, he became quite disturbed and accused the therapist of trying to shove dirty stuff into his head. Toward the end of this phase, he began to manifest surprising insights and talked openly of having always wanted to get rid of his father the "jerk" in order to keep his mother for himself. He admitted that he got pains in his stomach after he had been in bed with his mother. At this time, he brought masturbation fantasies in which a boy led a dangerous expedition through wild jungle country overcoming savage natives until he reached the temple of the naked goddess. It was this meeting that led to a high degree of excitement. As he brought more of this material into the analysis, his autonomous, learning ego was beginning to function more independently and effectively in the classroom situation. He brought new bits of knowledge to the therapist and would try and teach him. At one point, he said to the therapist: "If you want to learn this stuff, you have got to concentrate on it and not let your mind wander all over the place." With this comment, he burst out laughing as if highly amused.

He then began to question the therapist about what made therapy work: How did kids like him get better when all they did was to talk to each other? Was the therapist secretly teaching him without him being conscious of it? Was it a sort of hypnosis? He dismissed this and remarked that he was getting better for lots of other reasons: he was making friends at school; he was beginning to like his teachers; he no longer hated his father who was "not bad as fathers go"; he was paying much more attention in class; he was becoming really interested in history and wanted to do some historical research; abstract ideas no longer frightened him; it was no different from what he had learned in grade school except that "it was all in your head." For the science exhibition, he had constructed a very special science project for which he was awarded a first prize.

Toward the end of his treatment, he began to give his therapist lecturettes, about schoolwork, therapy, "psychology" and so on, and when his didactic approach was pointed out to him, he said with a smile, "It's my turn to teach and your turn to learn."

No case of a learning disability illustrates all the theoretical aspects that have accrued around this subject, but in Jamie's case, both his development and his treatment were richly illustrative of some of the leading ideas in the field, both from the psychoanalytic and the Piagetian viewpoints.

CONCLUSION

Learning is a magnificent adventure of the human spirit. It involves the taking in of the world, representing it structurally within the mind, making sense of it in the form of theories, reexamining it indefatigably, modifying it in the light of further experience, and applying it meaningfully and purposefully to further outside situations. To study the process of learning, one can examine the extent of attention, the competence of the response, growth of knowledge, and the capacity for recall. Most of all, one must consider the feelings that accompany learning, sometimes aiding and sometimes disrupting it. Throughout his development, the child invents more and more powerful searchlights to illuminate new experiences and clarify older ones. As he appears through the eyes of the psychoanalyst or through the more cognitive lens of Piaget, one fact is apparent: the child's mind is not a Popperian "bucket."

REFERENCES

Anthony, E. J. (1981), Psychoanalysis and environment. In: *The Psychoanalytic Perspectives on Human Personality Development Throughout the Life Cycle,* ed. G. H. Pollock & N. Greenspan. Bethesda, MD: National Institute of Mental Health.

Binet, A. (1894), The mechanisms of thought. *Fortnightly Rev.,* 55:785–799.

Bluhler, K. (1930), *Die Geistige Entwicklung des Kindes,* 6th ed. Jena: Fircher.

Bringuier, J. C. (1980), *Conversations with Jean Piaget.* Foreword by G. Voyat. Chicago: University of Chicago Press.

Erikson, E. H. (1957), *Childhood and Society.* New York: W. W. Norton.

Freud, S. (1895), Project for a scientific psychology. *Standard Edition,* 1. London: Hogarth Press, 1966.

Hartmann, H. (1964), *Essays on Ego Psychology.* New York: International Universities Press.

Inhelder, G., Sinclair, H., & Bovet, M. (1974), *Learning and the Development of Cognition.* Preface by J. Piaget. Cambridge, MA: Harvard University Press.

Piaget, J. (1946), *Play Dreams and Imitation in Childhood.* New York: W. W. Norton, 1962.

—— (1973), The affective unconscious and the cognitive unconscious. *J. Amer. Psychoanal. Assn.,* 21:249–261.

—— (1974), Foreword to *Learning and Development of Cognition,* by B. Inhelder, H. Sinclair, & M. Bovet. Cambridge, MA: Harvard University Press.

Popper, K. (1972), The bucket and the searchlight: Two theories of knowledge. In: *Objective Knowledge: An Evolutionary Approach.* Oxford: Clarendon Press.

Rapaport, D. (1950), On the psychoanalytic theory of thinking. *Internat. J. Psycho-Anal.*, 31:161–170.

——— (1952), Review on learning theory and personality dynamics. *J. Abnorm. & Soc. Psychol.*, 47:137–142.

——— (1959), The theory of attention cathexis: An economic and structural attempt at the exploration of cognitive processes. In: *Collected Papers*, ed. M. M. Gill. New York: Basic Books, 1967.

Szasz, T. (1963), Psychoanalytic treatment as education. *Arch. Gen. Psychiat.*, 9:46–52.

Chapter 5

Psychologically Informed Education: Historical Foundations

RALPH W. TYLER, Ph.D.

Schooling in America began in the seventeenth century as a minor component of an educational system largely based on learning in the home and in the workplace. The function of the school was to teach children to read, write, and compute, and thus to overcome the provincialism of an environment in which the child's learning was confined to experiences in the community and to the often superstitious and usually only partially correct views of the adults there. The colonial school was not expected to help students develop a constructive emotional life. Even as late as the beginning of the twentieth century, teachers gave little thought to the affective components of instruction.

I entered a Nebraska elementary school in 1906 and graduated from high school in 1917. What I remember from my experiences as a pupil are the strictness of the discipline, the catechismic type of recitation, the dullness of the textbooks, and the complete absence of any obvious connection between our classwork and the activities we carried on outside of school. The first editions of John

Dewey's two small volumes, *Interest and Effort in Education* (1913) and *The School and Society* (1899), had just been published and his profound influence on educational theory and practice was just beginning. The view then held by most teachers and parents was that the school was quite separate from the other institutions in society and its tasks should be sufficiently distasteful to the students to require strong discipline to undertake them and carry them through. Furthermore, they believed that while in school, children should not talk with one another; all communication should be between the teacher and the class as a whole or between the teacher and the individual pupil.

CHANGING ATTITUDES TOWARD STUDENT INTERESTS

My first experience with a different view of student interests was in 1915 when our history teacher introduced us to what she called the "Socialized Recitation." It operated as follows: for each major division of the history course, we first had the usual textbook study and class recitation. After this phase of our work was completed, each student was required to select a topic (with the approval of the teacher) which was germane to that division of the course. The student then developed a report, using not only the textbook but also other relevant sources of information. Finally, he or she presented the report orally to the class and then responded to questions asked by classmates.

This procedure is not unusual today, but it included features that were novel to us at that time. (1) Exercise of student initiative in selecting a topic; (2) use of several self-selected sources of information; (3) student responsibility for organizing, composing, and presenting an original report; and (4) interacting directly with other students in responding to their questions. The socialized recitation was a step toward informality in classroom behavior. It was also a small beginning effort to make the classroom a microcosm of the larger society. I liked this new technique and read more widely in the field of history than I had done in previous courses. I also enjoyed the quasi-debating character of the give-and-take with my classmates. Some students complained that they had to spend too much time in preparing their reports. Some parents protested that the relaxed and pleasant atmosphere of the history class indicated flabby discipline. Nevertheless, this innovation was continued until our teacher, Hazel Hempel, left teaching for marriage. Later, she was the first woman U.S. Senator (Mrs. George Abel) from Nebraska.

From the perspective of today, the socialized recitation may seem a very minor kind of innovation, but it had a real influence on the teachers who were being introduced to Dewey's writings. It demonstrated that at least some public school students would spend time and effort studying something in which they were interested. (Dewey's students were often viewed as atypical because they were in the Laboratory School of the University of Chicago.) It showed teachers that interest and effort in education were not always antithetical. It indicated that some students could take responsibility for questioning, and that discussion and debate among students could contribute to learning. It also established the fact that a classroom could be a learning society and need not be devoted solely to drill and catechismic recitation. These conclusions are now taken for granted, but in 1915 they were novel.

CHANGING VIEW OF INDIVIDUAL DIFFERENCE AMONG CHILDREN

Eighty years ago teachers, as well as the American public in general, viewed differences among children as either good or bad. Some children were bright, others were dull;

some were educable, others were not. Schools were expected to sort pupils beginning with the first grade. Those who performed school tasks satisfactorily were given good marks and encouraged to continue their schooling. Those who were slow or did not carry through the assignments and other school tasks were given low, often failing marks, and were discouraged from continuing their schooling. The Darwinian notion of the "survival of the fittest" was commonly accepted as the justification for the fact that in 1910 more than 50 percent of the children enrolled in the first grade had dropped out by the end of the sixth grade and only 10 percent graduated from high school. Three percent graduated from college.

One of those who was greatly stimulated by his observations of the variety of individual differences among school children was Frederic Burk, President of San Francisco Normal School during the second decade of this century. He believed that most children could learn what the school was expected to teach and set out to demonstrate this proposition. He conceived the idea of developing self-instructional materials that would enable children in the same classroom to study different assignments and work at different rates. In 1914, Carleton Washburne joined the San Francisco Normal School staff and participated in developing the curriculum plans and the self-instructional materials. Helen Parkhurst was also a member of the staff. After they left San Francisco—Washburne to become Superintendent of Schools in Winnetka, Illinois, and Parkhurst to found the Dalton School in Dalton, Massachusetts—they developed and published two plans for individualizing instruction. These plans became widely known and influenced many teachers and schools to use workbooks and other forms of self-instructional and partly self-instructional materials.

In 1919, shortly after Washburne became superintendent of the elementary school district of Winnetka, the staff began work on the curriculum and materials required for the type of individualized instruction they had adopted. The plan identified two distinct parts of the curriculum: common essentials and group and creative activities. Half of the morning and half of the afternoon were devoted to each. In the common essentials, individualization consisted of unit lessons with largely self-instructional materials on which the student worked at his own rate and then tested himself for mastery. When the student believed that the material of the unit had been mastered, the mastery test provided by the teacher was taken. If the test were passed, the student went on to the next unit; if not, a conference with the teacher provided guidance for further self-instructional work and retesting.

In the group and creative activities, individualization took the form of individual responsibilities in group activities and relevant individual projects. The classroom grouping was according to age and social maturity and not according to estimates of "ability," "intelligence," "scholastic aptitude," or earlier school marks.

Helen Parkhurst developed and introduced the Dalton Plan first in 1919 at a school for handicapped children in Dalton, Massachusetts. Later, in New York City she founded the Dalton School, which included both an elementary and a high school. As the school was originally established, the emphases were on providing opportunities for each child to pursue interests on his own terms, to study the fundamentals at his own rate, and to live constructively and cooperatively in the school community. The school employed contracts in which each child selected the interest he would pursue and stated what would be done during the contract period. In the study of the fundamentals, the contracts permitted the child to set his own pace, but was required to complete units in each of the subjects before going on to a more advanced unit in any subject. The student could not spend several weeks concentrating on only one or two subjects.

Henry C. Morrison, Superintendent of the Laboratory
Schools of the University of Chicago published a monu-
mental volume in 1926, *The Practice of Teaching in the
Secondary School,* which outlined a program for Mastery
Learning that had been demonstrated in the University
of Chicago High School. Because of the common opinion
that the Laboratory School students were not like those
in public schools, Morrison's program for Mastery Learning had less influence at that time than did the Winnetka
plan. However, nearly fifty years later, Benjamin Bloom's
work with Mastery Learning in public schools has received a good deal of attention and has been adopted in
several major school systems.

The Winnetka and Dalton plans are still operating,
although with changing personnel the modifications over
the years have been great. Nevertheless, the influence
of these two somewhat similar programs on views of individual differences among students were striking in the
1920s and 1930s, and many of the changes they stimulated have become part of the mainstream of education
in the United States. Some of the chief innovations were
(1) the development and use of workbooks designed to
provide relevant practice materials and other features of
self-instruction; (2) recognition of two major functions of
the school—instruction in basic skills and knowledge and
socialization through group living; (3) a plan for grouping
students for instruction that did not stigmatize the slow
groups nor magnify the feelings of superiority of the fast
groups; (4) a manageable procedure for providing for individual differences among students in rate of school
learning and in special interests related to learning activities.

PROJECT METHOD AND ACTIVITY SCHOOLS

After John Dewey moved from the University of Chicago
to Columbia University, he and his writings attracted

the attention of William Heard Kilpatrick, a professor at Teachers College, Columbia University. In 1929, Kilpatrick outlined a general methodology of teaching that he believed to be a faithful reflection of Dewey's ideas. He called it the Project Method, defining a project as "a purposeful activity carried to completion in a natural setting."

The idea that one learns through one's activities rather than from passive reception of instruction was already widely accepted among educational psychologists of that day. William James, Charles Judd, and Edward Thorndike, as well as John Dewey, based their experimental work and their theories of learning on this concept. However, the requirement that the learning activity be purposeful to the student and that it be carried to completion is clearly derived from Dewey's emphasis upon the child's interests and purposes and upon the continuity of experience, in contrast to the fragmentation which commonly resulted from rather miniscule topics of study and short class periods.

All of the major educational psychologists of that day were concerned with transfer of training; that is, the way in which what children learned in school would become part of their general repertoire upon which they would draw whenever and wherever it was appropriate. They· were all conscious of cases where the child could recite the lesson accurately and complete the practical drills without error but did not utilize the knowledge or skills in relevant occasions outside of school. Only Dewey, however, explicitly recommended that the school be part of society and not an isolated institution. Schooling would then be a part of the ongoing life of children, helping them to confront their problems, attack them, and thus make learning a central factor in living. This concept was the basis for Kilpatrick's definition of the project being carried on by the student in a natural setting.

Kilpatrick's summer courses in the philosophy of ed-

ucation attracted large numbers of educators. Teachers
were fascinated by his colorful lectures that depicted the
Project Method as a way to assure student motivation,
to turn routine schoolwork into a bustle of meaningful
activity and, at the same time, increase the knowledge
and skills of the students. His views were frequently attacked in public by William Bagley, another professor at
Teachers College, who argued that much of what children
needed to learn in school was the cultural heritage—the
knowledge and skills that had been developed over the
centuries and had been deemed essential to preserve and
maintain a civilized society. Whether or not children were
interested in all significant parts of the cultural heritage
was beside the point. Building on student interests and
purposes would, said Bagley, lead to a considerable waste
of time and a serious loss of learning.

These debates stimulated the formation of two par-
tisan educational groups: the Essentialists and the Progressives. The position of the Essentialists was largely
one of defending the status quo: no new programs or in-
ventions were constructed or well received from that
viewpoint. The position of the Progressives was that there
was need for educational reform. The Project Method was
an invention that attracted the Progressives, because
they saw the need for educational improvement and
wanted to try promising innovations.

Hundreds of schools set up Project Method classes, but
in only a few cases did the entire school program utilize
it as its sole instructional procedure, the methods Kilpatrick defined. The use of the Project Method, in this
true sense, was almost wholly confined to elementary
schools and to out-of-school educational institutions, such
as the 4H Club. Few high schools became involved, probably because high school programs are usually organized
in terms of school subjects—which limited the opportunities for carrying on "purposeful activities to completion
in a natural setting." Meriam's Project School, operated

by the College of Education of the University of Missouri, was a good example of a comprehensive adoption of the method throughout an elementary school. The Eighteen Activity Schools of New York City were illustrations of the adaptation of the Project Method to a large city school system.

The Meriam School no longer exists and there are now no Activity Schools as they were initially conceived in New York City or in any other large city. However, the influence of the Project Method still continues. The basic concept—learning programs that utilize student projects purposefully undertaken and completed in at least a quasi-natural setting—is now widely accepted as a sensible kind of program. Many out-of-school organizations for children and youth also base their educational programs on the Project Method. In junior and senior high schools, projects are common in almost every school subject. The development of the Project Method is part of the continuing movement toward schooling that encourages greater student initiative and responsibility.

THE EIGHT-YEAR STUDY

By 1930, several features of the typical elementary school in the United States were clearly different from those of 1915. The atmosphere of the classroom was more informal and more friendly. Children continued to study and work even when the teacher was busy in some other part of the room. Learning activities were more varied among members of the class as teachers made adaptations to individual differences. The contents of textbooks and workbooks used in the school were more relevant to their experiences and more interesting to the students.

The high schools, however, were still very much like those of 1910, particularly in terms of curriculum content and learning activities. High school staffs felt that they were prevented from making needed improvements because of the rigidity of college entrance requirements. Nevertheless, pressures for change in the high schools were mounting, coming in part from the students themselves. Many of the young people entering high school came from elementary schools that had given them greater freedom and more opportunities for self-direction in learning than they were permitted as high school students. Moreover, with the onset of the Great Depression in 1929, new demands for change came with such force that they could no longer be denied. Youth, in large numbers, unable to find work, enrolled in high school. Most of these new students did not plan to go to college, and most of them found little meaning and interest in their high school tasks. But still they went to school; there was no other place for them to go.

The high school curriculum was not designed for these young people. Most teachers and principals recognized this fact, and many favored a move to reconstruct the high school curriculum and the instructional program both to meet the needs of these Depression youth and to respond to the pressures to give greater opportunities for self-direction in learning. At the same time, however, they did not want to jeopardize the chances of college admissions for students who wished to go there. This was the dilemma.

The Progressive Education Association took the lead in attacking the problem. Its officers appointed a Commission on the Relation of School and College and charged it with the task of devising a way out of the impasse. The Commission consisted of twenty-eight members, including college officials, high school principals, and interested lay people. Wilford Aiken, then director of the John Burroughs School near St. Louis, Missouri, was appointed chairman.

The Commission served as a forum for the presentation of conflicting points of view. High school principals sought to eliminate or greatly reduce the requirements for taking particular subjects and courses for college admission. College officials, on the other hand, feared that if these requirements were eliminated, students who were unprepared for college work would be admitted, some argued for differential curricula that would separate, at the beginning of high school, the students who would go on to college from those who would not; some, including several laypeople, opposed this proposal because of its contribution to greater social stratification, noting that social mobility is increased when the options for college attendance are kept open as long as possible.

What the Commission finally recommended was a pilot program. A small number of secondary schools—ultimately thirty schools and school systems—were to be selected by the Commission, and for eight years they were to be permitted to develop educational programs that each school believed to be appropriate for its students, without regard to the current college entrance requirements. The schools would be responsible for collecting and reporting information about what students were learning—information that would help the colleges in selecting candidates for admission. The Commission would make sure that a comprehensive evaluation of the pilot program would be made and the findings reported.

The proposal was submitted to every accredited college and university in the United States, with the request that the plan be endorsed if the college were willing to admit graduates from the pilot schools during this period, admitting them without prejudice based on their lack of customary entrance requirements. Almost all of the major colleges and universities endorsed the proposal. In 1931, the Commission appointed a directing committee for the study. The committee selected the thirty secondary schools and school systems and continued throughout the eight years to be responsible for the supervision of the project.

The thirty schools included both public and private

schools. In the Chicago area, the participating schools were Francis Parker School, New Trier Township High School, North Shore County Day School, and the University of Chicago High School. The roster included large schools and small ones, suburban schools and inner-city schools, and every region in the country except the South, which had few members in the Progressive Education Association. A few years later, the Southern Association of Schools and Colleges established a similar study for the white schools of the South and the Negro Association conducted such a study among black high schools. In addition, the Michigan State Department of Public Instruction developed a project of this sort within the state. The initial support of the directing Committee of the Eight-Year Study was provided by Carnegie Corporation of New York. Thereafter, this project, as well as those in the South and in Michigan, received grants-in-aid from the General Education Board of the Rockefeller Foundation.

The schools of the Eight-Year Study began their pilot efforts in September 1933. It soon became apparent that they needed assistance, both in curriculum development and in evaluation. The Progressive Education Association established a commission on the secondary school curriculum which sponsored a series of studies of adolescents. These studies, under Caroline Zachry's direction, were to provide helpful information about the interests, needs, activities, and learning characteristics of youth. Under the leadership of Harold Albert, subject matter committees were formed to draw upon these studies and others and publish volumes that would furnish statements of overall objectives, subject matter and learning activities for these subjects. The publications included Louise Rosenblatt's *Literature as Exploration* (1938), Louis Zaner's *Language in General Education* (1942), Thomas Monroe's *Art in General Education* (1942), and the like.

To meet the need for assistance in evaluation, the

steering committee asked me to serve as director of evaluation and to assemble a staff to develop the procedures and the instruments. The curriculum associates and the evaluation staff worked closely with the schools throughout the pilot period. Learning how to develop and operate a curriculum and an instructional program designed to be serviceable to a wide range of high school students proved to be a highly significant experience for me.

In my opinion, among the most significant results of the Eight-Year Study were the following:

1. Widespread acceptance of the idea that schools could develop educational programs that would interest a large proportion of their students, that would help them meet some of their needs, and, at the same time, would provide them with the preparation essential to success in college.

2. Recognition by colleges that they could find among high school graduates who had not met specific subject requirements many who would succeed in their college work. They learned that they could identify successful candidates for admission on the basis of tests of their ability to read and to handle quantitative problems, and on evidence of strong interest in further education.

3. The freeing of high schools from the heavy domination in program development imposed by college entrance requirements.

4. The development of the in-service workshop which was "invented" during the study to furnish time and assistance to teachers in developing instructional programs and materials and in acquiring new knowledge and skills for their work. This device was recognized as an effective means for the in-service education of professionals.

5. The wide acceptance of the concept of educational evaluation as a procedure for appraising the attainment of the several main objectives of an educational program. This concept largely superseded the narrower concept of

testing in assessing education programs and student progress.

6. The recognition by educational practitioners of the value of defining educational objectives in terms of the behavior patterns students are encouraged to acquire. This process was shown to be helpful in defining objectives that could be used to direct curriculum planning, to guide instruction, and to furnish specifications for evaluation. It brought affective behaviors into the open as desirable educational objectives whereas previously terms like *developing appreciation in art or literature* were so vaguely defined that they were not given the attention they deserved in curriculum planning.

For example, in working with teachers of literature in the Eight-Year Study, I found that they would usually repeat some trite phrase like "the students should learn to appreciate literature." I would comment: "That sounds sensible. What do you mean? What have you observed that you are trying to help young people learn that you call 'appreciation.' Is it that they can tell you who wrote certain books? Is it that they can make critical judgments of a literary work in terms of such criteria as illusion of reality, unity, and so on?" We discussed this question until we reached a tentative agreement that in the teaching of literature the teachers sought to help students comprehend, interpret, and appreciate literary works. By appreciation they meant that the reader respond emotionally to the work and find life richer by reason of these emotional reactions. They saw appreciation as a response to reading which went beyond plain sense comprehension and cognitive interpretations. I believe that the Eight-Year Study had a significant impact in gaining recognition that affective behaviors called interests and those called appreciations are important objectives of schooling, and that they could be defined sufficiently to guide instruction and to appraise student learning.

THE CONTEMPORARY SITUATION

At present, we find that most teachers are accustomed to giving special attention to the cognitive components of arithmetic, science, reading, and social studies. They are concerned with the psychomotor components of handwriting, of physical education, of arts and crafts. But many have given little thought to affective objectives of school learning except in fields like art and music. Yet the development of children and youth into mature, responsible, loving, caring, happy adults requires a good deal of affective education in which they learn to express emotions in socially acceptable and satisfying ways, to find elements in their environment that can arouse interest, enhance pleasurable emotions, and serve continuously as stimuli for enjoying life rather than being bored. Although experiences in the home and other out-of-school settings contribute most to affective development, the school has a significant part to play.

Since the early 1920s, children's interests have been given increasing attention by teachers, most of the concern has been with interests as important sources for motivation to learn and major bases for the rewards pupils obtain when successful in learning. In these cases, the existing emotional reactions of children are means in the educational process. However, by the late 1920s, educators had found that skills in reading were not utilized by children who had not found reading interesting, and in terms of the content, subject matter learned was largely forgotten when children had found little of interest in a subject. Hence, in the 1930s, the curriculum of many elementary schools listed as objectives developing interest in reading, science, art, and other school subjects.

By the later 1930s, there developed a wide consensus on the importance of the objectives relating to appreciation; learning to respond with pleasant feelings to an increasingly wide range of aesthetic, social, intellectual, and physical aspects of the students' environment, and to respond in an increasingly varied way so that monotony and boredom do not take over the emotional potential of life. But even today, this general approval of affective objectives in the school curriculum is not widespread among parents and other community members. Furthermore, because these notions have not been analyzed and widely discussed among educators, there has developed a kind of cultism around the term *affective education*. It now seems clearly necessary to study, analyze, discuss, and demonstrate the ways in which elementary and secondary schools can constructively contribute to the emotional development of their students.

REFERENCES

Bagley, W. C. (1906), *The Educative Process*. New York: Macmillan.
———— (1934), *Education and Emergent Man: A Theory of Education with Particular Application to Public Education in the United States*. New York: Nelson.
Bloom, B. (1981), *All Our Children Learning*. New York: McGraw-Hill.
Dewey, J. (1913), *Interest and Effort in Education*. Boston: Houghton-Mifflin.
———— (1899), *The School and Society*. Chicago: University of Chicago Press.
Kilpatrick, W. H. (1929), *Project Method*. New York: Teachers College Press of Columbia University.
Monroe, T. (1942), *Art in General Education*. New York: Harper.
Morrison, H. (1926), *The Practice of Teaching in the Secondary School*. Chicago: University of Chicago Press.
Rosenblatt, L. (1938), *Literature as Exploration*. New York: Appleton-Century-Crofts.
Zaner, L. (1942), *Language in General Education*. New York: Harper.

Chapter 6

The Courage to Try—Self-Esteem and Learning

H. E. BERNSTEIN, M.D.

Everyone learns, but some learn more and some learn less. A few obvious factors contribute to those differences, such as opportunity, motivation, and innate capacity. Another factor, perhaps not quite as obvious, deserves attention, and that is the courage to try. Learning involves an active confrontation with the unknown and the unfamiliar, to some degree a fearful task for the mature scientist investigating nature as it is for the young child trying to learn to stand and walk. No matter how great the opportunity, motivation, or innate capacity, no learning will occur unless the individual finds within himself the courage to try.

I propose that the courage to try to learn directly reflects the level of self-esteem in each person. This will not be a novel idea to those involved in education whose experience repeatedly reaffirms the fact that those with high self-esteem are the most willing to try. But it does emphasize the importance of achieving a precise and accurate understanding of the meaning and the mechanism of self-esteem, a concept that has become clouded and confused by two fundamental errors. The first of those errors I believe to be the confusion of esteem with love; the second is the tendency to assume that self-esteem derives from and is maintained by the esteem or love of others.

The confusion of love with esteem has become deeply embedded in psychoanalytic thought and dates back at least as far as Freud's paper "On Narcissism, An Introduction" (1914), a paper about which Freud himself expressed great dissatisfaction. In this effort to describe the complex subject of narcissism he made a number of statements relating esteem to love, an example of which follows: "Complete object love . . . displays the marked sexual overvaluation which is doubtless derived from the child's original narcissism and thus corresponds to a transference of that narcissism to the sexual object. This sexual overvaluation is the origin of the peculiar state of being in love . . ." (Freud, 1914, p. 88).

Although one can surely acknowledge that overesteeming the object of love is common, one must just as surely take pause at his seductively simple statement that such is the origin of love. Later on in that paper Freud states that the lover has a lowered self-regard by virtue of having forfeited a part of his narcissism, which can only be replaced by being loved. That observation, I daresay, accords little with experience, for quite the opposite is usually true: the lover's self-esteem tends to be heightened. The lover whose love is rejected may suffer a fall in self-esteem, but then that is a consequence of rejection, not of loving.

Of course that paper represents an early phase in the evolution of Freud's psychoanalytic theory, a phase in which he was still attempting to explain psychological behavior in terms of ego instincts and sexual instincts (libido). Yet, what was wrought there became established and was carried forward by his contemporaries and by those who followed. To trace the evolution of that confusion to the present is beyond the scope of this chapter, but for those interested in pursuing the subject a number of critical review articles are available (VonDerWaals, 1965; Pulver, 1970; Spruiell, 1975; Dare and Holder, 1981).

It is more difficult to trace the second source of confusion back to its origin, for the mistaken notion that self-esteem derives from and is maintained by esteem or love from others is not exclusively psychoanalytic. It is a much more widely held belief that has been reinforced incidentally by the acritical acceptance of many psychoanalysts. It probably derives most directly from the feeling of well-being that accompanies the approval of others, and there can be little question that such approbation is widely sought for its pleasurable effect. What is overlooked is the transience of that effect which causes some to lead their lives in a never ending search for approval from others. They feel good as long as the applause is present, but when it stops they soon feel worthless again, and they must seek for more applause to bolster their feeling of well-being. These are the people who, lacking self-approval, attempt to compensate that deficit with the substitution of others' approval. When that particular form of psychopathology is mistakenly perceived as universal, as the "normal" state of man, it leads to theoretical distortions like Kohut's (1971) concept of the self-object (and thence to the unhyphenated selfobject) which holds that self-esteem is always dependent upon and derives from esteem or love from others.

Self-esteem is the evaluation of one's own worth, and it is the one critical judgment that everyone makes with remarkably consistent accuracy. In view of the prevalence of low self-esteem, it may seem harsh to conclude that all of those people are quite right in their judgments, that so many really are not worth very much. The key question here is, "Not worth very much to whom?" Whenever the subject of a person's worth arises there is a tendency to assume that some societal judgment is involved;

that is not so in this case. One can cite many examples of the "good" person who holds himself in low esteem and who persists in that view despite our repeated assurance that he is kind and considerate and contributes more than most to his society. We see him as a valuable person, but we are estimating different things. We are judging his worth to society, while he is describing his worth to himself, and the latter is the real meaning of self-esteem. He will be grateful for the expression of our esteem, may even feel better because of it for a while, but it will not alter his self-esteem one iota. As Alexander Pope put it long ago (1733–1734):

One self-approving hour whole years outweighs
Of stupid starers and of loud huzzas [Epistle IV, 1. 255].

To put it another way, I am suggesting that the popular concept of an "inferiority complex" is wrong. He who deems himself inferior does not do so because he is perversely hypercritical, nor does he distort and misperceive the truth about himself. If he sees himself to be inferior it is because, in some important way, he is inferior—not for you, not for me, but for himself.

What, then, is the basis upon which each person makes this critical and consistently accurate assessment of himself? Here accuracy and precision are lost, for it is rare to find someone who really knows why he judges himself as he does. Most people try to explain it in terms that fit some moral or interpersonal code. One person believes his low opinion of himself to be the result of having undesirable feelings, thoughts, or impulses, even though he is intellectually aware that these are shared by multitudes. Another explains that he has accomplished nothing substantial, has contributed nothing of significance, so he sees himself to be unsubstantial, insignificant. A third finds his explanation in his lack of sufficient intelligence or wit—or he believes himself to be physically unattractive or clumsy or unable to dance well—the list of rationalizations is varied and extensive. But they are rationalizations all, and none of them is the real basis of low self-esteem.

Perhaps an analogy will lead us most directly to the truth of the matter. You own an automobile that runs well. It starts when you want it to start, its brakes are good, and it stops at your wish. It steers easily, goes where you want it to go in all kinds of circumstances, and its gas mileage is high so that it gets you to your destination economically. I need not tell you that anyone who possesses a car of that description esteems it highly. On the other hand, if your automobile is difficult to start, if it tends to stall when you want to accelerate, if it has brakes that sometimes fail and guzzles gasoline in excessive quantities, then you will probably hold it in low esteem. If yours is the second car, no amount of praise of it by others will alter your judgment—no matter that they love its beauty, admire its power, respect its price. You know how it performs, and you will not esteem it well.

So it is with each person's judgment of his own self-organization. As he knows that he starts easily, stops at will, can rely upon himself in all kinds of situations, and that he can get where he is going with an economy of effort, so he will have high self-esteem. But as he knows that he cannot function well for himself, cannot depend upon his own performance, and that his performance requires excessive effort, then he will hold himself in low esteem. The assessment of how well one functions for one's self is the real basis of self-esteem. Even though we are rarely conscious of making that assessment, it is quite automatic and consistently accurate.

We lose sight of this simple and direct meaning of self-esteem when we confuse esteem with love and then proceed to equate self-esteem with self-love (narcissism), or see the one as some mysterious derivative of the other.

It is an easy confusion to fall into, for we do tend to esteem that which we love, and we do tend to love that which we esteem. Yet, their interacting effect does not make them a unity. Poets and philosophers have recognized for a long time that love is blind, and we accept that, recognizing that love is a feeling that follows no apparent logic or reason. On the other hand, *esteem,* a word that derives from the same root as the word *estimate,* refers to a process that is open eyed and judgmental. On that basis alone, we must conclude that loving and esteeming are two quite different processes involving very different psychological functions. Love is feeling, esteem is judgment.

Freud, as noted above, early described the general tendency to overestimate the object of love. The man who falls in love with a woman thinks that she is the most beautiful, the most perfect woman in all the world, and fond parents are impelled to see in their child all manner of perfections which sober observation would not confirm. It should come as no surprise, then, that he who loves himself, the narcissistic character, would also overestimate himself. How then can we square the narcissistic character and his often grossly exaggerated self-estimation with the assertion that self-esteem is a consistently accurate judgment? The answer lies in the narcissistic character's vulnerability, the ease with which its exaggerated self-estimation can be deflated, leaving him with the conviction of worthlessness. He behaves as though he holds two self-estimations, side by side, one very high and one very low. This, too, should be no surprise when we recognize that the narcissistic character is simultaneously the subject and the object of his own love: as object his esteem is exaggerated by that natural tendency to overestimate the object of love, but as subject he knows somewhere within that he is not functioning well for himself, and his self-esteem is correspondingly low. It is always self as subject that makes the accurate self-assessment.

The narcissistic character, however, is not the sole possessor of a double self-estimation. There is a far larger group of people who appear superficially to have a similar double self-estimation and who, because of that seeming correspondence, have been erroneously catalogued as narcissistic characters, too. But this latter and much larger group of people do not love themselves excessively, are not truly narcissistic. They simply have a low self-esteem that they attempt to hide beneath a defensive facade of haughty arrogance and cold superiority. While the narcissistic character vacillates between a *conviction* of high and low self-esteem, this larger group is always secretly aware of its low self-esteem and of the defensive nature of its haughty facade. They remind one of an insightful remark attributed to Groucho Marx. When asked if he belonged to a certain country club he replied, "I would never join a club that was willing to accept me as a member." Their apparently exaggerated self-regard is not the overestimation born of love, but is a defensive effort meant to convince others that they are, indeed, worthwhile.

The effort to convince others of one's own worth stems from the mistaken notion that self-esteem derives from and is maintained by esteem from others. It is an effort doomed to failure. That does not mean that the esteem of others is not, in itself, a pleasurable experience. Everyone enjoys the esteem of others, but that is not the route to self-esteem. Mark Twain (1906) suggested that the desire for self-approval may be called the "Master Passion," and everyone is aware, within himself, of how strong a wish it is. No wonder, then, that those lacking self-esteem would turn to the compensatory pleasure of winning the esteem of others. Adding confusion to confusion, they then often mistake esteem for love and believe that they are seeking the love of others, and so they *appear* to be always seeking to be loved, and are mistakenly labeled "narcissistic" on that account as well. Many of these people become quite adept at winning the esteem, or the love, of others. The proof of the failure of that quest lies in the outcome, for they consistently find their self-esteem unaffected by each victory. Instead, they are left with the hollow feeling of a lack of authenticity, characterized by the thought, "Well, I fooled another one!"

The only route to self-esteem is through the effective function of one's own self-organization, and it is here that a few definitions become imperative. By "self-organization" I mean the unique integration of all that constitutes an individual: his body and his mind, his physiology and his feelings, his intellect, attitudes, experience, impulses, and defenses. What we call his character is the expression of that self-organization, manifested in typical and habitual attitudes and modes of action and reaction. And the term *self* refers to a concept each person forms of his own functioning totality, a concept of his self-organization. In other words, the self-organization is a functional agency, character is its expression, and self is its conceptualization.

What we are dealing with is the issue of mastery—not in the usual sense of mastery of others nor of the external world—but mastery of one's self. Anything that interferes with mastery of self diminishes self-esteem. It makes some difference if that interference comes from outside or from within, but in the long run any interference with self-mastery lowers self-esteem. The slave will be abject, whether he be slave to another or slave to some unknown and unmanageable force within himself. To be helpless is the condition of lowest self-esteem.

The person with high self-esteem will appear self-confident, self-possessed, in contrast to the self-conscious person who acts as though he must always keep a wary eye upon himself to anticipate and prevent some cataclysmic loss of control. The self-conscious often strive to be cool, mistaking self-possession for coolness. The self-confident, the self-possessed, are not cool; on the contrary, they can be quite warm and feelingful, for they are comfortable with their feelings. The person who achieves coolness to be in control of himself has only deceived himself, for by locking his feelings behind a door of repression he has not gained control of them, he has only loosed those forces to push and pull at him behind his back. Now he must expend energy constantly to keep the door shut, and even then he does not know when one feeling or another might pour through a crack in the wall.

The issue of self-esteem joins the problem of learning as we recognize that the learner always faces the unknown and the unfamiliar on two fronts simultaneously. The external situation or problem is, by definition, unknown, for otherwise no learning could occur. The second front is the internal one, for the learner has never been in this exact position before and so cannot know precisely what to expect from within. As his self-esteem is high, he will experience some mild apprehension at what might occur, but confident in his self-mastery he can turn most of his attention to the external problem, reliant upon his self-organization to continue to work effectively. The learner with low self-esteem, lacking confidence in the effective function of his self-organization, must become his own diligent supervisor, warily watching for the first signs of trouble within, so that he might attempt to patch things up with whatever emergency measures he can summon. His attention must always be split between two potential sources of danger: the unknown externally and the undependable internally. Whoever finds himself in the latter position experiences the learning situation as dangerous and uncomfortable, and will tend to shrink from voluntarily exposing himself, thereby forfeiting the opportunity to experience the pleasure of learning.

Learning is a pleasurable experience, despite the apprehension that is always a part of it, for the learner, having learned, enjoys a double sense of mastery: mastery of what has been learned, and some extension of mastery of himself. For example, the student who learns to solve simultaneous equations with two unknowns enjoys his mastery of the subject and, at the same time, enjoys the discovery that he has within himself the means to master that subject. There are few things as satisfying as the realization that "I can do it!"

The intense desire for self-mastery, and the pleasure that accompanies it, probably derives most directly from the prolonged period of helplessness and dependency through the years of infancy and childhood. It is as though all of us, having started life experiencing the insult of helplessness, spend the rest of our lives striving for autonomy, for self-mastery. The infant has far to go.

For the sake of simplicity I would arbitrarily designate three areas or aspects of the self that require mastery. First, the individual must become familiar with, and through that familiarity, achieve mastery of his own body. Second, he must achieve mastery of his intellectual or cognitive function. Third, and I believe this is where most problems arise, the individual must achieve mastery of his own feelings. In each of these areas mastery can only be achieved through the familiarity that comes from prolonged actual experience. Usually, parents and other adults are willing to allow the child to develop control of his body at his own pace, but even here we have come to understand the damage to self-esteem that arises with premature and too rigid toilet training, for example. In the cognitive sphere there has developed a growing impatience in recent decades, so that we hear of experiments in teaching young infants to read, even though the words that they might learn have no content, no meaning, to the infant. But it is in the realm of feelings that adults have least patience and tolerance with children, and try to impose adult standards and controls upon them.

There are probably many reasons that the realm of feelings is the most problematical. Many adults, uncomfortable with their own feelings, become uncomfortable with the feelings of others, especially children, who tend to express feelings most directly and unabashedly. Underneath that there is a prevalent, often unconscious, view of children as little wild animals who must be trained to be human. But it is not only the parents or adults who are hostile toward children who interfere with the child's development of mastery of his own feelings. Many caring and loving adults who want only what is best for the child pursue a course that they mistakenly believe to be the child's greatest advantage; that is, to make the child be "grown-up" as quickly as possible. In their view, it is the "grown-up" who is most effective in achieving, so the precociously mature child is bound to have a head start over others. And all too often they succeed in creating high achievers—with low self-esteem, and a crushing chronic boredom. (A more detailed discussion of my views on this form of psychopathology, which I consider to be prevalent, may be found in "Boredom and the Ready-Made Life" [1975]).

The primary task of childhood is the development of a self-organization, and throughout life everyone strives to expand and improve that self-organization toward an ideal goal of autonomy. As the young child must experience his own arms and legs repetitively over time in order to learn to use those limbs effectively, so he must experience his own cognitive faculties to discover what he can do with those. Most people understand and accept that necessity, to a greater or lesser degree, so far as body and intellect are concerned. Feelings, however, receive short shrift. It is as though people do not realize that feelings, too, must be experienced by the individual who only in that way can become familiar with them and so learn to use them effectively. The ability to experience one's feelings and to use them effectively is a function of central importance to every individual, at least as important as the effective use of his body and of his intellect, for it is feelings, and feelings alone, that motivate us.

There is a tendency, especially in our culture, to attribute great motivational force to the realm of ideas, but about that we must be clear. Ideas give direction to our actions, but it is only the feeling that we have about an idea that moves us to action. An idea about which we feel nothing has no motivating force at all.

The development of a self-organization, then, is in great measure a matter of learning. We must learn to use our bodies, our intellects, and our feelings, and the degree to which we learn to do all of these things will determine the level of our self-esteem. What then are the conditions that will best facilitate the development of high self-esteem in the child? We all know the importance of parental love, yet love alone will not do the job, especially when that love leads a parent to devote himself to forcing the child to fit some preconceived image, no matter how noble or heroic that image may be. Empathy, a concept that has enjoyed a resurgence of interest in psychology of late, is also important, for it allows the caretaker to know what the child is feeling, and so respond. But it is respect that is essential; respect for the uniqueness of each individual that allows each child to develop into who he or she is. A note of caution! Respectful acceptance is not to be construed as total permissiveness. Infants and young children can do things that will be injurious, if allowed to, and that is one reason that the caretaker's presence is so essential. The caretaker's love and empathy will inform him of the limits to be set, and will enable him to set those limits in a way that will stop or discourage injurious behavior without squelching the feelings that gave rise to the behavior. The three-year-old must be allowed to experience his anger at the newborn addition to the family, but he can't be allowed to express it by hitting the baby with a hammer. There is a vast difference between experiencing feeling and expressing that feeling. That distinction does not yet exist for the young child, but if his excessive behavioral response to a feeling is controlled by his caretaker he will learn, in time, to make that distinction, and then will be able to experience his feelings while using judgment about their expression. On the other hand, the young child who is punished repeatedly for the expression of his anger will learn that it is the feeling, not only its form of expression, that is forbidden, and will compliantly attempt to repress it. Then he will grow up without access to his anger, will not know clearly how anger feels, and will miss the opportunity to learn effective ways of handling it.

Nor is the task of learning an effective self-organization complete when the child enters school. He has come a long way by the age of five or six. He has largely mastered the use of his body so that motility is possible, he has developed boundaries distinguishing self and not-self, he has developed language, and he has made a lot of progress toward achieving tension regulation. These are enormous achievements, not always recognized as such by adults who tend to believe that, if mere children can do it, the task cannot be very significant. Yet it constitutes the most important learning task, and perhaps the most intensive learning period, in every person's life. Still, the external world and the internal world of the self remain largely undiscovered at this stage. The child still approaches learning with a primary focus on discovering his internal capacities. For example, the first- or second-grade student beginning to learn arithmetic does not undertake that task with the express purpose of mastering that skill so that he can go to the corner market to swing an advantageous deal. He is much more concerned with discovering that he has, within himself, the capacity to master arithmetical concepts. Only later, when he is convinced of his own capacity to learn the subject, will he then turn his attention to the use of the skill to achieve mastery of the external world.

At every stage of development the learner is at risk.

What he risks is the discovery of his own helplessness. With increasing self-mastery, and the self-esteem and self-confidence that it breeds, the risk of helplessness diminishes, although for us humans it probably never wholly disappears. Even so, the more one achieves confidence in his mastery of his body, his intellect, and his feelings, the more willing will he be to face novelty.

It is my conviction that the teacher, especially of primary-school grades, who best knows how to protect and to foster the self-esteem of his students, will inevitably have the brightest, most involved, and most eager class of students in the whole world.

CONCLUSION

The learning ego stands, as it were, at the interface of the external world and the inner world of affects, exposed to both simultaneously. As there is familiarity with and confidence in the ego's mastery of this inner world of feelings, that individual will be free to invest his attention in the external novelty to be learned. Those who lack such familiarity and confidence will be forced to divide their attention in an effort to avoid being rendered helpless from either direction.

The familiarity with and confidence in the ego's mastery of the full range of one's own feelings is a central constituent of self-esteem, which is here defined as the subjective evaluation of the effectiveness of one's own total function. Esteem, an evaluative function of the ego, is to be distinguished from love, which is a feeling and, correspondingly, self-esteem is to be distinguished from self-love (narcissism).

The mistaken notion that self-esteem derives from and is dependent upon esteem from others is discussed and the tendency to attempt to compensate for low self-esteem by seeking others' esteem is described as a particular manifestation of a specific form of psychopathology.

REFERENCES

Bernstein, H. E. (1975), Boredom and the ready-made life. *Soc. Res.,* 42(3):512–537.

Dare, C., & Holder, A. (1981), Developmental aspects of the interaction between narcissism, self-esteem and object relations. *Internat. J. Psycho-Anal.,* 62(3):323–337.

Freud, S. (1914), On narcissism, an introduction. *Standard Edition,* 14:73–102. London: Hogarth Press, 1957.

Kohut, H. (1971), *The Psychology of the Self.* New York: International Universities Press.

Pope, A. (1733–1734), An essay on man. In: *Standard Edition,* Epistle 4, line 255, ed W. Elwin & W. Courthope. London: J. Murray, 1871–1889.

Pulver, S. (1970), Narcissism: The term and the concept. *J. Amer. Psychoanal. Assn.,* 18:319–341.

Spruiell, V. (1975), Three strands of narcissism. *Psychoanal. Quart.,* 44:577–595.

Twain, M. (1906), *What Is Man?* New York: DeVinne, Chapter 6.

VonDerWaals, H. (1965), Problems of narcissism. *Bull. Menn. Clin.,* 29:293–311.

Chapter 7

Supervision: A Teaching-Learning Paradigm

HYMAN L. MUSLIN, M.D.
EDUARDO VAL, M.D.

INTRODUCTION

Learning and teaching are synonymous with activities that dominate and define the existence of man. We are discussing here learning as an accretion of self-structure and teaching as those activities that promote the accretion of psychic structure. Learning and teaching are dependent on the capacities of the learner and teacher to empathize with each other so as to approximate and give or receive in tune with the other's self state. It is our argument in this chapter that all learning and teaching, and especially the learning and teaching involved in supervision of clinical work in psychiatry, reflects, wittingly or not, the functions that emerge from self/selfobject dyads: from mirroring functions to the functions of the idealized parent, to the merger-twinship functions (Kohut, 1977). It is of course a necessary aspect of these self-sustaining functions that they come into being as a result of empathy on the part of the teacher as well as the learner.

Supervision, the major teaching method in psycho-

159

therapy, has long been an object of interest from its beginnings in the early history of psychoanalysis (Schlessinger, 1966). While there is a wide variety of opinion in the literature on supervision, most authors agree that supervision should consist in the main of teaching rather than focus on the intrapsychic problems of the therapist. This point has been emphasized in two panels on supervision reported by Keiser and Sloane (Keiser, 1956; Sloane, 1957). DeBell's review of the analytic literature on supervision stressed these points in defining the purposes of the supervisor: clarification of the diagnosis and meaning of the case; providing a laboratory for technique; enhancing self-awareness in the therapist and facilitating the translation of the theoretical to the clinical (DeBell, 1963). Ekstein and Wallerstein (1958) in their monograph on supervision and Tarachow in his monograph on psychotherapy (1963) offer a difference in their approach to the supervisory situation. Ekstein and Wallerstein emphasize that the supervisor's task is to enhance the learning process and self-awareness as they relate to therapy. The focus is on the therapist's problems with the patient and the supervisor. At times, the therapist's problems with his patient parallel comparable problems he experiences in supervision (Ekstein and Wallerstein, 1958). By contrast Tarachow emphasized that supervision is to consist of the needs and problems of the patient expressed in the specific clinical phenomena to be understood by the supervisor and transmitted to his student. Tarachow emphasizes that the supervisor should avoid confronting his student with any intrapsychic problem which the student has displayed (Tarachow, 1963). As Fleming and Benedek pointed out, there are three models of supervision in psychotherapy teaching based on the supervisor (1) as demonstrator; (2) as corrector; and (3) as furtherer of the therapist's growth by helping him develop into a sophisticated instrument capable of evaluating the total system of therapeutic processes between therapist and patient, the "system sensitivity" of the therapist (Fleming and Benedek, 1964). Arlow and other writers on the supervisory process spoke of supervision as an experience of self-growth through the promotion of insight into inner mental processes (Arlow, 1963; Zetzel, 1953). While there has been little in the way of systematic research in supervision there have been some attempts to study the supervisory process in terms of the learning that takes place as observed in subsequent interviews (Muslin, Burstein, Gedo, and Sadow, 1967).

SELF/SELFOBJECT DYADS IN LEARNING AND TEACHING

It seems to us that learning and teaching involve in some measure the functions of mirroring. Further, it appears to us that learning at times requires the teacher to become a target for idealization.

The need to express the attitudes of the admiring superior to enhance or initiate learning, is, to be sure, a commonplace phenomenon, albeit neither a necessary nor a sufficient particular of the teaching or learning process. Certainly, learning can and does take place without echoing, approving, or confirming attitudes from the teacher. On the other hand, since the evidence of our senses provides in abundance instances where mirroring or other selfobject activities constitute the major impetus for learning, the notion emerges that the self-sustaining functions of mirroring are vital for some learners in some teaching-learning situations. Thus, there arises the necessity for the empathic diagnosis of the learner's selfobject needs by the teacher—who needs it, when, and in what form. To be sure, in a crisis of learning, when the learner is experiencing a major loss of esteem or a fear of loss of esteem, the teacher's empathy may urge him to repair the temporarily flagging self-regard by expressing the appropriate self-enhancing attitudes and language necessary to come to the aid of the learner's self-cohesiveness. Apart from such crises, however, the establishment of a milieu centered on the learner's need for mirroring is certainly a vital ingredient for the maintenance of the teaching-learning bond. Other mirroring functions such as the need to value the learner's perceptions, ideas, and courage may be essential in the learning dyad.

In teaching as well as in any relationship where one leads and one follows, the teacher is required at times to accept the status of being the target of the idealizations of the learner. The unique functions of the idealized parent—to guide, direct, calm, and soothe and offer standards—take on value once the learner transfers (i.e., invests) onto the teacher qualities of the idealized figures of his childhood. Teacher-learner dyads vary widely in the extent of idealization, so that some teachers are experienced as messianic figures who speak with omniscience while others are experienced as partners who offer suggestions. These various teaching-learning profiles are a reflection of the learner's need or lack of need to idealize, as well as the teacher's capacity for accepting idealization.

Finally, in this review of the functions performed in the main through the vicissitudes of the teacher's empathic diagnosis of the learner's needs comes the issue of the twinship type of relatedness and transference. This unique type of relationship deals with the experience of the other as oneself and thus lends itself to a merger with the "partner's" skills and ideals.

We have identified certain functions of teachers in adding to and maintaining the esteem of the learner (thus maintaining the cohesiveness of the learner [Muslin and Val, 1980]). The transmission of skills and knowledge, the goal of these relationships, proceed in this setting. While we have particularized on the specific functions of mirroring and the idealized parent functions, we have also pointed out that the posture of these dyads varies as a reflection of the learning and emotional needs of the learner's as well as the teacher's goals.

The essential point, however, in defining the nature of the learner-teacher dyad is that it is to be an outcome, not only of the needs of the learner and the capacities of the teacher but that it is to be an outcome of the empathic assessment of the teacher in the main as to the self-requirements of the learner at any given point in his development, and, of course, the goals of teaching. Teaching-learning dyads, of course, must respond to the changing needs of the material as well as to the changes in the psychological needs of the learner.

SUPERVISION AND THE TEACHING-LEARNING PARADIGM

Supervision is the major learning and teaching process in clinical psychiatry. It is in this arena that the learner is to acquire the skills and knowledge by which he is to become a practitioner in psychotherapy. Perhaps the most important medium in which the skills and knowledge are transmitted is within the dyad that is formed; the relationship entered into and its outcome constitute the model of learning in clinical psychiatry.

PHASE I—RAPPORT

The first phase of supervision, similar to the first phase of psychotherapy, has at its main task the understanding of the learner (Kohut, 1977). The supervisor's mission then is to appreciate the therapist's style of listening, understanding, and collating. More importantly, the supervisor becomes aware of the student's capacity for empathic observation and the resistance to the use of empathy. The pitfall to be avoided in the first phase of the supervision is that of telling the student what the clinical data mean, rather than recognizing the data from the side of the student's perceptions and encouraging the student to relate his understanding and reactions to the material he has gathered, all of which are to be valued. We are not unmindful of the necessity to relate to beginners in psychotherapy certain basic ideas of data gathering and collating and basic techniques of intervention. However, it remains in our view that the major goal of the first phase of supervision has as its goal the promotion of the experience of "safety" in the student so that he can express his percepts and responses without fear. Further, the learner, in this atmosphere can begin to experience the teacher as one toward whom it is possible to externalize one's inner mental life. The analogy to the first phase of psychotherapy, the promotion of the experience of trust is clear; in psychotherapy this initial aspect is necessary so that the patient will—after repeated reassurances of the noncritical surroundings of psychotherapy—begin to reveal his important hidden strivings to the benevolent therapist.

The experience of trust on the part of the learner implies that he experiences the teacher as one with whom he can expose, in part, his inner mental life since the teacher has demonstrated that he has valued his need for understanding. On the teacher's side, the establishment of rapport indicates that his empathy has resulted in a reduction of vigilance and defensiveness. The atmosphere is now filled with the benevolence which occurs when there is a mutuality of empathy; that is, empathy in which the learning and teaching needs of each other are appreciated.

THE FIRST PHASE OF STRUCTURE BUILDING IN SUPERVISION

The supervisor has a multitude of skills and a vast body of knowledge that he imparts to the therapist-learner over the course of his supervision. Regardless of the sophistication of the learner, the supervisor must always attend to the development or use of the skills involved in the method of psychotherapy. A partial listing of these skills include listening-following—cognitive and empathic observation; collating of the data into a model of the mind; focusing on the essentials in the data base—system sensitivities, use of interventions (Fleming and Benedek, 1966). The supervisor must, of course, transmit a large body of knowledge including at different times the theory of transference, the types of transferences and countertransferences, and their appearance in the data; the theory and usage of interventions—when do we intervene, what is to be rewarded, dosage factors. The teacher must also be reassured that the learner is possessed of a working knowledge of developmental theory, conflict theory, self psychology, and, of course, the various psychopathologic syndromes.

We are advancing a theory of learning that declares that learning—which we are defining as the accretion of self structure—will take place only as a result of the optimal functions performed within the special self/selfobject dyads of the teaching-learning milieu. Thus, in each teaching-learning milieu there is an optimal *learning self* which the learner enters into and an optimal *teaching selfobject*. As in any adult relationship, the self of the learner is in the main a mature self which does not depend on the selfobjects present to establish a cohesive nuclear self as is the case in infancy and childhood. Similarly, the selfobject of the teacher functions as a mature selfobject in the main, functioning not as a parental mirror or idealized parent but as a mature selfobject utilizing empathy to recognize learning needs. Thus, the mirroring or other selfobject functions of the teacher serve to *enhance* the formed self of the learner rather than establishing the self of the learner as would

be the case in childhood or in the treatment of a self
suffering from narcissistic defects.

SELFOBJECT FUNCTION AND ACTIVITY IN SUPERVISION

The learner of psychotherapy engages in supervision to
acquire the necessary tools and knowledge. Ordinarily
this amounts to the supervisor, from the outset, tuning
in on the therapist's particular manner of listening, collating, and interviewing. The supervisor makes an assessment of the learning needs in every segment of
materal; at times to be of assistance in listening-following
skills, at times to focus on collating-understanding, at
times to recognize an area of knowledge or theory that
is weak or deficient. In this manner the supervision proceeds, resulting in the learner ultimately acquiring the
necessary technical aids and knowledge to perform as a
therapist or diagnostician.

From the learner's side, the relationship is, from the
beginning, one in which the supervisor's functions will
include, apart from or together with the transmission of
tools and knowledge, those functions that emanate from
a so-called mature selfobject—either as noted above, a
mirroring selfobject, a twinship selfobject, or those functions which come from an idealized parent selfobject. In
fact our thesis is that the tools and knowledge that come
from the supervision can only be (or must be) internalized
within the context of an optimally functioning self/selfobject
dyad of learning.

From the side of the teacher, his diagnosis of the work
required during a particular session is based on his empathic assessment of the learner's self-needs. These may
include the need for amelioration of tension through
calming, or they may include admiring-confirming responses or the articulation of an important principle of
theory or technique.

Now what of our thesis that learning takes place with specific selfobject functions required for self-esteem regulation. The learner enters into supervision to learn; however, he also enters into a relationship which will, it is hoped, offer him self-sustenance and/or promote self-growth. Thus the learner comes to present his needs for skill and knowledge, to be sure, but he comes to have *himself* acknowledged (i.e., approved, confirmed). Must learning take place within this context of self/selfobject confirmation (e.g., an act of mirroring)? If the learner's work is not approved, that is, given value, *he* will not value it. Thus it is that at all stages of learning in psychotherapy supervision, the supervisor's functions of approving-confirming-admiring, the activities of mirroring, are important in what the learner will value, and, conversely, what he will discard in the way of a skill or explanatory concept. Of course, for the learner to value his teacher to the extent described means that the learner has become self-involved with the experience of the teacher as a selfobject, albeit a so-called mature selfobject whose value as noted previously is that of enhancing self-esteem not, as in the case of the archaic selfobject, experienced as the purveyor of self-esteem.

The mechanism of enhancing self-esteem in mature self/selfobject dyads, which Kohut referred to as empathic resonance (Kohut, 1984), involves the revival in the self of the experience of being with a selfobject who supports one's cohesiveness. Empathic resonance is the analogue in an adult of the archaic experience in childhood where, through a parent's empathy, the required mirroring and idealized parent functions are provided which ultimately, through optimal frustration, become internalized (transmuting internalization) to form the basic fabric of the self. Will the so-called mirroring functions of the teacher be internalized to add to the learner's self? It is a commonplace observation that the precepts of the hallowed instructor are a fixture of one's self in perpetuity, and so it is for the venerated teacher's confirmations. Apart from the empathic resonance offered by the instructor there is, therefore, as part of the learning experience, a measure—sometimes a goodly measure—of internalization of the mirroring functions of the instructor which adds to the learner's self.

In other instances, the self of the learner as previously described experiences the supervisor as an idealized parent imago. This situation is, of course, a commonplace in many learning situations, perhaps the supervisory experience lends itself to an idealizing process. The supervisor in psychotherapy learning must offer to his charge a variety of precepts based on his experience on the goals of therapy, the conduct of the patient and therapist, and many other articles of wisdom. He offers himself and his approaches as the standard which the learner will attempt to approach. However, not until the learner invests, that is, transfers onto the supervisor idealized properties, the specific properties of a vaunted (i.e., idealized) figure and becomes a supplicant to his target of idealization can we say that there is a self/selfobject relationship of an idealizing type. At this stage, the supervisor becomes a major figure to his student who now directs, leads, and serves as the purveyor of ideals. In other words, a self/selfobject relationship in which the supervisor becomes the target of one's idealization heightens or may be indispensable to the learning of the precepts which are being held out to the student. As in the case of the mirroring functions of the teacher, the ideals by the teacher are, in successful teaching-learning dyads, internalized to add to the self of the learner, specifically to the pole of ideals.

Another aspect of the teaching-learning situation is akin to the alter ego–twinship merger described by Kohut (1971) which involves an experience of sameness between the self and its selfobject. This relationship is experienced by the self as being a contact with someone whose experiences are similar to or the same as one's own. The gain from the side of the self of the learner is the experience of total acceptance through togetherness, the converse of loneliness. The supervisor, in describing his inner mental process, his "technique" of empathic observations, his method of following and evaluating—all these activities usher the student into the teacher's self workings and afford him the sharing of self states so as to enhance the value of his own responses.

Are the self/selfobject relationships described in teaching and learning akin to the self/selfobject transferences spontaneously formed in psychoanalytic therapy of people with self disorders? Clearly, the learner's relationships with an idealized teacher reflect the activity of the self of the learner transferring in a limited manner onto the teacher specific powers from parental imagos who were idealized parents. At times the learner's self is clearly involved in such a transference, which is similar to the transferences seen in psychoanalytic therapy. These learning transferences are diluted forms of the analytic-regressive transferences, since without the daily contact of an analysis the learning transferences are ordinarily diminutive in nature. The teacher's comments may then be experienced as possessing rectitude and certitude. In other instances a diluted form of idealizing transference is in process, the learner while valuing the teacher's precepts does not experience them as articles of faith which cannot be safely transgressed. However, for genuine learning to take place, that is, the process of structure building or enhancing, there must be a self/selfobject dyad that leads to internalization of the selfobject functions or through empathic resonance, the enhancement of one's self-functioning.

THE LEARNING OF EMPATHY

The learning of empathy involves many aspects of the learning paradigm that we have described. While people vary widely in their capacity to empathize over a wide range of situations and people, the basic skills of empathy can be taught, or at least initiated. As Kohut defined it most recently, empathy is the capacity to think oneself into the inner mental life of another person (Kohut, 1984). For the teacher in psychotherapy, the task is to encourage what is available to all but a few. The presentation by the supervisor, ordinarily by example, of the empathic mode of observation is sufficient, albeit with repeated emphases over time, to cause the therapist-learner to initiate an empathic attitude toward his observations and thus, it is hoped, to make it a major tool of understanding clinical data. The accuracy of the empathy, however, offers more difficulties in the supervision. To make an accurate empathic fit requires, among other variables, the freedom from transference distortions and projective identifications. It also requires that the therapist be capable of ferreting out a self state congruous with the object under scrutiny. Thus it is a truism that to think oneself into the inner mental life of another requires that one has had similar experiences. As an example, the capacity to think oneself into the inner mental life of a person in the senium or a person living through a protracted state of self-fragmentation may not be achieved by many.

The concern of the teacher to expand the use of the empathic mode of observation becomes quite complex at times. Once the supervisor has assisted the therapist-learner in the use of empathy to understand and by repeated emphases has helped the therapist in the persistent utilization of empathy, he must turn his attention to the accuracy of the empathy. He must recognize not only the resistance to the use of empathy but he must only be able to spot a transference in the observer masquerading as an empathic observation. He must be mindful of the learner's difficulty in empathizing with certain self states of his patient and thus be liable to a misunderstanding or lack of appreciation of a particular segment of data (Muslin and Schlessinger, 1971).

Example 1

> Ms. A. J. failed to appear for a therapy appointment. The resident, on confronting her with this absence in the following session, then heard the patient describe without shame that her appointment with the hairdresser had been delayed causing her to miss her appointment. The therapist, misunderstanding her failure to appear, confronted her with a statement of hostility against him, in his view probably a reaction to the previous session. The patient could not believe that the therapist had waited for her and was now showing interest, even irritation toward herself over missing the previous appointment. The therapist continued in his confrontation, however, insisting to her that the reaction was one of hostility.

In describing this material and even on repeated listening to the tape of the session, the therapist continued to "see" hostility at the core of the patient's reaction of avoidance. Only after the supervisor enumerated several examples of his experiences that were similar to those of the patient was the therapist able to revive a self state of his own experience in feeling unimportant so that he could now "see" that the patient could not experience her absence as important to her therapist.

This example, an ordinary occurrence in supervisory work, is described to set the stage for the understanding of the psychological processes that must be in place for the initiation and maintenance of the tool of empathy. The supervisor's focus is at first on the therapist-learner's resistance and how best to understand and alleviate it. Then the supervisor must attend to the nature of the teaching-learning dyad that is being formed so as to appreciate the learner's specific selfobject needs to promote learning.

The learner's resistance to the empathic appreciation of the patient's ineptitude is, of course, multidetermined and includes the variables of inexperience and rejection of the patient's authority—transference onto him as well his own transference onto an older person (the patient). However, the variable we wish to isolate in the supervision is his uneasiness in immersing himself, in the vignette described, into a memory of the self of inferiority, the central feature of his resistance. The supervisor's teaching diagnosis, centering on this variable, now permits him to address the problem in empathy, this time not by encouraging the student to focus on his resistance to empathizing with a state of ineptitude, but rather by asking him to find a self state in himself similar to the one the patient manifested, putting aside his subjective reaction of outrage to an "insult." The supervisor's functions are, on the manifest level, to demonstrate the method of data gathering, empathy. Further, in this vignette the supervisor was able to demonstrate how the patient's reactions allowed the therapist and supervisor to differentiate between the therapist's nonempathic subjective distortions and the more accurate empathic observations. The therapist's version of the material was able to move from the findings of the patient's "hostility" to the patient's feelings of inadequacy. On a selfobject level, the supervisor is now functioning as a leader who is encouraging emulation by inviting the therapist-learner to follow his lead and thereby acquire by this process the tools of the trade. The learner's experience is the urge to attach himself to the firm convictions of the supervisor in the use of the major tool of data gathering, empathy.

Example 2

An analytic therapist in supervision with his supervisor is describing a session of a patient who is in the fourth year of his analysis. The session has started out with the patient proclaiming that he is in good equilibrium even after a long weekend hiatus from analysis. He now states that it is due to "our work going well." Now he begins to falter and falls silent for a prolonged time. When he starts to speak again he becomes tearful and states that he wishes to leave, he is too anxious to go on. The analyst encourages him to continue, what is the fear? The patient says it must be that he used the term *our work* which made him uncomfortable. He again asks to leave and then says "you're keeping me here because of *your* needs, the time is over." Finally after another silence, he says: "I worried that when I got high, you wouldn't be able to calm me down, just leave me shaking." Then, the patient recounted his remembrances of being with his mother who could never calm or soothe, she was never available as a nurturer, always too caught up in her own private, agitated world.

The analyst's inner responses to the session were that he experienced the material as interesting and new. As he recounted the session, he stated that in actuality the material was not new and that his responses were curious and needed to be investigated. He knew in considerable detail the special childhood deprivations of his patient, a person who had to spend considerable time in bed during childhood suffering with rheumatic carditis. During these times, his mother avoided him and left him alone by always being in other rooms, only responding to him during times of acute stress, such as his calls for pain medication. The analyst and his supervisor now began to investigate the apparent lag in empathy. It turned out that the analyst's reactions to the patient's accusation "you're keeping me here for your needs" was central in the analyst's empathic lag. The analyst's reaction of surprise and shock thus revealed that the analyst experienced the transferential accusation as a valid indictment of his underlying motives toward the patient. Thus, he was unable to proceed with empathy in the unfolding of the subsequent data, the patient con-

tinued in the session by himself, so to speak, and performed well.

What had caused the derailment of the analyst? The
patient accusing him of being solipsistic effectively
checked his empathy with the image of the child who was
accusing the mother of inattentiveness and lack of compassion. He could not "see" the youngster crying out for
soothing and in his unconscious avoidance suddenly
found the "material" new and interesting. As the supervision proceeded, it became clear that the analyst temporarily could not immerse himself in the self of the
frightened boy petitioning for nurturance nor could he
accept the role transferred onto him of the distracted and
agitated mother.

The supervisor's functions were several. To begin the
investigation, he had to call attention to that point in the
session when the empathic lag started. He then was able
to ferret out the resistance in the analyst to immersing
himself in the childhood self of his maternally deprived
patient. Since the patient had revealed many times over
the material of his experience of maternal deprivation
now emerging ("you want to keep me here") transferen-
tially, why the sudden blockade to empathy? The central
finding was that this was the first time the *analyst* had
emerged as the culprit who would deny the patient his
much-needed calming. It ultimately became clear to the
supervisor that the transference material had evoked experiences in the analyst's own life which were then reacted to by the analyst through removing himself from
the material, that is, by *not* forming an identification,
albeit a transient one, with the self of weakness.

What next were the supervisor's functions? He engages his student in an in-depth investigation of the therapist's operational resistance to empathy with the special
self state being observed. The therapist would then, by
his associations, uncover the points of gross identification

with the patient's traumata which caused the temporary block in empathy. In this situation, the details of learning are concerned with the clinical theory of transference and countertransference in the psychotherapist. The supervisor is further concerned with helping his student become sensitized to his own experiences as the sessions proceed. These are the teaching matters in the supervision. From the learner's side, he experiences the messages of his supervisor in a fashion reflective of the unique learning transference in which he has become involved. To be sure there are supervisory situations in which no genuine learning transference takes place, the supervisee proceeding to attend to his teacher's precepts so as to avoid criticism or dismissal. In these situations in which no learning transference takes place, there is no addition or change in the learner's self, he simply goes along for as long as he must in a particular manner only to revert to his ordinary methods once the supervisor will not be observing him.

To proceed with the selfobject functions of the supervisor and its vicissitudes, the details of learning are experienced within the overall experience of the unique learning transference. Thus, as in this case, the learner's experience of his supervisor as an idealized figure ushers in the experience of the learning details imbued with the selfobject functions of guidance and makes for the uniqueness of the learning experience. This learning transference, carried out over a lengthy period of time, may result in accretions to the self in the learner; that is, permanent *additions* to the self of the learner manifest in his altered functioning as a therapist after supervision.

DISCUSSION

The process by which internalization of functions of the selfobject to become structures of the self has been described by Kohut on many occasions (Kohut, 1971, 1977,

1984). Kohut, who joins Freud on this matter, conceives of the internalization of self structure as the endpoint of a "learning" process which is initiated by the establishment of an empathic bond between a parent and the self of his child. This child experiences the parent as under his control responding without restraint to his need. Further, the child is conceived as experiencing the mother as the child experiences a part of his self, thus the designation selfobject. Once an intrusion onto this self/selfobject dyad, an interruption of nontraumatic proportions—temporally and spatially—a so-called optimal frustration, as contrasted to a traumatic frustration (e.g., a protracted absence) the child or infant will experience an intensification of the imago of the temporarily absent parent and the parent's selfobject functions. Ultimately these optimal frustrations and their sequelae—the internalization of selfobject function—become *self* functions (i.e., add to the self so that selfobject approval becomes self-approval).

In mature self/selfobject dyads which form between adult selves, such as in supervision, the learner's self certainly does acquire self structure, as in any learning situation, in a manner that is analogous to the fashion in which the original self structures are laid down. Thus the initial step is that a basic learning transference is formed which may have features of a mirroring or an idealizing transference. This basic self/selfobject learning transference has the features of an archaic self/selfobject bond *and* a mature self/selfobject relationship. It is not, of course, involved in the development of a nuclear self nor is it simply confined to a transitory infusion of support since it adds to the learner's self. What follows in the ordinary sessions of learning is that the learner's self accretes those structures that come from the body of material being taught with the addition of those selfobject functions that come from the selfobject teacher. This latter statement implies that the self of the learner, as noted above, is in an optimum state to receive the messages of his teacher. We are here speaking of structure as more or less persisting configurations of the self. These self structures of learning are not the self structures, the resultant of the archaic bonds that eventuate in the nuclear self, the basic tonus of the self that is already in place at twenty-four months or thereabouts. Those original self structures form the basic self experiences of one's worth, one's values, and result in the basic or nuclear self with its unique capacities for ambitions and its unique set of goals and values to live up to through the self's talents and skills. The self structures that are the result of the basic learning transference, however, represent *additions* to the nuclear self. A psychotherapist's *manner* of listening, collating, and integrating which derives from his unique interactions with his supervisor persists without his awareness of its origin through his life as a psychotherapist. The internalizations to the self that derive from the basic learning transference may be, as is usual, added to the self's pool of skills. In a learning transference that has features of the idealized transference, there may be additions to the learner's self of standards for his operations as a therapist or alterations in his goals for himself. In any learning transference where there has been mirroring, the learner's self may have become enhanced in its capacity to exhibit itself.

The additions to the self that result from the basic learning transference represent, as we have stated, additions to the nuclear self of the learner. They become, therefore, permanent increments to the bipolar self. The mechanism of internalization of these structures that arise from the basic learning transference, in our view, approximate the ordinary method of internalization of self structure in a self/selfobject dyad. In these instances after a self/selfobject dyad has formed either in the self's infancy or in a self/selfobject transference in psychoanalysis, an instance or instances of optimal frustration occurs after which the imago of the selfobjects and its functioning is intensified and becomes a permanent accretion to the self. Thus the supervisor's approvals or precepts now become, after optimal frustration, the learner's self-approvals or his experienced standards for devotion to the task at hand. The optimal frustration in these learning dyads most commonly lies in the fact that the learner receives only supervision. Once the supervision is ended, he must proceed with the psychotherapy on his own.

The fate of the internalized mixture of skills or knowledge laid down within the context of the selfobject learning transference will in this fashion become attached to the learner's nuclear self; not, therefore, as remembrances of one's teacher's words or approvals, but as therapeutic operations, the source of which one no longer remembers.

REFERENCES

Arlow, J. A. (1963), The supervisory situation. *J. Amer. Psychoanal. Assn.*, 11:576–594.

DeBell, D. E. (1963), A critical digest of the literature on psychoanalytic supervision. *J. Amer. Psychoanal. Assn.*, 11:546–575.

Ekstein, R., & Wallerstein, R. X. (1958), *The Teaching and Learning of Psychotherapy.* New York: Basic Books.

Fleming, J., & Benedek, T. (1964), Supervision: A method of teaching psychoanalysis. *Psychoanal. Quart.*, 33:71–96.

——— ——— (1966), *Psychoanalytic Supervision.* New York: Grune & Stratton.

Keiser, S. (1956), The technique of supervised analysis. *J. Amer. Psychoanal. Assn.*, 4:539–549.

Kohut, H. (1971), *The Analysis of the Self.* New York: International Universities Press.

——— (1977), *The Restoration of the Self.* New York: International Universities Press.

——— (1984), *How Does Analysis Cure?* Chicago: University of Chicago Press.

Muslin, H., Burstein, A. G., Gedo, J.; & Sadow, L. (1967), Research on the supervisory process. *Arch. Gen. Psychiat.*, 16:427–431.

——— Schlessinger, N. (1971), Toward the teaching and learning of empathy. *Bull. Menn. Clin.*, 35(4):262–271.

——— Val, E. (1980), Supervision and self-esteem in psychiatric teaching. *Amer. J. Psychother.*, 34(4):545–555.

Schlessinger, N. (1966), Supervision of psychotherapy. *Arch. Gen. Psychiat.*, 15:129–134.

Sloane, P. (1957), The technique of supervised analysis. *J. Amer. Psychoanal. Assn.*, 5:539–547.

Tarachow, S. (1963), *An Introduction to Psychotherapy*. New York: International Universities Press.

Zetzel, E. R. (1953), The dynamic basis of supervision. *Soc. Casework*, 34:143–149.

Part II

Psychoanalysis: Learning and Development

Introduction: Part II

Concern with the impact of past experience upon present actions and intents has become a defining characteristic of psychoanalytic inquiry. As Freud (1913) observed:

> [Psychoanalysis] implies more than the mere analysis of composite phenomena into simpler ones. It consists of tracing back one psychical structure to another which preceded it in time and out of which it developed. . . . [F]rom the very first, psychoanalysis was directed toward tracing developmental processes. It began by discovering the genesis of neurotic symptoms, and was led, as time went on, to . . . construct a genetic psychology which would apply to them too [pp. 182–183].

This genetic or epigenetic approach was outlined by Freud as early as his letters to Fliess, and expanded in the *Three Essays on a Theory of Sexuality* (1905), the case studies of Leonardo (1910a) and the Wolf-man (1914–1918), and summarized both in the Introductory Lectures (1915–1917), and the posthumous Outline (1940).

Subsequent elaboration of the genetic point of view (Rapaport and Gill, 1959) or approach (Schafer, 1976), through the work of Abraham (1924), Glover (1930), Spitz (1959), and, particularly, Erikson (1950, 1980) further extended Freud's initial formulation. This approach has been well summarized by Hartmann and Kris (1945) who noted that:

> The genetic approach in psychoanalysis does not only deal with anamnestic data, nor does it intend to show only "how the past is contained in the present." Genetic propositions describe why, in past situations of conflict, a specific solution was adopted; why the one was retained and the other dropped, and what causal relation exists between these solutions and later development. Genetic propositions refer to the fact that in an adult's behavior, anxiety may be induced by outdated conditions, and they explain why these conditions may still exercise influence [pp. 117–118].

This genetic approach has long influenced discussions of education. Much of the concern with problems of learning in the classroom has been focused on the extent to which such problems are influenced by the "outdated conditions" referred to by Hartmann and Kris, particularly those related to the nuclear neurosis. For example, a gifted college student was unable to complete assigned work in his college courses. His father, a distinguished scientist, had won international renown in his field. The college environment continually reminded the student of his father's success, including encountering his father's papers in assigned course reading. Paralyzed by fear that he could not equal his father's success, this student was unable to complete course papers, or laboratory assignments, and nearly failed a number of tests, making computational errors which he later recognized.

It is not difficult to realize the extent to which problems with academic achievement could be traced to the "outdated conditions" which Hartmann and Kris portray, including the father's demand that his wife devote her complete attention to him when he was home, leading the student to feel, even as a small boy, unable to attain his mother's attention when his father was present, and unable to equal his father's real worldly success. This sense of failure was relived in the classroom, shown not just in his failure to realize his talent, but also in his inability to ask questions or to compete for the instructor's time and attention with his fellow students.

The inhibition which this student showed in his work can clearly be traced to his experience of the past as relived in the present. Accompanying this inhibition, the student felt himself to be unequal to the demands posed by his studies and felt markedly lowered self-esteem. Within more traditional perspectives, these "outdated conditions" may be traced back to the time portrayed by Freud during which the child struggled to resolve the oedipal neurosis, resulting in positive identification with the same-sex parent, amnesia for the events of the childhood period, and liberation of energy for attainments in order to realize the coveted status of the same-sex parent. Indeed, as both Erikson (1950) and Parsons (1955) note, consolidation of positive identification fosters the child's desire to move from home and family into the larger community, and to gain necessary instrumental skills.

Questions have been raised regarding this portrayal of the events characterizing the resolution of the so-called oedipal or "nuclear neurosis" (Freud, 1910b). In the first place, it is clear that the resolution of this issue for little girls is markedly different from that for little boys. It will be recalled that Freud's initial formulation of this epochal transformation in the development of personality was inspired less by clinical or developmental observation than as a result of his own self-analysis (Sadow, Gedo, Pollock, Sabshin, and Schlessinger, 1968). Throughout the course of his work, Freud (1905, 1924, 1925, 1931, 1933, 1940) struggled with the problem of asymmetry in the origins and resolution of the nuclear neurosis among boys and girls. Emphasis upon bisexuality, distinctions between positive and negative aspects of the oedipal neurosis, and ultimately, recognition of the greater complexity of this issue for the development of boys and girls have provided psychoanalysis with a tangled theory not yet clearly resolved through observational study (Parens, Pollock, Stern, and Kramer, 1976; Roiphe and Galenson, 1981) or attempts at reformulation by feminist critics (Miller, 1973, 1977; Chodorow, 1978).

Freud (1933) had observed that problems in understanding what, today, would be called gender role identity were more an issue of psychology than of biology. In his discussion of femininity, Freud clearly pointed to the importance of considering socialization factors as the source of the difference in the manner in which issues of jealousy and the family romance were later reenacted among men and women. More recent study, beginning with Komarovsky's (1950) initial observation on socialization of little girls into interdependence, has suggested that girls are taught to think in contextual modes, while boys are taught to think analytically. Sex differences in the manner in which the nuclear neurosis is resolved are a part of early childhood socialization into quite different modes of thought. This differential socialization has important implications for concepts of self and for mental health, as well as for understanding problems of learning and of going to school, which are explored in this section.

Other problems remain in understanding the impact of development, viewed from psychoanalytic perspectives, upon problems in learning and going to school. For example, a number of developmental and clinical theorists have suggested that problems in learning, based on outdated conceptions, may derive from other sectors of development in addition to that portrayed as the nuclear neurosis. For example, problems in learning, such as those of the student described earlier, or the problems more generally observed among girls and young women in competing in school from adolescence onward, may be due less to issues related to consolidation of socially defined sex roles than to more fundamental issues of self-esteem, tension regulation, and consolidation of a sense of self, essential for realizing completion of psychological development. A number of theorists both in Great Britain and in the United States, including Winnicott, Khan, Kernberg, Balint, Mahler and her colleagues, Bion, Grotstein, and Kohut and his associates, have raised significant questions regarding the significance of the experience of sufficiency and satisfaction with early care as precursors of a later sense of the self as effective.

While there clearly are major differences in the assumptions of these several theorists and their students and colleagues, these formulations appear to agree that the child's experience of caretaking during the first years of life, prior to efforts at resolving the nuclear neurosis, may be of at least as much significance as the nuclear neurosis in determining later problems faced in learning. Outdated conditions which inspire problems in learning in school, reflected in a sense of lowered self-esteem, an inability to realize one's own talents and skills, may as much be traced to felt deficits in such early caretaking, as to the outcome of the nuclear neurosis itself. Indeed, the experience of the self as not equal to the task of competing with father itself may have its origins in much earlier life experiences. Events of the so-called oedipal period may be yet additional confirmation of a depleted sense of self engendered by failure to resolve critical issues in the first years of life, resulting in residual deficit states preventing most effective learning in school.

Related to the role of preoedipal as contrasted with oedipal origins of problems in learning is the issue of experiences earlier in childhood, as contrasted with those of the "nursery years" (Isaacs, 1932) as factors influencing the capacity to learn in school. Particularly across the past two decades, there has been interest in the work both of Piaget and the Geneva school of genetic epistemology and, more recently, Vygotsky and his Soviet colleagues as contrasting approaches emphasizing the significance of experiences in earliest childhood for later development. Although there are marked differences between these two approaches in terms of factors presumed to be most significant for later development, both theory and findings derived from this approach to the study of cognitive development in early childhood emphasize the extent to which child and environment must be linked if the foundations for later learning are to be established. In particular, the child's experience of caretaking, including the use of attributes of the caretaker as a part of the self, is essential in learning to learn.

The chapters in this section are united by a concern with issues of the genesis of psychological development as related to subsequent learning problems, and reflect a diversity of theoretical positions regarding both the significance of preoedipal and oedipal determinants of later learning problems, and the value of traditional and more recent perspectives on gender differences as related to manner of learning during childhood and adolescence. Four chapters deal with developmental factors in the learning process, based largely on normative rather than clinical perspectives, and emphasize the significance of learning as a process facilitating increased adaptation as a consequence of the development of psychological structure.

The chapter by Gerhart and Maria Piers, reprinted from a 1965 source no longer in print, portrays the points of correspondence between developmentally based theories of learning and psychoanalytic perspectives, emphasizing acquisition of insight. Stanley Greenspan summarizes several years of careful observational inquiry related to the means by which structure is realized, including differentiation of "inner" and "outer" in the boundary of the child and the external world, and including that of relations with others. Like the Pierses, Greenspan emphasizes the importance of intertwined intellectual and emotional factors in shaping the course of the learning process, understood in terms first of somatic learning, then of consequence learning, and finally of representational-structural learning. Greenspan emphasizes that elements from each phase contribute to the integration of learning in terms of biological, cognitive, and emotional learning. Effective learning results in the child's ability to integrate learning at different levels as, for example, the ability to reason effectively when confronted with an emotionally salient task.

Sussman's discussion of the response of young children to novelty, coordinating perspectives, and integrating cognitive and affective approaches carries further this concern with the integration of learning processes based largely on Piagetian perspectives. Sussman suggests that children learn successively increased mental structures fostering increasingly effective adaptation, including increased capacity to satisfy important desires. Sussman is particularly concerned with the means by which the child comprehends novelty, and of factors contributing to the child's willingness to undertake understanding of that which is unfamiliar. Encouragement by adults clearly plays a role in this process, as does the child's capacity to manage unfamiliar situations so as to permit exploration of limited aspects of the unfamiliar in ways which the child feels able to master. This capacity for "dosing" or organizing experience in manageable units presumably has its origins in experiences of earliest childhood, prior to struggle with the oedipal neurosis.

The significance of Piaget's approach is also shown in the chapter by Henderson and Kegan in their discussion of the constructive developmental view of learning. For these authors, the importance of understanding the capacities of a child at a particular age must include both reference to observable themes or processes and underlying assumptions or epistemological principles which organize or make meaning, enhance development of a

sense of self, and lead to new understanding of the learning process.

While Greenspan's, Sussman's and Henderson and
Kegan's discussions are informed by Piaget's conception
of emotional development, based on the assumption of
intrinsic maturational processes, and consistent with the
goal of Henderson and Kegan's discussion, Litowitz considers development of intelligence in terms of Vygotsky's
portrayal of learning as based on making social processes
a part of the personal world. Since initial publication of
the translation of Vygotsky's important report on acquisition of language, the work of this Soviet psychologist
has had great impact on the study of child development.
Litowitz emphasizes the significance of maternal involvement in the child's development as an important determinant of the child's capacity for using the social world
in the learning process. This discussion of learning focuses on the relationship of caretaker and child, and provides additional support for those theorists within
psychoanalysis and education who stress the significance
of experiences prior to resolution of the nuclear neurosis
as of singular importance for later experience of learning,
including formal education.

The perspective elaborated by Litowitz's discussion of
internalization as the basis for learning is extended in
Stott's observational report of a young girl's effort to learn
to write. Contrasting Piagetian perspectives with that
implicit in Vygotsky's work, and employing psychoanalytic perspectives stressing the importance of wishes and
intents as important factors inspiring the manner in
which learning takes place, Stott shows the manner in
which Jill was able to use the important persons in her
life as a means of learning to write, transforming the
context in which these persons used words into her own
perspective on the use of words and ideas; phrased in
terms important both for psychoanalytic perspectives,
and those employed by Vygotsky and the Soviet psy-

chologists, external speech had become internal speech. Writing had also become a means for extending and realizing increased meaning from these important relationships.

Garber also considers the importance of the parent as teacher, focusing on the problem of the means by which children learn to mourn or grieve the death of someone significant to them (particularly upon children confronted by the death of a parent). Garber shows the importance for the child's effort to make sense of this experience of the manner in which the surviving parent deals with the issue of loss, since the child's effort is derived from observation of the parent. Not just in the capacity to express grief, but also in the capacity to express feelings of anger at being left, the child learns from the parent how to cope with issues of grief and loss. Learning to express and accept feelings is as significant as cognitive learning in the developmental process and one, as Garber shows, about which we know very little.

Wolf's reformulation of the learning process in terms of the psychology of the self implicitly includes consideration of emotional factors in the earliest years of life as determinants of learning, as well as the major source of later learning problems. This approach builds both upon studies of learning in infancy and early childhood, as well as recent consideration of the child's experience of caretaking, as determinants of psychological structure making learning possible. Wolf's reconceptualization either explicitly or implicitly includes each of the preceding perspectives included in this section of the book, concluding that the child's capacity for effective learning presumes both the capacity to "dose" or manage learning in ways which are not experienced as overwhelming, and also the capacity to let others be of assistance in learning. Wolf discusses the ways in which the teacher can be helpful to the student, at least as experienced by the student, who both looks up to the teacher and learns by practicing and imitating the teacher's perspective on learning. However, his discussion goes beyond the student's role in learning, to consideration of determinants of the teacher's own contribution to the learning process, including the teacher's ability to tolerate students' admiration and his dedication to learning and to teaching in terms of his previous experience as a student.

Wolf extends this understanding of the student and teacher's contribution to the learning process to consideration of psychotherapy as a kind of teaching and learning experience, an issue also reviewed in Rocah's chapter on learning in psychotherapy. Again, as in Wolf's discussion, Rocah builds on the concept of development in earliest infancy as the basis for creating a system of self-regulation. Although her formulation of the processes contributing to deficits later apparent in psychotherapy conflict with the portrayal provided by Wolf, Rocah shares his concern for the factors leading to a stable and coherent sense of self, as well as factors leading to problems in learning, inspired not just by the conflict related to the nuclear neurosis, but also the child's experience of caretaking.

As Rocah shows, it is essential to appreciate the contribution of the child's experiences prior to the onset of the oedipal conflict, as well as the outcome of that conflict as a means of understanding the course of personality development. Indeed, the capacity for renouncing unacceptable wishes which accompanies the transformation to middle childhood is testimony to the capacity for self-regulation learned from experience with caretakers across the preceding years. The fact of personality as a complex of both cognitive and affective responses, in ways similar to those discussed earlier in the chapter by Greenspan, are echoed once again in Rocah's presentation of clinical examples where she demonstrates that personal crisis evident in psychotherapy reflects problems in each realm, and prevents the realization of a coherent sense of self.

Like Greenspan, Rocah emphasizes the significance of both cognitive developmental formulations, such as those of Piaget, and psychoanalytic formulations, in understanding the course of development. Indeed, Roach's work resonates with each of the preceding chapters in the section in an effort to understand both problems leading persons to seek psychotherapy, and, in particular, the contribution to subsequent development provided by psychotherapy and the person of the therapist. As in other chapters of this section, cognitive and emotional development are understood as intrinsically and directly interrelated in the study of learning and problems in learning and development.

Two chapters on learning and development complete the section. As already noted, much of what Freud had portrayed as the universal course of development through the oedipal phase of development was founded on his own self-analysis, and portrayal of the resolution of the castration complex in boys. Freud's later discussion (1925, 1931, 1933) may have further obscured rather than clarified discussion of development through the nuclear neurosis among little girls. More recent discussion, much of which has been inspired by the feminist movement of the past two decades, has provided little additional understanding of the significance of this developmental process among girls. Much of this work has focused nearly exclusively upon the developmental course itself, and upon the nature of the little girl's relations with her parents.

The chapters in the present instance are more directly concerned with the implication of the developmental course for differences in learning and in subsequent sense of competence as a student. Silverman suggests that much of the difficulty both among women in attaining success, and among men in accepting the views of women as deserving of equal opportunity for success, stems from unconscious sources. Reviewing factors contributing to gender role identity, attained during the second year of life, and consistent with other chapters in this section, Silverman argues that the character of the child's experience of caretaking is particularly salient as the factor shaping the subsequent sense of self as competent, regardless of the child's sex. The nature of this experience inevitably alters the child's experience of the oedipal conflict, including feelings of comfort with socially ascribed gender role identity and subsequent ability to learn in school.

Stiver focuses upon the outcome of this process in her discussion of work inhibitions among women. The tendency of many women to sabotage efforts at realizing increased success in the workplace due to conflicts between achievement and quality of interpersonal relationships further highlights socially defined, intrinsic differences in the manner in which men and women understand their place in society. Stiver endorses a view first expressed by McClelland (1965) and more recently emphasized by Miller (1973), Chodorow (1978), Cohler and Grunebaum (1981), and Gilligan (1982) that biology and socialization are intertwined in determining that the manner in which men and women understand self and gender role is inherently different, and that understanding of the girl's development, including development as a learner, cannot simply be understood as generalization from the position ascribed to boys. Academic achievement among boys is assumed to be autonomous and apart from home and family, while that of girls is more directly linked to the manner in which the girl's attainments may be significant within the household.

Since men and women have intrinsically different conceptions of such issues as self-reliance and interdependence, much of what appears to be lowered self-esteem in women is just a different mode of expressing wishes and intents. From this perspective, Stiver argues that it is difficult to discuss problems confronted by women in the workplace in the same terms employed for men. The concept of self-in-relation, important in understanding a definition of the situation among women at work is distinctively and fundamentally different from self-as-independent, as expressed among men at work.

These chapters raise many of the important contemporary problems in understanding development and later life experience among women. Clearly, much additional observational study is required in order to determine the role of both experiences prior to efforts at resolution of the nuclear neurosis, and those associated with the oedipal conflict, as factors shaping sense of self in relation to other among boys and girls. It is important that any discussion of contemporary psychoanalytic perspectives on learning and development be cognizant of the problems involved in understanding the development of gender role identity, recognizing that more traditional psychoanalytic formulations may have been unduly influenced by Freud's initial discussion of this issue in his own self-analysis.

REFERENCES

Abraham, K. (1924), A short study on the development of the libido viewed in the light of mental disorders. In: *Selected Papers in Psychoanalysis.* New York: Basic Books, 1953, pp. 418–501.

Chodorow, N. (1978), *The Reproduction of Mothering: Psychoanalysis and the Sociology of Gender.* Berkeley: University of California Press.

Cohler, B., & Grunebaum, H. (1981), *Mothers, Grandmothers, and Daughters: Personality and Child-Care in Three-Generation Families.* New York: John Wiley.

Erikson, E.H. (1950), *Childhood and Society.* New York: W. W. Norton, 1963.

——— (1980), Elements of a psychosocial theory of development. In: *The Course of Life: Psychoanalytic Contributions Toward Understanding Personality Development,* Vol. 1, ed. S. Greenspan & G. Pollock. Washington, DC: U.S. Government Printing Office, pp. 11–61.

Freud, S. (1900), The Interpretation of Dreams. *Standard Edition,* 4 & 5. London: Hogarth Press, 1958.

——— (1905), Three Essays on a Theory of Sexuality. *Standard Edition,* 7:1–243. London: Hogarth Press, 1953.

———— (1910a), Leonardo Da Vinci and a memory of his childhood. *Standard Edition,* 11:63–138. London: Hogarth Press, 1957.

———— (1910b), Five lectures on psychoanalysis. *Standard Edition,* 11:9–58. London: Hogarth Press, 1957.

———— (1913), The claims of psychoanalysis to scientific interest. *Standard Edition,* 13:165–192. London: Hogarth Press, 1958.

———— (1914–1918), From the history of an infantile neurosis. *Standard Edition,* 17:1–122. London: Hogarth Press, 1955.

———— (1915–1917), Introductory Lectures on Psychoanalysis. *Standard Edition,* 15 & 16. London: Hogarth Press, 1961–1963.

———— (1924), The dissolution of the Oedipus complex. *Standard Edition,* 19:173–182. London: Hogarth Press, 1961.

———— (1925), Some psychological consequences of the anatomical distinction between the sexes. *Standard Edition,* 19:241–260. London: Hogarth Press, 1961.

———— (1931), Female sexuality. *Standard Edition,* 21:221–246. London: Hogarth Press, 1961.

———— (1933), Lecture 33: Femininity (New Introductory Lectures). *Standard Edition,* 22:112–135. London: Hogarth Press, 1964.

———— (1940), An outline of psychoanalysis. *Standard Edition,* 23:144–208. London: Hogarth Press, 1964.

Gilligan, C. (1982), *In a Different Voice: Psychological Theory and Women's Development.* Cambridge, MA: Harvard University Press.

Glover, E. (1930), Grades of ego-differentiation. In: *On the Early Development of the Mind.* New York: International Universities Press, pp. 112–122.

Hartmann, H., & Kris, E. (1945), The genetic approach in psychoanalysis. *The Psychoanalytic Study of the Child,* 1:11–30. New York: International Universities Press.

Isaacs, S. (1932), *The Nursery Years.* London: Routledge & Kegan Paul.

Komarovsky, M. (1950), Functional analysis of sex roles. *Amer. Social. Rev.,* 15:508–516.

McClelland, D. (1965), Wanted: A new self-image for women. In: *The Woman in America,* ed. R. Lifton. Cambridge, MA: Houghton Mifflin, pp. 175–191.

Miller, J. B., ed. (1973), *Psychology and Women.* Baltimore, MD: Pelican.

———— (1977), Toward a New Psychology of Women. Boston: Beacon Press.

Parens, H., Pollock, L., Stern, J., & Kramer S. (1976), On the girl's entry into the Oedipus complex. *J. Amer. Psychoanal. Assn.,* 24 (Suppl.): 79–108.

Parsons, T. (1955), Family structure and the socialization of the child. In: *Family, Interaction and Socialization Process,* ed. T. Parsons & R. F. Bales. New York: Free Press, pp. 35–131.

Rapaport, D., & Gill, M. M. (1959), The points of view and assumptions of metapsychology, *Internat. J. Psycho-Anal.,* 40:153–162.

Roiphe, H., & Galenson, E. (1981), *Infantile Origins of Sexual Identity.* New York: International Universities Press.

Sadow, L., Gedo, J., Pollock, G., Sabshin, M., & Schlessinger, N. (1968), The process of hypothesis change in three early psychoanalytic concepts. In: Freud: The Fusion of Science and Humanism—The Intellectual History of Psychoanalysis, ed. J. Gedo & G. Pollock. *Psychological Issues,* Monograph 34/35, 2 & 3/9. New York: International Universities Press, 1976, pp. 257–285.

Schafer, R. (1976), *A New Language for Psychoanalysis.* New York: Basic Books.

Spitz, R. (1959), *A Genetic Field Theory of Ego Organization.* New York: International Universities Press.

Chapter 8

Modes of Learning and the Analytic Process

GERHART PIERS, M.D.
MARIA W. PIERS, Ph.D.

Man is the learning animal kat' exokhen. Born with a bundle of reflexes and the anlage to a number of drives, he has to learn how to integrate them with his experience into adaptive behavior. This is the meaning in which we shall apply the term *learning* throughout this chapter.

Space does not permit detailed discussion of even the most representative learning theories, neither the more naturalistic ethological ones of European observers, nor the experimental ones of American researchers, usually based on pure strains of laboratory animals, such as the maze rat and the college student. We freely admit to the clinicians' prejudice against the artifact of the experimental setup, the concentration on the smallest possible segment of behavior, and the extrapolation from the merganser and the rat to man, and question their broad applicability to the understanding of the human mind.

On the other hand, we have to agree with D. Rapaport

This chapter was first published in *Selected Lectures, Sixth International Congress of Psychotherapy* (1965), ed. M. Pines & T. Spoerri. Basel/New York: S. Karger.

(1960) when he takes psychoanalysis to task for failing to produce a learning theory of its own, one that would explicate the formation of abiding structures in the mental apparatus, resulting from normal growth, defenses against drives, and resolutions of conflicts.

In 1948 Hilgard indicted his own field with this lugubrious remark: "Watching a child learning to brush his teeth . . . makes most of our learning principles seem inadequate." At the same time he suspected that there may be several basically different kinds of learning, each with its own intrinsic laws.

We submit that there are *three* such *modes* of learning, clearly differentiable yet usually in varying combination with each other. We designate them as learning through conditioning, insight learning, and learning by identification.

Learning through conditioning is practically the only mode investigated by learning theorists and experimental psychologists. We include here all S-R systems, principles of reward (to reinforce) and punishment (to extinguish), and of trial and error (essentially forms of self-reward and self-punishment). Explanatory concepts of "contiguity" or "connectionism" appear to the clinician quite mechanistic until he remembers that "free associations" can be easily subsumed under these headings.

Those everyday learning processes of human beings which we regard as one or another form of conditioning show these common characteristics: they require a degree of repetition and they seem to lead to some measure of automatization. Not infrequently, the mood that accompanies this learning mode is that of a varying degree of dysphoria, or "unlust." Even though reward is the best taskmaster, punishing lurks around the corner; the granting of affection or approval seems only to signal the possibility of its withdrawal.

By insight learning, we mean a specific mode of learning through which "insight" is acquired. Among nonanalytic psychologies, the Gestalt schools may have come closest to an understanding of this "understanding"; and "insight learning" can probably be subsumed under "acquisition of a new Gestalt." In contrast to the slow conditioning mode, suddenness is a frequent characteristic of insight learning. A sudden light is thrust on something and seems to transform it, or make apparent what a moment ago was not there at all. A closure is reached— meaningless fragments are suddenly united into a whole which is different from its constituent parts. These learning acts are frequently accompanied by the so-called "Aha-Erlebnis," a distinct affect of ego gratification beyond mere tension relief. Again, this is quite different from the lingering dysphoria of the conditioning process. To be sure, sudden insight can be frightening as well.

Identification is the mode of learning most neglected by academic psychology. Only social psychologists have paid attention to it, though mostly in its external reflection, imitation, not as the unconscious basic ego function that analysts assume it to be.

We consider these three modes of learning to be in constant interaction, and perhaps none is ever found in "pure culture" in human beings under natural—not laboratory—conditions. Yet we strongly suspect that' they gradually evolve along different developmental lines, to use Anna Freud's (1963) felicitous concept, with different anlagen and precursors and with different peaks of growth for each. In passing, we point to the apparent preponderance of conditioning, particularly in the form of trial and error, in the toddler stage; the rapid development of insight learning after the establishment of symbolic language, and in latency; and the peculiar role of identification in adolescence.

Space limitations prevent us from even sketching the differing roles of superego, ego-ideal, and autonomous ego in the three modes.

We shall now illustrate action and interaction of the

three modes of learning in one complex learning act, the psychoanalytic (therapeutic) process. Since our emphasis is on modes of changes in ego structure, this analysis of analysis is of necessity limited—omitting, for instance, a discussion of transference or of technique and its theory; nor can we pay attention to considerations of emotional energies and their transformation.

In thinking of psychoanalysis as a learning process, one is tempted to subsume it entirely under "insight learning." In psychoanalysis "insight" has a very special meaning. We are not satisfied with mere "intellectual insight," mere cognition or comprehension, partly because we recognize the frequently defensive use of the purely intellectual act. The term *emotional insight* cannot quite satisfy us either. If this term is to designate insight into our emotions, it covers only one step in this learning mode. If, on the other hand, the emphasis is on the free experience of emotion, we get into the area of catharsis or abreaction, with their notorious limitations. Ultimately and ideally, the "analyzed person" should be one with that kind of "analytic insight" which permits the conflict-free fusion in the following three areas:

1. Insight into psychological cause and effect; that is, an awareness of the connection between one's motivating forces and one's behavior.

2. Between emotion and thought which, if in free interplay and not compulsively isolated, make for an enrichment of either.

3. (And this is perhaps the most specifically psychoanalytic form of insight) the connection between one's present and one's past which, if brought into fluid continuity by loosening the repression barrier, makes for that heightened sense of self-awareness which in turn is the basis of identity in Erikson's (1959) sense. Not only is this sort of threefold insight the ultimate goal of psychoanalysis qua therapy, but its elements are formed in day-to-day interpretations as well. The implicit partial goals

of insight are reflected by the various types of interpretation: confrontation serves mostly to establish links between affect and cognition, transference interpretation to establish the causal link between motivational conflict and resulting behavior or symptom, genetic interpretation to help make the past a part of the living present.

Yet we know that interpretation is not enough, and that insight is not achieved, let alone firmly established, unless something else takes place simultaneously.

We believe that the total psychoanalytic process requires participation by the other two learning modes, of identification and of some forms of conditioning.

Identification has come under psychoanalytic study as an intrinsic operant in the effect of interpretation. Grosser forms of identification with the therapist have come under observation as more and more so-called borderline cases have been shown to be amenable to analytic treatment, and even cases that have crossed the border between neurosis and psychosis. It has been claimed that identification in such cases is not analytic in the strict sense, not part and parcel of the analytic process, but rather a defense against it, or a contaminant. This is indeed frequently so, but not always. Although more easily observed in the borderline case or in that state of developmental psychosis called adolescence, identification in analysis deserves careful study as an intrinsic aspect of the process.

After all, the patient comes to us precisely because of unworkable identifications with early objects. To get an analysis going, the first phase of establishing a rapport or a therapeutic alliance is partly based on identification with the analyst's anxiety-free attitude. In more authoritarian or seductive forms of therapy, such as hypnosis or "suggestion," probably not much more than that happens, and has its limited effect. A weak or weakened ego identifies with the implicitly proffered image of the healer as a strong and hopeful object.

In analysis, these phenomena are underemphasized and frequently go unnoticed. From the just mentioned superficial identifications in the beginning phase of an analysis, identifications proceed to subtler and deeper forms. Lampl-de Groot (1956) speaks of the need that certain borderline characters have for narcissistic identifications, pari passu with their inability to channel constructively their liberated drive energy. The analysis may then take advantage of the fact that learning processes "run very much along the path of identifications." The patient learns to control his impulses by identifying with what he preconsciously perceives to be his analyst's attitude toward his own and/or the patient's drives. In this context, Lampl-de Groot also points to the importance of nonverbal communication.

We feel that identifications in the analytic process go beyond such borrowing of controls, that they occur also in the realm of autonomous functioning. We may not consciously admit it, but in one instance of our behavior we show that we are implicitly quite convinced of the presence and therapeutic effectiveness of identification; that is when we refer patients to other analysts. Not infrequently, we may try to make "the right match" by selecting analysts whose character is somehow either similar or complementary to the patient's. There are, to be sure, many reasons (or rationalizations) for such choices. Underneath, we might sometimes discover an ill-defined and usually unwarranted expectation as to something that could be called "corrective identification."

The reluctance to admit to identification as an operative factor in analysis and the consequent neglect of it in theory is perhaps based on two sets of reasons: the dread of our own omnipotence, and our lack of sophistication in regard to nonverbal communication.

Freud alludes to the former in a footnote to "The Ego and the Id" (1923). He speaks there of depressed patients whose "guilt complex" is a quasi-borrowed one; that is, the result of identification with a beloved object who himself had suffered from guilt. In such cases, Freud mused, therapy may be facilitated if the personality of the analyst were such that the patient could put it in the place of his own superego. This, however, Freud warned, may easily tempt the analyst to play the role of prophet and savior. The dread of our own magic omnipotence may be one obstacle in the way of recognizing, let alone better understanding, of identification in the analytic process.

The other obstacle may be the preponderance of nonverbal elements in identification. The patient gets his cues for identification not so much from what we say, but from how we say it, from the emotional undertones of our remarks, our nonverbal sounds, body movements, dress, and so on. This communications system, though more limited in analysis than in other forms of psychotherapy, is by no means absent. We mentioned our lack of sophistication in understanding and codifying this hidden language. Some patients use caricaturistic identification with our "paralinguistics" as a defensive attack. Is it not strange that we all know such patients, but that they are never *our* patients?

The presence of conditioning may be even more difficult to perceive in the analytic process. To repeat some of the characteristics of this mode of learning: automatization, often through repetition, reward, and punishment. The very ritual of the therapeutic analysis points in this direction: regularity, frequency, identical duration of sessions, same body posture, a degree of formalization of the intercommunication—all this suggests a conditioning setup. However, this framework merely facilitates the process; it does not cause it. More essential is the subtle and complex system which directs the process into "analysis" proper, representing a conditioning not unlike certain maze experiments with the hapless rat. Whenever the rat goes in the "wrong direction," a light flashes, a shock is applied; the "right direction" is rewarded with tidbits. Similarly, outlets of emoting, acting out, certain symbolizations or expectations of immediate gratification are blocked by frustration, silence, verbalization. The "right direction," which is recall, understanding, secondary process, is steadily and consistently reinforced by rewards which run the gamut from unconsciously experienced parental approval in the transference neurosis to the highest order of ego gratification.

One additional important aspect of the conditioning mode is the so-called *working through*. Unfortunately the term is used ambiguously. We are using it in Freud's implicit meaning; that is, the following through of the basic conflicts in all their derivatives—in character formation, thinking, feeling, acting. This persistent retracing of the infantile neurosis with the flashlight of the transference has certain marks of a conditioning (or unconditioning) process.

We trust that the recognition and careful study of the three modes will facilitate the understanding of learning on any level of development or task. In analysis qua therapy, it may help us not to put too much faith in one aspect alone as, for example, insight; it will remind us of the necessity of the occasionally dreary work of "conditioning" (i.e., repetitive working through); and may call our attention to facets of identification that are still too little known.

SUMMARY

The authors attempt to lay the foundations for a bridge between learning theory and psychoanalytic theory. Three basic modes of learning are postulated: conditioning (the one most investigated), insight learning (akin to acquiring a new Gestalt), and learning through identification (most neglected by both learning theorists and psychoanalysts). Conditioning in human learning is characterized by repetition, automatization, and—usually—a degree of dysphoria; insight learning by frequently sudden "closure" and ego gratification; identification is considered as different from imitation. There seems to be a developmental phase specificity for the three modes, as well as an affinity to different ego structures. The psychoanalytic treatment process, viewed as a complex learning act, is used to illustrate the functions of the three learning modes. Psychoanalytic insight provides connection between motivation and behavior, diminishes the isolation between emotion and cognition, and loosens the repression barrier between past and present; transference interpretation, confrontation, and genetic interpretation facilitate each of the three aspects of insight. Conditioning is shown as operative in many of the external aspects of the analytic setting and in the working through process, subtle forms of "reward and punishment" in the transference neurosis. Identification is stressed as a legitimate aspect of therapeutic analysis, and the role of nonverbal communication cues for identification is pointed out.

REFERENCES

Erikson, E. H. (1959), Identity and the Life Cycle. *Psychological Issues,* Monograph 1, 1/1. New York: International Universities Press.

Freud, A. (1963), The concept of developmental lines. *The Psychoanalytic Study of the Child,* 18:245–265. New York: International Universities Press.

Freud, S. (1923), The ego and the id. *Standard Edition,* 19:3–66. London: Hogarth Press, 1961.

Hilgard, E. (1948), *Theories of Learning,* 1st ed. New York: Appleton-Century-Crofts.

Lampl-de Groot, J. (1956), The role of identification in psycho-analytic procedure. *Internat. J. Psycho-Anal.,* 37:456–459.

Rapaport, D. (1960), The Structure of Psychoanalytic Theory: A Systematizing Attempt. *Psychological Issues,* Monograph 6, 2/2. New York: International Universities Press.

Chapter 9

Emotional Intelligence

STANLEY I. GREENSPAN, M.D.

Usually education is thought of in the limited context of impersonal learning, such as learning to read and write and do arithmetic. Most educational exercises, as well as tests of intelligence, focus on relatively impersonal contexts. Even high-level mathematical or literary interpretive problems are relatively impersonal as compared to the interpersonal emotional domains of love, dependency, assertiveness, anger, and competition.

Education is intended to prepare children for the challenges of life. Therefore it is paradoxical that most education focuses on instrumental and reasoning skills in relatively impersonal domains (i.e., the subject matter of school and college), while the work and family challenges of life involve using instrumental and reasoning skills in emotionally charged interpersonal contexts. "Life" involves thinking on one's feet. Whether the challenge is leading a company or balancing intimacy and dependence and assertiveness and independence in family life, intelligent thinking must be applied to emotional as well as impersonal domains.

Why has this obvious fact been largely ignored? In part, it has been ignored because we tend to view emotional and intellectual life as separate rather than interrelated domains. The fact that it is the same brain that processes information whether the information is of the order that because A is bigger than B and B is bigger than C, therefore A is bigger than C, or of the order that feelings like anger and love are not all or nothing phenomena but exist in gradations in relationship to each other (i.e., a seriation task) is infrequently addressed.

However, even though the same brain processes information, reasoning ability often does not develop equally in relationship to all "experiential domains." It takes practice and "learning" to develop reasoning capacities in different contexts. Generalization of abilities does not necessarily occur automatically.

In order to understand how impersonal and emotional learning are part of the same process, I have suggested (Greenspan, 1979) that the same mental structures develop in relationship to multiple experiential contexts, but that these structures may develop at different rates and to different levels, in part dependent on differential experience.

A UNIFIED MODEL OF "INTELLIGENCE"

In *Intelligence and Adaptation: An Integration of Psychoanalytic and Piagetian Developmental Psychology* (Greenspan, 1979), a relationship was proposed between the kind of structures studied by Piaget and the kinds of internal sensations considered by the dynamic perspective in psychoanalysis. It was shown that Piaget's cognitive psychology is compatible with the metapsychological points of view of psychoanalysis, including the dynamic point of view. Cognitive structures, it was suggested, may be seen as one of the multiple determinants of behavior.

In the discussion of the interrelationships between a hypothetical "external" cognitive boundary (that studied by Piaget) and the similarly postulated "internal" boundary, which deals with drive-related phenomena (emotions and drive-colored relationships), it was suggested that the processes operative at each "boundary" are symmetrical. The boundary of the structure differs only with regard to the stimulus world it encounters. The structure can exist at different developmental levels at each boundary and in different relationships to its stimulus world. It was pointed out that the different factors influencing the development of the internal boundary and the external boundary cause a relative differentiation of these two boundaries throughout development. The way in which these two boundaries are related, however, provides a synthetic link and permits us to integrate cognitive and affective contexts.

To amplify the relationship between cognition and emotion (the two boundaries), consider an illustration from early development. Means-ends differentiation and the capacity for figurative thinking may be highly dependent on early object relations. At the earliest stage, for example, there can be no development of psychic structure without the capacity for attachment. While there may be some development with compromised attachment, it cannot be the rich development that leads to optimal cognitive development, even in the impersonal realm. It is the infant's attachment to a human object that permits him to begin to differentiate means from ends and self from others. Severe lack of drive satisfaction, for example, deficiencies in physical contact during infancy, often lead to an increase in activity and in displacement of energy toward other stimuli. The young infant may turn to the inanimate world and, if there are objects available, may increase his involvement with them. Past a point, however, lack of drive satisfaction may lead to decreased activity and withdrawal, a type of giving up. The infant lies apathetic and listless.

The influence of the drives depends in part on the stage of development and the structure of the ego, and, in particular, on the relationship between the two bound-

aries. During early development, particularly during the
first few months of life, ego structures are relatively undifferentiated in terms of internal and external boundaries. Precursors of the external boundary are tied to
drive-related structures (the precursors of the internal
boundary). As development proceeds, there is a progressive differentiation, partly because of the different stimulus inputs or aliments from the internal and external
milieus.

This differentiation proceeds hierarchically, however,
so that at the base the internal boundary is intimately
tied to the external boundary. Further along the developmental hierarchy, relative autonomy prevails between
external boundary functioning and internal boundary
functioning, but a connection remains that can be called
into play under certain conditions.

To visualize the relationship between emotion and
cognition, consider the idea of a transitional operation;
that is, a series of gradients from primitive drive cognition to impersonal cognition. At one end of the spectrum
we find primitive drive-colored cognitions, then developmentally more mature drive-colored cognitions, then
cognitions only mildly colored by mature drive organizations, and eventually, at the other end of the spectrum,
impersonal cognitions only relatively or minutely affected by drive derivatives. What are the transformational variables that relate impersonal cognitive structures
to drive-colored cognitive structures?

The internal and external boundaries may develop to
different levels of cognitive operations. The degree of discontinuity (for example, the external boundary is at the
formal operations level and the internal boundary at the
preoperational level) may have an important influence
on the vulnerability to regression of the boundary at the
higher level. It is as though a backward pull were exerted
by the lowest level of development. With appropriate
stress (from the internal drives or external environment),

a new equilibrium may be found at the lower level of cognitive operations. We can observe this most clearly in a psychotic reaction in a "latent psychotic." His emotional cognition may have barely reached the concrete operational stage, and he may process much of his internal world in the context of preoperational processes (magical thinking). In the psychotic regression, particularly in response to a minimal stress, aspects of his external boundary, which may, in part, have reached a formal operational capacity, may regress to preoperational and early concrete operational modes of cognition. In a delusion about an "influencing machine," for instance, the machine may be given human qualities (preoperational) and have components that function in the context of concrete operational logic (in the secondary elaboration of the delusion).

To a lesser degree, regressions to the level of development of internal boundary are seen in all neurotic compromise formations, since they all use some preoperational and concrete operational thinking. In some phobias, for example, an inanimate object is experienced unconsciously as alive and dangerous and put through some complex transformations. To the degree that reality testing remains intact, only a small symbolized aspect of cognition is involved and the regression is therefore quite limited.

In order to resolve the oedipal situation, the youngster who has moved into it by being able to picture in fantasy one of the parents as a rival and take him on, so to speak, needs to be able to see that he "'can't have his cake and eat it too." The young girl cannot have the mother as her rival and father as the longed-for object of her desires and at the same time begin to develop a close identification with mother and expect support from mother. If she tries to do both, she gets involved in a series of covert, tricky relationships characteristic of those who have unresolved oedipal patterns. She also often gets involved in defensive neurotic formations. The same thing applies to the boy who is unwilling to relinquish his possessive feelings toward mother and rivalrous feelings toward father at the same time that he wants father to love him and wants to be the center of attention of both parents. He may refuse to resolve the situation, thinking he can have his cake and eat it too, but this will involve him in many defensive patterns.

To take a step away from this and look at it from a cognitive viewpoint, consider just the oedipal situation. In a sense, the child is unable to say "I cannot be a rival to this parent and also be a warm, secure, dependent lover of this parent." Thus, the young girl who stays in the middle of the oedipal situation often wants mother to be her supporter and to have all of mother's attention. From a cognitive perspective there is a failure here in *simple* classification. One person cannot be rival and nonrival at the same time. To wish for this state of affairs is to engage in egocentric, magical thinking that disregards logical classifications or categories.

The question is, What are the emotional bases for this alleged cognitive failure? The youngster with unresolved drive pressures, who never learned to give things up at the early dyadic level, has tremendous yearning and hunger to try to get some needs met in an oedipal configuration. He has trouble, therefore, in resolving his oedipal difficulties and gets stuck in the middle of the oedipal triangle. He may, then, because of the pressure of his drives, be unable to perform the simple cognitive tasks of forming mutually exclusive categories in human relationships, particularly with primary important objects that are closely connected to the drives. This inability may appear in impersonal relationships as well. On the other hand, if these drive pressures are not too great with, for example, nonfamily relationships, the child may be able to perform the task of mutual exclusivity in nonfamily settings.

Drive pressures may, however, affect not only the primary objects but also secondary objects, such as friends or peers, and yet not affect the inanimate world. In terms of manipulating blocks, the drives, since they are primarily placed on human objects, may not affect cognitive efficiency. There may be a progression from the primary objects, which are closer to the drives, to inanimate objects, which may be relatively removed from drive pressures. Nevertheless, if the drive pressures are intense enough, we may speculate that they would affect even the inanimate world. A general inability for classification, and therefore mathematics, may result from an internal boundary limitation in this area, or from a severe-enough fixation at the internal boundary. Drive pressure is therefore an important variable affecting cognition.

A third variable relating drive-colored and impersonal cognition is the degree of structure or the definition of the cognitive task. Where the inanimate external environment is highly delineated (e.g., round versus square pegs) and the cognitive task is also clearly delineated (e.g., classification), a high degree of structure is present. Such an instance is higher in structure than, for example, labeling human beings with different facial expressions.

The fourth variable to be considered is the organism's history of interaction among innate givens, maturational forces, and environmental influences. This variable includes the innate and developmental strengths of the cognitive structures and of the drive- and affect-modulating structures. If a person has basically intact innate equipment and good opportunities to act on his environment to develop psychological structures, and if there are no major early emotional insults to compromise them, one may assume very strong structures in relation both to inanimate objects and to tasks relating to human objects. Such structures are relatively resilient in the face of pressures from drives. They have a great deal of integrity and strength based on the original genetic and constitutional factors from which they evolved and on the environmental experiences that served to consolidate them.

A fifth variable is the situational context, which is partially related to the strengths of the drives and their related affects. In some situational contexts drive derivatives and affects are very active and tend to pervade cognition; in other contexts drive derivatives may be relatively inactive. For example, one could study a person's performance on certain cognitive tasks under situations varying in cues related to hunger, dependency, sex, or aggression, and observe their impact on cognition in relation to the personality organization.

A sixth variable is the degree of mutual enhancement between cognitive and drive-affect development. Mutual enhancement occurs when the development of the drives, object relations, and cognition is at the same level—for instance when there is oedipal resolution and, at the same time, the cognitive capacity for concrete operations. Out of this enhancement and mutual consolidation there may be a resistance to regression.

The symbolization of a cognitive task involves images that have a relationship to each other because of continuity along dimensions determined by drive investment. During the course of development, experiences become attached to initial drive-determined organizations, providing a secondary associative-experiential organization to memories or images. At one extreme of this hierarchy is the external configuration of reality, which may have features independent of a relationship to drives.

The degree to which an external boundary task is similar to stimulus configuration to issues at the internal boundary, however, may be another variable mediating the influence between the two boundaries.

Organic impairment or delay, as illustrated by biologically based mental retardation, raises some special issues. Where the cognitive structure does not develop, except in a rudimentary form, the capacities at both the external and internal boundaries will be severely affected. Consider, for example a retarded youngster who can develop cognitive structure only to the early phase of concrete operations. The limitations on his general intellectual functions are well known. It is also well-accepted clinically that many such youngsters develop emotional problems. While many reasons can be suggested for the development of emotional problems (e.g., a defective self-image), the model being developed here would offer a rather specific hypothesis.

The limitations in cognitive development restrict the flexibility of operations available to deal with stimuli at the internal boundary. The mildly retarded youngster has only the relatively simple mechanisms of early concrete operational cognition to deal with a developing internal milieu. As illustrated earlier, the early latency child, in contrast to his adolescent counterpart, has only a few cognitive operations and, in parallel, only a few defensive operations.

It is not surprising that retarded youngsters often develop or demonstrate emotional and/or behavioral difficulties in adolescence. Their internal milieu is becoming more intense and complex due to the biological and related psychological changes (e.g., drive-affect dispositions) of this period. Yet they have only the cognitive or, at the internal boundary, the parallel defensive and adaptive ego functions of early latency. The equipment, in a sense, cannot handle the stimulus input. Complex human relationships and their related drive-affect states, as well as the independent psychological changes of adolescence, are too much for the relatively inflexible system characteristic of the early concrete operational stage to cope with.

It should be pointed out that while retardation is often diagnosed by IQ scores, a more useful assessment of intelligence would be to observe the cognitive level attained. Marked biologically based limitations in cognition may restrict the development of the internal boundary as well as that of the external boundary. This hypothesis raises many interesting questions about treatment for such youngsters. Take, for example, the youngster with limited cognitive capacity who is relatively successfully using denials and reaction formations. Should these be interpreted or supported? What is the role of external boundary intelligence in treatment? Most important is the fact that most current support and treatment for retarded children rarely helps them achieve emotional maturity consistent with even their limited cognitive potential. (The fact that they rarely reach their cognitive potential is another issue.)

In the broader question of development in general, as we reach back into the first three years of life and try to facilitate ability to deal with the world, the present model of cognitive-affective interaction may prove useful. Those who are concerned with cognition cannot offer programs of cognitive stimulation without considering the underpinnings of human object relations and their drive-affect investments. A program of cognitive stimulation must take into account the child's capacity to reach a state of equilibrium, to attach to a human object, to develop a process of complex reciprocal interaction and organized social and emotional patterns, to develop representational capacities and differentiations, to move on to form triangular relationship patterns, and to move into latency issues. There may be ways to facilitate the cognitive aspects of these processes, but they would have to take into account early and later object relations and their associated drives and affects.

THE DEVELOPMENT OF EMOTIONAL
INTELLIGENCE: THREE LEVELS OF LEARNING

The human organism, it will be postulated, essentially learns according to three basic principles: somatic learning, consequence learning, and representational-structural learning.

Somatic learning will be suggested as an organizing principle for understanding learning that occurs in relationship to the human body, in particular the bodily or biological functioning which is accessible to variations in organization in the context of environmental experience. Such phenomena as general arousal patterns, overall interest in the world, specific autonomic nervous system patterns, bodily rhythmic processes (such as sleep-wake cycles, alert cycles, hormonal variations) will be seen to be determined in part by this very early type of "somatic" learning.

Consequence learning will be seen to be involved at both the somatic and the representational levels. This type of human learning which is evident in the stimulus-response approaches, for example, the operant learning paradigms (Skinner, 1938), is particularly powerful in demonstrating how learning of new behaviors and discriminatory capacities can occur as a result of behavioral consequences (the contingencies of reinforcement). While consequence learning can be applied to the level of ideas and meanings, its explanatory power is most useful when applied to observable discrete behaviors. In this context it is not surprising that operant approaches, developed from experiments with animals where discrete behaviors are easier to observe and control than in humans, help us understand a different level of human experience from experiences at the level of meanings. The reorganization of meanings into new meanings differs somewhat in character from changing behavior through altering consequences.

Representational-structural learning will be suggested as the way to account for "higher order" learning involving the formation and organization of mental imagery and symbols which ultimately fit into configurations that permit us to think and learn. This level involves "awareness" in the traditional sense (i.e., an awareness of ideas, or representational awareness).

Traditionally, learning is thought to occur only at the level of meanings. Through the capacity for forming, experiencing, and organizing and reorganizing mental imagery (mental representations), thinking and learning become possible. Perhaps the most complete theory to explain learning at the level of impersonal (nonemotional) meanings has been developed by Piaget and his colleagues (1969). Where meanings involve feelings and wishes, however, it is the psychoanalytic approach that has attempted to understand how learning occurs.

Before continuing to outline our basic model, a brief review of psychoanalytic approaches to learning may prove useful. A major challenge for psychoanalysis has been to integrate the cognitive and affective perspectives and to understand how learning occurs in relationship to both drive-affect–colored experience and reality-oriented experience. Early psychoanalytic conceptualizations of learning were predominantly drive- and conflict-oriented. The role of psychological structure and the learning which occurs in relationship to the external environment were understood only in the most general and global terms. Data and concepts from instrumental and cognitive learning theorists were for the most part outside the domain of psychoanalysis. Subsequent contributions focused on the need to understand how both the environment and drives influence the development, organization, and differentiation of internal psychological structures. While this interest opened the door to cross-fertilization and a more complete theory of learning (Hartmann, 1939; Rapaport, 1951; Wolff, 1960) it was recognized that a great deal more theory building was necessary. Recently a more complete model which integrates drive-oriented and reality-adapted experience in the context of the developmental sequence of intelligence and adaptation has been formulated (Greenspan, 1979, 1989).

While the three forms of learning suggested above are pivotal, there are also midway positions. For example, it will be seen later that between consequence learning and representational-structural learning there are processes of identificatory learning. We shall also see that representational-structural learning exists at different levels of organization. This model will therefore postulate three levels (and related sublevels) of learning occurring simultaneously, each accounting for different aspects of human experience.

In order to document the validity of this model, the evidence for the existence of each of these levels of learning will be presented by describing their emergence during the course of early human development. The organizations achieved, as well as the variations possible at each level, will also be described to show that these stages are not simply maturational milestones, but levels of learning open to change through experience. The relationships among the three levels will then be explored.

LEVELS OF LEARNING FROM AN INTEGRATED DEVELOPMENTAL PERSPECTIVE

SOMATIC LEARNING

At the first level, which occurs in the earliest stage in life, internal and external stimuli become processed according to somatic learning; that system which relies predominantly on the use of the physical (e.g., neurophysiologic) aspects of the human body.

This earliest and perhaps most basic kind of learning of which the human organism is capable is perhaps the most difficult to define. One way to approach it is through example—such as a neonate and mother in a rhythmical rocking pattern. There appears to be an early "fitting in"

originally described by Winnicott (1965) between the neonate and its nurturing environment, the key nurturing
caretakers. When this fitting in process is appropriate we
often see the infant begin to organize aspects of its somatic functioning. Thus the ability of the neonate to begin organizing patterns of sleep-wake and alertness is in
part related to environmental variables and is not solely
a maturational process (Sander, 1962).

That a special type of early learning does exist is also
indicated by the work on imprinting and critical periods,
which has recently been refined through research, showing that in certain animal species, even prenatally, selected "environmental experiences" act as inducers,
refiners, and maintainers for later behavioral patterns.
For example, the ability of a baby duck to respond preferentially to its mother's call is in part related to experiential factors a few days prior to birth (Gottlieb, 1976).
The synchrony between a baby's behavior and maternal
voice pattern is further evidence of a type of fitting in
between the neonate and his environment (Klaus and
Kennell, 1976). (It may be interesting to speculate that
later derivatives of this fitting in may relate to a sense
of organization, well-being, and accommodation as sometimes observed in certain types of one-time learning experiences [e.g., religious conversions, psychotherapies
that rely on hypnosis, and/or identification with a powerful charismatic figure].)

It should be pointed out that while we are postulating
a type of somatic organismic learning, early in life organisms also appear to be capable of responding to pain
and pleasure, and to have behavior shaped by consequences (Gewirtz, 1965, 1969; Lipsitt, 1966). We may also
postulate that the third level of learning, organizing internal representational experience, and therefore a primitive type of representational awareness, probably
begins very early on as well, since there is now evidence
that imitative behavior occurs during the earliest time

of life (Meltzoff and Moore, 1977). It should not, however, mislead us into assuming that either learning by consequences or by meanings predominates early in life. While learning of various levels may occur all the time, most relevant is the predominant type of learning in the human infant's natural environment at each developmental phase.

Somatic learning is consistent with what occurs during the sensorimotor period as described by Piaget (1969), and with empirical observations of the way infants use rhythmic patterns to deal with internal and external stimulation. It appears that the earliest phase of development does not have the quality of intentionality or "psychological life" that later stages will have. Somatic internal stimulation plays a larger role in determining behavior in this earliest phase than does differentiated social interaction which becomes more dominant later on. Early distress, for example, is related to internal physical and neurophysical events (Tennes, Emde, Kisley, and Metcalf, 1972).

Basic somatic systems, even at this early age, however, are complex and demonstrate individual differences among babies; for example, individual differences in state regulation, habituation patterns, crying responses, the establishment of homeostatic cycles and rhythms, and broad measures of temperament (Brackbill, 1958; Wolff, 1966; Thomas, Chess, and Birch, 1968; Parmelee, 1972; Brazelton, 1973; Emde, Gaensbauer, and Harmon, 1976). Under favorable circumstances we observe greater organization of somatic systems in infants in the first months of life. In the first two to four months of life, for example, we observe a number of processes in the neurological, cognitive, and affective development converge around an acknowledged nodal point; for example, the social smile (Emde et al., 1976). While the harmony between the infant and the caretaking environment plays a vital role in establishing the organization of these somatic patterns (e.g., basic rhythms and homeostatic mechanisms), there is still a great deal to learn about the way in which the very young infant perceives and experiences the world (Sander, 1962; Yarrow and Goodwin, 1965; Klaus, Jerauld, Kreger, McAlpin, Steffa, and Kennell, 1972; Yarrow, Rubenstein, Pederson, and Jankowski, 1972; Stern, 1974a,b; Lewis and Rosenblum, 1974).

Nevertheless, at this stage it appears that there are few detour or delay channels and the organism's capacity for entering into somatically based homeostatic rhythmic patterns, both with important figures in the environment and within itself, as an important adaptive tool providing protection during the earliest days, weeks, and months of life.

The capacity to achieve homeostasis (Greenspan, 1979), the earliest task of the somatic learning phase, is perhaps the first area in which we may observe variations in somatic learning. This task involves the ability to regulate states, form basic cycles and rhythms (sleep-wake, alertness), organize internal and external experience (e.g., implement certain stimulus thresholds, habituate to stimuli, organize initial response patterns, motor integrity, gaze, and so on), and integrate a number of modalities into more complex patterns such as consoling oneself and coping with noxious stimuli.

An optimal homeostatic experience in the early weeks and months of life involves achieving internal regulation in the context of initiating human relationships and interest in the world. For example, the infant who is alert, oriented, and engaged in the animate and inanimate world in an organized manner in the context of established patterns of sleeping-wakefulness and eating may be contrasted with the infant who can be calm at the expense of an optimal state of alertness and engagement. To the former, a mild stress (illness) may result in a temporary change in sleep pattern, while to the latter, a similar stress may result in intense apathy and lack of engagement in the animate world.

LEARNING BY CONSEQUENCES

A second step in the development of human learning involves learning by consequences. As the human organism develops, it begins to show that it is able to respond to consequences. It is able to repeat action patterns that bring it satisfaction. Eventually, it is able to distinguish patterns that lead to certain ends, distinguish means from ends, and is even able to use intermediary devices to achieve a desired end. The differentiation of means from ends and learning by feedback, as described by Piaget (1969), might more broadly be conceptualized as the capacity for learning by consequences.

There is enhanced potential for dealing with internal or external stimulation. To obtain certain gratifications, even complex patterns can be learned (e.g., the process of shaping described by learning theorists). The concepts of instrumental learning theory can also be applied to complex human behavior (Greenspan, 1975). Learning by consequences therefore provides more flexibility to adapt to a changing and complex environment and is closer than somatic learning to what we think of as intelligent behavior.

The phase of learning by consequences develops gradually and is evidenced by a number of observations and experimental findings. The young infant becomes more intentional and his interactions with the environment more differentiated. For example, still in the early part of the first year, the smiling response becomes less a product of internal stimulation and more a product of complex interpersonal cues (Wolff, 1963). Visual stimuli become more important (Sroufe and Waters, 1976). Events can begin to have a negative meaning (Brody and

Axelrad, 1970; Bronson, 1972; Tennes et al., 1972). Interactions slowly become more reciprocal and differentiated (Escalona, 1968; Lewis and Goldberg, 1969; Clarke-Stewart, 1973; Brazelton, Koslowski, and Main, 1974; Stern, 1974a,b; Sroufe and Matas, 1974; Emde et al., 1976).

Behavior at all levels—cognitive, affective, and social—becomes more differentiated and organized. For example, stranger anxiety (Spitz, Emde, and Metcalf, 1970) indicates a capacity to discriminate between the primary caregiver and others. The capacity for these discriminations, a product of learning by consequences by inference, leads to the impression that the infant now has greater capacity for differentiating various organizations of internal experience, including both memory and present perceptions. For example, the complex behaviors of surprise and anticipation appear between nine and ten months (Charlesworth, 1969), and affect and cognition appear more connected (Brody and Axelrad, 1966, 1970). With consequence learning we observe the shift from magical causality (e.g., an infant pulls a string to ring a bell which is no longer there) to consolidation of simple causal links (the string will only be pulled if it produces a noise), to the beginning of more complicated means-ends differentiation (e.g., use of substitutes, detours, intermediary devices).

The extent to which learning occurs at this phase may be illustrated by the variations in behavior and experiential organizations which are learned. For example, we may observe differences related to environmental factors in the achievement of the phase-specific developmental tasks of attachment and somato-psychological differentiation (Greenspan, 1979, 1981). There are infants who fail completely to develop age-appropriate contingent behavioral and emotional responses (e.g., withdrawn or behaviorally chaotic infants who fail to develop a basic sense of causality as the foundation of reality testing), either because of their own constitutional or genetic differences and/or because of a withdrawn or overly intrusive (projecting), noncontingent primary caregiver. There are also infants in whom only one aspect of emotional differentiation is compromised. Thus, assertiveness or anger may be ignored or associated with caretaker withdrawal, leading to a compliant or negativistic infant. Maladaptive psychologic patterns may come under the influence of specific environmental consequences (e.g., functional, gastrointestinal, dermatologic, eating, or sleeping difficulties).

Following the phase when consequence learning dominates, there is a transitional phase in the developmental process between the first two levels of learning and the highest level, the representational-structural level of learning; it is learning by internalization. This type of learning is related to the stage of behavioral organization, initiative, and internalization (Greenspan, 1979, 1981).

As the stage of consequence learning and somatopsychological differentiation reaches an organizational level with the ability of the infant to differentiate clearly and subtly the significant others in his interpersonal sphere, there is an increase in the process of "taking in" or internalizing, evidenced by increased imitative behavior. As this capacity becomes more developed we see the organization of certain emotional systems; for example, affiliation, separation, fear and wariness, curiosity and explorativeness (Ainsworth, 1973). The study of attachment (Main, 1973; Ainsworth, Bell, and Stayton, 1974) as a complex "high order" behavioral organization illustrates the development of constructs that match the infant's greater organization of behavior.

Initiative and exploration are enhanced by the capacity for combining schemata into *new* behavioral organizations that are goal directed (e.g., further use of detours, substitutes, delays, and intermediary devices). The infant's capacity to take initiative and organize behavior and feeling states is enriched by and in part further facilitates his capacity to internalize. For example, after eight to ten months of age we see progressively more imitative behavior which, in turn, facilitates organized exploratory behavior from the secure base of primary care-giver(s). The gradual individuation which occurs is perhaps best described by Mahler's representation of this practicing subphase of the separation-individuation process (1975).

The capacity for original or new behavior by combining known schemata, complex behavioral patterns (tertiary circular reactions), trial-and-error exploration, enhanced memory, and the gradual shifting from imitation to identification leads to a much greater sense of the toddler as an organized, initiating human being (e.g., child pulls parent to the refrigerator and points to a desired food). There is also evidence for the beginning of a psychological sense of self (Lewis and Rosenblum, 1974).

Variations in this type of learning are illustrated in situations where such enhanced organization does not occur and there are compromises in behavioral organization, initiative, originality, and the beginning of internal "psychological" life. Behavior remains fragmented, polarized (e.g., chronic negativism, disorganized aggressive behaviors), related to somatic or external cues. Intentionality and sense of self are "nipped in the bud." The capacity to use fantasy, and even thought in general, may be impaired.

REPRESENTATIONAL-STRUCTURAL LEARNING

As development proceeds further, the more organized transitional behavioral patterns lead to a capacity for new levels of organization; for example, identificatory behavior, the beginnings of a sense of self, person, and object permanence (Gouin-Dècarie, 1965; Piaget, 1969; Mahler, 1975).

A third phase in the development of human learning thereby gradually emerges—representational-structural learning. The capacity for psychological representation indicates the potential for a new order of intelligence. It enables the child to represent in an organized fashion aspects of external impersonal objects, as delineated by Piaget in his descriptions of object permanence, as well as external emotionally or affectively laden human objects, in whole or in part. It also enables the child to represent, in terms of psychological events, experiences from within; that is, beginning organizations of the self that call on various internal sensory experiences— proprioceptive visual, auditory—as well as other kinds of sensory and perceptual experiences reflecting events evolving from the organism.

The child, for example, can now hold a representation of an object and can call on this representation even when the object is absent. If there is stimulation from within, such as a yearning for physical contact with the mothering person, memories associated with the mother's sound, visual image, touch, smell, and so on, can be organized through mental representation, and some sense of satisfaction of the need for physical closeness with the mother can be gained. Thus sensations from within can be dealt with through this new capacity. Earlier in life the infant could only use fleeting sensations or imagery, imitative activity, and/or cry in protest and quiet himself with rhythmic experiences such as rocking.

The initial establishment of an internal sense of self and object, and the initial ability to conserve internal representations of animate and inanimate objects are evidenced by the increased behavioral, emotional, cognitive, and interpersonal repertoire of the two-year-old; for example, the ability to say "No," the development of personal pronouns, ability to recall, ability for organizing mental images and searching for inanimate and animate objects displaced in both time and space, memory for emotional experience, locating experiences that pertain to the self and nonself, the beginning of cognitive insight (combining internalized schemes), the ability to identify the various parts of self, relating in a diminishing need-fulfilling manner, and the beginnings of cooperation and concern for others.

Representational-structural learning is advanced by the growing ability to elaborate ideas and fantasy (symbols) and the continuing ability to learn by consequences, that is, the differentiation of means from ends, but now at a level of psychological representation. Paralleling what Mahler (1975) describes as "on-the-way to object constancy," there is the growing ability for reality orientation in both the cognitive impersonal realm and the emotionally laden interpersonal realm, at the same time that internal imagery is more available for elaboration. Symbolic play (e.g., using dolls to symbolize people or animals and language) becomes used for an ever richer, deeper, thematic elaboration.

With consolidation of representational capacity (object constancy [Mahler, 1975]) at ages three to four, there is the consolidation of basic personality functions such as reality testing, impulse regulation, integration and organization of affect and thought, delineation of self and nonself, mood stabilization, and capacity for focused concentration.

At this time there also emerges the capacity to construct *limited transformed derivative representational systems*. These are representational systems that are related to the existing representational systems in permanent and stable structures. This new capacity, described by Piaget (1969) for the impersonal realm in terms of the abilities for constructing inverse and reciprocal relationships, though not together in the same system (concrete operational thinking), and recently for the emotional realm (Greenspan, 1979, 1981) affords the youngster new capacities for learning as experience can be altered in accord with defensive and adaptive goals consistent with emerging principles of logic. New defenses and coping capacities are observed (e.g., use of rationalization and reaction formation). Transformations at this level (in comparison to more primitive levels) are fully reversible. Clinically, this is seen where an interpretation of a defense (a transformation) leads to greater associative depth and range (ideas and wishes emerge along a continuous associative pathway). Earlier levels of organization which do not reflect a capacity for representational transformation with reversibility are illustrated by patterns of ego splitting and the like.

If the capacity for self- and object representation is not reinforced by these transformations early in life, the youngster does not have much flexibility in dealing with stimulation from inside or outside. Mechanisms such as ego splitting, denial, and projection are used, indicating that the youngster cannot tolerate variety or intensity in terms of experience from his internal world or from his affectively laden external world.

The next substage in learning, and representative of human learning at a relatively optimal level is the capacity for constructing *multiple transformed derivative representational systems*. This occurs during the formal operational period as described by Piaget (1969). Here there is a capacity for creating multiple representational systems related to the original representational systems through a series of complex transformations. Systems can be constructed using the inverse and reciprocal together, along with the reciprocal of the inverse, the correlative, all in one system. This affords the capacity for constructing a multiple combinatorial system in the impersonal world and for relatively equivalent enhanced flexibility in the realm of affectively laden representations (Greenspan, 1979). There is a capacity for constructing systems of mental representations in relationship to the original representations via transformations that are rich in variety and flexibility. Clinically, one observes higher level defenses, synthetic potential, and associative capacities reflecting a wide range of depth and richness. Typically, transformations at this level are also reversible, providing the capacity for experiential continuity (at different levels of awareness or consciousness).

At this level there are more potential solutions to deal with ambiguity, conflict, and a wide variety of experience from inside and outside, leading to a vastly increased capacity for new learning.

At the representational structural level of learning, behavior is organized in relationship to the experience of mental imagery (representations). These are not just ideas, thoughts, or wishes, but refer to the entire range of internal experience (bodily sensations, affect tendencies, various sensory imputs, and so on) which can be organized in representational form.

THE RELATIONSHIP AMONG THE LEVELS OF LEARNING

We have delineated a model in the development of human learning which postulates three levels of learning occurring simultaneously (somatic learning, consequence learning, and representational-structural learning), each accounting for different aspects of human experience.

It is no longer necessary to conceptualize learning or education in terms of totally different realms of functioning, and therefore in different conceptual contexts (e.g., neurophysiological, emotional, and cognitive). It is now possible to consider a uniform framework of human learning where somatic or psychological events occur on a continuum of levels (i.e., somatic to representational learning) in a constant relationship to each other. The particular processes occurring at each level and the relationships among the three levels determine the nature of an individual's experience.

In more specific terms, however, we must consider how the three levels relate to one another; in particular, how somatic patterns relate in an ongoing manner to representational patterns.

Somatic patterns relate to representational patterns in three crucial ways. (1) Somatic patterns form part of the basic structure of the representational system; (2) they are part of the experiences which eventually become organized (internalized) at a representational level; (3) somatic experience is constantly perceived by the representational structures and is interpreted and transformed just as is external experience.

Somatic patterns are part of the basic structure of the representational system because of the constitutional and early developmental somatic differences that account for the individual ways in which infants process experience. For example, the early somatic pattern of arousal may form the basis for later intensity of internal representation. The early stimulus threshold (somatic pattern of shutting out stimulation) may form the foundation for later tendencies of the representational system *not* to experience certain noxious sensations. In her work on anorexia nervosa and obesity, Bruch (1973) postulated that because of experiences in early life, certain infants, toddlers, and young children do not ever become aware of such basic bodily sensations as hunger; on the other hand there are children who may be hyperreactive to minimal amounts of stimulation. Some adult individuals are acutely aware of sensations such as sexual longing and feeling; others may be totally unaware of such longings. In some instances, the denial of usually experienced sensations or feelings occurs secondarily for dynamic reasons. In other instances, because of early patterns where there are no confirmatory parental responses to the infant's expression of certain internal states, such as those described by Bruch, certain bodily feelings and impulses may never come to be available to representational awareness.

Somatic patterns are part of the experiences which eventually become internalized at a representational level.

During the second year of life when complex interactions are becoming organized and internalized, somatic patterns involved in these interactions may become organized and internalized at a representational level. For example, the toddler who experiences intense somatic patterns of irritability with stimulation (based on earlier somatic learning) may come to experience stimulating human relationships as "irritating," thereby forming mental images (representations) which combine the earlier somatic proclivity with the later complex human experience. A personal "meaning" is therefore established (e.g., human relationships are accompanied by irritation) incorporating the earlier proclivity.

Another example, the somatically very active infant may, in the second year of life, use this activity in the service of expressing rage. If as a consequence of this rage, mother or father withdraw, the toddler may internalize a representation associating activity and rage with loss of human contact. Again a meaning becomes organized which includes both the original somatic proclivity and the later interaction (e.g., activity and withdrawal). Similarly, early somatic pleasure patterns may become involved in complex human relationships which become internalized and reach a representational level.

As indicated earlier, the representational system once organized, in addition to evidencing distinct tendencies toward perception and interpretation of experience (including "somatic" experience), may also modify experience. For example, once there is the capacity to alter, recombine, and later transform internal representations (imageries) in accord with defensive and adaptive goals, we observe such events as the following. A vague sensation associated with protest behavior comes to be expressed as an angry feeling. This feeling may then be changed to a "loving feeling." Fears may be displaced from one object to another, and new fantasies may evolve from old ones. Through this process the original somatic experience may be hardly recognizable and its origins in early development easily obscured.

In summary then, the relationships between the somatic and representational levels of learning involve the somatic foundation of the representational system, the internalization of complex interpersonal experiences involving somatic proclivities, and the distinct styles of perception, interpretation, and transformation of the representational system in relationship to somatic experience.

IMPLICATIONS FOR PREVENTIVE WORK AND UNDERSTANDING THE DEVELOPMENT OF MALADAPTIVE OR ADAPTIVE CAPACITIES

The implications of this model for a general theory of learning relevant to both cognitive and emotional intelligence are especially important for preventive intervention approaches. This model would postulate, for example, that a highly adaptive organizational structure at a "higher" level of learning may compensate for a less adaptive organizational structure at a "lower" level or vice versa. This would work as follows: assume that a youngster has some mild difficulties in his early somatic-sensory organizations because of sensory processing difficulties. This leads to mild deviations in the early "somatically" based affective organizations (i.e., a youngster with difficulty in processing and modulating aggression and discharge of activity). Assume, however, that this youngster is in an unusually empathetic and sensitive environment which also sets effective limits. This envi-

ronment helps the child have confidence in and internalize fully his capacity for control, regulation, and
modulation of impulses and affects. More importantly, it
helps him develop a representational capacity wherein
sensations and affects are labeled, especially in the af-
fective-thematic areas that are vulnerable (i.e., aggressive feelings and discharge patterns) and can be
transformed in accord with adaptive goals. Such a
youngster, in spite of an early constitutional and maturational disorder in organizing sensory and sensory-affective experience, may very well develop a highly adaptive
personality structure because he has the capacity to perceive and interpret even usually overwhelming sensory-
affective experiences. He therefore makes "sense" out of
confusing messages. That such a proclivity, when interpreted and transformed, may later contribute to creative
or artistic endeavors is an interesting speculation.

Consider the other scenario. A youngster with similar
processing difficulties and limitations in the early "somatic" organization of affects has a very confusing family
milieu. He not only does not have an opportunity at the
level of prerepresentational interaction patterns to learn
to organize his early sensory-affect patterns, but at the
representational level develops confused meanings (because the family interaction patterns are filled with anxiety, conflict, inconsistent and undermining experiences,
and/or regression to concrete modes of thinking when anxiety is present). In such a situation there would be a
compromised organization of sensory-affect experience,
presumably "sending up" confusing signals and messages
for interpretation to the representational system. Only
in this instance the confusing signals are interpreted by
a representational system which would have difficulty
interpreting even clear sensory and sensory-affect patterns. The fact that such a youngster would look highly
disturbed, therefore, would not be surprising. He would

be vulnerable at both levels, the early somatic and the later representational level.

A most important hypothesis arising from this model is based on the fact that this approach focuses on levels of organization of experience. Therefore no one aspect of early somatic learning—a compromise in a sensory pathway or specific aspect of the early sensory-affective organization (i.e., an infant "learning disability")—need be decisive in determining the capacity of the youngster to organize at relatively more adaptive levels. Even youngsters with rather marked sensory processing difficulties may be capable of achieving highly adaptive levels of organization. In such instances, however, even intuitive caregivers may need to be aided by a specialized preventive therapeutic approach. Based on this hypothesis it may be assumed that the critical issue is to provide the child with the "phase-specific experiential nutriments" in whatever way possible so that the child can organize an appropriate level of experiential organization. In the case of deaf or blind children, for example, it is now well known that when the intact sensory modes were not used to provide the "phase-specific experiential nutriments," many of these children developed secondary sequelae and looked either retarded or autistic. However, when the blind children's hearing, touch, and other modes are used to provide the phase-specific experiential nutriments, they developed relatively competently. Similarly, deaf children do much better when their vision is used to help them have access to a range of phase-expected experience (e.g., early signing).

It is therefore intriguing to consider that the same principle may apply for severe processing deficits in auditory, tactile, vestibular, or other sensory pathways that are so important to early somatic learning. It is not far-fetched to assume that many of the severe emotional disorders, and even retardations, may involve a profound but highly specific disorder in the processing of infor-

mation (including affective information). In this context
it is interesting to note that studies of Down's syndrome
babies (Chiccetti and Sroufe, 1976, 1978; Butterworth
and Chiccetti, 1978) suggest that selected processing
problems may compound the overall cognitive deficits.
For example, to the degree that the care-giving environment continues to overwhelm the vulnerable sensory
mode, a youngster may experience the world as confusing.
Secondary phenomena, such as social withdrawal with
severe gaze aversion, extensor rigidity, sensory motor
delays, cross-sensory integration problems, may then result. Similarly, if the brain does not have access to "experiential nutriments" for structure building, cognitive
capacities may fail to develop, not necessarily because
maturation could not proceed, but because the information or the necessary opportunities for the youngster to
practice his potential abilities are not present. In other
words, the environment does not make available those
specialized experiences which could foster age-expected
levels of experiential organization through the intact sensory modes. Therefore it is constructive to speculate that
if a processing disorder did not initially interfere with
overall integrative functioning and did not involve all
areas of cognition, but only one or even two sensory pathways (such as the auditory and tactile or auditory and
vestibular) the prognosis might be quite good with appropriate patterns of care.

The above hypothesis leads to the preventive therapeutic principles of providing the phase-necessary information or "experiential nutriments" at whatever cost
through the intact modes and at the age-appropriate level
of learning (in other words, circumventing the impaired
mode; e.g., a severe auditory processing problem or severe
difficulty of handling a special type of affect, and making
the necessary experiences available to the other modes)
while, at the same time, gradually remediating the impaired mode. (This approach would be similar to the way

one works with an auditory-sensory processing difficulty in an older child.) With a baby, the prognosis might be significantly better because of the brain's greater plasticity in the early years. A suggested approach to assessing the early somatic organization and the later representational system is discussed elsewhere (Greenspan and Porges, 1984).

CONCLUSION

What are some of the practical implications of the view of learning we have discussed? Perhaps most important is the notion that education and learning begin at the beginning, with conception and the growth of the nervous system. From prenatal life and the early postnatal period, emotional, social, and "cognitive" learning must be viewed as occurring together. Programs must begin at the "beginning" to support all domains of "intelligence." Therefore education cannot wait until school age. There must be an integration of our educational, health, and human development policies.

An implication of this view for school-based education would be a shift from static to dynamic education. Children must be taught to reason in emotionally relevant contexts. Educational experiences should range from simulations of real life work challenges (i.e., running a company, a United Nations debate); simulations of interpersonal challenges (i.e., dealing with dependency, security, love, anger, curiosity), to greater emphasis on learning in multiple contexts such as having young teenagers learn about child development by working and learning in infant and child day care centers, through interacting with infants and children, not just reading about them.

These are only a few examples. "Learning" in emotionally relevant contexts offers the promise of helping infants and children learn to interact and reason with regard to those experiences that are most challenging and most "human."

REFERENCES

Ainsworth, M. (1973), The development of infant-mother attachment. In: *Review of Child Development Research*, Vol. 3, ed. B. Caldwell & H. Ricciuti. Chicago: University of Chicago Press, pp. 1–94.

—— Bell, S. M., & Stayton, D. (1974), Infant-mother attachment and social development: Socialization as a product of reciprocal responsiveness to signals. In: *The Integration of the Child into a Social World*, ed. M. Richards. Cambridge, UK: Cambridge University Press, pp. 99–135.

Brackbill, Y. (1958), Extinction of the smiling response in infants as a function of reinforcement schedule. *Child Develop.*, 29:115–124.

Brazelton, T. B. (1973), *Neonatal Behavioral Assessment Scale*. Philadelphia: J. B. Lippincott.

—— Koslowski, B., & Main, M. (1974), The origins of reciprocity: The early mother-infant interaction. In: *The Effect of the Infant on its Caregiver*, ed. M. Lewis & L. Rosenblum. New York: John Wiley.

Brody, S., & Axelrad, S. (1966), Anxiety, socialization and ego formation in infancy. *Internat. J. Psycho-Anal.*, 47:218–229.

—— —— (1970), *Anxiety and Ego Formation in Infancy*. New York: International Universities Press.

Bronson, G. (1972), Infants' reaction to unfamiliar persons and novel objects. *Monographs of the Society for Research in Child Development*, 37 (Serial No. 148). Chicago: University of Chicago Press.

Bruch, H. (1973), *Eating Disorders: Obesity, Anorexia Nervosa, and the Person Within*. New York: Basic Books.

Butterworth, G., & Cicchetti, D. (1978), Visual calibration of posture in normal and Down syndrome infants. *Perception*, 7:513–525.

Charlesworth, W. (1969), The role of surprise in cognitive development. In: *Studies in Cognitive Development*, ed. D. Elkind & J. Flavell. London: Oxford University Press, pp. 257–314.

Cicchetti, D., & Sroufe, L. A. (1976), The relationship between affective and cognitive development in Down's syndrome infants. *Child Develop.*, 47:920–929.

—— —— (1978), An organizational view of affect: Illustration from the study of Down's syndrome infants. In: *The Development of Affect*, ed. M. Lewis & L. Rosenblum. New York: Plenum Press.

Clarke-Stewart, K. (1973), Interactions between mothers and their young children: Characteristics and consequences. *Monographs of the Society for Research in Child Development*, 38 (Serial No. 153). Chicago: University of Chicago Press.

Emde, R., Gaensbauer, T., & Harmon, R. (1976), Emotional Expression in Infancy: A Biobehavioral Study. *Psychological Issues,* Monograph 37, 1/10. New York: International Universities Press.

Escalona, S. (1968), *The Roots of Individuality.* Chicago: Aldine.

Gewirtz, J. L. (1965), The course of infant smiling in four child rearing environments in Israel. In: *Determinants of Infant Behavior,* Vol. 3, ed. B. M. Foss. London: Methuen, pp. 205–260.

—— (1969), Some contextual determinants of stimulus potency. Paper presented at the meeting of the Society for Research in Child Development, Santa Monica, CA.

Gottlieb, G. (1976), Conceptions of prenatal development: Behavioral embryology. *Psychol. Rev.,* 83:215–234.

Gouin-Dècarie, T. (1965), *Intelligence and Affectivity in Early Childhood: An Experimental Study of Jean Piaget's Object Concept and Object Relations.* New York: International Universities Press.

Greenspan, S. I. (1975), A Consideration of Some Learning Variables in the Context of Psychoanalytic Theory: Toward a Psychoanalytic Learning Perspective. *Psychological Issues,* Monograph 33, 1/9. New York: International Universities Press.

—— (1979), Intelligence and Adaptation: An Integration of Psychoanalytic and Piagetian Developmental Psychology. *Psychological Issues,* Monograph 47/48, 3 & 4/12. New York: International Universities Press.

—— (1981), *Psychopathology and Adaptation in Infancy and Early Childhood: Principles of Clinical Diagnosis and Preventive Intervention:* Report No. 1. New York: International Universities Press.

—— (1989), *The Development of the Ego.* Madison, CT: International Universities Press, Inc.

—— Porges, S. W. (1984), Psychopathology in infancy and early childhood: Clinical perspectives on the organization of sensory and affective thematic experience. *Child Develop.,* 55:359–390.

Hartmann, H. (1939), *Ego Psychology and the Problem of Adaptation.* New York: International Universities Press, 1958.

Klaus, M. N., Jerauld, R., Kreger, N. C., McAlpin, W., Steffa, M., & Kennell, J. H. (1972), Maternal attachment: The importance of the first postpartum days. *New Eng. J. Med.,* 286:460–463.

—— Kennell, J. H. (1976), *Maternal-Infant Bonding: The Impact of Early Separation or Loss on Family Development.* St. Louis: Mosby.

Lewis, M., & Goldberg, S. (1969), Perceptual-cognitive development in infancy: A generalized expectancy model as a function of the mother-infant interaction. *Merrill-Palmer Quart.,* 15:81–100.

—— Rosenblum, L., eds. (1974), *The Effect of the Infant on Its Caregiver.* New York: John Wiley.

Lipsitt, L. (1966), Learning processes of newborns. *Merrill-Palmer Quart.,* 12:45–71.

Mahler, M. S. (1975), On the current status of the infantile neurosis. *J. Amer. Psychoanal. Assn.*, 23:327–333.

Main, M. (1973), Exploration, play, and cognitive functioning as related to child-mother attachment. Unpublished doctoral dissertation. Johns Hopkins University, Baltimore, MD.

Meltzoff, A. N., & Moore, K. M. (1977), Imitation of facial and manual gestures by human neonates. *Science*, 198/4312:75–78.

Parmelee, A., Jr. (1972), Development of states in infants. In: *Sleep and the Maturing Nervous System*, ed. C. Clemente, D. Purpura, & F. Mayer. New York: Academic Press, pp. 199–228.

Piaget, J. (1969), *The Psychology of the Child*. New York: Basic Books.

Rapaport, D. (1951), Toward a theory of thinking. In: *Organization and Pathology of Thought*. New York: Columbia University Press, pp. 689–730.

Sander, L. (1962), Issues in early mother-child interaction. *J. Amer. Acad. Child Psychiat.*, 1:141–166.

Skinner, B. F. (1938), *The Behavior of Organisms: An Experimental Analysis*. New York: Appleton-Century-Crofts.

Spitz, K., Emde, R., & Metcalf, D. (1970), Further prototypes of ego formation. *The Psychoanalytic Study of the Child*, 25:417–444. New York: International Universities Press.

Sroufe, L., & Matas, L. (1974), Contextual determinants of infant affective response. In: *The Origin of Fear*, ed. M. Lewis & L. Rosenblum. New York: John Wiley, pp. 49–72.

—— Waters, E. (1976), The ontogenesis of smiling and laughter: A perspective of the organization of development in infancy. *Psychol. Rev.*, 83:173–189.

Stern, D. (1974a), The goal and structure of mother-infant play. *J. Amer. Acad. Child Psychiat.*, 13:402–421.

—— (1974b), Mother and infant at play: The dyadic interaction involving facial, vocal and gaze behaviors. In: *The Effect of the Infant on Its Caregiver*, ed. M. Lewis & L. Rosenblum. New York: John Wiley, pp. 187–213.

Tennes, K., Emde, R., Kisley, A., & Metcalf, D. (1972), The stimulus barrier in early infancy: An exploration of some formulations of John Benjamin. In: *Psychoanalysis and Contemporary Science*, Vol. 1, ed. R. Holt & H. Peterfreund. New York: Macmillan, pp. 206–236.

Thomas, A., Chess, S., & Birch, H. (1968), *Temperament and Behavior Disorders in Chidren*. New York: New York University Press.

Winnicott, D. W. (1965), *The Maturational Processes and the Facilitating Environment*. New York: International Universities Press.

Wolff, P. H. (1960), The Developmental Psychologies of Jean Piaget and Psychoanalysis. *Psychological Issues*, Monograph 5, 1/2. New York: International Universities Press.

—— (1963), Observations on the early development of smiling. In: *Determinants of Infant Behavior*, Vol. 2, ed. B. M. Foss. London: Methuen, pp. 113–138.

———— (1966), The Causes, Controls, and Organization of Behavior in the Neonate. *Psychological Issues,* Monograph 17, 1/5. New York: International Universities Press.

Yarrow, L., & Goodwin, M. (1965), Some conceptual issues in the study of mother-infant interaction. *Amer. J. Orthopsychiat.,* 35:473–481.

———— Rubenstein, J. L., Pederson, F. A., & Jankowski, T. J. (1972), Dimensions of early stimulation and their differential effects on infant development. *Merrill-Palmer Quart.,* 18:205–218.

Chapter 10

Curiosity and Exploration in Children: Where Affect and Cognition Meet

RITA SUSSMAN, Ph.D.

> I sincerely believe that for the child, and for the parent seeking to guide him, it is not half so important to *know* as to *feel*. If facts are the seeds that later produce knowledge and wisdom, then the emotions and the impressions of the senses are fertile soil in which the seeds must grow. The years of early childhood are the time to prepare the soil. Once the emotions have been aroused—a sense of the beautiful, the excitement of the new and the unknown, a feeling of sympathy, pity, admiration and love—then we wish for knowledge about the object of our emotional response. Once found, it has lasting meaning. It is more important to pave the way for the child to want to know than to put him on a diet of facts he is not ready to assimilate.
>
> Rachel Carson, *The Sense of Wonder*

Recently, Richard Lewontin observed that the real message of evolution was that the only thing that was constant in nature was change. If, as he noted, this is particularly true for man, then how do motive and meaning develop in a world of constantly changing possibilities? What are the mechanisms and behaviors whereby young children not only learn to adapt to a varied and complex environment, but to anticipate it, make sense out of it, and change it to suit their needs and requirements?

This chapter focuses on one form of curiosity and exploration—the child's response to a novel object—as a way of modeling the intricate set of relationships between cognitive and affective processes. These principles and mechanisms, however, are applicable to children who explore in other ways—the child looking for mother, a student searching for the answer to a puzzling problem, a girl entering her new classroom for the first time, a scientist in a laboratory. In each of these instances a young person experiences uncertainty and a discrepancy between what she knows and what she wants to find out. Her response to that uncertainty (read "interest," "curiosity," "need") constitutes the substance of the exploratory process that we will be examining.

After reviewing the function of exploration for species survival and for human development we will consider the results of an experimental study designed to foster children's curiosity and quality of exploration. Highlighting some effects of intervention may provide clues to the ways in which motive and meaning develop out of the child's interaction with the environment and implications that can be drawn for optimizing the learning process.

DEVELOPMENTAL MECHANISMS

From infant to preschooler to self-directed learner, the growing child is both the product and increasingly the master of her own curiosity and exploratory activity. The more variation there is in the environment, and the more complexity to contend with, the more biological survival depends upon a flexible genetic blueprint (Rosenzweig, 1971). As it becomes more difficult to anticipate with the instinct model all possible environmental events and ways of responding to them, higher mammals and humans become more dependent upon learning to develop their capacities for knowing and acting in the world. Children accomplish this self-organization out of the very process of environmental interchange. From experience they build up links between stimuli they perceive in their world and rules for adaptively responding to them. These connections, in turn, serve as mental structures to regulate their activity and direct their behavior.[1]

At the simplest level this involves children's capacity to receive and transmit information, code it, and, as a result, modify their behavior in some appropriate fashion. It is also essential that they have some ability to know when new information is required and to learn how to obtain it through acting upon the environment. Developing the necessary coordinating structures, however, can only be accomplished if there is the possibility of feedback from the environment. Such feedback "instructs" or "teaches" the mental and physical capacities of the child to differentiate more finely among stimuli

[1] The functional model presented here is an amalgam of several theoretical and experimental perspectives. Piaget's developmental-structuralist approach provided the underlying conceptual framework (see *Biology and Knowledge* [1971] and Furth, *Piaget and Knowledge* [1970]). The ethological perspective of Lorenz (1969); the neurological contributions of Pribram (1971); information processing and cognitive processing models drawn from Simon (1969), Bruner (1973), and Olson (1970); the motivational theories best exemplified by the work of Berlyne (1960) are synthesized here to orient the reader briefly to those mechanisms most characteristic of the exploratory process.

Daniel Stern has utilized such a model in his pioneering work on the development of emotionality in infants (Stern, 1977). Most recently, discussions concerning the relationship between neurophysiological mechanisms, emotional states, and goal-oriented cognitive behaviors have demonstrated refinements in conceptualizing the elements of this basic model (e.g., distinguishing between tonic arousal and phasic arousal) that may lead to *qualitative* changes in emotional experience (see especially Stein and Levine, 1986, and Tucker, 1986). For a recent summary of the research literature on the psychology of curiosity, see Voss and Keller (1983).

and continually to adjust their behavior to be more competent and effective (Lorenz, 1969); that is, more "knowing."

Learning takes place, then, not only to modify behavior or reinforce it, but also to develop elaborated mental structures capable of recognizing and processing increasingly complex data about the world. As children's cognitive capacities become more sensitive to stimulus cues and their various meanings, they learn to make associations between cause and effect. They also begin evaluating the importance of these cues for their own emotional well-being and intellectual growth. Hence, by acting in their worlds and reacting to events, they learn the significance of mother's look, the multiplicity of functions associated with round objects like balls, what happens when you lift the receiver from a phone, and the excitement of pressing a button to ring the bell and make the cash register drawer pop open.

As the child responds to these environmental events, her activities provide "potentially useful knowledge" (Furth, 1970), in addition to satisfying immediate physiological need. The build-up of these structures of knowing and activity form sets, intentions, motives, and expectancies which take on the character of "acquired programs" that can be stored and used to reorganize a child's mode of response (Barbizet, 1970). If mother consistently engages in imaginary conversations when Sarah picks up the phone, rolls the ball back to her when she throws it, and smiles benignly as she takes pots and pans from the cupboard, then one might expect her to continue engaging in these sorts of activities with other objects in different environmental situations and to respond more competently and with pleasurable anticipation to the opportunity. If, to the contrary, her hand is continually slapped, and she hears "no, don't touch" from a frowning maternal figure, then we might presume that Sarah's mental set will be less inclined toward exploratory activities, more guarded in what she chooses to manipulate, and more concerned with ways of knowing and acting that do not incur mother's wrath.

It is also possible, however, that rather than utilize an exploratory program to gain information for the sake of knowing more about the world, a child may attach to it different motives. Hence Sarah may learn she can only get mother's attention by continuing to roll the ball or pick up the telephone. Or, rather than constraining her behavior in response to negative demands she may use these same behaviors to oppose mother's control over her. No longer, then, is she interested in the adaptive functions of the exploratory process. Nonetheless, in all cases, these secondarily acquired intentions and expectancies will select, condition, and constrain the types of information the child chooses to process and may function to direct and regulate behavior so as to satisfy other more compelling and immediate ends.

We can see, then, that exploration functions to build up affective as well as cognitive structures. As Simon (1969) notes, it is one means by which we build up a network of meaningful associations between the world as sensed and the world as acted upon which we can purposefully utilize to create a desired state of affairs.

CHARACTERISTICS OF THE EXPLORATORY PROCESS

Exploratory behavior is traditionally defined as "gradually exposing the receptors to portions of the environment" (Welker, 1961, p. 175), most often in response to the presence of novel or complex stimuli. If exploration describes the process by which children attend to novel stimuli and investigate them in the *external* environment, curiosity may be thought of as describing the *internal* state of the child who experiences perceptual-cognitive uncertainty generated by the presence of new and unanticipated stimuli.

A child experiencing curiosity is motivated to act upon it so as to reduce that uncertainty by acquiring information and extending her repertory of actions (Weisler and McCall, 1976). Whether she continues to attend to a stimulus and explore it will depend upon her mental organization and cognitive capabilities. Presumably a stimulus that can provide new information but is not so discrepant from what is familiar will receive the maximum amount of attention; it has also been suggested that stimuli that capture attention are also likely to be the ones most efficient in promoting changes in the cognitive system itself (McCall, 1971).

Each person is considered to have some "optimal level of stimulation" that maintains an intensity of excitation or arousal conducive to efficient learning (Hebb, 1955; Leuba, 1955). As shown in Figure 10.1, too low a level leads to boredom and desultory attention; too high a level gives rise to tension and anxiety. The advantage of such an arousal state is that it prepares the individual to receive information and alerts her to compare present stimulation with previously developed models of the world built up through past experience. As children develop images and categories of knowing, these begin directing attention and inducing their own "need to know." Arousal then is self-generated by an image of expectancy, an internal stimulation which then directs the exploratory process.

Researchers continue to distinguish between *specific exploration* and *play* (Berlyne, 1960; Sutton-Smith, 1970; Hutt, 1979); Hutt noted that investigative, inquisitive, or specific exploration is directional: the goal is "getting to know the properties" of an object or event. Play, in contrast, occurs only in a known environment, with a greater diversity and variability of activity and less of a sense of purpose. In play the emphasis changes from the

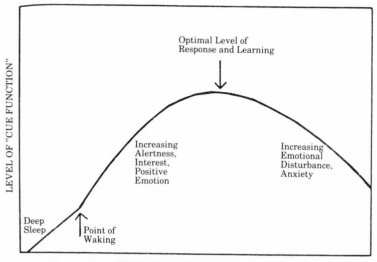

Figure 10.1. Performance as a Function of Arousal Level. (D. O. Hebb, Drives and the CNS. *Psychological Review,* Vol. 63, 1955, p. 250. © 1955 by the American Psychological Association. Used by permission.)

question of "What does this *object* do?" to "What can *I* do with this object?"

Thus the child's attitude is critical and determines her motivational stance: in exploratory play she has no clear set of priorities for valuing one set of actions over another. She is essentially exercising little control over what she or others expect the outcome to be or what types of information she might discover (Fagen, 1975). In contrast, specific exploration is more purposeful and efficient, seeking to gain information relevant to some task, be it testing for danger, searching for productive sources of food, finding out how an object works, or engaging in a science experiment.

Developmentally, control is exercised first by the ob-

ject itself which rivets attention and triggers a prepro-
grammed sequence of responses. Over time the child's
behavior becomes progressively more flexible and self-
directed so that she selectively determines not only what
is learned, but how she will act to obtain information and
how it is to be coded. Four stages in the development of
exploratory activity in young children have been delineated:

1. Chaotic exploratory attempts whereby manipulation has an accidental character and the child's
   interest wanes quickly. (We are all familiar with
   children who flit from one object to another without
   concentrating on any one thing.)
2. Movements and actions adapted to isolating inherent and practical features of an object and its
   functioning. (Children may learn to turn a handle,
   raise and lower a lever, and so on, but don't integrate each of the parts into a larger representation
   of the whole object.)
3. Planned investigation whereby manipulation is
   directed toward clarifying the significance of the
   individual parts to the whole and relations of each
   to the other. (In this stage a child may make things
   work through trial and error and figure out how
   things function.)
4. Planned, many-sided investigation in older children preceded by formulation of questions and visually orienting to the most important qualities of
   the object. (At this point children may observe
   something, question, and then proceed immediately to demonstrate how an object functions.)
   [After Boguslavskaya, 1961]

As Dewey observes, exploration is gradually transformed from "more or less casual curiosity and sporadic
suggestion into attitudes of alert, cautious and thorough

inquiry" (Dewey, 1909, p. 62). As children mature they explore less for the "raw sensory-perceptual feedback" of objects and events (McCall, 1974, p. 78; Stern, 1977). They begin instead to inhibit more primitive responses in favor of selective strategies which are governed by their own informational needs. This delay in responding not only allows for more flexible and systematic types of search: it also allows time for the child to "reflect" and utilize other information or meanings already encoded in her representational system (Kagan, Moss, Day, Alber, and Phillips, 1964; Maccoby, Dowley, Hager, and Degerman, 1965; Wright and Vlietstra, 1975). These earlier modes of behavior do not necessarily disappear; they are inhibited and "superseded" but may reappear as "regressive" behavior, the result of long- or short-term stress (White, 1964).

THE CHILD IN THE EXPLORATORY SITUATION

Several years ago I undertook a research project to see whether children could be helped to become more curious and learn how to explore better (Sussman, 1979). I was concerned that many children were being placed in day care centers which isolated them from a range of varied everyday life experiences. It seemed to me that children needed the stimulation of new and interesting events to keep intrinsically motivated curiosity alive and give them the opportunity to explore their environment verbally and physically. I hypothesized that continuous exposure to novelty would increase children's exploration of novel objects. Through frequent opportunities to interact with novel objects, I felt that children might become more inclined to expect their appearance, approach them more readily, and develop ways of interacting with them.

It also seemed that children needed the guidance and attention of a supportive adult to assist them in developing a more varied and complex repertoire of behaviors useful for manipulating new and familiar materials. Research has shown that particularly with disadvantaged students, enriching experiences alone may not be sufficient to bridge the gap between manipulative play with objects and the ability to transform newly acquired perceptions into generalizable and meaningful cognitive skills (Smilansky, 1971; Feitelson and Ross, 1973; Stokes, 1975). By highlighting various ways of investigating an object, adults might reinforce more productive behaviors with them and provide models of effective exploratory activity.[2]

The research focused on one subpopulation of children—three-year-old black, lower-income children in day care settings—to test whether a particular form of intervention utilizing novel materials and active teacher involvement with children could positively affect their approach to novel objects and foster their participation in a process of investigation and learning. Children were given different combinations of either novel or familiar objects and assigned to different groups. In some groups teachers worked with children helping them to explore objects. In others they remained responsive but made no effort to intervene in children's play. The children were

---

[2] The more complex an object, the more a child must attend to it, explore it, and utilize more finely differentiated perceptions and behaviors to "get to know" it. As children's responses become more complex, they use more information or more sophisticated information processing strategies to "make sense" of an object or encode it (Hutt, 1972; Nunnally and Lemond, 1973). Thus, combining or elaborating simpler behaviors, or demonstrating an awareness of some relationship between these behaviors and specific features of an object, for example, turning a crank to lower the ball of the crane into the crisper, may signify a more complex pattern of behavior than, for instance, a simpler response like pushing or pulling.

As conceptualized here, children are thought to explore more effectively or demonstrate more exploratory competence as their behavior is better organized, utilizes more complex activities with objects, and involves more symbolic and goal-directed activities.

tested before and after treatment by observing them individually for fifteen minutes in a free play situation with both novel and familiar objects.

What the data revealed was that a subtle balance exists among elements that comprise the exploratory situation such that intervention in any one area alters the network of relationships in other areas. The nature of the stimuli available for exploration, the context in which they are encountered, the effects of prior treatment or experience, help create differences among children that have implications for their personal learning.

THE NATURE OF PHYSICAL STIMULI

In order for children involved in this research to be "tested" for their level of curiosity and the quality of their exploration before and after treatment, two different sets of novel objects had to be used so each would be "novel" and, it was hoped, not previously encountered by the children. Four objects chosen in accordance with these criteria were divided into what appeared to be two comparable sets that were alternately used in pretest and post-test situations.

One set consisted of a wooden fire engine with removable people and ladders, accompanied by a colorful mechanical plastic juicer with removable bowl, and a dome that turned when cranked. Another set comprised a wooden crane with removable parts, manufactured by the same company as the fire engine, that had a ball that could be raised and lowered via a wooden crank; the second novel object in this set was a colorful salad crisper with an inside basket that turned when a cord was pulled. All of the objects had the potential for a variety of manipulatory behaviors, cause-and-effect results, and elaborated play situations.

The results showed that the character of the children's

activities varied considerably depending upon which set of objects were available to them. Part of the reason for such variation seems to lie outside of the children themselves and to reside in the nature of the external stimuli. Both sets of test materials could be considered "novel"; yet they could be shown to vary not only in the complexity of response which they invited, but also in the degree of their internal structuring and in their relationship to children's previous experience and associations.

The more representational fire engine and the juicer were objects that could be incorporated easily into existing schemata and be explored with some "sets" or "expectations" that were linked with preexisting behavioral patterns and cognitive structures, like firefighters climbing the ladders. Even the plastic juicer, which would have been uncommon in low-income areas, was often used for "pouring coffee," and thus could be included in fantasy or exploratory schemata. These initial and partial "matches," therefore, could provide a context of familiarity so that prior experience in other exploratory situations could be helpful and assert their effects within an extended play sequence that depended upon higher-level and sometimes creative mental activity.

The crane and the crisper, however, posed more difficult internal problems as to how they worked and fit together, and how to identify them. The greater degree of coordination they demanded directed the children's efforts to helping them master specific features of how the object worked. Although the children spent more time in exploring them with more complex behaviors, their behaviors were less sequenced and their exploration less competent than children who played with the fire engine and juicer.

Perhaps this illustrates how young children handle high levels of stimulus complexity that are too discrepant from what they already know (Nunnally and Lemond, 1973; Faw and Wingard, 1973). Just as children in this study may have attempted to make the complex situation more manageable and appropriate to their conceptual level by reverting back to simpler forms of interaction, so children in demanding or complex learning situations may fall back upon more primitive coping strategies, a form of regression in the service of the ego, when they have not fully mastered newly emerging schemata and rules for action.

Although the motive was the same for exploring both sets of objects (i.e., reducing the uncertainty in a strange situation), the two situations also may have had very different meanings for the children. With the more complex objects the children may have been trying to "solve the problem" of getting to know the object and what it was, by learning its function—manipulating individual features and mastering how it worked. With the simpler objects, each of the parts were more easily related to the others and then to an identifiable whole. This created a play situation that was invested with personal, creative meaning, incorporating both new and familiar toys in more symbolic, elaborated activity. The greater ability of the children to incorporate these objects in previously developed schemata enabled them to be more competent, more relaxed, and more flexible in their response to novelty.

THE EFFECTS OF PRIOR EXPERIENCE

The results of this study indicate that those children who had consistent opportunity to interact with novel objects were more curious and explored more competently. Experience with different novel objects and situations during the research thus may have prepared them to expect novelty more than children who played with familiar toys. It may have helped them learn to identify those features of the situation most productive of information, and be more organized in their response. These gradually acquired sets of expectancies acted as more than just perceptual filters: they were also competencies that enable children to adapt their actions skillfully to affect the outcome of events and in turn be modified by them, by knowing "what to do" and "how to respond."

TEACHING CHILDREN TO EXPLORE

There appeared to be a difference, however, in how children responded to novelty, depending upon the kinds of expectancies that were generated by prior experience. Deliberately teaching children to explore seemed to have very specific effects, biasing their perceptual set toward exercising those competencies for which it had been trained.

In all exploratory circumstances there is an implicit goal activated which may be termed the *reduction of uncertainty* and may be satisfied by choosing a set of alternative actions which provide information that ultimately "matches" what the child apprehends in the external environment. When organized, these actions may be termed *strategies;* when activated, they may have reinforcing properties. Thus knowledge of the object and the reduction of uncertainty is itself reinforcing; in addition, reproducing previously learned actions activated in accordance with a "plan" is both pleasurable and reinforcing of those actions. White (1959) speaks of these behaviors as being "in the ultimate service of competence" and motivated in their own right by the reinforcing "feeling of efficacy" (p. 329). They enable a child to feel in control of her own activity and to feel effectual in bringing about changes in the outside world too.

To the extent that certain strategies for exploring were reinforced through training in certain of the research groups, they may not only have taken precedence over other choices for action, but may also have influenced set and expectancy. Hence, they may have lowered the threshold for recognizing objects toward which these strategies could be applied; that is, helped children be more receptive to novel objects.

In addition, however, they also may have changed the conditions for labeling outcomes as "success" or "failure." Where previously information about the object—albeit obtained through many diverse behaviors such as in a play situation—may have been the desired end, when reinforced through additional ecological rewards such as adult approval, success, or failure may have been measured by the successful application of these strategies to the novel situation. Thus these strategies may have taken on the character of control mechanisms by directing behaviors toward ends which were not merely "implied" but "expected" and toward which the child had now become committed.

Consequently, training may place stress on children, prematurely reinforcing goal-oriented exploratory behaviors into a sequence of rigid control strategies. In this research, children who were taught to explore may have tended to respond to the appearance of novel objects with those behaviors previously reinforced in the teaching situation. These may have been adequate for dealing with less complicated forms of novelty like the fire engine and the juicer. However, the children's inability to organize their behavior effectively in the face of more complex and demanding objects like the crane and the crisper seemed to lead to a high degree of frustration and perceptual confusion.

The most distressing illustration occurred with children who were trained to interact with already familiar types of objects. When confronted by novel objects they functioned poorly on most qualitative measures of exploration and were significantly less competent in exploring them, whether the stimuli were simple or complex. Apparently, focused, directed teaching with familiar materials inhibited children's spontaneous interactions and in some instances confused their responses to novel toys. A possible explanation is that children would have received little orientation to exploring unfamiliar objects and would have been unprepared to deal with them. This finding is supported by Bruner (1949), who found that continual exposure of adults to the usual and familiar often leads to perceptual confusion when faced with incongruous or unexpected events.

In contrast, children who were given the same familiar toys but with no direct teaching may have experienced an optimal amount of stimulus variation and novelty without the intrusion of external reinforcers. In this study, they tended to show a flexibility of response that enabled them to explore competently regardless of the level of complexity they encountered in the novel objects.

In contrast, children without training who interacted with novel objects throughout the research tended to engage in less complex, nonsystematic reflex exploratory responses.

Hence, those children who were left to interact with objects on their own may have been more responsive to the basic elements of the exploratory encounter; they may have had the freedom to let their capabilities and experiences structure their activity with different sets of objects. Children, however, who learned strategies for acting on objects by responding to adult guidance may have been making a different set of connections to secondarily acquired motives where the meaning of the activity was also bound up in the ability to perform according to an externally induced set of standards.

IMPLICATIONS FOR LEARNING AND TEACHING

As polar opposites of educational theory, each of these models has its weakness, depending upon the unfamiliarity of the subject matter and the complexity of the materials. Lack of adult structuring and participation may encourage fleeting, short-term impulsive levels of interest and attention. Without the benefit of adult guidance, children may be denied the opportunity of developing a sustained in-depth involvement with the material so that at each level, new information or questioning provokes and directs renewed interest and exploration.

As we have seen, continous adult structuring has its own pitfalls. Olson (1970) demonstrated that successful training demands that the criteria for successful performance be anticipated by the teacher. Not only does she set the goals, but she also stipulates in advance a carefully sequenced program of skills that must be mastered to provide the information necessary for achieving these goals. While "education" may be thought of as transforming and reorganizing cognitive, intellectual, and motivational structures, training demands achievement of a particular end. By specifying certain behaviors and imposing desired outcomes, training supersedes the motivating qualities of personal interest, curiosity, and the need to be effective as they are expressed through self-regulatory processes of exploration. Consequently there is less opportunity through arousal of curiosity and personal interest to make widespread connecting links to associations in other parts of the self-system.

What appears to be called for is a more balanced approach than that utilized in this research. Children may need ample time to explore on their own. Judicious intervention is desirable, though, when children are frustrated, repetitive in their responses, don't know what to do next, or jump continuously from one activity to another (Smilansky, 1971; Feitelson and Ross, 1973). At that point adults can facilitate the learning process by stimulating further inquiry, pointing out unusual elements or apparent inconsistencies, and making suggestions at critical points.

Perhaps most important for a child is having the chance to learn and grow in companionship with an adult who keeps alive the sense of wonder, the joy and excitement of the mystery of the world (Carson, 1956). The process of exploration is a process of discovery, and the passion of that exchange with the world is infinitely more satisfying with someone who can share it and help a child to know it. Lillian Katz (1973) notes our current temptation to induce excitement in an effort to facilitate learning by gimmicks and one-time educational activities. She suggests, however, that a sound educative program is one which *"requires the children's sustained interest and involvement,"* by helping them to "develop and strengthen their own capacities for generating interesting, productive, or stimulating activities on their own" (pp. 108–109). Research and common sense suggest that, in addition, the attention of a supporting, guiding adult enriches the experience, nurturing and amplifying both cognitive and affective means of encountering and getting to know the world through their sharing of an emotional response together (see Stern, Barnett, and Spieker, 1983; Stern, 1986).

In this respect, then, novelty in the context of familiarity, particularly if familiarity includes the presence of a related adult, may help to foster an optimum environment for learning. Continuous exposure to novelty may be too exciting, too disruptive, too anxiety-producing for a child to make more than brief forays toward the source of stimulation. As we have seen, too, novel situations that are also complex and demanding may provoke defensive measures and reawaken past sets and expectancies that are reactive to feelings of personal incompetence and cognitive or emotional inadequacy.

Providing a context which is familiar, safe, and expectable may help a child to approach novelty and other types of demanding situations without the distracting, inhibiting effects of anxiety and stimulus overload. In this setting, motive is allied with personal interest and with the intrinsic desire to represent internally what exists externally, as well as to develop complementary ways of acting. In such a setting, too, the full adaptive capacities of the child can be marshaled to focus on the object of wonder and curiosity and to explore its meaning to her total sense of self.

Children encode their experience both intellectually and emotionally. There is no way of knowing in advance what the match will be between the child's encoded representations of the world as they currently exist in one moment of time, and objective reality as we choose to define it—through the medium of the physical object or the novel situation. We can compare objects and events as more or less complex or determine children to be at one or another developmental stage. However, the individual child's interaction with a particular stimulus event is a function of the characteristics and properties not solely of the events themselves, but of the events as they are experienced by the child.

SUMMARY

Curiosity and exploration are not isolated aspects of functioning elicited solely in response to the appearance of novel or complex stimuli. They manifest themselves as adaptational responses for survival in a complex world that cannot be programmed for in advance. They cannot be separated from the everyday interaction of children with their environment. Yet they may be supported and reinforced by certain environmental conditions.

As children develop meaningful conceptual networks they become more ready to recognize and anticipate new and unusual events. By manipulating objects in their environment and acting to gain further information, they develop conceptual networks and gain knowledge of the relationships between cause and effect, goal and activity.

As mediator of the environment to the child, the adult functions to structure an environment rich in content and as free as possible from anxiety so as to help the child experience pleasure in directing his attention outward to the social and object world.

REFERENCES

Barbizet, J. (1970), *Human Memory and its Pathology*. San Francisco: W. H. Freeman.

Berlyne, D. E. (1960), *Conflict, Arousal and Curiosity*. New York: McGraw-Hill.

Boguslavskaya, Z. M., (1961), Special features of the orienting activity of preschool children in the process of forming impressions of objects encountered for the first time, trans. K. Kaye. *Voprosy Psikholgii*, 3:93–101.

Bruner, J. S. (1949), On the perception of incongruity: A paradigm. In: *Beyond the Information Given*, ed. J. Anglin. New York: W. W. Norton, 1973.

———— (1973), *Beyond the Information Given*, ed. J. Anglin. New York: W. W. Norton.

Carson, R. (1956), *The Sense of Wonder*. New York: Harper & Row.

Dewey, J. (1909), *How We Think*. Boston: D. C. Heath.

Fagen, R. (1975), Modelling how and why play works. In: *Play—Its Role in Development and Evolution*, ed. J. S. Bruner, A. Jolly, & K. Sylva. New York: Basic Books, 1976.

Feitelson, D., & Ross, G. (1973), The neglected factor—play. *Human Develop.*, 16:202–223.

Faw, T. T., & Wingard, J. S. (1973), Conceptual development and its relationship to the effects of incongruity on exploration. Paper presented at meeting of Society for Research in Child Development, Philadelphia, PA, April.

Furth, H. (1970), *Piaget and Knowledge*. Englewood Cliffs, NJ: Prentice-Hall.

Hebb, D. P. (1955), Drives and the c.n.s. (conceptual nervous system). *Psychol. Rev.*, 62:243–254.

Hutt, C. (1972), Sex differences in human development. In: *The Process of Child Development*, ed. P. B. Neubauer, M.D. New York: Jason Aronson, 1976.

———— (1979), Play in the under-fives: Form, development and function. In: *Modern Perspectives in the Psychiatry of Infancy*, ed. J. G. Howells. New York: Brunner/Mazel.

Kagan, J., Moss, H. A., Day, D., Alber, J., & Phillips, W. (1964), Information Processing in the Child: Significance of Analytic and Reflective Attitudes. *Psychological Monographs*, 78 (578).

Katz, L. (1973), Education or excitement? In: *Talks with Teachers*, ed.

L. G. Katz. Washington, DC: National Association for the Education of Young Children, 1977.

Leuba, C. (1955), Towards some integration of learning theories: The concept of optimal stimulation. *Psychol. Rep.*, 1:27–33.

Lorenz, K. (1969), Innate bases of learning. In: *On the Biology of Learning*, ed. K. H. Pribram. New York: Holt, Rinehart & Winston.

McCall, R. B. (1971), Attention in the infant: Avenue to the study of cognitive development. In: *The Development of Self-Regulatory Mechanisms*, ed. D. Walcher & D. Peters. New York: Academic Press.

——— (1974), Exploratory manipulation and play in the human infant. *Monographs of the Society for Research in Child Development*, 39 (Serial No. 155).

Maccoby, E. E., Dowley, E. M., Hagen, J. W., & Degerman, R. (1965), Activity level and intellectual functioning in normal preschool children. *Child Develop.*, 36:761–770.

Nunnally, J. D., & Lemond, L. D. (1973), Exploratory behavior and human development. In: *Advances in Child Development and Behavior*, Vol. 8, ed. H. W. Reese. New York: Academic Press.

Olson, D. R. (1970), *Cognitive Development: The Child's Acquisition of Diagonality*. New York: Academic Press.

Piaget, J. (1971), *Biology and Knowledge*. Chicago: University of Chicago Press.

Pribram, K. H. (1971), *Languages of the Brain*. Englewood Cliffs, NJ: Prentice-Hall.

Rosenzweig, M. (1971), Role of experience in development of neurophysiological regulatory mechanisms and in the organization of the brain. In: *The Development of Self-Regulatory Mechanisms*, ed. D. Walcher & D. Peters. New York: Academic Press, 1971.

Simon, H. A. (1969), *The Sciences of the Artificial*. Cambridge, MA: MIT Press.

Smilansky, S. (1971), Can adults facilitate play in children: Theoretical and practical considerations. In: *Play: The Child Strives Toward Self-realization*, ed. G. Engstrom. Washington, DC: National Association for the Education of Young Children.

Stein, N., & Levine, L. (1986), Making sense out of emotional experience: The representation and use of goal-directed knowledge. Paper presented at the conference on psychological and biological processes in the development of emotion, sponsored by the Harris Center for Developmental Studies, University of Chicago, September.

Stern, D. (1977), *The First Relationship: Mother and Infant*. Cambridge, MA: Harvard University Press.

——— (1986), Sharing affective experience preverbally. Paper presented at the conference on psychological and biological processes in the development of emotion, sponsored by the Harris

Center for Developmental Studies, University of Chicago, September.

—— Barnett, R., & Spieker, S. (1983), Early transmission of affect: Some research issues. In: *Frontiers of Infant Psychiatry,* ed. J. Call, E. Galenson, & R. Tyson. New York: Basic Books.

Stokes, A. (1975), Applying research to play in the preschool classroom. *Childhood Ed.,* 51:232–237.

Sussman, R. (1979), Effects of novelty and training on the curiosity and exploration of young children in day care centers. Unpublished doctoral dissertation, University of Chicago.

Sutton-Smith, B. (1970), A descriptive account of four modes of children's play between one and five years. Unpublished manuscript.

Tucker, D. (1986), A modern neuropsychological model of the primary and secondary mental processes in emotion. Paper presented at the conference on psychological and biological processes in the development of emotion, sponsored by the Harris Center for Developmental Studies, University of Chicago, September.

Voss, H-G, & Keller, H. (1983), *Curiosity and Exploration: Theories and Results.* New York: Academic Press.

Weisler, A., & McCall, R. B. (1976), Exploration and play: Resume and redirection. *Amer. Psychol.,* 31:492–529.

Welker, W. J. (1961), An analysis of exploratory and play behavior in animals. In: *Functions of Varied Experience,* ed. D. W. Fiske & S. R. Maddi. Homewood, IL: Dorset Press.

White, R. W. (1959), Motivation reconsidered: The concept of competence. *Psychol. Rev.,* 66:297–333.

White, S. (1964), Age differences in reaction to stimulation variation. Unpublished paper.

Wright, J. C., & Vlietstra, A. G. (1975), The development of selective attention: From perceptual exploration to logical search. In: *Advances in Child Development and Behavior,* Vol. 10, H. Reese. New York: Academic Press.

Chapter 11

Learning, Knowing, and the Self: A Constructive Developmental View

ANN FLECK HENDERSON, M.S.W.
ROBERT KEGAN, Ph.D.

INTRODUCTION: LEARNING AND KNOWING—TWO DEVELOPMENTAL APPROACHES

Every teacher has had moments of surprise when students *learned* something quite different from what he or she had *taught*. The Sunday School child whose Christmas picture included "Round John Virgin" and the college student who "compared two authors" by listing personal facts about one and facts about the other, both gave their teachers this kind of surprise. As all learning is done in terms set by the learner's present cognitive system or way of making meaning the teacher must understand not only his or her subject, but to some extent the learner's "system" in order to facilitate learning; that is, in order to *teach*. The surprises constitute clues to that understanding. A teacher must know *whom* she is teaching in order to know *what* she is teaching; the students' meaning making is central.

Piaget's description of systems of reasoning from infancy to adulthood provides a general guide for understanding the capacities and constraints of meaning making at different stages. His work makes sense of many surprises by describing the logic underlying cognition, particularly among children and adolescents. Indeed, Piaget's lifetime of sensitive and scientific observations of children (1936, 1937, 1962) added a whole new image to the psychologist's collective memory. As Robert White wrote in a seminal essay on "motivation reconsidered" (White, 1959) this image could take its place alongside "the hungry animal solving problems, the child putting his finger in the candle flame, the infant at the breast, the child on the toilet, the youthful Oedipus caught in a hopeless love triangle" (p. 318). In contrast to these images of the child-who-learns-from-experience or the child-as-captive-of-instincts (or some combination of these two), Piaget's work yields an image of the child actively making sense, the child as a selective, interpretive, directed, constructive, and persistent organism who not only changes behavior as a result of experience (the classic definition of "learning") but changes experience as a result of a special kind of behavior, involved thus with knowing as much as with learning.

Piaget's work linked two powerful ideas evident in the psychologies of his day—the idea of development, prominent in psychoanalysis, that human personality itself evolves through qualitative eras according to regular principles of stability and change; and the idea of constructivism, prominent in Gestalt psychology, that human personality is constitutive of reality. His "genetic epistemology" amounts to, simultaneously, a developmental view of construction (that our meaning making itself passes through qualitative eras according to regular principles) and a constructivist view of development (that the very forms and processes of development are intrinsically meaning constitutive); "what an organism does," as William Perry says, "is organize, and the way a human organism organizes is called *meaning*" (Perry, 1970).

Piaget's stages of cognitive development are well known and their implications for curriculum design and a learner's intellectual capacities well discussed. What has not been much considered is that the same processes of self-invested knowing which give rise to stages of intellectual development may also set terms on such *psychological* issues in learning as: what is at stake for a person in learning or not learning? Where does the person place the locus of authority in a teacher-learner relationship? What is experienced as support to one's learning? What does it mean to the person to be a good learner? Recent work within the Piagetian tradition centering on the development of social cognition may have implications for the contexts of learning.

A given level of psychological development consists not only of a certain cognitive structure with the capacity for specifiable cognitive operations, but consists as well of an underlying epistemology. A given level of development is a living subject-object relation or *knowing system* which bounds and defines the entire psychological arena in which learning will go on. Although "the subject-object relation," a darling of sophomore philosophy classes, may seem a highly abstract notion, it is our hope in this chapter to suggest as educators how a wide variety of a student's learning behaviors and apparent experience may have a coherent unity, expressing as they do the same underlying epistemology or meaning system at work. That the same seventh grader, e.g., who is asked for a *definition* of "irony" and can only give *examples*, happens *also* to be less self-conscious about reading his essay in front of the class may be no accident; but why should such apparently disparate behavior be linked? This chapter will use two different approaches to the person as a knowing system. Both are Piagetian-based descriptions of unconscious underlying epistemology. Kegan

(1982) has explicated an evolution of stages of subject-object relation which are seen as the deeper structure behind social, moral, and scientific reasoning. Perry (1970) has described an evolution in the relation of knower and that which is known.

Perry's descriptive scheme was derived from interviews with college students. It charts a gradual shift in assumptions about the nature of knowledge and learning. In the earlier positions the learner sees knowledge as a matter of right or wrong, truth being located "out there," the teacher having special access to it. Learning is thus a matter of receiving, storing, and repeating what the teacher conveys, a matter of producing right answers. Subsequently the student discovers the possibility of legitimate uncertainty. It is not only *the answer* but the process of finding it that is now the "object" of the student's conscious attention. Some teachers or courses demand one way of thinking, and some yet another, an epistemology no longer strictly "dualistic" with regard to right and wrong. This evolves to systematic "multiplistic" thinking in which the student can take as object whole paradigms, sets of assumptions, or forms of knowing themselves. The shift to what Perry calls "contextual relativism" involves yet a further "objectification" of oneself as knower. The awareness that knowledge is relative to context demands both a new consideration of oneself as knower and a commitment to some position. Perry's scheme, outlined in Figure 11.1, is discussed more fully in the section "Inner Issues in Learning: Adolescence."

Kegan's stage descriptions, like Perry's, are structural in the sense that they are not about particular themes, issues, attitudes, or beliefs of a person, but something more abstract—the underlying epistemological principle which *shapes* a person's themes, issues, attitude, and beliefs. By "underlying epistemological principle," Kegan refers to a subject-object relation which a person's stage of development is said to compose. By "subject" Kegan refers to the structure of organizing, and by "object" he refers to the structures which *get organized.* "Subject" defines a system of making meaning, with which the person is identified; "object" refers to what is an element *of* that system. Similar to Piaget's notion of development as decentration, Kegan sees development as a process whereby that which was the very system of making meaning (subject) is differentiated from the self (made object) and integrated into a new system of which it is an element. Kegan's stages, summarized in Table 11.1, are thus a series of subject-object relations, or knowing systems, in which what is subject in any stage becomes object in the next. The "impulsive" preschooler (e.g., subject to her impulses and perceptions) grows into the "imperial" latency-age child, who is able to take control of and coordinate her impulses and perceptions into the more enduring dispositions of "needs" and the decreased egocentricity to distinguish points of view. In the same way, at adolescence typically, the self begins to give up its identification with its needs and a single point of view, and is gradually able both to coordinate its own needs with another, and hold multiple points of view simultaneously. This development, from an "imperial" to an "interpersonal" subject-object relation, brings into being the capacity for the *inter*personal experience of mutuality, and the intrapersonal experience of feelings as internal states rather than social negotiations. The several subject-object relations of personality development Kegan and his colleagues have researched and described (Kegan, Rogers, and Quinlan, 1981; Kegan, 1982, 1985; Noam and Kegan, 1982; Kegan, Noam, and Rogers, 1982; Souvaine, Lahey, and Kegan, 1989) are listed in Table 11.1, and more fully explicated in the next section.

In this chapter we propose that understanding something about the unconsciously constructed relation of knower and known, or subject and object, may serve to integrate psychological aspects of learning, and may il-

Figure 11.1: Scheme of Cognitive and Ethical Development (William Perry)

		Labels
Position 1	Authorities know, and if we work hard, read every word, and learn Right Answers, all will be well.	Basic Duality
(Transition)	But what about those Others I hear about? And different opinions? And Uncertainties? Some of our own Authorities disagree with each other or don't seem to know, and some give us problems instead of Answers.	
Position 2	True Authorities must be Right, the others are frauds. We remain Right. Others must be different and Wrong. Good Authorities give us problems so we can learn to find the Right Answer by our own independent thought.	Multiplicity pre-legitimate
(Transition)	But even Good Authorities admit they don't know all the answers yet!	
Position 3	Then some uncertainties and different opinions are real and legitimate *temporarily*, even for Authorities. They're working on them to get to the Truth.	Multiplicity subordinate
(Transition)	But there are *so many* things they don't know the Answers to! And they won't for a long time.	
Position 4a	Where Authorities don't know the Right Answers, everyone has a right to his own opinion; no one is wrong!	Multiplicity (solipsism) coordinate
(Transition [*and/or*]	But some of my friends ask me to support my opinions with facts and reasons.	

Dualism modified ⟶

Position	Description	Stage
Transition) *Position 4b*	Then what right have They to grade us? About what? In certain courses Authorities are not asking for the Right Answer; They want us to *think* about things in a certain way, *supporting* opinion with data. That's what they grade us on. But this "way" seems to *work* in most courses, and even outside them.	Relativism subordinate
(Transition) Position 5	Then *all* thinking must be like this, even for Them. Everything is relative but not equally valid. You have to understand how each context works. Theories are not Truth but metaphors to interpret data with. You have to think about your thinking. But if everything is relative, am I relative too? How can I know I'm making the Right Choice?	Relativism (contextual) generalized
(Transition) Position 6	I see I'm going to have to make my own decisions in an uncertain world with no one to tell me I'm Right.	Commitment foreseen
(Transition) Position 7	I'm lost if I don't. When I decide on my career (or marriage or values) everything will straighten out. Well, I've made my first commitment!	Initial Commitment
(Transition) Position 8	Why didn't that settle everything? I've made several commitments. I've got to balance them—how many, how deep? How certain, how tentative?	Orientation in Commitments
(Transition) Position 9	Things are getting contradictory. I can't make logical sense out of life's dilemmas. This is how life will be. I must be wholehearted while tentative, fight for my values yet respect others, believe my deepest values right yet be ready to learn. I see that I shall be retracing this whole journey over and over—but, I hope, more wisely.	Evolving Commitments

Relativism discovered ⟶   Commitments in Relativism developed ⟶

Drawn from Perry, (1981), hand out for lectures.

TABLE 11-1
Subject-Object Relations in Self Development (Robert Kegan)

	Stage 0 Incorporative	Stage 1 Impulsive	Stage 2 Imperial	Stage 3 Interpersonal	Stage 4 Institutional	Stage 5 Interindividual
Underlying structure (subject vs. object)	S—Reflexes, (sensing, moving) O—None	S—Impulses, perceptions O—Reflexes (sensing, moving)	S—Needs, interests, wishes O—Impulses, perceptions	S—The interpersonal, mutuality O—Needs, interests, wishes	S—Authorship, identity, psychic administration, ideology O—The interpersonal, mutuality	S—Interindividuality, interpenetrability of self systems O—Authorship, identity, psychic administration, ideology

drawn from Kegan, 1982

luminate a teacher's surprises and dilemmas in facilitating learning.

INNER ISSUES IN LEARNING: CHILDHOOD

"I know Big Bird isn't real," an earnest six-year-old wrote to *Sesame Street*. "That's just a costume. Underneath, there's just a plain bird inside!" What she "knew," she had figured out for herself, since it is unlikely anyone taught her this. Although *what* she knows is something of a surprise (one source of the amusement and delight we take in her words), *how* she knows, no less her own invention, is less surprising upon further consideration. Like many a six-year-old, she appears to be in the midst of reconstructing the way she knows the world: how things appear are no longer unreflectively taken as how things are (Piaget, 1936). That her surmise as to what does lie beneath the skin of appearance is itself not too "realistic" may be evidence that her new epistemological principles have not yet taken full control; but that she had distinguished *at all* between what is and what seems to be indicates a remarkable change, that the old epistemological principles have to some extent been outgrown. Though, at the moment, she could be said not to have *learned* much of anything, or not to know any *better* the truth about Big Bird (having swapped one misconception for another), from a developmental perspective she may well be expressing the effects of a gradual but qualitative transformation in the unconscious principles by which she actively constructs reality.

When children enter school at age five or six, like our young correspondent to *Sesame Street,* they are usually in the midst of an inner epistemological transformation. This transformation expresses itself in their cognitive, affective, interpersonal, and intrapersonal activities (Kegan, 1985).

Anyone who has spent time with both a four- or five-year-old and an eight- or nine-year-old cannot fail to note how different they seem, a difference which is clearly more than a child's "getting bigger." The older child seems to be functioning on a qualitatively different plane. She is not only physically larger, but seems physically more "organized," more "tightly wrapped." The younger child has a hard time sitting still for any length of time, moves continuously into and out of spaces with little predictability, and cannot attend long in any activity involving accommodations to others; the older child seems capable of adultlike forms of physical patience, "motoric propriety," and perseverance. The difference, most palpable and dramatic on a physical scale, appears over and over again on a score of more subtle dimensions. The younger child uses language as an appendage or companion to her means of self-presentation and social intercourse; for the older child, language is the very medium of interaction, central to the social presentation of the self. The younger child's life is filled with fantasy and fantasy about the fantastic (being Spiderman); the older child has taken an interest in things as they are and the fantasy life is about things that actually could be (being a doctor). The younger child will engage her parents in the middle of a conversation that she has already started on her own, as if she has trouble keeping track of which portions of a conversation she has actually had with you and which she has only imagined with you, or as if she takes it for granted that her private thinking is as public and monitored as her spoken thinking. The older child never does this, and, indeed, in her cultivation of a sense of privacy and self-possession she seems to have "sealed up" her psychic space. The younger children can roam neighborhoods moving in and out of houses with little or no observance of notions of private space or territoriality; older children ring doorbells, become shy, observe politenesses, and, indeed, post signs on their own bedroom doors, "Adults Keep Out." The younger children, asked to describe a movie they have just seen ("What is it about? What happened in the movie?") report discrete, unrelated episodes, discuss what particular characters did, and focus on actions and objects only randomly related to the story of the film; older children are able to construct a narrative of events, logically and causally linked, representing the movie's story line in a concrete but accurate fashion.

At a more global level, developmental stage theorists, from both constructive-developmental and psychoanalytic perspectives, make complementary generalizations about a basic transformation during the years of about five to seven. Piaget describes a shift, commonly occurring between five and seven, in the organization of the child's "scientific" knowledge about the physical world (Piaget, 1937). Prior to the shift, the child's thought is prelogical, or "magical," in which apparent or imagined events are confused with real events and objects, and perceptual appearances of qualitative and quantitative change are confused with actual change. After the shift, the child's thought is logical, organizing classes, relations, and quantities which maintain logically invariant properties in reference to concrete objects and events (Kohlberg and Gilligan, 1972). Kohlberg describes a shift, commonly occurring at the same time, in the organization of the child's moral judgment. Prior to the shift, children make decisions on the basis of what an outside authority deems to be right and wrong; after the shift, what is right is to meet one's needs, let others do the same, and be "fair," where fairness involves simple reciprocity and equal exchange (Lickona, 1976).

From the psychoanalytic perspective, Freud describes a younger child who is often intensely involved with both the opposite-sex parent (as a favorite); and the same-sex parent (as a rival for the attentions of the favorite); and an older child who is much less involved in this charged triangular relationship, and more turned outward from the home toward peers and personal skills. The younger child is at the mercy of his impulses and requires external controls and constraints on his longings; the older child has internalized these constraints, begun to take charge of his own impulses, and in the process has constructed a role for himself as "child" in relation to "parents" in a "family" which has changed from a context for romantic rivalry and longing into an institution of authority, hierarchy, and opportunity to demonstrate competent exercises of one's role built in part on new aspirations to emulate the same-sex parent with whom the child has become "identified."

Erikson describes a shift concurrent with the shifts thus far described. The younger child he depicts as in an "intrusive mode," intruding "into other bodies by physical attack . . . other people's ears and minds by aggressive talking . . . into space by vigorous locomotion . . . into the unknown by consuming curiosity" (Erikson, 1963, p. 87). The older child develops a sense of "industry": "He becomes ready to apply himself to given skills and tasks . . . learns to win recognition by producing things . . . to bring a productive situation to completion is an aim which gradually supersedes the whims and wishes of play . . . the child's danger, at this stage, lies in a sense of inadequacy and inferiority" (Erikson, 1963, pp. 259–260).

These extremely varied phenomena and multiple generalizations suggesting a fundamental shift between the ages of five and seven (White, 1970; Gardner, 1978) may find a unifying context in the idea of a reconstructed relationship of what, for the individual, is "subject" (the unconscious principle of self organization) and what is "object" (that which gets organized). Whether we consider Werner's "orthogenetic principle" (1940) of increasing differentiation and integration, or Piaget's notions of "decentration" and "re-equilibration" (1937), or any of several less explicit conceptions of development, a common evolutionary "rhythm" or movement emerges: when the organism develops, it undergoes a transformation by which the outgrown system of organization becomes a subsystem or element of the newly emerging system of organization. The old system (which was the way the organism was organized) is "differentiated" or "decentered" from what the organism has become, and it is "integrated" into the new system which thus achieves a new equilibrial state. The old system passes from the very principle of organization to *that which gets organized*. More precisely in this case, the child seems to be differentiating from a subject-object relation in which her very organization of inner and outer reality was *subject to* or embedded in her perceptions and impulses. The cognitive and emotional lability of the younger child may be a function of this embeddedness. While the child, unlike an infant, can recognize objects as separate from herself those objects are *subject* to the child's perception of them; if the child's perception of an object changes, the object itself has changed in the child's experience. In the famous Piagetian experiments, the younger child is unable to hold her perception of the liquid in one container with her perception of the liquid in the taller, thinner, container, precisely because she cannot separate herself from her perceptions. The same may be true of the structurally equivalent psychological category, the "impulse." The preschooler may have poor impulse control not because she lacks some quantitative countering force, but because she is composed in a qualitatively different way. Impulse control requires mediation, but the impulses are immediate to this subject-object balance. When I am subject to my impulses their nonexpression raises an ultimate threat; they risk who I am. Similarly, the preschooler's inability to hold two perceptions together (which is what gives the object world its concreteness, à la Piaget) is paralleled in the preschooler's inability to hold two feelings about a single thing together—either the same feelings about a thing over time which creates the "enduring disposition," needs, interests, which persist through time *in the child's experience of them,* or competing feelings at the same time. This latter suggests why the preschooler lacks the capacity for ambivalence and it understands the tantrum—the classic expression of distress in this era—as an example of a system overwhelmed by internal conflict because there is no self yet which can serve as a context upon which the competing impulses can play themselves out; the impulses *are* the self, are themselves the context.

One way of characterizing the *older* child's subject-object relation is in terms of the construction of the role. The child now has the social-cognitive capacity to overcome the earlier egocentricity and take the role of another person, as well as the affective differentiation within the impulse life of the family to take an appropriate role as a "child" in relation to a "parent." A distinguishing feature of this new subject-object relation is a self-containment that was not there before; the adult no longer finds himself engaged in the middle of conversations the child has begun all by himself; the child no longer lives with the sense that the parent can read his private feelings. He *has* a private world, which he did not have before.

It is not just the physical world which is being "conserved" but internal experience, too. With the constitution of the enduring disposition (what we call, for shorthand purposes, the "needs,"—but it should be clear we are not talking about any particular need as a content), there comes as well the emergence of a self-concept, a more or less consistent notion of a me, *what* I am (as opposed to the earlier sense of self, *that* I am, and the later sense of self, *who* I am).

With the capacity to take command of one's impulses (to have them, rather than be them) can come a new sense of freedom, power, independence—agency, above all. Things no longer just happen in the world; with the capacity to see behind the shadows, to come in with the data of experience, I now have something to do with what happens. As is the case with every new development, the new liberation carries new risks and vulnerabilities. If I now have something to do with what happens in the world, then whether things go badly or well for me is a question of what I can do. Looming over a system whose hallmark is newly won stability, control, and freedom is the threat of the old lability, loss of control, and what now appears as the old subjugation from without.

Perhaps it can be seen now how the same development which brings on the move from Piaget's "preoperational" stage to the stage of "concrete operations"—a change the consequences of which for intellectual capacity and curricular design are well understood—may also have considerable consequences for considering such *inner* psychological issues regarding learning as: What is experienced as support to one's learning? What is at stake in learning or not learning? Where is the locus of authority in the teacher-learner relationship? What does it mean to be a good learner?

In a study of children's experience of support to their learning, Zigler and Kanzer (1962) were impressed by the apparent difference between the younger children, five to six, and the older children, eight to ten. The younger children seemed to need responses from their teachers which were immediate, sensual, and communicative of praise, while the older children seemed to feel more rewarded by the information that they were correct. Support must in some way communicate *that the way the self runs* is confirmable, valuable, and approvable. How might the difference between support which is immediate, sensual, and praising, and that which provides the information that one is correct, be a function of the underlying subject-object distinction? When the self is still confused with its perceptions and impulses it has no point of view on itself or anything else which it understands as possibly distinct from someone else's point of view; it has no distinct point of view whose similarity or lack of similarity to another's view it might wonder about. It has no independent standard. Praise needs to be immediate and sensual because the self is embedded in the immediate and sensual; *joining* the younger self means being a participant in its impulse life and its egocentricity. Joining a self that takes perception and impulse as object means joining a self whose essential function is to take charge of its inner and outer experience. The self has become (1) a contained system with executive responsibilities; (2) creative of its own point of view or standard; and (3) able to recognize that there are different points of view people can take on a thing, including the self. As the self has become regulative of its own impulses, its confirmation or support is not a matter of finding an other to *gratify* its impulses, but finding an other who might *praise the way the executive system is itself gratifying* or dealing with the demand for gratification of its own impulses. As the self has become disembedded from its own perceptions it is interested in "reality," the correspondence of its own productions to how things "actually are," and it can see in the other's distinctness a source of this information.

As the self has become its own system, its experience of esteem is a function of the competent exercises of that system. Whatever other kinds of learning one might be told the primary grades are about, what they are most certainly also about is learning to *go* to school, learning to live in a world of rules and roles where egocentric behavior is less and less tolerated. For most children there is a good match between the developmental demands of the school's hidden curriculum and the evolutionary level of the child. The school is designed to fit exactly the individual the child has become. Children's love of ritual, order, bargain, making things, receiving the information that their manner of conducting themselves is correct, successful, or praiseworthy, is a love born of nothing less than the love for life itself, that ceaseless, creative motion which they are. It is a sacred celebration of the meaning they are. A school that is sensitive to the shame of failure at this age, especially public failure or public incompetence, is responding to something more than a peripheral, albeit humanizing, dimension of school life. It is dealing with an ultimate issue—a matter that impacts the child's very disposition toward the life project—and it is giving the issue the respect it is due. On the other hand, the school cannot be expected to meet the child wherever he or she is evolutionarily, and if the child is not ready to begin, however tentatively, the exercises of the new subject-object relation, if the child cannot play a role and take a role, then the school is left holding the child-to-come rather than the child-who-is, a frequently painful situation.

For the school-age child each learning exercise is another test of how well the individual works, and while each successfully accomplished assignment is a product *of* the self, each declaration, recognition, confirmation of its adequacy or excellence is a supply *to* the self. Carol Dweck's research on two styles of latency age learning (Dweck and Bempechat, 1983; Dweck and Elliott, 1983) shows us two faces of the same epistemological predicament. Dweck has taken an interest in the way children experience their *errors* in learning and observes that some children have a friendly feeling toward their mistake making, seeing this as a valuable means to their enhanced competence, while others regard the error as the enemy, incontrovertible evidence of their incompetence. As important as is the distinction between what Dweck calls the process-oriented and product-oriented learners (a difference psychodynamic psychology may be in a better position to help us understand) is the recognition that an identical epistemological structure is at work, defining the learning self as the solver of tasks, a kind of machine with "bugs" in need of ironing out. As we will shortly see, this differs considerably from the way either the process-oriented or product-oriented child will construct the meaning of learning in the adolescent years to come. By way of summarizing this picture of the psychology of learning in this second subject-object balance, consider these responses ten-year-olds gave us when we asked them what learning was, what a good learner was like, whether learning was important, what a good teacher was like:

A good learner knows how to draw well, how to do math, how to spell better than I can. A good learner reads a hundred books a year.

A good learner—it doesn't matter what you look like. It's about being able to listen real well to what the teacher says and taking in whatever he says, getting everything.

A really good learner can't be very popular because you'd have to spend all your time studying, go to bed about 8:15, and have no time to play with anyone.

A bad learner just does what he or she wants, doesn't listen to what the teacher says, and thinks everybody else will do it for them.

Bad learners don't care about school and they don't really think about what they're doing and they don't put any effort into their assignments and they're usually stupid.

You know you're learning when you get all the things pretty right.

The way I learn is just memorizing and keep reviewing.

Learning is when somebody teaches you something and then you memorize it and you get it.

Learning is important because if you didn't learn you wouldn't know what to do. (*Do what?*) You know, you wouldn't know how to comb your hair or brush your teeth.

A good teacher explains things clearly and is fair. (*What do you mean "fair"?*) He doesn't change his rules from one day to the next and he doesn't treat boys one way and the girls another.

A good teacher doesn't embarrass you in front of everybody.

A good teacher realizes you aren't babies and doesn't make everybody line up in a perfect line before you can leave the class.

What seems common to these views of different aspects of learning is both an embeddedness in the concrete (e.g., knowledge is a kind of *thing* that is transferrable from a teacher's mind to a student's, is understood in terms of what you literally do with it, cannot be defined by generalization but only by examples), and an attention to or interiorization of *activity*; that is, learning is about the control or discipline of personal action (listening carefully, doing what the teacher says). Put more abstractly, physical activity and concrete social information is *object,* differentiated from the self, controllable; and its control is *subject,* the very principle of the self's current organization. Perry's description of dualistic assumptions about learning fit the child at this point. The child construes the teacher as arbiter of truth, locus of authority and control. The teacher's task, as always, is to confirm the child's current way of knowing, embody more complex ways of knowing, and provide challenges to the current way of knowing. At this particular level, the teacher must provide concrete assignments, clear criteria for completion and success. She herself must coordinate competing

truths—whether in curriculum content or in the interpersonal struggle of children. The ability to reflect on and
coordinate multiple truths or viewpoints into a system
is, at this point, the teacher's alone. In the next development to come (beginning usually around eleven, twelve,
or thirteen) this whole "action and data controlling system" itself becomes object and the self is able to take *a*
perspective on "concreteness," competent doing, and the
exercises of the social role. The most familiar and well-
researched manifestation of this transformation in the
individual's subject-object balance is in the cognitive domain, the development of what Piaget called "formal operations."

INNER ISSUES IN LEARNING: ADOLESCENCE

The capacities to think abstractly, independently, and
relativistically—which appear to be implicit curricula of
much higher education—demand not only new cognitive
structures, but finally a shift in locus of authority and
responsibility in learning. In this section we will give
illustrations of characteristic learning dilemmas in the
high school and college years and try to understand how
Perry's understanding of epistemological development
and Kegan's subject-object balances may illuminate the
difficulties.

   With adolescence and the development of formal operations new methods of unconsciously scientific and
philosophical inquiry become available. The early adolescent ability gradually to think abstractly, make generalizations, hypothesize, test the logic of one's own and
others' thinking involves a fundamental development
which renders *relative* the concrete world of actuality,
and casts it from its former *ultimacy* to a place of one
among any number of possibilities. Piaget and Piagetians
have described these cognitive operations and their curricular implications. Selman (1980) has described a new

level of "mutual perspective taking" at this stage, in his investigation of the development of interpersonal and social understanding. If the child learned to take a role and play a role, the adolescent is more of a meta-role-taker and -player who must have a hand in the very definition of what the role shall be. Elkind's words about the early adolescent's relationship to his parents may be as true for his or her relationship to any authority, including the teacher.

> . . . the adolescent now sees a host of alternatives and decision making becomes a problem. He now sees, to illustrate, many alternatives to parental directives and is loathe to accept the parental directives without question. He wants to know not only where a parent stands but also why, and is ready to debate the virtues of the parental alternative over that chosen by himself and his peers. Indeed, the adolescent's quarrels with parental decisions are part of his own indecisiveness. While he is having trouble making decisions for himself, at the same time he does not want others making decisions for him. Paradoxically, but understandably, the adolescent's indecisiveness also frequently throws him into a new dependence, particularly on his peers, but also on his parents. The adolescent demands that his parents take a stand if only so he can rebel against it [Elkind, 1974, p. 101].*

This appreciation of multiple alternatives in any question of "truth" and its implicit relativizing of "what is" —including adult authority—is described also in Perry's positions of "multiplism." The teacher here has the task of confirming the student as meta-role-player or independent thinker by orienting to *ways* of thinking, decision making and problem-solving. It is true that this evolution

---

* Quoted by permission of Oxford University Press from "Egocentrism in Children and Adolescents," in *Children and Adolescents* (1974) by David Elkind.

into Kegan's third subject-object balance, especially in its transitional moments, can also involve a good deal of *resistance* to a teacher's authority and disenchantment with the institutional structures and rituals in learning. At the same time, the capacity to take the perspective of another taking the perspective of me can lead to more or less paralyzing self-consciousness about the public aspects of institutional learning. (Indeed it is this disenchantment and self-consciousness, every bit as much as the more popular saga of raging hormones, that make teachers of the eighth grade our least appreciated national treasure.) But it is *also* true that these new abilities (e.g., to role-take reciprocally) bring into being the capacity to construct interpersonal relationships oriented to empathy, expectation, and obligation, and with this new capacity, the new *need* to be connected with others who will be coexperiencers and cocreators in the activity of meaning making, a lifelong activity which has now become itself interpersonal. *Some* of the beneficiaries of this development can be the very same teachers who were earlier being politely and not so politely killed off. This "interpersonal" stage, in Kegan's terms, is characterized by an orientation to self-in-relationship arising out of the new capacity to reflect on self and other, or self as actor and object, simultaneously. The limit of this stage is the inability to reflect on interpersonal demands or on conventions and norms themselves and to coordinate competing ones. There is as yet no self system transcending interpersonal conventions, expectations, and norms. The person therefore has no "internal court" to which the dictates of social norms might be appealed.

The self-consciousness involved in the capacity to reflect on how one is seen also allows one to reflect on self as learner, to think about thinking for the first time. Early formal operations include nesting hierarchies of abstraction, liberating the student from the domains of the concrete and actual and from strictly trial-and-error experimentation or the application of assigned methods. New methods of scientific and philosophical inquiry thus become available. Learning can now proceed beyond surface or content understanding to reflection on the author's intent or the theoretical assumptions or the nature of argument. All such "deep" approaches to material involve abilities to shift levels of abstraction and to shift perspectives. They require the capacity to hold multiple perspectives on particular data—to see that a story can be told in a number of ways or that a narrative can be "ironic," for example, operating on more than one level at once. The same capacities enable the student to reflect on the teacher's purposes and to figure out "what they want."

Two college students speak of their experience with courses that demand an appreciation of multiple perspectives:

> 1. The most exciting course I had gave us different accounts of the same battle—written at the time. We had to figure out what the point of view was of the different writers. It was a whole new approach—not learning about the battle, but really seeing how differently it was seen and figuring out why.
> 2. When you learn related things and approach it differently in each course, no two professors follow the same track. . . . So I'm able to get a number of perspectives on this general body of theory . . . but I really don't know what's going on.

Clearly the two students *feel* differently about this business of multiple perspectives. Our guess is that the nature of their two learning *situations* is related to this difference. The first student's experience is contained within one course, and the teacher is seen as holding the varied perspectives in some coherent whole, which the student trusts. The student knows he is doing what he is supposed to do and learning what he is supposed to learn in this exercise in perspective taking and the relativity of battle accounts. The second student's experience is not contained within one course, and he feels lost:

> I have a reasonably comfortable grasp of this material from the number of these approaches, but I can't use each of these approaches to explain this material. Do you see what I am saying? When I arrived here from high school I felt that the body of material I'd been exposed to, I basically mastered. I really understood what was going on. I think that college work is substantially more difficult in that I don't understand what's going on.

The trouble here may be that no teacher has provided an integrating context, a context which this student cannot (yet) provide himself (the developmental transformation to come). He is willing and able to learn different approaches in different courses, and he feels the need for some integration—without the capacity to provide it. The result is a sense of *loss* of mastery, disappointment, and, in some moments, bitterness.

Orienting as she does toward relationship, convention, received norms and expectations, the learner in this balance is somewhat thrown by nondirective, unclear, or contradictory messages about what is expected. She is also likely to be bored or insulted by learning situations which demand memorization, regurgitation, and rote repetition. Such experiences are no longer self-confirming because the self they imply is no longer how the person is organized. Conscious of self as thinker she wants to *think*. In fact "learning" seems to mean to her most pointedly learning how to think on her own—but in a prescribed, circumscribed, and officially sanctioned way for which the teacher or some outside agent is responsible. Independent thinking, which to the concrete operational child meant "finding *the* answer myself," now means mastering ways to find answers. The process is as much the focus as the result (Knefelkamp, 1979).

A high school sophomore brings home a list of questions about the author's use of certain themes in a novel the class read. At first puzzled by this request for information not in the book, she begins with great difficulty to figure out how to answer the questions. The assignment is very near to the limit of her capacity to think abstractly, and she frequently asks a nearby adult if what she's coming up with is "right." A few months later she reports with glee, "I'm learning a new way to read a book." She is delighted with her independent thinking for which the teacher still provides a safe context, an authority to let her know if she's "doing it right."

The teacher of students in this epistemological balance has a delicate task of providing supports for the student to exercise judgment and develop ways of thinking without demanding that the student be able to construct the very context in which she thinks "for herself." A lot of "independent thinking" at this age has an "as if" quality, oriented as it is to producing "what they want" or conforming to a somewhat formulaic method of approaching particular learning tasks (Perry, 1970).

College students in this subject-object balance are vulnerable in a variety of ways. Not only are they often removing themselves geographically from their entire world of known relationships—an upsetting experience at most stages of life—but sometimes they enter classroom situations which are unmindful of their developmental needs. Such a class might consist of an extensive reading list, semiweekly lectures, a term paper, and an exam. The student being unclear, and anxious, about "what I am supposed to do" is likely to play it safe by trying to read everything and taking copious lecture notes, perhaps even tape recording the lectures. Without the supports of sanctioned procedures for the *exercise* of judgment and thought, the student experiences a loss of confidence and retreats to trying to "learn it all." Particularly vulnerable is the student whose high school did not provide structured opportunities for integration, judgment, and the articulation of opinion, and who has until college been orienting to expectations for associative learning and memorization at however complex a level.

This effort to play it safe by being obedient, dutiful, and thorough does not usually pay off. The student finds herself overwhelmed by quantities of material, undifferentiated detail, boredom, and lost time in an approach to study which has been aptly referred to as "improvident" (Entwhistle, 1981, pp. 93–103). The problem tends to compound itself as the very effort to insure success and build confidence jeopardizes success and lowers confidence. A college student, for example, went to a counselor with what the counselor soon saw were "improvident" study methods. The young man had pages and pages of detailed notes which he reviewed and underlined, but no sense of the main theme or important ideas in the course. The counselor explained carefully how to derive main themes and write summary paragraphs. The student was very impressed by these ideas, but suddenly blurted, "But *me*?! I couldn't do that. I can't change what I'm doing. I'm *failing*" (Perry, personal communication). The tendency here to defend one's present organization under stress, or retreat to a former safe method when anxious, may result in a stubborn allegiance to self-defeating methods. Experience with students caught in such dilemmas led counselors at Harvard's Bureau of Study Counsel to the creation of an ingenious developmental reading course designed to create the necessity for selection and judgment in reading as well as a safe context and guided procedures for using selection and judgment (Perry, 1950; Perry and Whitlock, 1954).

This Harvard Reading Course provides an example of a structured effort to support a "deep approach" to learning. The course design includes three components: films to illuminate written pages at increased speeds, exercises which provide the student with more reading than can be done word for word in the time allowed, and talks by the instructor. The film component is addressed to what could be considered students' conservative side. It implicitly promises increased ability to *get* every written word through practice in moving one's eyes. The exercises are addressed to the more radical side. They demonstrate the possibility of learning something from written material under conditions that require selectivity, and they develop the ability to do so through practice in using one's judgment. Students coming into this course frequently report that they have been habitually shutting off their minds when reading. Thought, they have supposed, is a process that happens *after* reading. They have seen reading as a passive-receptive exercise in absorption or reception rather than an active seeking of meaning. As the course demands that students try more active methods of reading, many students balk. They may indeed find that they *can* read through a page quickly, using techniques to find main points, and come out with a good comprehension of the material. However, this experience doesn't *feel* good. Typically, students report that they feel as if they have cheated or that they feel insecure about their learning, afraid they missed something. Reading slowly word by word on the other hand may result in noncompletion, boredom, distraction ("I can't concentrate"), and inferior comprehension, but it *feels* virtuous and safe. This tension is at the heart of the Reading Course. Resolving it requires of the student not only techniques, but also courage, the courage to take greater responsibility for what is to be learned. And this may amount to the courage to grow.

Perry and his colleagues interviewed randomly selected Harvard students in each of their four college years—in the 1950s and again in the 1970s. Open-ended interviews were tape recorded and analyzed for evidence of students' assumptions about learning. The first study led to formulation of the descriptive scheme of positions which students seemed to take in relation to their learning. The basic finding of this study was that students' assumptions about learning changed over the four years and that those changes took regular forms. Rather than finding different types of *students* or different learning *styles,* Perry found different "positions" in the evolution of naive epistemology. As we have mentioned, this evolution begins with a dualistic construction of learning, which sees knowledge as certain, answers as right or wrong, and learning as a process of accumulating quantities of knowledge or right answers. In this outlook authority is located in the teacher and the learning process is seen as one of transferring what is known from teacher to student. These dualistic assumptions "fit" the organization of young learners described earlier in this chapter. The positions following dualism are characterized by an increased tolerance for uncertainty—for some areas where there is no right and wrong. These positions Perry called "multiplistic," referring to their appreciation of the possibility of multiple answers or perspectives in a world seen as more uncertain. The students described earlier in this section illustrate a multiplistic perspective. Some problems do not have *an* answer, and the process or approach to a problem becomes important. The *way* to answers is more the issue, and learning is seen as implicating oneself and one's methods. Teachers are looked to as a source of methods and formulas, as guides. In that sense, responsibility is still invested in the teacher. To paraphrase a student in this position:

> I liked the course mainly because of the teaching fellow. He deemphasized formality and was really concerned with getting us to learn the subject matter. But it was up to us—he made us feel a sense of independence and

responsibility. Also the material interested me—once
I learned how to deal with it.

The sense of agency in this student's formulation has
an interesting split—"He made us feel independent"
—which perhaps captures some of the constraints on and
supports for independent thinking at this "multiplistic"
position. Students in this position are likely to respond
to a low grade with the disheartening (to many teachers)
protest, "But I thought this was what you wanted."

But multiplism can evolve to appreciation of the importance of perspective in which certainty becomes an
unusual special case. The student may arrive at this position through an adherent learning of systematic thinking and evidential support because it is "what they want."
Or he may question authority's right to be prescriptive.
Given the legitimacy of uncertainty he may see all opinions as equally good, truth as entirely subjective. In either
case he is vulnerable to the important shift to the next
position which Perry terms *contextual relativism*. In this
position the student fully apprehends that knowledge is
necessarily relative to context, that systematic thinking
is not just a teacher's demand, that thinking must be like
this, even for *them* (Perry, 1970), that there are criteria
for judgment among opinions in terms of quality of reasoning and fit with data and values. In this position authority shifts from being located in the teacher—or being
denied—to the student. The teacher is seen more as a
resource or model and less as the arbiter of truth or of
method. The student begins to see that knowledge implies
and requires a stance, and that the evolution of one's
stance will be a matter of personal judgment, responsibility, and choice. What this can mean in the broader
domain of the self is a collapse of the very foundations
of the "received tradition" and a placing of oneself, reluctantly or eagerly, in the role of having to judge the
truth value of any fact. Thus, Perry refers to this position

as "Commitment foreseen." The succeeding positions describe an evolution of commitment, of choices made in a context of uncertainty.

One beauty of Perry's scheme is that it points to the relatedness of learning and identity, of intellectual development and personality development. Complexity of thought and relation to authority change together as part of the same process. Thinking about thinking and examining assumptions behind any received wisdom or academic task (unless it is done as an intellectual game only because the institution demands it) would seem necessarily to disturb Kegan's "interpersonal" orientation. Even if it *is* done as a game, it would seem to provide the tools of its own upset; that is, a tendency to question the rules of the game. The interpersonalist's limit is the coordination of differing or conflicting conventions and relationships whose authority she has not yet relativized. Contextual relativists who foresee the need for commitment are transcending that limit. They need to appeal to some internal structure which would guide commitment, and which would constitute a more self-governing self-system, what Kegan calls the "institutional" subject-object balance, since the self has become an administrator of its own psychic institution.

Some excerpts from one student's reflections on her own experience will illustrate this transition to Perry's later positions and to an institutional self-system. This young woman sought counseling because she could not write her papers. In her conversation with a counselor she refers not only to her current dilemmas in learning, but to earlier crises and their resolution.

> Things go much slower. I used to be able to work so much more productively.... It's like ... what happened to me ... in high school.... I had much more push, in terms of if I sat down to do it, I sat down and I *did* it ... it's like then it was well I can *know* some-

thing, and now it's in terms of—who am I to judge if I know anything? (*Uh huh*) I mean it was like (sigh) I guess there's a difference in that then if I just read through it that would be enough. And now I have to read through it and judge like? . . . I'm doing two papers on Aristotle . . . they're judging things, you know, from primary sources.

(*It's not like you can just learn it.*)

Yeah . . . I don't now how to do it. It's like writing those papers in tenth grade. At least for me, tenth grade was the year we learned how to write a paper! (laugh) The first ones were weird because you had nothing to base your decisions on. Then you'd get the comments back and you'd listen to them and have a little more sense of what you were doing and you keep going back and forth. . . . Is there any way to go about learning how to trust your judgment and when not to trust your judgment? And when you have a good idea and when you have a bad idea? And when you think something that you should follow it, and when you think and you shouldn't follow it? And how to sort things in your mind? I feel like I can make all sorts of arguments either way. It seems like words are so—you can use them—they're not really valid. How do you decide when words are valid? It depends on [where you start], and so then you wonder and how do you get these things you start with? But that's not what they're asking for. (*Yeah. That's what you're asking. If it's the basic assumptions that determine the whole thing, where do I get them?*)

Yeah, so I don't know.

(*By then you come to a dead stop in writing the paper.*)

Yeah. Exactly.

It's a really important thing to me: What is science? So it's really hard to pin myself down and write something because I kind of feel like its (loudly), "O.K. Right now at this moment with this limited knowledge—with this, with this, with this—." This is what I kind of feel like. But that's not good writing. To be so *indefinite*! It feels so important to me. I'm really *scared* to. I don't want to commit myself.

I've got to start getting some definite opinions about things. I was a very opinionated kid until like ninth grade. And then I totally stopped using opinions and got tongue-tied. And I'm just wondering—when are you going to start being opinionated again?. . .

I think maybe things scared me away a bit, because in seventh grade I was reading things which no one else was familiar with, at least among my friends. When I talked to them it was like "What. Whoa! Hold back!" So I held back. And I've been holding back. And when am I gonna let go?

(*I'm waiting to stop my censoring?*)

I purposely stopped saying things for reasons that I wanted to be friendly with people. And so I guess, I'm not conscious of how I do it anymore. But I don't know how to go about doing this in terms of papers. . . . I don't know how to let go.

(*Is there again the thought that you know what you think?*)

Oh, I know exactly what I think. And I know exactly what I'm going to say.

(*It's just that you can't say it?*)

Yeah.

(*Have you started trying just to write?*)

You mean—not making an outline and writing?

(*That's right.*)

Just writing it? Oh no. I haven't. I can't. I've never done that . . . that sounds so weird. Like, so different than anything I've ever. . . . It's always been drummed into my head: Outline! Two examples for each statement! Highly organized! Transitional sentences!

(*Yeah.*)

It was a lot easier to write before I did it that way.

(*It's sort of like an analogy to the internal censor?*)

Yeah. That's really weird. Because I really started listening to the rules when the censor started in.

In Perry's terms this young woman has certainly seen

how relative truth is to context and she seems, at first, stumped by that. How then is one to know anything? She tells us she was an opinionated kid until junior high school. Until then she was a straightforward reader and had clear convictions. Perhaps she refers to a plateau in which she functioned as a concrete and dualistic learner. Between seventh and ninth grades she began to hold back and to be tongue-tied and passive out of concern for other kids' reactions. This seems to indicate a new sensitivity to how other people see and hear her, or a new level of ability to construct relationships. In tenth grade she seems to have leveled out again, this time not with direct expression of opinion, but with rules for acceptable thoughts (the internal censor) and methods for their acceptable expressions (outline and two examples). The former seems more psychological, the latter more pragmatic; but in a sense they are similarly interpersonally derived normative systems which shape self-expression. In one case she calibrated herself to peer responses, in the other to teachers' comments. But this interpersonalism no longer works at the time of the interview. The trustworthiness of her learned procedures for writing is thrown into question. The necessity for judgment and its implicit responsibility comes home. She can see that she needs to position herself and take a stand which is not derivative of others' expectations or definitions. This is "Commitment foreseen," in Perry's terms. She is profoundly uncertain about what to trust, but quite clear that it has to be something *in her*. The counselor is not really addressed as a source of answers. It is ironic that finally the counselor does respond with a new prescribed method . . . for writing without a prescribed method!

This student leads us to consider some of the characteristics and constraints of the "institutional" learner. The realization of contextual relativism, the apprehension that knowing is relative to one's own position, would seem to upset interpersonalism and imply a move toward a more institutional self. The converse may not be true; that is, a student who appears to have transcended interpersonalism might not be a contextual relativist in his studies. The transition to an institutional self-system involves the decentering from being determined by expectations, conventions, and norms. The capacity to reflect on relationships, conventions, and expectations allows the construction of a self-system that is more self-authoring and coheres across contexts. The person now has an "inner court" to which particular expectations and conventions are appealed. This capacity to relativize norms and relationships and to differentiate self from interpersonal demands often involves philosophical and systematic attention to questions about the self and values. It does not *necessarily* involve relativizing academic truths or paradigms. The learner in this subject-object balance may "buy in" to the received wisdom of his field without the radical doubt and questioning implied in Perry's move to "Commitment foreseen." One such student said:

> At college I learned how to play the game of learning *at that college*. If I'd been elsewhere, I'd have learned something a little different, but similar. The field I'm in has a set body of knowledge. What you learn—the information and concepts—is written down already. Teachers can be your guides and mentors.

For this student, unlike the earlier one we quoted at length, the frame and limits of knowledge are not open to question. His comment about learning how to learn at his college implies an *ability* to reflect on and relativize the assumptions of his teachers and his field, but he shows no signs of doing so. The institutional balance as described by Kegan (1982) involves a shift in social cognition and self organization which leads to a more internal locus of authority and responsibility. It seems, in a larger realm, analogous to the shift Perry describes. The institutional learner and the contextual relativist need less structure from teachers and are able to think independently with more internal criteria for the rightness of their thought. Though there need be no one-to-one correspondence between the developments described by Perry and by Kegan, it does seem that a realization of contextual relativism would tend to destabilize interpersonalism and call for the emergence of an "institutional self."

CONCLUSION

Kegan's successive subject-object balances and Perry's evolving epistemology both describe increasing objectivity, or, to use Piaget's term, *decentering*. The child who "looks behind" Big Bird's costume; the high school student who "looks behind" the author's story; the college student who "looks behind" her own reasoning are each becoming more "objective." Each is decentering from or reflecting on what was her very way of knowing. These moments when the terms of the knowing-system change, when what was the subjective ground of knowing can be seen as object, are particularly important and risky moments in learning. They involve a shift not only in what the student knows, but in *how* he knows, and in what supports and challenges his knowing. At bottom, they involve, to some extent, a change in *who it is the student is*.

But our discussion has proceeded as if this increasing objectivity were a personality development always showing coherence across all domains and contexts. To what degree real students exhibit such coherence is a matter of some debate. Probably students become able to coordinate perceptions, need systems, or relationships at different times, in different areas of their lives. Probably something like Perry's development from dualistic to contextual thinking and from external to internal locus of control happens again and again with new content and new learning situations.

Our hope is that these general descriptions of the relations of subject and object, knower and known, may make sense of surprises, serve as "maps" in terms of which individual differences may also be seen; sensitize us to the crucial moments of emerging new "objectivity"; and suggest ways to alter learning contexts so that they optimally fit those whom they are supposed to serve.

REFERENCES

Dweck, C. S., & Bempechat, J. (1983), Children's theories of intelligence: Implications for learning. In: *Learning and Motivation in the Classroom,* ed. S. Paris, G. Olson, & H. W. Stevenson. Hillsdale, NJ: Erlbaum.

——— Elliott, E. S. (1983), Achievement motivation. In: *Handbook of Child Psychology,* Vol. 4, ed. E. M. Hetherington. New York: John Wiley.

Elkind, D. (1974), Egocentrism in children and adolescents. In: *Children and Adolescents.* New York: Oxford University Press.

Entwhistle, N. (1981), *Styles of Learning and Teaching.* New York: John Wiley.

Erikson, E. (1963), *Childhood and Society.* New York: W. W. Norton.

Gardner, H. (1978), *Developmental Psychology.* Boston: Little, Brown.

Kegan, R. (1982), *The Evolving Self: Problem and Process in Human Development.* Cambridge, MA: Harvard University Press.

——— (1985), The loss of Pete's dragon: Transformation in the development of the self in the years five to seven. In: *The Development of the Self,* ed. R. L. Leahy. New York: Academic Press.

——— Noam, G., & Rogers, L. (1982), The psychologic of emotions. In: *Emotional Development,* ed. D. Cicchetti & P. Pogge-Hesse. San Francisco: Jossey-Bass.

——— Rogers, L., & Quinlan, D. (1981), Constructive-developmental organizations of depression. Paper presented at a symposium on New Approaches to Depression, American Psychological Association annual meeting, Los Angeles, CA.

Knefelkamp, L. (1979), Combining student stage and style in the design of learning environments using Holland typologies and Perry stages. Paper presented to the American College Personnel Association.

Kohlherg, L., & Gilligan, C. (1972), The adolescent as a philosopher. In: *Twelve to Sixteen: Early Adolescence,* ed. J. Kagan & R. Coles. New York: W. W. Norton.

Lickona, T. (1976), *Moral Development and Behavior*. New York: Holt, Rhinehart & Winston.

Noam, G., & Kegan, R. (1982), Social cognition and psychodynamics: Toward a clinical developmental psychology. In: *Perspektiv und Interpretation,* ed. W. Edelstein & M. Keller. Frankfurt: Suhrkamp.

Perry, W. G., Jr. (1950), A clinical portrait of a slow reader. Bureau of Study Counsel, Harvard College, Cambridge, MA (mimeograph).

—— (1970), *Forms of Intellectual and Ethical Development in the College Years.* New York: Holt, Rinehart & Winston.

—— (1984), Cognitive and ethical growth: The making of meaning. In: *The Modern American College,* ed. A. Chickering. San Francisco: Jossey-Bass.

—— Whitlock, C. (1954), A clinical rationale for a reading film. *Harvard Ed. Rev.,* Winter: 6–27.

Piaget, J. (1936), *The Origins of Intelligence in Children.* New York: International Universities Press, 1952.

—— (1937), *The Constructions of Reality in the Child.* New York: Basic Books, 1954.

—— (1962), *Plays, Dreams and Imitation.* New York: W. W. Norton.

Selman, R. (1980), *The Growth of Interpersonal Understanding: Developmental and Clinical Analyses.* New York: Academic Press.

Souvaine, E., Lahey, L., & Kegan, R. (1989), Life after formal operations: Implications for the psychology of the self. In: *Beyond Formal Operations,* ed. C. Alexander & E. Langer. New York: Oxford University Press.

Werner, H. (1940), *Comparative Psychology of Mental Development.* New York: International Universities Press, 1964.

White, R. W., (1959), Motivation reconsidered: The concept of competence. *Psychol. Rev.,* 66:297–333.

White, S. (1970), Some general outlines of the matrix of developmental changes between five and seven years. *Bull. Orton Soc.,* 20:41–57.

Zigler, E., & Kanzer, P. (1962), The effectiveness of two classes of verbal reinforcers in the performance of middle and lower class children. *J. Person.* 30:157–163.

Chapter 12

Patterns of Internalization

BONNIE E. LITOWITZ, Ph.D.

All theories seek to explain; developmental theories attempt to explain changes over time in human organisms. These explanatory theories themselves change over time as well; epistemology charts those changes, whether as paradigm shifts (Kuhn, 1970), as conjectures and refutations (Popper, 1959), or, modeled on human development, as genetic epistemology (Piaget, 1971). The topic of this chapter is a comparison of changes in two kinds of theories of developmental change: on the one hand, psychoanalytic theories describe the growth of affective attachment and the psychological emergence of the individual; on the other hand, cognitive theories take as their object of study the individual's accumulation and use of knowledge about the world. Language is a large part of the content and medium of acquiring and using knowledge, and, therefore, linguistic theories and cognitive theories are often imbricated. Both cognitive and linguistic theories take for granted those aspects of the

I am indebted to Drs. Theodore Shapiro, Arnold Goldberg, Michael Basch, and Norman Litowitz for their careful readings of earlier drafts of this presentation. Though not always incorporated in the final version, their insightful comments have helped to shape my understanding of this topic.

305

individual that psychoanalytic theories address, namely, what motivates a child to learn, and focus instead on what the child learns. Psychoanalytic theorists, for their part, use cognitive theories as a check against their own theories when inconsistencies occur. For example, Freud's notion of hallucinated wish-fulfillment came under attack when Piaget claimed the young infant incapable of mental imagery. Piaget's claim was based on his theoretical belief that imagery results from interiorized imitation. Interestingly, Piaget's position has been increasingly challenged by evidence that very young babies are indeed proficient imitators.

In spite of the different domains charted by the two kinds of theories, current versions of each have resulted from similar historical shifts and present us with amazingly consonant views of the development of the child. I will first present the roots of the current theoretical positions and then discuss what we might hope could result from such a fortuitous confluence of theoretical perspectives. Rather than attempt to discuss these theories in all their richness, I will focus only on the building up of the child's inner world by means of or as a consequence of his interactions with human and other objects in the environment; thus, my title: patterns of internalization. The questions these theories seek to answer are: How is structure—psychic, cognitive, linguistic—built up? How much naturally emerges? How much depends on the child's actions and how much on environmental responses?

For Freud, the child is born with instincts which provide energy, which in turn needs to be discharged in order to maintain an internal homeostasis or equilibrium. The child is portrayed as constantly regulating himself, controlling overstimulation from within through discharge of energy onto objects in the environment, and controlling stimuli from without which reach him via perceptions by cathecting only some and not others or by shutting out stimuli altogether in sleep. Freud's view has been criticized by other psychoanalytic theorists, critical of his importation of energy dynamics from hydraulic mechanics (Gill, 1976; Holt, 1976) and of his naive conception of perception (Basch, 1975). My mission is not to criticize but to sketch the portrait of the child which resulted from Freud's position.

The child thus viewed is object seeking because drives need discharge. Distinctions between inner and outer worlds are clearly drawn, and the inner world is built up by the internalized representations of the child's relationship to objects. During his lifetime, Freud posited and changed his models of the resulting psychic structure (e.g., the reflex⟶ the topographic⟶ the structural), some of which allow for individual development; for example, ego and superego development in the structural model. Developmental phases (oral, anal, phallic) and milestones (oedipal complex) were hypothesized as affecting the developing psychic structure.

For Freud, the major forces for change in the development of an individual come from within the child. The environment is present to be discharged onto; objects discharged onto can be human or not; and the results are internalized as object representations. The patterns of internalization which result from this viewpoint are secondary to the prior *ex*ternalization or discharge of inherent drives. As Freud's theory changed, he moved away from a general biological model (the reflex arc) shared by other organisms interacting with an environment. Freud moved to models more uniquely human where meanings could be built up via symbols, and conflicts within psychic structure were possible (Freud, 1915). Ultimately, adaptation and regulation characteristic of the whole earlier model were relegated to one agency, the ego, within a more complex internal structure (Freud, 1923). In a more complex model of psychic structure conflicts can arise internally between subparts as well as between whole organisms and their environment.

Along with the ego function of adaptation to an external environment, Freud opened up his basically biologically driven model in other ways to account for accumulated experiences; for example, in a later paper on signal anxiety (1926). However, I would agree with those who view these modifications in theory as a beginning shift to accommodate evidence on the significance of specific environmental factors for psychological development, but not as altering his commitment to a biological model. As Greenberg and Mitchell (1983) state in their perceptive documentation of the historical tension in psychoanalysis between theories of biological (libidinal) drives and theories of (interpersonal) object relations: "Freud moved from an early approach which has a great deal in common with later relational principles to the establishment of the drive model itself. Many of his later concepts—the reality principle, sublimation, narcissism, and the revised anxiety theory—represent his efforts to preserve the drive concept at the theoretical center, while granting an increasing role to early relations with others" (1983, p. 380).[1]

In cognitive psychology, Piaget most closely approximates Freud's position. Acknowledging his debt to Freud for theory and method (méthode clinique), Piaget also views the child as seeking an equilibrium. This equilibrium, however, is not internal but represents a balance between the child and the external environment. Motivation comes, not from energy inborn in each individual, but from the biological, adaptive principles of accommodation and assimilation common to all living orga-

[1] Greenberg and Mitchell (1983) establish through detailed analysis of psychoanalytic writers the shift in theoretical perspective that I have briefly outlined. My purpose here is not to repeat that documentation or to establish the parallel shifts in cognitive and linguistic theories. Rather, presupposing the existence of these shifts, my thesis is that (1) the history across fields is remarkably similar; (2) interdisciplinary efforts will be most fruitful among theorists of similar persuasions; and (3) similar perspectives are currently present.

nisms. These principles establish Piaget's patterns of internalization. Like the early Freud, Piaget takes his cue from the relationship of all organisms to their environment: the need for a homeostatic interaction. Piaget describes the two possible modes of such interaction —accommodation and assimilation—using the physical examples of retinal adjustment and alimentary absorption, respectively. Using these two modes, the child regulates himself in relation to his environment. For both Piaget and Freud, the child is active and the environment is reactive, providing objects for the child's needs. It is interesting that objects in psychoanalytic theories usually refer to people, particularly significant caretakers, while Piaget's focus is on nonhuman objects. The implication in Piaget is that the child's relationships to humans follow the same course as relationships to nonhuman objects. Actions and operations by the child in the world become internally represented by successively more abstract and social semiotic forms: interiorized imitations (i.e., actions), images, symbols, and verbal signs. For what remains of affective relationships not covered under this view of object relations and for purely internally arising conflicts, Piaget directs the reader to Freud.

In spite of Piaget's criticisms of the Freudian notion of symbolism (Piaget, 1962) and of the child's precocious capacity to hallucinate images of objects, these two major views of the child are compatible; not only because Piaget was influenced by Freud, but because for both men, the child's psychological-cognitive development sits on a neurological-biological base, the principles of which constrain later development. Both view change resulting from conflict but differ as to whether conflict is mainly internal or external. What is built up is an inner reality of the child in the form of psychic or cognitive structures, largely through an active child who constructs a universal reality for himself individually. Thus, all children everywhere at all times go through oral, anal, and phallic phases, and sensorimotor, preoperational, and concrete operational stages; individual variations result from different specific contents, developmental arrests, or decalages, and differences in congenital endowments or temperaments. Both Freud and Piaget are often criticized for not being interested in group differences (e.g., social or cultural differences) but only in the uniform developmental laws of an idealized child.

Linguistic theories which followed in the wake of Chomsky's revolution concerned themselves with the competence of an ideal speaker-hearer and attempted to show how an ideal child could acquire any natural language. Chomsky's view is that neurology constrains language. Language emerges, rather than is learned, on a neurological timetable tied to brain maturation; and thus constrained, language structure reflects the neurological base of a human language faculty. Children are hardwired (to use computer terminology) to seek and recognize language universals. These are learned earliest, followed by more specific rules of particular languages. This argument has been put forth for all aspects of language; for example, phonology, syntax, and semantics (Fodor, 1975; Jackendoff, 1983). If language reflects neurology, then psychological principles will need to conform to linguistic structure and not vice versa. This question has been the source of the major controversy between Chomsky and Piaget, obscuring the similarities in their positions (Piattelli-Palmarini, 1980). Piaget cannot accept that language is innate or that its structure serves as a boilerplate for other cognitive development. The controversy is over *what* is innate and universal—linguistic or cognitive structures—not that innate universals exist. In this latter sense, Piaget and Chomsky (and Freud) are compatible, and in many other ways as well. For example, to Chomsky's followers the specificity of the language environment adds specific content but it does not force any basic structural deviance. One has syntactic competence or not whether in Chinese or Spanish or English just as one conserves matter or not whether the material is rice or beans or playdough. For both theorists the role of the adult is to provide input the child can use as data, on the basis of which he confirms or refutes hypotheses about his language and his world.

One must acknowledge the existence of subtle differences that complete analyses of theories would bring to light. For example, linguistic theories following Chomsky are closer to Freudian than Piagetian theory in resolving the mind-body question with neurology rather than biology. On the other hand, such language theories differ from both Piagetian and Freudian theories in their total disinterest in equilibrium of the organism vis-à-vis its environment. Therefore, such linguistic theories are more strongly emergent than either the psychoanalytic or cognitive theories discussed. Nevertheless, I do not believe these variations dispel the basic thesis of similarities I am proposing.

While a few theorists remain completely faithful to the views presented thus far, the majority of theorists in each discipline have made alterations which have shifted our picture of the child. Most theorists have broken away from the isolated child as an individual actor. Earlier theorists had focused on the lone, asocial child building up an inner world as a result of his efforts to regulate himself in relation to his environment or to fine-tune inherent capacities. Now we discover the infant is not alone but is social from the start. Major theorists in all fields now tell us that the child is attachment-seeking, forming a complex, dyadic unit with the mother; that the child is incapable of self-regulation and must be other-regulated until it can gradually take over regulation and other functions as its own; that linguistic structure does not emerge but is extracted from functional contexts under the guidance of a more mature speaker. These later theories question the fiction of the individual as lone ar-

chitect of internal structure, and thus reestablish the importance of functional context(s). They redraw previous
boundaries which have isolated the child to one side and
the mother/other/object environment to another side; new
boundaries establish the mother-child dyad as the unit
of investigation. The patterns of internalization become,
not from child to environment or vice versa, but from
adult *and* child together to child alone.

In post-Freudian psychoanalytic theory, a shift occurred away from the domination of instinctual drives,
and the function of the ego inward in regulating instincts,
to the ego becoming an agency of functional adaptation
outward toward reality and the environment. In cognitive
psychology, Piaget is still consistent with this view since
the child, for him, adapts to reality via the two invariant
functions of accommodation and assimilation (which permit developing structures to become self-regulating). In
both views inner representations of objects (animate and
inanimate) build up in the child's mind as a consequence
of his actions on the environment.

Once having allowed the environment to become formative, however, the specificity of the external world and
its vicissitudes intrude themselves into theory. And later
post-ego psychological developments in psychoanalytic
theory, loosely categorized under "object relations theories," are devoted to the detailed description of the
changes in the relationship between the infant and a
specific environment—a significant other/caretaker/
mother. In some models drive apparatus is
functional—Klein, Spitz—while in others it becomes secondary—Mahler, Winnicott, Kohut (see Greenberg and
Mitchell [1983] for the place of drives in different theoretical approaches). Bonding and attachment become
most important and the relationship to the
mother/environment is central (Bowlby, 1969).

This view of the child pictures him as part of a global
whole, symbiotic or merged with the mother. Only grad-

ually, with good enough mothering, with empathy, with availability of a mother who allows herself to be used as the kind of object the child needs at each particular stage, does the child become differentiated, individual, and separate. One speaks of "environmental failures" and "breaks in empathy"; that is, the environment/mother does not or cannot provide what the child needs (Kohut, 1971; Winnicott, 1974). In other words, objects in the external world really *can* be good or bad. The environment is both specific and real, and its effects on the child influence his particular development. Although there are epigenetic developmental stages in how a child can deal with external objects, progression does not depend upon conflict alone, but rather on maturation in a specific context, each individual being affected by unique environmental responses.

Klein and Tribich (1981) carefully describe the differences between the original Freudian and later object relations theories: "Freud's theory holds no place for the primal need to be attached to another person" (p. 30). Quoting Kernberg, they agree that "Bowlby's hypothesis of attachment to mother as a primary drive contrasts with traditional psychoanalytic theory's consideration of the development of love as a secondary drive stemming from the need for nourishment and oral gratification" (p. 38). The difference in theories revolves around the following: "The question . . . that must be answered is not whether instinctual charges exist unrelated to internalized object relations, but whether at the onset of life such instincts exist independent of external object relations; or rather whether such instincts are the primary influential forces which shape the object relationship in the real world before such relationships become internalized" (p. 34).

What, then, is innate and primary: Freud's instincts, or Bowlby's attachment, separation, anxiety, anger, security, and so on; or Fairbairn's species-specific, instinctual object seeking (Klein and Tribich, 1981, pp. 37, 38)? Klein and Tribich (1981) rightly point out the connection of the later theories to learning theory which is concerned after all with how what was once external becomes internal.

When psychology moved away from the notion of an empty, passive child filled up with habits from a reinforcing environment (espoused by behaviorism), it gave up learning theories in favor of cognitive theories with an active child-learner of intentional behavior. Piaget's theory is such a cognitive theory, but one not compatible with this new shift in psychoanalytic theory because for him the child does not form a unit with the mother vis-à-vis the environment; the environment is not specific; development is not individual but universal; the mother provides only nourishment ("aliment") and not structure for the child. Instead, what is needed is another cognitive theory which will allow for environmental influence (i.e., learning), without returning to behaviorist conditioning. Soviet psychologist Lev Vygotsky has provided that theory.

Vygotsky's cognitive theory mirrors the view of the child-mother dyad professed by object relations theorists (1962, 1978). For Vygotsky and other Soviet psychologists, the child is part of a social and psychological unit with the mother from birth. To survive there is a species-specific need for the infant to maintain an attachment to the mother even over distance, which leads to development in humans of distance receptors of sight and sound earlier than motor capacities (Lisina and Neverovich, 1971). The infant is incapable of regulating himself and initially relies on the mother to perform these functions for him.

Vygotsky's famous maxim is that all development occurs twice: once on the *inter*psychic plane and again on the *intra*psychic. That other-regulation by the mother becomes self-regulation for the child himself through interiorization of such functions is, ironically, similar to Kahn's notion of the mother's holding functions in trust, as it were, for the child as a protective shield (1974). She relinquishes these as the child is ready to take them on himself. Kohut might describe similar data as the mother's functioning as a selfobject for the child until he can perform the functions himself through "transmuting internalizations" (1971). The irony resides in the *anti*-psychoanalytic bias of Soviet psychology (Volosinov and Bakhtin, 1973). Soviet criticisms focus on Freud's excessive individualism and supposed lack of interest in the social origins of psychological phenomena, as well as his purported disinterest in language. Never entirely accurate about Freud (Litowitz and Litowitz, 1977, 1983; Forrester, 1980), these criticisms hold even less for recent developments in psychoanalytic theory. Object relations theories are *entirely* concerned with the internalization (i.e., interiorization) of the mother-child dyad's interactions as these build up the inner psychological world of the child. And Lacan, for one, addresses both the role of language and social origins in psychological development (Lacan, 1977).

Vygotskian theory stresses the specificity of different environments—different environments require different responses—and the role of the adult in transmitting culturally appropriate responses. It particularly addresses motivation for learning or development as based on social, not biological, need (cf: Freud, Piaget, and Chomsky). Nor is Vygotsky alone in representing a shift in cognitive theories of development. In his article reviewing trends in psychology, Thomas (1981) stresses the "biosocial" matrix of development. Citing the enormous increase in our knowledge about infancy, Thomas hypothesizes an "interactionist conceptualization of development" (p. 597; also, "interactional," "transactional," p. 596) based on the infant as social and person seeking. Consistent with this new view which places importance

on context, Thomas criticizes earlier epigenetic conceptualizations of development, claiming that at different
times in the child's life the environment asks different
questions. It is the "goodness of fit" (p. 603) between child
and environment that matters.

For Vygotsky, however, the child's interaction with
the environment is mediated by an adult (his mother)
and the primary instrument of mediation is language.
The child and mother together act on the environment,
and he gradually interiorizes specific means of dealing
with the environment so he can ultimately do so on his
own. The difference between what one can do on one's
own and what one can do with another's help is called
the "zone of proximal development." The zone is the margin of growth that is available to a child (or adult, since
development never ceases) *if* he can use the knowledge
of a more advanced person. The zone of proximal development exists neither *in* the child nor *in* the adult but
as a potential for joint activity between them.

One can compare these ideas to Winnicott's "holding
environment" and "potential space" with the important
exception that for Vygotsky the other/mother is an active,
structuring participant rather than just a nurturing matrix (1974; Green, 1975). The same divergence in approaches can be seen concerning cultural objects and
language. For Winnicott, transitional phenomena provide prototypic experiences for the acquisition of culture.
The child must simultaneously discover and create the
transitional object, which the mother passively permits.
In contrast, Vygotsky claims that the structure that the
active mother provides most often involves: the identification of cultural objects and their functions; ways to
approach a task or problem; and the instrumental means
to accomplish or solve it. Such means usually require
language or other instrumental tools (Vygotsky, 1981).
The use of a particular tool or instrument totally transforms the activity, one's view of the world, and its internal

representation (i.e., thought). (For a more detailed comparison of Winnicott's potential space and Vygotsky's zone of proximal development, see Litowitz [1988].)

The introduction of context into linguistic theory has caused shifts similar to those described in psychoanalytic and cognitive theories: a widening of perspectives to include influences outside the child, most notably the mother; an interest in the child's interactions with the real world. In the past decade, the view of language as innately programmed, the structures of which emerge according to a neurophysiological timetable with minimal environmental-maternal intervention has begun to lose ground. Researchers have come to view language as based on prior cognitive development such as Piagetian preverbal sensorimotor intelligence (Brown, 1973); or on early (preverbal) social patterns of interaction between mothers and their infants (Bullowa, 1979; Uzgiris, 1979); or both (Moerk, 1977). Developmental psycholinguists who had thrown out mother's speech with Skinner's conditioning theory of verbal behavior (Chomsky, 1959) found themselves scrutinizing transcripts for Motherese in a baby talk (BT) register (Snow and Ferguson, 1977). Structuralism and the ideal (i.e., universal) speaker-hearer were replaced by emphases on the varied functions or uses of language by individual speakers, intending to communicate with others in specific contexts (Cazden, 1974). Next, studies of early language acquisition focused on the functional beginnings of language forms (Halliday, 1973); and on "language as a specialized and conventionalized extension of cooperative action" (Bruner, 1975b, p. 2).

I am not speaking here of the shift in developmental psycholinguists' emphases from syntax to semantics and currently to pragmatics correctly noted by several authors (Lock, 1980; Edgecumbe, 1981). In these shifts the view of the child may remain unquestioned, changing only from one who hypothesized linguistic rules, to one who hypothesizes about conceptual organization, to one who hypothesizes rules for communication and for problem-solving. The latest perspective, however, is even more radical, questioning not just the rules but the lone, hypothesizing child as well:

> [T]the infant's Language Acquisition Device (LAD) could not function without the aid given by an adult who enters with him into a transactional format. That format, initially under the control of the adult, provides a Language Acquisition Support System, LASS. It frames or structures the input of language and interaction to the child's Language Acquisition Device in a manner to "make the system function." In a word, it is the interaction between LAD and LASS that makes it possible for the infant to enter the linguistic community—and, at the same time, the culture to which the language gives access [Bruner, 1983, p. 19].

Everywhere but in isolated outposts of innatism (Wanner and Gleitman, 1982), the accepted fact is that language develops in the context of a prior interaction between an infant (literally, who cannot speak) and an adult speaker, between whom a social relationship exists; however imperfectly understood (Kaye [1982]; whether language necessarily depends upon that context is a debated question, e.g., Shatz, 1982). The adult/mother treats the child as a potential communicator; an expectation the child gradually fulfills. The mother carefully provides "scaffolding" of the speech situation so that the child can participate to the level of his current ability and even expand his competence without dropping out of the dialogue due to frustration or defeat. Ninio and Bruner (1978), Bruner (1983), and others have provided us with detailed analyses of these early verbal interactions in the same way that infancy researchers have given us microanalyses of prior preverbal patterning of mother-infant interactions (Trevarthen, 1980).

The mother treats the child as intending to communicate meanings and this has led some developmental psycholinguists to assume the existence of these intentions, taxonomizing them, studying their emergence and change as early intentions (Greenfield, 1980), functions (Halliday, 1975), or protospeech acts (Dore, 1975, 1977) or under the general guise of pragmatics (Bates, Camaioni, and Volterra, 1975; Bates, 1976). Efforts to show how early nonverbal patterns become transformed into specific verbal patterns usually rely on theoretical isomorphism (or at least analogy) of the two structures (Bruner, 1975a,b). Unfortunately, such "explanations" may evidence theoretical borrowing more than continuities in real behaviors; and we still know very little about how or why these developmental changes occur (Gopnik, 1981). Attempts to connect communicative and psychic structural development are equally problematic at this time (Freedman and Grand, 1977).

As one would suspect, there is most likely a little understood interplay between what is biologically given and environmentally learned in psychology, cognition, and linguistics. Furthermore, it seems that each capacity (e.g., language) will turn out to have a developmental line that is partially unique and partially shared with other general abilities (e.g., cognition) (Wanner and Gleitman, 1982). Stating his current position, Bruner claims:

> We can say, I think, that the last decade of research strongly supports the view that language acquisition *is* aided by the acquirer gaining world knowledge concurrently with or in advance of language, *is* aided by maturation, and *is* aided by a privileged social relationship between the child and an adult who is moderately well tuned to his linguistic level. But for all of that, the learning of a language *per se* still constitutes a unique problem space that the child must master beyond any world knowledge he may have gained or

beyond any skills he may have achieved in communicating nonverbally with an adult tuned to his needs
[1982, p. 3].

Researchers in all disciplines who focus on the mother
as context for development converge in their use of the
unit of analysis that includes both mother and child as
a dyad: the dialogue. Spitz's notion of an early (pre)dialogue
which becomes the prototype for and turns into real verbal dialogue has been much explored by current researchers (e.g., Spitz, 1963a,b; Stern, 1974; Brazelton, Koslowski,
and Main, 1974; Brazelton and Tronick, 1980; Kaye and
Charney, 1980). From the earliest days the child is
embedded in his mother's dialogue wherein he learns
about labeling objects, expressing intentions, choosing
topics, and making comments, turn-taking, reciprocity,
and so forth. The mother is responsible for structuring
and carrying the child in these dialogues well into the
preschool years, even when he is more active in his participation in them. (Like Molière's Bourgeoise Gentil-
homme, it seems that babies have been dialoguing for
years without knowing it!) Kaye and Charney (1980) sum
up this position: "Mothers are merely treating the child
as if he were already a full participant in dialogue, and
at the same time they are modeling his role for him. . . . it
is a basic aspect of mother-infant nonverbal interaction
and therefore not exclusively for language training. The
rules seem to be that if an infant gives his mother any
behavior which can be interpreted as if he has taken a
turn in a conversation, it will be; if he does not, she will
pretend he has" (p. 227).
  Even from these interesting and careful studies of
early dialogic continuity, however, it is not clear how or
why the child takes an increasingly responsible role (i.e.,
becomes more equal to the adult) in linguistic and cognitive tasks. Echoing Freud, Bruner states: "Where before there was a spectator, let there now be a participant"

(1983, p. 60). He learns how to participate, we now know, neither due to passive conditioning nor innate emergence, but rather as a consequence of his activities with others. But what motivates him to learn? This, it seems to me, is not only the topical question of this volume but the critical question at the moment for understanding children. Too often motive and meaning are temporally, sequentially, and therefore casually interpreted: early relationships are "social" (by which is meant, involve another person) or "psychological" (by which is meant, involve affect or emotion) and provide the base for cognitive and linguistic learning. Such a view of learning allows different disciplines to focus on their isolated domains: psychoanalysis on early affect; cognitive psychology on early thought; and linguistics on language. Each gives a sidelong glance to the others, acknowledges it, builds on it, but then settles down to till its own small plot of ground.

This "affect-leads-to-meaning" view of development is fallacious. The child is developing relationships at the same time as his cognition and language are developing. All three feed into and constrain the child's total development; in other words, what we call development are changes in thinking and speaking in relationships with others. Those very relationships are constituted in activities and dialogues. For example, acquisition of pronoun usage is instrumental in and reflects changing roles in the mother-child dialogue because the mother-child relationship is changing at the same time (Litowitz and Litowitz, 1983; Sharpless, 1985). The child is not *just* deciphering rules of his linguistic and communicational (pragmatic) systems, or mapping specific linguistic forms onto preexisting social patterns. Ability to feel a separate person and refer to himself as such must have something to do with the ability to view others as separate people who have different points of view; for example, social and cognitive decentering (Piaget, 1955, 1962; Shatz and Gelman, 1973). To speak of learning conversational rules, speaker roles, problem-solving strategies, or whatever, makes little sense without addressing uses of language in holding onto, while at the same time allowing separation from, the mother; or examining processes of identification, for example. On the other hand, introjected and projected maternal representations, the child's symbiotic relationship to the mother and eventual individuation, mirroring, and so forth need to be documented with cognitive and linguistic evidence. The time is past for theories of psychosocial, cognitive, or linguistic development that ignore or contradict each other.

This may be a particularly fortuitous time to address critical issues in child development since, across disciplines, our perceptions of the child are remarkably aligned. Due to very similar historical shifts within each discipline, psychoanalytic, cognitive, and linguistic theorists are struggling to create new, integrative paradigms in their fields. In psychoanalysis, instinct driven theories of ego psychology coexist uneasily with the attachment-based theories of Mahler, Kohut, and the British School (Tolpin, 1971; Kernberg, 1976; Klein and Tribich, 1981; Greenberg and Mitchell, 1983). In cognitive psychology, researchers speak of a post-Piagetian period and struggle to add Vygotskian perspectives on the importance of adults and semiotic mediation (Kaye, 1982). In linguistics, the state of the art (Wanner and Gleitman, 1982) finds developmental psycholinguists not ready to abandon language acquisition to psychologists, but unsure how to rescue an innate language acquisition device (LAD) for a separate language faculty from circularity and isolationism. While we await the messianic new paradigms, the current message across fields is clear: psychosocial, cognitive, and linguistic development must be related; and the child cannot be understood alone, apart from others in context.

A major challenge is to relinquish yet further the notion of the isolated person. We have widened our studies to include two persons—a mother and child dyad (or three: mother, father, and child triad)—at least insofar as the origins of development are concerned. Yet, we study these dyads as two individuals; one whole, the other an incomplete part on its way to spinning off as a separate whole. This basically embryological model (viz, the psychological *birth* of the human infant; Mahler, Pine, and Bergman [1975]) proposes the mother as context for the child until that time when the child can be context-free. But a new focus would examine the matrix in which both child and mother (and child and others) are embedded such that the child can participate in, initiate, and control increasingly complex contexts of activity. As Bruner comments: "The classical approach to the explanation of continuity was to say that with increasing mastery, the child's language moved from being highly dependent on its context of use to being, somehow, less and less context dependent. It is a view that is harder and harder to live with. At most we can say that adult language is context dependent in a different way than child language" (personal communication). Therefore, our challenge in defining new patterns of internalization has two sides: we need new units of analysis and new methodologies to understand functioning which transcends the individual; and we need to reinstate contexts not only as a source but as a goal of development.

The most painstaking microanalyses of mother-child interactions are still descriptions of the behaviors of two separate individuals, albeit mutually patterning, finely orchestrated, and unconsciously choreographed. What methodology will enable us to explore one individual as psychologically part of another? What methods will enable us to know when a child manipulates an object whether that object, separate to us, is in fact separate from himself for the child? All of the notions of external-internal relations which have been used in our explanatory theories to explain both motivation and learning may be ultimately attributable to a trompe l'oeil: that individuals ever become separate, bounded by their persons; and that cognitive and linguistic competence ever exists in a person's mind. We would cease to ask how psychic, cognitive, or linguistic structures are built up; how individuals grow up to be separate, mature adults who "know" formal operations and the full grammars of their languages. Rather, we would begin to ask: How do activities engaged in by a child and mother—or a child and teacher—change, with participation becoming more symmetrical; what are the continuities and shifts in exchanges and relationships which give the illusion of autonomous functioning; what are the processes by which activities and means of exchange are culturally given yet created anew. Answers to these questions will constitute the new patterns of internalization, or perhaps replace internalization altogether.

REFERENCES

Basch, M. (1975), Perception, consciousness and Freud's Project. *The Annual of Psychoanalysis,* 3:3–19. New York: International Universities Press.

Bates, E. (1976), *Language and Context: The Acquisition of Pragmatics.* New York: Academic Press.

———— Camaioni, L., & Volterra, V. (1975), The acquisition of performatives prior to speech. *Merrill-Palmer Quart.,* 21:205–226.

Bowlby, J. (1969), *Attachment and Loss,* Vol. 1. New York: Basic Books.

Brazelton, T. B., Koslowski, B., & Main, M. (1974), The origins of reciprocity: The early mother-infant interaction. In: *The Effect of the Infant on Its Caregiver,* ed. M. Lewis & L. Rosenblum. New York: John Wiley.

———— Tronick, E. (1980), Preverbal communication between mothers and infants. In: *Social Foundations of Language and Thought,* ed. D. Olson. New York: W. W. Norton, pp. 299–315.

Brown, R. (1973), *A First Language: The Early Stages.* Cambridge, MA: Harvard University Press.

Bruner, J. (1975a), From communication to language—a psychological perspective. *Cognition,* 3(3):255–287.

———— (1975b), The ontogenesis of speech acts. *J. Child Lang.,* 2:1–19.

———— (1982), The formats of language acquisition. *Amer. J. Semiot.*, 1(3):1–16.

———— (1983), *Child's Talk: Learning to Use Language.* New York: W. W. Norton.

Bullowa, M., ed. (1979), *Before Speech: The Beginning of Interpersonal Communication.* London: Cambridge University Press.

Cazden, C. (1974), Two paradoxes in the acquisition of language structure and functions. In: *The Growth of Competence*, ed. K. Connolly & J. Bruner. New York: Academic Press, pp. 197–221.

Chomsky, N. (1959), Skinner: Verbal behavior. *Language*, 35:26–57.

Dore, J. (1975), Holophrases, speech acts and language universals. *J. Child Lang.*, 2:21–40.

———— (1977), Children's illocutionary acts. In: *Discourse Production and Comprehension*, Vol. 1, ed. R. O. Freedle. Norwood, NJ: Ablex, pp. 227–244.

Edgcumbe, R. (1981), Toward a developmental line for the acquisition of language. *The Psychoanalytic Study of the Child*, 36:71–103. New Haven, CT: Yale University Press.

Fodor, J. (1975), *The Language of Thought.* New York: Thomas Y. Crowell.

Forrester, J. (1980), *Language and the Origins of Psychoanalysis.* New York: Columbia University Press.

Freedman, N., & Grand, S., eds. (1977), *Communicative Structures and Psychic Structures.* New York: Plenum Press.

Freud, S. (1915), The unconscious. *Standard Edition*, 14:159–215. London: Hogarth Press, 1957.

———— (1923), The ego and the id. *Standard Edition.* 19:1–66. London: Hogarth Press, 1961.

———— (1926), Inhibitions, symptoms and anxiety. *Standard Edition*, 20:75–175. London: Hogarth Press, 1961.

Gill, M. (1976), Metapsychology is not psychology. In: Psychology versus Metapsychology, ed. M. M. Gill & P. S. Holzman. *Psychological Issues*, Monograph 36, 4/9:71–105. New York: International Universities Press.

Gopnik, A. (1981), Review of Bullowa, M. ed. (1979), *Before Speech: The Beginning of Interpersonal Communication. J. Child Lang.*, 8:495–499.

Green, A. (1975), The analyst, symbolization and absence in the analytic setting. *Internat. J. Psycho-Anal.*, 56:1–22.

Greenberg, J. R., & Mitchell, S. A. (1983), *Object Relations in Psychoanalytic Theory.* Cambridge, MA: Harvard University Press.

Greenfield, P. (1980), Toward an operational and logical analysis of intentionality: The use of discourse in early child language. In: *The Social Foundations of Language and Thought*, ed. D. Olson. New York: W. W. Norton, pp. 254–298.

Halliday, M. A. K. (1973), *Explorations in the Functions of Language.* London: Edward Arnold.

———— (1975), *Learning How to Mean—Explorations in the Development of Language*. London: Edward Arnold.

Holt, R. R. (1976), Drive or wish? In: Psychology versus Metapsychology, ed. M. M. Gill & P. S. Holzman. *Psychological Issues,
Monograph 36*, 4/9:158–197. New York: International Universities Press.

Jackendoff, R. (1983), *Semantics and Cognition*. Cambridge, MA: MIT
Press.

Kahn, M. (1974), *The Privacy of the Self*. New York: International
Universities Press.

Kaye, K. (1982), *The Mental and Social Life of Babies: How Parents
Create Persons*. Chicago: University of Chicago Press.

———— Charney, R. (1980), How mothers maintain "dialogue" with
two-year-olds. In: *The Social Foundations of Language and
Thought*, ed. D. Olson. New York: W. W. Norton, pp. 211–230.

Kernberg, O. (1976), *Object Relations Theory and Clinical Psychoanalysis*. New York: Jason Aronson.

Klein, M., & Tribich, D. (1981), Kernberg's object-relations theory: A
critical evaluation. *Internat. J. Psycho-Anal.*, 62:27–43.

Kohut, H. (1971), *The Analysis of the Self*. New York: International
Universities Press.

Kuhn, T. (1970), *The Structure of Scientific Revolutions*, 2nd ed. Chicago: University of Chicago Press.

Lacan, J. (1977), *Ecrits: A Selection*. New York: W. W. Norton.

Lisina, M. I., & Neverovich, Ya. Z. (1971), Development of movements
and formation of motor habits. In: *The Psychology of Preschool
Children*, ed. A. V. Zaporozhets & D. B. Elkonin. Cambridge,
MA: MIT Press, pp. 278–366.

Litowitz, B. (1988), Early writing as transitional phenomena. In: *Sol-
ace Paradigm: An Eclectic Search for Psychological Immunity*,
ed. P. C. Horton, H. Gewirtz, & K. J. Kreutler. Madison, CT:
International Universities Press.

———— Litowitz, N. (1977), The influence of linguistic theory on psychoanalysis: A critical, historical survey. *Internat. Rev. Psychoanal.*, 4:419–448.

———— ———— (1983), Development of verbal self-expression. In: *The
Future of Psychoanalysis*, ed. A. Goldberg. New York: International Universities Press, pp. 397–427.

Lock, A. (1980), Language development. *Bull. Brit. Psychol. Soc.*,
33:5–8.

Mahler, M. S., Pine, F., & Bergman, A. (1975), *The Psychological Birth
of the Human Infant*. New York: Basic Books.

Moerk, E. (1977), *Pragmatic and Semantic Aspects of Early Language
Development*. Baltimore, MD: University Park Press.

Ninio, A., & Bruner, J. (1978), The achievement and antecedents of
labelling. *J. Child Lang.*, 5:1–15.

Piaget, J. (1955), *The Language and Thought of the Child*. New York:
Meridan Books/World Publishing.

———— (1962), *Play, Dreams and Imitation in Childhood.* New York: W. W. Norton.

———— (1971), *Psychology and Epistemology.* New York: Viking Press.

Piattelli-Palmarini, M., ed. (1980), *Language and Learning. The Debate Between Jean Piaget and Noam Chomsky.* Cambridge, MA: Harvard University Press.

Popper, C. (1959), *The Logic of Scientific Discovery.* New York: Basic Books.

Sharpless, E. (1985), Identity formation as reflected in the acquisition of person pronouns. *J. Amer. Psychoanal. Assn.,* 33(4):861–885.

Shatz, M. (1982), Relations between cognition and language acquisition. In: *The Child's Construction of Language,* ed. W. Deutsch. New York: Academic Press.

———— Gelman, R. (1973), The development of communication skills: Modifications in the speech of young children as a function of listener. *Monographs of the Society for Research in Child Development,* 38(5, Serial #152). Chicago: University of Chicago Press.

Snow, C. E., & Ferguson, C. A., eds. (1977), *Talking to Children: Language Input and Acquisition.* New York: Cambridge University Press.

Spitz, R. (1963a), The evolution of dialogue. In: *Drives, Affects and Behavior,* ed. M. Schur. New York: International Universities Press, pp. 170–190.

———— (1963b), Life and the dialogue. In: *Counterpoint,* ed. H. S. Gaskill. New York: International Universities Press, pp. 154–176.

Stern, D. (1974), Mother and infant at play: The dyadic interaction involving facial, vocal and gaze behaviors. In: *The Effect of the Infant on Its Caregiver,* ed. M. Lewis & L. Rosenblum. New York: John Wiley.

Thomas, A. (1981), Current trends in developmental theory. *Amer. J. Orthopsychiat.,* 51(4):580–609.

Tolpin, M. (1971), On the beginnings of a cohesive self: An application of the concept of transmuting internalizations to the study of transitional objects and signal anxiety. *The Psychoanalytic Study of the Child,* 26:316–352. New Haven, CT: Yale University Press.

Trevarthen, C. (1980), The foundations of intersubjectivity: Development of interpersonal and cooperative understanding in infants. In: *Social Foundations of Language and Thought,* ed. D. Olson. New York: W. W. Norton, pp. 316–342.

Uzgiris, I. C., ed. (1979), *Social Interaction and Communication During Infancy.* San Francisco: Jossey-Bass.

Voloshinov, V. N. & Bakhtin, M. (1973), *Freudianism: A Marxist Critique.* New York: Academic Press.

Vygotsky, L. S. (1962), *Thought and Language.* Cambridge, MA: MIT Press.

———— (1978), *Mind in Society*. Cambridge, MA: Harvard University Press.

———— (1981), The instrumental method in psychology. In: *The Concept of Activity in Soviet Psychology,* ed. J. Wertsch. Armonk, NY: M.E. Sharpe, 1981.

Wanner, E., & Gleitman, L.R., eds. (1982), *Language Acquisition: The State of the Art*. London: Cambridge University Press.

Winnicott, D.W. (1974), *Maturational Processes and the Facilitating Environment*. New York: International Universities Press.

Chapter 13

Making Meaning Together: Motivation for Learning to Write

FRANCES M. STOTT, Ph.D.

> Dear Nicole,
> I like School very much. How about you.
> (picture of a winter scene)
> Winter reminds me of you.
>
> Love Jill

This letter represents the first time Jill, five years and ten months old, initiated an activity whose function is unique to writing in that it is normally used to communicate across distance and through time. The idea of sitting down at home and writing this particular piece was Jill's; she only asked her older sister and mother for some spellings. Jill was experimenting with the medium of written language, yet she brought many assumptions about writing to the task. For example, she employed many of the basic principles of writing, such as the ideas that print stands for something besides itself, that there are a limited number of written signs, and that print is arranged on a page in a particular way. She also seemed to have the notions that writing is alphabetic in nature, that words need to be spelled correctly, and that there are linguistic conventions to be observed in writing letters. How is it that Jill, without formal instruction, at school or at home, came to be able to accomplish something so complex?

Working on the assumption that Jill's writing did not "just happen," this chapter considers the social context in which the development of early writing takes place. This is an observational study of some of the writing activities five-year-old Jill engaged in at home prior to her letter to Nicole.[1] It examines the various ways in which Jill's writing activities are structured or otherwise influenced by her mother and especially by her seven-year-old sister Nina. Moreover, in exploring the meaning for Jill of her early writing activities, this chapter joins psychological and cultural perspectives on development and learning.

Focusing on the social foundations of children's early writing is a relatively new line of inquiry. The prevailing view of the achievement of literacy has been based on the study of how school-age children develop specific skills in the language arts curriculum. Since the mid-1970s, however, the development of writing ability has been considered as an aspect of the larger process of language development. Learning to write, like learning to talk, is seen to involve more than receiving formal instruction. This recent emphasis on the preschool child's interest in and experimentation with early writing, however, has branched off into two different directions: one takes a Piagetian perspective and focuses on the child's constructing, more or less on her own, a personal representation of the principles underlying the structure and functions of written language; the other line of inquiry, which this chapter pursues, draws on the theories of the Soviet psychologist Lev Vygotsky (1962, 1978), which

[1] This project, in relation to two other observational studies, is described in R. A. Gundlach, J. B. McLane, F. M. Stott, and G. D. McNamee (1985), "The social foundations of children's early writing development." In: *Advances in Writing Research,* Vol. 1. ed. M. Farr. Norwood, NJ: Ablex. The author wishes to thank Bonnie Litowitz and Robert Gundlach for clarifying many of the ideas expressed in this chapter.

posit that the child's social interactions are of central importance.

Scribner and Cole (1981) conceptualize the achievement of literacy as not simply a matter of developing abstract skills, but as the use of reading and writing in the performance of the practices which constitute one's culture. The child's social environment therefore plays an extremely important role in influencing the development of his or her writing ability. In the Vygotskian perspective children develop competence in the sociocultural practice of writing through the internalization of social relationships. That is, children internalize the structure of the activities involving writing which they experience in their environment. This internalization presupposes an active role on the part of the child. Rather than simply observing other people writing and then copying that activity, the child must somehow act together with the other and share in the activity. The child then gradually internalizes or adopts specific means whereby he can ultimately appropriate written language and make it his own. The child begins to write because he has come to know about and value writing from these interactions with important people around him.

To say that Jill's writing developed out of earlier social interactions can be misleading. It was not just a matter of her mother or sister providing instruction or guidance, nor was it only a case of Jill's taking initiative and seeking to model herself after an available person. Interaction is more than two people involved at the moment—it encompasses their history and specific relationship with all of its permutations. It is the particular nature of the relationship which gives unique meaning to their joint activities (writing and otherwise). In order to consider what Jill brings to her writing interactions, I will attempt to discuss what psychological issues are important to Jill at this time in her life, as well as what is personally motivating to her. I will therefore employ psychoanalytic observations to explicate the themes (e.g., competition, identification, cooperation) that appear to run through her interactions. I will not use psychoanalytic theory in an attempt to understand the *content* of Jill's written language, but, rather, will use this theory to help explicate the *process* by which a young child comes to write without formal instruction. In terms of Nina's influence, I will describe ways in which her involvement facilitates or detracts from Jill's writing development.

The following examples are of writing activities Jill engaged in during the six months preceding her letter to Nicole. The observations were made primarily by the girls' mother, and in some cases by the author. While the order is roughly chronological, it is not based on a developmental continuum. The two major categories are "Mother and Sister as Models" and "Jill and Nina Joined in Purpose." These categories are descriptive and were developed according to the ways in which Jill's relationships contributed to making written language significant for her.

MOTHER AND SISTER AS MODELS

By the time Jill was five years old, she had had ample opportunity to develop a "literate orientation" (Scollon and Scollon, 1981). Her parents had always read books, played word games, and engaged in many kinds of language activities with the girls. In addition, Jill's mother had always valued writing as a medium of expression for herself. Jill undoubtedly watched her mother write, among other things, children's stories and her husband's social work reports. Nina, who had just begun second grade, like her mother, often engaged in writing activities and delighted in practicing what she knew.

Given Jill's many experiences with written language and her observations of her mother and sister writing, how was she able to make use of these encounters to further her own written language? The following three examples illustrate ways in which her mother and sister functioned as models of cultural roles.

"A HALLOWEEN STORY"

> Jill asked her mother for a piece of cardboard and said, "I'm going to write a story." She sat down and "wrote" a tale of a witch flying through the sky and a black cat. Her production consisted of parallel horizontal lines of cursive scribble, letters, words (BK CAT KIRA; JILL) and pictures (a witch flying over a box representing the sky with the moon and stars in it; a five-year-old's hieroglyphic).
>
> As Jill was "writing" her story she was telling it out loud. Yet she clearly did not want her mother to come too close, as her tale seemed to be disrupted when her mother did so. She didn't ask for any help and was unwilling to answer any questions about it. When Jill finished she asked her mother for a piece of tape and taped the story on the living room wall.

The immediate stimulus for this story was probably a similar Halloween story which Jill had heard at school. Her kindergarten teacher had a chart with the same combinations of pictures and words on display in front of the classroom. While Jill had this as a model and initiated the story at home on her own, there was still a profound influence that her mother undoubtedly exerted.

One way in which her mother regulated the writing activity was that she was available both to provide technical assistance (giving Jill the materials) and to receive the finished product. Perhaps more importantly, Jill's mother functioned as an object of identification. While Jill most certainly appreciated the value for her mother of writing in general, in this instance there was a more literal antecedent. When Jill was four, her mother had written a children's book about a witch. Jill not only listened to the story many times, but was able to recite it with impressive accuracy. The origin of her story can be considered to be in the interaction with her mother, and gives texture to Vygotsky's famous dictum of how an interpersonal process is transformed into an intrapersonal one:

> Every function in the child's cultural development appears twice: first, on the social level, and later, on the individual level; first *between* people (interpsychological), and then *inside* the child (intrapsychological). This applies equally to voluntary attention, to logical memory, and to the formation of concepts. All the higher functions originate as actual relations between human individuals [1978, p. 57].

First Jill participated with her mother by listening to the story; then she rehearsed it out loud. Finally, she used the memorized words as she talked to herself to guide her activity as she "wrote" her own story a year later.

Jill's Halloween story was important to her writing development as she was able to extract from all her previous experience and re-create a story of her own. In order to understand something of why she was motivated to do so, it is important to look at some of the unconscious issues involved in Jill's relationships. Based on psychoanalytic developmental psychology, it is assumed that the five-year-old is in the stage where he or she is negotiating oedipal issues; that is, the girl in this phase is thought to be more seductive with father while identifying with mother and competing for father's attention. By taking on one of mother's roles, Jill was able to successfully compete with her mother. In this framework, competition is the probable reason why Jill didn't want her mother directly involved in her story.

A related function for Jill in successfully writing a story on her own was that it enabled her to meet her need for control. As the youngest (by only eighteen months) of two children, a central issue for Jill is forever being in the least powerful and least independent position. As such, she is faced with having to compete with Nina, who is also identifying with their mother by taking over important activities. In this instance, mother and Nina were not writing stories, so Jill could be both powerful and independent. Only once she had completed an "acceptable" product was she able to present it to the world. This may also account for the fact that Jill historically (including the chronologically later example of her letter to Nicole) had few invented spellings. Unlike many young writers (Read, 1975; Beers and Henderson, 1977; Bissex, 1980), Jill had a strong desire to spell correctly. If Jill's need to be more adultlike in her writing is a function of sibling rivalry, perhaps it is the case that investigators of invented spellings have looked primarily at first or only children.

"KEEPING UP WITH NINA"

Nina was making a book called "Types of Plants" in which each page had a picture and label of a different plant. Jill asked her mother if she too could make a "book," and her mother stapled several pages together for her. Jill's text had the appearance of a book, parallel horizontal lines of letters and symbols. There were isolated words interspersed: MOM, JILL, KRA (Karen, a beloved babysitter). She incorporated many of the same symbols she used in her pictures of that era (a star, tree, and person).

There was no joining of purpose between Jill and Nina in this activity; rather they each worked independently. Jill tried to be a part of Nina's activity, but could not. For example, Nina would ask her mother a question about classifying the plants (which even she barely understood); Jill would attempt to ask a similar question and then become upset when it didn't work.

Jill became unusually demanding of her mother's attention, complained a lot, and broke into tears.

Once again, Jill's mother's influence was at work. Bookmaking was perceived by both girls as a valuable activity, and their mother's interest in horticulture (she was taking a course in it at the time) set the topic. Jill was taking the immediate culture of her family and making it serve her own purposes, one of which again included identifying with mother.

Nina's role in this activity added a new dimension because her influence was more direct—she had the idea of making a book which was something Jill could aspire to. What Nina was doing with her book, however (developing a rudimentary system of classifying plants) was too difficult for Jill. Jill therefore adapted what she knew to the new form of bookmaking: she drew familiar pictures and made isolated letters and a list of names that she had written before.

Things did not go well for Jill during this writing activity. She was far more conflicted while she was making her book than she was during other writing occasions (with or without Nina). She experienced many more upsets during the process and was not as pleased with her product (which also wasn't as good a production as were others of that period). In order to understand why this was a problematic experience for Jill, it is important to try to capture something of the meaning of it for her. While she simply may have been irritable that day, a real possibility is that she was feeling stymied in her attempts to identify with mother and compete for father. While somewhat of an elusive concept, the child's identification can be seen as the creation of a unique individual through shared activities (Litowitz, in preparation). For Jill, however, sharing in activities with, and trying to be like, her mother is complicated by having an older, more competent sister. She is often, as was mentioned earlier, faced with having to compete with Nina, as well as being third in line to father.

The primary motivation for Jill in this activity seems to have been to keep up with Nina. Bookmaking was obviously a highly charged, positive way to make contact with mother, please her, and be like her. Yet, Jill was faced with someone who could do it "better," and was therefore made keenly aware of her own limitations. Her conflict centered around her strong need to identify with her mother on the one hand, and the danger and pitfalls of competing with Nina on the other. It is probably not a coincidence that Jill omitted Nina's name from her list of important people (it is also interesting that Dad was not included; this may be evidence that the story was written *for* Dad).

From the standpoint of Jill's psychological development, the situation may have been a healthy means to sublimate her frustrations. The interaction was not optimal for Jill's writing development, however, in that she could not successfully negotiate her sibling rivalry issues. Because she did not feel a sense of mastery, Jill was unable, in this instance, to appropriate written language as an effective tool for herself. Rather, her attempt at modeling herself after Nina was comparatively unsuccessful. Thus, while Nina did offer a specific writing form (a "book") which Jill was able to adopt, it was a problematic learning experience, and how much Jill gained in terms of the development of her writing ability is questionable. As for all writers, however, it is important to note that ups and downs are part of the process.

"I 'AMN'T' GOING TO DO IT!"

In the preceding example Nina served as a role model which Jill was motivated to copy perhaps because of competitive feelings. The following is an example of an attempt by Nina to more directly influence Jill.

For some time, Jill had been using the word "amn't."
One day she used it in conversation with Nina. Nina
told her it was wrong and that she shouldn't use it. Jill
insisted that she *could* use it if she wanted to. She
launched some discussion of the word "ain't" to prove
her point. Jill was adamant. Nina was annoyed. Finally
Nina shouted, "Jill, don't use it. It *disturbs* me."

A few days later, Jill again used the word "amn't."
Nina again called her on it. "Jill, that's not *correct*."
Jill insisted, "I don't care." Nina told her that if she
continued to use "amn't" in the second grade, the kids
would make fun of her. Jill would not give an inch on
her right to use that word. Finally in exasperation,
Nina screamed at her, "Jill, if you keep saying that, no
one will want to marry you!"

This was followed by a less heated sisterly discussion about the desirability (or lack thereof) of marriage.

In this example Jill was insisting on controlling the
rules of her language and was not yet ready to accept the
culturally agreed upon usage—at least not as presented
by Nina. Nina's admonition that "no one will want to
marry you" vividly illustrates the recurring oedipal
theme. Rather than being outdone, however, Jill came
out of this exchange with an increased sense of autonomy
as well as good feelings about herself. While Nina was
unsuccessful as a role model in this instance, Jill's language learning was not hampered as she was well aware
of the incorrectness of her word. In fact, her feelings of
control over her language in this situation might well
have led to her being more receptive in later interactive
situations in which she could move toward making writing her own.

It is important to keep in mind that Jill *does* want to
be like her sister and mother, but must preserve her own
identity at the same time. There is a delicate balance
between feeling controlled by and in control of one's ac-

tivities, writing and otherwise. Far more frequently than not, Jill turns to her sister for writing and other cultural conventions.

JILL AND NINA JOINED IN PURPOSE

In the "bookmaking" example cited above, Nina's influence on Jill was rather indirect; she served largely as a model and the girls worked independently. While they were both writing for the same reason, to please and identify with their mother, they were cast in an adversarial position. There were other instances in which Nina played a far more direct and less conflicted role in the development of Jill's writing. The following two examples illustrate how, rather than just influencing the *occurrence* of a writing activity, Nina regulated the *degree of difficulty* of the tasks. In the bookmaking activity, Nina regulated the occurrence of Jill's writing simply by having the idea. The form of "books," however, and the process of bookmaking were not new to Jill. Her finished product was also not any more fully developed than were others she had made. In the following circumstances, Nina's involvement resulted in Jill's accomplishing more sophisticated or difficult pieces than she would have on her own.

A MAGIC POTION

> Each girl had a sheet of paper and they were talking about making a list of ingredients for a "magic potion." Nina wrote and spelled out loud, and Jill wrote the following:
> POCION UNGRINE PEPER, HAIR + HONEY + e
> GARLIK

In this example Nina functioned in an authoritative role much as a teacher. She had the idea, arranged for the materials, provided a model, and "spelled" words for Jill. (The invented spellings were Nina's—once again likely perceived by Jill as more correct than her own could be.) However, the quality of the interaction was very different from that of the bookmaking activity. Earlier that day Nina and Jill had actually concocted a "magic potion." Because the writing experience grew out of the earlier mutual play, and because it was not conflicted by competitive dynamics, the girls were able to enjoy working and talking together, as children often do.

This interactive event also differed from those with adults in a very important way. Nina was engaged in an activity that was pleasurable and meaningful to both herself and Jill. In that sense she and Jill had a "shared agenda." For both girls this writing activity was an extension of their earlier play. In mixing and then recording the ingredients, the girls were creating an imaginary situation which allowed them "emancipation from situational constraints" (Vygotsky, 1978). As such, they were able to explore and discover for themselves the forms, processes, and uses of both the potion and of written lists, without the pressure of producing a "correct" product. The experience shares the "paradoxical" quality of pretend play (Bateson, 1972) in that it was both pretend and real at the same time. This quality allowed the girls to feel that they had created their *own* meaning while involved in an activity that has a social, objective meaning (e.g., cooking, making shopping lists).

As a consequence of the girls' *mutual involvement,* Jill's written product was more sophisticated than her earlier work. While she had made lists of names before, they were always of the same familiar people. In the potion list, each word (some of which Jill contributed) was purposeful and consciously decided upon. Thus the mutuality which enhanced Jill's sense of control over her writing enabled her to produce something she would not have been able to without Nina's help.

"WRITING TO MAKE THE TIME GO BY"

> The girls had been talking about a brand of vitamins called "Flintstones" all morning. Their father then went out to the store and was going to buy some. He was gone a long time and the girls began to write notes. Nina wrote: "Dad put the flinsones on the table." Jill (with Nina's help with spelling) wrote:
> DAD DO YOU HAVE THE FLINST
> ONES?

Once again the writing activity for Jill can be seen as an outgrowth of the social interaction. They were mutually involved in discussing and playing with the "Flintstone" vitamins all morning, which were perhaps so important because of their symbolic value as characters. The girls were also joined in purpose in that they were becoming impatient waiting for their father. The primary motivation for both girls' notes seems to have been to express (and perhaps objectify) their impatience. While both notes served the same function, however, their level of sophistication was different. The notes differ in syntax; Nina's has an instrumental purpose, and, indeed, she taped hers on the door where her father would be sure to see it. Jill's note was less communicative in the sense that it was not as much a message as an expression of hope for the vitamins.

Like the preceding example, this writing experience was a highly successful and unconflicted one for Jill. It did enable her to allay her impatience while waiting, and once again the written product was richer due to Nina's influence. She discovered that writing was something she could do "to make the time go by"; she incorporated the word *Flintstones,* she used a question mark, and she experienced another form of writing (the note) used to communicate to others (as was her letter to Nicole, which was written soon after).

A SPECIAL CASE OF JOINT PURPOSE: JILL AND NINA AS COCONSPIRATORS

The preceding examples (with the exception of Jill's use of the word *amn't*) have all been activities in which writing was the primary medium. The purposes for writing letters, stories, books, lists, and notes are those served by the enduring aspects of writing; that is, they communicate across distance and through time, or record information. In all of these activities Jill was, to some degree or other, attempting to adopt the adult practice of writing and/or struggling with her own mastery of the written word. The following two examples present situations in which writing was secondary. The functions of these episodes were primarily served through other symbol systems (i.e., speaking, drawing, and play). What is of interest in these examples is that writing *was* included when it was not essential to the task.

"SOME SCATOLOGICAL MUSINGS"

Jill and Nina were in a room alone. Amid *much* hilarity Jill, with Nina's help (dictating and spelling) produced the following pages.

Page One: JILL DANIELS
                         PIS + PIS
                   NOW DID YOU
                   THINK OF LOOK
                     ING AT THIS
            SECR
      ET   ROBERT
   PAGE   GOING
                      PEE.

At the bottom of the page is a flower with a penis and a boy with an elongated penis urinating.

Page Two:
> JILL DANIELS
> ROBERT
> PIS + PIS
> NOW TAKE A LOOK AT TN

Page Three:
> JILL DANIELS
> KIRA (crossed out)
> BUTT
> ROBERT

There are several pictures of what appear to be penises.

Page Four:
> PI
> KIS SING
> LOVE ING
> e H

At the top of the page is a picture of a sun. At the side of the page is a boy crying and urinating.

This is a powerful example of the two girls banding together in order to deal with unconscious issues and their feelings toward a difficult neighbor. Robert, who is seven years old and lives down the street, appears to have serious emotional and learning problems. The girls are almost always angry with Robert for one reason or another.

Scatological musings are common for children of this age in that they help the child develop control or mastery over his or her feelings. In this case the girls were likely defending against oedipal feelings by berating and making fun of males, treating the penis as a liability rather than as an asset. The words and pictures served to both satisfy their voyeuristic impulses as well as to defend against underlying anxieties. The purpose was to be offensive both in the sense of being revolting and in the

sense of making an attack (Maria Piers, personal communication). The objects of the attacks were likely powerful adults *and* Robert, who so often upset them with his
unpredictable behavior.

While saying the words undoubtedly gave the girls
great pleasure and served as a sublimation, their scatology also took the form of drawings and written words.
Reenacting the scatology in other symbolic mediums
served to distance further the sublimation. Writing and
drawing allowed the girls to be able to both see and look
away, thus enabling them to maintain feelings of control.
Two things are interesting about the nature of the interaction and of each girl's contribution. First of all it
was Jill who did all of the drawing and writing; Nina
only provided spelling and some dictating. Nina was having Jill do "the dirty work." This may have been the case
because Nina was exerting her power as the older sibling;
or another possibility is that as a child more into the
latency stage, Nina was more concerned with social conventions.

A second aspect worth considering in this example is
the relationship between the drawings and writing. The
drawings were all done by Jill; the words, though recorded by Jill, were essentially Nina's contribution.
While the drawings might have been merely illustrations
to the text, it is likely that if she were alone, Jill would
have created her meaning only through drawing "dirty"
pictures. One can speculate that for Nina, the catharsis
was in the written word, while the pleasure for Jill was
in drawing. Support for this line of reasoning comes from
Gardner (1980). He states that the child who has not yet
learned to read or to write with some fluency is not yet
ready to "marshall her literary resources and to express
significant messages with. her pen . . . and so until the
task of writing has been mastered," Gardner continues,
"the system of drawing is the only one sufficiently elaborated to permit expression of inner life" (p. 155). Yet Jill

did, as an extension of Nina, write the words, and as a result produced a more sophisticated piece than was any of her other work of that time.

"THE SPYING GAME"

The last example is of a "Spying Game" that the girls and their friends played over a period of several months, culminating about the time Jill wrote the letter to Nicole "on her own."

> *Summer:* Jeannie, a playmate about two years older than Nina introduced the game of "spying" last summer. Several children were playing—Jeannie (entering fourth grade), Nina, Georgie and Kira (all entering second grade), and Jill (entering kindergarten). Jeannie had the idea of a "spying club." She organized the activity and set the rules. All the children met together in a group, made plans to sneak about the immediate neighborhood, observe people's activity, record their observations (each was supplied with paper and pencil), then return to a meeting spot and compile their findings. The only problem was that Jill wanted to play, but she couldn't write. So Jeannie said that Jill could either accompany one of the others and help them spy or she could go out on her own and come back and tell someone who could write her "spy." There was much discussion of who should go with whom, where they should spy, and where the meeting place would be. Whistles were distributed for some sort of signaling purpose. The game caught. It was played with intensity and enormous enjoyment.
>
> Some days after the game had been initiated, Jeannie and Nina decided that there should be a test to join the club. The two of them set about meeting to devise such a test. Jill was worried—how could she get in the club if she couldn't write to pass the test? Nina was pretty rigid ("Well then you can't be in the club") but

Jeannie prevailed in her decision that there should be *two tests,* one for those who could write and one for those who couldn't. She found out what Jill could do—"Jill can write her name, right? Well, then something like that will be her test."

Winter: Nina and Jill continued to play a modified version of the Spying Game. Usually this took the form of each of them writing down something they had "spied" on their own sheets of paper (e.g., DAD IS TALKING TO MOM). While Nina usually provided spellings, the content was often jointly arrived at.

Spring: Mother was folding clothes on Jill's bed. Jill pulled a slip of paper out of her desk, and, with Mother's help with spelling (and obviously pleased with her accomplishment), wrote:

> MOM IS
> FOLDING
> CLOTH
> ES

In the Spying Game, writing, though significant, was but one element of a complex activity. The game undoubtedly met the school-aged children's need for camaraderie and explicit rule-governed play. But more importantly, this game can be seen as the children's realization in play form of tendencies that cannot be immediately gratified (Vygotsky, 1978). Spying is a magnificent way in which to gain power over people—they can have no secrets you cannot discover. For children, who are continually striving to gain control and feel effective in an adult world, spying affords the wonderful opportunity to turn the tables and discover "what *they* are up to!"

In a further consideration of the Spying Game, it is interesting to speculate about why writing was incorporated into the game. It may be that the school-aged children had some notion that individuals who control the medium of writing have more power (Gundlach, 1982).

The children also had some recognition of the enduring aspects of writing and its potential for capturing and savoring experiences. When asked what the writing was for, Nina's response was "So we don't forget."

The influences of the Spying Game on Jill were many and complex. Obviously the whole notion of "spying" was as meaningful to Jill as to the others and she thoroughly enjoyed being a member of the older group. In some ways Jeannie, the oldest child, functioned as an adult for Jill. She structured the situation so that Jill could participate as fully as possible. First, she suggested that Jill could either accompany someone or dictate her "spy" to someone who could write. Then, unlike Nina, who was acting as the "upholder of the cultural standard" (or, as an older sibling), Jeannie suggested an alternative literacy test that Jill could "pass."

Nina's influence in the Spying Game over the course of the winter was much as it was in the examples of writing the list of ingredients for "The Magic Potion" and writing notes to Dad in order to "make the time go by." Jill and Nina were joined in purpose; as an outgrowth of their play they began to write, and in so doing discovered a new means to work out their cognitive and affective needs. Again, as a consequence of their mutual involvement, Jill developed a more sophisticated use for writing. Nina also served in somewhat of an authoritative role in that she supplied the spellings.

Finally, in the spring, Jill wrote her own "spy." While she did this independently of Nina, it is interesting that she transferred Nina's authoritative role to her mother, who was both the object of the "spy" and the provider of spellings. One possibility for this is that Jill was feeling guilty for "spying" and needed to let her mother know what they were up to—for her approval, because secrets are a heavy burden. Unlike the scatology, however, the Spying Game never had the same quality for the girls of doing the forbidden. While the children's voyeuristic tendencies were undoubtedly involved in the game, the overriding need seemed to be for a means of group identification. It seems that Jill's pleasure came from feeling like an effective member of that community. It may be that asking mother for spellings was a reflection of the fact that Jill needed technical assistance and no one else was around.

The Spying Game does illustrate a progression in how early literacy can be developed through social relationships. Through mutual participation in a very meaningful game, Jill experienced an activity which involved writing. Over a period of time, and with additional support from Nina, she was able to come to the point where she wanted to conduct this activity for herself. While she was still somewhat dependent on her mother, she was now in control in that she initiated the situation ("spying") and chose the symbol system (writing). It is quite likely that Jill came to write her letter to Nicole in a similar fashion.

DISCUSSION

Jill's activities and interactions involving writing illustrate the notion that the achievement of literacy involves more than the acquisition of abstract skills—the development of her writing ability was crucially influenced and promoted by the social context. Her parents and other significant people in her life helped determine her understanding of what written words are all about and what they are used for. Her relationships also influenced her desire to write; for Jill, writing was a way of becoming a more effective and powerful member of her family and community.

Focusing on the social context does not mean to discount the cognitive capacities that are involved in learning to write. Rather this focus seeks to understand what determines whether a child will encounter experiences of the kind that are necessary to produce change, and what factors shape the child's interpretation of his or her experiences. Michael Cole and his colleagues (Laboratory of Comparative Human Cognition, 1982) have addressed the issue of how culture organizes for the next step of development to occur, in any content domain. Building on Vygotsky's sociohistorical perspective, they suggest that culture influences the organization of children's environments in four ways: (1) it arranges for the occurrence or nonoccurrence of specific basic problem-solving events; (2) it organizes the frequency of these events; (3) it shapes the patterning or co-occurrence of events; and (4) it regulates the level of difficulty of the task.

Jill's immediate culture, her family, influenced the development of her writing in many ways. On one level her parents provide an environment which is replete with the tools of literacy, and they clearly value reading and writing as relevant and useful in their lives. They engage in countless language activities *with* their daughters, provide materials and assistance, and are an encouraging and appreciate audience for most of the girls' attempts at mastering written language (including the most remote of approximations). In these "substantive" ways, Jill was put in touch with the forms, processes, and functions of written language in her family in particular and in society in general (Teale, 1982).

On a deeper level, Jill's interactions with her family around literacy *motivated* her to learn to write, in that they served to forge links between Jill's internal psychological forces and writing. Still in the oedipal phase of development at age five, she primarily sees her parents only as they relate to her own self. The challenge of this phase lies in the recognition that one's self is not invariably part of every human equation (Basch, 1975, 1980). The child needs to master successfully her anxieties and come to grips with her separation in this sense of accepting realistic limitations to her power. Writing, for

Jill, is one way in which she can both hold on to and at the same time separate from her mother. Through sharing in activities and eventually taking them on as her own, Jill identifies with her mother.

What of the role of an older sibling in the development of early writing? Having considered the range of writing activities Jill engaged in "under Nina's influence," it appears that the presence of a sibling at home is a force to be acknowledged. Nina's influence did not always serve to facilitate or move Jill's writing development forward. If the girls were cast in an adversarial position where they were competing for the same role, Jill was generally frustrated. Nina's considerable edge over Jill in writing deprived Jill of the power and pleasure she experienced from writing on other occasions.

More often than not, Nina's influence was extremely beneficial to the development of Jill's written language. Nina often served as a model for Jill, and thereby arranged for the occurrence and frequency of writing activities. In their joint activities Jill learned that writing can co-occur with other symbolic mediums; one can play and write as with the "Flintstones," and writing and drawing can be used together, as in the "scatological musings."

At times Nina's collaboration regulated the difficulty of the activity by "stretching" Jill's writing, much in the manner Vygotsky (1978) speaks of in his discussion of the instructional area he called the "zone of proximal development." This is the distance between what the child can accomplish alone (the level of actual development) and what the child can do when helped by a more competent adult or peer (the level of potential development). It is interesting, however, to distinguish between the role of an adult and that of a more capable peer. Each time Nina's influence was positive, her role was not primarily instructive, but rather, the girls were joined in purpose and engaged in mutual *play*.

For Vygotsky play, like instruction, is a major source of development—indeed play *leads* development: "play creates a zone of proximal development of the child. In play a child always behaves beyond his average age, above his daily behavior; in play it is as though he were a head taller than himself" (1978, p. 102). Just as play led Jill's writing development, so did Nina. As Nina and Jill played together, they projected themselves into the adult activities of their culture and rehearsed their future roles. Play also enabled the girls to master their various conflicts, wishes, and fears. Thus, through mutual needs, the girls shared an agenda when they played. Because Nina is enough older (eighteen months), and because she has had more school experience critical to literacy (first and second grades), she was considerably further along in her writing development. As a writer who had already experienced some of the uses of writing, Nina, sometimes unwillingly, served to induce or entice Jill into writing. Nina usually provided the idea and the wherewithal to write. By being "carried along" in the context of play, Jill could participate in writing to her current ability and expand her competence without experiencing frustration or defeat.

In addition to regulating the occurrence, frequency, and patterning of writing in their play, Nina enabled Jill to experience new forms (lists, notes, etc.) of writing. Most importantly, through their collaborative efforts, Jill learned new and significant uses for writing. While concocting a "magic potion," for example, Jill learned a new way to represent the ingredients—and that a list is something you can consult later. By experiencing writing as another symbolic medium with which to express the potent themes involved in scatology or "spying," Jill advanced in her skill as a young writer. Thus Nina's influence is not that she "teaches" Jill how to write, but through mutual involvement the girls use writing to create shared meanings.

A brief final example illustrates how well Jill has learned the power of the written word. One evening (some months after the letter to Nicole), Nina was allowed to stay overnight at a friend's house. Jill was disgruntled and irritable for most of the evening. When it came to her bedtime, Jill protested, on the grounds that Nina was probably staying up later at her friend's house. Her mother insisted that Jill go to bed, and she was sent up to her room. Some time later, thirteen small slips of paper came fluttering down the stairs, each with the following message: "I HAT YOU." This written "Rain of Hate" vividly demonstrates that the medium is the message; and that this socially constituted medium (i.e., writing) can function in a personally meaningful way.

REFERENCES

Basch, M. F. (1975), Toward a theory that encompasses depression: A revision of existing causal hypotheses in psychoanalysis. In: *Depression and Human Existence,* ed. E. J. Anthony & T. Benedek. Boston: Little, Brown.
——— (1980), *Doing Psychotherapy.* New York: Basic Books.
Bateson, G. (1972), *Steps to an Ecology of Mind.* New York: Ballantine Books.
Beers, J. W., & Henderson, E. H. (1977), A study of developing orthographic concepts among first graders. *Res. Teach. Eng.,* 11:133–148.
Bissex, G. L. (1980), *GYNS AT WRK: A Child Learns to Write and Read.* Cambridge, MA: Harvard University Press.
Gardner, H. G. (1980), *Artful Scribbles: The Significance of Children's Drawings.* New York: Basic Books.
Gundlach, R. (1982), *How Children Learn to Write: Perspectives on Children's Writing for Educators and Parents.* Washington, DC: National Institute of Education.
Laboratory of Comparative Human Cognition (1982), Culture and intelligence. In: *Handbook of Human Intelligence,* ed. R. J. Sternberg. New York: Cambridge University Press.
Litowitz, B. (in preparation), Transitional writing.
Read, C. (1975), *Children's Categorization of Speech Sounds in English.* Urbana, IL: National Council of Teachers of English.
Scollon, R., & Scollon, S. B. K. (1981), *Narrative, Literacy and Face in Interethnic Communication.* Norwood, NJ: Ablex.

Scribner, S., & Cole, M. (1981), *The Psychology of Literacy*. Cambridge, MA: Harvard University Press.

Teale, W. H. (1982), Toward a theory of how children learn to read and write naturally. *Language Arts,* 59(6):555–570.

Vygotsky, L. S. (1962), *Thought and Language*. Cambridge, MA: MIT Press.

——— (1978), *Mind in Society*. Cambridge, MA: Harvard University Press.

Chapter 14

The Child's Mourning: Can It Be Learned from the Parent?

BENJAMIN GARBER, M.D.

INTRODUCTION

It has been said that therapy is like a song in that it has lyrics and a melody. The lyrics usually represent the content of the treatment while the melody represents the process. Most of the time the lyrics are interchangeable, in fact, popular songs are translated into different languages and still maintain their popularity. The melody, however, has to remain constant if the song is to be appreciated. This metaphor is imperfect, as is any generalization about human behavior. Certain lyrics have a tendency to remain unforgettable, while many melodies begin to sound similar and are easily forgotten. For any classic song to maintain its appeal over the span of generations the lyrics and the melody have to remain a constant pattern to be discovered, appreciated, and rediscovered by every individual.

The clinical data for this chapter originates from the research of the Barr-Harris Center for the Study of Parent Loss of the Chicago Institute for Psychoanalysis. The following constitute the staff of the Center: Sol Altschul, M.D., Helen Beiser, M.D., Benjamin Garber, M.D., Nan Knight-Birnbaum, M.S.W., Arnold Samuels, M.D. (Director), Joy Simon, M.A., and Colin Weber, M.A.

Most individuals who come for treatment are prepared to master the content of the therapeutic exchange. The language of psychotherapy, whether it has to do with issues of rejection, deprivation, oedipal longings, or low self-esteem can be memorized and used by most patients with a reasonable degree of skill and accuracy. Patients also become adept at using these words skillfully outside of the therapeutic setting. However, the melody of therapy (i.e., the process) is much more difficult to master. Numerous patients go from therapist to therapist reciting the now familiar lyrics, which may result in a temporary sense of well-being; however, they have not participated in a therapeutic process.

A somewhat parallel interaction emerges in the course of learning and teaching psychotherapy. The beginning therapist is usually well versed in the theoretical models which help him to understand the technique of the therapeutic approach. Consequently, he may be quite capable of appreciating the content of the patient's productions and possess the skill to respond therapeutically. However, an appreciation of the therapeutic process and some of its finer nuances is a lengthy process in its own right which is only mastered after much hard work and a certain measure of emotional distress.

In an attempt to bypass such painful learning, a patient as well as the beginning therapist may engage in an extensive and sometimes frantic search for textbooks and journals on "how to do it." Such an effort is primarily for the purpose of content learning and it may be rewarded with the discovery of more current and sophisticated formulations about solving certain problems. Nevertheless, one will be left with a sense of emptiness and incompleteness because the process elements of such important interactions have not been addressed.

A somewhat parallel interplay may also evolve in situations dealing with parent loss. The surviving parent will call the Barr-Harris Center to discuss with a professional what to tell the child and how to handle the events of the death. They will demand answers to a series of fairly standard questions, such as: "Should the child attend the funeral? Should the child be told the cause of death? How soon should he go back to school? Should the teacher and friends be informed about the loss?" In other words the surviving parent asks to be taught how to talk to the child about various interactions surrounding the loss. The more compulsive parent will have read books on the subject or have discussed these questions with friends, relatives, or other professionals. Some will even take notes and attempt to memorize the proper words and their sequence in anticipation of facing the child.

Although the professional's advice may prove reassuring to the bereaved parent, upon more thoughtful reflection most of those parents do know what to do and what to say to their children.

In all of the above situations the main thrust seems to be on the overpowering need to know and to learn the content component of the significant interactions. In all of the above incidents there seems to be a relative neglect of the process components of these meaningful encounters. In all of these situations there is the pervasive need to know the facts, to know what to do and say, or to know what is "going on"; however, this will often tend to obscure the affective components which seem far more crucial to the process.

This compulsive need to know seems to focus invariably on what the child is thinking or what he should think, in other words, the content. Seldom is one asked just what the child is feeling as a result of his loss; or more specifically, what the appropriate feelings may be at various times in response to the loss. While the parent insists on knowing the right words and how to say them, seldom does the parent care to ask about what a child should be expected to feel and how the parent is to respond to such feelings.

The patient who spends many hours discussing and dissecting the essential dynamics of his personality may have extreme difficulty in allowing himself to sense and to experience emerging feelings toward the therapist. The beginning therapist, who insists on knowing all the time what is going on, may have the same difficulty in allowing himself to experience and then use his own feelings as the essential instrument of knowing what transpires between him and the patient. Similarly the surviving parent, who demands to be taught what to say and do with his child in response to a loss, may be insisting on learning content when the real issue has more to do with the not knowing or appreciating the important affects, or the process.

It is indeed essential for the therapist to respond initially to the content presentation of the patient as that has a stabilizing and organizing function for someone in the midst of a crisis. However, it is our contention that the content component can be mastered or learned rather quickly and easily. In fact, most individuals, once they are calm enough, are capable of finding the appropriate words and constructing their own content. However, the process elements, which have something to do with the associated affects, are far more difficult to learn. Perhaps we are making a somewhat artificial distinction between the words and the feelings, between the content and the process, for ideally the two should be in harmony in any therapeutic exchange. Still, for a full appreciation and learning of the complexity of any interaction such a distinction is inherently useful and worthwhile. It is the appreciation of and learning about the primary affects of the child in response to a loss, and how these affects interdigitate with the feelings of the adult, that the rest of this chapter will attempt to delineate.

THE AFFECTS OF MOURNING

In the ongoing work at the Barr-Harris Center for the Study of Parent Loss at the Chicago Institute for Psychoanalysis we have encountered a number of latency-age children who seemed to be intensely involved in some type of mourning activity which is similar to what one would expect in the mourning of adults. These children were described more extensively in a previous paper (Garber, 1981). It was felt that they were a unique type of youngster who for reasons that were not readily apparent seemed to have hypercathected the image and the memory of the parent that died. They were intensely involved in remembering the absent parent, the events of the death, and the subsequent memorialization activities. They seemed overly invested in anything and everything related to the absent parent in a manner which seemed appropriate, realistic, and acceptable to the surrounding adults. Periodically the child's behavior tended to border on the pathological, but only transiently and in response to the loss. Although these youngsters seemed to be actively dealing with their loss by a repetitive attempt at mastering the trauma it soon became apparent that in certain ways these children seemed to be stuck; that is, in the sense that there was a constant repetition, reexamination, and reexperiencing of the events of the loss, with their associated affects, but these did not seem to be totally integrated into the child's personality.

In several instances, after lengthy, intensive therapeutic work, a number of such children were withdrawn from treatment. This usually occurred with little warning and seemed to happen while the child was in the midst of an intense preoccupation with the loss. The therapist in this type of situation invariably experienced a sense of disappointment, frustration, and often betrayal. It seemed puzzling as to how and why a surviving parent, who seemed to be committed to treatment, would choose to ignore the therapeutic contract and remove the child from treatment for no apparent reason. It appeared that in all these cases the sole precipitant for withdrawal was the fact that the child was dealing actively with his loss.

A closer examination of the clinical material seemed to indicate that in these instances the parent was beginning to sense that he or she had dealt with the loss and was ready to move on to other things. While some of the parents were in treatment, others had dealt with their loss by a plunge into activities and a seeking of a replacement. They felt that they were ready to pursue other interests. Meanwhile the child was stuck in and preoccupied with the full impact of the trauma. Consequently, the child's treatment continued to confront the parent with their loss and was a recurrent reminder of its presence. As the child became the conscience of the adult the treatment was experienced as the prime stimulator of pain, guilt, and loyalty conflicts. Given such circumstances, the child was removed from treatment, usually for nebulous external reasons. The covert message was that any further reactions to or feelings about the loss must be repressed, either permanently or perhaps to be reconsidered and dealt with at some later time and place.

From discussions at the Barr-Harris Center about the pertinent dynamics in such cases, it became apparent that the mourning of the child and the mourning of the surviving parent seemed to be out of phase with one another. For the child to be able to mourn effectively and productively it may be that one of the crucial prerequisites is that the mourning of the child should in some way be congruent with the mourning of the surviving parent. One would anticipate a certain parallel of mourning processes; otherwise one of the partners, more often the child, may have to curtail or abort their mourning work because it stimulates excessive guilt and creates conflict in the surviving parent.

While the ability to mourn necessitates the presence of a variety of cognitive and emotional skills, many psychoanalytic researchers have placed a strong emphasis on the role of certain key affects. Deutsch (1937) and Wolfenstein (1966, 1969) have equated the work of mourning with an affective experience, especially with a pattern of affective discharge. Mahler (1961) and Jacobson (1967) state that the very young child's handicap lies in not being able to sustain and express affects in a modulated piecemeal manner over a prolonged period of time. Most authors assume that with maturation there ensues an increase in the child's capacity to tolerate feelings.

Clinical experience with bereaved adults would tend to indicate that an impairment in the ability to tolerate strong affects is not uncommon; however, such individuals are usually seen as having other deficits also.

With children the emphasis has been on the child's developmental inability to tolerate powerful affects. There is much confusion and disagreement, however, as to which phase of childhood this may apply to as well as the inherent variations in terms of personalities and external factors.

In recent years there has emerged, based on the work of cognitive psychologists, a greater appreciation of the complexity of the young child's mind. Just as the child's cognitive abilities have received greater recognition, there has been a parallel increase in the awareness of the child's ability to appreciate complex affective states.

Surbey (1979) found that three- and four-year-olds have an awareness of the logical relationships between events that are causal antecedents and logical consequences of emotional states. Positive emotions are less well differentiated than negative emotions. The essence of Surbey's work was the finding that three- to four-year-old children are capable of complex adultlike thought about emotions.

Demos (1974) has found that as age increases so does the ability to make distinctions between emotions. It seems that the largest increase in this ability occurs between the ages of six and nine. It also appears that females are generally better than males at making distinctions between affects.

Schwartz (1981) detected a developmental shift that may occur in children ages six to eight in their ability to make distinctions between emotions. It seems that by age eight, children's ability to discriminate between affects approximates that of older children and adults. Older children's facility for language production appears to account for much of the emphasis that has been placed on the developmental differences between older and the young child's comprehension of emotions.

Contemporary research on young children's (six years or younger) understanding of emotions has in general tended to lead to the conclusion that young children are not able to understand emotions in complex ways. Researchers on this issue state that young children may exhibit some understanding but that their understanding is relatively simplistic or not like that of adults.

While parents spend large amounts of time teaching the child certain cognitive skills, whether they are the naming of colors or the tying of shoes, one has to wonder how much effort is expended by a parent in trying to teach the child about his emotions. It may well be that children learn from parents about feelings, what they are and what is permitted, primarily by example. Perhaps the tangible rewards for cognitive mastery are more apparent, while the rewards for affective mastery are rather subtle and evanescent. Consequently, the child's ability to understand and to communicate his own feelings is to some extent dependent on the mother's ability and comfort in differentiating affects for the child by labeling them and helping him become aware of them.

The child may then differentiate for himself the observed feelings and relate them to specific circumstances. Ultimately, one hopes that the child will not only differentiate his feelings for himself, but also categorize them and then begin to compare them with the feelings of others.

In mourning the loss of a significant love object, the most commonly differentiated affects have been longing, grief, sadness, and anger. Anxiety and shame have frequently been included as integral parts of the clinical picture. The experience of longing for the lost object is a basic innate elemental response which all children are capable of experiencing irrespective of how the environment supports, reacts to, or does not react to their loss. Consequently, it would seem that most children are able to experience longings, to a greater or lesser extent.

Grief has variously been defined and described as a feeling of deep sorrow. It has been labeled as an integral part of mourning as well as one of the outward manifestations and components of the mourning process. Grief is an affect that accompanies mourning although it may occur in situations which do not involve a mourning process. Grief is generally connected with an irretrievable loss, while in separation anxiety hope persists that the loss is not irretrievable.

The most characteristic feature of grief is not prolonged depression but acute and episodic pangs; these pangs are associated with severe anxiety and psychological pain. Such episodes are usually triggered by a memory of the lost object and the reality confrontation that the object is gone. At such times the person is strongly missed and the survivor sobs or cries out for him. Having done that, there may follow anger at the object for its absence, but more commonly there sets in a sadness with the gradual realization of the object not being there.

The episodes of grief have been likened to severe somatic distress which has been localized in various parts of the body, whether it be the pit of the stomach or the chest. It is also experienced as a "knotlike" quality or a "tearing away." It is the physical-like somatic sensation of grief that may account for the expression of "dying from a broken heart." The higher incidence of physical illness as well as death in survivors after a loss has been well documented in the psychiatric literature.

The experience of grief for the child probably has more of a somaticlike component due to the immaturity of the psychic apparatus. One would assume that for the younger child, whose secondary process thinking has not been fully developed, the sensation of grief will most likely be experienced as somatic pain and bodily distress. It is not surprising then that most children would be wary of any situation which might potentially induce this type of bodily pain. It is also not surprising that the younger child who has just experienced grief would more than likely try to distract himself from such stimuli; whether it be by words, activities, somatic complaints, and more than likely a thrust into hyperactivity.

Grief often tends to resemble a physical illness or injury; it has often been described metaphorically as a physical wound that heals gradually and painfully. Episodes of grief are very frequent immediately after the loss as they seem to occur spontaneously. With the passing of time they occur less frequently and only when something brings the loss to mind. One could almost conceptualize that the episodes of grief in and of themselves constitute a discrete process within every mourning process. Grief episodes may occur because of a variety of reasons: a preoccupation with thoughts of the lost person, they may derive from an urge to search for the lost person, or an attempt to make sense of the loss and to fit it into the scheme of things. Although grief may include any and all of the above elements, the one unifying thread is that grief is triggered by painful repetitions and recollections of the loss experience.

The general clinical impression has been that children do have the ability to grieve. They may experience the full impact of grief in its most basic and elemental forms. The child may also choose to erect various defenses to ward off the intensity of the grief, or at least to diminish the acuteness and the severity of the accompanying pain. To what degree a child will be successful in accomplishing this task will depend on the nature of the defenses as part and parcel of the preloss personality organization. One would assume that the child's innate ability to tolerate pain would be a crucial determinant in the ability to deal with grief. The child's experience with anticipatory grief might be another contributing element to the ability to experience grief. One would assume then that the parent's ability to enhance or to interfere with the child's grief is rather limited.

Children and adults probably encounter the greatest difficulty in expressing anger toward the person that died. There is something about allowing oneself to sense anger, especially to feel it and to say it toward the person that died that suggests crossing over into forbidden territory. One can talk about being angry at the dead, one can even make a list of reasons why one would be justified in being angry, but to combine the content and the affect in the here and now is a formidable task.

Bowlby (1960) and Pollock (1961) regard anger and frustration in grief as inevitable and relate it to the initially primitive and insatiable nature of the yearning for the lost object. They attribute a special constructive role to the presence and discharge of anger in the mourning process.

One of the more memorable clinical experiences that I have encountered was an incident involving a rather morose, withdrawn seven-year-old boy whose father had died two years prior. After a prolonged discussion about his father's death he became silent and remained so for a long time, after some prodding he jumped up and yelled, "Okay, okay, so I hate his guts for dying on me like that, so what am I supposed to do, go to the cemetery and stomp on his grave?"

The intensity of the reaction and my resultant uneasiness about the explosiveness may well portend some hint as to why the adult tends to become uncomfortable with the child's anger. Children, far more easily than adults, acknowledge anger at the dead both for having died and for their shortcomings when still alive. Children are far more likely to direct their hostilities not only at the death itself but at the love object's deficiencies prior to the death.

Children often have an overriding need to recount and remember the flaws and the disappointments they experienced with the person that died. Such an expression has a driven, self-propelled quality, an urgent need for discharge as a part of mourning. The surviving adult, however, may have an extremely difficult time in allowing the child to express the anger because of its intensity, its lack of disguise, and its directness. In addition to the anger expressed, the child may also need some acknowledgment as well as validation of the objective reality that stimulated the complaints. If the surviving parent ignores this, or dismisses such questioning as fabrications of an impressionable mind, then not only will the child remain silent and turn the rage inward, but his reality testing as related to the internal image of the lost object may well become impaired.

The surviving adults, in their need to maintain an idealized picture of the one that died, may hide their own expressions of anger and disappointment from the child. This in part is due to the need to protect themselves from the open and direct manifestations of the child's rage.

Furman in her monograph *A Child's Parent Dies* (1974) has made the rather cogent point that the prelatency child needs permission from the surviving parent before he can allow himself to experience and particularly discharge sadness and anger in regard to the object's loss.

The child's anger toward and about the loss is expressed in a number of differing styles. The chronic sulking and grumbling, as expressions of anger in an indirect manner, are probably the ones that most adults find acceptable. On the other hand, anger that is expressed by the child in sudden, direct, intense outbursts is more than likely to stimulate parental anxiety.

The expression of anger toward the lost object by the child is interfered with by the surviving parent more than any other affect. Such an interference is probably doubly motivated. The child's hostility toward the lost object elicits anxiety in the surviving parent; it is almost as if the primitiveness and directness of the child's rage could actually hurt and destroy the lost object. In addition, the anger may elicit a retaliatory response from the lost object or perhaps some higher unknown power. The second motivation for the parent's interference stems from the anxiety that the intensity and undisguised nature of the child's rage could also hurt the surviving parent. Consequently, the interference is an attempt to deflect the anger in the service of protection of both parents, the one that is lost and the one that is still grieving.

Since much of the anger toward the lost object is interfered with and in turn deflected, one can assume that guilt is a prominent component that accompanies the hostility. Shame over the anger may also become a part of the clinical picture. However, a sense of shame about the loss is a separate response that has been documented in the psychoanalytic literature (Wolfenstein, 1969). The feeling of shame is not that obvious, but it does occur as an extension of a sense of being different due to the loss. The child feels a mild sense of embarrassment whereby the loss spotlights him as being set apart from his peers. This may be observed directly when the child tries to talk about the loss or it emerges indirectly as the child works at making it known that he is just like the other kids. Such an overemphasis on sameness and averageness may become accentuated in the adolescent who lost a parent. Since the feeling of shame is so subtle, most parents will not recognize it or respond to it. Even if they do become aware of it, the usual response is: What does he have to be ashamed of anyway?

It is with the expression of *sadness* that there seems to emerge the most consistent sense of congruence between the affects of the adult and the affects of the child. The sadness of the child is responded to, appreciated, and supported by significant adults whether it be the surviving parent or the child's therapist. Consequently, the child is more perceptive to, aware of, and far more expressive of his sad state. Whether the sadness is grieving for the lost object, identification with mourning relatives, or a reaction to the withdrawal of grieving adults, the child shows and is usually able to express his sad feelings.

For many children sadness, which may be expressed via crying and sobbing, could perhaps be seen as the beginning of relief (Furman, 1974). In some children prolonged and inconsolable sobbing can frequently be observed as a function of their age and inherent preloss personality structure and defenses. Initial weeping in response to the loss seems to increase with age. Children under five years of age cried little, if at all, or at best they did it sporadically. Latency-age children seemed to cry more consistently but still on a rather sporadic basis while children over ten seemed to cry copiously and for prolonged periods of time.

Some young children's pain, as manifested via longings and sadness, can be so poignant that adults do not allow themselves to observe it. This may be due to the surviving parent's inability to mourn or the anxiety about the regressive wishes stirred up in the adult. However, the adult's inability to observe and empathize with the child's sadness is far more difficult to understand. Might it not be possible that the intensity and directness of the child's feelings represent a threat to the surviving adult's precarious defenses?

Still, the sadness of the child whose parent has died elicits the most compassionate and empathic response in the adult. Within certain limits the child's sadness is probably the most prominent emotional state available for recognition and empathy. It seems that the child's interactions with significant adults are facilitatory toward the expression, understanding, and integration of sad feelings far more than any other affective state.

Although we have touched on grief, sadness, and rage as primary affective components of the mourning process, there are other affects which may be equally important. Although they may not always be associated with mourning per se, they are nevertheless a significant part of the clinical picture.

Anxiety is a crucial component of any mourning process. Since the child has lost one parent there is generally the fear that he may lose the other parent also, either by death or perhaps in some other way. The child may express this anxiety by a constant need to know the parent's whereabouts, schedule, and plans. There may be much emotional and physical clinging to the surviving parent, especially during periods of stress and at night.

The child's anxiety may then be complemented and compounded by the anxiety of the surviving parent. The parent feeling alone, abandoned, and guilt-ridden may experience anxiety via physical symptoms and an excessive preoccupation with his or her own health and well-being. The parent's anxiety about being alone and their well-being may have something to do with why so many parents find themselves sleeping in the same bed with their children after a loss. Anxiety, probably more than any other affective state, may exhibit an additive effect between the feelings of the child and those of the parent. It is also a basic affective state which is readily transmitted from the parent to the child and vice versa. The hypochondriacal concerns, the phobias, and the general anxieties of the mother have a way of being transmitted to the child. They may be expressed in a different form and elaborated by the child's own personality characteristics. Still there is a complementary relationship and a mutual feeding and fueling of the anxieties of both partners.

It may be that the surviving parent is not the initiator of the child's anxiety; but it does seem that the parent has a rather active part in perpetuating it.

CONGRUENCE OF AFFECTIVE STATES

Brenner (1974) has indicated rather cogently that all the different words that connote the general and specific categories of affects cannot be defined except in approximate terms. Affects are not precisely the same in any two individuals indeed, they are radically different from person to person. Each affect is unique for each individual, and such differences may have something to do with developmental differences in childhood. In addition, such differences in affective states in the child may also have something to do with how significant adults help the child in observing affects in others, perceiving affects in themselves, differentiating and labeling them, as well as allowing permission to experience and to express them.

From early life children are witnesses to how their parents, relatives, and other significant adults handle traumatic experiences and their associated affects. Children are acutely sensitive to how significant adults handle loss. The child's capacity to deal actively with these experiences may reflect the nature of their passive experiences in these situations as well as their learning. If the environment is emotionally open and feelings are expected to be expressed, he will participate more fully in the bereavement process. If the opposite situation is presented to the child, then he may enter into the adult conspiracy and conform to the expectation of seeing no sorrow, hearing no grief, and expressing no sense of loss. Children are quick to perceive the signs and signals so that when a parent stays silent, the child, due to his compliant nature, will stop asking questions. When a parent demonstrates a fear of feelings then the child may proceed to hide his own.

To find the proper words to describe his feelings the small child needs help from his parents; he needs to be taught. The child quickly learns that adults are often far more concerned with how he expresses his feelings than how he feels. The child may also have trouble having his feelings understood since certain words may be forbidden because of their undesirable associations.

Children under five years of age and through their early latency years still need a love object's help in recognizing, verbalizing, and tolerating affects. Such teaching by the adult not only facilitates the child's cognitive appreciation of affective states, but it also contributes to an identification with the adult's permissive stance in dealing with painful feelings. The midlatency child may not necessarily have the need to learn how to identify emotional states; however, the model for openness with one's painful feelings is still necessary.

It has been variously suggested that one of the most crucial elements in the child's ability to mourn the death of a parent may be a certain parallel between the mourning of the child and the surviving parent. In other words, if the parent has more or less completed the mourning work then it would be helpful for both if the child has reached a similar stage. It is indeed useful for each one if the mourning process of the parent and that of the child are in rhythm or in phase with one another.

Kliman (1969) expressed a similar idea when he indicated that one of the crucial therapeutic approaches with the surviving parent may be some child guidance whereby the parent is taught to appreciate the different rhythms of his child and the child's mourning.

Such an idea emphasizes the possibility that there evolves a congruent series of interactions between the mourning activity of the child and the mourning process of significant adults. What we are suggesting is that on a more microscopic level there also ensues a congruent relationship between the affective experience of the child and that of the parent. If the parent is experiencing anger and hostility toward the lost object while the child is in the midst of profound longing and sadness, then such a variance and dissonance of affective states may lead to conflict between the surviving parent and the child.

Although there is an awareness that affective states are fluid and dynamic rather than fixed entities, we are addressing ourselves to the notion that these are more or less valid approximations which are constantly changing in the day to day interaction between parent and child.

Since the cognitive and emotional development of the child is more fluid than that of the adult, the parent then has to be aware that the child may not sustain a particular affective state for a long period of time. While a specific affective state of the parent may remain stable—the younger child may shift in his feelings about the lost object rather easily and frequently. The child may also shift in his activity level and his interests as a means of defending against the painful affects related to the loss. As development has a certain back and forth or to and fro rhythm, the parent should not be surprised that the child may have to go back and rework a previously seemingly mastered position. Just because something has been dealt with in a satisfactory manner previously does not preclude the possibility that the younger child has an all-pervasive need to return to the same painful issue and rework it all over again. The net result is a situation in which the parent has the need to impose closure on certain mourning-related issues while the child still feels driven to open the wounds with painful questions and equally painful statements about the loss. One may conclude then that perhaps the most common interferences in the child's ability to complete the work of mourning are the various dissonances between the affective states of the grieving adult and the grieving child.

LEARNING ABOUT MOURNING

In the work with parent loss cases at the Barr-Harris Center we have attempted to examine those clinical situations in which children were removed from treatment before the therapeutic work was completed. One of the repeated findings has been that in situations where the child was withdrawn from the treatment prematurely there may have been a certain dissonance between the mourning of the child and that of the surviving parent. Consequently, there has emerged an increasing appreciation for the notion that the child and the surviving parent should be able to mourn together, whether this be for the sake of mutual comfort, permission, or the validation of mutually experienced affective states. If the child and the parent were at the level of experiencing incongruous affective states it is indeed possible that such would interfere with the child's ability to mourn. We assume that the child is in a more dependent, helpless, and compliant state vis-à-vis the needs of the parent. If there is a dissonance between these affective states it is plausible that the child would withdraw and mourn in complete solitude and isolation.

Since congruence between the mourning of the parent and the affective state of the child is a theoretical ideal and practical impossibility, then what can be accomplished to make the two more compatible?

It might perhaps be considered a useful therapeutic undertaking if the bereaved parent were to be taught something about the mourning process of the child. The parent needs to learn that the child is indeed capable of engaging is some type of mourning activity, but that the child does it differently from the adult.

The content aspect of the mourning work that the

grieving parent needs to know in order to respond reasonably to the child's questions and requests can be taught and it can be learned. For the content has to do with data accumulated by professionals over many years as well as with commonsense issues that most individuals are capable of arriving at on their own. The bulk of the initial therapeutic interventions are content oriented, for that is the most comfortable manner of initiating meaningful interactions between patient and therapist.

Once the parental anxiety has diminished and the parent has achieved the sense of knowing what to say and how to say it, then the process components need to be addressed.

The process aspects of these interactions are far more difficult to master by the patient and just as difficult to teach by the therapist. The reason for such a difficulty is rooted in the evanescent nature and vagueness of the therapeutic process. To teach another person how to feel, what to feel, and when to feel is an extremely difficult if not an impossible task. The only way this can be done is via the leverage of an ongoing therapeutic relationship.

However, there is something that the parent can be taught, and in turn the parent can teach the child. The parent can be taught to listen, to observe, to notice, and to identify for the child what he is feeling. The parent needs to know something about what, how, and why the child feels certain things. Most importantly, the parent has to learn just how the child's feelings about the loss are very different from his own. One of the main points that one can transmit to a parent is that the intrinsic rhythm of mourning is different for the child and the adult. Once the parent can understand that and perhaps even accept it, he will permit and facilitate the child's expression of his own feelings. The parent will then teach by his awareness of these basic differences and also by example.

It can also be taught that often the adult and the child

will be out of phase with one another in what they think and remember about their mutual loss, in addition to what they feel about it, so that the feelings of one may make the other uncomfortable, but that is expected and appropriate. For even though there may be such dissonance of affective states, it is still crucial that parent and child should be able to know, to appreciate, and perhaps even understand some of the differences. It is also important for the parent to know that the child cannot mourn as the adult does, nor as the adult says he does. For the parent to be aware of such distinctions may keep him from interrupting or interfering with the varieties of mourning activities experienced by the child. If that should indeed happen, then the child will know that he has the choice to mourn together with the adult as well as to mourn alone. That is something that is very important to learn and to know; in fact, it seems that such a freedom is one of the most crucial elements of this complex process called mourning.

REFERENCES

Bowlby, J. (1960), Grief and mourning in infancy. *The Psychoanalytic Study of the Child,* 15:9–52. New York: International Universities Press.

Brenner, C. (1974), On the nature and development of affects: A unified theory. *Psychoanal. Quart.,* 43:532–556.

Demos, E. V. (1974), *Children's Understanding and Use of Affect Terms.* Unpublished doctoral dissertation. Harvard University, Cambridge, MA.

Deutsch, H. (1937), Absence of grief. *Psychoanal. Quart.,* 6:12–22.

Furman, E. (1974), *A Child's Parent Dies. Studies in Childhood Bereavement.* New Haven, CT: Yale University Press.

Garber, B. (1981), Mourning in children: Toward a theoretical synthesis. *The Annual of Psychoanalysis,* 9:9–19. New York: International Universities Press.

Jacobson, E. (1967), Introjection in mourning. *Internat. J. Psychiat.,* 3:433–435.

Kliman, G. (1969), *Psychological Emergencies of Childhood.* New York: Grune & Stratton.

Mahler, M. (1961), On sadness and grief in infancy and childhood:

Loss and restoration of the symbiotic love object. *The Psychoanalytic Study of the Child,* 16:332–357. New York: International Universities Press.

Pollock, G. (1961), Mourning and adaptation. *Internat. J. Psycho-Anal.,* 42:341–361.

Schwartz, R. (1981), *A Developmental Study of Children's Understanding of the Language of Emotions.* Unpublished doctoral dissertation, University of Chicago.

Surbey, R. (1979), Self knowledge and emotional development. In: *The Development of Affect,* ed. M. Lewis & L. Rosenblum. New York: Plenum Press.

Wolfenstein, M. (1966), How is mourning possible? *The Psychoanalytic Study of the Child,* 21:93–123. New York: International Universities Press.

———— (1969), Loss, rage and repetition. *The Psychoanalytic Study of the Child,* 24:432–460. New York: International Universities Press.

Chapter 15

The Psychoanalytic Self
Psychologist Looks at Learning

ERNEST S. WOLF, M.D.

INTRODUCTION

Over sixty years ago, in 1925, in a preface to August
Aichhorn's pioneering volume on the psychoanalytic approach to education, *Wayward Youth,* Freud made his
famous remark about the three impossible professions,
namely, educating, healing, and governing. I think one
can safely say that Freud's comments, which he repeated
fifteen years later in his *Outline of Psychoanalysis* (1940),
are just as true today as they were in his own time. Yes,
the demands made on teachers, healers, and governors
are often just as unreasonable and impossible to fulfill
today even though, indeed, both teachers and healers
perform with a great deal more competence and effectiveness than their predecessors in former generations
were able to do. As a people we are better educated and
healthier than ever before. Psychoanalysis, to the extent
that it is a healing profession (beyond it's primary raison
d'etre of being a science of subjectively experienced mental states and a method for researching in this scientific
field) probably has become a mite less impossible as a
result of the advances made during the last two decades

through the introduction by Heinz Kohut of the selfobject concept.

In this chapter I shall look at the contributions that the introduction of the selfobject concept has made, or can make at least potentially, to the theory and practice of the teaching-learning process. The significance of referring to these activities neither as teaching nor as learning but as a teaching-learning process lies in the recognition—now almost generally accepted though not always acted upon—that information is not passed from teacher to learner via language and writing like milk passes from cow to child in a pail, but that teaching-learning is a process in which at least two people actively participate. Teacher and learner function as a unit sharing and creating not only information about the world around them but simultaneously and *necessarily* also share, create, and participate in each other's inner experience of themselves and of the other. This sounds like deceptively simple common sense that every good teacher knows, but admittedly it is very difficult to conceptualize clearly this very complex intersubjective experience. Moreover, the active participation of both partners in the educational enterprise is not mere decorative icing to sweeten the essentially bitter pill of knowledge being dispensed by the teacher for swallowing by the student. Rather, the fundamental proposition here is that without a mutually responsive active relationship there can be no learning. As Anthony says in chapter 4, "the child, as he appears through psychoanalytic eyes or through the views of Piaget, is never a bucket."

THE SELFOBJECT CONCEPT AND ITS APPLICATION TO EDUCATION

The newborn baby is a living, breathing, metabolizing, and experiencing organism. In order for it to survive these processes of life, the breathing, the metabolizing, and the

experiencing have to be maintained. The baby's environment has to supply what is needed for the baby's life to
continue. In other words, the baby is born preadapted for
a certain environment and it begins a physical and a
psychological interchange with its surroundings from the
moment of birth, in fact, it continues an interchange that
already began in utero. Without oxygen, nourishment,
warmth, and so on the baby cannot survive, and it is
equally true that the baby requires an active response
from one or more persons, a psychological response that
takes the form of holding, touching, rocking, smiling,
making soothing noises, talking to the baby, stimulating
the baby to respond in variety of ways. Without an adult
actively responding to the baby in a mutually interactive
age-appropriate pattern in such a way as to give the baby
the psychological experience of being cared for and thus
creating a certain psychological ambience the baby will
not survive. Even if these psychological responses are
present but in an inappropriate or faulty or distorted form
the baby will be damaged, sometimes very seriously. Such
children grow into psychologically deficient and handicapped adults. It is here that the origins of much of mental
illness, emotional illness, and behavior disorder are to be
found.

Sometime during the second year of life the child becomes aware of being a person, an "I," a self. In order for
this sense of self to emerge a subtle dialogue has to have
occurred between the child and the person or persons of
his surround. The most important of these persons usually is the mother, and for convenience sake I will talk
about child and mother without mentioning each time
that there are often other persons in the surround who
can be just as important for the child's development.

What is it that the child needs for the self to emerge
and to become strong enough so that we, as outsiders,
can say without a doubt in our minds: this child is a
person, it has a secure sense of itself or, even better, a

sense of its self? Kohut (1984) discovered that the child needs to have two kinds of psychological experiences. (1) It needs to be made to feel that its being here as an important member of the family is taken for granted, unconditionally. In other words, the child must feel accepted for what it is, for what it experiences itself to be, for what it has been, and for what it is going to be: its being is unconditionally good and wonderful—an experience of bliss in knowing itself to be the apple of mother's eye. The activity of the mother that brings about this blissful state is often called mirroring. But the child is not a passive onlooker to this activity of the mother. Indeed, the child actively participates by mirroring itself in the mother's warmly responsive demeanor. The blissful state is called the *grandiose self*—a rather misleading term perhaps, because it represents the point of view of the detached adult outsider, an "objective" observer and not the point of view of the child. (2) The child must have available to it the experience of becoming part of a larger, stronger, calmer, better "other." The child partakes of this elevating experience when, for example, it is being held close, or lifted up by the strong hands of the beautiful, perhaps one should say "godlike" creature, the mother. The mother's activity here we call availability for idealization. The child's bliss here is the result also of its own psychological activity of *merging* with the idealized selfobject, of experiencing itself as part of the idealized selfobject.

In the first kind of experience the child becomes a self by feeling itself mirrored in the mother's responsive glow, and in the second kind of experience the child becomes a self as part of the idealized other. Both kinds of psychological experiences are necessary for the child's self to emerge and to remain cohesively whole, just as both oxygen and nourishment are needed for the child's body to live and to remain healthy. But, of course, both kinds of experiences do not have to be present simultaneously all the time, they may oscillate and one may predominate over the other.

Since it is objects, at first mother and father, and later teachers and others, that perform the functions which allow the child's self to exist and to emerge and to be whole, we call these functions selfobject functions, or selfobjects for short. When we say, rather imprecisely, that a parent or a teacher has become a selfobject for a child we always mean that the teacher or parent performs functions for the child which let the child experience itself as a self. It is important to distinguish the selfobject functions from other psychological functions performed by objects such as parents, teachers, or others. Thus a teacher may fulfill all kinds of needs for the child which are not selfobject needs. For example, the child needs information which the teacher supplies. To function as a source of information is a legitimate activity and can develop a useful interpersonal relationship between two people. However, I think by the activity of teaching we understand something different, something that involves both teacher and learner in a more actively and mutually responsive relationship. Teaching, in my view, is at least in part a selfobject function. To mention some other examples, teachers may help children with a variety of skills, such as putting on their boots, or drawing a house, or writing a sentence. The teacher here performs a function within a context of an interpersonal relationship that fulfills the psychological need to be instructed in a skill, and which usually is not experienced as self-sustaining: therefore, this is primarily an interpersonal and not a selfobject relationship. The teacher is not needed to respond to selfobject needs. Nevertheless, it is common for certain interpersonal relationships to take on selfobject functions. For instance, a student may have a music teacher who instructs him in the playing of a musical instrument. Twice a week the student goes to have violin lessons, let us say. The teacher instructs, he praises, and he criticizes. Gradually, the student seems to need more than mere instruction in skills because the teacher has taken on an additional meaning for the student. The student's feeling of well-being begins to depend, to some extent, on how he perceives the teacher feels about him: "He is frowning, he doesn't like me anymore, I feel terrible, what have I done, he hates me because I said. . . ." Psychoanalysts will recognize the clues to an emerging transference relationship. The teacher has taken on a selfobject function; that is, the student's self needs to feel mirrored by the teacher, or needs to feel the teacher is available for merging the self into an idealized selfobject. No longer can the student easily take himself and his violin elsewhere to another teacher like he might take his shoes to a different shoemaker or his car to a different mechanic. A situation has developed that in crucial respects is analogous to that outlined above as constituting the self/selfobject relation between child and parent. When this occurs in a psychoanalytic treatment it becomes the pivot around which the treatment process revolves. We call it a selfobject transference. In the learning-teaching situation this occurrence is usually not as regularly recognized as in the analytic situation and both participants probably try as best they can to ignore or somehow get around this "emotional involvement." The essence of this involvement consists of an interpersonal relationship having taken on the functions of a selfobject relationship. Most students are ready to form such a selfobject transference with teachers very quickly, just as they are transference ready with their doctors or with their counselors. Fortunately, these selfobject transferences ordinarily do not become intense enough to disturb seriously the teaching-learning process. The specially constructed psychoanalytic situation with its own rules and rituals is designed to facilitate the emergence of these transferences in intensely amplified form for their analytic and therapeutic usefulness. However, I have observed in a few instances the disturbing emergence of such intense transference reactions in educational situations. I have seen both teachers and students become extremely upset on such occasions because they did not know what was happening nor did they know how to cope except by fleeing from the anxiety which was aroused. Some teachers after a few such experiences develop a protective style of distancing themselves emotionally from their students. Such defensive postures do aid in protecting the teacher, albeit at the price of losing the intuneness necessary for good teaching.

In summary, the child-teacher relationship, as an interpersonal relationship, fulfills many interpersonal needs of the child. These are not selfobject needs. It is only to the extent that the teacher supplies a needed selfobject function which is experienced by the child as a confirmation of its self that we can talk about a selfobject relationship with the teacher.

Should teachers be concerned about their students' selfobject needs? Why should they bother? After all, teachers are there to teach and not to heal.

Unfortunately, it is not that simple. We do worry about the child's physical needs lest they interfere with the capacity for learning. We make sure, for example, that the classroom is appropriately aired and heated, we try to make sure that the child had something to eat and is not sick. We know that a child whose body is not functioning well, a sick child, will not learn very well.

The same is true of the child's psychological well-being, the well-being of its self. Unless we make sure that the child's sense of self is secure, that it has a minimum of self-esteem, it will not learn well either. The child needs a steady supply of selfobject responsiveness, its "psychological oxygen," in order for its self to be cohesive and functioning well. A cohesive self is curious, eager to learn, and we think of such children as well motivated for learning. In contrast, a child whose self has not had sufficient selfobject nutriment will come into the class-room with a fragmenting self. This psychologically starved child will be overwhelmingly concerned with its self cohe-sion, with satisfying the various selfobject demands that imperiously assert themselves in the form of all kinds of symptoms among which the inability to concentrate on his studies is prominent. We think of such children as poorly motivated for learning, as indeed they are because they are primarily motivated for psychological survival.

Furthermore, what I have been saying about children is true also of all adults. We continue to need selfobject responses from our environment until the day we die. It is only the form of these selfobject needs which changes. Whereas infants need the concrete presence and activities of the parents, and later children need the sibling or the peer friend, or the teacher, as adults we gradually come to substitute more symbolic and less concrete selfobject functions. For example, quite in addition to our intimate relationships with family and friends, we may derive part of our experience of being mirrored by belonging to a professional community that gives us recognition and affirmation of our professional selfs. We usually have available to us also a variety of experiences of merging with idealized selfobjects. We may merge our selfs into an admired author by reading his novels, or into an ad-mired character in the novel. We may immerse our selfs into the grandiosity of a Beethoven symphony or into the magnificent structure of a Bach fugue. We may merge into the ideals of our country or our religious beliefs or our *Weltanschauung*. For each stage in life there exist appropriate selfobject functions to be experienced. With-out these, one begins to deteriorate psychologically, one becomes insecure, feels anxious or depressed, and one's general functioning in life deteriorates along with the falling apart of one's self.

Thus, as teachers, we also need our students to confirm our teachers' selfs, to mirror us. We use them also to look up to as having great potential, to be available to us as potential idealizable selfobjects, for our idealizing needs. Perhaps we need our students less than they need us—let us hope so. But unless we can get a dialogue going, a dialogue within a mutually responsive and reciprocally self-sustaining ambience, there will be precious little education.

LEARNING AND THE ACQUISITION OF STRUCTURE

What do we mean when we say that the child has learned something? For me this is a very difficult question. Sometimes we mean that the child has acquired a skill; for example, he can tie his shoes. Sometimes we mean that the child has acquired some knowledge. For example, he knows the dog's name is Chelsea and he can use this knowledge when calling the dog. Sometimes we mean that he now acts as if he knew something; for example, as if he were afraid of someone without consciously being aware of this. Perhaps whenever his Uncle Edgar comes to visit the youngster is very subdued and manages to disappear; yet when asked he will assure us of liking his uncle and seems totally unaware of his peculiar behavior when this man is present.

One could enumerate other kinds of learning but for our purposes that is not necessary. Let us make one assumption: all learning represents the acquisition of some psychological structure. Some experience has taken on an enduring form in the child's mind so that now it patterns the child's relationship to those elements that made up the experience. Of course, when speaking about psychological structures we are using a metaphor. Structures in the sense of three-dimensional objects cannot exist in psychological space but only in physical space. A psychological structure is an enduring configuration of relationships with a past, a present, and a future. Enduring means that it normally changes only very slowly, perhaps comparable to the growth of a tree. I know of no other way of talking about psychological concepts than in such metaphors.

So our original question about what we mean when we say that the child, or the adult, has learned something has now become "what do we mean by conceptualizing that the child has acquired some new psychological structure?"

I shall now attempt to illustrate how this process of acquiring new psychological structure occurs in a psychoanalytic treatment. In doing so I am proposing a second assumption, namely that the basic processes of structure formation are the same whether they occur within the psychoanalytic situation or out of it. The psychoanalytic situation is distinguished from most others by setting up conditions and rules which favor the formation of structures that emerged crippled or not formed at all during the normal developmental process. The teaching-learning situation is set up in such a way as to facilitate the age-appropriate acquisition of certain cognitive capacities of the self by increasing the self's structuralization.

Of course, the fact that selfobject relations can give structure to the self does not in any way deny or diminish the facts about the constitutional givens which are the basic substrate upon which experience works its effects. Psychoanalytic self psychology does not ignore heredity and constitution any more than the physician does who prescribes diet and exercise to build up his patient's body. We deal with those aspects that we can modify and try not to waste too much time on what we cannot alter.

> A young woman during the second year of her analytic treatment was complaining bitterly about her boyfriend whose interest in attending certain sports events with his school buddies while she was sitting at home

left her feeling alone and abandoned. As I listened I
was able to resonate with her experience of disappointment and anger and let her know that I understood.
But my thoughts also wandered to the usefulness to
her if she could gain some understanding of what made
him act in this strange manner (which I did not find
strange at all) and I began to explain to her something
about *his* needs to feel part of his group of buddies and
I conjectured about *his* need not to be thought of by
them as being under the thumb of his girlfriend. My
explanation was received with cold silence and an unmistakable aura of tension had entered the room. I
knew, almost immediately, that I had made one of those
unavoidable faux pas where seemingly from the best
of intentions the analyst momentarily abandons the
stance of empathy with the analysand and assumes,
perhaps for very good reasons, a different posture. In
this case I had become empathically understanding of
him rather than of her and, in addition, had become
educational (about him) rather than analytical. The
silence did not last long but for the remainder of that
session the tension persisted. The subsequent analytic
session opened with an angry outburst by the analysand—I cannot recall precisely to which of my various
shortcomings she had displaced her outrage. I accepted
her rage as clearly justified from her point of view and
so indicated to her without apology or feeling any regret. I reviewed what I thought had happened, rather
matter of factly, and—this is the crucial step—she was
able to pull herself together and begin to participate
in this mutual exploration of the sequence of psychological events leading to the disruption of the previously reigning harmonious selfobject transference.
While I did *not* explain to her my (to me reasonable)
motivation for my break of empathic understanding of
her, she spontaneously began to see it also from my
point of view and to credit me with the benefits she
derived from understanding her boyfriend better. By
this time the tension had vanished and we both knew
we understood each other better than before this in-

cident, an incident that from the point of view of the
"objective" outside observer may indeed appear to be
quite trivial.

Subsequently, similar "empathic breaks" commonly
recurred with renewed outbreaks of rage though the
latter seemed to diminish each time. Eventually, it was
possible to examine her relationship with her boyfriend
from all sides without inordinate anger at me or at him
and concomitantly with a gradually deepening relationship between the two of them.

I propose that in the above clinical vignette one can
discern the process of structure formation underneath the
surface manifestations of a disrupted and then healed
intersubjective relationship. However, the kind of structure formation described has been variously criticized as
not really being psychoanalytic but as representing a
kind of "corrective emotional experience" as advocated
by Alexander (Alexander and French, 1946, pp. 66–70).
Alexander suggests planned reexposure of the patient to
emotional situations he could not handle in the past. To
achieve this the therapist attempts actively to assume
attitudes modeled to be in contrast to those of the parents.
Such active role playing is not part of the armamentar-
ium of the self psychologically informed psychoanalyst.
Self psychology recognizes the spontaneity and inevita-
bility of the transference repetition regardless of what
the therapist is really like and regardless of how the
therapist actually acts. However, self psychology emphasizes the recognition of the fact that the transferential
repetition is experienced by the patient as *real* in the here
and now and that cure can come only when the empathic
understanding of this reality is joined by insight into its
etiological precursors. The latter insight usually is facilitated by the analyst's interpretation. Furthermore, self
psychology stresses the necessity of providing a warmly
neutral and responsive ambience that avoids giving the
patient actual reasons in the present for his always in-

evitable transference response. Thus the patient will find it more and more difficult to avoid the conclusion that he is overreacting to a rather stable and mostly benign analyst. He gradually begins to realize that his real feelings are being evoked so strongly in the present because he experiences the analyst as if he were acting like a figure from the past regardless of the analyst's actual demeanor. This insight must come from within the patient and cannot be imposed by the analyst. For this insight to occur the analyst must refrain from actually acting in the cold, or rejecting, or noxious, or overbearing, or domineering, or know-it-all, or seductive manner that the patient accuses him of. The analysand must begin to realize that the analyst is attempting to understand his, the analysand's, subjective experience, no more and no less. In short, the analyst is there, available to understand the analysand, but not to impose any part of himself.

To be really understood by another human being is, indeed, a gratifying experience. It is not a gratification of either sexual or aggressive instincts or their derivatives. It is a positive response to a self's need for a confirming ambience.

How can we conceptualize the formation of psychological structure as a result of the sequence of emergence-disruption-restoration of a selfobject transference? Do concepts like "internalization" really clarify or do they beg the question of how and what is being internalized? It seems to be more productive to expand Kohut's concept of "empathic resonance" (Kohut, 1984). He suggested that empathic resonance means replacing the archaic selfobject need with the analyst's empathic understanding. Certainly we can observe in our analytic practice every day how feeling oneself understood becomes such a self-sustaining and self-confirming experience for our patients that the old and terrible need for some particular *archaic* selfobject response begins to fade away. The analysand who at one time was always terribly upset when

I did not greet him at the door with a warmly inviting smile can now accept my friendly but mainly matter of fact manner because he knows and feels himself understood by me. But in order to claim that this observable change represents an increment of new structure one would have to demonstrate the relative permanence of this change and its persistence in my absence. Indeed, the notable improvement in this analysand's relations with people outside of the analytic situation allows one to infer such an accretion of new psychological structure. Still, I cannot easily conceptualize how this new structure got there from his experience of being understood. Does he now carry with him at all times an image of being understood by me? Is this what we mean by internalization? Is the new structure, therefore, the memory or the image of being understood? What alternate possibilities of conceptualizing these changes can be constructed? I do not know. Clearly, this would be an important area for further clinical and theoretical research in psychoanalysis.

CONCLUSION

I propose to extend my earlier assumption of the analogy of teaching-learning to psychological structure formation by assuming that the sequence emergence-disruption-restoration may be just as crucial in the educational situation as in the analytic one. At first glance this looks quite artificial and not at all in accordance with the usual way we think about good teaching and easy learning. Can we not all think back on having had some wonderful experiences with great teachers where almost literally we sat at their feet and took their words and their thoughts into ourselves to make them our own? Identification, yes; internalization, yes; but disruption-restoration, no!

But let us not give up so quickly. For now let us confine

our discussion to formal educational settings. What is the actual and typical sequence of events when a child leaves home to go to school or even when it does not leave home but the tutor comes to the child? In either case the child leaves one ambience for another. The "home ambience," whatever its possible shortcomings, is a context that has become familiar to the child. The child has adapted, more or less successfully, to the tensions and conflicts as well as to the opportunities for enrichment and growth open to it. It has learned how to obtain at least some minimal selfobject sustenance and how best to avoid or to defend against fragmentation threats. In fact, one might well say that in normal circumstances the child has become so familiar as to have become part of the family, of the very ambience in which it finds itself. All this changes radically as the child leaves the "home ambience" to enter the "school ambience." No longer does everything and everybody feel familiar, nor does the child still feel fully part of the new surround. School represents not the family but the outside world, education is about those strange and wonderful and threatening and exciting things and people out there. Even the most secure and emotionally healthy child will experience some loss of self cohesion upon entering this alien milieu until it adapts to the newly offered, self-sustaining selfobject sources. The child's anxiety and the hope for needed selfobject support focus on the teacher. The stage is set for the kind of disruption-restoration sequence that in the analytic situation we have identified as the nuclear experience in the acquisition of structure (i.e., of knowledge).

Let us follow the child into the classroom. The well tuned-in teacher will make some appropriate comments to support the child's self-esteem and both teacher and child will respond to each other in a mutually self-sustaining dialogue. The latter need not necessarily be all verbal. The child will begin to relax as the positive aspects of the relationship with the teacher grow. The anal-

ogy to the gradually established selfobject relationship
in an analytic situation is obvious. Similarly, we can discern the inevitable disruptions in the educational settings also. There occur the unavoidable expectations and
disappointments that both participants experience. For
example, the student is not ready to "learn" as well and
quickly as the teacher might expect, or the teacher, without doubt, will fail to understand the student as intimately and as responsively as the latter feels he absolutely
needs. Probably the intensity of the selfobject relationship, and consequently the disruptions of this relationship, cannot be nearly as intense in the educational
situation as in the analytic one because usually teacher
and student cannot be as intimately involved with each
other; and that is fortunate. The goal of education is not
to affect the deep structures of the personality, as in a
psychoanalysis, but more toward the surface oriented
structures that determine a person's skills and cognitive
capacities. Nevertheless, in both situations the success
of the enterprise depends on the healing of the disruptions. The responsibility for this falls most heavily on the
professional, whether analyst or teacher. It requires empathic sensitivity, thorough grounding in the theory and
practice of his professional mission, and patience and determination to stick it out through the inescapable ups-
and-downs.

Let me stop here without attempting to play out the
infinite variety of student-teacher interactions that have
the potential for creating the intersubjective experience
of mutually and reciprocally participating in spiraling
sequences of disruptions and restorations. Litowitz points
out in chapter 12 that we still are describing "the behaviors of [two] separate individuals, albeit mutually
patterning, finely orchestrated and unconsciously choreographed." Indeed, I join her in calling for a reversal
of perspective where we will look at the mother-child unit
or the teacher-learner unit from within the intersubjec-

tive space and try to study the "illusion of autonomous functioning." As Basch and I have suggested on previous occasions we must shift from self psychology to selfobject psychology (Wolf, 1983). But for now I am satisfied if we can add the self psychological perspective to our examination of the teaching-learning process.

REFERENCES

Alexander, F., & French, T. (1946), *Psychoanalytic Therapy.* New York: Ronald Press, pp. 66–70.

Erikson, E. (1959), Identity and the Life Cycle. *Psychological Issues,* Monograph 1, 1/1. New York: International Universities Press.

Freud, S. (1925), Forward to August Aichhorn's *Wayward Youth. Standard Edition* 19:273–275. London: Hogarth Press, 1967.

——— (1940), An outline of psychoanalysis. *Standard Edition* 23:209–254. London: Hogarth Press, 1964.

Kohut, H. (1984), *How Psychoanalysis Cures.* Chicago: University of Chicago Press.

Rapaport, D. (1960), The Structure of Psychoanalytic Theory: A Systematizing Attempt. *Psychological Issues,* Monograph 6, 2/2. New York: International Universities Press.

Wolf, E. (1983), Empathy and countertransference. In: *The Future of Psychoanalysis,* ed. A. Goldberg. New York: International Universities Press.

Chapter 16

The Organization of Resistances to New Learning in Psychoanalysis: A Developmental Perspective

BARBARA ROCAH, M.D.

Psychoanalysis is a process through which new knowledge—insight—is gained through interpretation of unconscious transference and resistances. Freud (1926, 1937) discussed two different theories of resistance to insight. His 1926 theory was a comprehensive structural formulation that described resistance as the unconsciously motivated defensive organization against infantile instinctual derivatives that were remobilized in the psychoanalytic situation. Freud described five types of resistances, each motivated by one of the three structural systems of the mental apparatus—id, ego, and superego. Interpretation of the infantile wish and the fear of retaliation that lay behind the resistance, plus the inadequate solution made by the immature ego of the child to coping with that danger, as well as the primary and secondary gain from infantile fixations and regressive adaptations, were supposed to lead to increments in self-knowledge through a process of working through.

However, Freud's discovery of instances in analysis where interpretation did not result in expectable structural change led him to make, in 1937, his now-famous statement about bedrock resistance. He stated that uncovering a woman's wish for a penis and a man's masculine protest signifies "that all psychological strata have been penetrated, that bedrock has been reached, and all analytic activities are at an end" (p. 252). He regarded bedrock resistance as biologically determined. Freud theorized that this type of resistance was beyond interpretation and could be attributed to the death instinct. This resistance functioned as a limitation to the overall effectiveness of psychoanalysis since it restricted the assimilation of new psychoanalytic knowledge by the individual. Sedler (1983) states that neither the life nor the death instinct has specific contents for consciousness. Both Freud and Sedler describe the aim of instinctual life as either to establish new unities and growth or to establish status and resist all change. Sedler, in agreement with Freud's views, sees the death instinct as exerting a force that opposes the psychoanalytic project of revision.

In this chapter, as in a previous paper (Rocah, 1984a), I shall also explore factors that oppose the psychoanalytic project of revision. I shall detail some cognitive factors that interact with perceptual and affective factors which contribute to resistance to new learning through psychoanalysis. The specific areas that I will examine are, first, presymbolic sensorimotor organizations, second, the synthesis of a symbolic self-schema, third, the synthesis of a symbolic object-schema, and fourth, transformation of the magical, phenomenalistic thinking of the two- to six-year-old to more logical frames of reference. The study of impairments in these four perceptual-cognitive-affective syntheses provides an alternative explanation based on biological factors that are consistent with modern developmental theory to account for the resistance to new learning that Freud called bedrock and attributed to instinctual sources. The available level of cognitive development determines how the child initially organizes its experience and later organizes its symbolically represented conscious and unconscious wishes and fantasies. The use of a cognitive frame of reference permits understanding of the influence of presymbolic organizations as well as later symbolic organizations on pathogenesis.

My plan in this chapter is as follows. I shall first summarize developmental research that is pertinent to understanding of the four perceptual-cognitive-affective syntheses involved in sensorimotor functioning in infancy, the development of a self-schema, the development of an object-schema, and the transformations of the magical phenomenalistic thinking of the two- to six-year-old to more logical frames of reference. I shall then present four clinical examples that demonstrate impairments, originating in each of the organizations I am considering, that opposed the psychoanalytic project of revision. I shall then discuss these examples and some additional ideas about the role of cognitive development in pathogenesis and reconstructive work in psychoanalytic treatment.

SENSORIMOTOR ORGANIZATIONS OF EXPERIENCE

The first perceptual-cognitive-affective synthesis that I shall examine is based on sensorimotor learning in a social context. It includes development of stable states of sleep-waking, hunger-satiation, and alertness-inattentiveness as described by Sander (1983). In addition Basch (1976) has described differentiated affect expressions in the infant that are stabilized by predictable environmental responses to inborn affect schema. Spitz (1959) and Emde, Gaensbauer, and Harmon (1976) have described the synthesis of two organizers of development: the smile response and stranger anxiety. These organizers signify syntheses of perceptual-cognitive-affective factors that

function as perceptual sets to facilitate specificity of infant social interaction and anticipation of events. Piaget
(1936, p. 216) proposes that development proceeds in infancy as a function of increasingly complex sensorimotor
schemata that govern action upon the world. In the repeated process of action and feedback, the infant assim-
ilates (internalizes) new information to existent structure.
Growth occurs as new assimilations change inherent sensorimotor schema to permit new, more complex adaptations.

Psychoanalysts have been interested in the integrations that take place through the internalization of regulatory interactions within a social infant–care-giver
system. Interactions within this system provide a context
in which learning takes place. Motives for continued interaction arise from the infant as well as the care giver.
Motives that have been attributed to the infant do not
assume knowledge of goals or symbolic self-awareness of
action. Motives are based on the infant's constitutional
prewiring (Shapiro and Stern, 1980) to behave and interact in specific ways. Freud (1911) postulated that tension reduction was one motive of this type. Others are
information searches (Kagan, 1974), resolution of perceptual discrepancies (Steckler and Carpenter, 1967), resolution of polarities determined by incomplete assimilation
and accommodation cycles (Piaget, 1936; Sander, 1975),
effectance motives (White, 1959), and alert attentiveness
(Freedman, 1979). These noninstinctual motives for interaction may emerge at different times throughout the
first year. They are patterned by appropriate environmental responses so that they become actual, serviceable
functions.

The care giver appears to be motivated by the infant's
alert attention (Freedman, 1979) and by the nonreflective, inborn, communicative affective signals (Basch,
1976; Emde, 1980) that communicate the infant's state
and guide the care giver's intervention. Differentiated

feedback by the care giver, who also provides novelty and stimulation to the infant (Steckler and Carpenter, 1967; Basch, 1976; Dowling, 1977) patterns this early perceptual-cognitive-affective integration.

This early phase of sensorimotor learning and internalization of social interactions illuminates those aspects of human behavior that are beyond verbalization of symbolic mental functioning and wishes. Any psychoanalytic reconstruction of these early states is inferred from residues of presymbolic action patterns which forestall disorganization, and Case 1 illustrates symbiotic patterns relied upon for that reason.

THE ORGANIZATION OF A SELF-SCHEMA

G. Klein (1976) defines the self-schema as a "supra-ordinate cognitive organization that functions as a reference point for subjective experience of integration and failure of integration [conflict], as well as constituting the locus of assimilative and accommodative activity [learning], motivation, and of ordering feedback" (p. 282). Observational data that pertains to the ontogeny of the self-schema have, in my opinion, been offered by Sander (1983) and Piaget (1966).

Sander (1983) describes naturalistic observations of infant–care-giving couples over a period of thirty-six months. In Sander's view the self is a holistic organization that guides the child in intentional interactions with others via mediating predispositions. These predispositions are organized in the first thirty-six months of life through negotiation of adaptive issues within the infant–caregiver system. Up to eighteen months the issues are negotiated presymbolically, and prerepresentationally, guided by increasingly complex sensorimotor combinations. Of interest to the present discussion is the fourth negotiated issue (twelve to fourteen months of age) that Sander terms *focalization of aims*. Focalization extends the manipulation of inanimate objects established in the third negotiated issue to the manipulation of other humans. The infant pressures the mother to accommodate to its activity. This intentionality is prerepresentational. Piaget (1966) uses the term *exercise play* to describe a similar phenomena. Exercise play is a presymbolic form of play that repeats sensorimotor activities for their own sake. These activities have been acquired elsewhere in the course of adaptation; they are motivated by effectance pleasure (Broucek, 1979) and confirm a newly acquired skill.

The significance of exercise play or focalization for the developing infant is that it permits, through active repetitions in new combinations, assimilation of what the child has perceived and passively experienced into the child's existent self-schema. The self-schema at this level of maturation is a presymbolic, nonrepresentational sensorimotor schema organized through repetitions (G. Klein, 1976; Gedo, 1979, 1981a) that cause an effect and repetitions that reverse passive experiences into active ones. In addition the self-schema is organized through infant initiative that is eventually transformed into intentional action toward real and symbolic goals. According to Sander (1983) infant initiative flowers in periods in which the infant's activity is not preempted by endogenous (drive, need) requirements or exogenous (social) requirements. Sander's investigations on these open spaces seem to confirm G. Klein's (1976) assertion that continuous conformity to social requirements skews development and is pathogenic insofar as it distorts expression of infant initiative, one of the foundations of a self-schema.

With the maturation of symbolic capacity the quality and form of the child's intentionality and initiative change. Sander (1983) describes an adaptive issue that he terms *reversal* which occurs between eighteen and thirty-six months of age. This adaptive issue, Sander feels, helps the child establish (self-consciously) that he is an active organizer of his own experience. Sander reports his observations of the intentional disruption of the established harmony in the care-giver system by the toddler followed by restoration of the harmony at either the care giver's or the infant's initiative. This behavior, in contrast to focalization, is dependent upon the child's cognitive capacity for imaging (interiorized action) a sequence of events that form a causal chain. In these sequences, as in the former sequences of focalization, the motive for the toddler's behavior is not adaptation to reality. On the contrary the motive is, as in focalization, assimilation of reality to the self-as-active-agent. Piaget (1966) terms this type of sequence *symbolic play*. In this symbolic play the child relies upon imitation of caretaking adults as signifiers of meaningful transactions that the child has experienced elsewhere. Although Piaget (1966) describes imitation as an accommodation to reality, in this instance these "deferred imitations the basis of symbolic play, are the instruments through which reality is transformed by assimilating experience to the self through construction of subjective signifiers" (Piaget, 1966, p. 492).

A further evolution of self-schema is suggested by Lichtenberg (1982), who states that "for the infant to emerge from the interactional matrix, the toddler is required to carry out intention in response to desire and at the same time monitor the sequence of events in relationship to mother's encouragements and prohibitions" (p. 22). This new factor, self-monitoring use of remembered feedback, indicates that self-continuity is a synthesis of desire (intentionality) and environmental pressure for conformity and accommodation. Self-continuity withstands auto-manipulation in thought (symbolic play, deferred imitation) as well as environmental influences that temporarily co-opt the child's open space and autonomy. Continuity or conservation of the self-schema would seem to be an equivalence of object conservation (Piaget,

1937), which I shall discuss below. In brief, internal continuity or conservation of self-schema withstands automanipulation in thought and the external influences that impinge on the child's open space.

The synthesis of self-schema, and object-schema, next to be described, are considered to be the basis of psychologically motivated behavior. Early affectively charged sensorimotor adaptations are transformed, with the aid of symbolization, into subjective organizations of experience that can be manipulated in thought and fantasy. Various interacting patterns associated with these subjective organizations can be inferred from dyadic transferences in analysis. Case 2 demonstrates a poorly organized self-schema in which contradictory schema were not ordered into unified goals.

THE ORGANIZATION OF AN OBJECT-SCHEMA

In the previous section I reviewed the origin of a child's self-schema from observational data. I shall now review parallel developmental complexities associated with what I term an *object-schema*.

An object-schema is a complex synthesis of three aspects of mental representation. An object-schema includes factors of object permanence and conservation of objects (Piaget, 1937). It also includes what has been termed *object constancy* (A. Freud, 1968; Hartmann, 1953). Finally, the term *object-schema* includes internalizations of learned interactive patterns that function as both self-regulatory and motivational structures.

The terms *object permanence* and *conservation of objects* were introduced by Piaget (1937) to describe stages in the epigenesis of reality. Object permanence is the end point of sensorimotor development. By eighteen months (stage 6 of sensorimotor development) the child is able to retain an image of an object's existence in the absence of perceptual cues and independent of direct action by the infant. Piaget infers that at this point action has been interiorized by the infant and the infant is capable of imaging. In Piaget's theory, this maturational advance modifies a child's naive egocentricity. This means that the child conceives of himself as well as the object as one among many, rather than viewing events as the results or extensions of one's own actions. In addition this maturational advance of imaging permits deferred imitation of experience and imaginative play. Although psychoanalysts have not been directly interested in the phenomena of object permanence, Kohut's (1971) definition of a differentiated other as an independent center of initiative is a psychoanalytic developmental concept based on cognitive object permanence.

In Piaget's developmental scheme the concept of conservation of the object is a later developmental advance belonging to the stage of concrete operations (ages six through twelve). Conservation is an immutable law that extends beyond objects recently handled, perceived, or invisibly displaced. It is a concept that describes the indestructability of matter as an abstraction beyond phenomenalism and subjectivity. Applied to other humans, it refers, it seems to me, to the child's capacity to perform mental operations on symbolic representations of interactions without destroying the representation.

Object constancy is an additional aspect of an object-schema. It is a term associated with Hartmann (1953), A. Freud (1968), and Mahler, Pine, and Bergman (1975). However, each of these authors defined the term differently. Hartmann (1953) defined object constancy as the neutralization of the aggressive and libidinal cathexis of an object. This was both an outcome of ego development and a contribution to further ego development. A. Freud (1968) defined object constancy as the capacity of a child to cathect an object image irrespective and independent of instinctual wish. Mahler and her colleagues (1975) defined the term as the child's capacity to maintain a stable, evocative image of the mother irrespective of either the child's need state or the mother's presence. This development is necessary as a prelude to the child's ability to tolerate separations from the mother. All of these authors are attempting to find a term to describe the stability of schemata pertaining to the mother in the absence of need states or wishes because psychoanalytic developmental theory includes the hypothesis that the child initially awakens to the world of objects insofar as he is driven by need. This model implies that need satisfaction extinguishes longing for contact with other humans. Sander's (1980) work on an infant's alert attentiveness and object-seeking behavior during periods of quiescence which he terms *open space* is a challenge to this psychoanalytic developmental theory. Although there are many who have challenged the psychoanalytic hypotheses of infants driven by instinctual needs and desire for tension relief, the term *object constancy* persists in the literature to describe the onset of the child's capacity for evocative memory and the relationship of subjective wish to the stability of mental representation. These considerations are important aspects of the child's eventual capacity to distinguish between action and wishful fantasy as well as to tolerate frustration of wishes.

The third aspect of the object-schema is based on the internalization of patterns of interaction with others that evolve into motivational structures and self-regulating structures. The level of cognitive development determines the significance of the internalization. For example, during the sensorimotor phase of cognitive development the partner is perceived as an extension of the child's action. In the preoperational phase the capacity to perceive another human being as a reciprocal partner develops along with the child's capacity to differentiate and symbolize qualities of partnership with other humans and their rections to the child's assertions and demands. The child learns to relinquish unacceptable erotic and aggressive aims based on his maturing capacity to remember responses from the environment to wishful expressions. Gedo (1979, pp. 222–223) proposes that the basis of the child's foregoing these aggressive and erotic aims is his acceptance of moral standards by virtue of his capacity to idealize parents and their authority. This is in contrast to Freud's view (1924) that the child's aggressive and sexual aims are relinquished on the basis of castration anxiety. Cases 3 and 4 in this chapter demonstrate derailments in both of these factors, which in my view are not mutually exclusive.

THE TRANSFORMATION OF THE MAGICAL, PHENOMENALISTIC THINKING OF THE TWO- TO SIX-YEAR-OLD CHILD INTO MORE LOGICAL FRAMES OF REFERENCE

Between eighteen months and six years there occurs a nodal phase of cognitive development that has been called by Piaget (1952) the preoperational phase in the development of logical thought. This period has special significance for psychoanalysts because it spans the period in which the Oedipus complex originates and is resolved. I shall direct my discussion to some speculations about the noninstinctual structure of the Oedipus complex as well as the cognitive complexities that are associated with its resolution.

I shall briefly review some material pertaining to cognitive development before discussing the Oedipus complex from this perspective. The preoperational phase of thought, from eighteen months to six years, replaces sensorimotor practical intelligence by the maturational capacity for symbolic representation of self and object schemata, imaging, and imagination. These representations are initially egocentric, affectively patterned, and are able to be manipulated in the child's fantasy in the absence of perceptual cues. This period of preoperational (prelogical, verbalized) thought is characterized further by the child accommodating his thinking processes to the appearance of things available to direct observation without concerning himself with the laws of transformation, conservation, reversibility, reciprocity, and relationships between systems. These just-mentioned laws form the basis of concrete operations, the next cognitive stage which begins between six and seven years and lasts until adolescence. Although within the preoperational stage, the child is able to grasp the notion of groupings and shift from static imaging about perceptions to more symbolic, subjectively organized meanings, the child typically perceives the end state of a group without concerning himself with the (invisible) transformations that led to the end state. One consequence of interest to psychoanalysts of this mode of prelogical mental functioning is that both boys and girls misinterpret the significance of difference between the sexes. Typically, children perceive the end point (presence or absence of penis) without concerning themselves with how that state came into being. It is interpreted in a magical-phenomenalistic manner by attributing absence to loss—as loss of the fecal column or loss of the urinary stream. What psychoanalysts term *castration anxiety* is an expression of uncertainty connected with prelogical thinking. It is universal because stages of cognitive development are biologically determined. Children differ in the capacity to resolve uncertainty by further investigation and integration. This difference is due to inherent factors of intelligence as well as environmental interference with learning (such as parents who undermine children's sexual curiosity).

By the time the child enters the concrete-operational phase of thinking, at six or seven years, subjectivity and personal satisfaction are gradually suspended in favor of accuracy. The child achieves objectification and decentering. Piaget terms the final phase in the development

of logical thought *propositional*. In this phase, which begins in early adolescence, the child is able to deal with
hypotheses about objects rather than requiring the presence of the objects themselves. Hypothetical deductive
reasoning becomes possible and with it the constitution
of a formal logic that is applicable to any kind of content.
Mutative insight that is associated with structural change
requires the capacity for propositional logic.

Although psychoanalysis is not the study of cognitive
development, there are nonetheless a growing number of
authors (G. Klein, 1976; Basch, 1977; Shapiro, 1977;
Gedo, 1979) who regard cognitive development rather
than hypothetical instinctual development as the biological continuity that underlies increasingly complex psychological behavior. These authors feel that psychoanalytic
emphasis on the significance of sexual wishes throughout
the life-cycle does not have to be accounted for by postulating a sexual instinct. The importance of sexuality
in early childhood can be accounted for by new cognitive
capacities that record sensual, pleasurable experience in
the motivational history of people from birth to adulthood. G. Klein (1976) states that

> [T]he occasions of sensual experience in activities, and
> positive and negative values which such experiences
> acquire are recorded in a cognitive structure or schema
> whose activation ever after helps to shape sensual ex-
> perience. The evolving cognitive record of sensual ex-
> perience is thus both a product of past sensual experience
> and a framework which shapes the content of current
> sensual experience. Experienced through that frame-
> work, the current sensual occurrences gather meaning
> beyond simply the affective sensual tone [p. 83].

In the preoperational phase the emergence of language
permits the child to inquire into the nature of his body
and those of adults. The responses to questions are subjectively organized into the infantile theories of sexuality

that Freud recognized. Kleeman (1965, 1966) demonstrates that learning about genitalia, feces, and urine is accompanied by confusion and uncertainty which is resolved unless the environment interferes. Comprehension of the significance of the anatomy and body products appears to be a discontinuous rather than linear process.

From the perspective of this discussion the Oedipus complex is a complex, perceptual, cognitive, affective organization of wishes directed toward specific individuals whom the child imagines will respond in predetermined fashion either by gratifying the child or punishing him. The child succumbs out of fear to this idealized authority. The child at this point is said to be self-regulating because he has adopted the adult point of view in regard to the expression of forbidden wishes. Such wishes are hereafter inhibited by arousal of affectual signals of guilt and shame. Resolution of the Oedipus complex depends upon the child acquiring a system of lawful rules governing human relationships.

Not only is the oedipally aged child expected to experience his or her own wishes, but to imagine simultaneously the prohibitions and reactions of the parent to manifest or latent wishes. According to Piaget (1937) a child between two and six is capable only of magical, phenomenalistic thinking, whereas the inferences of the type described require thinking on the basis of propositions independent of the objects themselves. The oedipal child is expected to know that wishes are not the same as actions. The oedipally aged child is expected to be able to renounce phenomenalistic hypotheses concerning his understanding of relationships between people and to realize that action is no longer at the service of wishes. The defense mechanisms of doing and undoing, isolation of affect, and splitting are pathological versions of this concept. The oedipally aged child is expected to know that a wish continues to have a predispositional effect even though it is invisible and not conscious (i.e., repressed).

Change in location, from conscious to unconscious, does not change the essential qualities of the wish.

It becomes clear that the Oedipus complex, whatever else it is, is a complex configuration of wishes and cognitive operations that traverses preoperational, concrete operations, and propositional stages of cognitive development through its inception and final resolution. Case 4 will be discussed from this speculative point of view.

I shall now turn to case demonstrations of impairments in each of the four nodal organizations that I have described.

IMPAIRED SENSORIMOTOR ORGANIZATIONS

In the phase of sensorimotor organization of experience mental functioning is presymbolic. Mental representation occurs through interiorization of action and results of action (Piaget, 1936). The care giver is defined as a psychobiologic object who provides tension reduction, stimulation, opportunities for attachment, and contexts for informational feedback. The care giver is not the target of instinctual wishes since the infant is, at this stage, incapable of wishing.

Impairments attributable to sensorimotor organizations of experience are presymbolic. They result from either a handicap that hampers the infant's capacity to engage the environment (Engel and Reichsman, 1956; Fraiberg and Freedman, 1964; Freedman, 1979) or from failure of the environment to supply facilitative contexts and accommodations to the infant's communications and growing maturational capacities (Spitz, 1945; Kohut, 1971; Sander, 1975; Emde et al., 1976; Dowling, 1977).

I shall now offer a clinical example illustrative of an impairment in one aspect of sensorimotor organization of experience. This patient demonstrates a problem in supplying herself with meaningful contexts. She had trouble understanding her own actions as well as the responses of others. In this particular patient the vulnerabilities associated with this deficit emerged in her treatment in the midst of structured conflicts.

CASE EXAMPLE 1

An unmarried young woman began treatment while in the throes of a personal crisis. As the youngest child in a family consisting of an older brother, parents, and an elderly grandmother, she was, from all appearances, dominated by the adults in her family. She permitted self-fulfillment only in the limited area of her lifelong interest in figure skating. She had planned to enter the Olympics and had worked on perfecting her talent most of her life. A major defeat in a competition was followed by a prolonged period of anxiety, depression, irritability, and withdrawal from competition. During this period her family actively made decisions for her. After a period of isolation she attached herself to a man of whom her parents disapproved. When her parents pressured her to renounce this relationship her negativism became transformed into open defiance. It was at this point that she sought help.

In our work over a period of two years I became aware of some unusual aspects of her mental functioning. She had profound difficulty in perceiving her feelings and ideas in a meaningful context. For example, she had difficulty in expressing or experiencing appropriate affect, although intellectually she understood that she was angry or sad and so on. She attributed the source of this problem to her parents' abhorrence of emotionality. In most situations she either felt nothing or substituted an inappropriate feeling for the one she was experiencing, such as smiling when she was angry. For a time we considered this phenomenon to be the result of repressive forces motivated by wishes to mislead people about the nature of her true affects. It turned out, however, that her smile when she was angry was, more accurately, a shallow engagement of another person that produced a stereotypic response in return. I found myself, for example, tempted to smile when she was smiling inappropriately. I learned to "disregard" her vacant smile and substitute the appropriate emotion. My behavior alerted me to a pathologic interaction around affect patterning and expression. Complications arose in our work when, in an attempt to discover what she was feeling, I appeared to be suggesting affects that she could experience.

Her difficulty in participating in a dialogue and establishing meaningful contexts in which we could understand one another was further complicated by what I came to recognize as her concretization of thought. She had a practical rather than an imaginative, symbolic, or metaphorical intelligence. My metaphorical statements were taken literally by her with expectable chaotic effects on mutual understanding and further communication. Early in her treatment, for example, I interpreted her inertia as a resistance against family pressure. I said, "You are afraid that if you begin to do things you will become an ornament on your mother's Christmas tree." From the context of my statement it was clear that I was speaking to her about the defensive aspects of her inertia, flatness, and depression. She did not comprehend my meaning, however. To be hung on her mother's Christmas tree meant to her that she was a pretty, sparkling ornament, a concept that did not fit her self-awareness of depression, obesity, and apathy.

Her dreams provided further evidence of her deficient capacity to supply herself with meaningful contexts for her emotions. When she experienced intense sexual or aggressive wishes she did not represent these dream images holistically. Instead they consisted of raw and undisguised, disembodied parts of her body or the bodies of others in bloody, fragmented states. These bizarre images frightened her, and she became increasingly confused when she tried to think about them. She feared she was losing her mind.

When the following dream was reported some progress had been made in our recognition and understanding of these factors. This dream illustrates both a new capacity for representing ideas symbolically and the persistence of her difficulty in supplying herself with meaningful contexts for her emotions.

> I was in an old building. I was on the top floor and the wood floors were rotten. I was afraid the floor would not support my weight. Then I was at home with Jack. (Jack was her boyfriend who had recently told her he wasn't interested in continuing a relationship with her.) Jack went into my brother's room. There was a strange boy in the room who looked queer. Jack went over and grabbed this boy's penis. I was shocked and felt guilty. I started to wake up, and I had this bizarre image of a mouth with a huge tongue moving in and out.

As she began to associate to her dream she noted with satisfaction her new capacity to cry over the loss of her boyfriend. She commented that her tears reflected her sadness as well as her defiance of her parents who continually told her to stop feeling sorry for herself. I commented that I thought she had problems connecting her defiance or annoyance to herself and thus dreamed of these feelings as disembodied body parts. She shifted to thinking about a conversation she had recently had with her father who reproachfully said he thought she was too dependent upon her treatment. She had said to herself she didn't want to become too dependent on me because her parents would be upset. She resented my implying that her problems had something to do with her relationship with her parents. She suddenly became openly angry and said she didn't want to talk to me anymore.

She was silent for a prolonged period of time. When she resumed speaking she related an incident illustrative of her older brother's rebelliousness and her parents' anxiety and repressive measures. I asked her about that part of the dream in which she felt guilty and responsible for her boyfriend's aggression toward the unknown boy in the dream. She could not explain her guilty response. She said the unknown boy in her dream was a homosexual friend of Jack's. I said she attempted to experience her aggression vicariously through her relationship with her older brother. She became very angry with me. "Why," she demanded to know, "was I pushing her to be angry? Why did I insist that she not talk with her parents anymore? What difference did it make if she were dependent upon them or me?" I said she remained dependent upon someone because she was fearful of knowing and experiencing her own affects. This helped her calm down enough to contemplate the source of her dependency rather than the object of her dependent longings.

DISCUSSION

The exchanges between this patient and myself were not experienced by her as a "creative amalgam" (Sadow, 1979) to which we both contributed. She experienced what I said to her as perscriptions for how she must think. In a contradictory manner her open defiance and anger in the transference emphasized her differences with my understanding and, at the same time, asserted her congruence with her actual parents' attitudes. Thus, even her manifest defiance maintained her entanglement with her parents' attitudes.

Sander (1983) presents empirical evidence to demonstrate that symmetrical participation within the infant–care-giver system permits interactive patterns of behavior to be modified in both partners. This allows the

infant to develop flexibility and increases his or her capacity to accommodate to novel situations. On the other
hand, nonsymmetrical participation in the infant–caregiver dialogue leads, in the most extreme case, to symbiotic attachments to the care giver and rigid reliance
upon a more efficient partner to provide stability of functioning and a comprehensible environment. It is this latter type of pattern that I believe to be demonstrated by
the patient I am discussing. She required external assistance to compensate for her confusion, concretization
of thought, difficulty in experiencing her own emotions,
and understanding of other people's communications to
her. Symbiosis, defined as the infant's rigid reliance upon
a care giver, is not a normal aspect of this early phase
of development since development proceeds symmetri-
cally and bidirectionally between a prewired infant
(Shapiro and Stern, 1980) and an adequate caretaking
environment. The description of Mahler and her colleagues (1975) of an infant "hatching" from a symbiotic
cocoon is an alternate model of early development. Mahler's model places symmetrical interactions as a late development (thirty-six months) after individuation has
taken place. Others (Sander, 1980; Litowitz, see chapter
12) see symmetry fostered by infant initiative from the
beginning of life.

This patient's symbiotic attachments to her parents,
brother, as well as to myself, in the transference, were,
in my opinion, evidence of impaired assimilative and accommodative capacities that normally mature in the
phase of sensorimotor organization of experience. This
patient's need to maintain multiple symbiotic attachments indicated, in my opinion, impaired capacity to provide self-regulation of basic homeostatic systems. I
attributed pathogenic significance to her parents' continued willingness, for their own reasons, to substitute their
thinking and decision-making capacities for hers.

The brief clinical material that I have presented demonstrates that her impairment was not restructured by a later developmental epoch as suggested by Shapiro (1977). The dream that I have reported demonstrates her deficit in the midst of latent dream thoughts concerning phallic wishes and conflicts. The day residue for her dream was her reaction to her boyfriend terminating their relationship when he could no longer tolerate her manifest seductiveness that ended in frustration for him. She had seduced him to rescue her from her bondage with her parents through engaging in a sexual escapade which her parents would vehemently oppose. However, her underlying fear of a sexual relationship had led her to demand that her boyfriend take care of her as a baby rather than have a relationship with a sexual woman. The latent content of her dream was determined by her unconscious wish for a penis, as well as by her competitiveness with and envy of her brother. In her dream she dissociated herself from these wishes by representing her boyfriend as the person who acted for her. Her feeling of guilt in the dream revealed the true origin of her aggressive wish. Her symbiotic partnership with her brother as well as other men functioned to gratify her unconscious wish for a penis, as well as to provide her with an illusion of independence from her parents. It was as if she were saying in her dream, "That homosexual boy doesn't need his penis. His penis might supply me with what I need to be rebellious like my older brother." Thus she symbolized in her dream her goal for independent functioning in a disavowed wish for an anatomical part that she coveted and guiltily envied.

Analysis revealed that she could not place her wish for separateness from her parents in an appropriate context. In her view envy and competitiveness were emotions that would shake the foundations of her symbiotic attachments. She clung to her partnerships with men as a means of establishing both a semblance of detachment from her parents as well as defensively disguising her aggression toward men. Frustration in the transference resulted in covert aggression and competitiveness that contributed to her dream image of the collapsing floor. She attacked me and the therapeutic work for threatening the existing basis of her homeostatic balance.

This patient's active attempts to restructure her symbiotic needs into sexual relationships with men did not result in her being able to dispense with developmental problems connected with communication, regulation of her affects, and her concretism. Instead, sexual relationships, as long as they existed, provided her with a compensatory cover for her deficit in these areas. Sexual relationships and bodily intimacy with another person became a tool that helped her dispense with communication on a verbal symbolic level. In addition, through providing a path of excitement and discharge of tension, they temporarily reduced her need for symbolic regulation of her affects and reduced the frequent appearance of bizarre fragmented images in her dreams. Discussion of her dream revealed she experienced problems in learning about the sources and function of her dependency upon me as well as others. Fragmentation occurred when I interfered with the patterns that protected her symbiotic relationships with her parents and brother. Fragmentation was also a nonreflective signal that she required my assistance in order to maintain an optimal level of integrated behavior.

IMPAIRED SYNTHESIS OF A SELF-SCHEMA

Impairments in self-schema have been conceptualized in accordance with the author's developmental theory. Ego-developmental theories describe weakness in specific ego functions such as establishing separate self and other representations. Developmental theories that stress infant-caretaking interactional systems describe deficiency states called fragmentation and disintegration. These are states of psychophysiologic overstimulation and disorganization in which the care-giving environment is deficient or pathological. In Kohut's (1971) formulations, these psychophysiologic states are more similar to actual neuroses than to a psychoneurosis. Deficits in the self/selfobject amalgam are postulated, in this theory, to exert a continuous effect on development in the form of arrestations patched over by sexualized and aggressivized patterns which disavow the existence of the deficit. Developmental theories that describe the evolution of a supraordinate self structure (Erikson, 1959; G. Klein, 1976; Gedo, 1979, 1981a) that has continuity across a lifespan describe deficits that distort expectable epigenetic transformations. Erikson, for example, describes psychosocial crises in ego identity. Identity emerges as the end point of negotiated crises based on societal pressures and individual maturation readiness throughout the life cycle. Each crisis is epigenetically related to the one preceding or following it. Although Erikson postulates that the ultimate integration of identity occurs at adolescence, deficits appear as identity diffusions in any period of expectable life-cycle transformations. G. Klein (1976, p. 177) describes crises in integrity of the self schema due to failure of the individual to maintain continuity of self in the face of increasing environmental pressure for accommodation. Continuity is maintained through maturation of symbolic thought that elaborates presymbolic experience in different modes. Gedo (1981a) sees the foundations of the self as the sum of those psychobiological patterns that become obligatory components of the compulsion to repeat. Crises are determined by the level of developmental organizations. In presymbolic organizations "the crucial issue is that of maintaining optimal levels of stimulation. The crucial issue of the transitional mode is the capacity to regulate behavior in terms of a coherent hierarchy of aims" (p. 313). He sees symbiotic needs as a secondary consequence of an analysand's developmental deficit in the prepsychological organization.

I shall now present some clinical data that illustrate a woman's incapacity to organize her behavior coherently consistent with a hierarchy of aims. Contradictions were managed through reliance upon mechanisms of denial and disavowal although each of the multiple self schema were interchangeable motivational systems. Insight gained through her analysis into the complexity of her character structure led to a paradoxical increase in her anxiety as she became aware of the necessity to choose between contradictory plans of action.

CASE EXAMPLE 2

A thirty-three-year-old woman sought analysis ostensibly because of marital problems. She obsessively ruminated about grievances that had occurred in her marriage and threatened her husband with divorce. As her analysis proceeded she revealed a complex character structure that included multiple impressions of herself that were at variance with each other. She appeared unaware of the contradictions in her thinking and acting. Her chronic low self-esteem and anxiety experienced in interpersonal relationships appeared inconsistent with her prevailing fantasies concerning her perfect beauty, her goodness, and her unchallenged ability—if she applied herself. In the hour preceding the one I am about to report, she had given a detailed account of an encounter with a potential employer whom she characterized as a "jerk." I had interpreted that her preoccupation with this man's behavior was a defense against self-awareness in the situation. She left her hour feeling angry that I had not agreed with her views. In the next hour she reported the following dream.

I was looking in a mirror and I did not see my reflection

until I squeezed a blackhead and pushed out an enormous fecal-like string. Then the scene shifted and I was
with the man I was telling you about yesterday. He
proposed anal intercourse. I don't know what I did.
Then I was standing beside a swimming pool. A woman
who was beside me said "put a stick into the pool and
determine it's depth." I did so reluctantly. The woman
then sat down and said nothing. I felt angry that she
didn't congratulate me.

Her initial associations recalled how angry she felt
during her session the previous day. She assumed I had
correctly confronted her with her failure to observe herself in the situation she had described to me. She recalled
feeling angry during her job interview due to her failure
to impress this man with her ability and motivation to
work. She felt defensive and wished to attack him. She
realized that she reversed this in her dream and portrayed the man wishing to attack her from behind. She
recalled a game from childhood in which she would invite
her baby brother to watch her sit on the toilet and de-
fecate while telling him that there were snapping turtles
in the toilet. When he demanded to see for himself she
would stand up as if to show him and then quickly flush
the toilet and tell him that he couldn't see them after all.
She enjoyed his frustration and his willingness to be
teased again and again. Her potential employer was not
as interested in her as her brother was in her childhood.
I said she had reversed that detail in her dream as well.

She then shifted to thinking about her grooming activities in her dream. Lately she has been preoccupied
with her appearance and cannot pass a mirror without
looking at her reflection. Sometimes she watches other
people looking at her in the mirror and thinks to herself
that they are impressed with her beauty. She remembered how she and her mother spent pleasurable time
together sitting in the bathroom and grooming each

other. I inquired about her thoughts concerning the blank mirror in her dream. She said petulantly that the mirror was blank because I had sounded so critical yesterday. Her parents always reassured her that she was better than most people. Anyone who challenged this family consensus was, by definition, a jerk. Her parents could be critical of her also. They did it by seducing her to perform better. They said "you are so smart, you could work harder." Her parents told her that her husband was not good enough for her. She didn't listen to them, but they were correct. In her opinion he isn't good enough for her but she can't leave him. She doesn't understand why she can't separate from him. She hopes her analysis will assist her in becoming strong enough to live on her own. I said I thought the blank mirror not only symbolized my not agreeing with her but something about herself as well that she didn't wish to see. She became silent and recognized that I was repeating the same interpretation as on the previous day. She continued by stating that her analysis has become too important. If analysis was just a grooming procedure it would be pleasurable, safe, but noninformative. She said she had to find out about all that stuff she dreamed about and she needed my help. I said that the last part of her dream conveyed more than her awareness that she felt dependent upon my help. "That is right! I didn't want to do what you said, but I had no will of my own. I was your dip stick. I wanted you to be grateful that I did it for you."

I interpreted her dream as her wish to disguise through reversal aspects of herself that she regarded as flaws. I thought she was tempted to dismiss me as a jerk because I called attention to her flaws. She defended against that awareness by the blank mirror in her dream which only reflected her image after she removed her flaws. She pictured herself in her dream as an extension of my will. This was a complicated compromise consisting of her wish to identify herself with my flawlessness, and her fear that she would be exploited by me in the transference.

Discussion

I shall limit my discussion to issues connected with her multiple self schemata and forego discussion of the origins and vicissitudes of the anal and phallic aims of her exhibitionistic and voyeuristic wishes that were aspects of her psychoneurotic compulsive character structure.

Her associations to this dream revealed multiple fantasies that were aspects of her unintegrated self schema. She simultaneously imagined herself to be impressive, inferior, independent, tough, and attached to someone who could enhance her performance. She wanted to be free to both depreciate her partners and to idealize their capacity to assist her by covering up what she subjectively experienced as phallic and intellectual deficits. In childhood she impressed her family by mundane activities which they typically overestimated. This was represented in her dream thoughts by her capacity to produce an enormous bowel movement. Although her bowel movements may have satisfied her family and gained the awestruck admiration of her baby brother, it hardly served as a program for achieving acclaim in her adult life. It was equally possible that at other times in her life she had overestimated their interest in her toileting activities and used it as a screen for her envy of adult sexual activities and envy of her brother's maleness. In her adult life she attempted to impress her public by her beauty and her compassionate nature. These characteristics were present to some degree but did protect her against feeling flawed. In many respects this woman experienced relief through discovering her psychological complexity and acquiring a more accurate picture of her unconscious motives. On the other hand this information faced her with the task of establishing priorities. For most of her life she had relied upon pseudoconsensus with idealized care givers to establish achievable goals. (Her dream represented her consensus with her mother as a grooming partner.) Characteristically in these relationships she felt competitive with the partner she leaned on and defeated any attempt to actually accomplish what she had agreed to do. Preservation of the relationship through self-defeating behavior substituted for competition. In the dream I have reported she attempted to defend herself against awareness of her pseudoconsensus with my psychoanalytic goals of insight as well as defend herself against her dawning awareness concerning her wishes to damn me as a jerk when I failed to reestablish a partnership with her. Reliance upon defenses of disavowal and denial interfered with her capacity to think deductively about herself. In the face of deductive reasoning she relied upon transductive mental operations (Piaget, 1924) as she moved from schema to schema without logic and without hierarchical organization.

IMPAIRED SYNTHESIS OF OBJECT-SCHEMA

Object-schema as well as self-schema are built up as a result of interaction between intrinsic cognitive maturation and experience. The level of cognitive development prevailing in the child at any time determines the significance for the child of what has been internalized from their relationships with other people. I am suggesting that the influence of early experience upon later experience is not only through the effects of frustration, gratification, or trauma. In addition one can observe these subjective qualities through examination of the child's changing inherent capacity to process the significance of personal events.

Impairments in the object-schema may emerge as either problems in differentiation of self and object-schema or as problems of psychological motivation connected with internalized relationships with others. Clinically impaired differentiations are patched by compensatory structures such as symbiotic partnerships (Mahler et al., 1975). Kohut's (1971) postulate of a self/selfobject amalgam is another way of describing hidden partnerships that disavow separateness and permit stable or even creative functioning in some individuals. Of course in Kohut's developmental psychology separateness is not a goal of development. He emphasizes instead (1977) maturation of the self/selfobject bond to include more abstract qualities of interaction such as wisdom, humor, and objectivity as eventual self-regulating principles.

I shall turn now to clinical material that describes problems of psychological motivation that resulted from disavowal of the emotional significance of disturbed object relationships. Sam was an eight-year-old boy who lived in a psychological universe that was filled with unmasterable tension and peopled by malignant presences. He shifted rapidly between deferred imitation and enactments based on his introjects and longings to be subdued by someone he could admire. His underlying problems in age-appropriate idealization of both parents interfered with structure-building internalizations of objects and with the development of stable self-regulating structures.

CASE EXAMPLE 3

Sam was described by his family as a tyrant. He had a history of uninterrupted bed-wetting since infancy and was painfully shy with strangers.

When I first met Sam he confided to me that he had been sad and mad since the birth of Mark and Bill, his younger twin brothers. He made a direct appeal for help and quickly agreed to come four times a week. When I saw him again after a four-week interval he appeared changed from my initial impression of a bouncy, engaging little boy to a lethargic, isolated, withdrawn, uncommunicative child. He picked and tore at his body and clothes.

He began to bring pictures of his heroes—huge wrestlers and muscle men. He identified himself with one of the most ferocious-looking men: LeRoy Brown, the meanest man in town. This character was one of several unintegrated introjects that I shall describe. Sam admired LeRoy Brown for his physical powers, and he feared him as someone who might injure Sam if he didn't act right. When Sam saw men who resembled LeRoy Brown at wrestling matches he attended with his father and twin brothers he would flinch and cling to his father in a frightened manner. However, at home Sam acted like LeRoy Brown. He abused both of his brothers regularly and reduced them to tears. Significantly, mother adopted a policy of letting the boys fight it out—a policy that was obviously unrealistic as far as Mark and Billy were concerned. I interpreted his meanness as a defense against the depression that he had let me know about when he started to see me. To my surprise, it was his tyranny rather than his depression that emerged full force in his sessions.

He began a repetitive interaction which we eventually referred to as the genie-in-the-bottle game. I was Sam's genie in the bottle who had the sole function of bringing a smile to Sam's lips through performing under his direction. I was also to leave him free to ignore me. Repetition of this game eventually led to my understanding that the genie was a character modeled on his interaction with his mother. He provided details about the multiple ways in which he pushed his mother around until she became so angry she exploded in rage and eventually refused to serve him. When she exploded, he felt free to ignore her fury and continue doing as he wished.

The genie-in-the-bottle game alternated with another interaction which Sam called his shutout game. The shutout game took the place of his lethargic, self-defeating manner of playing board games that he demonstrated when we started our work. In the shutout game I was quickly forced to surrender my men in hopeless and helpless defeat. At the moment of unconditional surrender Sam insisted that I must play the game and *not* give up. I initially interpreted this interaction as Sam's way of asserting that he did not need help. This proved to be an error. The game was part of an intensely ambivalent father transference in which Sam asserted the unlimited power of his aggression. At the moment of his victory he wanted me to be stronger and subdue him (that is, not surrender). Sam thought his father was a weakling who could not effectively subdue Sam.

Sam became very excited when his father expressed disbelief that Sam won all the checker games in his sessions. Although Sam bitterly complained that his father was competitive with him, and that his father didn't believe him when he was telling the truth, Sam seemed reassured that his father could put him down in this fashion.

The fourth unintegrated pattern of interaction based on his relationship with his parents emerged in stories and play that Sam called sneak attacks. If I moved in the room while he was busy with something, he appeared frightened as if I were going to attack him. If I occasionally won a game Sam accused me of a sneak attack. Eventually, Sam told me that he feared sneak attacks from his father. He showed me a scar on his finger which he said he acquired when he was eighteen months old on an outing with his father. The outing took place when his mother was in the hospital delivering the twins. Sam had reached up to take his father's hand and did not notice father's cigarette. Sam burned himself and attributed the cause of this injury to his father's sneak attacks.

Sam was intensely ambivalent about his father. Over the years he managed to hang on to features of his father that he seemed to admire, such as his father's love of expensive gadgets. Sam shared his father's pride in these objects, and they spent time together learning about them and using them. This activity never compensated for Sam's bitter disillusionment toward his father who in Sam's view used Sam in place of himself to fight his wife and who was capable of sneak attacks.

In spite of prolonged effort Sam appeared unmoved and unaffected by the treatment process except paradoxically to intensify his LeRoy Brown enactments with his brothers, increase his coercion of his mother and myself as his genie, and insist on fierce shutout games with me. The fierceness of his struggle finally led to my surrendering. I gave up treating him after four years. He did not protest. He seemed relieved that I would leave him alone to do as he wished. As a compensation for my not being strong enough to subdue him, Sam seemed to extract a victory from this failed opportunity of correcting his problems through treatment. The ending seemed to confirm, from his view, his grandiosity and his unlimited capacity to defeat a rival.

Discussion

This clinical fragment demonstrates the multiple introjects that peopled this child's psychological world. Each introject had a motivational effect on Sam's behavior. Retrospectively, I can understand Sam's fierce negativism and impenetrability as a statement of his mistrust based on his unending entanglement in his parents' psychopathology. Negativism as well as grandiosity passed for organized self-determined goals.

Sam's screen memory of his father burning him when he was eighteen months old condensed his despair over the birth of the twins and unconscious fantasies of retaliatory castration by his father for his oedipal fantasies of successfully conquering his mother. Sam's boast to his father concerning his power to conquer me in the transference was both an expression of his phallic aim as well as a depreciation of his father. There was also evidence that he admired his mother's competitiveness and success at games. As the eldest of eight children her intellectual talents had received little admiration and attention from her family because of their preoccupation with multiple younger children. She encouraged Sam's competitiveness, to his own detriment, because she regarded it as a trait that would, in her view, save him from feeling displaced, as she was, by younger siblings. Sam's admiration for his mother as well as her refusal to protect her young twin sons from Sam's LeRoy Brown enactments fostered his grandiosity. She used Sam to express her suppressed rage against her younger siblings.

Sam's shutout game and his magical genie were overdetermined constructions that defended him against enmeshment in my psychoanalytic world of understanding and learning as well as providing a vehicle for enacting his sadomasochistic fantasies of conquering me. Sam's negativism did not yield to interpretation. My poor performance at games seemed to be a crucial context that permitted Sam to ignore what I said to him. Sam could not rely upon me as a strong person because he concluded from the evidence of my poor performance at games that I was a beaten weakling who had nothing to offer him. I frustrated Sam's longings to submit to a powerful LeRoy Brown. I represented both his depreciated father and his angry competitive mother who had been beaten by her younger siblings. His depreciation of me was also understood as a defense against his castration anxiety, although interpretation of that dynamic proved to be no more successful than interpretations of his disillusionment in me. Sam seemed incapable of making the leap between my explanations of his behavior with me and understanding the origin of these behaviors in his relationship with his parents. These were two different universes as far as Sam understood. He seemed tied to his immediate perceptions and actions and could not infer absent causes, or sequences. This made analytic reconstruction of genetic sequences an almost useless enterprise.

The relationship between idealization and confidence in caretakers and structure formation has been explored in psychoanalytic literature primarily in relationship to superego formation. That Sam's superego development had been markedly interfered with was evidenced by his inability to understand the meaning of the word *no*. Initially, the word *no* establishes in the context of dyadic interactions that neither the child nor the adult has unlimited power over the other. Spitz (1959) termed the word *no* as the third organizer of the psyche. He attributed significance to this verbalization beyond the capacity of communication to replace action. Correct use of *no* reconfirms through the use of verbal symbols, bilaterality and symmetrical participation within dyadic transactions that had previously been learned in action. Sam used the word *no* to assert his grandiose fantasies of power over other people, and he experienced other people's use of the word *no* as a similarly murderous act. This derailment within dyadic interactions appeared to be based on his profound disillusionment with each of his caretakers. This interfered with later superego internalizations of an idealized authority to contain his aggressive competitive wishes.

This clinical fragment demonstrates the significance of subjective organizations of object relationships in the child's memory as a motive for deferred imitations in active and passive modes. Sam's enactments disavowed the emotional experience of profound disillusionment with and mistrust of his parents. This mistrust was revived in the course of analysis and interfered with learning within a psychoanalytic context. Efforts at interpretation were futile in the face of the child's phenomenalistic thinking which prevented him from considering absent causes, displacements, and re-editions of his problems in his work with me.

IMPAIRMENTS IN THE TRANSFORMATION OF THE MAGICAL PHENOMENALISTIC THINKING OF THE TWO- TO SIX-YEAR-OLD CHILD INTO MORE LOGICAL FRAMES OF REFERENCE

Basch (1981) asserts that the mechanism of disavowal affects the transformation from sensorimotor to preoperational thinking. Repression affects the transformation of preoperational thought into concrete operational thought. This later transformation, under normal circumstances, permits the child to relinquish egocentric, magical phenomenalistic thinking in favor of logical relationships. Psychoanalysts know, however, that renunciation of this early form of thinking is not absolute. The earlier form of thinking continues to exist in another location (i.e., in the unconscious), where it continues to have a predispositional effect on behavior.

In Basch's (1981) view deficits attributable to oedipal conflicts are due to mental contents, which, though symbolized, cannot participate in the transformation of the next stage. In his view deficits appear when the child functions on more than one level of cognitive operations stimultaneously. In this reformulation, internalized conflict arises due to discrepancies between persisting unconscious preoperational and sensorimotor actions and logical frames of reference attributable to concrete operations and propositional logic. This definition of conflict differs widely from the usual psychoanalytic definition of structural conflict. The difference between the two definitions is that in the first instance conflict is regarded as a disorder of thought whereas in the second instance

the components of conflict arise from incompatible unconscious instinctual wishes (intrasystems conflicts), or
unconscious wishes opposed by ego and superego structures (intersystemic conflict).

The following case material will be discussed from
this speculative viewpoint.

CASE EXAMPLE 4

Tom was a ten-year-old boy whose unresolved infantile
neurosis was an extremely complicated one. In the foreground was behavior that revealed his rivalry with his
father, intense jealousy of his younger sister Ann, as well
as his possessive tyrannical claims in his mother. This
typical oedipal configuration screened a more deeply repressed triadic conflict that involved his mother, his older
half-brother Steve, and himself. Analytic work reconstructed these interrelationships and their significance
for Tom's psychopathology.

Tom was referred for analysis because of fierce battles
with his mother that had continued unabated since Ann
was born, as well as persisting behavior problems in
school, and nightly enuresis. His analysis was complicated by my becoming pregnant and delivering about a
year after we started our work. At the time of my pregnancy his half-brother Steve came to live permanently
with Tom's family following Steve's father's death. Steve
had previously lived with his father and his stepmother.

The early part of Tom's treatment consisted of his
trying either to seduce me or tyrannize me. He was frightened of retaliation from imagined rivals. He seemed to
"know" I was pregnant before I told him. He wanted to
"shower me with seeds" and get inside "my magic box."
His first dream in his analysis connected themes of birth
and conception with Ann's birth and Steve coming to live
at his house. In his dream, Steve pushed Tom out of a

tree, and Tom broke into a thousand pieces. I interpreted the dream as revealing that Tom felt shattered and pushed out by my baby as well as by Steve and Ann. Tom became increasingly tyrannical in his hours before my delivery.

He was angry and sad when he resumed analysis after my delivery. He made a direct appeal to me to admire his "stick, that was 30,000 miles high." He said "no woman has such a stick!" I interpreted his phallic exhibitionism and grandiosity as a defense against his experiencing his smallness in comparison with adult men, such as my husband and his father, who could shower a woman with seeds. He shifted away from this interpretation of competition with adult men to his more immediate competition with Steve. He asserted that his mother thought that Steve was perfect, whereas Tom was categorized as a troublemaker. Tom reported dreams which represented him forced by external forces or his internal grandiosity to perform impossible tasks. From his associations to these dreams we understood that he felt he had no right to succeed at anything he did. If he were to succeed, he might replace Steve as the perfect child. Even though his mother now had Steve with her permanently, Tom now felt his mother was willing to sacrifice him in order to protect her relationship with Steve.

Tom became aware of his fury toward his mother who disavowed her knowledge that Steve was not a perfect child. He gradually gained insight into the frustration connected with his attempts to compete with a perfect child. He attempted to hide his competition with Steve, as well as his wish to kick him out of his mother's life, by failing in things he did. His failures saved his rivals who could then push him out. Tom began to refer to himself as a "home-wrecker." This was a reference to his previously repressed fantasy that his mother's pregnancy with him had been the "cause" of Steve choosing to live with his father. It was also an expression of his wish to

wreck my home (my office was in my home) and coerce
me to leave my baby for him.

In his hours he begged me to make him good by taking
away his aggressive and competitive strivings. He insisted that I wanted him to be good so I wouldn't have to
worry about him and I could return to my baby. Abandonment was the punishment for his wish to reverse the
manifest content of his first dream and kick my baby out
of the tree and make him fall into a thousand pieces. By
wishing to be good, he was in effect giving me permission
to leave him and not worry about him. Tom dealt with
his internal ambivalence about me and the impact of my
pregnancy upon him through obsessive preoccupation
with being punished.

An approaching summer vacation brought forth a new
storm of regressive behavior. He chanted "who cares" in
response to anything I said. Eventually, he told me about
his father who was never home and "didn't care." He was
afraid that his mother would abandon him in my office.
His mother had permitted one child to remain with his
father—that proved in Tom's view that his mother "didn't
care" either.

He was assaultive when he returned from vacation.
I restrained him and he yelled that I was murdering him.
He dreamed about a monster who was torturing him because he was so bad. He said the monster was his father.
He told me that he fought with his mother when his
father was not home. I interpreted his longings for a
"murdering father" who could restrain him. He said he
never wanted to get married because women didn't let
men be strong. He thought his father left home because
his mother wanted him to be weak and under her power.
He wavered between defensively idealizing his father by
imagining him to be a murderer, and hating him because
he didn't help. He became increasingly defiant in his sessions. In interpreted his defiance as a wish to have me
subdue him, as well as an attempt to hide his fear that

I would overpower him and make him weak. He said he didn't want to come and see me anymore. His parents also wanted him to stop treatment because his behavior was worsening. I bargained for another year of work.

Tom expressed both relief and surprise over the news. He had never anticipated that his treatment might stop or that he would ever grow tired of "torturing me." He told me that he had never forgiven me for betraying him when I had my child. Sadly, he said "everyone has someone they love or who loves them. I have no one at all. If I had wanted to see you when you were home with your baby, you wouldn't have wanted to see me." Not unexpectedly, Tom got expelled from school.

He reported a dream.

> My mother gave me medicine which made me small enough to ride Steve's HO train. I thought I was invisible but a policeman stopped me; I didn't have a ticket for the train. I also dreamed that you were a witch. Your house was haunted. I ran away and stole a bicycle with a friend.

From his associations his ambivalence became clearer. In the transference I represented, along with his mother, a powerful, phallic woman who overpowered men and wouldn't let them be strong. In Tom's dream he substituted himself for his half-brother Steve, who had been made perfect, by submitting to a phallic mother who transformed him into a baby or a miniaturized adult. His dream image of becoming invisible was an overdetermined symbol of his magical escape from my phallic power over him. In the transference he felt determined to run away from his fear of submission to me as well as his longings to stay with me. As was his pattern, he dealt with my informing him that we had a year more to work by taking an active role and abandoning me in his dream. His emotional insight into his fear and longings led to a grim determination to leave both home and treatment. He asserted he never consciously wanted to hitch a ride on Steve's HO train. He didn't believe in Steve's perfection or in my child's perfection. He did think that he had to be perfect in order to have a right to be with someone. He continued to be outraged over Steve's exclusive relationship with his mother. He longed for his father to spend time at home and befriend him. He became sullen and silent during his sessions.

After many silent sessions an unexpected change took place in Tom. On the day Martin Luther King died Tom came to his session in tears. He was anxious and frightened. Who was the King who died, he wanted to know. Did we have a King in the United States? When I clarified what had happened Tom asked me, "How do you feel about me? Do you like me? Do you value anything about me? Will you miss me? Will you remember me?" Tom seemed to be breaking into a thousand pieces and putting himself back together again. He told me that he had wanted my unconditional admiration. He said, "I don't want to have to work, but I guess I will have to."

Tom had many talents and a superior intellectual endowment from which he had never profited. His phallic grandiosity had defended him against knowing about himself and about the peculiar interrelationships in his family. His grandiosity had prevented him from accepting any limitations on his capacity to appeal to his mother. As the disavowals that maintained his grandiosity were analyzed, Tom felt overwhelmed by the complexities of his life, and he was determined to leave home. As long as he lived with his parents he wanted to torture them for disappointing him. He ended treatment with some insight into his need to be punished by expulsion to relieve him of his guilt over wanting to destroy his rivals through successful competition and achievement.

Discussion

Psychoanalytic work with Tom, as we understood his reaction to my pregnancy, led to beginning insight into his
symptoms. His anger and tyranny were only one aspect
of his repressed grief-stricken reaction to the loss of
father, who turned away from his family when faced with
additional responsibility, and the loss of his mother, who
throughout his life had remained preoccupied with her
oldest child. Although any personal event or qualities of
the analyst influence the direction of the patient's associative work, this particular case demonstrates that what
we term a re-edition of the neurosis in the transference
is indeed an amalgam of factors that include the reality
of the analyst as well as the patient's infantile neurosis.

Resolution of the Oedipus complex requires an internalized solution of conflict of sexual and aggressive
wishes directed toward ambivalently loved parents at the
level of symbolic functioning as opposed to action. Maturationally, transformation of affective-interactive schemata initially learned through action is normally reworked
and relearned on a symbolic level in the phase of preoperational functioning. In Tom's case this gradual transformation appeared incomplete. For the most part Tom
lived in a world of action and reaction as opposed to introspection or verbal discourse. On the level of action he
inferred sequences of retaliatory aggression (abandonment, castration) to manifest expression of his aggres-
sive-competitive wishes. His autonomous solution to this
dilemma was actively to provoke environmental restric-
tions and explusions that were then used as justification
for his continuing to torture his parents and analyst.
Although Tom manifestly feared punishment for expression of his unconscious wishes, his fear was never assimilated in such a manner as to constitute an internalized
authority mobilized by signals of guilt and shame that

would guide his behavior. On the contrary, his inferences about punishment were based on an internalization of his parents' aggression which perpetuated his sense of entitlement to ignore responsibility and remain self-centered and to use coercion or seduction when faced with events not to his liking. Identification with parental aggression interfered with Tom's appreciation of himself as the person who required restraint.

Resolution of the Oedipus complex also depends upon the child acquiring a set of lawful rules that describe the interrelationships among family members as well as the ordering of these relationships by gender, generation, and preferences that limits the number of combinatorial possibilities within a family. Piaget (1937) describes the child's capacity to decenter his perceptions (relinquishment of subjectivity governed by perception and wish) based on the modification of magical-phenomenalistic explanations of events in favor of considerations of reality. Freud was also concerned with structuralization of the psychic apparatus at the time of the resolution of the Oedipus complex that differentiated primary- from secondary-process thought. Analytic work demonstrated that Tom was acutely aware of exclusions that were determined by his parents' relationship with each other, as well as by his mother's preoccupation with Steve. In his analysis Tom became aware of his fury toward his mother who disavowed her awareness that Steve was not a perfect child. We reconstructed that his failures disavowed his competitiveness and saved his rivals so that they could exclude him. Eventually, he faced his grief in the transference about his father who "did not care" and his mother who was so preoccupied with others. As we began our last year of work he said he never thought he would stop torturing me for having a baby. His experience of grief led to some objectivity and insight about his parents' motives for excluding him. It also led a fierce determination in Tom to leave home because he felt hopeless about loving and being loved by his parents and analyst.

The continuing effect of his overwhelming grief pushed Tom to rerepress his conflicts and attempt a premature attempt at adolescent detachment and search for new people whom he might love and who might love him. In all probability this would constitute another impossible task in which he would reexperience his frustration and longings and unconscious conflicts.

Tom's repetition compulsion to seek punishment from ambivalently loved parents could be understood to be motivated by unconscious guilt over his competitive and aggressive "home-wrecking" wishes or his phallic sexuality, or regressive changes in his superego. However, there is little evidence that Tom internalized an impersonal, lawful authority based on sufficient idealization of his parents. He reacted to my pregnancy by feeling betrayed and could foresee no end to his wish to torture me even though he feared my retaliation. I understood this to mean that superego development was impaired in Tom because of insufficient idealization of his caretakers who betrayed him by their inconsistency, their irresponsibility, their preoccupation with others. In place of an internalized idealized authority Tom relied upon malevolent omnipotent figures as regulators of his tension and unconscious wishes. This was evidenced in his last dream in his analysis in which he is shrunk by his mother, apprehended by a policeman, and threatened by a witch whom he identified as me. His intense reaction to the death of Martin Luther King initiated his first inquiries about what qualities he had that I could admire and what Martin Luther King had done to deserve the outpouring of grief at the time of his death. These inquiries were a hopeful sign of Tom's nascent interest in conducting himself in a manner to preserve his self-esteem rather than leave it in the hands of omnipotent caretakers who "didn't care."

Piaget has charted the successive steps by which the child develops a sense of reality of inanimate objects and properties of physical matter. The stages in the child's sense of reality of human relationships have received much less systematic attention (Ferenczi, 1913). This case suggests that the precursors to realistic appraisals of self and others are based on the integrated experience of ambivalence toward differentiated others, sufficient idealization of appropriate restraining authority, and the capacity to see events from another person's point of view (i.e., empathy with caretakers).

RECAPITULATION, DISCUSSION, AND QUESTIONS

In this chapter I have considered patients in whom interpretation and working through have not resulted in an expectable degree of learning and change. I agree with Rangell (1981) that there are two types of insightful learning in psychoanalytic work. The first involves the revelations and discoveries made by interpreting the resistance of defenses against infantile anxiety. The second involves the integrating, synthesizing efforts of the patient which result in working through and structural change. Rangell states that the resistances against this type of insight lie in the repetition compulsion which repeats "the chronic neurosis and various secondary gains that have become integrated into the life pattern as a whole" (pp. 653–654).

Investigations of how things change through insight or why things fail to change because of resistance require psychoanalysts to become familiar with developmental factors beyond our usual interest in unconscious mental processes. We need to understand the interaction between cognitive development that determines the conceptual range of the child, anxiety, and trauma as composite pathogenic factors.

Work with these patients indicated to me that it was necessary to comprehend fully how their minds worked as well as the specific contents of their unconscious mental life. It was necessary to explore the factors that shaped perception and comprehension of the analytic work itself. I have used the terms *deficit* or *impairment* to cover those repetitive, maladaptive limits to comprehension of experience that seem to operate in addition to those defenses motivated by unconscious wish and anxiety. I have attempted to define the expectable process of cognitive development that underlies each of the synthesized integrations that I have discussed.

Sensorimotor thinking and functioning is the basis of early organizations of affectively charged interaction. Preoperational thinking is the basis of the child's capacity to construct subjectively organized symbolic self and object schemata. Finally, the shift to logical thinking that underlines the resolution of the Oedipus complex in middle childhood corresponds to the transition to the phase of concrete operations. The maturational, biological continuity of cognitive development has been differentiated from the specific contents of traumata, fantasies, wishes, contexts, and events that each patient organized within any one of these stages of cognitive development.

Before turning to the interrelationship between learned experience and arrests in cognitive development I will make a few general remarks about the psychopathology of these patients. The psychopathology of the patients that I have been discussing has been understood as an impairment in their integrative capacities, rather than an outcome of internalized conflict between unacceptable wishes and restraining factors (Sander, 1975, p. 131). Each of these patients demonstrated conflicts of the latter sort as well as the deficits that I have described. Resistance to new learning and integration of self-knowledge has been attributed to disruption of expectable synthesis. Resistance has not been understood as a defense against instinctual anxieties or regressive evasions of more advanced conflicts. Resistance has been interpreted as a cognitively derived interference in the patient's ability

to assimilate new information and permit new accommodations and adaptations to take place (Gedo, 1981b).

Each of the patients challenged the analyst to discover
how to shape interventions appropriate to the level of
cognitive organization that was manifested in the course
of his or her regressive transference neurosis.

The first patient's impaired ability to construct contexts through which she could understand communication emerged in the transference whenever she was
deprived of external assistance from a symbiotic partner.
Although she longed to dispense with her symbiotic partners she resisted learning about what function they
served in her overall psychic economy. I postulated a continuity between early environmental intrusiveness in her
life which had continued to the present and puppetlike
attachment to others who thought for her and directed
her actions. The perpetuation of this factor throughout
her development was attributed to repetitive instances
in which the need for intervention to correct states of
fragmentation occurred when she was bereft of the stabilizing influence of symbiotic partners. In a cyclic manner she regarded these interventions as intrusions (i.e.,
actions) that forced her into more dependent relationships. Her clinical resistance was based on a cognitive
deficit. Her concretization of thought, her fear of her affects, her inability to conceive of absent realities, and the
absence of decentering led me to infer that she was fixated
in the sensorimotor organization of experience, at least
in the area of human relationships. Her concreteness
made interpretive work almost impossible. (Parentheti-
cally, she had trouble integrating information in other
situations.) Insight was initially limited to modification
of action patterns that increased her self-sufficiency.
Gradually, there has emerged an increasing capacity to
deal with her feelings on a symbolic level.

The second patient's deficit in the synthesis of a hierarchically ordered self-schema dramatically affected

her capacity to set goals and achieve them. This problem emerged in the transference after her pseudoconsensus with my analytic goals became more apparent to her. As a result she experienced both fears of and longings to be influenced by the analysis. Her anxiety about this new psychoanalytic influence revived memories of pathogenic factors in her upbringing. Her multiple, often contradictory, views of herself were interchangeable, and transductive mental operations interfered with learning about sequences of causes and effects as a means of resolving the contradictions that existed. Her rapid shifts between contradictory goals limited the effectiveness of any interpretation that touched, by necessity, on only one aspect of her subjective world. Her reversals were a pathological undoing rather than a logical mental operation. She was unaware of contradictions in her behavior and could not hierarchically order contents of her thought. Piaget (1924) terms this *transductive operations* as opposed to inductive or deductive reasons. He understands this type of mental function to be essentially a motor action rather than a mental operation. It is an aspect of thinking characteristic of the preoperational stage of cognitive development.

The third patient's incapacity to manage intense disillusionment in both his parents without reliance on splitting and disavowal mechanism resulted in an impaired synthesis of an object-schema. In his analysis these problems arose in the context of a disrupted idealizing transference which I could not effectively interpret. He was sensitive to my poor performance at games which indicated to him that I, like his father, was not strong enough to subdue him. I inferred that structuralization of self-regulating patterns from internalization of regulatory interactions with parents was interfered with by insufficient idealization of his care givers. Cognitively, this child was phenomenalistically bound to his perceptions and had an impaired understanding of time, displacements, repetitions, causes, and so on, making reconstruction of absent events almost impossible. His almost delusional self-certainty did not yield to any psychoanalytic intervention.

The fourth patient seemed best able to utilize interpretive activity. His difficulty in understanding the complexity of his life and relationships within his family emerged in the context of a transference revival of the birth of his younger sibling. His insatiable desire to torture his parents for their limitations in caring for him led to resolve to leave his home and attempt to find new people to relate to. His painful and stormy treatment eventually resulted in his recognition of the necessity to be restrained, his capacity to decenter his perceptions, and his beginning to relinquish his magical, phenomenalistic explanations of his complicated existence. Disavowal and repression lessened as he began to enter the concrete operational phase of thinking. His problem with idealization of his care givers and their displacements and problems with aggression remained a significant source of potential pathology. He attempted to find an accurate picture of himself and to contemplate preserving his own self-esteem by planning to work and achieve in his own right.

I shall turn now to some questions raised by this investigation of resistance. I shall first discuss the relationship between anxiety and the conceptual range of understanding that is available to a child. Secondly, I shall discuss trauma as a pathogenic factor in development. Thirdly, I shall discuss reconstruction of continuities and discontinuities in development.

Speculatively, I have begun to think that the level of cognitive conceptualization available to a child determines the regular appearance of developmental anxieties that we, as psychoanalysts, have learned to expect. (I mean, of course, separation anxiety, anxiety about loss of love, and castration anxiety.) As I tried to point out in my discussion of the cognitive organization of an oedipal child, castration anxiety appears to be based on preoperational thinking. Perception of anatomical differences between sexes is understood by the child preoperationally; that is the child perceives the end point, the presence or absence of a penis, without concerning itself about how such a state came into being. In a subjective rather than a logical manner the child invents an explanation: in one sex the penis was lost, or invisibly displaced, and it must reside somewhere (in a woman's vagina, and so on). What Galenson and Rophie (1971) have described as early castration anxiety in girls would be better understood, I think, as an expression of uncertainty (Kleeman, 1965, 1966) when the child is faced with perceptions which are unfamiliar and which cannot be easily integrated into an existing schema. This uncertainty should not be confused with what we term *anxiety*. Factors of internalized predispositions, wishes, and fantasies interacting with environmental response may interfere with the resolution of uncertainty in children.

I have further inferred that each of these patients suffered both acute and chronic trauma in his or her early life. Developmental observations of infants and older children suggest that there are self-righting, resilient, biobehavioral tendencies to get back on the track after deviations have occurred (Emde, 1981). Such resiliency is most pronounced in younger children after environmental conditions have been changed to supplant precipitating stressful conditions with conditions conducive to reintegration and growth (Kagan, 1974). If, as the work with these patients illustrates, environmental conditions do not change after prolonged or intense stress, then the critical-period hypothesis described by Spitz (1959) is applicable. From an external vantage point we have no sure means of predicting the ultimate fate of what appears to be stressful. We rely upon reconstruction to determine how stress acted on development and what segmented

aspect of development was affected. The influence of
stress appears to be determined by how it is encoded in
the person's memory system. However, Freud (1899) discovered that the child had enormous potential for constructing fantasies after the capacity for imagery and
representation had matured. Fantasies can act as memories and unconscious motives for future actions. These
factors make reconstructions of early events as determinants of current transference reactions a highly questionable procedure (Gedo, 1981b). Any reconstruction
must account for discontinuities as well as continuities
in development. Freud bypassed this issue by relying
upon the continuity of instinctual fixations rather than
memories as a way of describing the continuous action
of trauma in the life of an individual. He asserted that
trauma induced instinctual fixations that acted as predispositions to later neurotic symptom formation.

In this chapter I have attempted to offer a model of
relativity to describe the action of trauma on maturation
and development. This model of relativity suggests that:
(1) trauma in infancy refers less to an event and more to
an environmental context which fosters maladaptive
functioning or interferes with synthesis and elaboration
of maturational potential. Work with patients 1 and 2
demonstrates this action of trauma. (2) Trauma refers to
the arousal of anxiety or disequilibrium at the time new
functions are emerging (Murphy, 1980) or at times of
biobehavioral shifts (Emde et al., 1976). This stress results in interference with the consolidation of maturational gains or produces regression. Work with patients
3 and 4 illustrates this aspect of trauma. (3) Trauma is
associated with the presence of pathological models from
whom the child learns maladaptive ways to cope with
life's contingencies. Patients 2, 3, and 4 exemplified the
action of this factor. Models that stress the relativity of
any event in a total field of forces (Emde, 1981) are more
in accordance with principles of normal development

than models that describe certain and lasting effects of acute or chronic stress.

Turning now to the final problem raised by investigations of the sort I have been engaged in, I shall comment upon the influence of hypotheses of continuity and discontinuity in development on a psychoanalyst's reconstructive work. Development is neither totally continuous nor totally discontinuous, it is both; discontinuous syntheses interact simultaneously with continuous factors in development.

Models that emphasize continuities in development describe epigenetic sequences in which early organizations are superseded by more complex organizations. Early organizations remain potentially active through regression. These are linear models in which more complex development is thought to arise from primitive precursors. Cognitive development, as described by Piaget (1936), affective development as described by Basch (1976), and the developmental lines of A. Freud (1968) are examples of continuities in development. Discontinuous models describe somewhat differently how competencies arise in the infant. In contrast to linear, continuous models, discontinuous models describe the maturation of separate independent factors which are eventually synthesized into new competencies in a manner prescribed by the genetic code. These syntheses result in new functions which are qualitatively different from the sum of the component parts. Freud's hypothesis concerning biphasic sexual development is an example of discontinuous development, as are Emde et al's. (1976) concept of biobehavioral affective shifts in infancy and childhood, Freedman's (1979) discussion of development of affects and object relatedness, and Gedo's (1979) concept of nodal rearrangements of goals and ambitions.

In this chapter I have examined the relationship between the continuity of cognitive development (from sensorimotor thought, to preoperational thinking, to the beginnings of concrete operations) and the appearance of discontinuous, synthesized constructions of somatic organizations, self and object-schemata, and the synthesis of an Oedipus complex and its resolution. I have suggested that cognitive development is the foundation of these synthesized organizations. In addition each organization also reflects the influence of perception and the internalization of affectively charged interactions with other people. When environmental factors have been pathogenic so as to impinge upon developing self schemata, or where there has been an arrest in cognitive development (as with patients 1, 2, and 3) these synthesized constructions are impaired and clinically function as resistances to new learning within psychoanalytic treatment. It is difficult to assert accurately whether the arrest in cognitive development determines the impairment in the synthetic organizations that I have described, or vice versa. Perhaps the sequence is not as important as the amalgam of the two factors in forming what Freud (1937) called bedrock resistance to change through psychoanalysis. Although with each of the patients I found it plausible to reconstruct the early environmental contexts from transference data (recapitulated earlier), these environmental factors interacted with inherent factors that appeared to lead to difficulties in their capacity to conceptualize. The reconstructions I have made are speculative inferences about both presymbolic and symbolized experience. In a previous paper (Rocah, 1984b) I discussed a developmental perspective, used here and in psychoanalysis in general, as one which raises a number of questions.

One, we do not know the hierarchical ordering or regulatory principles that determine the patterning and internalization of early transactions between caretaker and infant. Two, we do not know how early experience with others acts as an organizer of future encounters:

continuously, discontinuously or at critical periods in the development of an individual. Three, though developmental research is a predictive tool, we do not have the means to predict what aspects of the infant's subjective experience within the infant caregiver system will influence later symbolizations and eventually be patterned into meaningful motivational systems [p. 11].

This chapter has been an attempt to respond to specific aspects of these questions through examining impairments in expected synthesized perceptual-cognitive-affective integrations which are formed in development through an amalgam of inherent factors and experience. These impairments are memorials to maladaptations in development and not only, as I have demonstrated, contribute to pathogenesis, but also provide an area through which the nature and action of continuous and discontinuous factors in development can be examined postdictively.

Progress in treatment was dependent upon assisting my patients in acquiring a capacity to comprehend how they thought as well as the conscious and unconscious contents and conflicts of their subjective world. The most meaningful learning was in understanding the factors that shaped perception and comprehension of the analytic work itself.

REFERENCES

Basch, M. (1976), The concept of affect: A re-examination. *J. Amer. Psychoanal. Assn.*, 24 (4):759–777.
——— (1977), Developmental psychology and explanatory theory in psychoanalysis. *The Annual of Psychoanalysis*, 5:229–268. New York: International Universities Press.
——— (1981), Psychoanalytic interpretation and cognitive transformation. *Internat. J. Psycho-Anal.*, 62 (2):151–177.
Broucek, F. (1979), Efficacy in infancy. A review of some experimental studies and their possible implications for clinical theory. *Internat. J. Psycho-Anal.*, 60(3):311–316.

Dowling, S. (1977), Eleven esophageal atresia infants. *The Psychoanalytic Study of the Child*, 32:215–256. New Haven, CT: Yale University Press.

Emde, R. (1980), Toward a psychoanalytic theory of affect. I. The organizational model and its propositions. In: *The Course of Life*, Vol. 1, ed. S. Greenspan & G. Pollock. Washington, DC: U.S. Department of Health and Human Services, pp. 63–85.

——— (1981), Shaking of the foundations: Charging models of infancy and nature of early development. *J. Amer. Psychoanal. Assn.*, 29(1):179–220.

——— Gaensbauer, T., & Harmon, R. J. (1976), Emotional Expression in Infancy: A Biobehavioral Study. *Psychological Issues*, Monograph 37, 1/10. New York: International Universities Press.

Engel, G., & Reischman, F. (1956), Spontaneous and experimentally induced depression in an infant with a gastric dia fistula. *J. Amer. Psychoanal. Assn.*, 4(3):428–451.

Erikson, E. H. (1959), Identity and the Life Cycle. *Psychological Issues*, Monograph 1/1. New York: International Universities Press.

Ferenczi, S. (1913), Stages in the development of the sense of reality. In: *Contributions to Psychoanalysis*. New York: Basic Books, 1950, pp. 213–239.

Fraiberg, S., & Freedman, D. (1964), Studies in ego development of the congenitally blind child. *The Psychoanalytic Study of the Child*, 19:113–169. New York: International Universities Press.

Freedman, D. (1979), The sensory deprivations: An approach to the study of the emergence of affects and capacity for object relationships. *Bull. Menn. Clin.*, 43:29–68.

Freud, A. (1968), Report of panel discussion held at the 25th Congress of the International Psychoanalytic Association, Copenhagen, July 1968. *Internat. J. Psycho-Anal.*, 49(2–3):506–512.

Freud, S. (1899), Screen memories. *Standard Edition*, 3:303–322. London: Hogarth Press, 1962.

——— (1911), Two principles of mental functioning. *Standard Edition*, 12:213–226. London: Hogarth Press, 1958.

——— (1924), The dissolution of the Oedipus complex. *Standard Edition*, 19:173–182. London: Hogarth Press, 1961.

——— (1926), Inhibitions, symptoms and anxiety. *Standard Edition*, 20:77–178. London: Hogarth Press, 1959.

——— (1937), Analysis terminable and interminable. *Standard Edition*, 23:216–254. London: Hogarth Press, 1964.

Galenson, E., & Roiphe, H. (1971), Impact on early sexual discovery on mood, defensive organization, and symbolization. *The Psychoanalytic Study of the Child*, 26:95–216. New York: Quadrangle Press.

Gedo, J. (1979), *Beyond Interpretation*. New York: International Universities Press.

——— (1981a), Measure for measure. *Psychoanal. Inq.*, 1(2):289–316.

————— (1981b), *Advances in Clinical Psychoanalysis*. New York: International Universities Press.

Hartmann, H. (1953), *Contribution to the Metapsychology of Schizophrenia—Essays on Ego Psychology*. New York: International Universities Press, 1964, pp. 182–206.

Kagan, J. (1974), The form of early development: Continuity and discontinuity in emerging competencies. *Arch. Gen. Psychiat.*, 36:1047–1054.

Kleeman, J. A. (1965), A boy discovers his penis. *The Psychoanalytic Study of the Child*, 20:239–266. New York: International Universities Press.

————— (1966), Genital self discovery during a boy's second year: A follow-up. *The Psychoanalytic Study of the Child*, 21:358–392. New York: International Universities Press.

Klein, G. (1976), *Psychoanalytic Theory: Exploration of Essentials*. New York: International Universities Press.

Kohut, H. (1971), *The Analysis of the Self*. New York: International Universities Press.

————— (1977), *The Restoration of the Self*. New York: International Universities Press.

Lichtenberg, J. (1982), Reflections on the second year of life. Paper presented at the American Psychoanalytic Society Meeting, May 1982, Boston, MA.

Mahler, M., Pine, F., & Bergman, A. (1975), *The Psychological Birth of the Human Infant*. New York: International Universities Press.

Murphy, L. (1980), Psychoanalytic views of infancy. In: *Infancy and Childhood*, ed. S. Greenspan & G. Pollock. Washington, DC: U.S. Department of Health and Human Services, pp. 313–364.

Piaget, J. (1924), Judgement and reasoning in the child. In: *The Essential Piaget*, ed. H. Gruber & J. Voneche. New York: Basic Books, pp. 89–117.

————— (1936), The origins of intelligence in children. In: *The Essential Piaget*, ed. H. Gruber & J. Voneche. New York: Basic Books, pp. 215–239.

————— (1937), The construction of reality in the child. In: *The Essential Piaget*, ed. H. Gruber & J. Voneche. New York: Basic Books, pp. 250–296.

————— (1952), Logic and psychology. In: *The Essential Piaget*, ed. H. Gruber & J. Voneche. New York: Basic Books, pp. 445–481.

————— (1966), The semiotic or symbolic function. In: *The Essential Piaget*, ed. H. Gruber & J. Voneche. New York: Basic Books, pp. 483–508.

Rangell, L. (1981), Panel report: Contemporary problems of psychoanalytic technique, reported by R. Simons. *J. Amer. Psychoanal. Assn.*, 29(3):643–658.

Rocah, B. (1984a), Fixation in late adolescent women: Negative Oedipus complex, fear of being influenced, and resistance to change.

In: *Late Adolescence: Psychoanalytic Studies,* ed. D. Brockman. New York: International Universities Press.

———— (1984b), Introduction to panel: The origins of motivation. In: *Psychoanalysis: The Vital Issues,* Vol. 1, ed. J. Gedo & G. H. Pollock. New York: International Universities Press.

Sadow, L. (1979), Discussion of M. Tolpin and H. Kohut paper "The disorders of the self: The psychopathology of the first years of life." Paper presented at Chicago Psychoanalytic Society, May 22.

Sander, L. (1975), Infant and caretaking environment. In: *Explorations in Child Psychiatry,* ed. E. J. Anthony. New York: Plenum Press, pp. 129–165.

———— (1980), Investigation of the infant and its caregiving environment as a biological system. In: *The Course of Life,* Vol. 1, ed. S. Greenspan & G. Pollock. Washington, DC: U.S. Department of Health and Human Services, pp. 177–202.

———— (1983), Polarity, paradox, and the organizing process. In: *Development in Frontiers of Infant Psychiatry,* ed. J. Call, E. Galenson, & R. Tyson. New York: Basic Books, pp. 333–346.

Sedler, M. (1983), Freud's concept of working through. *Psychoanal. Quart.,* 52(1):73–98.

Shapiro, T. (1977), Oedipal distortions in severe character pathology: Developmental and theoretical considerations. *Psychoanal. Quart.,* 4:559–579.

———— Stern, D. (1980), Psychoanalytic perspectives on the first year of life: Establishment of an object in an affective field. In: *The Course of Life,* Vol. 1, ed. S. Greenspan & G. Pollock. Washington, DC: U.S. Department of Health and Human Services, pp. 113–128.

Spitz, R. (1945), Hospitalism. An inquiry into the genesis of psychiatric conditions in early childhood. *The Psychoanalytic Study of the Child,* 1:53–74. New York: International Universities Press.

———— (1959), *A Genetic Field Theory of Ego Formation.* New York: International Universities Press.

Steckler, G., & Carpenter, G. (1967), A viewpoint on early affective development. In: *The Exceptional Infant,* Vol. 1. Seattle, WA: Special Child Publications, pp. 163–189.

White, R. W. (1959), Motivation reconsidered: The concept of competence. *Psychol. Rev.,* 66:297–333.

Chapter 17

Gender Identity, Cognitive Development, and Emotional Conflict

MARTIN A. SILVERMAN, M.D.

INTRODUCTION

Relatively few women have benefited so far from the progressive opening up to them of greater job and career opportunities which has taken place in recent years. There have been three women prime ministers in the world, and the number of white upper-class women in certain professions and in nonclerical business positions has increased significantly in a number of countries. The *overall* distribution between women and men of work opportunities and earning power has not changed to any great extent, however. Reflection upon some of the psychological factors that may have contributed to this is in order.

Vast social and economic changes have taken place in our society since the turn of the century. These have provided women with unprecedented opportunities for personal achievement and success in a broad range of business, professional, and creative activities which previously had been reserved almost exclusively for men.

451

With the shift from a predominantly rural, agrarian society to an urban, industrial, and increasingly technological one, the role of manual labor and, with it, the premium placed on sheer physical strength and endurance have decreased enormously. Vastly improved health care has led (except among the most disadvantaged socioeconomic strata) to greatly reduced infant and child mortality rates. Together with improved birth control methods, heightened awareness of the dangers of overpopulation, and vast improvement in the salaries of individual workers as the result of unionization and changed governmental attitudes, this has greatly decreased the birth rate and the size of the average family. Today's women are required to devote much less time and energy than their predecessors to the tasks of childbearing and child rearing at the same time that they are living much longer lives. This has freed them to pursue other avenues of achievement without necessarily having to give up the realization of maternal ambitions.

A number of factors have combined to promote an unheralded degree of openness to shift and change in societal values and attitudes, including those that bear upon the relationship between the sexes. There has been a revolution in the speed of communication and of travel. The explanatory power of investigative science has blossomed at the expense of religion, which is a much more conservative force acting in the direction of acceptance and maintenance of the status quo. The role of the extended family as a mediator of traditional roles and values has been reduced to such an extent that it is all but threatened with extinction. Stimulated in part by the startling revelations resulting from Freud's investigations into the depths of the human psyche, there has been a trend toward reexamination of personal motives, goals, and individual possibilities. The net effect of all this has been a great diminution in the impact of tradition in shaping people's lives and an unprecedented openness to reassessment, redirection, and change in personal goals and aims.

The widening of the range of channels of self-realization available to women in our society has coincided with a burgeoning financial incentive to take advantage of them. People's appetites have been whetted for an increasing share of the abundance of material goods, services, and recreational opportunities which has become available in technologically successful societies to fill the expanding leisure time available to workers at all levels. At the same time, it is difficult for most families to obtain all that they want with the income that can be provided by a single worker.

As a result of this combination of factors, women have become more and more able, inclined, and at times even pressured to go beyond their traditional roles as helpmates to breadwinning husbands and as the main force in raising children and maintaining the family home. A broad opportunity has opened up for women to go out into the business and professional world to develop their talents and capabilities in the pursuit of personally and financially rewarding careers of their own. Yet far fewer women have availed themselves of this opportunity than might have been expected; and of those who have done so relatively few have attained positions of significant power and leadership.

It might have been expected that men would be quick to recognize the advantages of sharing the burden of earning a living with their wives. Yet men have proved to be a good deal less than eager to avail themselves of the opportunity to ease their burden and increase their families' material and recreational advantages by supporting their wives' entry into the economic marketplace. Instead of welcoming the possibility of reducing their own grueling workloads or of increasing family income without working any harder themselves, they have tended more often than not to oppose the idea of their wives seeking

jobs and developing their own careers. Rather than viewing the latter option as offering advantages to the two of
them, they have tended instead to perceive it as endan-
gering the man's status and prestige (i.e., as a threat to
masculine pride and self-esteem). At the same time, many
women have been suspicious of a more egalitarian attitude toward job and career opportunities, fearing that it
will shrink their area of traditional privileges, deprive
them of their exemption from hazardous responsibilities,
and threaten the earning power of their husbands. The
Equal Rights Amendment has not been opposed by men
alone.

Many men resent women who "invade" what they
have come to view as their rightful territory in order to
"usurp" the roles and prerogatives they regard as belonging more or less exclusively to them. Many women,
on the other hand, fear that their femininity will be compromised if they enter occupations that in the past were
available only to men or if they assertively pursue promotion and advancement in competition with men. They
worry seriously about the accusation that they are seeking to dominate and "castrate" their male counterparts
rather than merely seeking an egalitarian place of their
own in accordance with their own talents and capabilities. Couples pursuing the personal and material rewards
available in a dual-career, dual-income marriage run a
considerable risk of having their union come undone.
Households in which husbands and wives share both the
breadwinning function and the domestic and childrearing
tasks turn out statistically to be relatively unstable. A
marriage in which the wife earns a larger income than
her husband is in particular danger of foundering.

Why is this so? Why are women and men having so
much difficulty making the adjustments necessary for
them to take advantage of all the new opportunities available to them? Some disappointed feminists have explained it in terms of a male-female power struggle that

involves external, sociological factors alone. They claim that men are reluctant to give up the prerogatives and advantages that accrue to them when power and economic strength are concentrated in their hands and women are relegated to a dependent status in which they are obliged to please the men upon whom they rely. Women who shrink back from pursuing personal achievement in the economic marketplace do so according to this point of view because they are bullied, brainwashed, and blocked from realizing their potentials by men who do not wish to see their ability to dominate and control women come to an end.

Analysis of women who attribute their failure to pursue personal achievement to male suppression, however, reveals that beneath this conscious point of view are much deeper, far-reaching, unconscious sources of inhibition that are hindering them from pursuing accomplishment, satisfaction, and pleasure in *multiple* areas of their lives. The analysis of men who oppose changes in the traditional allocation of roles among male and female members of society similarly reveals far more important unconscious reasons beneath their more acceptable, conscious reasons for doing so.

EMOTIONAL AND COGNITIVE DEVELOPMENT

To understand the unconscious factors involved it is necessary to look at the complex developmental pathways that lead to gender identity, gender role identity, and the male and female attitudes and expectations that determine the relationship between the sexes. A complex interaction between emotional and cognitive elements is involved in this developmental process. To begin with, it is evident that learning plays a major role in the development both of core gender identity, that is, one's view of oneself as male or female, and of gender role identity, the set of views and attitudes one holds about the roles to be played by each sex, separately and in relationship with one another (for a detailed examination of the difference between core gender identity and gender role identity see Tyson [1982]). As I have indicated previously (Silverman, 1981), parents harbor very different feelings about, attitudes toward, and expectations of their male and female children from the moment they are born. By acting and reacting differently toward boys and girls from the very beginning, they teach them not only to which sex they belong but also what is expected of them for belonging to that sex. These differences in parental approach have very little to do with actual differences between newborn boys and girls.

Male and female neonates do exhibit certain intrinsic differences, but they are quite minor (Lichtenstein, 1961; Stoller, 1968, 1976; Green, 1976; Kleeman, 1976; Sander, Julien, and Burns, 1976). According to Annelise Korner (as cited by Konner [1982]), for example, newborn boys exhibit somewhat greater muscle strength, as indicated by more head lift in the prone position, while newborn girls exhibit somewhat greater skin and taste sensitivity, more searching movement with their mouths, more reflex smiling, and a quicker response to light flashes. Maccoby and Jacklin (1974), in a review of hundreds of careful studies of children, found no consistent pattern of sex differences in general intellectual ability, discriminative learning, social memory, competitiveness, motivation to achieve, imitation, conformity, suggestibility, or self-esteem. They found very weak evidence of greater tactile sensitivity, timidity, and compliance in girls, and of greater assertion of dominance in boys. In the cognitive sphere, they found good evidence only for superior visual-spatial and quantitative ability in boys and men (the recent observation by de Lacoste-Utamsing and Holloway [1982] that in the nine male and five female brains they dissected, the rear portion of the corpus callosum, the region which is believed to play a role in transferring visual and spatial information between the right and left cortical hemispheres, was larger and more bulbous in the males; this is the first anatomical evidence of possible differences between male and female brains) and for superior verbal ability in girls and women. The strongest evidence they found for gender differences was for a greater tendency for girls to develop nurturant attitudes toward infants and for much more aggressive behavior in boys. Even here, however, it is unclear to what extent these observations reflect intrinsic, inborn differences and to what extent they derive from differences in parental handling and expectations of their male and female children.

There certainly may be intrinsic physical, including hormonal, factors that contribute to "masculine" and "feminine" attitudes and self-perceptions. The studies carried out by Stoller (1968), Money and Ehrhardt (1972), and others certainly point in this direction, although not unequivocally. A unique condition being studied by Julianne Imperato-McGinley (cited by Konner [1982]) and her colleagues at New York Hospital–Cornell Medical Center has afforded an opportunity to observe both the impact of hormonal factors and the capacity of human beings to undergo remarkable adjustments when hormone effects go awry. Thirty-eight individuals from twenty-three, interrelated families in three rural Dominican Republic villages have been found who, because of a genetic defect, lack the enzyme 5-alpha-reductase, which converts testosterone into dihydrotestosterone. Because of this, they have normal levels of testosterone, but almost a total lack of dihydrotestosterone. Since *both* are needed for the development of male external sex characteristics the boys are born looking like girls, and they are raised as girls. Pubertal changes raise the level of dihydrotestosterone sufficiently for phallic growth, testicular descent, deepening of the voice, and development of a masculine muscular pattern when they reach the age of twelve years or so. Seventeen of eighteen such boys who have been studied have demonstrated the ability to transform themselves from female to male gender identity and gender role identity (though not without considerable emotional strain and years of confusion along the way), without any formal outside assistance. The investigators reason that the testosterone circulating within these boys during gestation and throughout their childhoods had had a masculinizing effect on their *brains,* even though their external sexual characteristics had misled them as to their gender (the familial occurrence of this disorder, of course, must contribute significant cultural assistance). The basic plan of brain structure appears to be a feminine one in mammals, with testosterone producing a masculinizing effect, while in birds it is just the reverse.

Another group that demonstrates the apparent effects of this upon gender role identity consists of girls born with adrenogenital syndrome. Erhardt has reported that they tend to be more tomboyish and less interested in dolls and in eventual marriage and childbearing than other girls when they reach ten years of age. They attribute this to the masculinizing effect on the brain of the unusually high level of testosterone circulating during gestation, since surgical correction after birth restores a normal level thereafter (again, the impact of the attitudes of parents and other family members toward them from the time of their birth probably plays a significant role as well).

THE DEVELOPMENT OF GENDER IDENTITY AND GENDER ROLE IDENTITY

The development of a person's self-perception as male or female, together with what it means to belong to one sex or the other, is a learning experience whose nature is determined by a combination of cognitive and emotional

factors that change and evolve over the course of childhood and adolescence. Core gender identity (i.e., the
child's self-perception as a boy or a girl), which develops
as an integral part of the self-representation that emerges
out of cognitive maturation and development, is clearly
observable by the time the child is walking, and achieves
stability by the middle of the second year, according to
Kleeman (1971, 1976) and Money and Ehrhardt (1972).
It is irreversible by three years of age, according to Stoller
(1976), though Roiphe and Galenson (1981) question this.
Since it develops within the preoedipal, separation-individuation process that takes place during the child's
first three years, it is marked by the vicissitudes of all
that takes place between mother and child and by the
oral and sadistic-anal conflicts through which the child
passes during that period of time. Kohlberg's (1966) contention that cognitive maturation alone determines gender identity is reductionistic in its ignoring of other
factors.

Human infants are born in an immature (secondarily
altricial) and therefore helpless state, and they come into
the world with sex-related, biological differences that are
very subtle and slight. The initial balance of forces, therefore, is heavily weighted in favor of parental influences
as the predominating factor (even as the child matures
into a more effective initiator, parental input will continue to be a vital force).

Parents bring with them all their own complex feelings and attitudes about male and female as they handle,
respond to, and present their infant children with sets of
expectations and requirements that reinforce some behaviors and discourage others. As they hold, administer
to, and play with them, they speak and act differently
with their male and female offspring, thereby offering
them very different signals and instructions as to what
is fitting and what is not for a boy and for a girl. These
interactional details of ongoing experience become codi-

fied within each child as more or less patterned engrams of coenesthetic self-perception that constitute the beginnings of the sensorimotor awareness of self. Cognition is organized at first primarily in the reproductive assimilations and accommodations and the circular reactions that take place in the course of interaction between infants and their caretakers. The earliest influences that ultimately lead to self-perception, self-image, and self-regard inevitably are affected, therefore, by the experiential reflection of the different feelings and attitudes which parents bring to their male and female offspring.

Even newborn infants demonstrate a remarkable capacity for learning, via rapid accommodation to variations in external stimuli. They mold and pattern themselves to their caretakers' holding behavior, ways of ministering to, and expectations of them, even as the latter more or less empathically read and respond to the infants' rhythms, cues, and variations (see Bennett [1971] for a striking commentary on the degree to which caretakers can distort their perceptions of infants on the basis of preconceived notions and personal biases, which then influence their way of relating to them).

Infants' experience of life is so intimately intertwined with what is brought to them by their mothers in the course of their ongoing, reciprocal interaction that, psychologically speaking, infants do not have a separate, independent existence apart from them (Mahler, 1963, 1968, 1974; Jacobson, 1964; Winnicott, 1965; Kohut, 1971). The impact of the initial, soothing "primal identification" (Freud, 1926) with the mother is longstanding and fateful, although it is somewhat different in boys and in girls. It is disturbed by the gradual ascendancy of the infant as a force within the mother-infant dyad, because of central nervous system maturation during the first year (Sander, 1969).

As the infant develops an appreciation of separateness from the mother, during the latter half of the first year and into the second year, he or she experiences considerable distress (the prototype of expulsion from the Garden of Eden and of nostalgia in general?). At first this distress is organismic and sensorimotor in nature. It is observable in the form of the five-month-old baby crying and reaching toward the mother who is leaving the room, and then in the stranger anxiety of many eight- to ten-month-old infants. Symbolic mental imagery and evocative memory begin to appear toward the end of the first year and during the first half of the second year, as a result of the sensorimotor explorations and imitative actions that have occupied the baby in waking hours until then. They convert the organismic distress that has accompanied the sensorimotor realization of separateness from the mother into the beginning of truly psychological selfobject differentiation. This produces fear of the loss of the mother, the first of the three great fears (of object loss, loss of the object's love, and castration) that Freud (1926) described as central motivating factors in human psychology. The anxiety and sadness that the infant in this developmental phase experiences as a result of separation from the mother is poignantly evident in the sleep disturbances (characterized in particular by refusal to go to sleep unless the mother is present), periodic fretful moods, and the use of transitional objects and phenomena (Winnicott, 1953) to create an illusion of oneness with the absent mother, especially at bedtime or when the child is ill or unhappy. These observations apply equally to male and female infants and toddlers, although there has been little study of the ways in which boy and girl infants may differ with regard to them, and further investigation into differences in the ways in which mothers relate to their male and female infants would be very welcome.

The enormous pull toward identificatory union and oneness with the all-giving, all-powerful mother presents the same kind of problem for the boy and for the girl at

first, but eventually it will become very different for
them. The toddler necessarily undergoes a crisis of ambivalence with regard to his or her awareness of separateness from the mother, for alongside the distress that
comes with the knowledge that the mother is a separate
being with a will of her own, so that intermittent loss of
her is inevitable, is an equally powerful, aggressive wish
to be free from the weak and helpless dependence upon
her that characterizes their relationship during the first
year or so after birth. The ascendancy of symbolic mental
imagery (and, hence, representational intelligence and
the beginnings of language) during the first half of the
second year occurs pari passu with the acquisition, at
long last, of bipedal locomotion. Toddlers become intox-
icated with their newly gained mastery of space and
newly achieved capacity for independent, self-reliant assertion of their own will. As Mahler and her colleagues
have clearly demonstrated, young toddlers in the "practicing subphase" of the separation-individuation process
become so entranced with the exercise of these new abilities that they lose interest in their mothers and in what
their mothers provide for them, with consequent major
impact not only upon themselves but also upon their
mothers.

Observation indicates that practicing toddlers periodically are stirred out of their absorption in the independent exercise of their motor, sensory, and intellectual
capacities by the disturbing realization that it has taken
them away from the mothers who are so important to
them emotionally. Indeed, the mothers apparently are
still viewed in a blurry way as a part of them, that is, as
so important that they cannot be fully accepted as indi-
visible from them. Children in the practicing period require the mother's presence (and they develop an apparent
"low-keyed" sadness if she removes herself from their
vicinity). They are observed periodically to interrupt the
independent exploratory activity that preoccupies them

in order to make brief, physical contact with the mother. This "emotional refueling" (Mahler, 1974; Mahler, Pine, and Bergman, 1975) appears to be necessary if the toddler is to be able to continue to function independently of her for a while longer. The mother is a necessary audience to the toddler's seemingly independent, narcissistic-exhibitionistic exercise of his or her newly acquired ability to function alone.

There appears to be a to-and-fro, dependent-independent, ambivalent conflict in which urges to bite, push, and dart away from the mother vie with a powerful insistence upon closeness and union with her that, in accordance with the egocentric orality of that period of life, provoke fantasies of fusion and mutual engulfment. The toddler requires the mother's presence but becomes enraged when she interferes with his or her assertion of independence and self-will. The crisis of ambivalence taking place in the child is more or less matched by one that occurs in the mother. The bearing and raising of children forms an integral part of what is viewed as the essence of femaleness. A mother harbors mixed feelings toward the infants who were created by her and have developed within her body (so that psychologically they were perceived as a part of her), only to part from her in pain and then, after a time of total dependence upon her, increasingly "reject" her ministrations, her offerings, and her leadership to move off on their own, away from her. She both values and resents the infants' dependence upon her, with all the demands that go with it, and she tends to be equally ambivalent about their movement away from her, toward independent self-assertion. A certain amount of hurt at finding herself becoming apparently less important and less needed by her child (who even tends to lose interest in food during the practicing period) is more or less inevitable. At the same time, her child's lessening dependence upon her has to be relatively welcome, and the necessity to curb the toddler and impose rules of behavior, in the interest of safety and order, leads to friction that both reinforces their awareness of their separateness from one another and heightens the ambivalent tension between them.

The result is, as Mahler terms it, an intense *rapprochement crisis* between mother and child, in which they must come to terms with their separateness and togetherness, their independence and interdependence, their mutual hate and mutual love, the vicissitudes of the power struggle going on between them and the problems presented to them by their excitement with each other and with other animate love and hate objects in their lives. In the midst of all this, gender-related attitudes and expectations that will form the essence of the child's gender role identity develop out of the intersection between parental (especially maternal) perceptions and attitudes and the child's emerging perception of itself as a boy or a girl. The latter at first is a simple learning process that takes place without awareness of anatomical differences between the sexes.

Beginning somewhere in the middle of the second year, in the midst of increasing awareness of anal and urinary functions, however, children begin to develop an increased genital awareness associated with a focused interest in the sensations they experience in their genitals. Both an endogenous, maturational factor and an exogenous factor consisting of external stimulation appear to be involved in this. Sooner or later, boys and girls are confronted with the anatomical distinction between the sexes, which they quickly incorporate into their perception of their gender identity as a boy or girl. This places them under considerable cognitive and emotional strain. The preoperational cognitive organization of the preschool child does not permit the construction of a clear, logical, complete understanding of anatomical differences based on the coordination of criteria of inclusion and exclusion of all details. Instead, the preschool child thinks syncretically, concretely, and physicalistically (Piaget, 1932, 1947, 1950; Silverman, 1971), defining what is seen by means of the immediate, global perception of surface features to which meaning is ascribed in an egocentric, global fashion that disregards discrepant details and blurs physical, causal, and psychological relationships with one another. The young child confronted with the anatomical differences between the sexes at first cannot clearly and logically understand that there are two classes of beings with equally valuable, useful, and important sexual organs, nor can he or she readily apprehend features that are not directly observable and/or palpable, with the preoperational thinking that is available to the preschool child. The boy and the girl alike, therefore, become swept up at first in a phallocentric point of view in which penis, scrotum, and testicles are prized as large, external, readily observable, valued genital organs and the primarily internal, unobservable, impalpable female genital organs cannot be readily apprehended, conceptualized, or valued. The little girl's discovery that she does not possess the genital structures she sees on her father or brothers is experienced as a major narcissistic injury, especially as it usually takes place during a phase of intense narcissistic-exhibitionistic pride in bodily skill, strength, and prowess (Tartakoff, 1966). The little boy reacts with shock to his discovery of beings that do not possess the genital organs he prizes and with fear that he might lose them. Neither the boy nor the girl can imagine that the preoedipally perceived, all-powerful mother lacks these organs, and direct observation of her penislessness is greeted at first with disbelief or denial. The belief that the mother does possess those organs somewhere within her contributes to an interest in the insides of the mother's body that already had begun with fascination with her capacity to produce babies from within her. In the boy, this interest in the insides of his mother's body combines with impulses to

obtain pleasure in his tumescent penis by thrusting it
against something to lead him toward a dawning perception of heterosexual genital activity. In the girl, it combines with her self-exploratory discovery of her vaginal,
urethral, and anal openings, her own fascination with
her mother's ability to give birth, and her syncretic
awareness of her similarity to her mother and her
mother's body. These pull her toward what Kestenberg
(1968) has characterized as the central importance to the
little girl of inner genital sensations and an inner-genital
body space.

FLIGHT FROM THE PREOEDIPAL MOTHER TO THE FATHER AND OEDIPALITY

As the little boy and the little girl gradually realize that
their mother does not possess the penis and testicles they
at first have insisted upon attributing to her, they are
faced with a dilemma that impels them away from her
and toward the father as an object of their narcissistic
desires. The boy's castration anxiety reinforces his need
to struggle against the pull toward identification with
the powerful, dominating, and controlling, preoedipal
mother in the interest of separation-individuation and
independence. He turns toward his father as a narcissistically endowed love object with whom he can identify
on the basis of their common possession of male genitalia.
When he does so, however, he finds that possession of a
penis and testicles is all they have in common, and that
he has a much smaller and therefore inferior replica of
his father's genitals at that. He is not big and strong like
his father, and he possesses a high-pitched voice and soft,
smooth skin that more closely resemble those of his
mother than the deep voice and hairy, rough exterior of
his father. The net effect is for boys to emulate their
fathers, who by and large have been handling them much
more roughly than their more empathic, gentle mothers

from the time they were little babies, as Brazelton's films, for example, readily demonstrate. They renounce their maternal, inner-directed tendencies and put a premium on being rough, tough, big, and strong, as they perceive their fathers to be. (This is exemplified by the two-and-a-half-year to three-year-old boy who excitedly hurried his father through dinner every night so that they could box with inflated, "socker-bopper" boxing gloves, explaining "I'm little and you're big; I want you to help me get big and strong," adding after a while "so I can knock you down!") This tends to be reinforced by the differential attitudes of parents toward their male and female children, in which mothers and fathers alike tend to expect their little sons to be more aggressive, resistant, and hard to handle than they expect their little daughters to be.

The latter tend to turn away from their mothers to their fathers as the source of rough, tough strength and power, which they too perceive them to be. The little girl's pull toward oneness with the mother that hinders her in her quest for individuation and independence is even greater than is the boy's because of her identification with her mother as another female, so that she has a great deal to overcome. She has a powerful need, furthermore, to find the strength to struggle against her mother's forcible domination of, control over, and forcible removal of her valuable "insides" in the course of toilet training. It is probable that girls become toilet trained earlier than boys not only because of their intrinsically more precocious rhythmicity, frustration tolerance, self-control, and educability, but also by the tendency for mothers to be more stringent in their requirements that their daughters be neat and clean than they are with their sons, because of the unconscious residue of their need to master and overcome their cloacal confusion over their own vaginal and excretory body openings. (I am indebted to Dr. Sara Vogel for calling my attention to this important dimension of mother-daughter relationships.) It is important to keep in mind that the neat sequence of oral, followed by sadistic-anal, and then phallic, and finally oedipal psychosexual phases described by Freud are actually far less discrete and sequential than he heuristically described them. In actuality, as Marianne Kris (1957) has cogently pointed out (Silverman and Neubauer, 1971), there is a large degree of overlap and simultaneity among these various developmental dimensions.

When the boy's attention is drawn to his father as a source of phallic pride and strength, this brings with it the realization not only that his father is better endowed than he is but also that his father is the preferred object of his mother's sexual desire. His rough, tough emulation of his father is heightened by intense rivalrousness that spurs him to the wish to battle against, outdo, and take away his father's masculine strength so as to replace him as his mother's favorite, in a positive oedipal victory. The terror of castration that results from the combination of projective fear of retaliation and fear of the homosexual fantasy of sexual submission to his father in order to take in and obtain his larger genital organ, impels him to repress his oedipal urges, internalize his father's prohibitional and punitive voice as a more or less strict, internal voice of conscience, turn away from his genital concerns and his sexual interests, sublimate his aggressive, competitive strivings into athletic and (via displacement upward) scholastic rivalry with his male peers, and deny his excited interest in females by disparaging them and turning away from them in order to band together with his male peers in a world from which females are excluded. Deflection of the dangerous, aggressively rivalrous, oedipal impulses into defensive reassurance of the intactness of the boy's masculinity by acting rough and tough, but only within an exclusively masculine world, produces an outwardly desexualized, hypermasculine, aggressively macho, fidgety school-age boy who not infrequently has difficulty settling down, behaving himself, and submitting to domination by the predominantly female teachers he encounters in school. It is not surprising that boys are found so much more often than girls to present behavioral and learning problems during the early school-age years.

When a little girl turns to her father for the phallic strength she desires, she is propelled first into a negative oedipal phase in which she hopes to obtain from him the phallus with which she can compete with him as her mother's preferred sexual object. She fantasies using it to fill up her mother's inner genital space, at the same time obtaining a narcissistically acceptable way of reuniting with the mother with whom she once had been one. This quickly leads to a positive oedipal rivalry with her mother to be loved preferentially by her exciting father and to have her own inner genital space filled by his penis. The latter wish becomes interwoven with the preoedipal wish to contain and produce babies like her mother as it is transformed into the wish to be lovingly impregnated by the father and outdo her mother in the production of many, many babies. A powerful impetus to suppress and repress the negative oedipal fantasy derives from the need to struggle against the urge to fuse and reunite with the mother and thereby lose the separateness, independence, and self-reliance she has labored so hard to achieve. It is reinforced by anxious dread of the aggressive impulse to castrate her father to punish him for possessing the idealized and coveted phallus which she lacks and to steal it away for herself (in part, she is pressured by intense strictures, at first imposed by her mother and then internalized, to control herself and hold in the dangerously dirty, messy, destructive substances within her, which in the syncretic, preoperational child are equated with aggressive, destructive psychological urges, as Melanie Klein [1932] has vividly described).

She is impelled to suppress and repress her positive

oedipal inclinations by equally powerful psychological forces. Not only does her positive oedipal rivalrousness threaten her with the loss of the love and protection of her primary love object, but the aggressiveness involved conflicts with the enormous pride she has built up in being soft, gentle, nutritive, caring, and caretaking like the mother to whom she has been acutely aware of being similar. Furthermore, she feels woefully deficient as a rival to her mother, possessing none of the curves, breasts, pubic hair, and feminine know-how she perceives her mother as possessing. Even after she moves beyond the fantasy that her mother's pubic hair conceals a hidden penis and testicles, she is acutely aware of her inability as yet to produce babies from her insides the way her mother has done, and is preoperationally unable adequately to appreciate the value and wondrousness of her internal, unobservable, all but impalpable internal female sexual organs (Silverman, 1981). She can only be terrified by her wishes to be overpowered and raped by her father, whose huge penis she fears would tear her apart. Perceiving her intralabial cleft as a wound, she egocentrically interprets it as evidence of punishment for her evil fantasies and deeds and a sign of worse punishment to come (Ernest Jones [1927] referred to this as aphanisis) if she does not control herself henceforth. The superego development that ensues, as part of the repression of her oedipal strivings as she enters the school-age years, is more complex than is that of the boy, because of the greater complexity of her pathway toward it. In some ways her suppression and repression of her aggressive, oedipal inclinations is greater than that of the boy. This is evidenced in the degree to which she must suppress her aggressivity (which is at least as important as intrinsic, biological differences between boys and girls in rendering the school-age girl so much less aggressive than the boy) and in the extent to which she turns it back upon herself, leading to a much greater degree of inhibition and depression in girls of latency age (Beller and Neubauer, 1963) and beyond. At the same time, the need to deflect sexual impulses away from her mother toward her father leads to a greater degree of consciously aroused positive oedipal excitement than is observed in a boy of the same age. She suppresses her competitiveness, with boys as well as with girls, and devotes herself to the skillful management of interpersonal conflict. In deference to the complex juggling act she must maintain, she becomes much more sophisticated in matters of conscience, exercising care and flexible attention to individual personalities and relationships, as compared with the more primitive, global applications of rigidly codified rules and regulations that are typical of the boy's superego activity. Unlike boys, who tend to band together in group activities that reassure them as to their masculinity via mutual support and control of intragroup competition by imposing strict rules upon it and by redirecting it against the superordinate, common enemy of opposing groups and teams, girls tend to congregate in small numbers and to maintain precariously balanced individual relationships that are as motherly as they are sisterly in the caring, guiding, helping dimension that plays such an important part in them.

Adolescence provides an opportunity for boys and girls to revise their attitudes toward themselves and toward each other, and to reconstruct the ground plan that governs the relationship between the sexes. Patterns that have been built up out of fear and pain and then have been systematized by years of practice do not come apart easily, however. Despite shifts during this transitional period that permit male and female teenagers to more or less shed the constraints that until then have kept them apart, they enter adulthood with patterned gender role attitudes and inclinations, largely defensive in origin, that more often than not continue to influence them as they pair off in heterosexual unions. The cycle of intergenerational transmission of social patterns that dovetail with individual, unconscious, psychological systems has provided young adults in our society with a social structure that has defined the distribution of gender-related roles in compliance with the solutions reached by the individual members within it of the developmental struggles they have had to negotiate en route to adulthood.

As social patterns change, a great deal of stress is placed upon the individuals who make up the society to rearrange the ways in which their personal psychological solutions interweave with the societal solutions into which they have to fit. This is especially so during a time of transition from one pattern of interaction to another. We currently are going through such a period of social change. Traditional patterns of gender-linked role distribution have been changing relatively rapidly. It should not be extremely surprising that men have been finding it difficult to adjust to the loss of traditional male sanctuaries from which women are excluded, to having to compete with women in professional and industrial activities which women are beginning to enter in significant numbers, to earning jointly with their spouses instead of for them, to sharing in household duties that until recently had been labeled as feminine ones, and so on. Nor should it surprise us that individual women have been finding it difficult to overcome the restriction and inhibition of the aggressivity they have built up in order to become assertive and competitive in the job market instead of keeping the peace and maintaining workable relationships, to compete with men instead of relying on them for strength and protection, to jeopardize their complex femininity by engaging in activities traditionally labeled as masculine, and so on. It will take time to make the changes that have to be made, and it is inevitable that there will be casualties along the way.

The course boys and girls traverse on their way to adulthood is a complex one, in which cognitive and emotional developmental factors take part in integration with one another. The complexity is so great that it is difficult to apprehend fully all that is involved, and this attempt to encompass it all within one small, unified net does not truly do justice to the intricacies and complexities that are involved. But it is useful to try to embrace the total picture in all its complexity. A tendency to which some investigators in the social sciences fall prey is to reduce the overwhelming complexity of the field being observed by looking at only part of it, leading them to reductionistic and simplistic formulations. If one looks only at external, social, and economic factors, for example, one can ascribe reluctance to make changes in gender-related, social role distribution to a simple power play between those who do not want to relinquish advantages they hold to an oppressed, weaker sex that is reluctant to continue to maintain the status quo. If one looks only at the psychosexual conflicts with which children grapple, one can conceptualize it entirely in terms of the social expression of oedipal conflicts. If one looks only at cognitive factors, that can lead to a constructivist formulation that ignores emotional conflict and explains the adoption of gender-related traits and characteristics in purely cognitive terms. Ullian (1981, 1982, 1984), for example, following Kohlberg's cognitive approach, accepts the responses made by four- to seven-year-olds to questionnaires at face value and attributes the differentiation they make between male and female characteristics to their physicalistic observation of surface features alone. She seems not to recognize that by the age of four, children have turned their conscious attention away from deeper emotional sources of their feelings and attitudes about themselves in relation to their mothers and fathers.

A POSTSCRIPT ON PATTERNS OF LEARNING

If one looks at certain intellectual differences observable in boys and girls and men and women, one can devise simple (i.e., simplistic) explanatory hypotheses that appear to be acceptable but are misleading in their one-sidedness. It is well known, for example, that boys tend to excel in mathematics and science, areas of learning in which girls and women tend to be less adept, while girls and women tend in general to excel in the areas of study that are interpersonal and "soft" rather than "hard" and mechanical. There is a tendency to attribute the differences entirely to biological factors, such as variations in male and female brain functioning (either intrinsic or due to hormonal effects). And there very well may be biological differences between male and female brains, as de Lacoste-Utamsing and Holloway's observation (1982) of differences in the thickness of the portion of the corpus callosum in male and female brains that carries nerve fibers involved in spatial and visual information (however small the number of brains examined) may indicate.

Nevertheless, biological factors are far from all that are involved. As Erikson (1950) noted, for example, little girls and little boys have very different preoccupations in the play activities they utilize to puzzle out and master the mysteries and problems that confront them in their lives. Little girls tend to construct containers and enclosures with blocks, he noticed, while little boys tend more often to build tall towers. My own observation of three- and four-year-old nursery school children selecting a toy to take with them to their cots at naptime points in the same direction. Boys tend to choose trains, cars, airplanes, and so on, to propel across the cot and through the air. Girls tend to select little animals or dolls, or boxes that nest within each other. That there is a connection between these choices and the need of children of this age to explore and understand, on themselves and via the manipulation of symbolic materials, their genitals and the masturbatory impulses associated with genital sensations is corroborated by child analytic observations.

The need of little boys to figure out the meaning of move- ments and changes in the size and shape of their penis and testicles (penile tumescence and detumescense, tes- ticular retraction and scrotal wrinkling) undoubtedly contributes to their interest in mathematical measure- ment, the laws of physics, spatial relations, mechanical devices, and so on. Little girls need to puzzle out and understand their complex genital anatomy by minutely examining and sorting out all the little bumps and folds and openings of their external genitalia and attending vigilantly to faint, difficult to define, inner genital sen- sations, in turn contributes to their sensitivity to subtle details, nuances of meaning, intuitive hints, and the per- sonal as opposed to the concrete and inanimate. It is not surprising that men find their way by consulting road maps, while women tend to be adept in using landmarks to negotiate the route from one point to another—"I don't know where it is on the map, but you turn right when you get to the big stone church with ivy on it, go up the hill for a while, turn left when you get to a corner where there's a white house with a big tree on one side and a gray Cape Cod with a bluish roof on the other side." These differences tend to become more or less generalized and codified into patterns of gender-related expectations (e.g., "boys are good at math and science but girls are not"). These hinder children and adolescents from transcending the impact of their early preoccupation with the myster- ies of genital definition and functioning as they develop beyond it by imposing influential social restraints and guidelines upon them. They contribute to the perpetua- tion of sexist categorization and to fear of jeopardizing one's femininity or masculinity by pursuing interests that are identified as belonging to the other sex.

CONCLUSION

If current and future generations of men and women are to succeed in their efforts to adjust to changing conditions in such a way that they realize the new opportunities available to them, improve the quality of their lives, and reduce rather than increase the degree of strain and tension under which they operate, they will need to struggle against the forces of inertia, resistance to change, and fear of the new and unknown that express themselves within the confluent impact of social pressure and individual psychological struggle. The complex nature both of social forces and of individual developmental pathways encourages reductionism, simplification, and scotomization in order to reduce the field of view to what seems like more manageable proportions in an attempt to understand the factors involved. This only leads to distortion, however, that impedes rather than facilitates understanding.

Neither biological factors nor psychological ones are more important than the other in human development; neither cognition nor emotional conflict is more important than the other. What makes human personality fascinating is the multiplicity of interwoven, undulating threads and materials of which it is constituted. We need not fear the complexity of human beings, nor should we deny it. It is only by respecting and appreciating that complexity that we can put ourselves in a position to comprehend and master it.

REFERENCES

Beller, E., & Neubauer, P. (1963), Sex differences and symptom patterns in early childhood. *J. Amer. Acad. Child Psychiat.*, 2:417–433.

Bennett, S. L. (1971), Infant-caretaker interactions. *J. Amer. Acad. Child Psychiat.*, 10:321–335.

de Lacoste-Utamsing, C., & Holloway, R. L. (1982), Sexual dimorphism in the human corpus callosum. *Science*, 216:1431–1432.

Erikson, E. (1950), *Childhood and Society*. New York: W. W. Norton.

Freud, S. (1926), Inhibitions, symptoms and anxiety. *Standard Edition*, 20:75–174. London: Hogarth Press, 1959.

Green, R. (1976), Human sexuality: Research and treatment frontiers.

In: *American Handbook of Psychiatry*, ed. S. Arieti. New York: Basic Books, pp. 665–691.

Jacobson, E. (1964), *The Self and the Object World*. New York: International Universities Press.

Jones, E. (1927), The early development of female sexuality. In: *Papers on Psycho-Analysis*. Boston: Beacon Press, pp. 438–451.

Kestenberg, J. (1968), Outside, inside, male, female. *J. Amer. Psychoanal. Assn.*, 16:457–520.

Kleeman, J. A. (1971), The establishment of core gender identity in normal girls. *Arch. Sex. Behav.*, 1:103–129.

———— (1976), Freud's views on female sexuality in the light of direct child observation. *J. Amer. Psychoanal. Assn.*, 24:3–28.

Klein, M. (1932), *The Psycho-Analysis of Children*. New York: Grove Press, 1960.

Kohlberg, L. (1966), A cognitive-developmental analysis of children's sex-role concepts and attitudes. In: *The Development of Sex Differences*, ed. E. E. Maccoby. Stanford, CA: Stanford University Press, pp. 82–173.

Kohut, H. (1971), *The Analysis of the Self*. New York: International Universities Press.

Konner, M. (1982), *The Tangled Wing*. New York: Holt, Rinehart & Winston.

Kris, M. (1957), The use of prediction in a longitudinal study. *The Psychoanalytic Study of the Child*, 12:175–189. New York: International Universities Press.

Lichtenstein, H. (1961), Identity and sexuality: A study of their interrelationship in men. *J. Amer. Psychoanal. Assn.*, 9:197–260.

Maccoby, E. E., & Jacklin, C. N. (1974), *The Psychology of Sex Differences*. Stanford, CA: Stanford University Press.

Mahler, M. (1963), Thoughts about development and individuation. *The Psychoanalytic Study of the Child*, 18:307–324. New York: International Universities Press.

———— (1968), *On Human Symbiosis and the Vicissitudes of Individuation*. New York: International Universities Press.

———— (1974), Symbiosis and individuation: The psychological birth of the human infant. *The Psychoanalytic Study of the Child*, 29:89–106. New Haven, CT: Yale University Press.

———— Pine, F., & Bergman, A. (1975), *The Psychological Birth of the Human Infant*. New York: Basic Books.

Money, J., & Ehrhardt, A. A. (1972), *Man and Woman, Boy and Girl*. Baltimore, MD: Johns Hopkins University Press.

Piaget, J. (1932), *The Moral Judgment of the Child*. Glencoe, IL: Free Press, 1960.

———— (1947), *The Psychology of Intelligence*. Patterson, NJ: Littlefield, Adams, 1948.

———— (1950), *The Child's Conception of the World*. London: Routledge & Kegan Paul, 1951.

Roiphe, H., & Galenson, E. (1981), *Infantile Origins of Sexual Identity*. New York: International Universities Press.

Sander, L. (1969), The longitudinal course of early mother-child interaction. In: *Determinants of Infant Behavior*, Vol. 4, ed. B. M. Foss. London: Methuen, pp. 189–227.

——— Julien, H., & Burns, P. (1976), Primary prevention and some aspects of temporal organization in early infant-caretaker interaction. In: *Infant Psychiatry: A New Synthesis*, ed. E. N. Rexford, L. W. Sander, & T. Shapiro. New Haven, CT: Yale University Press, pp. 187–204.

Silverman, M. (1971), The growth of logical thinking. Piaget's contribution to ego psychology. *Psychoanal. Quart.*, 40:317–341.

——— (1981), Cognitive development and female psychology. *J. Amer. Psychoanal. Assn.*, 29:581–605.

——— Neubauer, P. (1971), The use of the developmental profile for the prelatency child. In: *The Unconscious Today: Essays in Honor of Max Schur*. New York: International Universities Press.

Stoller, R. (1968), The sense of femaleness. *Psychoanal. Quart.*, 37:42–55.

——— (1976), Primary femininity. *J. Amer. Psychoanal. Assn.*, 24(5):59–78.

Tartakoff, H. H. (1966), The normal personality in our culture and the Nobel prize complex. In: *Psychoanalysis—A General Psychology*, ed. R. M. Loewenstein, L. N. Newman, M. Schur, & A. J. Solnit. New York: International Universities Press, pp. 222–252.

Tyson, P. (1982), A developmental line of gender identity, gender role and choice of object. *J. Amer. Psychoanal. Assn.*, 30:61–86.

Ullian, D. (1981), Why boys will be boys: A structural perspective. *Amer. J. Orthopsychiat.*, 51:493–501.

——— (1982), The child's construction of gender: Anatomy as destiny. In: *Cognitive and Affective Processes: A Developmental-Interactionist Perspective*, ed. E. Shapiro & E. Weber. Hillsdale, NJ: Erlbaum.

——— (1984), Why girls are good: A constructivist view. *Amer. J. Orthopsychiat.*, 54:71–82.

Winnicott, D. W. (1953), Transitional objects and transitional phenomena. *Internat. J. Psycho-Anal.*, 34:89–97.

——— (1965), *The Maturational Processes and the Facilitating Environment*. New York: International Universities Press.

Chapter 18

An Examination of Work Inhibitions in Women: A Special Problem for the Female Teacher and Student

IRENE P. STIVER, Ph.D.

Work as an important source of identity and self-esteem is not always integrated easily into women's lives, and women's experience with work-related issues differs quantitatively and qualitatively from that of men. Indications of low self-esteem and low confidence about work performance become evident in women very early, and clear differences between girls' and boys' attitudes toward their school performances have been demonstrated. Teachers, then, need to be alert and responsive to this crucial issue. Because many schoolteachers are women, their relationship to their own work needs to be clarified to help them in turn help their female students.

Two studies illustrate the ways in which low self-confidence is expressed in women at all ages. Crandall, Katkovsky, and Preston (1962) found that with latency-aged children, the brighter the boy, the better he expected to do in the future and the more he thought his good scores were a result of his competence. In contrast, the brighter

the girl, the less she was apt to think her good performance was a reflection of her own capacity. In another
study, Ruth Moulton (1977) surveyed 200 psychoanalysts,
150 men and 50 women. They were asked the simple
question, "Would you refuse an invitation to speak publically?" Fifty percent of the women said they would refuse to speak, contrasted to 20 percent of the men. This
is particularly surprising since the subjects were women
psychoanalysts who were presumably sophisticated and
self-aware.

While this chapter will focus on particular manifestations of work inhibitions in adult women, in the postschool world, there are some interesting findings with
elementary, high school, and college students which show
that female students are more vulnerable than male students to the development of significant work inhibitions.

It is well known that girls get better grades through
the school years; even at the high school level when girls
begin to "hide" their abilities more, in the service of gaining more popularity with boys, they continue to do as
well or better than boys (Maccoby and Jacklin, 1974, table
4.4, p. 136). At the college level no differences are found
between female and male students' grades (Crandall,
1969) and in some studies (cited in Maccoby and Jacklin
[1974]) females continue to do somewhat better than
males. Also, investigations comparing achievement motivation, task persistence, approach behaviors to intellectual goals, all demonstrate no sex differences during
the school years (cited in Maccoby and Jacklin, 1974,
table 4.4, p. 143; Crandall, 1969). Comparisons of IQ
scores indicate no significant differences, although girls
tend to be somewhat higher in some studies (cited in
Maccoby and Jacklin [1974]). If then females *perform* as
well or better than boys throughout their school years,
and are similar in achievement motivation, why do they
seem more disadvantaged after they finish their formal
schooling and move into the workplace?

One area of investigation helps clarify the situation to some extent. Research on "expectancy" of academic and intellectual achievement does reveal that at a very early age, sex differences emerge. In one study (Crandall, 1969), children aged seven to twelve years were given six different kinds of intellectual tasks, each with graduated levels of difficulty, from which estimates were obtained of their expectations for future performance. For each individual task the girls' estimates were lower than those of the boys. The girls approached these intellectual tasks with a significantly lower assessment of their intellectual skills than did the boys; IQ comparisons between the sexes yielded no significant differences. At the college level, another study (Crandall, 1969) demonstrated that while female grades were higher than those of the males, initial estimates of their probable grades in their first courses were significantly higher for the males than those for females. Yet for females the estimates of the grades for each quarter were slightly higher than their own past grades. Males were well above the past feedback they received and *overestimated* from past data more than did females in each quarter. Even more suggestive was the finding that at the end of their academic careers, more females actually estimated lower than their past grades would warrant, while males continued to estimate higher than their preceding grades. Another study (Sontag, Baker, and Nelson, 1958) found significantly fewer girls than boys whose intelligence tests scores had risen over the elementary school years and significantly more girls than boys whose mental test scores had declined.

The assumption then that females only begin to demonstrate work inhibitions in the postschool world is belied by the data which indicate that females from an early age demonstrate significantly less confidence in their abilities, despite evidence to the contrary; and there does seem to be a gradual and persistent trend toward feeling less and less confident over the college years and toward performing less effectively on intelligence tests. Even when one addresses the work inhibitions that become apparent in adult women, in the postschool years, on the job and/or in a career, the indications of difficulties are not especially evident in how these women actually perform their jobs. Rather, they are reflected more in underlying attitudes and assumptions that continue to sabotage efforts to move ahead, and contribute to considerable internal tension and conflict. Again teachers need to be alert to the significance of the early signs of low expectation for success in girls and other indications of the kinds of issues to be described below, found so often in adult women.

As a therapist, I am impressed on the one hand by how frequently and pervasively women experience conflicts and varying amounts of distress in their jobs and on the other by how rarely women come into therapy with a presenting problem around work. Men who have difficulties at work seem to see them as legitimate reasons for entering therapy. Women more typically come into therapy because of a concern about a personal relationship, and it is only as the therapy progresses that work issues come into focus.

Are women's problems about work different from men's and if so, how? What is immediately apparent is that for men, work has been a means of enhancing their experiences of themselves as men, supporting their identities as men, and work has always been an important source of their self-esteem. The successful man is perceived as more masculine than the man who is less successful. Many women, on the other hand, experience considerable conflict between their sense of self at work and their sense of self and feminine identity in their personal lives. Typically for women, work has not been a primary source of self-esteem; instead, success and failure in personal relationships has been the major monitor of women's self-esteem.

In reviewing the difficulties women experience in the work setting, one finds a wide range of types and degrees of inhibitions. Some women experience so much anxiety about entering or reentering the work arena that they do not try to get a job, even though they may have a strong interest in doing something which would use their talents and abilities. Other women working out of economic necessity and feeling dissatisfied with their jobs often feel helpless about their ability to move into work which might be more meaningful. Then there are those women who do pursue work interests and prepare for a career but get stuck at some point and cannot go further; for example, a graduate student who does well until she has to write the doctoral dissertation and then becomes blocked and cannot complete her work; or a woman in industry who reaches the middle management level and then sabotages her own chances to move ahead, and does not take advantage of opportunities for advancement. Even women who are clearly successful, effective, and competent often feel privately that their horizons are limited significantly by the kinds of anxieties and difficulties they experience in their work situation.

In reading the literature (Hennig and Jardim, 1977), a common recommendation for resolution of this dilemma for women is to help them learn more about the competitive situation that is presumably called for in their work, to help them learn to take power more effectively, to become more task-oriented than people-oriented, to become more impersonal than person-oriented in their work situations, to learn to become more invulnerable to feedback because we know that women are much more "sensitive" to getting approval from others, and to help them become more "analytic" in their thinking. This strategy of resolution contains in it some of the very problems with which women are currently struggling and does not recognize some significant and unique aspects of the psychology of women.

In recent years the writings of Jean Baker Miller (1976), Janet Surrey (1982), Carol Gilligan (1982), Jordan (1982), Stiver (1983), and others have brought to our attention the fact that much of our understanding of female experience and development has been based on a masculine model and data from samples in which men were represented more than women or women were not included at all. Drawing from research with women and from clinical experience with women patients in psychotherapy, these authors have presented us with a different vantage point which has highlighted some of the differences between men and women and has identified the intrinsic value of women's distinctive qualities.

Carol Gilligan's work (1982) on differences between men and women in moral development is illustrative of this point of view. When Kohlberg (1981) applied his stages of moral development to a sample of women, the women appeared to be deficient in moral development since their judgments on the tasks he devised to measure it seemed to exemplify the third stage; at this stage morality is conceived in interpersonal terms and goodness is equated with helping and pleasing others. Kohlberg felt that women failed to advance and progress like men to higher stages where relationships were subordinated to rules and rules to universal principles of justice (stage 6). Gilligan noted that Kohlberg's stages were based on a study of eighty-four boys whose development he followed for a period of twenty years; there were no females in the sample. When Gilligan included women in her samples, she found significant differences in the ways each sex struggles with moral dilemmas and attempts to resolve them. For Gilligan, the psychology of women is distinctive in its greater orientation toward relationships and interdependence, which implies a more contextual mode of judgment and a different rather than lesser moral understanding than that of men.

Current developmental theory has stressed the importance of separation, individuation, and achievement of independence as the hallmarks of maturity (Mahler, Pine, and Bergman, 1975). Yet this model seems more applicable to male than female development. Again, just as women were seen as lacking in moral development when compared with Kohlberg's data obtained from men, so are women often described as immature and dependent, based on the traditional concept of female development as simply a variant of male development. This understanding of women overlooks the significance of human relationships as a propelling force in their psychological growth. It does not sufficiently take into account an understanding of women's sense of self, as observed through research and clinical practice. In her book, *Toward a New Psychology of Women*, Jean Baker Miller (1976) emphasized the significance of personal relationships to women. A central theme of her book is that "women's sense of self becomes very much organized around being able to make and maintain affiliation in relationships" (p. 83).

Such conceptualization of the female experience has led to a new theoretical understanding of female development which we refer to as "self-in-relation" theory (Surrey, 1983). This theory identifies the "relational self" as the core self structure in women, and offers a new model of growth and development for women. In this model, the developmental process is seen as that of relationship differentiation, rather than separation-individuation, which assumes an increasing self-differentiation in women within a context in which the maintenance of relational ties remains central. This significant assymetry in the different developmental paths followed by men and women, as they move from their earliest relationship to their mothers and fathers through adolescence into adulthood, has differential effects on men's and women's experiences in all aspects of life, and certainly in the work arena.

Since for women the need to feel emotionally connected to others, to be caring and empathic and attentive to the needs of others, is central to their sense of self, their developmental goals are different from those of men. For men the goal of development is the assertion of differences and separateness, autonomy and independence; for women it is rather to achieve "increasing levels of complexity, structure . . . and of articulation within the context of human bonds and attachment" (Surrey, 1983, p. 10). Self-esteem in women is more a function of their ability to be effective in establishing and maintaining relationships which are emotionally gratifying, than of achievement and mastery in relative isolation. Women's search then is for interdependence, rather than independence, in their significant relationships, with a need for mutual empathy and understanding of these relationships.

SELF-DOUBT

We already saw in the data about expectancy with young children, as well as with college age students, how low self-confidence and self-doubt are evident very early. However, in the school setting, females continue to perform well despite their self-doubt, which may suggest that there is perhaps less intense inner conflict between self-image and intellectual performance in the school setting. After all being "good" in school has been a means of getting approval and acceptance for the female student and achievement does not yet conflict with the sense of female identity. Adult women, on the other hand, struggle more acutely with their lack of self-confidence and inner conflicts.

It is noteworthy how often women express enormous doubts about their abilities and their competence. Women still underestimate and negate signs of their effectiveness. They minimize their intellectual worth and their inner ambitions, and tend to hide their abilities. Occasionally, their intelligence and good ideas motivate them to speak up publically, but they begin to ruminate afterwards about the value of their contributions. They worry about whether they were too aggressive; should they have said this, should they have said that, perhaps they shouldn't have spoken so long or so little or so much. If they are recognized for saying something worthwhile, they are gratified at the moment but then they begin to feel that they "fooled" others, believe that they are "phonies" and frauds, and are fearful that people will find them out eventually. Also, women typically attribute their successes to chance events and believe that they "happened" to be at the right place at the right time, or were just "lucky." While women are often aware that they belittle and devalue themselves and are annoyed with themselves for doing it, they continue to hold on to the conviction that they are inadequate and that their accomplishments are deceptive.

What is particularly interesting is how much women resist changing such attitudes about themselves in the face of contrasting information and other dynamic interpretations (Applegarth, 1972). When women talk about their sense of inadequacy, it is often in the context of how defective they feel. They usually overvalue men, undervalue women, and feel that they are lacking something. Psychoanalytic theory might interpret these feelings as reflections of penis envy, or envy of men's power position, at least in the work situation. Such interpretations are, however, no more effective in changing women's attitudes than other kinds of interpretations. We must ask then, Why do women hold on to their sense of themselves as incapable and inadequate, which often keeps them in dependent and subordinate positions at work?

In a book called *The Cinderella Complex*, Dowling (1981) takes the position that women use their helplessness and dependency in the service of their wishes for the strong man to come and rescue them; but, since he will never come, she urges women to become instead more "independent," "strong," and "self-reliant." Certainly, there is some truth to the idea that our culture supports a woman assuming a dependent role and presenting herself as helpless, with the seductive promise that she will be taken care of, even though she is typically disappointed. The seductive fantasy may itself be so gratifying to some women that they continue to hold on to a helpless, dependent position even though it is so damaging to their self-esteem. Yet, in a more general sense, this is an oversimplification of the meanings of women's dependency (Stiver, 1983); also it is another reflection of the masculine model which emphasizes the goal of independence as "the index" of maturity.

A more general expression of this point of view in our culture is seen in a tendency to equate the need to be related to other people with dependency. The self-in-relation theory, however, offers a different perspective. If a woman's sense of self is a relational one, and she needs to feel related to others as a crucial aspect of her identity, it is not surprising that she may have learned to present herself in ways which will allow for a greater likelihood of feeling connected to others. It is certainly true that assuming a dependent position has been the major mode available to women, in relating to others, mothers, teachers, and certainly to men.

In her 1983 paper, Harriet Lerner discusses how women's display of passive dependency often has a protective and systems monitoring function. For example, in the family system, the underfunctioning of one spouse can allow for the overfunctioning of the other. Thus the helpless, dependent stance of one partner has an adaptive, ego bolstering effect on the other. For the woman to move out of this position is often perceived by others, and consequently by herself, as aggressive and hurtful. She may then hold on to or stay in the position of relative weakness for this most significant relationship to survive. This dynamic can of course apply to other relationships outside the family. At an early stage, in school settings and elsewhere, differences between girls and boys have been noted, which reflect the greater importance of relationships to females, as compared to males, and the greater reinforcement of "dependent" behavior among girls than boys.

At the elementary school level, such differences between girls and boys have been noted. Girls seek more physical contact with their teachers, stand closer to them (Beller and Turner, 1962), and seem more frequently to seek help from adults and peers (Crandall and Rabson, 1960). Mothers are reported as being more overprotective of their daughters than sons, and keep their daughters closer to them. They begin very early to distance themselves from their sons, pushing them more into the world of school and activities outside of the home (Bing, 1963; Block, 1981).

The degree to which the term *dependent* is used pejoratively in our culture may be related to a tendency to see dependency more often as a female than a male characteristic. Yet, we know that both men and women are vulnerable to regressive pulls and seductive promises of being "taken care of." Women are more apt to acknowledge it more because it is more permissible. Yet the successful woman is considered to be someone who can take care of herself. As we shall see later in this chapter, women often experience the consequences of success at work as alienating and distancing them from their colleagues, and thus expect little support from others in the work arena. At home, women often assume much of the caretaking of others, despite the fact that they may be carrying significant responsibilities at work; they often feel it is selfish to expect others to respond to their needs, when they are not available "full time" to those at home. Paradoxically men are more likely to be "taken care of" in their marriage since emotional dependency needs are more apt to be gratified by the wife than by the husband. Women are better trained than men to be nurturant care-takers. In particular, successful men often feel "entitled" rather than selfish about their expectation to have their needs met without openly acknowledging these needs or directly asking that they be gratified. At work, too, the successful man is frequently catered to and "taken care of" by those more junior in the organization.

ASSIGNING PRIORITIES

Another issue with which women struggle at work is how to assign priorities to a task. Again, the literature tells us that women have blind spots about recognizing op-portunities and challenges. In *The Managerial Woman* by Hennig and Jardim (1977), we learn that women rarely seek opportunities for advancement; indeed, they often experience such opportunities as burdensome ob-ligations and feel resentful rather than grateful. As these authors investigated how women function in industry, they surveyed women in business settings and sat in on numerous meetings. They report the following vignette to illustrate how women fail to recognize the challenges that are right in front of them.

In a meeting where a young, up-and-coming woman presented an impressive plan, the executive vice presi-dent of the organization responded very positively, say-ing:

> "If you give me a draft by Friday I can discuss it with the president when I see him over the weekend." For a moment she looked staggered and then she said, "I can't. I'm going to an out-of-state conference on Fri-day." He looked at her and then said very carefully, "Well, I wouldn't object to having it on Thursday." She said, "But the problem is, I'm making a presentation at the conference and there are a lot of visuals involved.

I'm going down on Thursday to rehearse the whole thing," He said, "Then make it Wednesday." She said, "But tomorrow is Tuesday and I've got everything on my desk to clear up before I go." He said, "Look, it doesn't really matter how you arrange this, I *want* that draft by Friday." As they left the room she said to the authors, "Did you hear him? Drop everything! Forget about priorities. Do what I say! and it's a draft for God's sake!" Then they explained to her that she had a great opportunity to be heard by the president, and she blew it. "My God" she said, "I never saw it!" [pp. 27–28].

What was left out in these authors' discussion was a consideration of other options in this situation. No one thought that perhaps the president could hear the woman's plan a week later. It was assumed that her advancement should come first and that nothing else mattered. The possibility that "the other things" on her desk might have been tasks which she felt involved obligations to others was not considered.

Is it as simple as the authors of *The Managerial Woman* suggest? Are women more naive in the working world? Have they not been trained sufficiently as competitors? And do they have blind spots about recognizing new possibilities? Again an understanding of the concept of "self-in-relation" helps to highlight other reasons women have difficulties assigning priorities to their tasks at work.

One of these reasons is that women are taught that they should do for others before doing for themselves. Consequently, if they do something for their own advancement ahead of something for other people, they are apt to feel selfish and opportunistic, which is threatening to their self-esteem. At the same time, women also feel discouraged and resentful when they see themselves bypassed or somehow miss taking advantage of opportunities. Another factor to take into account is that women's self-doubt and sense of inadequacy may make them much more timid about risk-taking and moving into new areas.

Again this phenomenon is evident early in the school years. Block (1981) reports that girls are more reluctant to deviate from existing structures, while boys do take the initiative more in moving into unfamiliar territory. This may in part be a function of girls' low self-confidence, which may contribute to their anxiety about trying new things. There are other considerations, however. Boys, who have less of an investment in relationships than do girls, can more easily move away from others and "go-it-alone"; they are also less inhibited by considerations of expectations of others, teachers and peers, which may allow them more freedom to explore other approaches or other interests. Girls do seem to place a higher priority on maintaining their relations with others than on discovering new things which often involves going off on one's own. Compared to boys, girls may use their initiative and demonstrate innovative skills in their interpersonal relationships more than in their schoolwork, again demonstrating the higher priority girls give to relationships over achievement.

Another reason women have difficulties with establishing priorities is that at home women continue to carry significant household responsibilities, even when they are working, despite the changes in some households where men have assumed more domestic responsibilities. In addition, women's involvement in these family tasks is often not understood sufficiently. Family tasks are, in fact, more than the sum of hours required to execute them. In listening to women discuss these concerns in therapy, it is apparent that the emotional bonding and the intensity of the bonding with those "at home" involves significant emotional energy. Thus the "wrenching away" from home to work and from work to home takes more of a toll on women than men. Because of this struggle, women often develop a precarious balance between what they do at home and what they do at work. If anything occurs to threaten this balance, for example, one more demand at work, many women experience enormous anxiety and begin to feel that they do not have things sufficiently under control. Every new obligation and every new task carries the potential of creating disequilibrium in that balance.

PROFESSIONAL BEHAVIOR

In talking about work women often worry excessively about whether or not they have behaved "unprofessionally." Men who are successful in work rarely worry about whether somebody did something that was "unprofessional." As one explores what these women mean, it is apparent that they believe that to behave professionally is to behave "like a man." The fantasy seems to be that men move through every work situation strong, confident, and self-sufficient and clearly not emotional; to be emotional is the worst kind of unprofessionalism. Women believe too that it is not appropriate at work to take into account personal feelings, associated with their relationships with their colleagues and others. Again this reflects the woman's belief that in order to be effective at her job and in dealing with her male colleagues, she must adapt to the masculine model, which places high value on the maintenance of a logical, rational, and unemotional stance.

This self-in-relation perspective of female experience helps us understand why women feel so conflicted between their need for emotional expressiveness in their interactions with others and the demands to be relatively unemotional in the work setting. Jean Baker Miller (1976), in her discussion of the importance of relationships to women, stresses the affective component of relationships and believes that women serve as carriers of certain aspects of human experience, such as nurturance, caring for others, and emotionality, since these are so often experiences men need to defend against in themselves. For Miller, these female characteristics are seen as closer to certain human essentials which need to be acknowledged by both men and women and not denied.

In most work settings, men are more numerous and more often in power positions which sets the climate for "acceptable" behavior. Women have difficulty adapting to what they believe are the expectations for "professional" behavior, which often conflict with their own experience, inclinations, and talents. Recently a woman who has a high administrative position said to me, while agonizing over an important personnel decision, "I have to separate my professional from my personal opinions." When I asked, "Why?" she was startled, and replied, "That's what men do." This premise needs to be questioned, however. In fact, men do allow personal considerations to influence their decisions at work. But men and women differ on the types of personal concerns which motivate them at work. What this woman was struggling with was her need to separate what she felt was her objective appraisal of a particular employee's performance from her positive feelings about him personally. The relationship was very important to her; yet, she believed, it would be unprofessional for her to allow liking or not liking someone to influence her decision. Men, however, do give more legitimacy for personal considerations which enter into the making of decisions, but these considerations are not typically in the context of maintaining relationships. More often the personal considerations for men at work are around issues of power and competitiveness. For example, a male colleague who wanted to fire someone explained with anger and forcefulness that this was because "he does not accept my authority." This was clearly a decision based on "personal" and emotional considerations, since the employee's competence was not at all in question; yet he felt perfectly comfortable in believing it was a good reason to fire this employee.

In attempting to adapt to the work setting, many women tend to internalize a set of values about acceptable behavior at work which is often polarized, with rather stereotyped masculine characteristics at one end of the continuum and feminine on the other. Masculine characteristics are considered "good" at work and feminine are "bad," and they must be kept separate. For women to show too many feminine characteristics at work feels dangerous. Women often believe that if their feelings somehow escape, their heads will stop working or people will expect them to stop working and they will be perceived as "unprofessional."

In this connection, one of the greatest fears a woman has, the worst act of unprofessionalism, is to cry on the job. Thus women learn to curtail emotional expressiveness at work, particularly in their communications with male colleagues. Often in a group discussion, women who have strong feelings about an issue are fearful that if they speak up they will become upset, angry, or possibly tearful, and believe that they will either not be heard and/or be labeled "hysterical," and then feel humiliated. As a consequence they often withdraw and remain silent. This perception is validated frequently enough to reinforce women's reluctance to put themselves forward around emotionally charged issues. A woman executive reported that a young woman who was recently hired to a high-level position, asked her during the orientation where the ladies room was, "because that's where I'll be doing my crying."

Communications, however, are often emotionally loaded by the degree to which one is invested in the issue, how urgent or important it is considered to be, and so on. Men's response to emotionally toned communications, however, is often to dismiss and at times not even hear the content, since men tend to be threatened by the strong emotions expressed. Yet what women require in their relationships with others is some validation of what they are feeling, with a recognition of the importance of what they are saying in order to feel encouraged to continue to make important communications to others.

COMPETITION

Another troublesome area for women is competition. It is possible that competitive issues become more salient for women after elementary school, in college, graduate school, and the postschool years. It has been suggested that grades are not generally seen as competitive by young children, since they do not see achieving a high grade on tests as affecting other children getting a high grade (Maccoby and Jacklin, 1974). This may in part account for the ability of latency-aged girls to work toward a high standard of excellence in the academic sphere and continue to do well, despite their low self-esteem. Adult women, however, compared to men, are very alert to competitive issues and are more likely to avoid competitive situations, less likely to acknowledge competitive wishes and not likely to do as well in competition. In a paper on "Female Self-Development in the College Years" (Kaplan and Klein, 1985), the authors note that the emphasis on competitive success in college may be experienced by college women as an inherent threat to relational ties and therefore can undermine the development of both the sense of self and self-esteem. Based on observations of female college students who were members of specifically designed discussion groups, they found that these women experience the competitive atmosphere of college as threatening to their relational self, and that contributes to the likelihood of becoming depressed and developing eating disorders.

The prevailing assumption in our culture is that to be as openly competitive as men are is a good thing. Again the writings on women and work urge women to learn to become more openly competitive and more skillful at being competitive. For several reasons, it is difficult for women to be competitive. When a woman is openly competitive, she frequently experiences herself as aggressive and destructive. Fearful that others will perceive her that way, she feels that the worst thing she can be called is a "castrating woman." However, it goes deeper than labels other people give. Women are trained to be concerned about others and sensitive to their feelings, so that it is very hard to enjoy vanquishing a rival if one is at the same time empathic with that rival.

Another problem around competition which is more complicated for women than for men is: Whom does one compete with? Interestingly, although women are not given permission to compete the way men are, women are allowed and even encouraged and groomed to compete with other women for men. Men struggle in competing with men, perhaps a symbolic competition with their fathers over their mothers, in which success may carry fear of retaliation, guilt, and anxiety. Accordingly, some men have difficulties with work and fear success.

For women there are more complications. When they compete with men, several problems arise. First there is the danger of being considered unfeminine, aggressive, and destructive, and potentially being called "castrating." Second, because some women need to idealize men and see them as stronger and more powerful for the sake of the "rescue fantasy," it is too threatening to "do better" than the man one wants to idealize. Yet when women compete with women, they also are competing with the very people they want for support. Also, they are competing symbolically with their mothers, and that raises other complications in terms of guilt and anxiety, which are different from those of men with their fathers and mothers.

SEPARATION FROM MOTHER

Perhaps the most important area to address is the issue of identification with and separation from mother, as women move toward work and a career. For many reasons work issues highlight the ways in which women identify with their mothers. These issues often reveal women's struggle against identification with mothers, who are seen as devalued, and women often feel alone and lost as a consequence.

The following two examples are illustrative. One woman physician told me that, as a resident, during rounds, she made a rather dramatic correct diagnosis. People were surprised and impressed by her ability to do this. While she was exhilarated at first, she suddenly experienced enormous anxiety and had to retreat to her office; she felt acutely alone and isolated. Another woman who had recently returned to her teaching career in her forties was timid in work situations, but began to speak up more and more. At one conference where she expressed her thoughts more fully, her contributions were appreciated, and she felt encouraged and pleased. But that night she had a nightmare in which she was lying in bed, helpless and immobilized, calling out desperately for her mother. Her mother had died about two years earlier.

In order to explore the role that separation from mother plays in women's difficulties at work, it is necessary to elaborate further on the "self-in-relation" understanding of female development. This involves examining the differences between the types of attachment men and women develop with their mothers and the ways they mature and change that relationship. As noted above, current theory speaks of this process of development in terms of separation-individuation. Chodorow (1978), in exploring the unique characteristics of female development, notes that little girls in growing up are not encouraged toward separate strivings, nor are they encouraged to achieve a separate identity from their mothers, as little boys are. Since mothers tend to experience their daughters as more like and continuous with themselves, there develops a particular bonding of mothers with daughters with expectations of mutual caretaking and mutual empathic interactions and interdependency (Surrey, 1982). Daughters can then experience more continuity with past relationships such as early dependency on their mothers without seeing it as a threat to their growth and maturity. Surrey's (1982) paper on the development of the self in women talks about the identification with mother as "mother," which contributes further to women playing a more nurturing role than men in most relationships and becoming highly sensitive and vigilant to the nuances in interpersonal interactions. This can also be seen as the earliest precursor to the development of empathy; studies have found that women are generally more empathic than men.

The dynamic of the mother-son relationship follows another developmental path. Mothers experience their sons as different from them and are under both inner and outer pressure to affirm this difference. The cultural expectations of how boys should be are internalized by many mothers; and they believe that in order to help their sons develop a strong masculine identification, they need to encourage aggressive behaviors and separate strivings. However, a mother's sense that she must help her son achieve individuation and independence through pushing him away from her conflicts often with her natural inclination to maintain attachment, while affirming the differences between them. While the mother feels very torn as a consequence, the pressures to conform to social expectations are usually strongly supported by the father. Fathers' attitudes and behavior toward their sons serve to reinforce and underline the pressures on the mother to push the little boy toward separation and on the little boy to negate his wishes to maintain more open and continuous contact with his mother.

It is not surprising then that girls continue to experience strong attachments to their mothers with a much deeper sense that they must be like their mothers and truly take care of them psychologically, with all that that implies. Women, consequently, have different kinds of problems than men do in separation from their mothers.

Mothers in turn often feel the need to continue their role as mothers. It has been an integral part of their female identity, and they often can continue to play the role more comfortably with daughters than with sons. Since mothers feel they need to help their sons to separate and develop more independence, they can fulfill their needs for more direct interpersonal connectedness through maintaining attachments with their daughters. The more positive aspects of the mother-daughter bond, however, are countered by the mother's tendency to project feelings of inadequacy onto her daughter. While this may give the mother more license to hold on to the daughter and to "mother," it contributes to the highly ambivalent aspects of mother-daughter interrelations. Thus, mothers may express their ambivalence by holding on to their daughters at the same time that they are quite critical of them. Also mothers can become competitive and fearful, as well as gratified, as they see their daughters move forward in a positive and competent fashion. And daughters, as one often hears in psychotherapy with women, often struggle to defend against their identification with their mothers, whom they see as critical, devalued, and unhappy. Yet these same women fear betraying their mothers and experience considerable guilt if they move ahead and demonstrate "differences" from their mothers. In attempting to break this bond, women may feel that the only alternative is complete independence, which is again an attempt to identify with the more valued masculine goal. But the woman is left feeling absolutely alone in the world, without any support and with a significant sense of loss in disconnecting from her mother. A woman's attempts to resolve this dilemma by looking for a strong man who will take care of her results frequently in considerable disappointment. Yet, efforts to gain vicarious gratification through identification with "the powerful man" only leaves a woman with longstanding resentments and low self-esteem.

I would like to suggest that this dynamic between mother and daughter may get played out to some extent in the classroom. This would then serve to intensify for girls the conflict between maintaining their connection and identification with their mothers and teachers, while at the same time asserting their own individuality in pursuing academic and work interests with confidence and effectiveness.

Just as the mother often does not serve as a positive role model for her daughter, because she feels devalued, and often is devalued, so may the female teacher subtly communicate her self-doubts to the girls in her class. Mischel (1974) found that both men and women, boys and girls, devalued work labeled as done by women over the same work labeled as done by men. Since teaching is often seen as a female profession, women teachers are aware of how they tend to be devalued and they, in turn, devalue themselves. It seems very possible too, that, like the mother, the woman teacher may project her feelings of inadequacy onto her female students; at the same time she is apt to appreciate their "good" behavior, since it is often in the service of gaining the teacher's approval and feeling related to her. The teacher's "pet" is more often a girl than a boy, and while this may become an enviable position for the girl, it is paradoxically devalued since boys who might be so chosen would be considered "sissies." While teachers talk fondly of their girl students and appreciate their compliant and accommodating behaviors, they are apt to hold more extended conversations with boys, and provide more extended directions than they do in response to girls' requests (Serbin, O'Leary, Kent, and Tonick, 1973; Block, 1981).

One woman who has been teaching third grade (Hutchings, personal communication, 1983) for more than ten years observed how mothers of very bright, gifted sons become very invested in their school performance, helping them with projects, visiting the school often, and so on, apparently in the service of their ambitions for their sons' success in school; while clearly proud of their bright and talented daughters they do not become as invested in their "outside the home" activities.

Another area highly relevant to the issue of women and work is the conflict women face between having children and having a career. It is such a complex topic, however, that it would require a separate paper even to begin to explore all the pertinent issues. It is clear that women face harsh difficulties in this area, and I don't think one can overemphasize the degree of anguish women experience in their struggle to resolve the conflict. They sometimes tend to minimize the struggle because it seems so impossible, sometimes overstate one side of the conflict and understate the other.

FEAR OF SUCCESS

The influence of the notion that success jeopardizes women's femininity and attractiveness to men cannot be overestimated, but it also merits reexamination. Again and again women report the feeling that a successful woman alienates herself from both women and men. Single women often feel that the more successful they get, the narrower will be their choice of acceptable men.

The literature suggests that women who have very supportive fathers typically are more successful (Hennig and Jardim, 1977). But in my clinical experience, when the daughters begin to face the conflict between their personal and professional lives, these fathers suddenly stop being very supportive.

> One woman whom I was seeing in therapy was very successful in her work, and her father had always been supportive, encouraging her to pursue her career and taking pride in her success. She had earned an important promotion in her job with increased obligations and responsibilities and she was bringing her work home evenings and weekends. She also had trouble with her marriage, the original reason for her coming into therapy a year earlier. After the promotion, the marriage had become more troublesome, and she finally talked to her parents about her marital difficulties. Her father became enraged. He told her that the recent promotion had been too much, that she was putting work ahead of her family and her husband should come first. Further, if she stopped all this nonsense and put her energies in her marriage and not her work, things would be different. She was devastated. Her father's reaction was unexpected, but it confirmed her belief that her personal life was compromised by her getting ahead in her career.

The notion that "fear of success" jeopardizes women's personal lives is part of the thesis put forth by Matina Horner (1972). Working with high achievement women, she found that the anticipation of success in competitive activity was countered by the anticipation of negative consequences; for example, social rejection, disapproval, not being liked, and loss of femininity.

Another way to understand this fear of success is to recognize how much the relational self is threatened in women, since success often carries with it the danger of feeling disconnected from others. Do women have to emulate the masculine model for success in order to obtain gratification from their work, and what particular problems do they encounter when they try to do so? I have chosen two clinical case examples to illustrate some of the dilemmas women are faced with when success at work is experienced as threatening to their personal connections.

> Susan is a woman of thirty-five, divorced with two young children, who during the process of psychotherapy completed the requirements for a bachelor's degree which she had postponed for more than ten years. It was around that time, too, that she was able to divorce her alcoholic husband and apply to graduate school. After finishing a master's degree, she was encouraged by faculty to pursue a doctorate at a much more prestigious university. She did this with some trepidation, still feeling unsure of her ability to juggle the responsibility of running a one-parent home and becoming part of a very competitive program. Nonetheless, she entered the program and began a strenuous course of study. During this time she also became involved with a man who was already an established professional in his field. He, too, was divorced with two children. Since his wife had custody of the children, he lived alone in a bachelor-type existence, was hard working and ambitious. This relationship was especially significant, for it was her first truly intimate relationship with a man. In one session, she reported that over the past weekend her ex-husband had taken the children, and for the first time in a long time she had unlimited free time to catch up on her work. However, she and the man with whom she was involved typically spent weekends together, since the weekdays were so busy for each of them. She knew he expected to relax and for them to enjoy each other. He had quite an unemcumbered week devoted entirely to work, but she had gone to class, run errands, visited her daughter's school, stopped in on her mother who was ill, helped out a friend in distress, and so on. She wanted to tell him that she couldn't spend all the weekend playing, but felt this would seem selfish and too ambitious. Still, she mustered her courage and did tell him. His reaction was surprising. "Of course," he said,

"work would always come first with me." He was very accommodating, helping her use much of the weekend to do her work.

The other case was somewhat different:

> About one year after Joanne had terminated therapy she returned to see me about a crisis at work that had caused her considerable anxiety and obsessive preoccupation. She had an executive position with a company she had been with for twelve years, and she supervised a large staff. I knew she had given birth to a baby six months earlier, because she sent me an announcement, but she spoke only of the issues at work. She was troubled by the hostility she felt from her junior staff, and she thought it centered on her having recently been given more responsibility in the company. There was so much upheaval that she feared the corporation president would see her as unable to do her job effectively. She expressed considerable anger at members of the junior staff, whom she felt had always been her friends, and she was quite upset at the thought that they disliked her now. After two sessions of talking about this, I noted that she had hardly said anything about her new son. Even she was startled by how little she had mentioned him, since she had intense feelings about him and about dividing her time between home and work. What soon emerged was that the complaints from her staff were that she had become aloof and uncaring, in sharp contrast to her style before her son's birth. She became aware that she had considerable difficulty leaving her baby to come to work, as well as proving she could combine motherhood and a career. At home she had almost handed over the care of her son to a housekeeper and to her husband. At work she curtailed her nurturing, sensitive feelings toward her staff in order to prove her ability to continue her career after having the child.

These two women illustrate different facets of the

problems addressed here: Susan wanted to be responsive to the man in her life and feel connected to him, and at the same time to be able to put herself forward without feeling she was hurting or harming him; a common dilemma for women. To act for herself made her feel she was being selfish and destructive to the other person. Although she was relieved at his response, she felt she could not fully accept his premise that "work would always come first" for herself; and one would have to question whether this made her a less effective person than the man. Joanne felt she had to suppress her concerns for others to prove that she was effective, and, in fact, became less sensitive to her staff and more alienated and less effective as a consequence.

A paper by Lois Hoffman (1972) says, "Driving a point home, winning an argument, beating others in competition and attending to the task at hand without being sidetracked by concern with rapport requires subordination of affiliative needs" (pp. 136–137). These aggressive strategies are typically seen as necessary for women to learn in order to get ahead in the area of "work." Are there alternative ways for women to deal with work situations and gain gratification without experiencing so much threat to their sense of self and without experiencing so much guilt, shame, frustration, and alienation?

One can, perhaps, consider different models of success for women, which may not be fully consistent with success as defined in our culture. For example, women can learn to value their relational and empathic skills and emotional expressiveness and use these adaptively at work. Surrey (1983) suggests that rather than offering "assertiveness training workshops" for women, one might develop instead more advanced "relational training courses" emphasizing the utilization of collaborative processes in the work setting, for both men and women. Other goals women may begin to envision, which would allow more expression of their relational self, might be: to achieve freedom to pursue work interests in a cooperative context, to use their talents and powers to develop other people's abilities for getting the job done; to be affirmed as an effective person and still maintain relatedness with others, with all the richness and complexities that relatedness encompasses. Women also need to feel entitled to pursue their work interests without feeling selfish and destructive. In the end such feelings add to women's resentment and interfere with their ability to respond effectively to the needs of others.

At the same time, we must recognize that most work settings present women with a masculine model which emphasizes independence and autonomy; and it places high value on impersonal, nonemotional, objective as well as competitive attitudes toward the tasks involved. This kind of setting stresses women both intrapsychically and interpersonally. The core sense of self, feminine identity, and self-esteem are threatened when a woman feels that success at work conflicts with her needs to feel connected to others, to maintain her ties with her mother, to foster the development of others, and to feel empowered and validated by these connections with others. In women's daily interpersonal encounters at work, with their colleagues and others, they often experience their style of approaching their work and relating to others as devalued; and if they are effective in what they do, they often experience anxiety about being seen as too aggressive or are afraid of hurting others. Finally, they experience themselves as selfish and uncaring when their investment in their work conflicts with demands from others, both real and imagined and both explicit and implicit. It is not surprising then that women are reported to experience more stress at work than men, in some settings, and that work inhibitions are so prevalent among women at all levels of functioning in the marketplace.

We have seen that the origins and signs of conflicts adult women experience in the work situation are evident

already in the early years of elementary school. How can
teachers address the problems outlined in this chapter to
help both themselves and their female students? If
women teachers recognized that there is indeed an intrinsic conflict between success as defined in our culture
and the qualities women value for themselves, they would
be able to understand their own legitimate confusion in
attempting to harmonize such discrepant "realities." Typically, women experience this confusion as simply another indication of their inadequacy rather than the
inevitable consequence of being a woman today in our
culture. Such self-awareness in teachers could in turn
encourage them to help their students, both male and
female, appreciate this dilemma. Women teachers also
need to see how much they, and women in general, have
internalized assumptions, attitudes, and stereotypes of
what is better, worse, valued, and not valued, based on
a masculine model of success which may sometimes be
destructive and often inhumane. They could then encourage both female and male students to consider other
models to pursue.

Male students, in their needs to adapt to the more
masculine model of success, do often overestimate their
expectations for future success, which creates its own
problems and sets them up to experience different kinds
of failures and blows to their self-esteem. Teachers can
help both their female and male students to consider possible alternatives to our cultural definitions of success by
modifying teaching techniques and classroom milieu. The
development of group projects with emphasis not only on
the task itself but on the interpersonal interactions, for
example, could utilize the relational competencies girls
have so well developed and could help boys realize more
their potential for sensitivity and empathy to others; a
focus on modes of helping others to achieve the goals of
a task and attention to the value of cooperative endeavors
could be evaluated and even "graded," as well as the

particular skills required to execute the task itself. Such innovative methods would be beneficial to the growth and development of both boys and girls as effective people and learners.

REFERENCES

Applegarth, A. (1972), Some observations on work inhibitions in women. In: *Female Psychology*. ed. H. P. Blum. New York: International Universities Press.

Beller, E. K., & Turner, J. A. (1962), A study of dependency and aggression in early childhood. From a progress report on NIMH project M-849, National Institute of Mental Health, Washington, DC.

Bing, E. (1963), Effects of childrearing practices on development of differential cognitive abilities. *Child Develop.*, 34:631–648.

Block, J. H. (1981), Gender differences in the nature of premises developed in the world. In: *Cognitive and Affective Growth: Developmental Interaction*, ed. E. K. Shapiro & E. Weber. Hillsdale, NJ: Erlbaum.

Chodorow, N. (1978), *The Reproduction of Mothering: Psychoanalysis and the Sociology of Gender*. Berkeley: University of California Press.

Crandall, V. J. (1969), Sex differences in expectancy of intellectual and academic reinforcement. In: *Achievement-Related Motives in Children*, ed. C. P. Smith. New York: Russell Sage Foundation.

——— Katkovsky, W., & Preston, A. (1962), Motivational and ability determinants of young children's intellectual achievement behaviors. *Child Develop.*, 33(3):643–661.

——— Rabson, A. (1960), Children's repetition choices in an intellectual achievement situation following success and failure. *J. Genet. Psychol.*, 97:161–168.

Dowling, C. (1981), *The Cinderella Complex*. New York: Summit Books.

Gilligan, C. (1982), *In a Different Voice*. Cambridge, MA: Harvard University Press.

Hennig, M., & Jardim, A. (1977), *The Managerial Woman*. Garden City, NY: Doubleday.

Hoffman, L. W. (1972), Early childhood experiences and women's achievement motives. *J. Soc. Iss.*, 28(2):129–155.

Horner, M. (1972), The motive to avoid success and changing aspirations of college women. In: *Readings in the Psychology of Women*, ed. J. Bardwick. New York: Harper & Row.

Jordan, J. (1982), Women and empathy. *Work in Progress*, 1:2. Wellesley, MA: Stone Center Working Paper Series.

Kaplan, A., & Klein, R. (1985), Women's self-development in late adolescence. *Work in Progress,* 17:2. Wellesley, MA: Stone Center Working Paper Series.

Kohlberg, L. (1981), *The Philosophy of Moral Development.* New York: Harper & Row.

Lerner, H. (1983), Female dependency in context: Some theoretical and technical considerations. *Amer. J. Orthopsychiat.,* 53:697–705.

Maccoby, E. E., & Jacklin, C. N. (1974), *The Psychology of Sex Differences.* Stanford, CA: Stanford University Press.

Mahler, M., Pine, F., & Bergman, A. (1975), *The Psychological Birth of the Human Infant.* New York: Basic Books.

Miller, J. B. (1976), *Toward a New Psychology of Women.* Boston: Beacon Press.

Mischel, H. (1974), Sex bias in the evaluation of professional achievements. *J. Ed. Psychol.,* 66:157–166.

Moulton, R. (1977), Some effects of the new feminism. *Amer. J. Psychiat.,* 134(1):1–6.

Serbin, L. A., O'Leary, K. D., Kent, R. N., & Tonick, I. S. (1973), A comparison of teacher responses to the preacademic and problem behavior of boys and girls. *Child Develop.,* 44:796–804.

Sontag, L. W., Baker, C. T., & Nelson, V. L. (1958), Mental growth and personality development: A longitudinal study. *Monographs of the Society for Research in Child Development,* 23 (Serial 68). Millwood, NY: Kraus Reprints & Periodicals.

Stiver, I. (1983), The meanings of "dependency" in female/male relationships. *Work in Progress,* 11. Wellesley, MA: Stone Center Working Paper Series.

Surrey, J. (1982), The relational self in women: Clinical implications. *Work in Progress,* 1:2. Wellesley, MA: Stone Center Working Paper Series.

——— (1983), Self in relation: A theory of women's development. *Work in Progress,* 3:1. Wellesley, MA: Stone Center Working Paper. Series.

Part III

Clinical Perspectives on Learning: Applications

Introduction: Part III

The authors in this section deal with clinical issues, some noting the implications of emotional disorders for learning, some noting the implications of learning disorders for the treatment of troubled children. Here the multi-faceted interface between education and psychotherapy is explored. Areas of similarity and difference between the two endeavors in reference to issues such as purpose, theoretical framework, specific interventive technique, and expected outcome are presented and discussed.

Sally Provence, in her chapter on the relationship between education and psychotherapy in the treatment of very young, developmentally delayed children, emphasizes the confluence between education and treatment. In such a treatment situation, educational methods may be therapeutic, and psychotherapeutic interventions educational. The totality of the young person, growing both cognitively and emotionally within the guiding influence of a positively experienced therapeutic relationship is emphasized. Several case vignettes demonstrate Dr. Provence's combined psychoeducational approach, which is adapted in each case to the needs of the individual child. In this very young age group then, it is proposed that education and therapy are inextricably combined in any comprehensive and effective treatment effort.

Donald Schwartz's chapter focuses on resistances to learning arising in conjunction with psychopathological development during the oedipal phase. He presents a detailed account of the complexities of cognitive and emotional growth during the phallic-narcissistic, oedipal, and latency periods, but emphasizes the particular importance of the oedipal complex and its appropriate resolution both for character formation and for development of the capacity to learn. He contends that the vicissitudes of the infantile neurosis integrate preoedipal influences into oedipal level organization and determine overall psychological structure. The latter, of course, includes the self representation as a person capable of learning, or, in pathological circumstances, as one who should not, ought not, or cannot learn. Dr. Schwartz gives clinical examples showing various ways in which intrapsychic conflict stemming from the oedipal phase of development interferes with the acquisition of knowledge. For example, he shows how a child may identify with the parent's unconscious wish that the child *not* learn. In another instance he describes how a child's inhibited curiosity and pseudostupidity were related to her mother's specific wish that the child not learn about sexuality. He demonstrates in a compelling way the powerful influence that the developmental issues of the oedipal phase (the infantile neurosis) have for either facilitating or compromising the capacity to learn.

Richard Kaufman emphasizes the necessity for careful diagnostic differentiation between those cases of school failure associated with developmental deficits and those cases associated with neurotic conflict. The modes of clinical intervention differ, as he points out in his cogent discussion of the clinical theory applying in each instance. He presents three cases of developmental deficit, and, for contrast, one example of a neurotically structured learning disorder. Dr. Kaufman's primary purpose in this chapter is to highlight the role of neurophysiological deficits in making it impossible for children so afflicted to assimilate information and growth enhancing experience as offered by parents and teachers. He demonstrates a form of treatment for these children which allows them to understand and acknowledge the early developmental disturbance, to reinstitute an early positive maternal bond, and to do what they had never had the opportunity to do before; that is, to establish those self-regulatory and cognitive functions which permit learning.

Benjamin Garber investigates a fascinating clinical finding, namely, that many children with learning disorders also have a deficit in the capacity for empathic understanding of the feelings of others. Dr. Garber explains how this lapse in development is associated with the immaturity of the nervous system, just as is the primary learning disorder. He shows how this "genetic given" adversely affects the interaction between mother and child, resulting in the failure of the child to learn about his own feelings and the feelings of others. Such children, stunted in emotional responsiveness, feel only a sense of emptiness and are convinced that something is wrong with them. They may develop a compensatory "as if," mechanical, social responsiveness, perhaps saying the right things, but remaining incapable of true empathy. They are often "found out" by peers and rejected, accentuating their isolation and sense of "wrongness." Dr. Garber presents clinical material demonstrating how, in the treatment of learning disabled children, they may be helped to learn about their own feelings and eventually to develop a genuine capacity for empathic intuneness with others.

Gil Noam presents a social-developmental framework for the understanding of normal and pathological adolescent development. He offers a life span perspective encompassing, integrating, and expanding the formulations of Piaget, Mahler, and Kernberg. He emphasizes the importance of progressive transformations of the self and the self in relation to others over each successive phase of development. Every separation-individuation conflict in adolescence or adulthood, Dr. Noam argues, is influenced not only by one's early separation experiences but by these later, more complex psychological organizations as well. His goal is to show the importance of such a life span perspective both for education and for treatment. To illustrate his thesis, he presents three very different borderline adolescent cases, the physical borderline adolescent, the instrumental borderline adolescent, and the mutual borderline adolescent. For each type of personality organization he explicates the appropriate and effective forms of clinical and educational intervention. Dr. Noam sees a life span developmental perspective as an overarching theoretical framework which can act as a bridge between education and clinical practice, enriching both disciplines in their shared goal of stimulating developmental transformation.

Finally, Blom, Ek, and Kulkarni, eschewing the traditional psychoanalytic view that physical disability invariably contributes to psychopathology, argue that a normative and adaptive approach to such handicaps is essential to the effective education of this large group of children.

Although the chapters in this section have a largely clinical orientation, all of them address various aspects of the interdigitation between educational and clinical concerns. They highlight the essential unity of cognitive and emotional development. They suggest the efficacy of a shared developmental theoretical framework in the treating and teaching of emotionally and learning disordered children and adolescents.

Chapter 19

Some Relationships between Education and Psychotherapy in the Treatment of Developmentally Delayed Infants and Toddlers

SALLY PROVENCE, M.D.

If one believes that education is much more than promoting the child's cognitive development it is difficult at times to draw a dividing line between what is education and what is psychotherapy for infants and young children. Such an effort is likely to be artificial and nonproductive because all continuing adult relationships with infants and very young children, of necessity, inform and educate. Under one name or another, the support and facilitation of certain of the autonomous functions of the ego—the most obvious being perception, memory, intelligence, speech, and motility—and such adaptive functions as self-regulation, modulation of affect, and the capacity for delay of discharge are the concern both of the psychotherapist and educator. Special educators of children with handicaps expect to facilitate the child's mental and physical development through providing appropriate and individualized educational experiences. What is sometimes lacking is a social-emotional environment

517

that is facilitating for the individual child. Similarly, psychotherapists of the very young, while sophisticated about mental health issues, may not fully appreciate the importance of or take responsibility for helping the child acquire skills as an essential part of psychotherapeutic work. The importance of educational methods has been most widely accepted for the neuropsychiatric disorders of early onset, particularly childhood autism, infantile psychoses, and other moderate to severe impairments. But I am proposing that enabling the young child to learn, and supporting the development of competence, are important components of the psychotherapeutic treatment of all infants and young children. The task for the therapist, then, is to decide on the context, timing, and content of the educational measure and how these are integrated with other elements of the therapeutic plan for an individual child. If a child cannot talk, his therapist must, for a time at least, talk for him as well as with him. If knowledge of himself, of others, and of the world about him is impaired, information must be provided; if movement is achieved only with difficulty or is under poor control, practice in its use becomes part of the treatment; if perception is distorted because sensory systems are impaired, efforts to minimize the distortion are essential. Such needs involve the therapist in becoming a teacher in a sense, but the teaching will not be therapeutic unless other talents and insights are also a part of her or his preparation.

In this chapter I will describe some aspects of an approach to working with developmentally deviant or disturbed infants and young children which has evolved in the Child Development Unit of the Yale Child Study Center over the past thirty years. It has been influenced by the work of others as well as by our own research and clinical experience. Constructs that guide diagnosis and treatment are derived from pediatrics and psychiatry, psychoanalysis and developmental psychology, clinical social work and early childhood education. The need to draw upon the knowledge and practices of these various disciplines reflects the fact that as yet there is no single theory that is adequate for understanding and treating the disorders of the earliest years. And yet a coherent and useful approach can be made to them through integrating clinical and developmental constructs derived from the above fields.

The value of careful diagnostic evaluation in the earliest years as a basis for therapeutic intervention for the psychopathological and maladaptive states of infancy and early childhood can, in my view, hardly be overemphasized. Some of the unique characteristics of the early years make differential diagnosis difficult and therefore the specificity of treatment also. The closeness of the psychic and somatic systems in infancy along with the relative lack of differentiation of both are reflected in the common finding that the younger the child the more likely he is to react to adversity with global responses and multiple symptoms rather than the more circumscribed and specific ones characteristic of older ages. Moreover, a noxious influence is highly likely to disturb or cause delay in more than one area of the infant's development and in the organization and integration of emerging functions. As development proceeds through successive phases and there is increasing differentiation and structuring of the signs and symptoms of psychological distress or illness; we find ourselves on more familiar ground and are less likely to misunderstand the causes and course of developmental and behavioral disturbances. In the very young, psychosocial stress commonly finds expression in somatic symptoms; deviation in motor development induced by experiential factors may be confused with neurological disorders; distortions of emotional expressiveness and delays in acquiring language, cognitive development, and social skills, due to adverse environmental influences, are frequently misdiagnosed as primary mental subnor-

mality or other biological defects. The fact that some infants are inherently more vulnerable than others to
environmental stress must also be taken into account.
Conditions such as prematurity, traumatic birth, neonatal illness, genetic disorders, and sensory defects such
as deafness or blindness, when combined with problems
in the nurturing environment, are especially hazardous
for the developmental process and for behavioral organization.

It is important that diagnosis be careful and comprehensive for the reasons referred to above. Specific assessment measures will vary but will fall short of what
is needed unless they include diagnostic data gained from
interviewing the parents, from pediatric evaluation of the
child, from observations of child behavior and of parent-
child interaction, and from formal assessment of developmental and behavioral levels and characteristics. Recommendations for alleviation of the child's problems,
while anchored in accumulated knowledge and wisdom
about what is likely to be good for infants in general,
must be individualized for a specific child and those who
take care of him. Global recommendations such as "find
a nice, warm foster mother" for a child who has been ill-
cared for, or "Mrs. A., play with your baby more" to the
mother who suffers from depression and whose child is
lagging in development, are clearly inadequate to meet
the therapeutic needs of infants and toddlers who come
to the attention of early childhood specialists. Obviously
an individualized prescription for a unique child with his
unique characteristics and his unique parents requires
that one carefully assess him and his environment. With
that plea for diagnosis as the basis of therapeutic planning I will turn to some considerations about treatment.

Before discussing aspects of the direct work of the
therapist with the child, which is the main focus of this
chapter, I wish to emphasize that the work with the parent or other primary care giver is crucially important in

efforts to alleviate the child's problems. The dependency of the young child on adults for the love, protection, and guidance necessary for healthy development make it essential that parents be helped to carry out these nurturing functions at least reasonably well. Only when that becomes an integral part of the therapeutic work can infant specialists expect to have a lasting beneficial influence. The work may involve parent and child together or separately. At times it may be primarily developmental guidance for the parent; at other times or in other cases therapy of the parent may be important before changes can take place. In other instances tangible supports to parents may be necessary before they can utilize a psychotherapeutic contact. The parents' need for support, guidance, or treatment must also be closely coordinated with work with the child. And what is learned by the therapist in contact with the child is translated into suggestions to the parents or points the way to paths of further exploration. At its most effective, the therapeutic effort becomes an alliance of the adults in behalf of the child. The severity of the problems of the parents, or to put it more positively, their capacity for change, determine whether this working together will be very influential or much less so.

The most effective therapy for disturbed infants and toddlers requires that the therapist be part mother, part teacher, and part dedicated weaver who helps the child to gain, as Kestenberg (1969) has suggested, a meaningful integration of units of achievement, memory fragments, body feelings, words, and concepts. Because this period of life (the first two-and-a-half years or so) is one in which speech, our usual mode of communication in therapy, is minimally available, and because of the very nature of psychological development during infancy and toddlerhood, we find ourselves having to rely heavily on behavioral cues to try to understand the mind and emotions of the child. In discussing analytic work with chil-

dren ages two to four years Kestenberg spoke of the task
in this way:

> In tracking a pre-oedipal child through the land of his
> illusions, one feels like an explorer encountering a jun-
> gle tribe whose means of communication are different
> and strange. . . . In order to understand the child we
> have to devise means to reach the inhabitant and cre-
> ator of the illusory land and help him grasp the intent
> of the outsiders who invaded it. These procedures are
> designed to give insight and as such they may be con-
> sidered educational. They are analytic when they help
> to form an alliance between analyst and child in the
> common task of removing obstacles to ego building [p.
> 360].

The achievement of the therapeutic alliance with the
child, as Neubauer (1972) has emphasized, has two components—forming a relationship and making it work for
the therapeutic aim. In order to proceed with analytic
work, Neubauer says, the achievement of separation-individuation is a necessary developmental step as are the
achievement of object constancy and the internalization
of conflict. The analyst's first task may be to assist the
child in achieving these steps.

Children under age two-and-a-half years, approximately, are not sufficiently advanced in intellectual and
emotional development to fulfill these criteria for entering into a psychoanalytic treatment and yet psychoanalytic developmental psychology has much to offer in
guiding effective therapeutic work with infants and toddlers. First and foremost are constructs regarding the
importance of the child's object relationships because of
their powerful influence on immediate experience as well
as on the processes that determine his future. The development of object relationships is facilitated by the biological readiness of the neonate for social contact and
the predisposition to respond and become attached to oth-

ers which are coordinated with the responsiveness of the parent to the infant's needs and with phases in their own development. A conviction about the crucial role of human relationships for the child's development will, of course, have immediate applicability to planning and carrying out therapeutic and preventive intervention work. One begins by assuming that the adult must be both source and mediator of the stimulation, guidance, love, and understanding that enable a child to develop normally or to recover from a psychopathological or maladaptive disorder.

Of special relevance for the early years also are constructs from ego psychology, including Hartmann's (1939) propositions regarding the existence of an ego constitution, the preadaptedness of the newborn infant to an "average expectable environment," the ego as the "organ of adaptation" through which man comes to terms with his environment, and the crucial role of learning and of social relationships in the formation and stability of these adaptation processes. Serious attention to the interdependence of object relations, ego, and drive development familiar to psychoanalytic theorists and clinicians is a useful perspective through which data of observation of infants and toddlers can be examined, explanations proposed, understanding facilitated. Valuable, too, in their applicability to practice are the seminal contributions of Mahler and her colleagues (Mahler, Pine, and Bergman, 1975) regarding the psychological birth of the human infant and the separation-individuation process.

Four additional contributions from psychology and education provide ideas that I have found particularly useful in thinking about the treatment of the very young: Piaget's propositions about the development of the infant's intelligence and the crucial role of sensory motor experience in its formation; Escalona's coordination of Piaget's work on cognition with aspects of ego psychology; current views on the significance of competence (mastery motivation) stimulated by Robert White's (1959) ideas; and, from scholars of early childhood education, the philosophy of the developmental-interaction approach articulated by Barbara Biber and her colleagues (Biber and Franklin, 1967; Shapiro and Biber, 1973; Biber, 1977, 1984).

Piaget emphasized the necessity of the infant's acting upon his environment for learning to take place on the sensory motor level which leads to ideas and structures on the psychological level (1952). Escalona (1963), following Piaget's thought about cognition, has proposed on the basis of her research that other adaptive ego processes, among them "communication, modulation of affect, control over excitation, delay and aspects of object relation, and hence identification, all are the result of a developmental sequence in sensory motor terms before they can emerge as ego functions in the narrower sense" (p. 198). These ideas are compatible with my observations and those of many others who work with infants and toddlers, namely that helping the infant to be active—motorically, socially, affectively, intellectually—and doing so carefully and with sensitivity often brings about impressive improvement. It is well known that difficulty in being active in these various modes is frequently found in psychologically vulnerable infants due to biological or experiential factors, or both. Therapy which enables the infant to be active toward the outside world and in his inner world is often reflected in a reduction or disappearance of symptomatic behavior, improvement in various dimensions of development, increased coping behavior, and, it appears, diminished vulnerability (Provence, 1974). We assume that the observable changes in development and behavior reflect and further contribute to internal psychological structural change. Improvement is most dramatic in those suffering from deficits in the environment such as deprivation, discontinuity, inconsistency, disorganization, and so on, but is also seen in infants with sensory defects and other handicaps (Provence and Lipton, 1962; Brazelton, Young, and Bullowa, 1971; Fraiberg, 1971, 1977, 1980; Provence, 1972, 1978). The advantages to the child's adaptive capacities of experiences of mastery were emphasized by White (1959) who noted that competence has high adaptive value in man who has so much to learn about dealing with the environment. Others (Harter and Zigler, 1974; B. White, 1975; Yarrow and Pederson, 1976; Harter, 1978) have contributed further to views on the origins of competence in the child, motivation for mastery, and relationships between motivation and cognition. Experiences of mastery in the infant and toddler are as a rule accompanied by great pleasure at the moment and even more significantly are believed to be experiences that positively influence the ways in which psychological energies invest ideas, feelings, and actions and contribute to the capacity for interacting successfully with the human and material environment. One of the things that can be said to be both a goal and an indication of successful treatment of the very young child is the steady aggregation of experiences in which those feelings of mastery occur.

The philosophy of education of the very young articulated by Biber and her colleagues has as a central tenet the view that "the growth of cognitive functions . . . cannot be separated from the growth of personal and interpersonal processes, the development of self-esteem and a sense of identity, internalization of impulse control, capacity for autonomous response, relatedness to other people" (Shapiro and Biber, 1973, p. 689). Educational practices with young children are guided by this philosophy and I chose this developmental-interactional approach as an example of what is encompassed in a wise and comprehensive educational philosophy. Expressed in these terms, education and therapy for the very young clearly partake of one another and are not necessarily distinguishable. For the infant, education can be therapeutic; therapy can and probably must be in part educational.

To summarize some of the essentials of the work of the psychotherapist of infants and toddlers: Whatever the history of the child's disturbance, the therapist's work begins with establishing a relationship with the child because the acceptance of the therapist as a benevolent adult who meets many of the child's needs and who provides the child with experiences that build ego development and expand the affective life is at the center of successful therapy. Infants and toddlers are, of course, still very dependent on the primary object, and if a child has been unable to rely on a primary object long enough and securely enough, the relationship to the therapist will reflect that experience. For infants who have been deprived, neglected, mistreated, or handled with great inconsistency the therapist may be the first reliable, trustworthy adult. If the mother has been insufficiently available or there has been much discontinuity of care for any reason there may be minimal cathexis of the human object.

Another important task of the therapist of the very young child is to understand the level of development of the mind. In the second year, for example, the mixtures of presymbolic and symbolic thinking, magical thoughts and wishes, verbal and nonverbal communications and expressions may not be easy for the therapist to understand, and yet it is important to be able to tune in on the child's feelings and forms of expression. This requires a flexibility, a capacity to be both empathic social partner and observer, to be able to identify, as well as an adult can, with the child's view of the world. That we achieve this only imperfectly there is no doubt. And yet, for therapists, as well as for parents rearing children, the child's willingness to partake in our world as we try to understand him helps to build a working relationship through which change can take place.

The case material to follow is offered in illustration.

CASE EXAMPLE 1—BOBBY, AGE SEVENTEEN MONTHS

Bobby, the firstborn of parents who were college graduates, was admitted to the hospital at age seventeen months with a presumptive diagnosis of mental retardation. The referring physician who had known him only for four months had become increasingly concerned about his delayed development, small size, and a feeding disturbance. A full-term, healthy baby he had grown normally, according to his parents' record, for the first eight months. The feeding situation, however, had been lacking in satisfaction both for infant and for his mother from the first. He sucked efficiently on his bottle but fed slowly and fell asleep during feedings. His mother recalled thumping his feet to keep him awake and being annoyed at having to spend the forty-five minutes or so required for each feeding. There was no vomiting, spitting of food, diarrhea, or pain. Solid foods were started when he was three months of age and at first were taken well; later his mother could feed solids only by distracting him. Forced-feeding and verbal insistence alternated with attempts at persuasion or removal of the food in anger, and feeding became a situation around which the child and his mother actively struggled. The atmosphere during feeding for the three or four months prior to admission was charged with feelings of anger or anxiety; she often felt disgusted, defeated, or indifferent; Bobby had very few opportunities to be fed by a person who could enjoy him and make the feeding situation pleasant. He often pushed away the feeding hand and had been throwing food or spoon when attempts were made to encourage self-feeding.

During the first days of hospitalization Bobby was often irritable in the presence of staff members and ap-

athetic, sad, or depressed when left alone. He reacted to
the appearance of any new person by crying or looking
apprehensive. He was invariably upset for a few minutes
by a change from one situation to another; for example,
if he were moved from crib to high chair, from chair to
floor, or picked up or put down. But once the transition
was made he was again comfortable. He had a bit of
interest in play materials which he used partly for his
own amusement and partly in a game with the adult in
which he threw the toys to the floor looking at the adult
as though to say, "What are you going to do about it?"
He enjoyed being held and talked to and made some attempts to initiate social contact by smiling, vocalizing,
or offering a toy after he had familiarized himself with
a particular adult. On the formal developmental examination Bobby's gross motor development was six months
below his age level while fine motor development including grasping patterns and eye-hand coordination were
adequate for his age. On nonverbal problem-solving tasks
appropriate for his age he had some success at or slightly
above his chronological age level and failures at age level
and below. Language was three to four months delayed.
His responses to people consisted of initial fearfulness
followed by tentative attempts to initiate social contact
and by provocative casting of objects with obvious intent
to elicit some kind of response from the adult. Careful
medical evaluation revealed no physical disease process.
Of diagnostic significance in the history of Bobby's first
year were these facts from the parents' report: Bobby was
an infant who from birth was content to spend a greater
part of each day in his room alone while his mother
worked in another part of the house. She could recall no
pleasure in caring for him as a young infant. When he
was four months of age she became pregnant for the second time. When he was seven months of age her father
died, a death that was a great shock to her, and there
followed a prolonged period of grief and depression from

which she found it difficult to arouse herself sufficiently to take care of Bobby. When he was about eleven months of age, during the sixth month of her pregnancy, she shifted some of his care to his father: she described her husband as willing to help but finding little enjoyment in child care, preferring to spend his time working around the house rather than with the baby. Some warmer and more spontaneous contacts occurred during his weekly visits with the grandparents. At a year of age he had three words which he stopped using following the birth of his sibling.

The diagnostic impression of Bobby was that he was not a mentally retarded child as had been feared, but an emotionally deprived, insufficiently stimulated child whose most enlivening interactions with the adults had come to occur in the struggle around the feeding. A three-week therapeutic trial was carried out in the hospital setting with the specific purpose of trying to find ways to alleviate the feeding problem and to provide social, emotional, and physical stimulation. Ideally, the way of providing this therapy would have been to make one interested and constant mother substitute responsible for his total care. While this could not be arranged in the hospital setting it was approximated by limiting the mother substitutes to two warm and skillful nurses one or the other of whom was responsible for all of his care during his waking hours. They helped Bobby with feeding but did not force-feed; he was permitted to get his hands in the food and to feed himself as he was ready to do so. At first there was much messiness and throwing both of food and spoon, he ate little, and at first lost weight, but within a week he gave up the throwing behavior and, after patient and friendly demonstrations from the nurse, and her presence to assist him, he became actively interested in self-feeding. Feeding became a much less charged situation and he demonstrated some pleasure in self-feeding as long as one of his two nurses was present

to encourage and lend a hand. Because there were many
times apart from the feeding situation in which his interactions with adults could be stimulating, interesting,
exciting, or comforting as the need arose, he became strikingly less apathetic, used more language, smiled and
laughed more, and his interest in toys became more sustained and constructive. With demonstration and good-
natured encouragement from his two nurses, he came to
realize that toys offered many opportunities for exploration, manipulation, and discharge of feelings. He
moved about much more freely and with greater vigor
and enjoyment so that in all areas of development in a
relatively short period he had become more active, had
many more experiences that included pleasure in mastery, and had enlarged the dimensions of his social interaction with maternal figures. It was an exciting,
expansive period for Bobby and while the provocative
interaction was occasionally seen it did not cause problems. Meanwhile both of Bobby's parents, noting his improvement, were able to give up their terrible fear that
he was mentally retarded and to gain new hope. They
were helped to participate in his care in the hospital and
agreed to continued counseling and developmental guidance after he left. They believed that Bobby's mother's
long period of mourning was largely past and that they
would need no help with that.

It was clear that the benevolent, supportive, and
emotionally nurturing atmosphere created the conditions
under which Bobby could improve. In addition he was
provided an opportunity to learn that one could enjoy food
and the pleasure of feeding oneself and did not have to
fight with an adult over it. He learned also that self-
initiated action could lead to interesting happenings and
pleasure and that there were many dimensions of social
contact that were possible and could be relied upon at
least from one day to the next. He learned that specific

words at his command could be followed by predictable responses from the adults and that speech could be useful to him.

CASE EXAMPLE 2—JAMES, AGE TWENTY-ONE MONTHS

James, age twenty-one months, was referred for evaluation by his physician because his parents were concerned about his delayed speech and what they called his shyness. He had been a difficult baby from the beginning, one whose mother remembered his first year as one of almost continuous crying. While free of illness he was difficult to comfort, often irritable, and produced in his mother feelings of helplessness, anger, and concern about herself as a mother. While the crying had lessened appreciably when James was about a year old these intelligent parents were aware that they were still in need of some assistance. At the time of the evaluation they described James as a child who could be a charming companion at times but also was often hard to please, "whiny," and easily frustrated. The first impression of James was of a passive, highly anxious child, but over a few play and testing sessions it was possible to understand that if one could make him more comfortable and provide toys he could be enabled to play and to enjoy the social interaction. The diagnostic study, which included exclusion of organic factors, led us to formulate the problem as follows: James, as a neonate and young infant, had suffered more than most from internal distress and heightened internal tension, possibly also from hypersensitivity to external stimuli. We reasoned that he would not have been easy for any mother, but for this particular mother who felt insecure and inept in his care, had very little assistance in her maternal role, and was disappointed that her first child was not a girl, James

was impossible. He developed a pattern of crying episodes, alternating periods of sleep, and wide-eyed watch-
fulness. Neither of these conscientious parents felt
successful with him. It appeared that the physical discomfort and physiological instabilities of the earliest
months of James's life had led into psychological discomforts of some magnitude. The therapeutic task was to
remove the obstacles to the forward thrust of development
through helping James and his parents. One of our nursery school teachers began to see James in individual session, at first with his mother in the room. This gentle,
skillful teacher, respecting James's sensitivity and gear-
ing her actions to his need, helped him to play and led
him very quickly to expand the areas in which he felt
competent and could enjoy action. As he gradually became more active, more verbal, and more competent he
also became less anxious and developed active strategies
to cope with frustration and stress. Experiences of satisfaction and pleasure between parents and child increased as both they and James could relate differently
to one another. The balance shifted in their behavior to
a predominance of attitudes and interactions that supported development, and by the time James was three
years old, though still a sensitive child and somewhat
anxious, he was well able to cope with and benefit from
a regular nursery school program. His superior intelligence became increasingly apparent and was both a
pleasure to his parents and a source of strength and satisfaction in his own psychological economy. In every way
he appeared more robust, more active, more trusting of
his parents and others, and possessed of an increased
repertory of adaptive and defensive abilities. He had
learned, moreover, from his teacher, and then from his
parents, not only a set of skills involving action in regard
to people and inanimate objects, but also learned how to
recognize some of his own feelings and to talk about them.

CASE EXAMPLE 3—MARY, AGE NINETEEN
MONTHS

The process of helping a young child feel comfortable, coming to trust new adults enough to accept, however tentatively, an invitation to interaction and communication, often comes about with very sensitive, psychologically fragile children in surprising ways. Far from being able to accept the physical and social contact they need so much, many of them seem terrified of it. Mary, age nineteen months, was a passive, inhibited, watchful and anxiously apprehensive girl who refused to walk, though she was able to, and appeared comfortable only in her crib. When first evaluated because of parental concern about mental retardation, she was very wary of any direct physical contact or vis-à-vis social interaction and also quite passive as though fearful of the play materials as well. Asked to evaluate her the consultant reported as follows:

> I tried all my tricks to make the materials attractive to Mary but she would accept them either not at all or would hold them briefly and drop them, though not crying or objecting actively. After fifteen to twenty minutes of this, a fortuitous event occurred. This effort to evaluate Mary was taking place in a large room in the hospital in which smoking was permitted, and one of the interns, waiting for something to happen, had lighted a cigarette and was idly blowing smoke rings. When I noted Mary's immediate visual interest in them and her reaching out toward them I asked him to blow smoke rings her way. She became fascinated as they floated toward her and tried to take them in her hand. After a few moments of grasping at the smoke rings with clear signs of interest and pleasure, she was willing to accept from my hand some small, light plastic rings with which she began to play. After some time of playing with the rings manipulating them, smiling

about them, looking at me with some pleasure, she then
accepted the formboard and various others of the test
materials utilizing them with a fair amount of interest.
Each day for the ten remaining days of hospitalization
I went back to see her and spent time with her each
day during which time, primarily because I was the
source now of some toys that interested her, she began
to accept and relate to me. As long as I respected her
need for distance and her need to determine when she
would be active in the contact, she seemed to begin to
accept and trust me, and the basis for the later work
which continued over a period of three years was laid.
For months I had always to be careful to be certain the
toys she was accustomed to were there because she
could react to any absence or even a small blemish,
sometimes with anger, sometimes with near panic.
Slowly she learned, that is, she came to understand,
that I was the same person even when I had new
glasses, that when I talked to her on the telephone I
was the same person whom she saw when she came to
the clinic, that the bigger of two blocks or the biggest
of three could be understood as relative characteristics,
that some things were safe and some were dangerous,
and so on. I became for her the person who could tell
her about how she seemed to be feeling, about such
diverse matters as how a day could be marked, about
what one could try to do when upset, what was real
and what imagined. Much of this she at first committed
to memory and repeated before she could really understand; that is, she accepted my statements because
she trusted me and, when she was able, she incorporated them in a different way into the psychological
system. This was reminiscent, of course, of a normal
child's learning from parents about his expanding inner
and outer worlds.

Therapists of very young children give them all kinds
of information. This can be viewed in part as the adult's
"lending ego" to the child whose ego is not equal to the

tasks imposed on it. We also convey our intent to be protective of the child who is in danger of hurting himself: "The corner of the table is sharp. It would hurt you if you fell against it, and I don't want you to be hurt," to the child who is flailing about the room and indeed in danger of hurting himself; the need for caution to a child who is climbing too high or getting too close to the street. Much information about objects in the real world is conveyed if we feel the child needs such information. And there is much about the world of human and inanimate objects and about cause and effect that the child needs to know and will often inquire about. There are also informative comments about such things as the child's feelings or what we have noted that he does when he is particularly afraid, or sad or angry. Indeed, the use of books and stories that can be read to the child about other persons or about animals, among their other meanings, have the advantage of allowing the child to know that certain feelings and connections and relationships are possible and even that there can be a favorable outcome. Such information-giving, educational measures in treatment must be geared to the therapist's understanding of an individual child, his central problems, and his changing needs and capabilities.

While little has been said in this chapter about the emotions of child and of therapist, their relevance for the therapeutic effort is implicit. The therapist, in order to assist the young child must, in addition to other talents, be able to communicate affectionate interest in a variety of ways. He or she must be willing to become a real object for the infant-toddler, and able to regulate the intensity of the social-emotional interchanges in accordance with the child's needs and the therapeutic aim. To be able to supplement or complement the parents in their nurturing roles, to provide corrective experiences, whether social, cognitive, or emotional, to help the child become more competent is no easy task. In addition to the ability to understand the therapeutic implications of the level of development of the young child's mind and his "illusory world" as Kestenberg calls it, it seems probable that the therapist's ability to participate in a rich emotional communication with the observing ego always in operation is of utmost importance. For the child this is education and a great deal more.

REFERENCES

Biber, B. (1977), A developmental-interaction approach: Bank Street College of Education. In: *The Preschool in Action*, 2nd ed., ed. M. C. Day & R. K. Parker. Boston: Allyn & Bacon, pp. 423–460.

——— (1984), *Early Education and Psychological Development*. New Haven, CT: Yale University Press.

——— Franklin, M. B. (1967), The relevance of developmental and psychodynamic concepts of the education of the pre-school child. *J. Acad. Child Psychiat.*, 6:5–24.

Brazelton, T. B., Young, G., & Bullowa, M. (1971), Inception and resolution of early developmental pathology: A case history. *J. Amer. Acad. Child Psychiat.*, 10:124–135.

Escalona, S. K. (1963), Patterns of infantile experience and the developmental process. *The Psychoanalytic Study of the Child*, 18:197–244. New York: International Universities Press.

Fraiberg, S. (1971), Intervention in infancy: A program for blind infants. *J. Amer. Acad. Child Psychiat.*, 10(3):381–405.

——— (1977), *Insights from the Blind*. New York: Basic Books.

——— ed. (1980), *Clinical Studies in Infant Mental Health: The First Year of Life*. New York: Basic Books.

Harter, S. (1978), Effectance motivation reconsidered: Toward a developmental model. *Hum. Develop.*, 21:34–64.

——— Zigler, E. (1974), The assessment of effectance motivation in normal and retarded children. *Development. Psychol.*, 10:169–180.

Hartmann, H. (1939), *Ego Psychology and Problems of Adaptation*. New York: International Universities Press, 1958.

Kestenberg, J. S. (1969), Problems of technique of child analysis in relation to various developmental stages: Prelatency. *The Psychoanalytic Study of the Child*, 24:358–383. New York: International Universities Press.

Mahler, M., Pine, F., & Bergman, A. (1975), *The Psychological Birth of the Human Infant*. New York: Basic Books.

Neubauer, P. B. (1972), Psychoanalysis of the pre-school child. In: *Handbook of Child Psychoanalysis*, ed. B. B. Wolman. New York: Van Nostrand Reinhold, pp. 221–252.

Piaget, J. (1952), *The Origins of Intelligence in Children*. New York: International Universities Press.

Provence, S. (1972), Psychoanalysis and the treatment of psychological disorders of infancy. In: *Handbook of Child Psychoanalysis*, ed. B. B. Wolman. New York: Van Nostrand Reinhold, pp. 191–220.

———— (1974), Some relationships between activity and vulnerability in the early years. In: *The Child in His Family*, Vol. 3: *Children at Psychiatric Risk*, ed. E. J. Anthony & C. Koupernik. New York: John Wiley, pp. 157–166.

———— (1978), Application of psychoanalytic principles to treatment and prevention in infancy. In: *Child Analysis and Therapy*, ed. J. Glenn. New York: Jason Aronson, pp. 581–596.

———— Lipton, R. (1962), *Infants in Institutions*. New York: International Universities Press.

Shapiro, E., & Biber, B. (1973), The education of young children: A developmental-interaction approach. In: *Children with Learning Problems*, ed. S. Sapir & A. Nitzburg. New York: Brunner/Mazel, pp. 682–709.

White, B. (1975), Critical issues in the origins of competence. *Merrill-Palmer Quart.*, 21:243–266.

White, R. W. (1959), Motivation reconsidered: The concept of competence. *Psychol. Rev.*, 66:297–333.

Yarrow, L. J., & Pederson, F. A. (1976), The interplay between cognition and motivation in infancy. In: *Origins of Intelligence*, ed. M. Lewis. New York: Plenum Press, pp. 379–399.

Chapter 20

Implications of the Infantile Neurosis for Learning Problems in Childhood

DONALD D. SCHWARTZ, M.D.

From its inception by Freud psychoanalysis has had as its goal the attainment of knowledge; self-knowledge for the patient; knowledge of the psychology of his patients and knowledge of the mind of human beings for the analyst. The theory and method of making such knowledge manifest has changed, for example, from "id analysis" predicated on a toxic theory of anxiety due to dammed up (repressed) libido, to the analysis of unconscious resistance, "ego analysis," based upon a structural theory of the mind and ego psychology. The intention of the analyst, however, has been to facilitate the patient's becoming aware of what has been, for him, psychologically unknowable. This is the case whether the psychology of the id, ego, self, or object relations is the issue. Through the interpretation of resistance, transference (and countertransference) as a "remembering" via repetition (Freud, 1914b), and construction of the past predicated on transference experiences in the present, the patient comes to learn about what has been dynamically maintained as unknown.

Knowing, the attainment of knowledge, the quest for "truth" has been a prominent feature in mankind's myths, fairy tales, drama, religion, and philosophy. The Old Testament story of the Garden of Eden is focused around what Adam and Eve were permitted to learn, and the consequences of their disobeying the injunction against eating of the fruit of the Tree of Knowledge; and the biblical use of knowing as sexual intercourse, carnal knowledge, is relevant to a study of learning problems. Robert Graves in *The White Goddess* (1948) remarks that in ancient times if the secret name of a god were known by the enemies of his people, they could perform destructive magic against them. He presents his thesis that the subject of an ancient Welsh myth, Cad Godden (The Battle of the Trees), fought between Arawn King of Annwm and the two sons of Don, Gwydion and Amathaon, represents a battle for religious supremacy. Graves's version is as follows: "There was a man embattled who unless his name were known could not be overcome, and there was on the other side a woman called Achren ('trees'), and unless her name were known, her party could not be overcome. And Gwydion of Don, instructed by his brother Amathaon, guessed the name of the woman . . . " (p. 373). According to Graves the battle of the trees was a struggle between the white goddess and Apollo who was challenging her. The trees are a tree-alphabet, the secret of which Gwydion and Amathaon stole from the god Bran; and it was the knowledge of the secret sacred name that brought victory, the overthrow of female dominated religion by a male dominated one. The power of knowledge, of the word, is frequent in fairy tales; for example, Rumplestiltskin, and the poet warns us that:

A little learning is a dangerous thing;
Drink deep or taste not of the Pierian spring:
There shallow droughts intoxicate the brain,
And drinking largely sobers us again

[Pope, 1711]

Knowing or not knowing is central in Sophocles' Oedipus plays. Oedipus did not know that the man he met and killed was his father or that Jocasta was his mother. Oedipus became king on the strength of answering the riddle of the Sphinx, and a reasonable interpretation of Oedipus' gouging out his eyes is that in blinding himself he expressed the wish that he had remained in the dark, that he did not see, as in the expression "I see" means "I understand, I know." In their more mundane, everyday lives, children, and adults, too, unconsciously struggle with desires, ambitions, fears, and conflicts similar to those of Adam and Eve, Oedipus, and the adherents of the White Goddess; and these all too often result in disturbances of the process of learning when it becomes involved in unconscious psychological meanings and motives.

A psychoanalytic consideration of the implications of the infantile neurosis in learning problems of children must take into account the interrelationship of the innate biological, neurological, cognitive development, and psychic development including autonomous ego functions, sexuality, aggression, and object relationships as they result in the formation of the psychic structure of psychoanalysis as well as cognitive structures, and their relationship to knowing and learning.

It is necessary to understand how these factors result in a latency level of maturation, cognition, and psychosocial development. Latency is important in relationship to formal education and learning as it is in this phase that we need to know what the child requires developmentally to enable him to learn as an autonomous function in relationship to the internal and external environment, to use the knowledge attained, and to be further motivated to further learning. This developmental level can be used as a baseline from which to consider the interferences with learning, the pathological influences on learning which are the result of the child's ontogenetic passage through preceding stages of development. To do this, it is first necessary to differentiate the infantile neurosis defined as a childhood neurosis from the infantile neurosis as developmental, and in my view, inseparable from the oedipal phase of development and its central intrapsychic and interpersonal configuration, the Oedipus complex. It is also necessary to differentiate these from the manifestations of preoedipal psychopathology in contrast to the preoedipal aspects of the infantile neurosis. The oedipal phase is not only an organizer of preceding phases of development but its own psychosexual object relations and cognitive organization are influenced by the normal and pathological resolutions of these earlier stages of maturation and development. Developmentally, the infantile neurosis is the ongoing process of this oedipally oriented psychic reorganization and the establishment of a superseding system of psychological function, including those cognitive structures relevant to the quality of learning for which the latency-age child will be responsible. It is the nature of the resolution of the Oedipus complex which may prove vital in determining the capacity or incapacity for learning in an academic setting to which the child will be progressively exposed.

A children's book entitled *The Boy Who Could Enter Paintings* (Valen, 1968) dramatizes the shift from fantasy to reality leading to late and postoedipal cognitive development. In it the author tells the story of a boy named Edward who lives in the loft with his father, an artist. Throughout the story there is no mention of his mother, and early on the reader learns that Edward has discovered that he can hop up the stairs to his father's studio and considers this a measure of his growing strength, that there are no other children in the building, and that Edward spends much of his time in watching his father paint. No age is mentioned; however, as the story takes place between winter and Edward's awaiting his attendance at school for the first time, he is probably between ages four-and-one-half and five when the story begins and five to five-and-one-half years old when it ends. One winter day he passes a copy his father has made of a jungle scene (it is a painting by Henri Rousseau) and feeling warmth from the bright sun in the painting, he closes his eyes, hops toward it, and with the third hop finds himself in the painting, on the grass beneath the hot sun with chattering monkeys who drop him an orange from which Edward sucks the juice. When his father comes looking for him, the boy calls out and waves; but realizes his father can neither hear nor see him, so snowsuit and shoes in hand, he hops back into the cold room. In answer to his father's question, he explains that he has been in the painting to keep himself warm, to which his father, with bemusement, responds that now that he is back Edward should put on his clothes.

Subsequently, while at the museum with his father who is copying Manet's *In a Boat*, Edward hops in and out of Goya's *Don Manuel*; and there is an exchange between the boys in Spanish and English and Don Manuel allows Edward to hold a string tied to a black bird. On another occasion at the museum Edward ends up playing catch with Suzanne, the girl wearing a rose-colored dress in Seurat's *La Grande Jatte*. (Edward has found that it is increasingly difficult to enter the painting, requiring five hops this time.) After several adventures, including losing his ball in the water, Edward hears the bell indicating closing time at the museum and rolls out of the painting onto the floor where he is found by his father. Edward asks his father if a speck in the picture could be a ball, and when his father answers that it could be, Edward, putting his hand in his pocket and finding that his ball is not there, concludes that he's "pretty sure" that's what it is.

In the following weeks important things happen in Edward's life. A family with a son Edward's age moves into his building, and for the first time Edward has a playmate. Instead of going to the museum with his father, Edward spends most of his time playing with John and thinking about school, which his father has informed him will begin in a few weeks. The story comes to a close after Edward's father finishes his copy of Manet's *In a Boat* and goes into the kitchen to have tea. Edward examines the painting and in response to the awareness of his desire to join the man and woman in the boat, he closes his eyes and starts hopping. After three hops nothing has happened; by the sixth hop he hears his friend John calling him; and after an eighth hop there is a tearing sound and Edward has gone through the canvas and is on the floor of the studio. To his horrified father Edward explains that he had been hopping with his eyes closed and fell through the painting. His father explains that he must not hop around paintings and that this must never happen again. Edward sadly acknowledges that he understands and says, "I know that. I don't think it can ever happen again," and runs downstairs to play with John without hopping even once.

Bettelheim (1977), in his book about the meaning and importance of fairy tales, writes that wisdom and a reasoned understanding of one's existence in the world in which one lives are achieved gradually over time by experiences in that world, beginning with irrational ideas (from a mature adult's view) and becoming increasingly maturely intelligent and realistic. Bettelheim contends that fairy tales offer a child conscious presentations of unconscious fantasies and developmental conflicts and anxieties in structured forms which facilitate the child's mastery of the inevitable problems of being a child and growing up. The emergence into awareness of the unconscious in derivative and displaced forms allows the child to contend with them through imagination and by identification with the hero (often a child) who struggles through the vicissitudes of dealing with the human experiences of good and evil. Bettelheim comments on the role of the parents in offering and participating in the reading of fairy tales to their children, and I would add that beside providing the security of their presence and acceptance the parent offers the child a more secondary process language and the validation of the child's age appropriate conceptualizations of the fairy tale's content. He emphasizes that while the fairy tale has features of the everyday world, its essential value is the externalization of internal processes of the individual which the child can experience and contemplate more consciously.

The Boy Who Could Enter Paintings offers a child some of the advantageous features of fairy tales highlighted by Bettelheim in regard to primary-process, fantasy, and secondary-process thinking. These are illustrated through Edward and the vicissitudes of his "ability" to enter paintings, those experiences in his world (internal and external) over time which enable, even force him, to become more reality oriented. This whimsical story can serve as the basis for a psychoanalytic perspective of the author's intuitive understanding of the developmental requirements for the child's introduction to formal learning in a school setting. For my purposes, the consideration of the infantile neurosis in relation to problems in learning in children, I will somewhat freely interpret the story as if Edward, a late oedipal child, was early in the story an even younger child, and at the end about to enter first grade rather than kindergarten, that is, closer to latency. In Edward we can see the interrelationship of cognitive and psychological development, the interpersonal experiences with his father, and the social world outside of the home and parents which are the necessary attributes for the task of formal learning and the personal and social use of attained knowledge. The active fantasy of entering paintings and his "belief" in the actuality of his experiences are creatively presented testimonials to the quality of "reality" in the young child which goes unquestioned

by the reader (child and adult) and by young children and
adults in such a child's actual life. (Although such "reality" might well be sorely questioned by a ten-year-old
latency child.)

Edward's entering the four paintings can be viewed
as stages in psychological and cognitive development,
from early psychological experience and capacity for
thinking to an oedipal-latency readiness for intrapsychic
interpersonal growth and learning in a school setting.
The entrance into the first painting (which has a "primitive" quality) is accompanied by a sense of warmth and
comfort; with no clothes or food and no human beings;
while his interaction with Don Manuel is a dyadic relationship with another very young boy, limited in verbal
communication and primarily involving physical acts. In
La Grande Jatte there is not only Suzanne, a girl, but
also experiences with adults, both men and women. In
regard to entering the first painting, there is seemingly
no question about the actuality of the occurrence and no
hesitation in saying so to his father who intuitively accepts his son's statements without trying to explain that
it is an impossibility (much like a parent reading a fairy
tale to a young child does regarding the magic and mir-
acles often found in them). By the third painting, Edward's maturation and development psychologically and
cognitively make it increasingly untenable for him to
continue to maintain the fantasy he has until then so
readily been able to enter. The more idiosyncratic, highly
personal "reality" is giving way to more socially related
communication and consensual validation. In general
this is represented by the increased difficulty, the greater
number of hops necessary, for him in entering the paintings. More specifically, he says to himself when Suzanne
speaks to him in French (though he's able to comprehend
that she's telling him her name and responds by telling
her his name) that he must remember to go into paintings
where they speak English. He also experiences some un-

certainty about whether he has "actually" been in the painting and has really lost his ball in the water (i.e., there is an increased capability for differentiating imagination and actuality). Regarding this, it is after his father's affirmation that a speck in the painting could be a ball that Edward is only "pretty sure" it is a ball. The psychic development with increased capacity for reality testing, autonomy, and independence, self and other differentiation, and cognitive development, which reinforce each other, are significantly influenced by the involvement of the parents in regard to their appreciation, affirmation, and validation of the child's internal shifting from lesser to greater reality testing and secondary process thinking and conceptualizing. This is illustrated in the difference between the father's response to Edward's explanation that he'd been in the Rousseau painting (as a three- or four-year-old might assert), and the exchange between father and son regarding the ball and *La Grande Jatte*, in regard to realistic possibilities.

The culmination of this story of a boy who in his imagination entered paintings coincides with the culmination of psychic and cognitive development in the young child, the resolution of the Oedipus, the establishment of triadic object relations, the relatively stable cohesive organization of ego and superego, the basis for the capability of self-esteem regulation, autonomy, social interaction, and formal learning in school. At this point I treat Edward as if he were a latency-phase child.

The intrapsychic developmental state and the interpersonal social relationships are combined in the dramatic failure of Edward's last attempt to fantasize himself into Manet's *In a Boat* to join the man and woman in the picture, as Edward, aware that it is more difficult than ever before, hears his friend John calling him just before reality holds sway over fantasy and he goes crashing through the canvas. His father reacts appropriately to his son as a child who should know better than to hop around paintings with his eyes closed and admonishes him that it must never happen again. Edward, as if mourning for a developmental time now past, sadly realizes he can't do it anymore; and he expectantly turns to the succeeding developmental phase, his friendship with John and the anticipation of attending school.

I have used the story of Edward to elucidate the progressive psychic and cognitive development from primary to secondary process, from idiosyncratic personalized fantasy to reality testing and dealing with facts which are the usual psychological accompaniments of the child's entrance into the psychosocial latency phase. As an example of a potential problem in learning related to knowing that Edward does not have a mother living with him, a question could be raised about whether his entering into paintings was a fantasy about finding his preoedipal and oedipal mother. If this were so, would his curiosity have been interfered with, would there be an inhibition in regard to finding out; that is, learning in school? If he unconsciously experienced his teacher (especially a woman) as his (fantasied) mother, this might prove detrimental to the neutralized quality necessary for a teacher-student relationship. On the other hand, Edward's experience with his father, which fostered idiosyncratic fantasy-oriented learning on his own, might make him ill-prepared for the greater secondary process reality-oriented attention required for formal learning in school. Were Edward to continue his active fantasy life in response to the content to be learned, the oedipal boy's "creative" thinking would become a serious liability to the latency boy and interfere with his efforts at learning and problem solving. The difficulties he might encounter because of failures in the resolution of his infantile neurosis could be due to unconscious symbolic meanings and conflicts associated with learning, the subject to be learned, and the person from whom he would be learning. The concepts presented by Flavell (1963), Klein (1967), and Schwartz (1973) are useful in understanding the effects of these on Edward's capacity to learn.

Shapiro and Perry (1976) state: "We place special emphasis on the remarkable fact that the chronological age of 7 ± 1 is referred to so frequently as to suggest a milestone marking discontinuous development . . . the longer view of history and sociology of childhood antedating Freud's work indicates that empirically many cultures had discovered the unique competence of 7-year-olds that permitted them to assume new roles not available when they were younger" (p. 80). It is not merely coincidental that societal and parental expectations that a child is ready and capable of learning in the formal sense of learning is concurrent with the latency phase of development. It is usually by the second grade that teachers take note and parents become aware of a child with difficulty in learning in general or in regard to a specific subject; and if it persists into third or fourth grade, that child is identified as having a problem in learning. In order to examine the influence of the infantile neurosis on learning, it is necessary to first take into account the factors involving learning and in what ways the interrelationship of those factors result in that autonomous, conflict-free capacity to learn which is a concomitant of the latency phase.

Intelligence, the ability to acquire and retain knowledge, to learn and understand, is grounded in phylogenetic inheritance, innate constitutional endowments, and the integrity of the central nervous system. While central nervous system maturation is an obvious necessity for an increasingly complex intelligence, the maturation of the peripheral nervous system of all physiological functions is of importance in learning. Beyond those reflex responses, for example, the sucking reflex, the infant and the young child learn with and through their bodies and bodily functions and these "learning" experiences are progressively established and elaborated psychologically.

The anatomical form and mode of physiological function influence the child's experience and learning about the world within and without himself, in part shaping fantasies and relations with others (Erikson, 1950), and ultimately the child's approach to academic learning.

Taking in, retaining, or spitting out by mouth and retaining and letting out associated with anal sphincter control are correlates of learning, and disturbances in learning and utilizing knowledge are readily demonstrated clinically with children and adults in relation to conflicts associated with oral intake and anal retention or expulsion and the attendant fantasies and object relations. The maturational abilities of bringing his hand, and what it holds, to the infant's mouth involve hand-eye coordination, touching and grasping with fingers and hand, the sensations in his hand, lips, tongue, and mouth, as well as experiencing the object visually and tactilely. Simultaneously the infant is learning about and establishing psychic representations of what will become knowledge of himself and what is not himself. My point is that anatomy and physiology, form and function, are destined to contribute to psychic development in general and cognition more specifically. These developments are initially nonconflictual, maturationally determined aspects of the process of psychic structure formation including cognitive structures.

It is for the purpose of emphasis that I may seem to differentiate cognitive development from psychic development such as psychic structure formation, self and object representations, object relations, sexuality and aggression, conflict, defense, and so on. Sandler and Flavell attest to Piaget's view of cognition as psychological. Sandler (1975) states, "Piaget sees the development of the various aspects of intelligence as a psychological outcome of the interaction between the biological organism and the social environment. He sees the interaction as a process of progressive psychological adaptation, involving the development of increasingly sophisticated and complex psychological 'structures' or 'schemata' " (p. 365). Flavell (1963) writes, "Intellectual functioning is a special form of biological activity . . ." (pp. 42–43). This biological substrate upon which intelligence is based involves specific hereditary organic structures and physiological functioning; for example, those involved in perception which allow and also limit the establishment of fundamental concepts. Our biological endowment also includes capabilities which enable humans to develop intellectually and to go beyond the limitations inherent in organic givens. This is the mode of intellectual functioning which "generates cognitive structures [which we do not inherit] which develop as the result of functioning, and this mode of functioning . . . remains essentially constant throughout life . . . despite the wide varieties of cognitive structures this functioning creates" (pp. 42–43). The invariant functions basic to intellectual functioning and intelligence are organization and adaptation, the latter comprised of assimilation and accommodation. Elsewhere Flavell notes that "intelligent activity is always an active, organized process of assimilating the new to the old and of accommodating the old to the new. Intellectual content will vary enormously from age to age in ontogenetic development, yet the general functional properties of the adaptational processes remain the same" (1963, p. 17).

For Piaget cognitive structures are mediators between the invariant functions of assimilation and the accommodation and the multiform behavioral contents from which cognitive structures are inferred. Cognitive structures change with age and development and because of the influence of the many variables in any stage of development, there is no correlation of stage and a specific age. In the outline of Piaget's concepts of intelligence that follow, I will rely in the main on Flavell.

The sensorimotor period, stage 6 (18–24 months),

shades into the onset of the preoperational period of
thought (1-1/2–2 years to 5–7 years). In contrast to the
sensorimotor infant who uses direct action, the preoperational child uses mental representations of various schemata involved in any act to be performed enables
increasing intellectual adaptation via conceptual symbolic means. This is a significant contrast to performing
the actions in the sensorimotor period; that is, there is
a transition from overt sensorimotor acts of intelligence
to preoperational thought which becomes increasingly a
function of internal symbolic manipulations of reality.
Representational thought allows the establishment of a
mental organization of separate events and for the child
to recall the past, represent the present, and anticipate
the future. It enables the child to be free from concrete
reality and to consider "entities which are not tangible
and can't be pictured, such as scientific and mathematical
thought. Conceptual intelligence, in contrast to the privacy of sensori-motor cognition, becomes socialized through
a system of symbols which the whole culture can share"
(Flavell, 1963, p. 152). The initial symbols are private
and nonverbal, predicated on the symbolic function, "a
basic acquisition which makes possible the acquisition of
both private symbols and social signs. . . . Language is
the vehicle par excellence of symbolization. . . . But
thought is far from being a purely verbal affair. . . . Language, first acquired through the auspices of a symbolic
function which has arisen earlier, will . . . lend tremendous assistance to the subsequent development of the latter" (pp. 154–155). (These comments and those following
about symbolization, language, and verbalization are of
importance in the role played by the parents in relation
to the infantile neurosis, in facilitating and promoting
progression, or interfering and delaying the child's increasing utilization of symbolic socialized thought.)

   An outstanding feature of the preoperational child's
thinking is what Piaget termed *egocentricism,* by which

he referred to the child's inability to put himself in another's place, to recognize another's viewpoint, and consider his own as one possibility. Nor can the child consider correlating his view with others. He finds no need to justify his reasoning to others or take into account contradictions in his own thought. The preoperational child does not differentiate play and reality and there are "different cognitive realms [or preoperational and concrete operational thought] possessing distinct and different internal ground rules" and Flavell concludes with a quote from Piaget on child's play as an "autonomous reality" which is opposed to the "true reality" which for the child is "considerably less true for the child than for us" (p. 161). In psychoanalytic terms the same can be said for a child's imagination, fantasy, and his psychic reality in contrast to "actual" reality. In the fifth, sixth, and seventh year, the preoperational qualities of thought are superseded by those more characteristic of concrete operational thinking. The child of later preoperational, early concrete operational thinking in Piaget's theory is the psychoanalytically perceived child of the oedipal–early latency phase of development with the associated ongoing and resolving infantile neurosis.

Concrete operations occur between six and seven to eleven years of age. The most significant difference between the preoperational child and one of middle childhood is the nature of the latter's "coherent and integrated cognitive system with which he organizes and manipulates the world around him" (Flavell, 1963, p. 165). This cognitive system is stable and flexible, enabling the child to relate the present to the past, without disruption and contradiction; it is a complex internal, symbolic representational system of cognition. A cognitive act as an operation is defined as "any representational act which is an integral part of an organized network of related acts [and] all that is implied in common mathematical symbols like $+, -$; $\times, \div$; $>, <$; etc., belong to, but do not exhaust, the domain of what [Piaget] terms 'intellectual operations' " (p. 166). (In relation to learning problems, if an intellectual operation is symbolically a part of a psychological system which involves it in conflict, causes anxiety, and so on, it may well result in an interference in some aspect of learning in regard to that operation.) While the preoperational child's propensity is to function primarily in terms of the immediate actual reality, the concrete-operational child has developed the beginning capability of extending his thought from the actual to the possible, although such organizing, ordering, and extrapolation to the not immediate events and things in the present is limited. The extension of this aspect of cognitive development is the hallmark of the subsequent phase of formal operations which are established during adolescence from about age twelve onward and whose essential characteristics include the consideration of what is real and what is possible. In the seven- to eleven-year period, concrete objects and events are cognitively organized; in formal thinking, the results of these concrete operations are put in the form of propositions, and the further operations involve various logical connections and relationships between them as well as combinations of them. Such combinations are hypotheses to be confirmed or disproven.

Psychoanalysts have given some attention to learning and psychoanalytic theories of thinking. Rapaport was interested in and wrote several papers and one book on the psychoanalytic theory of thinking (1950, 1951, 1957). Rapaport defined cognitive structures in the following way: "By cognitive structures I mean both those quasi-permanent means which cognitive processes use and do not have to create de novo each time and those quasi-permanent organizations of such means that are the framework for the individual's cognitive processes" (1957, p. 631). For Rapaport, a theory of cognition must concern itself with man's ways of obtaining information regarding internal and external motivating stimuli and how this information was organized so it enables him to control and gratify needs and to deal with the environment. It should include "conscious and unconscious, perceptual and memorial, imaginary and veridical, self-expressive and reality-representing, dreamlike and waking, ordered and freely-wandering, productive and reproductive, normal and abnormal cognition" (p. 632). Rapaport notes that a psychoanalytic theory of cognition was explored by Freud (1900, 1911, 1915a,b). Freud's theory of thinking was presented in his conceptualization of the topographic model of the mind and Rapaport considers various states of consciousness as having particular forms of cognitive organization. Freud's views on the psychoanalytic theory of thinking are concerned with the differences between and transitions from the pleasure principle to the reality principle; primary and secondary process thinking, the external world, thinking as trial action, thought instead of action, the control of motor discharge by cognition, and the use of secondary process to gratify primary process impulses in accordance with reality. He provided theories in regard to conscious, preconscious, and unconscious thought organizations, the transition between them and the influence of each upon the other, especially of the repressed unconscious on the preconscious conscious. Freud (1900) stated:

> The primary process endeavors to bring about a discharge of excitation that, with the help of the amount of excitation thus accumulated, it may establish a "perceptual identity" [with the experience of satisfaction]. The secondary process, however, has abandoned this intention and taken on another in its place—the establishment of a "*thought* identity" [with that experience]. All thinking is no more than the circuitous path from the memory of a satisfaction (a memory that has been adopted as a purposive idea) to an identical cathexis of the same memory which it hopes to attain once

more through an intermediate stage of motor experience. Thinking must concern itself with the connecting paths between ideas without being led astray by the *intensities* of those ideas. . . . [T]hinking must aim at freeing itself more and more from exclusive regulation by the pleasure principle and at restricting the development of affect in thought-activity to the minimum required for acting as a signal. . . . As we well know, however, this aim is seldom attained completely even in normal mental life, and our thinking always remains exposed to falsification by intelligence from the unpleasure principle [pp. 602–603].

Predicated on the psychoeconomic point of view and the instinct-discharge theory, Freud postulated that when instinctual drive was prevented from discharge, the instinct was transformed and manifested itself as either affect or thought, and he attributed to the sexual instinct an important motivation for curiosity and learning. Regarding Hans at age three and a half who when at the zoo excitedly said, "I saw the lion's widdler," Freud (1909) remarks, "There can be no doubt about Hans's sexual curiosity; but it also roused the spirit of inquiry in him and enabled him to arrive at genuine abstract knowledge" (p. 9). The abstract knowledge that Freud is referring to is clarified in his comments about Hans at age three and three quarter years who, upon observing water being let out of a train engine, determined that "the engine's widdling. Where's it got it's widdler?" He then reflected, "A dog and horse have widdlers; a table and a chair haven't." On this Freud commented, "He had thus got hold of an essential characteristic for differentiating between animate and inanimate objects.

"Thirst for knowledge seems inseparable from sexual curiosity. Hans's curiosity was particularly directed towards his parents" (p. 9). What followed—questions by Hans of his mother and father about their having widdlers and the same in regard to his newborn sister—was understood by Freud as an indication of Hans's involvement in (phallic) phase concerns about the positive and negative differentiation of the sexes, castration anxiety, and attempts to deny that possibility, for example, by the belief that both mother and sister had a penis. Freud relates this to his earlier idea about Hans's discovery of characteristics by which to differentiate between the animate and the inanimate. Here is an illustration of the mutual influences of cognitive development (the ability to establish criteria for making differentiations is a significant intellectual attainment) and psychosexual development. While the former enables the latter to occur, at the same time the content, conflicts, and anxieties of the phallic phase (in this instance) serve to interfere with the utilization of the cognitive capability to comprehend a particular reality.

The Freudian view of thinking is determined on the one hand by metapsychological theory emphasizing the psychoeconomic instinctual frame of reference, the topographic model, repression, and discharge-delay model as well as the pleasure principle and reality principle, and concepts pertaining to primary and secondary processes. On the other hand Freud's views about thinking and learning were derived from a clinical-theoretical perspective centering around concepts related to psychosexual development and childhood sexuality; for example, his comments that curiosity and the desire for knowledge are inseparable from sexual curiosity. From 1914 through 1940 (Freud, 1914a, 1917, 1921, 1923, 1926, 1930, 1937, 1940) Freud's psychoanalytic theorizing increasingly involved the structural point of view (in conjunction with the economic-instinct point of view), with psychic structure conceptualized as a stable, though changing, abiding configuration, and identification was the process by which psychic structure was established. The formation of such psychic structures, for example, memory, concept, ego, or superego was the result of interaction between the internal and external world; between the innate instincts and objects, between psychic reality and "true" reality. The ego became less synonymous with the person, one's self, and more often represented a depersonalized psychic structure defined by its functions, and this resulted in the increasing attention given to the ego in analytic theorizing and clinical application, the prominence of ego psychology and the influence of the external world. Ego psychology and concepts such as primary autonomous ego functions which were innate and in the beginning conflict free, secondary autonomous ego functions, which though at first involved in conflict become conflict free, and automatization as well as ideas regarding adaptedness (Hartmann, 1939, 1952) had important influences on the psychoanalytic theory of thinking, for example, in regard to perception, memory, concepts, organization, and synthesis. Erikson's work (1950, 1959) correlated the influences of organ modes of function and that of the social milieu in which a family lives and a child grows up. This focus on the interaction between psychosexual and psychosocial aspects of development has implications for the study of learning and learning problems as they involve the influence of organ modes (e.g., oral incorporation, anal retention and elimination, and so on) on the psychological modalities of human existence and relationships.

George Klein investigated cognition and motivation psychoanalytically (Klein, 1967), and basing his original ideas on Freud's theoretical views (Freud, 1900, 1911, 1915a,b) he conceptualizes motivation as a behavioral unit which includes ideation, affect, and action. He contends that discussing drive as separate and interacting with thought is not clarifying, and that drives are recognized as motivations "only as structured affective-cognitive-motor events . . ." (p. 84). He also makes correlations with Piaget's processes of assimilation and accommodation in learning, for example, in his statement that motivation gives "meaning to what we see and do (assimilation in Piaget's terms), or it causes us to revise what we think we know (accommodation). . . . To the extent that a thought records a directed relationship of knower to object, to event, to self, to other, it is a unit of motivation" (p. 84). He points out that in psychoanalytic therapy the primary source of information about drives are thoughts which can be interpreted in relation to unconscious ideas about sexuality and aggression and their influence on behavior. While internal (or drive) or external stimulation may activate behavior, they become motivations only when they are cognitively represented, for example, as a wish. I am going to summarize certain aspects of Klein's paper at some length because his theories, which are embedded in the psychoanalytic theory regarding the functioning of the psyche, along with those of Fred Schwartz in regard to attention, cognition, learning, and motivation, are most cogent in regard to a psychoanalytic perspective of problems of learning in children. Klein says about this paper, "My topic is the power of a train of thought; the capacity of an idea to take hold of behavior, exerting influence on perception, imagery, symbolic construction, gesture and action" (p. 80). The term *peremptory* refers to the imperative quality of ideation involved in conflict and repression. The intensity and urgency of a train of thought may increase when it is kept from conscious awareness and acknowledgment and it may manifest itself when one's intention is quite different so that an intentionally developing thought will also express the unintended one. Klein includes unintentional, repressed, unknown thoughts in that group of motivating forces such as unconscious fantasies, wishes, and memories. When these are repressed and unconscious (unknowable), there is an interference with conscious awareness and attention related to them and the perceptions, memories, actions, and verbal links (sometimes increasingly distant derivatives) are included in what is not to be known. Obviously this is a statement relevant to repression, analysis, resistance, and the analytic efforts to make the unconscious knowable consciously during psychoanalytic treatment. It is also relevant to interferences with learning as the result of a failure in conceptual comprehension which serves as a defense against knowing anything which might gratify an unconscious wish or evoke anxiety. Forms of disturbances in comprehension can be various; for example, perceptual, awareness of causal relationships, recall, and so on.

CASE EXAMPLE 1

The analysis of a nine and one half-year-old boy whose parents tended to lie by omission, ostensibly so as not to burden him emotionally, can serve as an illustration of such an interference with perceptual and conceptual comprehension. As this behavior by his parents and the boy's acting as if he was not aware of it became apparent in his sessions, and he was able to become conscious of what he had known all along, he would confront them with direct questions about what had been left out and they would answer him honestly. On one occasion his mother was very upset about the serious illness of a close friend; and when her son asked about it, she gave him partial answers and was unable to tell him. The boy, identifying himself with his mother's wish to not acknowledge that she was distressed because she would then have to tell him the reason, quickly provided a nonserious illness which his mother confirmed. Over several weeks the analysis of this defensive identification as the one who doesn't know and his own anxiety about knowing allowed him to speak with his mother. She responded, with some relief, by telling him the truth about her friend's illness and how upset she was, and that she had mistakenly tried to spare him from knowing what was all too obvious. The boy was relieved of the necessity of "not seeing" what he saw and "not knowing" what he knew.

It is Klein's contention (1967) that the peremptory nature of repressed ideation makes it, in Piaget's terms, assimilative, and he astutely notes the observable fact that "a repressed train of thought is usually impervious to changes wrought by interaction with the environment; it colors encounters with objects and events [and one can add for the purpose of this chapter that the object may be a teacher and the event a learning experience] with its own meanings—the internal 'pull of the repressed' as Freud referred to it—rather than itself being much modified by such encounters . . . " (p. 110). In this view, the accommodative aspect of intelligence is interfered with when what can be learned or what one is supposed to and consciously intends to learn is associated with a repressed fantasy, memory, or idea. On the other side of the coin displacements can be the cause of intense affective interests in anything which unconsciously represents that which is repressed. Fascination, curiosity, and a particular absorption may be manifestations of such displacements. Continuing with these ideas based on Freud's insights presented in his paper on repression, Klein, using the unity of unconscious fantasy embedded in an unconscious cognitive structure, suggests that this "serves both as programmer and a coder of experience; in terms of it events are understood and meanings are assigned and symbolized . . . " (p. 124). This could present a problem because in defensive and symbolic modifications of the environment the cognitive activity is mainly assimilative and reality is experienced, comprehended as that of internal psychic reality (which is unconscious) rather than the logical intellectually derived reality of the external world, including facts and information.

In the context of my subject, the influence of the infantile neurosis on learning problems in children, Klein has some thoughts about the process of learning which are germane. He writes that "an unconscious fantasy can affect the learning process or produce a different kind of learning from the sort that is intended to bring about accommodative changes in cognitive schemas, as in the school room" (1967, p. 126). Unconscious fantasy may organize perceptions in idiosyncratically personal ways and so interfere with conceptualizations that need to be learned in the classroom (Blanchard, 1947). This is of utmost significance because in learning by accommodation personal meanings have to be minimized. The Blanchard paper provides examples of idiosyncratically symbolized facts such as the letters of the alphabet; however, personal meanings to a child can prove an interference with learning when they involve the person of the teacher and learning or the subject matter to be learned. It is a commonly observed phenomenon in the classroom that there are students whose ability to learn is compromised because of a teacher who is personally unpleasant. In fact, in the case of a very young child this is usually considered to be appropriate and the responsibility is attributed to the teacher. It is regarded as a sign of maturity for a child to increasingly learn a subject outside the influence of the personality of the teacher. We also recognize the opposite, that learning only under the influence of a positively experienced teacher has significance in considering healthy and pathological development. Where learning is conflictually involved with parental approval or love as well as disapproval and even more potentially damaging when these are unconscious, or the parent maintains an unconscious, often ambivalently held image of the child as one who doesn't, can't, or shouldn't know or learn, the likelihood of disturbances in learning are increased. Klein concludes with the observation that repressed fantasies are potentially positive in their influences as they may lead to interests in areas of reality in ways that are intellectually creative. Repressed ideas may induce "innovative restructurings or symbols" which, while they serve as a personal resolution of an unconscious fantasy, may also achieve insights into the reality on which these elements of the fantasy had been introduced (p. 127).

Fred Schwartz (1973), in his paper on the psychoanalytic theory of attention and learning, utilizes the hypothetical concept of limited central capacity (that there is a limited capacity for processing information), a concept originally postulated in terms of information theory. This is reality understood in psychoanalytic terms of psychic structure, consciousness, attention, and conflict, which Schwartz uses in applying the concept to short-term memory and he assumes that it is an inborn capacity which is modified by experience. Schwartz's hypotheses correlate well theoretically and clinically with George Klein's ideas, especially in regard to Klein's exposition on the effects of unconscious repressed fantasy and thought on learning, on conceptualization, and on comprehension. In a summary statement, Schwartz presents the proposition that conscious experience is bound by a limited capacity, that internalization of experience extends that capacity, and what he terms *overlearning* automotizes response which frees capacity and enables one to carry out complex acts without conscious awareness. A clinically oriented hypothesis (in part concerned with learning in psychotherapy) was put forth "that motives and intentions imposed boundary conditions on the operation of an underlying mechanism. This conception combines the principle of multiple function with the principle of hierarchical levels . . . dynamic factors influence the role of capacity limits and preconscious automotisms in determining behavior" (p. 213). Learning decreases a necessity for actively attending to information in the present and a large part of everyday behavior is based on knowledge that is preconscious so that one may be involved in a wider range of experience. Following Rapaport's ideas regarding the psychoanalytic theory of

motivation, the proposition that consciousness involves
a limited quantity is based on observations that cognition
is interfered with when one is preoccupied, involved in
acute conflict, or experiencing strong affect. The mind is
limited in how much it can process in a limited time. It
is difficult to simultaneously give attention to two stimuli
or tasks, for example, what a child is supposed to learn
or is reading in school and intrapsychic fantasies, concerns, conflicts —conscious or unconscious—which may
or may not be specifically related to knowing and learning. The ability to selectively limit attention can increase
or decrease in relation to psychopathology and development (as an example of the latter, the preoedipal child's
primary process associational thinking in contrast to the
more secondary process thinking of the latency-phase
child). Schwartz views short-term memory psychologically as an active thought process which places a demand
on central capacity. He applies the hypothesis of limited
capacity to learning during which "one rehearses, thinks
about, organizes, or otherwise works over the presented
material. . . . Once such learning is completed all the
complicated activities of thought . . . drop out . . . " and
the repetition of what has been learned becomes essentially automatic. What has been learned can serve as
"tools of cognition" which expand the limits of capacity.
"Extended practice [that is over learning] . . . makes for
the most efficient behavior" (p. 205).

The concepts and hypotheses of cognition postulated
by Klein and Schwartz in these papers provide an interrelationship with psychoanalytic theory and clinical observation as well as a correlation with Piaget's concepts
of assimilation and accommodation as the essential processes in progressive intelligence. Taken together, they
can be viewed as an organizer of the preceding discussion
of psychoanalytic theories relating to the motivation and
the processes of thinking and learning—instinctual-drive,
anxiety, conflict, defense, a genetic developmental frame

of reference regarding psychic structure formation (ego and primary autonomy and cognitive structure), object relations, external reality, and psychic reality. These pertain to what is disordered—intelligence, cognition, knowing, learning. The causes of disorders in learning germane to psychoanalysis are the results of disturbances in psychological development affecting an otherwise autonomous, conflict free capability of the human mind which has become involved in unconscious conflict and has taken on unconscious meaning inappropriate to the act of learning about the subject in question.

Psychoanalytic theories of development are predicated on the interaction and mutual influences of phylogenetic determinants and ontogenetic experiences, nature and nurture, the internal and external worlds of an individual. The innate endowments, primary autonomous functions (including intelligence and the capacity for progressive learning), "instinct," manifestations of affective states, adaptedness, the interrelatedness of psyche and soma, relations with objects, nonconflict-related and conflict-related experience, ubiquitous and idiosyncratic, and so on, are basic to a psychoanalytic understanding of development as a progressive establishment of one's self, character, psychic agencies, and the relative autonomy from internal and external stimuli, with corresponding capacity for self-regulation. Psychosexual phase development, aggression, and narcissism, which are influenced by biological as well as psychosocial experiences culminate in self and object constancy with relatively well-stabilized self-other differentiation. The psychoanalytic theory of psychic development involves the interrelationships, reciprocal influences, on conscious, preconscious, and conscious levels, of the object world and the internal world of the infant and child; the actual reality and psychic reality. This interrelationship, which is present from birth, results incrementally in the establishment and the organization of psychic representations

of such repeated experiences and via the process of identification, the formation of structure. (In this conceptualization memories, mental images, wishes, and fantasies
are psychic structures as well as the ego and the superego.) Identification and psychic structure formation continue throughout development in an increasingly secondary
process mode. Those identifications and psychic structure
formations which take place during and at the resolution
of the oedipal phase of development are most decisive to
the infantile neurosis, its outcome, and its potential influence on disturbances in learning which may become
manifest during latency. The intrapsychic heir to the
Oedipus complex, the cohesive superego, repression and
other defenses, identifications, the degree and the nature
of conflict, neutralization, and so on, are determinants of
the meanings and symbolizations unconsciously assigned
to knowledge and learning.

A frame of reference with which to consider the interrelationship of individual psychological development,
cognitive development, and the influences of the infantile
neurosis on learning is that of the concept of developmental lines first formulated by Anna Freud (1963). Sigmund Freud's view of normality and neurosis was
consistently developmental, most clearly postulated around
progressive hierarchical levels of libidinal drive organization as psychosexual phases, oral, anal, phallic, and so
on. Anna Freud extended this developmental point of
view to include a number of developmental lines which,
though they were mutually related to one another, could
be evaluated somewhat individually and whose developmental course could be delineated and followed alongside and in conjunction with other lines of development.
Van Dam (1980), commenting on the special developmental significance of the oedipal phase, emphasizes its
influence on:

[O]bject choice and aspects of ego development, such as

memory, ego organization, defense, and other structure formations: Identifications, superego and ego-ideal development are all strongly influenced by the oedipal libidinal strivings. Therefore more than any other line of development, sexuality continues to deserve a special position in human development. The oedipal phase remains an organizer—a momentous event in the child's life. Its outcome determines . . . not only libidinal and aggressive development, but also the child's capacity to participate in such latency tasks as academic learning, the ability to relate to peers, and to continue to modify the contents of a superego and ego ideal. Therefore, the outcome of a child's oedipal conflicts remains nuclear for later neurotic solutions [p. 576].

Using as an example the line of development from an infant's play with his own body to the ability to work, van Dam concludes that such oedipally related conflicts as castration anxiety, penis envy, masculine or feminine identifications may act to interfere with the conflict free aspects of work and achievement; and children in analysis demonstrate how unresolved oedipal conflicts may result in disturbances in learning.

One aspect of development which is not specifically taken up in the concept of developmental lines is verbalization, the use of words and speech and the culmination of communication via language by the developing young child and those in his world, especially his parents. Verbalization as a means of understanding and expressing thought and concepts becomes essential in intrapsychic and interpersonal exchanges and in the process of learning. Furman (1978), in a paper on the developmental aspects of the verbalization of affects, cites Annie Katan and Margaret Mahler. Katan's three major conclusions were that: (1) verbalization of perceptions of the external world occurs before verbalization of affect states and the child's learning is facilitated by verbalization and accompanying parental encouragement; (2) verbalization

of affects furthers ego controls, decreases conflict interpersonally and in relation to superego precursors; and
such verbalization delays acting on feelings; (3) verbalization facilitates differentiation of fantasy and reality
with increased secondary process functioning. Furman
refers to Mahler's hypothesis that autonomous ego functions, including memory, reality testing, and cognition,
required the mother's presence and positive interaction
in order to develop in an optimal fashion. The development of conflict free functions such as learning are influenced by the caretaking person as well as by the conflicts
in which they may become involved. Furman suggests
that oedipal–latency phase–appropriate maturity includes the ability to selectively not verbalize anything
and everything, and that this is an aspect of progressive
psychological development into latency. It is necessary
for the oedipal child's thoughts and feelings to become
private and undergo repression, sublimation, and so on;
and the child and his parents may delay resolution of the
Oedipus complex by the use of verbalization as a means
of continued oedipal involvement and gratification. He
notes in this context the reluctance of mothers and fathers
to give up this relationship with their child which includes access to the child's inner feelings and thoughts.
Even without more than these brief references to a complex subject, the relevance of verbalization (and its vicissitudes as it is interrelated with psychic development)
to the facilitation or interference with learning is obvious.
In this regard, besides the object-related aspects of a
child's verbalization, there is the continuum of attention
to isolation, or of the use of intellect to intellectualization,
as well as the not uncommon multiple possible unconscious meanings of speech or certain concepts which result in conflicts, inhibitions, and interferences with a
child's thinking and learning.

Nagera (1966) presents a developmental organization
beginning with developmental interference on through

developmental conflicts, neurotic conflicts, and the infantile neurosis. He assumes that there is a continuity in development, both normal and pathological, that "early disturbances [as a result of developmental interferences] . . . will determine the outcome of subsequent developmental conflicts, neurotic conflicts, the infantile neurosis, and the neuroses of adulthood" (p. 37). Nagera defines developmental interference as detrimental interactions between the child's impulses and needs and his environment which result in disturbances of the typical unfolding of development. These may be due to inappropriate, unreasonable demands or excessive stimulation beyond the child's ability to manage or to a lack of stimulation and experience between the baby-child and his mother, father, and more general environment. Clearly the development stage of the child is a determinant in the response to such developmental interferences. Developmental interferences contribute to the variable normal and abnormal aspects of character and are significant factors in the nature and severity of subsequent conflicts. Developmental conflicts are ubiquitous, experienced by every child when he attains certain maturational and developmental levels usually associated with specific expectations from the environment; and an otherwise developmentally usual conflict may become a significant developmental interference. The readiness of a child for environmental demands "implies his having reached the required physical maturity, the appropriate phase of instinctual development, the necessary ego development, and the corresponding stage of object relations" (p. 42). The specific developmental conflict disappears when the external expectations, for example, toilet training, have been essentially internalized. Because the internal processes of the child are in flux, particular interpersonal experiences may take on particular meanings which may set off a neurotic reaction or establish the basis for later neurotic disturbances.

Nagera restricts neurotic conflict to internalized conflicts that occur between id, ego, and superego; however, as he includes superego precursors, before the establishment of a cohesive superego organization, it would seem that he considers as neurotic those conflicts involving the ego without superego involvement.

> Developmental conflicts which have not been resolved by sublimation, reaction formation or the formation of character traits may become manifest as neurotic conflicts. Neurotic conflicts will influence subsequent personality development . . . including conflict-free and autonomous aspects. Once an ego function, for example, attention is caught in the neurotic conflict and is affected, then other related functions (memory, thinking, etc.) are also likely to show interference. The tendency to withdraw into fantasy as a defense against unpleasant aspects of reality will eventually affect the subject's perception of external reality as well as his memory. . . . [If] perceptual processes [are] affected . . . this may pave the way for later deferred ways of assimilating information (visually or auditorally) [pp. 49–50].

Nagera also remarks on the potential for neurotic conflicts to become integrated into the subsequently established infantile neurosis, which the neurotic conflicts themselves have in part shaped, as well as their participation in later adolescent and adult neuroses.

A four-year-old boy in therapy illustrates the concepts discussed above as they relate to the intrusion of developmental interference into his psychological development and the interference with his age-phase appropriate curiosity and his need for factual information. Chester was a bright, verbal boy with an excellent vocabulary who indicated he had traversed the anal phase and separation-individuation reasonably well and demonstrated his involvement in the intrapsychic and interpersonal aspects of the phallic phase. The latter included a lively imagination and an intrusiveness which extended to his curiosity. Coincident to the concerns for which the parents sought a consultation, he presented himself at our first meeting as if he did not have knowledge of things one would expect of a four-year-old boy (which he actually did have); and he asked many questions about things when he obviously knew the answers; for example, about items in my office with which he was already familiar. During one of the consultations, he behaved as if he didn't know that a piece of clay he was using had fallen under the table although when I mentioned the clay, he knew immediately where it was. Later, after therapy sessions on a regular basis had begun, he would ask, "Where is it?" regarding such things as his box of materials, always kept in the same place in a cabinet in my office; and "What is it?" as if he didn't know about something he'd made of clay and then, in response to my asking him what it was or telling him I thought he really knew, he would show that he did know. At times he would spontaneously tell me that he was fooling or teasing me about not knowing. One example was about babies which came up in association to his asking me where the dolls were when he knew that they were in his box. After wondering about a baby inside his mother, he said that babies are not inside a woman's stomach, that babies were inside a man's stomach following which he laughed and said he was only fooling me, that he knew babies were inside women. Then he wanted to play a game in which I would pretend to fool him in the same way and he would then correct me.

Chester's conflict about knowing–not knowing diminished during therapy but would return following experiences with one of his parents which were traumatic for him but about which he was told he must not tell the other parent or me. He would behave in a pseudoignorant way and in his associations verbally and behaviorally would, via displacement, relate to me as with the parent.

Chester himself was anxious and the concerns expressed
were in regard to his penis in relation to his mother and
father, mother and me, and castration anxiety was much
in evidence. At the same time his attention span decreased and unlike other sessions he was not able to listen
to me or learn about himself. Related to this was a defense
against the anxiety by identification with me as he perceived me to be. While this defense contained an identification with the aggressor, it also contained an
identification with me as the parent who didn't want him
to know or for him to tell what he knew to anyone including the parent.

Chester demonstrates a boy with phase-appropriate
curiosity, primarily relating to phallic-phase interests
such as his penis, differentiating male and female, and
his own sexual identity but also including elements of
the Oedipus complex and a developing infantile neurosis.
The latter did in fact become more cohesive with continuing therapy and his progressive development and his
curiosity was focused in regard to ideas and fantasies
about the relationship of his mother and father as well
as about the triadic relationship of child and parents,
including theories concerning babies, how they're made,
where they grow, how they come out, and so on. The
interference with what should have been Chester's relatively conflict free curiosity (or at least what might be
described as conflictual because of the normal interferences due to the child's level of development, fantasies
associated with it, and his cognitive capabilities) resulted
in a pseudoignorance, a conflict about knowing or learning or showing what he knew. His conflict was genetically
related to past experiences at age two to three in which
he "knew" too much and was thereby traumatized psychologically, and to his present life experience where the
content was somewhat different but associated with the
earlier events in his life. Added to this was the expressed
injunction against telling what he knew which increased

for him the anxiety associated with his perception of knowing and revealing what he knew as being dangerous. Integral aspects of the problem for him were on the one hand that he couldn't allow himself to receive information when it was offered and on the other a failure of verification and confirmation or modification of what he did know, factually, imaginatively, or combinations of both. The developmental conflicts were transformed into developmental interferences and he was involved in neurotic conflicts in regard to knowing which were associated with developmental conflicts (of the phallic and oedipal phases) and their unconscious and repressed aspects. The child indicated that the nature of his phallic phase and oedipal development were pathologically skewed and the influence on his infantile neurosis could have been significant without therapy. It is not too speculative to assume that without therapy one likely pathological result would have been an intelligent latency child with conflicts and manifest problems in learning in which the infantile neurosis was implicated.

In the preceding discussion I have repeatedly referred to latency as that phase in a child's development when conflicts about learning become manifest and are recognized as a problem by the child, his parents, and his teachers. The parental and societal expectations that a child is capable of learning in a more formal, academic setting (actually this includes nonacademic, though still formal learning experiences such as art, drama, gymnastics, dance, organized sports, or learning to play a musical instrument) converge upon and are intuitively responsive to the level of the latency child's neurological, cognitive, intrapsychic, and psychosocial maturation and development. In terms of Anna Freud's concept of developmental lines, there is an environmental expectation in correspondence with the child's development from play to work as well as a child's level of object relations which enable him to attend to the task of learning. As it is this otherwise relatively conflict free capacity to learn and utilize knowledge that is interfered with by pathological vicissitudes of the preceding infantile neurosis, it will be useful to describe what the average expectable latency child is like in these respects.

Pine (1980) is in concert with Anna Freud's concept of developmental lines in describing the latency child as follows:

> By 7 or 8, the child is normally, solidly involved in the world of school and peer relations. . . . At home, in early childhood, the pre-schooler is ordinarily in close proximity to the mother and other family members for much of his day; the sights, sounds, smells, and feel of family members are at all times in the background, and often in the foreground, of life and contribute percepts and memories to the thought processes from which fantasy and wishes are formed. The learning that takes place is in considerable measure learning on and about their own body and the bodies of others. From early self-other differentiation through self-feeding, bowel/bladder control, self-toileting, and self-dressing, critical learnings have an intimate relation to body and mother. Additionally, family members in general have no peer in their significance as extended others in the life of the child.
>
> But entry into school brings major changes. While family members remain central figures in the psychic life of the child, teachers and peers begin to assume importance as representatives of a wider world, affectively a bit more neutral, less intimate, providing new avenues for identification and attachment. Learning, too, changes. While motor skills continue to develop, learning linked to the body itself is less intimate and less central. And non-body learning assumes enormous importance—reading, writing, arithmetic, social studies (the world of school), and chance, games, tricks, rules (the world of childhood). The learning process itself is less tied to the parents; not only are they not

always the teachers, but things may be learned (formally, from the teachers; informally by observations
of others) that the parents do not even know or do not
do . . . the child's physical proximity to mother is less,
as he spends time in school and has the after-school
skills and inner achievements to go out of the house
without mother to play with peers. . . .
  The formation of new relationships (with the opportunities they provide for displacement and reworking of old familial relationships) and the achievement
of new learnings are major psychological tasks of the
period [pp. 165–166].

Pine goes on to state that for the latency-age child it is
necessary that learning be neutralized, conflict free, autonomous, and automatic enough to allow for new learning. Learning is seen as the work of the school-aged child
and success or failure in learning has profound effects on
the child's self-esteem in relation to himself, parents,
teachers, and peers.
  Freud introduced the concept of latency as a developmental phase involving clinical observations, and biological, phylogenetic, cultural, and ontogenetic factors.
His references to latency were numerous and, in one
(1926), his view of latency was of a phase "characterized
by the dissolution of the Oedipus complex, the creation
or consolidation of the superego and the erection of ethical
and aesthetic barriers in the ego" (p. 114). Castration
anxiety was the motivating force in the establishment of
repression and the resolution of the Oedipus complex and
the increasing importance of guilt (although in girls he
thought this less powerful and that conflict with her
mother and attendant anxiety about the disturbances in
their relationship and potential loss of love were significant factors). Latency follows the resolution of the Oedipus complex and the establishment of the superego with
concomitant reaction formations, sublimations, and significant identifications which allow sexual curiosity to be

transformed into learning. In a maturational developmental description of the latency child, Schecter and
Combrinck-Grahm (1980) point out that by age seven a
child has attained 90 percent of his brain volume and has
progressively matured and developed to:

> (1) an ability in the gross motor area; (2) an ability in
> the fine motor as well as visual-auditory motor areas;
> (3) an ability in the language sphere (to track visual
> and auditory stimuli, imitate language, define
> words . . . express ideas, differentiate make-believe
> from reality with an ability to convey these differences
> verbally, count . . . ; begin punning and enjoying ver-
> bally expressed humor . . .); (4) an ability in the per-
> sonal-social spheres (to separate from parents for
> considerable periods, dress himself, relate with peers,
> express needs and desires verbally, be a participant in
> some group activities . . .) [p. 90].

They note that concurrent with the stage of concrete operations (Piaget) and the resolution of the Oedipus complex there is an increase in electroencephelographic
alpha activity which probably indicates further delineation and specificity in function and localization of the
central nervous system.

   In regard to biological underpinnings of development
at the latency phase, Shapiro and Perry (1976) present
data and suggest conclusions to be drawn from the concomitant level of neurological maturation. They consider
biological maturation to be a very significant variable
determining the changes in the 7 ± 1 child and they
propose that rather than the biphasic nature of sexual
drive, it is the maturation of the nervous system and the
associated cognitive capabilities and organizations that
may provide latency with its biological timetable. According to Shapiro and Perry:

> The greater stability and invariance of mental pro-

cesses and the new cognitive structure at 7 . . . *permit the inhibitions and control of drives* and the postponement of action. The intrusive animism of the pre-oedipal child [the pre-operational thinking of Piaget prior to concrete operations], which is based on associative thinking, is no longer as intrusive. Stable structures have replaced earlier instabilities and can now be used in the service of new cognitive skills which keep sexual drive components in greater isolation. What we call repression may rest upon the splitting and reorganization of archaic and more integrative forms of thinking which complement each other and are simultaneously present in different organizational frames within the same apparatus. . . .

Psychoanalytic theory has defined a number of factors that facilitate the socialization characteristic of the latency child's functioning. Among these are the transition from primary process to secondary process modes of discharge; the cognitive basis for the structuralization of the mental apparatus, which includes the possibility of resolving the Oedipus complex; infantile amnesia; and the establishment of an invariant, internalized superego to direct and modulate behavior without the constant need of external controls. We recognize that man in conflict is the essential datum of psychoanalytic clinical practice, but man in conflict depends upon opposing internalized structure, which in turn are a feature of the new abilities of the 7-year-old [p. 97].

The quotations from this paper have been selective to suit the purpose of my discussion and it is necessary to add that Shapiro and Perry are fully aware of and ascribe to the central importance of the influence of the child's psychic reality and the human environment on the psychological development of the latency phase.

On October 15, 1897, Freud, in a letter to Fliess, wrote:

I have found love of the mother and jealousy of the

father in my own case, too, and now believe it to be a
general phenomenon of early childhood. . . . If that is
the case, the gripping power of *Oedipus Rex*, in spite
of all rational objections to the inexorable fate that the
story presupposes, becomes intelligible. . . . [T]he Greek
myth seizes on a compulsion which everyone recognizes
because he has felt traces of it in himself. Every member of the audience was once a budding Oedipus in
phantasy, and this dream fulfillment played out in reality causes everyone to recoil in horror, with the full
measure of repression which separates his infantile
from his present state [1897, pp. 223–224].

In *The Interpretation of Dreams* (1900), after recounting
the story of Sophocles' dramas about Oedipus; Freud
writes:

His destiny moves us only because it might have been
ours. . . . Here is one in whom the primeval wishes of
our childhood have been fulfilled. . . .
     There is an unmistakable indication in the text of
Sophocles' tragedy itself that the legend of Oedipus
sprang from some primeval dream—material which
had as its content the distressing disturbance of a
child's relation to his parents owing to the first stirrings
of sexuality [pp. 262–264].

The oedipal phase with the Oedipus complex as its
central psychosexual content is in my experience ubiquitous in human development. With the exception of primary disturbances such as early infantile autism, evidence
of oedipal development is present in the lives and in the
transferences of even those patients whose major psychopathology is preoedipal in origin and whose oedipal
phase is markedly influenced or distorted by preceding
developmental abnormalities. The oedipal phase is organized by and is itself the superordinate organizer of
preoedipal developmental organizations. During this
phase of development there are significant achievements

in regard to self-object differentiation, separation-individuation, object and self constancy, and the differentiation of the sexes, with the establishment of a basic sexual identity accompanied by the enduring capacity for triadically experienced object relationships. There is, associated with the formation of a cohesive superego, increased autonomy in relation to the external world (e.g., parents) and the internal world (e.g., sexual and aggressive impulses, fantasies) with progressive capabilities for self-esteem regulation. In regard to ego functions, a shift from primary process to greater secondary process occurs with the utilization of sublimation, neutralization, defenses, and ego control. The ego's capacity for organization, synthesis, and differentiation as well as the decreasing influence of the child's psychic reality, allows for the furthering of reality testing and the readiness for formal learning. Probably the most descriptive presentation of a phallic and oedipal child (and I would add *the* infantile neurosis as well as *an* infantile neurosis) is Freud's regarding Hans during the child's living experience of those phases as reported by his father (Freud, 1909).

For Freud the term *infantile neurosis* was essentially interchangeable with the conflicts inherent in the oedipal phase of development (A. Freud, 1965; Nagera, 1980). The concept of the infantile neurosis has been understood to refer to the normal developmental conflicts as well as to a psychopathological neurosis which may develop during that phase of development. "Infantile neurosis is Freud's term for the disturbances and stresses that he considered to be the common fate of all human beings when they pass through the phallic-oedipal phase of development" (Nagera, 1980, p. 54). While this statement refers to the infantile neurosis as a manifestation of the oedipal phase, a quotation from Freud indicates the reference to the infantile neurosis as psychopathology: "Infantile sexuality, which is held under repression, acts as the motive force in the formation of symptoms; and the essential part of its content, the Oedipus complex, is the nuclear complex of neurosis" (1919, p. 204). There is an intimate relationship between the two, the infantile neurosis as those conflicts, with symptomatic manifestations, of the oedipal phase of development and the infantile neurosis as a neurosis of childhood; the differences between them being determined by the intensity of the conflicts, the influence of preoedipal developmental interferences and conflicts, and the nature of the child-parent relationship. Although Freud and analysts subsequently used the term *infantile*, it is obvious that the term and the concept of infantile neurosis refer not to infancy but to childhood and it would be terminologically, conceptually, and developmentally more accurate to refer to the conflicts, neurotic symptoms, and neuroses of the oedipal phase as conflicts of childhood and childhood neuroses when it is in evidence. Keeping in mind the continuation or influence of earlier preoedipal conflicts, the major conflicts of the oedipal phase are inherent in growing up and are developmental conflicts typical for that phase and age group. Developmentally the conflicts associated with the infantile neurosis can appear because of the maturational and psychological levels attained, involving the multiple lines of development including cognition and the capacity for synthesis and organization. The regressive and progressive shifts ultimately result in a superordinate psychic organization of great complexity with the oedipal phase—the Oedipus complex, triadic object relations, and the formation of a cohesive superego—becoming predominant. Neurotic symptom formation and the formation of an infantile neurosis (i.e., a complex pathological psychic constellation) are possible because of the relatively high level of psychological organization enabling conflict to occur interpsychically between id, ego, and superego (although the interaction between a child and his parents remains significant) and establishes the Oedipus complex as the nucleus of neurosis (A. Freud, 1971; Loewald, 1974; Ritvo, 1974). The "normal" and potentially pathological resolution of the Oedipus complex and infantile neurosis has been the subject of consideration by analysts (Freud, 1924; Loewald, 1979), and Loewald writes:

> [N]o matter how resolutely the ego turns away from it [the Oedipus complex], and what the relative proportions of repression, sublimation, internal "destruction" might be, in adolescence the Oedipus complex rears its head again, and so it does during later periods of life, in normal people as well as in neurotics. It repeatedly requires repression, internalization, transformation, sublimation, in short some forms of mastery in the course of life—granting that the foundation for such repeated mastery are established during latency . . . [p. 753].

Tolpin (1970), noting the ambiguous and imprecise use by Freud and other analysts of the term *infantile neurosis* in its meaning of a psychopathological configuration, provides a significant clarification, differentiating the clinical symptomatic manifestations of the oedipal phase from the "underlying motive force" (p. 274). As evidence of this distinction she cites Freud's 1919 paper and quotes a passage from his comments on Little Hans.

> [L]et me say in Hans' favor . . . that he is not the only child who has been overtaken by a phobia at some time or other in his childhood. Trouble[s] of that kind . . . are extraordinarily frequent. . . . In later life these children either become neurotic or remain healthy. Their phobias are shouted down in the nursery. . . . In the course of months or years they diminish, and the child seems to recover; but no one can tell what psychological changes are necessitated by such a recovery, or what alterations in character are involved in it. [Although a seven-year-old boy repeatedly experienced inordinate fear of being alone in his bedroom, his parents, after

checking his room, told him there were no ghosts, and so on, and he had to remain in his room by himself. When seen in consultation one year later the anxiety, somewhat modified in content, was evident although he did not complain to his parents about it; and the ostensible reason for the evaluation was a problem related to learning.] When, however, an adult neurotic patient comes to us for psychoanalytic treatment (and let us assume that his illness has only become manifest after reaching maturity), we find regularly that his neurosis has as its starting point of departure an infantile anxiety such as we have been discussing, and is in fact a continuation of it; so that, as it were a continuance, an undisturbed thread of psychical activity, taking its start from the conflicts of his childhood, has been spun through his life—irrespective of whether the first symptom of these conflicts has persisted or has retreated under the pressure of circumstances [Freud (1909, pp. 142–143) quoted in Tolpin (1970, p. 274)].

Not quoted by Tolpin is Freud's statement that "it seems to me we concentrate too much on symptoms and concern ourselves too little with their causes" (p. 143). For Tolpin, "Freud's concept of infantile neurosis as the endopsychic structure which is the model of the transference neurosis is the metapsychological construct which underlies his clinical findings regarding the Oedipus complex in normal development and in the psychoneuroses . . ." (p. 273). She makes explicit that the term *infantile neurosis* should not be used to refer to the psychopathological manifestations in all phases of childhood; that it should be limited to the "repressed, potentially pathogenic oedipal conflict (associated with the phallic-oedipal phase) which is central in the pathology of the transference neuroses" (p. 278). In this view the infantile neurosis as an unconscious psychic organization (the Oedipus complex) is to be distinguished from clinically observable symptomatology, for example, neurosis, for which it is the motive force. Tolpin's clarification does, in her words, "enhance the theoretical consistency and the clinical usefulness of the concept of infantile neurosis" (p. 279) so vital in psychoanalytic understanding of normality and pathology and is relevant to considering the relationship of the infantile neurosis to learning problems in children. Her discussion furthers the psychoanalytic view that there is no adult neurosis (I would add adolescent or childhood neurosis) without a preceding infantile neurosis; that both are motivated by conflict and the same psychic mechanisms are involved in the formation of symptoms that adult and infantile neuroses are the result of: "conflict, followed by regression; regressive aims arousing anxiety; anxiety warded off by means of defense; conflict solution via compromise; symptom formation" (A. Freud, 1971, p. 80). It is an elaboration on the comment made by Greenacre that "the term infantile neurosis may be used in two somewhat different senses; one meaning the outbreak of overt neurotic symptoms in the period of infancy, i.e., approximately before the age of 6; a second meaning the inner structure of infantile development with or without the manifest symptoms, which forms, however, the basis for later neurosis" (Kris, 1954, p. 18).

I concur with Tolpin's differentiations regarding the infantile neurosis; however, I believe that she has continued the usual presentation in analytic writings of the phallic and oedipal phases as being synonymous and most often hyphenated as phallic-oedipal. Freud did not differentiate between them (although as I noted earlier, his discussions of Hans from ages three to five are probably the most accurate descriptions of the phallic boy developing into an oedipal boy to be found in the analytic literature) and this has tended to persist in the papers of subsequent analysts on the subject. Freud and Nagera (1966, 1980) considered the oedipal phase to occur between the ages two and five. Continued psychoanalytic investigation, via clinical analyses and child observations, has made it obvious that the onset of the oedipal phase is at about ages four-and-one half to five and comes to a close at about ages six to seven. There is reason to differentiate the phallic phase from the oedipal phase (theoretically and clinically) as Edgecumbe and Burgner (1975) have done. They differentiate the quality of the object relations found in the phallic and oedipal phases and point out that the former is dominated by exhibitionism and scoptophilia. They use the term *phallic-narcissistic* for the preoedipal part of the phallic phase and *oedipal* for the later aspect when triadic object relations are formed; and emphasize that in the "phallic-narcissistic" phase, the genitals are a primary source of erotic pleasure in boys and girls. In relation to the matter of disturbances of learning in children they write:

> With entry into the phallic-narcissistic phase . . . curiosity becomes sharply focused . . . on questions of sexual differences and sexual activities; the wish to look now has the urgency of a drive derivative, which distinguishes scoptophilia as a sexual activity from more general curiosity. It is well known that this is an important period of development for the child's future learning capacity; in favorable circumstances . . . [it] can boost the child's ego functioning, increasing his wish and capacity to learn; whereas unduly severe conflicts over scoptophilia can result in generalized inhibition of curiosity and can drastically reduce his learning capacity [pp. 168–169].

The oedipal phase, coextensive with the infantile neurosis, is that phase of development whose resolution results in the unconscious psychic organization involving impulses, objects, and fantasies, which may be manifest clinically as neurotic symptoms or a neurosis (infantile/childhood neurosis, e.g., Hans). It forms the basis for neurotic character formation or later psychoneuroses in which a disturbance in learning may be one overt manifestation. Problems of learning in children do not stand alone; they are not, in my experience, discrete neurotic aspects of a child's personality. Within this larger psychological context, a learning problem will be over-determined in its formation and expression as well as in its unconscious meanings. The unconscious erotization or aggressive meaning of learning; the anxiety, guilt, or shame unconsciously associated with learning are activated in the transference and transference neurosis. It is only in such patient-analyst experiences that the unconscious meanings, motivations, conflicts, and defenses in relation to impulses, objects, and fantasies can be comprehended in their genetic, dynamic, and adaptive aspects. The infantile neurosis of development and the transference neurosis of psychoanalytic therapy are intimately associated, as has been discussed previously in regard to the oedipal phase–Oedipus complex. Descriptively and dynamically the two are similar, centered around the oedipal phase with regressive and progressive shifts and changing transferences and identifications (so well described and discussed by Freud [1909] and Nagera [1966]). One can observe in transference relationships and via reconstructions the interrelationships and mutual influences of successive preoedipal and oedipal phases of development as well as the modifications which occur as the result of developmental passage through latency, adolescence, adulthood, parenthood, and so on (Loewald, 1979). An analogy can readily be drawn between the influence of the parents during the developmental infantile neurosis and the analyst during the resolution of the analytic transference neurosis and facilitating the transformation of more primary-process to increasing secondary-process functioning and thinking. As the resolution of the oedipal phase/infantile neurosis establishes a higher level superordinate organization of psychosexual and cognitive development, similarly work-

ing through and the resolution of a transference neurosis
through interpretation and insight (learning) enables the
patient to reorganize previously unintegrated unconscious repressed aspects of his personality. I do not mean
to imply that the transference neurosis in the analysis
of an adult or child is a recapitulation of the genetic
historical developmental infantile neurosis (although the
structure and dynamics are essentially the same in both),
or that the analyst is a psychoanalytic reincarnation of
the parent (whether as the parent was actually or might
optimally have been) in relation to the patient. It is
through the transference neurosis that the infantile neurosis, that unconscious psychic organization presents itself so that it is possible to understand the psychology of
disturbances in learning—in knowing, in demonstrating
that one knows or what one knows, and in the utilization
of knowledge by its applications in various ways and as
the basis and stimulus for further learning.

The period of the oedipal phase is marked by a notable
increase in conceptual intelligence, the use of representational symbolic images of the past, present, and the
anticipation of the future, and the capacity for organization. Developmental conflicts, primarily those involving the Oedipus complex, the progressive and regressive
processes of the infantile neurosis, are reflected in the
curiosity, interest in relationships (especially within the
family), questions regarding origins and causality (how,
why), and an intense desire to learn about everything.
While some analysts noting these characteristics of the
oedipal child have attributed to the psychological experiences of that phase a positive inducement of thinking
and progressive intelligence (Freud, 1909; Ritvo, 1974),
my focus has been on the implications of the infantile
neurosis as a neurotic intrusion on the child's intellectual
functioning.

Throughout this chapter I have introduced clinical
examples, my own and from the literature, to augment

theories of psychic development and cognition and to relate them to the implications of the infantile neurosis on
learning problems in children. What follows are a more
extensive series of clinical experiences which demonstrate the potential neurotic influences on learning and
illustrate some of the various possible psychodynamic
configurations which can be manifested as disturbances
in learning.

CASE EXAMPLE 2

I accompanied a five-and-three-quarter-year-old boy and
his father (both friends of mine) to a favorite museum,
a museum of natural history. Father and son had a generally positive relationship although the boy's engagement in his Oedipus complex, evident for some time, had
become increasingly tinged with competitiveness and rivalry. One source of satisfaction for both of them had
been the father's "teaching" his son (e.g., about sports,
the exhibits in the museum) and they shared a mutual
pleasure and pride in the son's learning and showing off
that knowledge. On this day, however, it was to be otherwise. As he moved briskly through the museum trailed
by the two adults, he "lectured," informing us of what he
knew (it is pertinent to what followed that prior to going
to the museum the three of us had, at my request, been
to a liquor store where his father, who is well informed
about wine, advised me on my selection and had "lectured" on various wines), and all went well until his
father, as on other occasions, called his son's attention to
an exhibit and began to read to him the information provided. The boy's reaction was to abruptly turn away with
the announcement that he was leaving. On the way to
the exit his father once again attempted to engage his
interest in an exhibit only to be once more rebuffed by
his son who, behaving as if he hadn't heard, made it quite
clear that he had no intention of learning anything his

father had to offer and continued his determined march out of the museum. In this instance an oedipal boy's normal developmental conflicts temporarily disrupted a relationship with his father which had usually fostered learning because being taught by, learning from, his father became momentarily unconsciously implicated in his on-going infantile neurosis involving oedipal triadic competitive strivings, fantasies, and conflicts which seemed colored by a phallic, narcissistic exhibitionistic aspect as well. I'm reminded of Little Hans (Freud, 1909) and the competitive exchanges between him and his father, often around who was the better analyst or who could be more clever. On one occasion with what might have been a dig at Freud, thus killing two birds with one stone, Hans told his father to write to the professor who would certainly know what things were all about. Not so normal was the effect on learning in a latency-age boy of a pathological resolution of the infantile neurosis.

CASE EXAMPLE 3

Fred, at age ten-and-one half, was an intelligent boy whose problems included chronic underachievement in school since first grade where he had performed very well academically. During his analysis his learning problem became better delineated; and it could be recognized that he had more difficulty in demonstrating what he knew than in learning per se. He would frequently do well in the beginning of a school semester only to once again do poorly on homework, tests, and assignments; he would do well in some subjects and not in others, yet in the next semester or year this would be reversed. Over time we were able to understand via transference experiences several conflicts that were involved in his learning problem including that which centered around those of the oedipal phase. Regarding the latter, a preoedipal dyadic "symbioticlike" relationship with his mother, in which the mutually insufficient psychic separation was experienced by the child as their being of one mind, was organized oedipally so that he and his mother understood each other while his father was excluded. This would occur when he and his mother would have discussions about psychological experiences as both were in therapy and his father was not. When Fred would speak in a mumble which his father couldn't understand but his mother could, his father would repeatedly have to ask what was said and she would "translate." Although at one level this was an "oedipal victory" for Fred, it was not without consequences because for him it included an unconscious identification with his mother who was looked upon by her husband and son as "stupid" and unable to convey ideas in an organized logical manner. A further complication of this identification was its contribution to the castration anxiety related to his negative oedipal longings and rivalry with his mother. It also served as a defense against the unconscious castration anxiety associated with his positive oedipal hostile competition with his father whose physical strength and the tendency toward angry aggressive behavior evoked awe, admiration, and fear in his son. Simultaneously, his academic difficulties enabled him on one hand to present himself to his father as "self-castrated" and on the other it represented a masculine identification with his father who himself had been a bright but poor student.

Fred's analysis continued through middle adolescence and certain aspects of his problems in learning became prominent, partly stimulated by the realistic changes in him; he was now bigger and stronger than his father and he had surpassed his father in an activity in which his father had a long-standing interest but which he had never pursued with energy and diligence equal to that of his son. The comparisons and competitiveness between them reevoked the oedipal conflicts and anxieties (reenacted in the transference) and the identification with his father and his father's learning problem was intensified. An unexpected development was the understanding that this identification also represented the adolescent boy's enactment of his unconscious oedipal view of his father's unconscious wishes (that Fred not achieve academically) as well as unconsciously showing this to his father via Fred's disturbances in learning. Behind this was his unconsciously maintained relationship with his preoedipal and oedipal father, seen as a superhero, to avoid hurting his father in the present and to avoid his own disappointment in and disillusionment with his father.

Although examples could be presented from late adolescence and early adulthood, I will complete this developmental-psychopathological continuum with a vignette from the analysis of a lawyer in his early thirties who had been dealing with conflicts which interfered with his professional performance.

CASE EXAMPLE 4

He came to a session complaining of a teaching-learning problem which interfered with his advancement within his law firm. He had begun working with a senior partner who thought well of my patient who recognized that this was an excellent opportunity for him to learn and to demonstrate his own knowledge and competence. He was consciously aware of his competitiveness with the older lawyer whom he respected as an experienced, well-informed authority. My patient's presentation and discussion were so conflicted and inhibited that he appeared not to comprehend the legal issues involved and at the same time he was resistant to learning from the older man. An exchange would occur in which after the senior attorney would explain a point to the younger man, the latter would say he had actually considered that himself, which in fact he had but had not mentioned during his presentation. Besides threatening the positive relationship with his employer, my patient limited his learning experience by putting the older attorney in the position of discussing matters which my patient already knew rather than discussing with him the more intricate legal issues which would have deepened and expanded the younger man's knowledge. In his analysis he would repeat the same interactions described in relation to the senior attorney and with both of us he was intensely involved in an oedipal paternal transference competition with narcissistic undertones, and unconsciously experienced guilt about who was better informed and the wish to show he knew everything and that neither I nor the older attorney had anything to teach him. He would then put himself in the position of feeling humiliated and treated as if he didn't know as much as he really did, which was a repetition of experiences with his father whom he had actually far surpassed in professional achievement. Increased resistance to my interpretations, to learning anything from me that he hadn't already figured out himself, were accompanied by associations relating to ages five to six, around the time of his mother's pregnancy and the birth of a sibling. During that period he had undergone diagnostic proctoscopies and lower intestinal barium x-rays. To learn from his analyst was to have me put interpretations into his ears, into his mind, from behind. He unconsciously experienced this as a homosexual submission which was intolerable. Even more unconscious was his negative oedipal fantasy regarding his father and an identification with his pregnant mother. The unconscious meaning of learning from an older, better informed man interfered with his conscious intention to learn, in his professional work and in his analysis.

I have presented a continuum, from an actively oedipal boy to a latency and adolescent phase boy and a mature adult man, whose disturbances in learning (as they were manifest in their lives and in their analyses)

were influenced by psychopathological resolution of the
oedipal phase which had characteristics similar to those
of the five-and-three-quarter-year-old boy living through
his developmentally normal infantile neurosis with its
particular developmental conflicts. Oedipal conflicts, and
the preoedipal elements both organizing and organized
by and included in them, figured significantly in their
learning problems. The positive aspects of the triadic
Oedipus complex with conflicts and anxieties regarding
sexual and aggressive impulses and fantasies associated
with competitiveness as well as the negative oedipal constellation in which rivalry with his mother also raised
the danger of castration for the boy are, in particular
ontogenetic circumstances, powerful determinants of potential learning problems in children. Identification with
a parent or with his or her conscious or unconscious (actual or as perceived by the child) image or preference
regarding the child as a nonlearner during the oedipal
phase can be utilized defensively in reaction to conflict
and anxiety. These vignettes from the analyses of a child,
adolescent, and adult demonstrated the narcissistic aspects of the infantile neurosis as they become imbricated
in the neurotic reaction to learning and performing with
preoedipal exhibitionism prominently included. The intrusion of the curiosity about sexual oedipal relationships
into a child's desire to know can result in complications
in what would otherwise be a neutralized desire to learn.

CASE EXAMPLE 5

A nine-year-old girl at the beginning of her psychoanalytic therapy told me she was stupid, and indeed she
spoke and seemed to think as if she were a five- or six-
year-old and sometimes a younger child rather than a
latency-age girl. There was a pervasive interference with
the use of her intellect in all aspects of her life; in learning
at school, socially, and at home. Disavowal was closely

connected with not wanting to know, and it was soon evident that she knew much more about many things than she could allow herself to be aware of consciously and intentionally, and an outstanding transference repetition was her belief that someone did not want her to know. Her history (from her and her parents), her associations, and her transference indicated the probability of serious traumatic experiences in the earliest years of her life; but there were also other associations and memories clustered around ages five and six which suggested that while the psychological obstacles to knowing were preoedipally rooted, there was reason to consider that these had become organized and entrenched characterologically in response to the experiences involving the infantile neurosis. Repeated confrontations and interpretations effected some amelioration in her symptomatic pseudostupidity. Soon after this, about one and one-half years after her analysis began, she was clearly preoccupied with sexual fantasies, curiosity about her own body, particularly her vagina, and the bodies of others, especially the penis of males—all of which was accompanied by excited giggling. Her resistance (which took the form of insisting that she knew nothing about the obvious meanings of her verbal and behavioral associations, denial after she had herself understood them and said so or had agreed with my interpretations, and an exacerbation of her pseudostupidity) gave way to interpretations of the maternal transference in relation to her certainty that I did not want her to know. What emerged was her curiosity about intercourse with indications that what she knew about the parts played in it by the penis and vagina may have been learned too soon, at an age when she could neither comprehend nor effectively manage the excitement. Her response to taking responsibility for what she knew about sex was a dramatic increase in her awareness that she knew, and of what she knew in regard to herself and in relation to me; and the manner in which she communicated became more verbal, logical, straightforward, and informative. There was also some improvement in her schoolwork. In this girl, although her psychodynamics were quite complex, an academic learning problem, which was one facet of a pervasive interference with knowing involving mainly her mother experienced as not wanting her daughter to know about sexuality, was related to the infantile neurosis both in regard to conflicts associated with the Oedipal complex and secondarily as it was influenced by her unresolved conflicts of the preoedipal phase. In some ways the object relations aspect involving her image of her mother as well as an identification with the mother who didn't want to be confronted with what she didn't want to know was more overtly prominent than the "instinctual" aspect of her conflicts about knowing and making known what she knew.

It is during the developmental infantile neurosis that identifications, enhancement of ego and superego formation, and the basis of one's character are established. If during this period the parent fails to validate what a child knows (especially when the parent denies what is apparent to both) this may become secondarily involved in intrapsychic conflicts, the resolution of the oedipal phase, and learning (Blos, 1960; Berger and Kennedy, 1975). These sources and the girl discussed above are relevant to a particular form of interference with learning which involves a secret which may become intertwined with the curiosity, developmental conflicts, and ongoing process of the infantile neurosis. It has been my experience that such secrets and the unconscious meanings to the child may compromise a child's ability to learn in school and act as a resistance (to learning) in analysis. This is of importance psychologically and cognitively because an oedipal child's increasing capacity for awareness of secrets, of differentiating truth from lies, reality from fantasy is vulnerable to a lack of verification by a parent (Schwartz, 1982).

Pervasive disturbances in learning occur when the child's primary psychopathology is the result of pre-oedipal experiences, even when they are integrated into the oedipal phase of psychic organization. The child's insufficient self and object differentiation with unstable self and object constancy is accompanied by excessive primary process thinking, less than adequate reality testing, and the influence of psychic reality and fantasy which intrude upon the process of learning. In contrast, learning problems, in which the infantile neurosis of the oedipal phase is causal and where learning has taken on unconscious meanings and become involved in unconscious conflicts, are less profound and involve inhibition, identifications, anxiety, and guilt in relation to sexual and aggressive impulses.

In discussing disturbances in learning I have confined myself to the pathological influences of the infantile neurosis. I have not taken up the effects of organic deficits or damage, retardation, learning disabilities, or those children with average intelligence whose parents have expectations of academic achievement which are beyond the child's intellectual capacity. Nor have I considered preoedipal psychopathology, such as psychosis or borderline conditions, in which disorders of learning are secondary and do not involve the unconscious symbolic meanings, as is the case in children whose learning difficulties are based on conflicts of the oedipal phase. It is on those unconscious meanings and motives associated with the developmental conflicts and object relations of the infantile neurosis that I concentrated my attention, primarily from a psychoanalytic intrapsychic perspective, in regard to the implications of the infantile neurosis on learning problems in children.

REFERENCES

Berger, M., & Kennedy, H. (1975), Pseudobackwardness in children. *The Psychoanalytic Study of the Child*, 30:279–306. New Haven, CT: Yale University Press.

Bettelheim, B. (1977), *The Uses of Enchantment: The Meaning and Importance of Fairy Tales*. New York: Vintage Books.

Blanchard, P. (1947), Psychoanalytic contributions to the problems of reading disabilities. *The Psychoanalytic Study of the Child*, 2:163–187. New York: International Universities Press.

Blos, P. (1960), Comments on the psychological consequences of cryptorchism. *The Psychoanalytic Study of the Child*, 15:395–429. New York: International Universities Press.

Edgecumbe, R., & Burgner, M. (1975), The phallic-narcissistic phase. *The Psychoanalytic Study of the Child*, 30:161–180. New Haven, CT: Yale University Press.

Erikson, H. (1950), *Childhood and Society*. New York: W. W. Norton.

———— (1959), Identity and the Life Cycle. *Psychological Issues*, Monograph 1, 1/1. New York: International Universities Press.

Flavell, J. (1963), *The Developmental Psychology of Jean Piaget*. New York: Van Nostrand.

Freud, A. (1963), The concept of developmental lines. *The Psychoanalytic Study of the Child*, 18:245–265. New York: International Universities Press.

———— (1965), *Normality and Pathology in Childhood*. New York: International Universities Press.

———— (1971), The infantile neurosis, genetic and dynamic considerations. *The Psychoanalytic Study of the Child*, 26:79–90. New Haven, CT: Yale University Press.

Freud, S. (1897), Letter #71 to Wilhelm Fleiss, October 15, 1987. In: *The Origins of Psychoanalysis*, ed. M. Bonaparte, A. Freud, & E. Kris. London: Imago, 1954, pp. 223–224.

———— (1900), The Interpretation of Dreams. *Standard Edition*, 4 & 5. London: Hogarth Press, 1953.

———— (1909), Analysis of a phobia in a five-year-old boy. *Standard Edition*, 10:3–149. London: Hogarth Press, 1962.

———— (1911), Formulations on the two principles of mental functioning. *Standard Edition*, 12:218–226. London: Hogarth Press, 1958.

———— (1914a), On narcissism. *Standard Edition*, 14:67–104. London: Hogarth Press, 1957.

———— (1914b), Remembering, repeating and working through. *Standard Edition*, 12:145–156. London: Hogarth Press, 1958.

———— (1915a), Repression. *Standard Edition*, 14:146–158. London: Hogarth Press, 1957.

———— (1915b), The unconscious. *Standard Edition*, 14:166–215. London: Hogarth Press, 1957.

———— (1917), Mourning and melancholia. *Standard Edition*, 14:237–258. London: Hogarth Press, 1957.

———— (1919), A child is being beaten. *Standard Edition*, 17:175–204. London: Hogarth Press, 1955.

———— (1921), Group psychology and the analysis of the ego. *Standard Edition*, 18:67–144. London: Hogarth Press, 1955.

———— (1923), The ego and the id. *Standard Edition*, 19:3–68. London: Hogarth Press, 1961.

———— (1924), The dissolution of the Oedipus complex. *Standard Edition*, 19:173–179. London: Hogarth Press, 1961.

———— (1926), Inhibition, symptom and anxiety. *Standard Edition*, 20:77–174. London: Hogarth Press, 1959.

———— (1930), Civilization and its discontents. *Standard Edition* 21:59–148. London: Hogarth Press, 1961.

———— (1937), Analysis terminable and interminable. *Standard Edition*, 23:141–208. London: Hogarth Press, 1964.

———— (1940), An outline of psychoanalysis. *Standard Edition*, 23:209–254. London: Hogarth Press, 1964.

Furman, R. (1978), Some developmental aspects of the verbalization of affects. *The Psychoanalytic Study of the Child*, 33:187–211. New Haven, CT: Yale University Press.

Graves, R. (1948), *The White Goddess*. New York: Vintage Books.

Hartmann, H. (1939), *Ego Psychology and the Problem of Adaptation*. New York: International Universities Press, 1958.

———— (1952), The mutual influences on the development of the ego and id. *The Psychoanalytic Study of the Child*, 7:9–30. New York: International Universities Press.

Klein, G. (1967), Peremptory Ideation: Structure and Force in Motivated Ideas. *Psychological Issues*, Monograph 18/19, 2 & 3/5. ed. R. Holt. New York: International Universities Press.

Kris, E. (1954), Problems of infantile neurosis: A discussion. *The Psychoanalytic Study of the Child*, 9:16–71. New York: International Universities Press.

Loewald, H. (1974), Current status of the concept of infantile neurosis. *The Psychoanalytic Study of the Child*, 29:183–188. New Haven, CT: Yale University Press.

———— (1979), The waning of the Oedipus complex. *J. Amer. Psychoanal. Assn.*, 27:751–775.

Nagera, H. (1966), Early Childhood Disturbances, the Infantile Neurosis, and the Adulthood Disturbances. *The Psychoanalytic Study of the Child*, Monograph 2. New York: International Universities Press.

———— (1980), The four-to-six-years stage. In: *The Course of Life*, Vol. 1, ed. S. Greenspan & G. Pollock. Washington, DC: U.S. Department of Health and Human Resources, pp. 553–561.

Pine, F. (1980), On phase characteristic pathology of school-age children. In: *The Course of Life*, Vol. 2, ed. S. Greenspan & G. Pollock. Washington, DC: U.S. Department of Health and Human Resources, pp. 165–203.

Pope, A. (1711), An essay on criticism. In: *A Treasury of Great Poems: English and American*, ed. L. Untermeyer. New York: Simon & Schuster, 1942, pp. 530–531.

Rapaport, D. (1950), On the psychoanalytic theory of thinking. In:

Collected Papers, ed. M. Gill. New York: Basic Books, 1967, pp. 313–320.

——— (1951), *Organization and Pathology of Thought*. New York: Columbia University Press.

——— (1957), Cognitive structures, In: *Collected Papers*, ed. M. Gill. New York: Basic Books, 1967, pp. 631–664.

Ritvo, S. (1974), Current status of the concept of infantile neurosis. *The Psychoanalytic Study of the Child*, 29:159–183. New Haven, CT: Yale University Press.

Sandler, A.-M. (1975), Comments on the significance of Piaget's work for psychoanalysis. *Internat. Rev. Psychoanal.*, 2:365–377.

Schecter, M., & Combrinck-Grahm, L. (1980), The normal development of the seven-to-ten-year-old child. In: *The Course of Life*, Vol. 2, ed. S. Greenspan & G. Pollock. Washington, DC: U.S. Department of Health and Human Resources, pp. 83–108.

Schwartz, D. (1982), Discussion: The Institute for Psychoanalysis Teacher Education Program Conference: The World of Learning: From Motive to Meaning, Chicago, IL, May. Unpublished.

Schwartz, F. (1973), Psychoanalytic research in attention and learning. *The Annual of Psychoanalysis*, 1:199–215. New York: International Universities Press.

Shapiro, T., & Perry, R. (1976), Latency revisited: The age 7 plus or minus 1. *The Psychoanalytic Study of the Child*, 31:79–105. New Haven, CT: Yale University Press.

Tolpin, M. (1970), The infantile neurosis, a metapsychological concept and a paradigmatic case history. *The Psychoanalytic Study of the Child*, 25:273–305. New York: International Universities Press.

Valen, H. (1968), *The Boy Who Could Enter Paintings*. Boston: Little, Brown.

van Dam, H. (1980), Ages four to six—The Oedipus complex revisited. In: *The Course of Life*, Vol. 1, ed. S. Greenspan & G. Pollock. Washington, DC: U.S. Department of Health and Human Resources, pp. 573–587.

Chapter 21

The Inability to Learn in School: The Role of Early Developmental Deficiencies in Learning Disabilities

RICHARD KAUFMAN, M.D.

INTRODUCTION

I wish to call attention to a group of children whose school failure and learning disturbances are the consequence of abnormalities of neurophysiological maturation. The current interest in infancy and early childhood presents an enormous challenge and opportunity to the psychoanalytic clinician to deal with the effects of preverbal, non-libidinal, nonstructural, archaic traumatic states created by deficiencies, lags, and imbalances in the unfolding of biological endowment (Weil, 1978).

Freud was well aware of constitutional and developmental implications. In the theoretical section of *Studies on Hysteria* he referred to the individual's innate disposition and described how "resistances which prevent the passage of intracerebral excitation to the circulatory and digestive apparatuses vary in strength from one individual to another" (Breuer and Freud, 1895, p. 203). If we define learning as environmental influences on behavior, some of Freud's earliest definitions of trauma cannot easily be improved: "an occurrence of incompatibility took place in their ideational life—that is to say, until then ego was faced with an experience, an idea or a feeling which aroused such a distressing affect that the subject decided to forget about it because he had no confidence in his power to remove the contradiction between the incompatible idea and his ego by means of thought-activity" (Freud, 1894, p. 47). Although he used an electrical-hydraulic metaphor and did not extend his inquiries to observations of infants, nonetheless his concept of inborn variations of the ability to master experience is entirely compatible with that of most contemporary researchers: "As the shape of the oceans delimits the land, and the map of land delimits the shape of the ocean, so a proper grasp of genetics tells us more precisely the shape of what we have to explain by learning" (Cattell, 1982).

Freud wrote in his important article "On Narcissism" that "all our provisional ideas in psychology will presumably some day be based on an organic substructure" (p. 187). In that same article he discussed the difficulties of bringing a purely psychological inquiry into the area of the "actual neurosis" and hypochondria which brings us "to closer quarters with the idea of a damming up of ego libido. . . . [W]e have recognized our mental apparatus as being first and foremost a device designed for mastering excitations which would otherwise be felt as distressing or would have pathogenic effects" (Freud, 1914, p. 85).

Hartmann continued Freud's interest in the biology of the mind. He referred to neurobiological functions—motility, cognition, language, sensation—as "autonomous factors." In his 1950 essay, "Comments On the Psychoanalytic Theory of the Ego," Hartmann stated:

> We have to assume that differences in the timing or
> intensity of their growth enter into the picture of ego

> development as a partly independent variable, e.g., the
> timing of the appearance of grasping, of walking, of the
> motor aspects of speech. . . . [T]he presence of such fac-
> tors in all aspects of the child's behavior makes them
> also an essential element in the development of his self
> experience [Hartmann, 1950].

Neuroanatomical, physiological, and biochemical research has demonstrated that different segments of the
central nervous system develop and are myelinated over
widely differing time sequences (Meyersburg and Post,
1979). Differences in adequacy and evenness of the unfolding sequence of neural maturations have important
implications for the child's capacity to deal with stimuli,
to tolerate frustration, to experience competency, and to
establish a repertoire of defense, object relations, and a
sense of self. The effects of disturbances in the organization, competency, phase, or evenness of maturation
form the basis of the earliest learning disorders through
interfering with the reciprocity with the environment
necessary for further engagement, interaction, and adaptation. In a sense the drastic alterations in the personality caused by sensory, motoric, linguistic, or integrative
flaws can be viewed by the clinician as arrests in development based on failure to learn from experience which
have implications for all future learning.

In otherwise "good enough" environments the child
with developmental damage, disorganization, or uneven-
ness experiences helplessness accompanied by some degree of rage, failure, and dread. The earlier such
developmental aberrations occur the more the child turns
toward the environment. The case illustrations demonstrate clinical distinctions between the child whose distress results from disturbance of autonomous factors and
those children whose personality arrests resulted from
failures in the areas of "unification" and "pacification"

(Gedo and Goldberg, 1973) caused by a malign or unsatisfactory environment.

The importance of these findings to the educator and learning diagnostician is that there are emotional inhibitions and reactions against learning that are caused by intrinsically biological deviations in maturation and their sequellae in personal, family, and community life.

I will offer here the case examples of three children whose inability to learn at school was the result of developmental defects and deficiencies. Their diagnoses were diverse—one child was a fragile borderline-psychotic, the others showed psychoneurotic and depressive features. They were typical of many children in my practice who suffered from massive interference with thinking. For some, the primary way of coping was by nearly complete avoidance of thought. Other, less defended children were unable to focus or organize their thinking and were constantly in a wild and overstimulated state. Each child's developmental history revealed some early deficiency in what has been termed the *stimuli barrier*. Each child had an area in which he was unappeasable, inconsolable, or unsoothable. A fourth child whose learning disturbance was psychoneurotic was included to contrast endowment, history, and clinical course.

CASE EXAMPLE 1

Marv was eight when he was referred to me for "spells" in school where he would stare into space, thumb in mouth, inert and withdrawn. When not withdrawn his behavior in the classroom was disruptive. He refused to work or turn in assignments, yet he was found to have fourth-grade reading skills when he was tested at the end of first grade.

Marvin was a child who could not be comforted by his mother. Marvin's biological clock never established a twenty-four-hour cycle. He was constantly held and rocked for his first two-and-one-half years. His sleep was short, fitful, and unsatisfying. At age eight Marv was able to fall asleep at an appropriate time but only with the use of the radio.

Both parents would be considered extremely brilliant. Mother had had various kinds of anxiety symptoms most of her life which have taken the form of excess worry, fearfulness, or fears of certain foods or illness.

Marv began the first interview by telling me my office was cozy and just right for two people to talk. Very soon afterwards he began to take in all of the details of the furniture, books, and pictures with an exhilarating sense of curiosity mixed with distraction. He told of his need to be in total charge of his life by keeping everything well planned. He felt like a tightrope walker in the circus, always on the brink of falling, or a monkey riding a motorcycle. Not understanding something in school gave him the same feeling of danger, jeopardy, and panic.

In the fourth session he told a dream about trying to fix a neighbor's hot-water heater. The damage to the water heater was based on an error in the construction which caused it to overheat. His associations dealt with the effects of the floods resulting from ruptured water heaters.

Marv's behavior became more and more disrupted. He would squirm and wiggle about on the couch in a restless tension state. Eventually he assumed a head-butting posture on his hands and knees which we learned had been his way of attempting to fall asleep by banging his head against his pillow when much younger.

I was amazed to learn that Marv carried the head-butting behavior, which was a defense against helplessness and anxiety, into school in the form of certain mental activities, which he coupled with certain imperceptable physical movements. He had an elaborate way of spending the entire school day "planning" each movement that he would make. Each thought would be planned in advance. If he were to change his position in the chair, pick up a pencil, open or close a book, change the pressure on the pencil, shift his weight in the chair, look at the teacher, look away from the teacher, these activities were anticipated and charted out in advance.

As treatment continued, Marv switched from "head-butting" to escape into the closet where he closed the door to shut me out. "Closeting" became a substitute for "planning." Marv's ability to ignore me and to shut me out filled him with great pleasure. Closeting became his way of handling the tensions in our relationship. When he was angry with me he would head for the closet.

Marv was shocked when I eventually told him that the closet, which was his haven of safety, was, after all, a part of my office, and to a certain extent, something that I provided for him and wished him to have (i.e., I understood he was using me for support as an early maternal object).

Within several months Marv began talking about his experiences and his feelings with the intention of making sure I knew how he felt. He now wanted me to know what was going on "in his mind." Over the next several months I was able to watch an expansion of the process of thinking. "I don't want to tell you," alternated with his fervor that I understand.

Marv realized he was choosing not to think. He was able to understand that he was overexcited. He could describe his overexcitement in language to himself and to me. Marv was able to perform with his own mental functions what he had previously accomplished by using the couch or by "planning." Marv's school career improved. His reading skills were several years advanced when he was tested at the end of third grade. The reduction of Marv's self-preoccupation at home heralded the arrival of a number of family and developmental conflicts. Marv changed from being a fairly helpless baby to being a rather bratty and obnoxious latency child. Long-term follow-up has shown an excellent school record but many social and family problems have persisted.

CASE EXAMPLE 2

Steven was ten years old when he was referred for psychotherapy because of total inability to participate and learn in school. Steven had been in special education classes throughout his school career where his nonperformance was accepted because of a marked perceptual disarray. Motivation for referral came when follow-up IQ testing revealed a surprisingly high IQ (127) in a child whom the teachers had assumed to be of borderline average intelligence.

Steven weighed two pounds when he was born, three months prematurely, and dropped to one pound, seven ounces before beginning to gain weight.

Steven did not cuddle or mold until he was nearly one year of age. The smile response was considerably delayed. Steven continued to be clingy and relied on physical contact as his main source of comfort and soothing.

Steven progressively shunned any sort of intellectual task. He gradually wandered into his own little world in school. Steven's basic posture in school was to ignore everything that was going on around him.

Steven presented himself to me as an amorphous, blank, mindless child, without worry, pleasure, or mentation. He described his life as being devoid of interest or involvement.

Several months passed in which Steven would sit with me and complain that his mind was blank and that he had no thoughts. Or he would talk in a monotone about obscure details he noticed in the office decor. Eventually, my interpretations that he was using all of his energies not to think kindled a small flame of curiosity. As Steven's willingness to ask questions and to tell me about himself came into view, he became anxious. Several ad-

ditional months were spent in helping him to deal with
his fear of getting punished by me or of doing something
distructive in the office were he to use any of the toys.
He eventually made a "garbage ball" which at first he
used very shyly, and ultimately threw about the office
with wild abandon.

The nature of Steven's progressive excitement turned
out to be connected to highly charged sexual thoughts,
worries, and impulses. The next year in treatment was
dominated by Steven's constant questioning about and
drawings of intercourse, penises, vaginas, breasts, and a
host of derivative images. He drew automobile races,
space ships, tunnels, and locomotives to illustrate every
sadistic and dangerous pregenital and genital relationship. Curiosity about my wife, my sex life, how babies
were made, competitive themes with me were all churned
up this year. However, looking back on the treatment I
believe that the major cause of improvement was not so
much interpretation as that the sexual and aggressive
frenzy burned itself out. While there were obvious transference implications, Steven seemed to benefit most from
the abreactive experience. He developed the ability to
talk about sexual issues without exploding in overexcitement.

Needless to say, school performance changed. Steven
went from being the class punching bag to somewhat of
a bully. From being almost mute in class he became gar-
rulous and frequently obnoxious. Assignments were completed, he participated in classwork, and toward the end
of our work together he went from a special-ed to a regular classroom.

My follow-up extended for three years. Steven picked
up a musical instrument and played in the school band.
At times of stress he tended to fall back on his retreat
and detachment; he tended to be rather possessive of his
friends, and at times still had his original dreamy quality.
However, he was achieving at grade level, he was pop-

ular, and for the most part he was indistinguishable from his peers.

CASE EXAMPLE 3

Jerry began analytic treatment with me when he was seven years old because of total refusal to work in school. Jerry was a charming, ingratiating, precocious child who totally resisted authority, felt he could do anything regardless of his own limitations, and was intolerant of any direction, advice, help, or authority. Efforts to get Jerry to work met with gross failure. At home Jerry was oblivious to any request or demand. Discipline was accomplished only by virtue of sheer physical force.

Jerry experienced auditory and visual hypersensitivity from birth. The rays of sunlight falling on his eyes as he was taken home from the hospital caused extreme distress. The hypersensitivity to light remitted in about six months. However, he continued to have distress from noises. Jerry also experienced a disturbance in his bowel function from his very first days of life. From infancy up to the present Jerry suffered alternating diarrhea and constipation. The pediatrician felt that the most likely cause was a food allergy of undetermined source.

Jerry's first year was also marked by precocious motoric and intellectual development. He was using full sentences by his first birthday, and before the first year was eager to acquire new words and expand his vocabulary.

Jerry's attempts to play were futile. His efforts were disrupted by "tornados" that turned his cities and villages into ruins. "Storms" struck, objects were hurled through the air, and in a frenzy Jerry would himself become a holocaust, a process which he described as "going crazy." My interventions were to help him monitor his levels of excitement, anticipate for him the emergence of loss of control, and to provide restraint when necessary. As he began to acquire dominion over the office with immense constructions, giant spider webs, ski lifts, and machines which would connect all the objects in the office to me and would be under Jerry's control.

As we proceeded Jerry was able to describe the effect of overexcitement as the loss of mental content, that is to say, loss of the ability to think and use his mind.

One facet of the treatment was Jerry's concern and fear about "emergencies." "Emergencies" came from worries and worries brought him to a state of panic and collapse. These "emergencies" came about when he was helpless to control his own emotions and impulses. Fear, rage, and excitement would drive him into abrupt action, which typically would begin as full-fledged recklessness, and rapidly escalate to total disruption. As we looked at his failure to "stop and think" as a way of dealing with his drives and with his fears, Jerry made an astounding discovery: "I'm not able to pretend." His inability to anticipate the future, to use trial thought, to anticipate, to plan actions came from his inability to use his imagination.

There were several problems in using words that became obstacles to the treatment. Words to Jerry were often a source of overstimulating noise. Many interpretations could not be handled because of the retraumatization they produced. My words were often abrasive. Jerry would hide in the toy chest and post a "do not disturb" sign. A second problem in communication was Jerry's conflicts around passivity which eroticized the listening process. As opposed to his early grasping at new words which probably was defensive, Jerry would be unwilling to tolerate the receptivity, openness, and vulnerability to the outside world which listening required. Jerry loved to build cities and landscapes with blocks. He invariably would be frustrated at the end of each session because he would not know how to reconstruct his "layouts" in the exact fashion upon his return. The idea of making a blueprint brought great delight. He now preoccupied himself with drawing, mapping, and diagramming. After several months of these activities and going through several reams of paper, Jerry triumphantly announced, "I don't need to put this onto paper, I can do it in my mind."

Jerry could now anticipate occasions where he would "lose his mind." For the first time in his life he began to feel in charge of his own mentation and behavior. Jerry began to seek out ways to increase the excitement and stress so that he could master his newly gained thinking function. In contrast to previous times when he would jump into overstimulation because of a basic sense of underprotection, he now chose to test himself against experiences with the development of mastery, confidence, competence, and a sense of challenge. He began to resemble a healthy toddler going out into the world to seek out adventure.

I presented only one highlight of a unique and complicated clinical case. Because of outside circumstances the treatment was interrupted. I do know that a year after we stopped Jerry was enrolled in a private school where he was appreciated for his superior writing skills and use of poetic imagery.

CASE EXAMPLE 4

John was a child I saw intermittently from the time he was seven through fifteen. He, too, was referred in part because of complete and absolute refusal to perform or learn in school. He also had exaggerated nighttime fears and did not feel safe sleeping in his own bed, preferring to hide on the floor in a sleeping bag. Developmental history did not reveal abnormality until the age of three when John suffered a massive setback following his mother's fulminating depression. Mother had had a series of very mild depressive disturbances previously, but suffered a near-psychotic collapse in the context of severe marital tensions several months after the birth of her second child. She was virtually unable to function for the next three years. She sought relief for her despair with alcohol, and it was her alcoholism which eventually brought her to psychiatric treatment. During the time that I worked with John, mother remained in treatment and demonstrated progressive improvement.

The epitome of the child that "didn't know anything," John's sole purpose in life was to be entertained. Throughout most of the time we worked together he had no active interest in anything in the world. His day was divided into those times when he was passively narcotized by loud rock-and-roll music or those times when he would actively evade thinking and feeling by wild, driven, physical activity. John was tormented by the occasion to sit and talk and think reflectively. "This is boring, let's do something," was his perpetual lament. The years came and went; tutors came and went; learning therapists came and went; learning diagnosticians and psychometricians came and went. John remained refractile, oblivious, walled-off, and unproductive.

John's isolation from thought and experience was virtually total. He was content to accept his failing grades year after year without protest or objection. Therapy was intermittent over much of this time.

When John was fifteen we began another trial of therapy. My interpretation that thinking and feeling were being warded off at all costs could now be understood. With paroxysms of affect, John expressed anger toward his mother and younger sibling. Transference implications appeared and interpretations were now effective. We learned how the three-year-old child's helplessness was reduced by his identifying with the unresponsive, paralyzed, and nonfunctional mother. Thereafter, the world could helplessly attempt to get a response from John, as he had helplessly attempted to communicate with his depressed mother. John defeated and castrated me by thwarting the treatment—he controlled, dominated, and tortured me by his stubbornness, negativism, and withholding. His homosexual yearnings and passive receptive and feminine attitudes were warded off by his nonreactivity and inertness. Panic, separation-anxiety, and the dread of incorporation were defended against by maintaining autonomy through his immutable oppositionalism. The wish and fear for surrender, submission, and giving up of his own will were finally put into words in the context of developing a massive overidealization toward me which represented the lost parental attachment prior to his mother's depression. We were able to gain insight into the libidinal overload of his early years when mother clung to him to dispel her own loneliness and despair, and the sudden loss of this exclusive relationship following mother's depression and the arrival of a sibling. This sibling, an adorable and bright girl, consumed all the available attention of the household, and what little energy mother had left now went toward her. The termination process revived the loss of mother and the deflection of father's interest to his "little princess." John's improvement would mean loss of my attention and my turning away from him toward my other patients as father had left him emotionally for his darling baby daughter. Finally, we saw how producing in school was an occasion for John to attempt to perform unconsciously as a woman for me and, via his grades and achievements, bring me a daughter. The recognition of these passive feminine longings as well as his feminine identification allowed John to take an active interest in schoolwork for the first time in his life. Conduct at home improved; John began to read for his own relaxation and pleasure. At the time of this writing he is a high school senior. His academic work is mediocre, based in large part on his impoverished background; however, he studies diligently, has made friends, and intends to go to college.

DISCUSSION

I have presented three children whose failure to learn
was an aspect of an original failure to grow, adapt, and
thrive. Each of these children had a biological impedi-
ment to becoming a "good enough infant" capable of making use of an average, expectable environment. Thus,
their failure to deal with "good enough" parents was not
the result of conflict, per se, with the world, nor the direct
result of ungratified libidinal drives, but was the product
of the various intrinsic neurophysiological discrepancies
which rendered them more or less unparentable. Greenspan has examined the therapeutic strategies of dealing
with such infants in great detail (Greenspan, 1981). My
work demonstrated the problems encountered by the clinician at a much later date when an early arrest in development has been incorporated into character.

To work psychotherapeutically with such children we
must return for guidance to one of Freud's earliest definitions: trauma is an experience that cannot be mastered
by thought activity. We can then understand the clinical
process as recovery of a past situation of the collapse of
homeostasis, a forgotten learning failure, a warded off
and therefore ongoing inability to adapt; in short, a potential opportunity to resume growth. The three children
I described who had massive developmental abnormalities and deficits continued to live unconsciously in the
past. Their recovery did not follow from the interpretation
of a pathological conflict to an observing ego, nor from
the gratification of "snack-bar psychotherapy" (Winnicott, 1963). The therapeutic interventions addressed the
missing self-regulative functions, and by doing so correctly and honestly, allowed the reinstitution of an early
maternal bond. The intrinsic accuracy of the communication process, especially where failure of homeostasis
was recognized, brought about a renewal of "learning":

the therapist, by being a thinking person (Bion, 1965) became a serving person as well.

To paraphrase Winnicott (1963), in the end the patient succeeds by discovering failure (i.e., the concept of failure). By discovering an unacceptable truth about an unacceptable situation, language is created. There is return of the early, undifferentiated, positive attachment when the child can experience helplessness and collapse and then communicate the feelings of vulnerability, frustration, mortification, and failure.

In cases 1, 2, and 3 the healing process involved the recognition and alleviation of the early developmental disturbance which allowed the recovery of a positive transference. In contrast, the fourth case showed the role of transference as resistance and the interpretation of this transference as the means of restoring health. For the most part, transference interpretations were neither useful nor indicated in the first three cases where the life experience of the children did not contain collapse of the environment. The strongly positive transferences which emerged were the result of the treatment and were indications that a developmental arrest had been successfully altered. With the continuing expansion of competence the transference became unnecessary and was, so to speak, abandoned. In each of the first three cases reliance upon the therapist diminished spontaneously. In the fourth case the transference resistances became more extreme until they ultimately culminated in an interpretable transference neurosis.

In contrast to the neurotic, where the treatment process returns a chance to revise the effects of something that happened, the therapeutic benefit treatment brings to the child with a deficiency is to allow something to happen that never before occurred. The patient does not recover a time of conflict, rather a chance to leave a time of urgency, powerlessness, and nothingness. The neurotic child gains an opportunity to revise and resolve old problems. The developmentally damaged child recovers an opportunity to have a problem. The neurotic must eventually come to terms with the impossible and forbidden loves and hates of childhood. The damaged child must ultimately mourn the lost competency that others possess which can never be his. He must bear true witness to those areas of severe flaw, limitation, and vulnerability which are his lot in life. Such as the neurotic child must replace repression by condemnation, the damaged child must reconcile his missing or deficient functions through transcending helplessness. The termination phase brings bereavement for those persistant peculiarities, liabilities, and hypersensitivities which will make his portion unique and different.

The importance of this series of cases for learning diagnosticians is that although each child had extreme interference or erotization of thinking, the causes and the optimal types of intervention were different. The clinician must be specifically aware of the age specific, biological, adaptive tasks and the unfolding of successive, age appropriate interactions, organizations, and structures.

By the time school problems have become compelling there is always an aggravated tangle of intra- and interpersonal maladaptation. Learning disabilities became complicated by both conscious and unconscious avoidance of the learning situation. The child with severe disturbance in phase, evenness, or organization of development faces annihilation anxiety in attempting to produce and achieve with a defective center of initiative, inability to regulate tension, and hypersensitive self-esteem. Parents, teachers, and school administrators find difficulty conceiving of such abysmal and early faults in the personality. Most often the rage, helplessness, and anger such children experience is so profoundly archaic that the caretakers' repression interferes with understanding and empathy. And often the child's needs for protection, insulation, structure, appeasement, encouragement, and soothing are so infantile and regressive that they cannot be supplied in the ordinary classroom or family setting. I have tried to emphasize the significance of developmental status in evaluating adaptation, particularly in such a highly complex area as the school learning situation where associated social and environmental disturbances tend to camouflage and overshadow enduring biological alterations in phase, organization, and evenness. Our task as learning diagnosticians and therapists is to integrate the plethora of information about early cognitive, physical, and affective development into our clinical practice. To do so will demand revision of our methods of history taking and assessment as well as alterations in the theory and practice of consultation and therapy.

REFERENCES

Bion, W. R. (1965), *Transformations*. London: Heinemann.

Breuer, J., & Freud, S. (1893–1895), Studies on Hysteria. *Standard Edition*, 2. London: Hogarth Press, 1955.

Cattell, R. B. (1982), *The Inheritance of Personality and Ability Research Methods and Findings*. New York: Academic Press.

Freud, S. (1894), The neuropsychoses of defense. *Standard Edition*, 3: 41–61. London: Hogarth Press, 1962.

———— (1914), On narcissism, an introduction. *Standard Edition*, 14:67–102. London: Hogarth Press, 1957.

Gedo, J., & Goldberg, A. (1973), *Models of the Mind: A Psychoanalytic Theory*. Chicago: University of Chicago Press.

Greenspan, S. (1981), *Psychopathology and Adaptation in Infancy and Early Childhood*. New York: International Universities Press.

Hartmann, H. (1950), Comments on the psychoanalytic theory of the ego. In: *Essays on Ego Psychology*. New York: International Universities Press, 1964, pp. 113–141.

Meyersburg, H. A., & Post, R. M. (1979), An holistic developmental view of neural and psychological process: A neurobiologic-psychoanalytic integration. *Brit. J. Psychiat.*, 135:139–155.

Weil, A. P. (1978), Maturational variations and genetic-dynamic issues. *J. Amer. Psychoanal. Assn.*, 26:461–492.

Winnicott, D. (1963), Dependence in infant-care, in child-care and in the psychoanalytic setting. *Internat. J. Psycho-Anal.*, 44:339–344.

Chapter 22

Deficits in Empathy in the Learning-Disabled Child

BENJAMIN GARBER, M.D.

INTRODUCTION

A number of children that were diagnosed as learning disabled and subsequently seen in consultation and psychotherapy were often described by teachers and parents alike as being self-centered and selfish.

If egocentricity is defined as a heightened importance placed on feelings toward the self with a seeming callousness toward the sensitivities of others, then indeed several of the youngsters observed could be described as strikingly egocentric.

Although they were labeled as "good kids," meaning not malicious in intent or acting out, they were often described as insensitive to the feelings of others and consequently hurtful to an extreme degree. This seeming insensitivity and callousness was often counterbalanced by an exaggerated concern for the well-being of others, especially adults. They were equally hypersensitive to the hurts of younger children or animals yet they possessed a limited genuine sensitivity for the pain that they inflicted upon peers. When such youngsters were confronted with the results of their words or actions the usual response was one of puzzlement, perplexity, or confusion.

While some attempted to gloss over or rationalize such incidents, the clinical impression was that such a child just did not know the nature or the extent of the hurt that they inflicted on another youngster.

Learning-disabled children are constantly preoccupied with concerns about how damaged they are as well as how others see them and what other people think of them. Such a pervasive concern about one's self-image and self-esteem may result in a constant state of tension and anxiety. Since so much emotional energy is invested in determining the answers to these ever present questions, there may be much less energy available for an investment in the consideration and concern for others.

Concomitantly the presence of a learning disability implies the limited availability of certain basic cognitive skills, whether due to a slower rate of development or an immaturity in the skills that are present. Due to the overinvestment in one's own emotional pulse as well as the limited availability of certain cognitive equipment, it is suggested that some learning-disabled youngsters demonstrate an impairment in their ability to be empathic with others.

LITERATURE REVIEW

While the study of empathy in psychoanalytic practice has been an ongoing process since Freud (1921) stressed its centrality in analytic work, the study of the developing empathic capacity in the child has been a relatively recent undertaking.

Empathy in the sense of the ability to feel what another person feels is probably one of the most fundamental prerequisites of mature sociability. In *Group Psychology and the Analysis of the Ego* (1921) Freud stressed the significance of empathy. In the chapter on "Identification" he mentioned empathy in the following footnote: "A path leads from identification by way of imitation to empathy, that is to the comprehension of the mechanism by means of which we are enabled to take up any attitude at all towards another mental life" (p. 110).

While the psychoanalytic literature on understanding, as well as the uses and misuses of empathy, has been extensive, almost all of it has emerged from the psychoanalytic treatment of adults. Although there have been numerous conclusions about the adult's empathy with the child as well as the empathic capacity of the child, the field of observation has usually been the empathy of the adult. Numerous studies have made global inferences about the development of empathy in the infant; however, what promotes or interferes with the development of empathy in the oedipal and latency-age child has been relatively neglected.

Olden (1953) first called attention to the development of empathy when she addressed herself to the various interferences that prevent the adult from being empathic with the child. In a later study Olden (1958) speculated that the primitive mother-child fusion, which is partly biological, should be regarded as the starting point of the phenomenon of empathy.

Definitions of empathy have often attempted to include some reference to the genetic origins of this capacity. Burlingham (1967) considered the infant's sensitive response to the mother's affective state as the beginning and perhaps even the foundation for the developing empathic capacity. A related view is that empathy is a primitive and archaic skill which means that it is at its peak in infancy and then gradually diminishes as the child becomes older.

It is extremely difficult to pinpoint exactly when the individual develops the capacity for empathy; however, if our ideas about development are semiaccurate then it is not plausible that such a complex emotional instrument is present in the infant. Since empathy, by its very nature, requires a certain capacity to be able to separate the self from the nonself, and since stable self and object representations are not established until later, then it is essential that the child would have at least completed the necessary separation-individuation (Mahler, 1968).

Most psychoanalytic researchers have approached the question of how the child develops an empathic capacity from various observational vantage points. Nevertheless they all seem to converge within the very early interactional matrix between mother and child.

Normally, as the child develops he becomes aware that various feelings are not experienced only by himself but also by others. Burlingham (1967) in her sensitive observations on mother-infant interactions stated: "[W]e say the child is an acute observer of all those overt reactions of the mother which betray what happens in the depth of her mind. The child draws conclusions from what he has observed and bases actions on these inferences" (p. 771). Shapiro (1974) in a similar vein noted: "As a child begins to read another's facial expressions and body attitudes, he must bring them into coordination with his own growing repertoire of emotional states in order for empathy to emerge" (p. 18). Easer (1974) in her study of "Empathic Inhibition and Psychoanalytic Technique" seemed to elaborate a similar point of view: "The child becomes aware that feelings are experienced not only by himself but by others. He can begin to validate and label his feelings through the recognition of them in others and by his mother's empathic response to him. On the one hand the child integrates his mother's mode of perceiving his feelings and on the other he is able to perceive her feelings apart from his own" (p. 567).

Whatever the affective components of the mother-child interplay may be, all the authors imply that the child requires the availability of certain basic ego capacities, such as perceiving, observing, comparing, integrating, and validating complex psychological data.

EMPATHY AND COGNITIVE DEVELOPMENT

Basch (1983), in his thoughtful review of the concept of empathy, felt that a type of autonomic mimicry, rather then the mechanism of identification, explains the affective resonance (described here as a biological and not yet psychological experience) that has been noted by all observers to be an essential part of the empathic experience; consequently there may be an important genetic link between early imitation and later empathy.

What developmental achievements are necessary in order to acquire an object-centered empathy? In all probability they are those same neurological and psychological developments that enable the child to become more autonomous in terms of narcissistic need fulfillment and more able to learn about his objects in their own right, to love them with object love, and to be concerned about them. Empathy involves reasoning with the other's unconscious affect and experiencing his experience with him while the empathizer maintains the integrity of his self intact. Consequently, beginning in early childhood and continuing throughout life we continue to develop and evolve a variety of internal resources which need to be used for the purpose of making such sophisticated comparisons. These resources may involve memory, fantasy, conceptualization, and other cognition in relation to impulses, affects, body sensations, superego pressures and gratifications, defenses, and need-satisfying as well as gratifying introjects. All parts of the psychic apparatus participate as they necessarily must if we are to encompass in an empathic experience the full range and complexity of various states of mind. Consequently, the capacity for empathy would require highly developed ego functions such as thought, memory, comprehension, and conceptualization for the purpose of integrating the affective cues.

Schafer (1959), Kohut, (1959, 1971), Beres and Arlow (1974), Sawyier (1975), and others have emphasized that empathy involves complex cognitive processes by which we form certain hypotheses about another person's inner experience, hypotheses that are open to further study so that the judgments that were made about the other person's state of mind can be confirmed or proven false.

Empathy has been studied extensively by psychoanalytic researchers and developmental psychologists, and as a result there have been a variety of descriptions and multiple definitions of the concept. Thus, we may also define empathy as a vicarious emotional response to the perceived emotional experience of others.

Because empathy, as all who have concerned themselves with the topic seem to agree, depends on the transmission of affect, it is not surprising that a satisfactory explanation of this process has continued to evade us, for it could not reasonably be expected to be forthcoming as long as the psychology of affect itself was not sufficiently understood (Basch, 1983).

PSYCHOSOCIAL CONSIDERATIONS

Cultural bias, the opportunities for learning and for expression, the presence of intrapsychic conflict, as well as arrests in development, all play a part in determining on what level and with what freedom any one person can perceive, transmit, organize, and utilize affective signals in a given situation.

For example ghetto children seen in large city hospitals are not capable of defining many emotional states, and the finer nuances of sadness, anger, or hurt go largely unnoticed. This does not suggest that their repertoire of affects is less full than those of middle-class children. It means only that the flexibility of response to affects is limited because they are categorized in a limited way or may be used primarily as signals for action (Shapiro, 1974). By the same token, their range and/or variety of empathic responses may be quite different from what we would see in a middle-class child.

In spite of ongoing difficulties confronting our constant attempts to grasp the essence of what constitutes empathy we do know a number of its basic characteristics.

The reliability of our empathy declines the more dissimilar the observed is to the observer, so it is very difficult for us to be empathic with the very young child as well as with our own earlier mental organizations.

The more empathic an individual is the more likely he is to share his feelings with a wide range of individuals; consequently he is more accepting of a wider range of people from diverse groups.

While both males and females may be equally adept at affective perspective taking, females have most frequently been reported as more empathic in their vicarious affective responses.

Where the empathy measure includes a social comprehension component, consistent and significant age effects have been found, most likely reflecting the developmental changes in cognitive skills. Age effects may also reflect the accumulation of emotional experiences.

CLINICAL DATA

While the ability to be empathic is based on a certain sensitivity to and mutuality of emotional responses with another human being it is equally obvious that certain cognitive skills are essential so as to sense, compare, validate, and to integrate the affective elements. If a child is damaged in the area of being able to sense, to integrate, and to make comparisons between his affects and those experienced by someone else, then his ability to be empathic immediately and accurately will be impaired.

Some clinical vignettes will illustrate this clinical impression:

Donald, a six-year-old, accidentally broke Ellisa's favorite toy, a delicately carved glass elephant. Ellisa cried hysterically when she realized her loss, while Donald stood there mute, with a blank and puzzled look on his face. Even though he knew that this was Ellisa's favorite toy, he could not understand why she was so upset. Even after it was explained to him he nodded in understanding yet his facial features betrayed a blankness and a lack of comprehension.

Mike, a bright ten-year-old, would become awestruck and then silent whenever I would comment that he seemed happy, unhappy, anxious, or angry at the beginning of the hour. He eventually told me that he was dumbfounded by my ability to know how he felt without his saying anything. At first he thought that perhaps I was guessing; however, he discarded that explanation when he realized how accurate I was in my assessments. He would then become silent because he felt inferior and dumb because he could not figure out my moods while I could discern his so easily. For weeks he demanded to know how I could do this.

Paul, a rather articulate twelve-year-old, assumed that the only way I could tell how he felt was that I probably took classes on learning how to know people's feelings in Psychiatry School. He hoped someday to be a psychiatrist just like me so that he also could find out how to know about the feelings of others.

All three of these youngsters were demonstrated to have learning disabilities for which they were receiving special education placement as well as individual tutoring. While their school performance fluctuated, they all had a marked difficulty in comprehending how another person felt. Concomitantly their ability to perceive their own feelings about themselves in a particular situation was also impaired. In social situations in which others could assess the nature of the various interactions immediately and accurately they frequently found themselves puzzled, confused, and eventually overwhelmed.

In recent times Kohut (1971) has probably been the most significant psychoanalytic researcher to suggest a variety of possible impediments in the child's ability to develop an empathic capacity.

Kohut, as well as other psychoanalytic observers, has assumed that most frequently the empathic disturbance in the child is primarily related to a parental lack of empathy or faulty or unreliable empathy.

The potential for the acquisition of a special talent for empathic perception is usually interfered with in early life. A depressed mother who meets her child's needs with uniformly unenthusiastic behavior does not provide a model for mirroring a variety of emotional states. Or the depressed mother who has learned to utter the proper words with the same consistent flatness may equally well transmit an emotional response that can only elicit confusion in the child.

Similarly, a child whose moods are invariably interpreted according to a pat definition may retreat in disappointment and expect that he will not be understood (Kohut, 1971). This same child, because of his innate learning limitations, may then not know how to define his own state of feeling and may experience a sense of uneasiness or tension; consequently he will also feel that there is something wrong with him that keeps him from understanding others.

While Kohut and a number of other researchers have also alluded to certain genetic factors as being responsible for the so-called primary disturbance in empathy, such factors have been discussed in rather global and vague terms. When the etiology of a particular psychopathological constellation is expressed in global terminology then it is relegated to a kind of pseudo-organic never-never land which is placed beyond the scope of psychological inquiry.

Kohut (1971) described the following primary deficits in empathy: the emotional coldness of the mother, the absence of consistent contact with the mother, the baby's congenital emotional coldness, and the mother's withdrawal from an unresponsive baby. The result from any of these situations may be a stunting of the important first stages of the baby's empathic interplay with the mother.

While the extremes of the above-mentioned disturbances would be a mother who is severely depressed or a child who may be autistic, our interest was focused on the less extreme forms of disturbance which contribute to deficits in empathy. The earliest maternal observations on their children had to do with an impression that the child was "different" from other children. Such an impression may have resulted from the parental disappointment with a child that did not measure up to an idealized image of the perfect baby, or from a very basic appreciation that in some subtle way the child was indeed different. This difference defied specification initially, and only later did it crystallize into elements of a learning disability. In either instance one cannot exclude the possibility that the mother was depressed and the disappointment with the child (whether actually damaged or not) was indeed a vital contributing element to such perceptions.

While these children were not always seen as difficult to mother or regulate, they were ultimately assessed as being erratic in their developmental progression. Although their learning was age appropriate, perhaps their peer relations were of a more infantile nature. Some of these children were very social but may have had some visual-motor perceptual problems. However, it is only when the child enters school and is looked at more objectively by teachers and mental health professionals that a learning disability, which is in essence a developmental lag in the maturation of the central nervous system, is often pinpointed. Consequently it may well be that the maternal perception that the child was different from the very beginning was indeed accurate.

While it is infinitely easier to focus on the environmental determinants of the child's psychopathology, the child's deficits in such an interplay are frequently discounted or dismissed. The parental depression and disappointment with a youngster who is learning disabled may indeed be a powerful element in the child's inability to develop a stable empathic capacity; nevertheless certain deficits within the child himself may be equally significant in the evolution of such a limitation. The parental depression may not necessarily remain a constant to which the child is exposed, as parental moods change and fluctuate; however, a cognitive deficit within the child is a far more pervasive constant to contend with. The youngster whose mother is depressed may often turn to other significant adults for an empathic response and may indeed learn from others about empathy. However, the child who is inherently limited in his ability to sense and understand the feelings of others has no one to turn to except his own sense of confusion and perplexity.

While children are taught how to act and to behave toward others, they are not necessarily taught about what others may feel in response to their pronouncements. The focus in teaching the child is usually action or performance oriented, for these are tangibles that one can observe and evaluate. However, it is much more vague and difficult to teach the child what another may feel in response to his actions or words. The child who breaks another's most cherished toy will only think in terms of how he will replace the destroyed object, but he may not necessarily sense the intensity of the loss that the other child is feeling.

Given the evanescent nature of empathy it is not surprising that a parent may not be inclined to teach such a process to the child. The parent may conclude that empathy is something that is just there, or that the child should learn about empathy from parental examples; that is, if we assume that parents are usually empathic. Although it is easier to call the child selfish and self-centered, most children will respond to such name-calling defensively. If the child responds to such labeling with perplexity and confusion then the result may be only slightly less palatable, for then he is exposed to the possibility of being called "stupid." Given such alternatives it is not surprising that the more perceptive youngster will choose to act "as if" he is in tune with the feelings of others while continuing to hide an inner conviction that something is wrong with him.

ADAPTIVE RESPONSES

As the child matures and reaches a higher level of intellectual development then he may find more subtle means of compensating for his deficit. It is within the nature of the human organism that when one becomes aware of a particular limitation or deficit then certain compensatory and adaptive mechanisms tend to come into play. The child who becomes aware that something is amiss in how they react to others will attempt to compensate for such a limitation, even though he may not know its exact nature.

Such compensatory responses will originate from two sources; from the significant adults as well as from within the child. The child may observe and learn from his parents by mimicry and imitation as to how one should respond in a particular emotionally charged situation. So that if the child is informed that someone of consequence has died his initial response may be a lack of response until he realizes that he is supposed to act sad even though he may not feel that way. By the same token the child may also exaggerate his emotional response to such an extent that it will be just as inappropriate as if he did not respond at all. The youngster who imitates or who acts "as if" he is feeling for others will be quickly discovered by his peers and will be shunned. While adults are occasionally taken with the "little actor" other children are not fooled by shallow imitations.

Nevertheless, those youngsters who possess limited intellectual and adaptive resources will continue to pick up cues on how to feel for someone in a particular situation and they will act accordingly. As they become older the repertoire of emotional responses may increase; however, at the younger level their shallowness will be easily discovered.

As the child becomes older, there is a concomitant maturation of most cognitive skills and abilities. Those youngsters who are intellectually superior will use their intellect in the service of adaptation to environmental stresses and demands. Since the child is aware that on a preconscious level he has difficulties in figuring out how others see him and how he should be sensitive and attuned to another person, then he will attempt to think out or figure out how he should behave in response to another person's feelings.

At this state in his development, having determined directly and indirectly that his empathic skills are limited, the more intelligent youngster will make use of his cognitive equipment to compensate for the emotional deficits. Such a youngster will collect a variety of data before he arrives at some consensus about how he feels or for that matter how the other person feels.

Mike, an intelligent thirteen-year-old, was eventually able to tell me that as soon as he saw me he scrutinized my face, especially the eyes, and then he would examine how I greeted him. That was only the first step, for as I walked to my chair he would watch the expression on my face and then he noted how comfortably I sat in the chair. After that he would observe how quickly I settled in, then he noticed my clothing, and eventually the facial expression. If that was not enough, he would wait silently to see how soon I would initiate the conversation and then he noted the content. If I was silent then he noted how restless I became. He would then go through all these evaluations like a checklist after which he would decide as to whether I was glad to see him. If he concluded that I was happy to see him then he would initiate a discussion or ask a few questions; however, if he felt that I was not happy to see him then he would remain silent or ask some indirect questions after which he would reassess my feeling state. Besides the checklist that he was consciously aware of, he felt that there was probably other data that he was collecting subconsciously to monitor how I felt about him.

What gradually emerged was the impression that he was like a computer collecting bits of observational data which he then put together into an impression about how the other person feels, which in turn influenced how he should act and behave, and ultimately how he felt about himself. His perceptions were so egocentric that he immediately assumed that any and all of my reactions were related to him and only him.

If the thought-out behavior is inappropriate then the youngster may have a ready-made rationalization to cover the anticipated exposure and embarrassment. The more inventive youngster may prepare a variety of responses so that one never knows what the real response may be, for there is more than one. It is the variety of responses to a particular emotional situation that betrays such a youngster and makes him appear shallow. Since their responses to an emotionally charged interaction seem so changeable and unreliable, then an objective observer may assume that these are not genuine reactions but that the youngster is only acting as if he is feeling something. Those adolescents who are the more talented with such acting will continue to do so beyond the point when the behavior is necessary or useful, for there is a certain inherent pleasure and excitement in one's ability to deceive. They may do so because they assume others expect it or because it has become such a habitual and integral part of their functional self, that anything different would create a sense of tension. Such an adaptation may seem reasonable and probably useful, since often how one acts and behaves is more important than what one is, nevertheless it may result in rather serious problems. In spite of mastering the art of acting empathic and concerned, the youngster will continue to struggle with a sense of emptiness or more specifically feeling like a fraud or a sham. They will continue to demand reassurance that what they sense and feel about others and themselves is genuine and can be validated. If such reassurances are not forthcoming because the demands are too frantic, then such an adolescent may feel worse and may then turn to drugs or sexual acting out as a means of feeling temporarily intact and genuine.

A somewat related problem is that since such youngsters may become quite fluent in what Kohut (1971) described as cognitive empathy, excessive amounts of emotional and intellectual energy are tied up and invested in such a process. The youngster then tends to function as a computer that collects huge amounts of data so as to engage in and deal with daily interpersonal interactions. Since so much of their intellectual capacities are concerned with this kind of constant intellectual exercise one may wonder just how much of their intellect is available for learning. It may well be then that such youngsters learn in school in a rather cursory and superficial manner, without really mastering the essence of a particular subject. They act as if they have learned something when in reality they have accumulated superficial disconnected facts and have then laced them with the conviction that they know a particular subject. It is only when they are confronted by someone knowledgeable and more aggressive in his knowledge that they will feel exposed, trapped, and embarrassed. At those times they may indeed revert to covering up with the same superficial rationalizations that have served them in the past.

TREATMENT CONSIDERATIONS

A number of years ago a book by Haim Ginott (1968) enjoyed great popularity with adults who were experiencing difficulties in parenting. This book, like others before and since, emphasized a variety of commonsense approaches in dealing with a child in distress. However, one of the recurring suggestions was that no matter what the child is distressed about the parental response should be one of understanding. The relevant prescription for any discussion between parent and child should be prefaced by a statement "I understand how you feel but . . . " While to understand another human being is essential in any interpersonal interaction, to sound or act as if one understands is somewhat of a sham. It is impossible to order another human being to be understanding; however, it takes minimum effort to act as if one understands. While such an act may impress the peripheral observer, most children will sense such verbalizations as shallow and meaningless because the actions will contradict the verbiage.

A nine-year-old girl told me once that her softball coach acted very nice and understanding when she had a conflict about participating in a game, yet, she reasoned that he could not really be that way because he got mad and mean when she arrived late.

The treatment approach with the child who has a deficit in empathy is the treatment approach used in dealing with more broadly based conflicts. Nevertheless there are certain treatment considerations that one needs to keep in mind when approaching a patient with such a deficit. If indeed such a problem has been identified, it is not too far-fetched to assume that the child may know very little about something that we call affects. When a child is puzzled and confused by an emotional response it may well be that he needs to be taught about feelings, their combinations, and the fact that one feeling state may cover an underlying feeling that is different.

However, it is even more important to focus in the transference on how the child's words and actions may make the therapist feel. If a youngster comes to his appointment around dinnertime eating a delicious looking candy bar, then it may be important to discuss the multiple possible effects of such behavior on the therapist. This child may not know that another human being may have a variety of emotional responses to his seemingly innocent behavior. While parents will attempt to teach the child about such things the therapist has the luxury of doing it at a leisurely pace without being punitive or judgmental. At the same time it is important to recognize that the child's act does not necessarily imply hostility, provocativeness, or selfishness, but indeed results from not knowing the other person's full range of emotional responses.

CONCLUSION

This chapter is an attempt to pinpoint some of the genetic determinants for a child's defective empathic capacity. Children with diagnosed learning disabilities have often been described as insensitive, selfish, and callous with their words and actions toward peers. It is suggested that the child's learning disability contributes directly and indirectly to this deficit in empathy. The direct contributions stem from the unavailability of certain cognitive integrative skills which are so essential for the emergence of an immediate and accurate empathic response. The indirect contributions of the learning disability to a lack of empathy is based on the impression that in such children a huge amount of intellectual and emotional energy is invested in attempting to discern their own state of well-being. Since they are so preoccupied with their sense of intactness and stability, then there is limited psychic energy available for the sensitivity and concern about others.

Those younger children that are intellectually gifted, as well as adolescents, develop a variety of compensatory mechanisms to cover over their deficit. It is suggested that within the treatment one of the initial tasks with such a youngster is to teach them some of the basics about the range of human affects.

REFERENCES

Basch, M. F. (1983), Empathic understanding: A review of the concept and some theoretical considerations. *J. Amer. Psychoanal. Assn.* 31(1): 101–126.

Beres, D., & Arlow, J. A. (1974), Fantasy and identification in empathy. *Psychoanal. Quart.*, 43:26–50.

Burlingham, D. (1967), Empathy between infant and mother. *J. Amer. Psychoanal. Assn.*, 15:764–780.

Easer, B. R. (1974), Empathic inhibition and psychoanalytic technique. *Psychoanal. Quart.*, 43:557–580.

Freud, S. (1921), Group Psychology and the Analysis of the Ego. *Standard Edition*, 18. London: Hogarth Press, 1974.

Ginott, H. (1968), *Between Parent and Child*. New York: Macmillan.

Kohut, H. (1959), Introspection, empathy and psychoanalysis. *J. Amer. Psychoanal. Assn.*, 7:459–483.

———— (1971), *The Analysis of the Self*. New York: International Universities Press.

Mahler, A. (1968), *On Human Symbiosis and the Vicissitudes of Individuation*, Vol. 1. New York: International Universities Press.

Olden, C. (1953), On adult empathy with children. *The Psychoanalytic Study of the Child*, 8:111–126. New York: International Universities Press.

———— (1958), Notes on the development of empathy. *The Psychoanalytic Study of the Child*, 13:505–518. New York: International Universities Press.

Sawyier, F. H. (1975), A conceptual analysis of empathy. *The Annual of Psychoanalysis*, 3:30–47. New York: International Universities Press.

Schafer, R. (1959), Generative empathy in the treatment situation. *Psychoanal. Quart.*, 28:342–373.

Shapiro, T. (1974), The development and distortions of empathy. *Psychoanal. Quart.*, 43:4–25.

Chapter 23

Marking Time in the Midst of the Hardest Movement: Educational and Clinical Implications of Adolescent Borderline Disorder in Life Span Perspective

GIL G. NOAM, Ed.D., Dipl. Psych.

> ... We take on
> everything at once before we've even be-
> gun
> to read or mark time, we are forced to
> begin
> in the midst of the hardest movement,
> the one already sounding as we are
> born. ...
>
> Adrienne Rich
> *Transcendental Etude*

INTRODUCTION

Psychoanalysis has made great inroads into an understanding of the educational process by applying developmental theory and concepts of psychopathology to the school setting. From the beginning education posed important challenges for the founders of the field. Freud's

Acknowledgment: I thank Maryanne Wolf, Barbara Panza, David Miranda, Laura Rogers, Copeland Young, and Lawrence Kohlberg for supporting this project.

dictum on education remained the guiding principle of psychoanalytic pedagogy: to enable the individual to take part in culture and to achieve this goal with the smallest loss of original energy (Freud, 1909). Erik Erikson's (1935) entry into psychoanalysis began as a teacher in the psychoanalytic preschool in Vienna and his experiences there remained formative for the development of his epigenetic theory. Aichhorn (1925), Anna Freud (1935), and Erikson's other teachers were in the process of writing their seminal papers on psychoanalytic educational theory and practice. Meanwhile, the socialist school experiments of Vera Schmidt (1924) and Bernfeld (1925) gave new directions to psychoanalytic education which were to influence a future generation of postwar educators in the 1960s, especially in Europe. Zulliger's psychoanalytic pedagogy (1957) influenced liberal American and European education.

With the advent of behaviorism in America, educational practice turned away from psychoanalysis to the point at which it was a rare exception in the educational literature to find systematic and innovative contributions of psychoanalysis to education. Learning machines and reinforcement procedures, including social learning theory, had shaped the psychological perspectives of the 1950s and 1960s, and these learning approaches eventually influenced educational practices. With the emergence of Piaget and his encompassing theory of the development of intelligence and his paradigm of adaptation in childhood and adolescence came a cognitive-developmental revolution of educational theory and practice (e.g., Kohlberg, 1969; Furth and Wachs, 1975; Elkind, 1976). Psychoanalytic ideas receded even more. These developments were reinforced by the strong medical orientation of American psychoanalysis, which by and large explored psychopathology in the treatment situation rather than normal developmental processes in real life context.

Important developments within psychoanalysis (e.g., Kernberg's integration of ego psychology and object relation theory and Kohut's self psychology) make very timely the renewed theoretical discussion around the contribution of psychoanalysis to education and the equally important but usually ignored contribution of education to psychoanalysis. This chapter argues that the new phase of psychoanalytic theorizing in the area of education, including the role of the teacher, needs to embrace the important contributions of Piaget's paradigm and the American expansion of his ideas into a social-developmental framework. A dialogue between psychoanalysis and developmental psychology requires more than the currently obligatory reference to "Piaget, 1926." That the Piagetians have traditionally remained aloof to psychoanalytic thinking, even though Piaget himself had tried on a number of occasions to demonstrate bridges and argued for an integration of the two great theories into a general psychology (Piaget, 1973), has contributed equally to the artifical separation of these disciplines (Edelstein and Noam, 1982).

This chapter attempts to describe the need to apply a social-developmental[1] framework in the tradition of Piaget to a psychoanalytic understanding of psychopathology. It will focus on the adolescent phase of development, distinguishing the different adolescent worlds which are defined by levels of social development, and describing the psychoanalytic contribution to education of the study of life history, unconscious motivation, regression, and transference. A study of a severe pathology such as the borderline personality disorder serves to

---

[1]*Social-development* is used here as a term to address social-cognition in the Piagetian tradition and not all other forms of social-development theory. Cognitive developmental or structural-development are also used in the literature, but are too strongly tied to cognition (rather than affect-cognition) and to objects (rather than person-objects) to underline our research attempts.

illustrate the reemergence of earlier developmental problems at higher levels of development. The framework presented here uncovers a process of separation-individuation struggles at a number of conceptually and empirically relevant stages of the life cycle. I propose the need to understand the genesis of borderline personality disorders, not only in terms of developmental arrest at an early age, but also in terms of a predisposition to manifest separation-individuation (*and* affiliation-integration) difficulties. These later difficulties can begin at the separation-individuation period (although they do not have to), but take different forms at different developmental points.

Three cases of adolescent borderline personalities exemplify three of the evolving positions of the self organization.[2] At each of these three developmental stages (and their respective transitions to the next stage) a social-cognitive theme prevails for which the terms *subjective-physical* (stage 1), *reciprocal-instrumental* (stage 2), and *mutual-inclusive* (stage 3) have been coined. For each stage I will demonstrate how the symptom clusters differ on the dimensions outlined in *The Diagnostic and Statistical Manual* III (DSM-III) (American Psychiatric Association, 1980) and I will explore the different *forms* of interpersonal difficulty, identity problems, impulsivity, and depression. I will focus on the clinical and educational implications by arguing that the social-developmental levels in concert with the reemerging of earlier vulnerabilities provide a grid for the educator, clinician, as well as for the student and patient.

---

[2] I use the term *self organization* to mean the "biographical and transformational self and other" in order to distinguish it from the traditional psychoanalytic ego with its ego functions. But the use of *ego* by psychologists such as Loevinger (1976) as a frame of reference of self and other makes these terms almost interchangeable. For more elaborate discussions of this question, see Lee and Noam (1983).

THE BORDERLINE PATIENT: SOME PSYCHOANALYTIC CONTRIBUTIONS

Early literature on borderline conditions shows that clinicians sought to situate the syndrome along a continuum from neurosis to psychosis. Borderline patients were often called primitive hysterics (Zetzel, 1971), impulsive characters (Reich, 1925), as if personalities (Deutsch, 1942), or latent schizophrenics (Bychowski, 1953). It was Knight's work (1953) that paved the way for a systematic and empirical effort to study this group of patients (Grinker, Werble, and Drye, 1968; Gunderson, 1977; Perry and Klerman, 1980). Still controversial, the term *borderline personality disorder* has been included among other character disorders in DSM-III. We find the following descriptions:

1. Significant impairment of a sense of identity.
2. Inability to build and retain important and meaningful relationships.
3. Varying degrees of impairment of the capacity to reality test, associated with inadequate coping and defense styles.
4. Overt or covert depression, disabling anxiety states, and unmodulated rage reactions.

I embrace these current descriptions of borderline psychopathology. Of course, psychoanalytic discussions about the etiology and severity of borderline pathology continue (Buie and Adler, 1973; Robbins, 1976). The Kohutian perspective, on the borderline syndromes, for example, differs significantly from the theories described in this chapter (Kohut, 1971; Wolf, 1976; Tolpin, 1980). My focus on the self and on its transformations relates closely to many of Kohut's assertions. Self psychology, however, focuses on the early development of the self and thus the adolescent and especially adult self continue to be unexplored. Also, the method of analysis presented here for borderline patients can be applied to narcissistic pathology across the life span.

Mahler calls the first few weeks of life the autistic phase. The infant perceives external stimuli, though he does not differentiate any external objects, and is more attuned to internal stimuli.

In the second month the child has a vague perception of the mother as a need-satisfying object. The child then develops a strong attachment to the mother and enters the symbiotic phase. This attachment is expressed, for example, through preferential smiling at the mother. The child perceives two entities, the symbiotic unit of mother-child and the outside world. This phase peaks around the age of four to five months.

The next phase, separation-individuation, is of central concern to our topic and is marked by specific subphases. The general characteristics are a move to physical separation from the mother and to actualization of the child's potentials. The first of these is differentiation, which is characterized by development of a body image, exploration of the mother's body, and an increasing attachment to transitional objects which substitute for the mother in her absence. This subphase is also characterized by comparative scanning in which the child checks back with the mother to compare new objects to her, and by both interest in strangers and anxiety toward them.

During the next subphase which Mahler calls practicing, two events occur: the physical movement away from the mother, and the accomplishment of this movement by walking. Most prominent in this subphase (especially between ten to twelve and sixteen to eighteen months) is a fascination with exploration of the world. New adults are more readily accepted, and the child will actively run away from the mother, gaining the assurance that the mother will not be far behind, eagerly trying to catch the child.

The third subphase, rapprochement, brings not only increased mastery to the child, but also the awareness of the separateness of self from the parents. This may take the form of a developmental crisis. Mahler points to two especially important patterns in the child: "shadowing," or the watching and following of the mother, and "darting-away" while expecting to be recaptured by the mother. The child, Mahler notes, fears the "loss of the love object" and demonstrates heightened sensitivity to approval and disapproval by the parent during this phase. Mahler calls the fourth subphase the "consolidation of individuality and the beginnings of emotional object constancy."

Masterson (1973), Kernberg (1975), and most other psychoanalytic theorists who have studied borderline psychopathology (Giovacchini, 1973) argue that the borderline patient has not successfully negotiated the separation-individuation phase. We might now ask how the difficulties that arise for the twelve- to eighteen-month old are responsible for adolescent and adult psychopathology. We do not know what the processes are that continue to exert influence over adolescent and adult thought, feeling, and behavior. At a time when we are expanding our knowledge about important personality shifts over the life span, we will have to rethink the relationship between unresolved conflicts from childhood and their changed adolescent and adult manifestations. Kernberg, for instance, takes an extreme position regarding the adolescent crisis. He argues that identity diffusion is not a normal part of the adolescent phase and relates it back to early pathology.

I think that the syndrome of identity diffusion *always* reflects serious psychopathology related to borderline personality organization which stems from vicissitudes of very early development; the underlying intrapsychic structures which reflect such psychopathology are

probably crystalized within the first five years of life
[1975, p. 39; emphasis added].

However, Kernberg never states how the *shape* of the
conflict is different for the adolescent than for the preschool child. I have stated earlier that in a post-Piagetian
era, in which the governing structures of adolescent
thought have been rigorously studied, it becomes hard to
hold to the position that central psychological functions
remain unaltered throughout life.

Masterson argues that the fear of engulfment and of
abandonment in borderline patients relates to the rap-
proachement subphase as described by Mahler, Pine, and
Bergman (1975). The earlier the age at which the presumed arrest occurs, the more prominent will be the fear
of engulfment; the later it occurs, the more prominent
will be the fear of abandonment. Further development
throughout the life cycle, which normally encourages continued separation and individuation, will aggravate borderline symptomology, such as acting out and abandonment
depression (see Table 23.1). Such symptomology often
remains "subclinical" or masked until the person is
stressed in relation to normal dependency needs. As adolescence normally accentuates the drive toward separation, the borderline disorder may become prominent at
that time. Masterson (1973) states:

> All adolescents go through a second separation-indi-
> viduation phase in prepuberty, owning to the matur-
> ational spurt of the ego. In some borderline patients
> this alone is able to precipitate a clinical syndrome, in
> others this internal event combined with an actual ex-
> ternal environmental separation exposes the patient
> to the experience he has been defending against since
> early childhood, separation from the maternal partner
> to whom he has been clinging. This, in turn, reactivates
> with great intensity, his defenses against his feelings

of abandonment, which wax strongly at this point. The environmental separation precipitates the intrapsychic feelings of abandonment [p. 251].

As an adult, the borderline personality is confronted with the need to experience individuation as well as separation. Some individuals will refuse, by remaining at home. Others may leave home and obtain quasi-independence, choosing in their working lives activities that permit the experience of independence which is inhibited in the personal realm because of overwhelming fears. With the onslaught of interpersonal relationships and consequent issues of intimacy, fears of engulfment and abandonment often culminate in borderline conditions.

The issue of intimacy both directly stimulates the fear of engulfment and indirectly stimulates the fear of abandonment, since the threat of separation is inherent in an intensifying relationship. The extent of such fears vary, but both are characteristically evident in the borderline personality.

Masterson and Rinsley (1975) have introduced a life cycle orientation to the study of early vulnerabilities of the separation-individuation phase. Their view of the life span, however, is a modified version of phasic life cycle theory. Certain life tasks trigger the core borderline vulnerability, as if it exists as a "time-bomb" inside the person, ready to explode when difficult separations or "intimacies" are impending. Table 23.1 shows the eras in the life cycle, the precipitating events and the clinical picture of the borderline syndrome.

Masterson and Rinsley's life cycle orientation to borderline pathology does not share with Erikson and the Piagetian model an understanding of transformation of psychic reality. The handicap induced early in life will manifest itself in the life spheres across time. No mention is made of the "maturing ego" which integrates earlier vulnerabilities with new ones, and enhancing experi-

TABLE 23.1

Masterson's Borderline Syndrome and the Life Cycle

Time in the Life Cycle	Precipitating Event	Clinical Syndrome
Childhood	Leaving home for school Leaving home for camp	School phobia Phobia
Prepuberty	Leaving the local school for the high school	Abandonment depression with its defenses
Middle Adolescence	Sex functioning	Abandonment depression with its acting out defenses
Twenties	1. College graduation or leaving home for work	Abandonment depression and acting out defenses
	2. Difficulty with work, avoiding individuation	Lack of satisfaction
	3. Challenge of intimacy	Fear of loss of self or object
Thirties	1. Difficulty with work, intimacy, husband or wife, marital conflict	Avoidance, clinging, or distancing due to fear of loss of self or object

	2. Difficulty parenting	Anxiety, depression
Forties	1. Difficulty as parents with adolescents who rebel against depersonification or who comply at cost of individuation	Anxiety, depression
	2. Promotions at work where a previously encouraged dependency is lost	Anxiety, depression
	3. Lack of work satisfaction due to avoidance of individuation or acting out	Acting out
Fifties	Failures in work and heterosexual relationships as opportunity runs out and fantasy meets frustration	Abandonment depression
Sixties and Seventies	Extraordinary difficulty with changes and with loss of loved ones, friends, work	Abandonment depression

ences in work and love. Even Kernberg, who builds on
Mahler's observations, disagrees with Masterson's "strong
fixation" on the separation-individuation phase. Kernberg maintains that Masterson as well as other authors

> . . . apply a theoretical frame of reference derived from
> Mahler's work to the psychotherapeutic treatment of
> adolescent and adult borderline patients that, in my
> opinion, treats these patients as if they were fixated at
> the conflicts of separation-individuation to the exclu-
> sion of the developments and transformations that
> these conflicts undergo under the influence of oedipal
> developments [Kernberg, 1980, p. 31].

But if developments and transformations are conceded
for the oedipal period, why not for all the transitions of
the life cycle? Is everything that follows the preoedipal
and oedipal years a recapitulation of these two early life
transitions?

When Kernberg disagrees with Masterson about an
overdetermined fixation theory of separation-individuation, he too exposes himself to criticism. As I have argued
earlier, the transformations of the self continue *throughout life*, reshaping psychological experience in ever new
and complex structures. Any fixation theory that stops
at the preoedipal or oedipal years misses these major
reorganizations in human development. The position
taken in this chapter is that there is no separation-individuation conflict in adolescence or adulthood that is
not under the governance (or at least part governance)
of these later psychological organizations.

Mahler's own point of view is more cautious. She
aligns herself potentially with a broader developmental
orientation, embracing concepts of transformation and an
understanding of the past as, at least partially, a construction of the present. This position asserts that genetic
orientations which retrospectively uncover childhood dynamics run the danger of interpreting memory traces as

real events. Kaplan (1980), a colleague of Mahler, wrote a thoughtful review on this topic in which she agrees with Freud that childhood recollections of adults are governed by a process in which time is turned upon itself. "There is in fact no direct line," she argues "from the adult present to the infantile past" (p. 537). She also criticizes the simplistic application of Mahler's observations to adult psychopathology. Psychoanalysts "fail to take into account the variety of developmental vicissitudes between infantile and adult mental organizations. . . . [T]he clinical outcome of the rapprochement crisis of children depends as much on later development as it does on the immediate effects of the separation-individuation phase" (p. 575).

Mahler observes that already in the preoedipal phase there is a restructuring of the earlier experiences: "early and preverbal sensorimotor patterns had already been integrated by the middle of the second year, solidly enough, so that derivatives could not be reconstructively traced back, step-by-step, by means of deduction" (1971, p. 414).

This is due to the integrating capacities of the ego; Mahler notes: "the progressive forces of the growing ego are astonishingly successful, often they tend to even out most of the discrepancies and minor deviations" (1971, p. 414). Mahler does, however, attribute psychogenetic significance to the separation-individuation phase. She maintains that vulnerabilities from unresolved conflicts can lead to more trauma in the oedipal years and throughout life.

More specifically she states:

[I]n those children with less than optimal development, the ambivalence conflict is discernible during the rapprochement subphase in rapidly alternating clinging and negativistic behaviors. This process may be in some cases a reflection of the fact that the child has split the object world more permanently than is optimal into "good" and "bad". . . . These two mechanisms—coercion and splitting of the object world—if excessive, are also characteristic of most cases of adult borderline transference [Mahler, Pine, and Bergman, 1975, p. 226].

But the relationship between separation-individuation vulnerabilities and transference relationships in psychotherapy remain unexplored. Mahler never clarified the two positions she embraces, which are tied to the two roles she is performing: the developmental researcher engaged in prospective studies and the psychoanalyst involved in reconstructive work in treatment. Thus, there is continued puzzlement over the similarities and differences between the original separation-individuation phase and later separation-individuation manifestations.

Mahler, Pine, and Bergman (1975) preface their classic book with a statement which defines the object of their study:

We wish to emphasize our focus on early childhood. We do not mean to imply, as is sometimes loosely done, that every new separation or step toward a revised or expanded feeling of self at any age is part of the separation-individuation process. . . . An old, partially unresolved sense of self-identity and body boundaries, or old conflicts over separation and separateness, can be reactivated (or can remain peripherally or even centrally active) at any and all stages of life; but it is the original and infantile process, not the new eliciting events or situations, to which we shall address ourselves [1975, pp. 4–5].

Any attempt to understand the influence of early vulnerabilities of separation-individuation throughout life requires a theory of the life span.

THE SOCIAL-DEVELOPMENTAL FRAMEWORK

Jean Piaget, the most important and far-reaching developmental psychologist, never focused on a theory of ego or self however, it was his starting point. He states, "in estimating the child's conception of the world, the first question, obviously is . . . can the child distinguish the self from the external world?" (1926, p. 33). But his lifelong preoccupation centered around the "epistemic self," which is based on the generalized universal *structures* of cognitive development. From such a position, ego development was of secondary importance. Similarly, the domain of emotional development so central to an ego theory never was a focus in Piaget's work, although he did address *emotions* in their relationship to cognitive structures (e.g., Piaget [1973]). Piaget posits a parallelism in the development of cognitive structure and affective energies and argues that emotions are the phenomena that indicate disequilibrium and stage transition. But Piaget's position, even with the detailed elaboration of emotional development at each stage of cognitive reorganization has left a central question unanswered. What is the mediation between the cognitive and affective domain? Does this mediation follow structural lines? What is the understanding of clinical phenomena?

Piaget's great contribution was to present a developmental structuralist model involving an integration of the concepts of (1) wholeness; (2) internal regulation; and (3) developmental transformation. Kohlberg (1969) has transformed Piaget's model into a social-cognitive one in which the person's understanding of social norms and rules become the focus. This line of work has opened the way to very productive work in the area of the developing self. Some of the principles will be summarized before describing the stages of the self in social-developmental perspective.

Structures refer to whole systems rather than to

groups of independent elements. Elements are defined by
the laws governing the roles played within the whole.
Thus, the elements derive their power as phenomena only
as parts of this whole. The structure orders the elements
and raises them to a form not possessed in isolation. In
this respect, a Piagetian view shares much with psychoanalysis; that is, behaviors are interpreted in both paradigms as part of an underlying system, although the
system itself is conceptualized quite differently.

Some examples of structural accounts are found in a
new area of psychology that bridges developmental and
personality psychology. Most prominent in this effort are
Loevinger's model of ego development and theories building on Kohlberg's theory of moral development. For Loevinger (Loevinger, 1976) the ego is the master personality
trait around which the whole personality is constructed.
Her concept of ego development draws on the theoretical
traditions of interpersonal, cognitive, and character psychology. Loevinger's perspective emphasizes the individual's integrative processes and overall frame of reference.
The assumption is that each person has a customary
orientation to the self and world and that there are stages
and transitions along which these frames of reference can
be organized. Her stages are differentiated along dimensions of impulse control, conscious concerns, and interpersonal and cognitive styles.

In a tradition more directly linked with Piaget's paradigm is research in structural-self or self-other psychology. These theories build mainly upon the work of
Kohlberg and expand it in areas relevant to a theory of
the self and the life span; for example, perspective-taking
(Selman, 1980). One group of theorists is working on more
explicit developmental theories of the ego, the self, or self
concept (e.g., Kegan, 1982; Damon, 1983; Noam, 1985).
These theorists attempt to define the self in terms of an
underlying logic.

One important way of thinking about the logic organization of the self is through role-taking; that is, forms of social perspective–taking (Baldwin, 1902; Mead, 1934; Selman, 1980). The notion here is that activities of the self always involve role-taking; the awareness that the other is in some way both like and unlike the self, and that the other knows or is responsive to the self in a system of complementary expectations. Social perspective also has an intrapsychic counterpart, a process I term "internal perspective taking." Developmental changes in the understanding of the social world are paralleled by changes in the psychological understanding of internal processes. These include the self-reflective capacities, the experience and labeling of emotions, as well as the distinction between conscious and unconscious motivations. Also, what is defined as self, as the boundary between internal and external, between intrapsychic and interpersonal, is importantly related to the underlying logic of the self.

Structural-developmental psychology posits that role-taking, much like morality and cognition, develops throughout life in a progression of qualitative stages of equilibration (and disequilibration). These stages give the variety of social experiences cohesion. The development of the self always means moving toward greater equilibrium in the organism-environment interaction. This balance—between external objects and internal assimilating and accommodating structures—represents perspective, knowledge, logic, and adaption. New and more complex forms of understanding of the relationship between the self and the other also bring out new motivational systems, such as wishes and desires, needs and gratifications. Inherent in interpersonal relationships, conflict emerges as something new at each developmental position. Each new stage is defined by a particular logic and is associated with surface manifestations and typical motivations related to the underlying perspective.

Because of the combination of its strong social-developmental orientation, its link to the cognitive logic in the Piagetian tradition, and its empirical strength I build upon Selman's perspective-taking levels in the descriptions of stages of the self's social and internal perspective. Table 23.2 summarizes stages of the developing self with their internal perspectives.

Table 23.2
Noam's Self Stages Relevant to the Adolescent Phase

1. The Subjective-Physical Self-Other Stage

At the subjective-physical stage there is no consideration of the other's interests and desires as different from the self's. There is an emerging awareness of the distinction of physical and psychological characteristics in people, but, mostly, actions are evaluated in terms of physical consequences. Impulsive responses are typical and feelings are expressed in action language. Strength is the ability to distinguish between fantasy and reality, to show strong will, and to demonstrate an independent curiosity. These strengths are in part based on at least a partial achievement of object constancy. The weakness is an emphasis on wish fulfillment, seeing others as suppliers and being very dependent on them. The concrete perspective on the self leads to a dichotomous view of being good or bad. In the process, the self hides from or submits to powerful authority figures that can inflict physical harm.

2. The Reciprocal-Instrumental Self-Other Stage

At the reciprocal-instrumental stage there is the possibility of understanding self interests and goals as separate from the intent of others. Conflicting interests between self and other are usually resolved through instrumental exchange. The person can step out of the concrete bounds of the self and thus create "two-way" reciprocity. This perspective also changes the internal perspective-taking ability. There now is the conceptual distinction of outer appearance of the "public self" and "inner hidden self." This creates the possibility of planned deception, through which the self can affirm its boundaries. Conflict usually does not lead to submission or impulsive action, but to self protective assertion of control. The negative outcome is opportunism, exploitation, and manipulation. The positive outcome is the mastery of the tool world, the ability to control feelings and to concentrate on tasks. The limitation of the reciprocal-instrumental stage is the isolation of two exchange-partners whose relationship is not guided primarily by trust and altruism but by interest.

3. The Mutual-Inclusive Self-Other Stage

At the mutual-inclusive self perspective, others are understood in a relationship coordinated through a more generalized perspective. The person experiences different points of view through the "Golden Rule" of seeing reality also through the eyes of another person. This perspective creates the context for altruistic actions and surpassing the bounds of self-interest. Attitudes and values are seen as persisting over time often leading to stereotypes like "I am that kind of person." These "self-traits" in addition to the new internal perspectives lead to more complex self-observational capacities. The limitations of this stage are, however, an over-identification with the views of the other, and the dangers of conformist social behavior. It is very crucial for the self to be liked and appreciated in order to feel a sense of esteem. Typical feelings of low self-esteem and a proneness to experienced depression and anxiety are linked to a sense of abandonment and feeling "lost" in the world.

4. The Systemic-Organizational Self-Other Stage

At the systemic-organizational stage the societal point of view is distinguished from the interpersonal one. Multiple mutual perspectives can be integrated into a broader systems view. When the self takes a systemic perspective on relationships, the communication between people is seen as existing on a number of levels simultaneously. Individual relations are interpreted in terms of their place within a larger system of consciously defined roles and rules. System-maintenance of the self becomes the hallmark of Stage 4. The person views the self as having control over his or her destiny. It is also the point, however, at which the person realizes the existence of parts of the self not easily managed by the system's control, i.e., the discovery of unconscious motivations. The societal perspective also brings out strong motivations of achievement, duty, and competition. The limitations of the systemic self-other perspective is the attempt to overcontrol self and other, to reflect on social relations too much in terms of power, role, and status, and to take so many perspectives on self and other that obsessive-compulsive indecision can result. These contradictions are reintegrated into a new whole at the Integrated (5) and Universal (6) self-other perspectives. These are, however, positions not relevant to the adolescent phase.

THE NEED TO INTEGRATE: PSYCHOANALYTIC
AND SOCIAL-DEVELOPMENTAL THEORIES

The Piagetian framework turned into a theory of self provides the psychoanalyst and psychoanalytically informed clinician and teacher with very important concepts. As I have noted, psychoanalysis has provided us with a form of structural analysis of the preoedipal and oedipal years. It has not been able, however, to describe satisfactorily similar developmental dramas and their complete or incomplete resolutions on other developmental stages. It is here that developmental psychology has major potential contributions to make. Each stage is defined by a new and qualitatively different logic. A social-developmental perspective brings us a step closer to a life-span approach, in which we can uncover new patterns which go beyond repetition of the archaic parts of our lives.

Another important contribution of a social-developmental orientation is that it is a cognitively based theory. Because each new level of development creates a new potential for self-observation, it is possible to describe not *the* observing ego, but a variety of ever more complex and encompassing observing selves. Only if the interpretations and clarifications made to the patient or student are consonant with the observing capacity will they be used and generalized over time.

The attempt to expand a theory of the self into a method of understanding clinical phenomena poses a number of interesting questions. The Piagetian transformational model of the self, building on Piaget, does not account for unintegrated earlier vulnerabilities, forms of "regressions," and ego weaknesses. This is not an oversight, but is inherent in the model itself. Thus symptoms and conflict dynamics are interpreted solely as part of a process captured through a stage-developmental perspective.

I have chosen here to concentrate on the borderline patient, to illustrate in the extreme case the need to focus both on early and unresolved vulnerabilities, and on continued development in adolescence and adulthood. It is at this central point of connection that psychoanalytic psychology and social-developmental theory can most strongly influence each other's future. The emergence of earlier conflicts such as the oedipal triangle, which continues to shape the adolescent's object choice (e.g., unattainable others, jealousies, and competitions with a stronger person of the same sex), has been excluded from the Piagetian models described earlier. This demonstrates a lack of understanding, and even more importantly a lack of theoretical constructs that could describe and explain the notion of regression or recapitulation, a return to earlier forms of functioning under stress. Yet the concept of regression, ill-defined in psychoanalysis, is one of the most important developmental ideas, since it relates to unconscious motivation and affective development. The regression induced in treatment, connected to the transference idea, is one of the most powerful tools for the understanding of human development. The application of Piagetian concepts to psychotherapy will be severely limited without these central psychoanalytic insights. But more importantly, these practical omissions can lead us to more general theoretical reorganizations.

In my own work of developing a model of the self, I have found two dimensions to be of central importance. These ideas are elaborated elsewhere (Noam, 1985), but for the purpose of addressing some pertinent clinical and educational questions in adolescence, I will briefly describe them as an interpretive grid for the case material. They are (1) functional phases and structural stages, and (2) biography and transformation.

STAGE AND PHASE

Erikson is not only one of the great pioneers of a life-cycle approach, but also a reference point for the psychoanal-

ytically trained. The comparison of Piaget's theory with
that of Erikson might clarify similarities and differences
between a social-developmental orientation and an epigenetic one.

Although Erikson's model shares the Piagetian principle of invariant universal sequence of development, it
differs on a number of counts: (1) the definition of the
stages of ego development; (2) the view that each stage
is linked to social phases of development, and that each
crisis is connected to an age-specific functional requirement that makes new adaptational modes necessary; (3)
the premise that each of the crises exists from the beginning but has its focal crisis phase and its key potential
for resolution at a given time in the life cycle. This theoretical position allows Erikson to relate old crises to new
ones as well as to retain the important concepts of regression and multiple functioning that psychoanalysis has
made meaningful. If old crises have not been resolved,
they will reemerge at a later stage. This approach generates the possibility, close to my own views, of tracing
thought and action to their precursors for an understanding of clinical and everyday phenomena, and giving us
new avenues to a scientific study of regression.

While Erikson organized his stages of the ego around
ages of development, a structural self theory conceptually
dissociates stages and ages; stages refer to processes and
levels of understanding of self in relationship to others,
while age refers to a culturally organized timetable of
tasks (Noam, Kohlberg, and Snarey, 1983).

This dissociation allows for the study of the relationship between phases and stages: the self perspective described earlier refers to the process and structure of
meaning attributed to self, other, and life task. That there
is coherence to this experience and that it is organized
by core principles which are derived from social-developmental theory makes the concepts of *meaning organization* and reorganization useful. Thus an adolescent

can be organizing adolescence at a variety of different stages of meaning organization (stages). Adolescents can function at stages of the subjective-physical self, the reciprocal-instrumental self, the mutual-inclusive self, and the systemic-organizational self, ranging from pre- to formal operations in Piaget's theory. I view these different meaning organizations within this single life phase as an exciting possibility to subdivide adolescence from a developmental perspective and to explore the concept of "different adolescent worlds." All adolescents, as participants in important social interaction, pushed forward through biological growth, have to face important occupational, educational, and interpersonal shifts which are best described as socially mediated tasks around love, work, and learning. The self system will determine the meaning given these shifts and the ways the person will respond to these demands. The distinction between stage and phase in adolescence can enhance our understanding of different adolescent worlds. For this reason, I chose adolescent borderline cases, rather than patients at different ages. Figure 23.1 shows the meaning organization in relationship to life tasks as central dimensions of the developing self. The understanding brought to the phasic tasks is one side of the self dynamic; the other consists of the new life tasks, such as intimacy in adolescence requiring new and more complex ways of structuring reality. (Masterson's chart shown earlier is of limited value since it only addresses the *life task* aspect of life span development.)

BIOGRAPHY AND TRANSFORMATION

When we distinguish adolescence as a phase from the underlying self perspectives, we can concurrently interpret the highest level of social and cognitive functioning.

DIMENSIONS OF THE DEVELOPING SELF

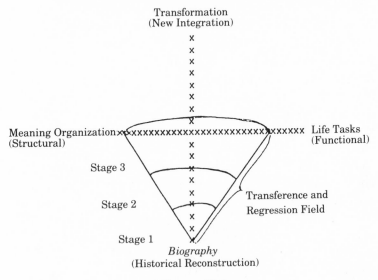

Figure 23.1

This in turn provides us with the opportunity to distinguish another set of dimensions: biography and transformation.

Biography refers to those aspects of the person's history and psychological adaptation which point to unresolved conflicts in the past and to the ways in which past experiences shape present-day thinking, feeling, and action. It is an attempt at understanding the repetition compulsion in which the person goes back to those parts of the past not worked through and repeats them. These repetitions have both an adaptive and maladaptive side. On the adaptive side, our "lawful regressions" are continuous efforts to subsume earlier events and less developed ways of being in the world into the more complex structures which can best be described through the social-developmental self. These returns to earlier forms and times also contribute to the more creative ways in which people link adolescence and adulthood with childhood, the intrapsychic aspect of family tradition, and the history of important objects which continue to be guideposts in a person's life. The maladaptive side of repetition and recapitulation is known to most psychotherapists: the person is condemned to repeat the self-destructive and painful patterns of the past until they are reworked. Borderline pathology is partly shaped by these unresolved aspects of a person's history, as was described in the earlier part of this chapter. The unresolved separation-individuation phase, the first one in the person's life, creates vulnerabilities and motivational maps which continue to influence (at times even to take over) a person's adolescence and adult experience. The other side of the vertical in Figure 23.1, transformation of the self, points to the continued developmental pattern of the self and the system which "does" the integrating, the working through of earlier conflicts, and the self-observation. Regression is the field between the transforming self's highest forms of organization and the unresolved conflicts. Figure 23.1 shows the regression or transference fields which differ depending on the person's most advanced self system. (The general theory has been elaborated in a variety of papers [e.g., Noam, 1988a,b].)In the case of the borderline patient, the return is usually to the earlier levels of development described in detail by Margaret Mahler. But in the course of treatment, *all* developmental positions, from the earliest to those of the present day, become part of the therapeutic relationship. The cases to be discussed will show that these early separation-individuation vulnerabilities are experienced and worked out differently at different stages of development. I will develop the clinical and educational themes from the cases, so that the implications for the clinician and teacher of the borderline student come to life. Though each person I worked with confirmed the model, each individual life *was* its own narrative, *was* its own history, more powerful, creative, and hidden than any heuristic could uncover.

EDUCATIONAL DIMENSIONS

I will describe in detail the clinical aspects of borderline psychopathology in adolescence because the clinician's in-depth understanding of problems, their causes, and their change patterns can help the teacher in addressing some basic educational questions. By and large, the therapist has traditionally been too uninvolved in understanding the educational process and the role of the teacher. I hope that a life span developmental perspective can add to a bridge between the clinical and educational worlds. An overarching developmental framework speaks to both pathology and education, and sees the teacher and psychotherapist as agents of change who act "in the best interest of the child." That both teacher and therapist are implicit developmentalists is an underlying assumption shared by psychoanalysis and clinical-developmental psychology. The teacher is the provider of social experiences around a set of goals (achievement of skills, manipulation of tools, and enhancement of a work-oriented future), but since learning consists of the interaction between the developing organisms in relationship with the body of knowledge in the world, the most basic aspects of learning are developmental in nature. In this regard, learning is transformation of psychological structures, reconstructed in the Piagetian tradition through the stages and their transitions of levels of social intelligence.

The therapist also provides a set of social experiences around a set of goals, only these are quite different in nature. Learning in therapy is about reflection on behavior, about the overcoming of symptoms, and the resolution of interpersonal problems. In the psychoanalytic tradition the focus of this learning is the establishment and recognition of an important relationship in which earlier problems are reenacted. In this regard the new experience of relationship and the new form of reflection potentially lead to transformations of the self's relationship with itself, which again can partially be captured by underlying developmental progress addressed by a Piagetian perspective.

Anna Freud's little-known paper on psychoanalysis and education published in the *Harvard Educational Review* (A. Freud, 1952) can be viewed as cautionary remarks to the educator who has incorporated psychoanalytic concepts. Anna Freud criticizes the emerging psychodynamic practices of teachers and argues that the role of the school is to help a child overcome the regressive element of the oedipal conflict with a goal of concentrating on new tasks. These basic learning tasks require the ability to repress impulses and to distinguish between settings in which emotional expression is appropriate and those in which it has to be put aside. The teacher who confuses the classroom with a group therapy setting encourages intense psychological conflicts and the transfer of sibling rivalries and oedipal conflict from the family into the school. Anna Freud's clear and characteristically uncompromising position might surprise the psychoanalytically oriented teacher, but is one of the logical expression of the psychoanalytic interpretation of child development.

In a thoughtful analysis of psychoanalytic pedagogy written in 1939, Michael Balint states that a phase of psychoanalytic critique of educational practice was followed by a recognition that there was no positive psychoanalytic theory of education. He attributes this fact, almost as true today as it was in his lifetime, to an overemphasis in education on superego factors (shame, morals, discipline, cleanliness, and so on). Balint argues that both ego psychology and pedagogy in psychoanalysis were dominated by the superego analyses. He suggests that education and psychoanalysis need a true ego theory. He defines learning as: "Lernen heisst im ursprunglichen Sinn erfahren werden, d.h. das Ich bereichern und entwickeln" ("Learning means in its original form to be experienced, i.e., to enrich and develop the I [ego]"). The strong and exploring ego should be the goal in psychoanalysis and education. He states, "One has in my opinion focused too much attention in recent times on the early developmental stages of the ego, the never observed origins of ego formation. I believe the time has come where we should study more precisely the daily observable ego changes" (p. 102). Nowhere else could a clinical-developmental analysis of psychoanalytic and Piagetian make-up contribute more and so enrich the clinical and educational discussions.

From the perspective presented here, Anna Freud's and Michael Balint's ideas continue to be relevant, but in a new fashion: each new developmental position requires a different form of task orientation and a different rationale for sublimating intense emotional states that usually emerge in the family context. The teacher and student engage in intense and important interactions. This relationship needs to be reflected upon with emotionally healthy and, even more importantly, with disturbed adolescents such as the group I will describe here. Each new developmental position brings with it new struggles around repression and sublimation, requires new strategies of conflict resolution and different forms of explanation to the student about the boundaries of the relationship. Without a significant relationship there is no lasting learning process.

The teacher's provision of learning materials and support of the developmental progress requires knowledge about the emergence of the unintegrated parts of the self and the transformational capacities of the person.

SOCIAL-DEVELOPMENTAL CONTRIBUTIONS TO THE BORDERLINE PERSONALITY DISORDERS—EDUCATIONAL IMPLICATIONS

I will now describe the three groups[3] of borderline adolescents by proceeding from the least advanced position, "the subjective-physical borderline patient," to the next developmental level, the "reciprocal-instrumental borderline patient," and finally to the "mutual-inclusive borderline patient."[4] At each stage the separation and individuation fears take a different form, a different narrative with its own specific requirements for text analysis. This does not imply that earlier and more primitive breakthroughs do not exist. Anyone who has worked with borderline patients in a clinical or educational setting knows about the fluctuations in ego states, the short psychotic episodes, the overdetermined rage reactions. I want to show, however, that even with such a confusing and diverse clinical group, a clinical-developmental model can add to our theoretical and practical understanding. As mentioned before, my model does not assume that all thought, feeling, and action is regulated by the highest stage of organization a person has achieved.

The patients have a number of other features in common—all have been hospitalized and were followed by me in evaluation or intensive psychotherapy. I chose this form of case presentation, although it introduces a number of biases due to the intense clinical relationships

[3]We know only of one other attempt to apply a Piagetian model to the study of borderline personality disorders (Weinberger, 1978). He proposes that borderline adults are preoperational thinkers. We feel that he has accepted the premise that all borderline patients are arrested "early." To translate orality into preoperational thought contributes to our understanding but loses the transformational character of thought throughout life.

[4]There is, however, no conceptual reason to assume a priori that borderline disturbances could not exist beyond Stage 3 and the stages three to four transition. Only future empirical work in this area can clarify the relationship between more advanced stages of the self and borderline disorders.

which are not primarily geared toward research goals because I was able to make very important observations during the course of the work. Ongoing research will establish the three groups more rigorously. The clinical method presents a certain advantage by enabling me to observe my own thoughts, feelings, and behaviors triggered in my intense work (three to four sessions a week). I learned about the patient's future hopes, present despairs, and past disappointments in ways no research interview could ever capture. The slow-moving process of a relationship that brings out past and present is an ideal ground to make observations about the developing person. For purposes of this discussion, I reviewed carefully the educational progress of these patients as it was described in the medical records and as it emerged in the treatment. Table 23.3 can provide an overview of the different developmental levels of the borderline adolescent and the educational implications expanded on within the text.

THREE CASE STUDIES: THREE LEVELS OF BORDERLINE DISORDER

THE SUBJECTIVE-PHYSICAL BORDERLINE PATIENT: DANIEL

Daniel was hospitalized at a major psychiatric hospital in the northeast. He was then fourteen years old, a son of Italian parents, a brother to a five, a seven, and a twenty-year-old sister. Daniel was a chubby, pre-adolescent-looking boy who had been in intensive, individual psychotherapy for treatment of his severe depression, school phobia, and psychosomatic milk allergy. The referral to the intensive adolescent and family treatment center was made by his psychiatrist because he felt that Daniel's problems were very strongly related to unresolved family difficulties and because his condition was deteriorating.

The hospitalization, as one would expect, was a major trauma for Daniel and his family. The fact that he was admitted to an adolescent and family treatment center was a relief to his family, though. In contrast to most other families with hospitalized adolescents, this family felt that they as a group needed help, though Daniel was seen as their problem member, the identified patient.

In the first phase of psychotherapy, Daniel felt very threatened by the closeness and the intimacy of the setting; illustratively, he wore a green T-shirt that covered his body from nose to toes. Even that protection, however, was insufficient. Quite frequently Daniel would hide behind a big chair pointing its four legs at me like guns. He seemed threatened by what he perceived as my wish to control him and to guide his mind and felt persecuted by the staff and by me. Whenever he appeared to experience closeness, he would immediately become worried about homosexuality and death.

Daniel had begun to enter what Masterson calls "the testing-out phase" of treatment. He wanted to leave the hospital and often ran impulsively to his parents without hospital permission, knowing that his parents would take him to dinner in a good restaurant. They, too, as was discovered in family and couples and multiple family therapy, were enraged at the treatment team, and tried to split the "good" and giving workers from the "bad" and withholding ones. Although relieved that they had found a place in which Daniel was taken care of, the family suffered greatly from the separation. Since time—especially the connection between past, present, and future—was a major difficulty for this family, the present state of separation was seen as final. Thus, Daniel was not only acting out his own anxieties but also those of his parents. Any attempt by Daniel to settle down in the center led to signals of disapproval, for he was then seen

TABLE 23.3
Borderline Disorders in Life-Span Perspective

Borderline Adolescent	Shape of Problems	Educational Implications
The Subjective-Physical-Borderline Adolescent	Physicalist expressions of separation fears. No system to interpret anxieties as psychological. Key problem: impulsive expression of conflict—not preplanned manipulation. Need authority to curb action. No understanding of motivational connections, self and other taken at "face value."	Impulsivity, inability to concentrate, hyperactivity require concrete tasks, frequent one-to-one supervision, focus on impulse control and small tasks which slowly help in the process of delaying gratification and attend to goal-oriented activities.
The Reciprocal-Instrumental-Borderline Adolescent	Concrete interpretation of problems trying to get "what I want," preplanned manipulations, power struggles over who is in control. Impulsivity has explosive quality (rather than tantrum) and is connected with self-protective stance. Usually feels victimized, little *felt* anxiety and depression. It's others' fault.	Teacher-student power struggles. Challenge of authority. Need to reduce risk of breakdown of relationship by supporting peer-interaction, group learning, and practicum experience. These activities are geared toward combining self-control with emerging trust in adults and peers alike.

The Mutual-Inclusive-Borderline Adolescent

Psychologic reality of others experienced on their terms. Self can experience itself through the eyes of others. Self merges into other and experiences its loss when separation occurs. This is due to self definition as relational. Anger and other differentiating feeling cannot be tolerated because of experience of self-hate and abandonment as result.

Teacher needs to accept need for strong relationship and know about the danger of hypersensitivity and feelings of rejection. Support task orientation in one-to-one and support in peer group ties. Help in containing feelings to be able to focus.

as a family betrayer, breaking the bonds of family loyalty. On the other hand, the family had made it clear that a return was not an avenue open to Daniel or themselves. After their expensive dinners, Daniel was brought back to the hospital and "handed over" to the staff. The staff, in turn, was criticized for not having ensured that Daniel couldn't leave this open-door unit.

Daniel escalated his behavior during these months of treatment and fluctuated in individual therapy; moments of appreciation for the attention and help that he was receiving were interspersed with long spans of time in which he was furious, bored, covertly sadistic, and incoherent. He needed very structured interview sessions and was able to respond only in very short units of thought. He saw the therapist as judgmental, the way he also saw his parents. He externalized his fears of being rejected by the group to a hatred of the group. Whenever treatment progressed to a point at which he became in closer touch with his underlying sense of desperation, his fears became so intolerable that he had to run away from the place that "caused" his problems. Psychological well-being was attached to the physical space; if one has painful feelings at the treatment center, then one has to change settings and the problems will disappear.

The testing-out phase ended with something of a personal crisis: Daniel had not received the privileges to leave the hospital grounds, but his family and he had made plans to go on an important visit to Chicago. This confrontation between the unit, the therapists, and the family led to the parents' decision that Daniel was to stay in the hospital. That afternoon, after the parents had told him about their decision, he cried bitterly about the first real acknowledgment of a process of separation that was occurring within the family. Daniel came to his therapy appointment feeling sad, but at the same time relieved. It was the first time that I had heard an ambivalent statement of acknowledgment from him. He said that he hated to stay in the hospital, but that at the same time his parents had finally made a decision that they wanted him to be in the hospital. Now, he said, he could begin with *his* work.

Daniel's family unconsciously recognized this first and major achievement of separation and individuation by giving him a watch as a present. When asked about the meaning of this gift, Daniel responded: "Now I am in charge of my own time. Before I did not want that. Whenever I wanted to be sure my parents, my parents . . . that I could talk to them, I asked what time it is. You can't ask people what the weather is like every five minutes, but time changes all the time!"

Daniel began to translate the new sense of responsibility into other areas of his life. He became a good student at the hospital school and slowly moved into the group of adolescents that he had detested earlier.

Daniel focused in therapy on work competency, got a job at a local restaurant, and decided that he wanted to become a restaurant owner and a cook. After a year of hospitalization in which he could work through aspects of the "abandonment depression," give up much of the self-destructive behavior, build a better inner structure which protected him from unmanageable impulses and affect, Daniel was discharged. He had gained enough inner separateness from his parents, siblings, therapist, and peers that relationships felt less threatening and engulfing.

At the first-person self-perspective, inner and outer reality is experienced in physical terms. Thus Daniel did not realize that outer actions could reveal inner feelings. When he lost his privileges, always shortly before the weekend, members of the treatment staff suggested to him that he might be getting into trouble, so that he would not be allowed to go home. He looked at them in utter despair, since he had never in his life heard anything so "ridiculous." At this level of self-development, motives are taken at face value, the unconscious has not yet been uncovered, and the concept of self-deception is not part of the person's lexicon. At this social perspective, the person is lacking the capacity to control and distance himself from the impulses that guide his behavior. Daniel was at the mercy of intense feelings of annihilation without the security of adults to control them. Daniel's fears and thoughts were the real events in the world: his fears of accidents were experienced by him as if they had in fact taken place. Since other people were not seen as having a mind of their own, his own thoughts were seen as open to the world and readable by the therapist. Thus, protection from overwhelming adults was found only through physical hiding or running away. Given Daniel's age, it is quite remarkable that he was still functioning on a level of self-organization typical of children around the age of six. The case illustrates the importance of subdividing age and stage, or, as I have earlier described, the distinction between phase (functional tasks) and stage (meaning organization). But even with this massive arrest, his intense fantasies of death and explosion at any important point of separation cannot be explained from within the social-developmental level alone. These fears point to the *replay* of separation-individuation fears from an earlier era, within the physicalist position of stage 1. Not every person at that level experiences separations as final and avoids self-assertion because of the danger of separation and annihilation. The expression of boundary (hiding behind a chair), the impulsive expression of desires and anxieties without understanding their symbolic value point to a physicalist expression of the separation-individuation fears. The interpretation of the hospitalization as a final separation of the family and the impulsive running between family and hospital also support this position. One can, however, also interpret Daniel's behavior as an attempt at resolving these fears within a physical-social developmental level. Most regressive phenomena are attempts to *resolve* them, and the area in which this happens is the transforming self. Daniel's change during the year-long hospitalization can be traced as a transition from the physical self-perspective to the instrumental one. His impulsive behavior got *worse* when we look at the dangerous results, but it can be viewed as an attempt to gain control by moving from unreflective impulsivity to preplanned manipulation. That the transition did not only lead to a more complex pathology at a new developmental level can be attributed to the skill of the treatment staff and the partial cooperation of patient and family. In the entry to the reciprocal-instrumental level Daniel had found more adaptive ways of dealing with a new set of problems: work, relationships, and school.

Educational Implications

When Daniel came to the hospital, I was able to observe the ways in which he made use of the school. He continued his pattern of anxiously avoiding any school tasks and whenever possible skipping school. No loss of privileges could convince him that school was an important institution relevant to his future, and that he needed to work and learn. Assignments were left undone even though he was ambitious and ashamed enough to try to hide the fact that he did not know how to solve the problems at hand. It was only after the changes that occurred in the treatment when the family allowed for more separation that Daniel changed his attitudes toward work and school. Rapidly after the separation occurred, his grades went up dramatically from F's to B's. The hospital's school provided important experiences which, only then, was Daniel able to use. He reported that he could concentrate in most subjects except math, which continued to be a problem because he remained convinced that he was not smart enough to do the work. The individualized tutoring

approach together with small group activities which were
not geared toward competitive achievement provided new
opportunities for Daniel to experience himself as mastering tasks and receiving important positive feedback.
That this feedback was behavioral in nature and concrete
(written up in weekly reports together with points he
could receive) made it possible for Daniel to connect his
behaviors with direct experiences of success. Much to the
amusement of the other treatment staff, in my work with
Daniel we began to chart as a ritual the weekly progress
and regress of Daniel's school achievement. In his free
time Daniel charted the weeks and brought in the concrete reflections of his week's work in different subjects.
While he had always blamed all disappointments and
failures on the blatant omissions and stupidities of the
teachers, he began to observe his own part in the process
of learning. These charts led to many discussions in therapy about Daniel's special skills, his weaknesses, and his
future aspirations. The mixture of behavioral orientation
with psychodynamic reflection (at least in the mind of
the therapist) provided experiences consonant with the
level of understanding of self and other at which Daniel
had begun to operate. This transition led to a new level
of concentration and impulse and motor control, which
are really the prerequisites for successful learning. This
new stage was also paralleled by a new work ethic in
which Daniel began to work toward the goal of earning
money. The teacher too allied herself with this important
goal. This alliance is especially important when, as in
Daniel's case, the goal of learning is connected with the
mastery of new independence from authority figures and
with ways to internalize the rules set by adults into generalized and more internalized rules systems. The sublimation of important urges, needs, and impulses into
delay of gratification, mastery, and skill provides one of
the important and lasting developmental transitions in
the lifelong transformation of the self.

Daniel's developmental shift brings us to the level at which Richard was operating when he was hospitalized in the same institution. The description of his problems will show that a higher developmental level does not guarantee better school adaptation, but provides new challenges in learning and in the relationship between student and teacher. The hope, however, is that, in the developmental transformation, a shift toward better coping much like in Daniel's case can be achieved.

THE INSTRUMENTAL-BORDERLINE PATIENT: RICHARD

Richard, a fourteen-year-old adolescent, was admitted to a psychiatric hospital by a juvenile court waiting for a recommendation from the hospital before deciding his case. The parents had asked the court to intervene since they could not control his "acting-out behavior at home." He was frequently truant from school, ran away from home on several occasions, was involved in drug and alcohol abuse, and had threatened his parents on numerous occasions.

Richard was the second of two sons of a father who was a wealthy lawyer and a mother who was a teacher. Richard described problems with his parents as long as he could remember. He felt they never understood him, were belligerent toward him, and tried to enforce inappropriate rules at home. The major problems occurred when his brother was found to have an incurable illness and his grandmother died. Richard, eleven at the time, was very depressed and scraped his wrist and hurt himself with a knife. He described his father as a weak man and his mother as cold, manipulative, and aggressive. He remembered with pride his physical fights with his father.

During the course of the hospitalization, Richard

wanted to return home on his parents' terms, if they would retract the court petition. To the treatment staff, the proposal seemed like a way to negotiate himself out of the hospital more than a genuine change of direction. Richard refused to talk about himself and his parents in detail, so that most of the information came from observation in family therapy which he had begun to attend with interest. Richard felt close only to the family dog. He became very sad when he described his relationship with *his* dog, whom he missed greatly. "She is the only one who really is happy when I come home." He often shared his room with her and took her on long walks. Richard, however, had many friends and found it easy to make new ones. But they found pleasure mainly in the shared distribution and consumption of drugs and alcohol: "We go out, have fun, and get high." He liked to talk about one friend, who was different; "He is someone who is really there when you need him, and I am there for him." The friend left the area and Richard missed him. Because his mother disapproved of this friend, Richard would make occasional phone calls to him only in secret.

Although he did well academically, Richard never liked school very much and began to stay away frequently. He rarely cooperated with the teachers and did not develop any real plans for the future.

I term Richard's orientation *reciprocal-instrumental* because it connotes a second level of self-perspective more complex than Daniel's subjective-physicalistic level. Richard shares with the subjective-physical stage the "externalized" and concrete interpretation of self and social reality. The subjective-physical orientation has been transformed, however, into a higher order system which Kegan (1982) calls the impulse over time—the need system. The reciprocal-instrumental borderline patient can usually curb and control immediate impulses and act in a more planned fashion. Associated with this increased impulse control is the ability to view oneself and others at what Selman (1980) calls the second-person perspective-taking level. Individuals at this cognitive level are able mentally to leave the self and view their thoughts and actions through this outside perspective. This capacity to self-reflect provides the individuals with a more constant sense of themselves over time than was evident in the subjective-physical orientation. However, the reciprocal-instrumental borderline patient is less complexly organized at the interpersonal level. The individual at the second-person perspective-taking level is unable to integrate his needs with those of others, resulting in a self-protective (Loevinger, 1976) or nonmutually oriented stance. Kohlberg's description of the "I scratch your back, you scratch my back" morality captures this social perspective. It is in the transition to the interpersonal level that the self in its core self-definition becomes more mutual. The ways in which the separation-individuation concerns reemerge are dramatically different when compared to Daniel. Richard's needs for closeness expressed itself in rage against his parents ("I am going to kill them") and a sense of frustration that "they don't understand, anyway." His fear of abandonment remained largely unconscious, although he was always sure people would not care and took the parents' appeal to the court as the last sign. Only in the relationships with his brother and friend was he able to express the wish to be close and be taken care of. But his experience was that they, too, became ill or left him. The only one he could really turn to was his dog, a stable and unthreatening object. In Richard's case the fear of engulfment was much more visible, the need to distance himself, to be isolated and removed and not to trust any adult. He was afraid adults would take over and he would have to submit. While he was not aware that this could have also been a wish, he consciously struggled for independence from the family, but in ways that would re-create the child's fantasies of running away and being brought home (by the courts).

Richard could not see any use in our meetings; he came because he had to. It was part of required activities. He would lose privileges if he did not come to therapy. As a result, he tried to find ways to avoid coming and not lose privileges; for example, by becoming ill just before our therapy hour and getting well soon thereafter. The initial period of therapy was actually quite positive. He described in greater detail, with much focus on the concrete actions, what he most liked to do and why he hated the hospital, parents, and all other authorities. While he could not understand what talking would do to help him, he began to see me as an ally against the other authorities. He did not consider our meetings therapeutic since he did not feel that he should be in the hospital in the first place. His definition of his problem was that he was getting in trouble with the law and his parents and it was their inflexibility that led to this "punishment." Richard stated a number of times that he would plan an escape, if there was nothing in the hospitalization for him. However, he wanted the hospital's protection from the judges. Given the choice between a psychiatric institution and a setting for juvenile delinquents, he preferred the "plush" grounds of an institution "with class." As he saw it, our meetings were negotiations, with an implicit deal in which I was to help him in the legal actions.

It is here that in almost all the cases with acting out borderline patients the therapy breaks down—in the initial implicit or explicit contract. The relationship is defined as "helping me out." If that does not occur, but limit setting and exploration set in, then the power struggles which are the hallmark of the acting out adolescent are soon to follow. If the patient has a choice, he stops coming; if the therapist has a choice, he usually stops performing the services. Usually the break-up of the relationship occurs with the adolescent storming out. The calmer, yet equally angry therapist labels the patient as primitive. This process is repeatedly observable in the supervision of trainees. Ready to do insight-oriented psychotherapy after reading much psychoanalytic literature, they are confronted with a reciprocal-instrumental borderline patient. They ask psychologically oriented questions that go far beyond the level of self understanding of patients at this level. The focus soon shifts into a control struggle which leaves the therapist helpless and hopeless. It is problematic to call this behavior resistant on the part of the patient, since the patient usually follows his basic understanding of the situation and applies his usual forms of coping. In other words, the patient is teaching the organization of his experience to the therapist. If a breakdown of the therapy does not occur, usually because the adolescents are forced to continue and the trainees force themselves to continue, a new level of compromise is found. The therapist and patient are seen walking together to the cafeteria and talking as they eat. This is experienced by both as a compromise; both share in an activity which is a comfort to each. Often these activities are expanded into sports activities which become very useful ways to build a relationship.

Therapy is not only about helping a person adapt within a given psychosocial stage. Each new level of self and interpersonal development brings a possibility for the reworking of past vulnerabilities and their integration into a new self system. This integrating focus is especially difficult at the reciprocal-instrumental level since the therapist has to hold on to a biographical view of the person while the patient is concretely embedded in the present and the near past. The therapist has to store much information and to become the "biographical keeper" of the relationship. As history is written in the relationship (having done things together) and a new self-complexity emerges, the joint experience will be of invaluable help to the patient, especially in terms of confronting inevitable conflicts in intimate relationships. In the later struggle around the actual ideological creation of the self through the identity crisis, the new integration will be based on the internalization of this biographical point of view.

Educational Implications—Richard

Richard had severe educational problems but they were different in shape from those of Daniel. For Richard the problem did not pose itself as an inability to curb impulses of the moment, to understand that the school was an important part of preparing for a future. Thus one would not expect the same form of attention-deficit problem with which Daniel had to struggle. As with Daniel, separation problems with the family were at the forefront of the psychopathology and also encompassed the work in school. But in Richard's case, the school problems revolved around preplanned attempts to undercut the authority of the teachers and the school as an institution, much like, and maybe even in delegation, of the parental authority that he was so disappointed in. These authority struggles led to the participation in a counterculture of drugs and violence which used the home as a refuge from school in a very different way: to be with peers who are "like me" and who have similar wishes to disobey the authority of the people who are "not like me." This struggle makes a smooth integration into the school impossible, especially since at this level of development the student continuously feels manipulated, "pushed around and treated unfairly." Since there is not yet an ability to understand both the self and the teacher on their own grounds, decentered, and through the eyes of a third person, each intervention of authority, especially if it is not seen as of direct benefit, is interpreted as a harmful and self-interested activity. What is left for Richard to do is to fight the system and then to retreat when it becomes clear that the system is ultimately stronger. At that point, the retreat into the peer group with its orientation toward pleasure connected with breaking the law seems like an adequate resolution. Much like the problem that the therapist encounters in treating these adolescents, the teacher is faced with an impossible situation: he is tested and will be seen as a friend "if he helps me get what I want." If, however, he asserts the authority of an adult who is part of the school system and enforces rules, "he is my enemy and has to be fought." In both cases, the learning process breaks down: if the teacher permissively seduces the adolescent, he has given up his role as a model and as an authority figure who teaches skills, knowledge, and interpretive schemes. If he rigidly follows the regulation of the school, he will not be able to engage in a relationship of trust and respect which is so important to any learning. What is the way out of this dilemma? Important for the learning process is the recognition of the teacher that the student needs a great deal of autonomy to pursue his goals. The teacher should avoid wherever possible the traps of the power struggle which cause the student to feel victimized and result in a breakdown of communication, since the student feels victimized. Autonomy is best enhanced by that which works least in the position Daniel was in: to help the establishment of the peer culture within the classroom in which the students can learn from each other and in which the teacher can work through the group to reach the individual. Discussions about fairness and rules within the classroom have proven very successful in the Kohlberg tradition (Kohlberg, 1985). In addition the teacher should try to see himself much like the therapist, as a consultant to the educational problems of the student. What are the student's educational goals? How can he be helped by the teacher to reach those goals? Creative and innovative ways of learning within practicum settings in which the student can learn through identification with adults who are somewhat outside the traditional hierarchy are needed to support the more traditional student-teacher

role. Most important is the attempt to work against the
sense of victimization that the student suffers and to
counterbalance it early through work and learning experiences that have a direct immediate value. It is here
that grades should be replaced by other forms of achievement review more rational and comprehensible to the
student. While Daniel needed the point system in order
to experience the success of concentration and delay,
Richard needed to be helped to develop relations with
peers and adults and to begin to see learning as an interpersonal activity which bears the fruits of a task
shared, of a vision that connects, and of knowledge which
supports. That this process is at the same time relevant
to both the processes of psychotherapy and learning
should have become clear from the case description. The
ideas presented here are most difficult to implement because of the difficulties the teacher encounters as part of
the school system when trying to experiment with new
and hence suspect methods. There are, however, many
examples of school systems that have allowed for these
principles to be implemented. Ultimately the teacher
must be a model for the student, showing that there are
possibilities within the system for combining courage and
caution in the process of dealing with seemingly un-
bending and intolerant institutions. If the teacher is only
a passive tool in the machine of regulations, he cannot
expect to be a model for the students who are trying to
find ways of breaking with tradition, of leaving the important authority figures of the past and experimenting
with new ways.

THE MUTUAL-INCLUSIVE BORDERLINE
PATIENT: DENISE

Denise was fifteen-years-old when she was admitted to
an adolescent psychiatric treatment unit following a suicide attempt.

Six months prior to the suicide attempt, Denise's parents had separated. Her mother and father had argued often, with Denise taking the role of mediator. Following the separation, Denise isolated herself socially and withdrew from friends. At home alone during the evenings, she sat in the basement of the house. She was afraid of the sounds made by the tenants in the apartment above, whom she had never met. It was at such times and in this setting that Denise first began to think about killing herself.

Denise had anxiety attacks and felt she "was losing herself" after her father left the house. She began drinking while alone in the apartment in an attempt to dull her pain. She also felt a deep yearning for someone "who knew just how I felt." She said that she felt "miserable all the time" during this period and began to feel that "it would never stop." Her fantasied solution, a savior-prince, had not appeared and she doubted that such a person would ever save her.

Denise's response to a desperate need for acceptance by others, combined with almost constant anxiety and despair, was to drink the remainder of a bottle of her mother's vodka, combined with a large dose of tranquilizers. She did this approximately one half hour before her mother's return home from a visit with a male friend. When asked why she did so she replied, "telling with words wasn't enough."

This was a planned suicide attempt with a reasonable chance of discovery by her mother, since Denise knew approximately the time she might expect her mother to return home. However, Denise did not know exactly how lethal this overdose could be, and commented later that she would "rather be dead than to go on feeling miserable."

Denise has reached the third level of social development. She can step outside her own perspective and view herself and "the self" through the eyes of a third person.

A mutual-inclusive organization of relationship creates intimacy and the definition of self as interpersonal. Thoughts and feelings are shared within relationships which are seen as ongoing and developing. Denise developed a more complex self organization than Richard (and of course than Daniel), even though there were no age, class, or intelligence differences between the three adolescents. Her ability to understand and coordinate the psychological reality of others on their terms and to view herself from their perspectives opened the way for true empathy. She was depressed about the break-up of her parents' marriage, "understood" the father's yearnings for the mother (and shared them), and respected the mother's need for a new life with someone she could "really love." In each of these *relationships* her self was located—which also created an important vulnerability. Anger and other differentiating feelings could not be tolerated because the distance was experienced as a loss of self (one could call this a "loss of mirror" at a later developmental stage than Kohut focused on). The break-up of the parents became a dissolution of self and a wish to kill herself. This is a frequent danger with adolescents (and adults) at the mutual-inclusive level who are dealing with separations from significant others. The loss of the mirroring other leads to grave self-doubts and self-hate. The anger cannot be expressed toward the loved object and turns against the self.

Denise became strongly engaged in therapy. The appointments with me were an important part of her life in the hospital. She talked easily about her disappointments and the many rejections she experienced and cried in most of our meetings. She frequently wanted to know what I thought about her situation and the decisions she had to make (e.g., whether to live with her father or her mother). Her helplessness paired with her hypervigilance around rejection made it necessary to spend much time discussing the reasons I would not make the decisions for her. She often interpreted my rejection of her wish as a sign of lack of interest, withdrew into herself, fell into a silence, and became convinced I would not be interested in meeting with her again. It took much patient and empathic work, encompassing both her need to experience intimacy with me as submitting to my "all-knowing powers" and her need to explore separateness. That she could begin to feel more separate after many months of treatment without retreating into depression (i.e., "basement") strengthened our relationship. Eventually Denise began to see patterns and develop observational skills in her therapy.

There are few therapeutic models for the borderline adolescent at the third level of self-development. The experience of self through the eyes of other is usually interpreted as "early pathology," yet the rapid progress these patients make in a good therapeutic relationship puzzles the therapist who is focusing on early deprivation and primitive merging. The attempts at self-observation and self-reflection are often experienced as cold and analytic, especially when they are geared toward a self system that *can* observe the patterns and meanings of relating: this observing self emerges only in the transition from the mutual-inclusive perspective, which began in Denise's case after almost eight months of treatment. The mixture of supportive therapy and insight orientation which is appropriate to the self system (i.e., observation of the fluctuations of the feelings and thoughts *in* the important relationships of the patient including the therapist) requires a further understanding of the self's transformational capacities in adolescence and adulthood. But again, the early and recurring themes of separation, abandonment, and depression create a life narrative in which the earlier fears resurface within the context of the later self. The focus on biography and meaning organization as shown in Table 23.2 give this tension a transformational direction in which the self integrates itself within a more complex and encompassing structure.

Educational Implications: Denise

We have seen that Daniel needed help in curbing his impulses and in beginning to develop an orientation toward learning which went beyond the moment and created moments over time, namely dispositions, goals, and aspirations. These dispositions could help him free himself from external enmeshment with the family, and also its internal counterpart the enmeshment with his anxieties, those thoughts and feelings which hinder the concentrated orientation toward the world of skills and mastery. For Richard the main problem revolved around his feelings of being manipulated by the authority of teacher and school and the need to help him create relationships with peers and adults alike which could help him in the transition toward an interpersonal orientation of cooperation and trust. For Denise the educational implications are quite different. She views herself through the eyes of others, especially close friends and her peer group and is continuously concerned with how other people might see her. She has removed herself from others because she could not tolerate the disappointment and confusion that came with two sets of expectations and self views which were diametrically opposed: that of her mother who hurt her father and that of her father who felt abandoned by her mother. She could understand both positions but because the core of her self definition resided in those relationships, she began to experience the loss of each parent and herself. Retreating from school and friends she was trying to get comfort through drinking. Denise was endangered; it was only the seriousness with which she contemplated suicide that led to her hospitalization. Hospitalization had become necessary because the school and the home were not able to provide the external structure she needed. The focus of the hospitalization was her wish (and that of her father and maybe even of the whole family) to bring the parents together through her treatment. But even though the school, the teachers, and the learning process were not central to the patient, it might be important to analyze what their roles were in the process of recovery and how the teachers could help this adolescent in ways that were consonant with her developmental position.

Denise's educational problems were also ones of concentration, but she differed dramatically in the school setting from patients such as Daniel and Richard since she did not share the temper tantrums or the premeditated manipulations and escapes. Instead, she retreated into a world of sadness and despair in which she thought of the important relationships in her life and the disappointment she was experiencing. Metaphorically speaking, she brought her basement to the school. It was an important step forward that she had to leave the alcohol at home. The teachers took on the task of setting limits which the parents were not able to provide. On the other hand, Denise's inability to "drown her sadness" put a great burden on the teacher and the classroom. Denise's need to be held was great even though she communicated on a conscious level the wish to be alone and the belief that "no one could help her anyway." Given Denise's wish to indulge in her sad experiences, it would have been easy for the teacher to enter the world of relationships and intimacies in fantasy and reality. By doing so, the teacher would have responded to a strong wish, but would probably have lost the ability to fulfill the teaching functions. Denise wanted to avoid breaking away from her anxieties and sadness and needed to be shown that even under difficult circumstances when others were suffering she could perform and orient herself to learning without abandoning them or being abandoned.

Given the mutual-inclusive self-perspective, Denise

was not a behavior problem in the traditional sense; she could always understand the other side and needed to be accepted and loved by the teacher. Thus it was important to deal with her often in a one-to-one context which addressed her relationship needs without making the relationship itself the center: it was the schoolwork that provided the joint focus and taught her that relationships can also be the vehicle toward an orientation outside the self and its intimates. Because Denise was easily hurt, the teacher had to guide her cautiously and keep her engaged. The hardest part in Denise's learning process was to help her integrate herself into the peer group which she saw as a hostile environment. She preferred developing a close relationship with another student and to share experiences with her through long letters and talks.

The movement beyond this position which was enhanced by the separation from her parents, her therapy, and the subsequent freeing from the conflicts that had led to the hospitalization, was observable over time. The transition involved more reflection about the ways in which she was bound into the needs and wishes of others, precluding her own ways of protecting herself. In this transition, which parallels Erikson's identity crisis, she began to reflect on the questions of her own destiny and her ideological commitments which were already foreshadowed in her loneliness and retreat. What was she to stand for? How was her school helping her figure out where she wanted to be in five or ten years? Was it a career she wanted? Was it children and a husband? Now she needed teachers who were partners in dialogue and guided her through asking important questions; not the learning of facts but the tools of interpretation became central at a time when she had begun to see herself in relativistic terms (Perry, 1968) and was not capable yet of seeing herself committed to one view of who she was in the world. Again, the dangers for the teachers centered around the establishment of the therapeutic relationship rather than a focus on the learning of skills, the use of tools, and interpretation which follow their own logic rather than the uncovering of psychodynamic motivation. Again, the teachers helped in the process of sublimation and repression and the development of ego strength as discussed by Anna Freud and Balint. But what was being sublimated and repressed? Who did the sublimating and for what purposes? Who did the observation and the insight that lead to development and strength? What system integrated the separation vulnerabilities? The arc between biography and transformation gives these dimensions a life span rationale.

CONCLUSION

Richard did not make use of our intensive therapy meetings the way Denise did. For Denise the relationship was central. She was looking forward to therapy sessions and would have less depression and less loneliness to contend with when we were meeting. Denise's self system was too open. She experienced herself in the context of her relationship, merging with the important others of her life. Her third-person perspective was the basis for her experience of hurt for others. She had, one could say, decentered too much and had begun to believe that she could not exist without the view of the other. Richard's system was too closed off and self-protective. At the second perspective-taking level he could understand that others have needs too and are out to get them fulfilled. The interpersonal negotiations of these needs are regulated through the exchange principle. Daniel's self-organization was open again. Much like Denise he was oriented very strongly toward important others, the family. These similarities often lead to calling both Daniel and Denise "borderline mergy." But we lose some of the general differences between them if we don't focus on the self systems that coordinate this merging. Daniel's boundaries were open on a much more basic and physical level. When anxious he hid behind a chair. When separated from his parents, he was convinced they blew up in a car accident. When he had the urge to leave the unit, he just took off. There was no planned aspect to his impulsivity (as in Richard's case). He literally thought I or anyone else who was close could read his mind. Denise's problems were of a different sort. She felt she was going to lose her *sense of self* when losing the relationship. It is not the physical other that is in the center of her concerns but the psychological other. Her system is open but on a hierarchically more advanced level. She had a period in her life in which her self system had closed much like Richard's. Daniel was still struggling to set these early boundaries.

I have presented the outline of work bridging both developmental psychology and psychoanalysis. By choosing one of the most difficult and confusing diagnostic categories in psychiatry, the borderline personality disorders, I have left myself open to numerous criticisms. Developmental psychologists might argue that our construct building on Piaget and Kohlberg has addressed cognition in normal development. They can, with some justification, argue that the pathology in borderline patients creates sufficient "noise" to impair the overall structure making the application of the theories unwise. Psychoanalysts might argue that theories addressing the overall development of the self are too broad and fail to get at the core of borderline pathology, namely specific ego deficits and early developmental vulnerabilities which express themselves throughout life. Psychiatrists might add to the confusion by stating that the theorizing of this nature is not useful since borderline pathology has a biological base.

Each of these views has certain convincing features. Why then did I embark on this seemingly hopeless enterprise? An emerging clinical-developmental psychology which attempts to bridge psychoanalytic and Piagetian principles of development is based on a number of assumptions which were outlined earlier. I have tried to demonstrate through the case discussions that even with severely disturbed patients a most striking aspect of their existence is a coherence of self organization which I have described along a developmental line. This underlying structure of the self, which gives meaning to life in general (or dissolves meaning), is a missing key to an understanding of borderline patients in treatment. I have tried to demonstrate in the cases that the positions of self accounted for important differences of self-perception, interpersonal relations, and conflict resolution. The self-transformations are not only cognitive in nature but are about the mediation between cognition and affect and forms of self-reflection. That these levels of self are connected to intrapsychic and interpersonal conflict is becoming more and more evident in research, educational, and clinical intervention.

Only through a search for underlying principles of self and interpersonal relations in any patient group will it be possible for us to discover systematic developmental patterns and apply them to the school and the clinic. Our problem, however, is that we lack any convincing theory of developmental psychopathology. Empirical studies applying developmental measures to clinical populations are still the exception in psychiatry and psychology. Extensive investigation with different patient populations is necessary to shed light on some of the unrecognized aspects of human development. The specific focus on the borderline patient may have contributed to the growing field of clinical-developmental psychology in several ways. Mainly, it has facilitated the exploration of two developmental principles, one derived from psychoanalysis, the other derived from developmental psychology. The first is the Freudian notion that until we have worked through our greatest vulnerabilities from the past, we are destined to relive them. Second, and equally important are the conflicts of the separation-individuation period, such as the first experiencing of boundaries, aloneness, and the comfort of the holding other. They set the stage for many more separations and individuations throughout life as well as many affiliations with important others. Too much holding or too much rejection can lead to abandonment fears, clinging, and a sense of engulfment throughout life. Developmental psychology makes it possible for us to learn more about these conflicts at different times of life. A theory of self transformation in which earlier psychological forms get integrated into a larger and more complex structure is a useful model to explain how these early vulnerabilities can be worked out at later stages of development. Transformations in life are only partial in that they present human dilemmas which are never solved but only integrated into a more encompassing attempt at resolution. The earliest dilemma between closeness and dependency is not solvable. The dilemma of longing for the parent of the opposite sex and not attaining him or her is a more complex form of the same conflict. This dilemma also leads to only partial resolution. Every new dilemma across the life span between the wish for affiliation and intimacy and the wish for individuation and identity will put into question all other only partially resolved dilemmas of the past. Biography is a constant process of creation in the bounds of history. This tension makes us truly human and prone to the most human conflicts: that we have to mark time—always—in the midst of the hardest movement contributes to many of the borderline vulnerabilities but it also creates the metaphors and narratives of experience and reflection; "the one already sounding as we are born" and transforming with the other psychological births of our time.

REFERENCES

Aichorn, A. (1925), *Wayward Youth*. New York: Viking, 1953.

American Psychiatric Association (1980), *Diagnostic and Statistical Manual of Mental Disorders*, 3rd ed. Washington, DC: American Psychiatric Press.

Anthony, E. (1976), Freud, Piaget and human knowledge: Some comparisons and contrasts. *The Annual of Psychoanalysis*, 4: 253–277. New York: International Universities Press.

Baldwin, J. M. (1902), *Social and Ethical Interpretations in Mental Development*. New York: Macmillan.

Balint, M. (1939), Ichstaerke, Ichpaedagogik und "Lernen." In: *Int. Zeitschrift Psychoanal.* and *Imago*, 24: 417–427.

Basch, M. (1980), Psychoanalytic interpretation and cognitive transformation. Unpublished manuscript. Center for Psychosocial Studies, Chicago.

Bellak, L., Hurvich, M., & Gediman, H. (1973), *Ego Functions in Schizophrenics, Neurotics and Normals*. New York: John Wiley.

Bernfeld, S. (1925), *Sisyphos; or the Limits of Education*, trans. F. Lilge. Berkeley: University of California Press.

Blos, P. (1962), *On Adolescence*. New York: Free Press.

Buie, P., & Adler, G. (1973), The uses of confrontation in the psychotherapy of borderline patients. In: *Confrontation in Psychotherapy*, ed. G. Adler & P. G. Myerson. New York: Science House.

Bychowski, G. (1953), The problem of latent psychosis. *J. Amer. Psychoanal. Assn.*, 1:484–503.

Damon, W. (1983), *Social and Personality Development*. New York: W. W. Norton.

Decarie, T. (1978), Affect development and cognition in a Piagetian context. In: *The Development of Affect*, ed. M. Lewis & L. Rosenblum. New York: Plenum Press.

Deutsch, H. (1942), Some forms of emotional disturbance and their relationship to schizophrenia. *Psychoanal. Quart.*, 11:301–321.

Easser, R., & Lesser, S. (1965), Hysterical personality: A reevaluation. *Psychoanal. Quart.*, 34:390–405.

Edelstein, W., & Noam, G. (1982), Regulatory structures of the self and post formal operations in adulthood. *Hum. Develop.*, 25:407–422.

Eisenstein, V. W. (1951), Differential psychotherapy of borderline states. *Psychiat. Quart.*, 25:379–401.

Elkind, D. (1976), *Child Development and Education—A Piagetian Perspective*. New York: Oxford University Press.

Erikson, E. (published under Erik Homburger) (1935), Psychoanalysis and the future of education. *Psychoanal. Quart.*, 4:50–68.

——— (1950), *Childhood and Society*. New York: W. W. Norton.

——— (1959), Identity and the Life Cycle. *Psychological Issues*, Vol. 1. New York: International Universities Press, pp. 133–134.

Freud, A. (1935), *Psychoanalysis for Teachers and Parents*. New York: Emerson Books.
——— (1952), The role of the teacher. *Harvard Ed. Rev.*, 22 (4):229–234.
Freud, S. (1909), Analysis of a phobia in a five-year-old boy. *Standard Edition*, 11:163–175. London: Hogarth Press, 1962.
Fromm, E. (1976), To Have or To Be. *World Perspect.*, 50(Series). New York: Harper & Row.
Frosch, J. (1964), The psychotic character: Clinical psychiatric consideration. *Psychiat. Quart.*, 38:81–96.
Furth, H. G., & Wachs, H. (1975), *Thinking Goes to School*. New York: Oxford University Press.
Giovacchini, P. L. (1973), Character disorders with special reference to the borderline state. *Internat. J. Psychoanal. & Psychother.*, 2(1):7–20.
Greenspan, S. (1979), Intelligence and Adaptation: An Integration of Psychoanalytic and Piagetian Developmental Psychology. *Psychological Issues*, Monograph. 47/48, 3 & 4/12. New York: International Universities Press.
——— Lourie, R. (1981), Developmental structuralist approach to the classification of adaptive and pathologic personality organizations: Infancy and early childhood. *Amer. J. Psychiat.*, 138(6):725–735.
Grinker, R., Werble, B., & Drye, R. (1968), *The Borderline Syndrome*. New York: Basic Books.
Gunderson, J. (1977), Characteristics of borderlines. In: *Borderline Personality Disorders*, ed. P. Harticollis. New York: International Universities Press.
Guntrip, H. (1971), *Psychoanalytic Theory, Therapy and the Self*. New York: Basic Books.
Hoch, P., & Polatin, P. (1949), Pseudoneurotic forms of schizophrenia. *Psychiat. Quart.*, 23:248–276.
Hulsizer, D., Murphy, M., Noam, G., & Taylor, C. (1981), On generativity and identity: From a conversation with Joan and Erik Erikson. *Harvard Ed. Rev.*, 51(2):249–269.
Jacobson, E. (1964), *The Self and the Object World*. New York: International Universities Press.
Kaplan, L. (1980), The developmental and genetic perspectives of a life history. *Contemp. Psychoanal.*, 16 (4):565–580.
Kegan, R. (1982), *The Evolving Self*. Cambridge, MA: Harvard University Press.
——— Noam, G., & Rogers, L. (1982), The psychologic of emotions: A neo-Piagetian view. In: *Emotional Development. New Directions in Child Development*, ed. D. Cicchetti & P. Hesse. San Francisco: Jossey-Bass, pp. 105–128.
Kernberg, O. (1972), Early ego integration and object relations. *NY Acad. Sci.*, 193:233–247.
——— (1975), *Borderline Conditions and Pathological Narcissism*. New York: Jason Aronson.

Knight, R. (1953), Borderline states. *Bull. Menn. Clin.*, 17:1–12.

Kohlberg, L. (1969), Stage and sequence: The cognitive developmental approach to socialization. In: *Handbook of Socialization, Theory and Research*, ed. D. Gosline. New York: Rand McNally.

————— (1985), The just community approach to moral education. In: *Moral Education*, ed. M. Berkowicz & F. Oser. Hillside, NJ: Lawrence Erlbaum.

————— LaCrosse, T., & Ricks, D. (1972), The predictability of adult mental health from childhood behavior. In: *Manual of Child Psychopathology*, ed. B. Wolman, New York: McGraw-Hill.

Kohut, H. (1971), *The Analysis of the Self*. New York: International Universities Press.

Lee, B., & Noam, G. eds. (1983), *Developmental Approaches to the Self*. New York: Plenum Press.

Loevinger, J. (1976), *Ego Development*. San Francisco: Jossey-Bass.

Mahler, M. (1971), A study of the separation individuation process and its possible application to borderline phenomena in the psychoanalytic situation. *The Psychoanalytic Study of the Child*, 26:403–424. New Haven, CT: Yale University Press.

————— Kaplan, L. (1977), Developmental aspects in the assessment of narcissistic and so-called borderline personalities. In: *Borderline Personality Disorders*, ed. P. Harticollis. New York: International Universities Press.

————— Pine, F., & Bergman, A. (1975), *The Psychological Birth of the Human Infant*. New York: Basic Books.

Masterson, J. (1973), The borderline adolescent. *Adol. Psychiat.*, 2:249–268.

————— Rinsley, D. (1975), The borderline syndrome: The role of the mother in the genesis and psychic structure of the borderline personality. *Internat. J. Psycho-Anal.*, 56:163–177.

Mead, G. (1934), *Mind, Self and Society*. Chicago: University of Chicago Press.

Noam, G. (1985), Stage, phase and style: The developmental dynamics of the self. In: *Moral Education*, ed. M. Berkowitz & F. Oser. Hillside, NJ: Lawrence Erlbaum, pp. 321–346.

————— (1988a), A constructivist approach to developmental psychopathology. In: *Developmental Psychopathology and Its Treatment*, ed. E. D. Nannis & P. A. Cowan. New Directions for Child Development, 39, Spring. San Francisco: Jossey-Bass, pp. 91–122.

————— (1988b), The self, adult development and the theory of biography and transformation. In: *Self, Ego and Identity*, ed. D. K. Lapsley & F. C. Powers. New York: Springer, pp. 3–29.

————— Higgins, G., & Goethals, G. (1982), Psychoanalysis as a developmental psychology. In: *Handbook of Developmental Psychology*, ed. R. Wolman. Englewood Cliffs, NJ: Prentice-Hall.

————— Kegan, R., (1982), Social cognition and psychodynamics: Towards a clinical-developmental psychology. In: *Perspektivitat und Interpretation*, ed. W. Edelstein, & M. Keller. (1983), Frankfurt: Suhrkamp.

———— Kohlberg, L., & Snarey, J. (1983), Steps toward a model of the self. In: *Developmental Approaches to the Self*, ed. B. Lee & G. Noam. New York: Plenum Press.

Perry, J., & Klerman, G. (1980), Clinical features of the borderline personality disorder. *Amer. J. Psychiat.*, 137(2):165–173.

Perry, W. (1968), *Forms of Intellectual and Ethical Development in the College Years*. New York: Holt, Rinehardt & Winston.

Piaget, J. (1926), *The Language and Thought of the Child*. New York: Harcourt Brace & World.

———— (1932), *The Moral Judgment of the Child*. New York: Free Press, 1965.

———— (1973), *The Child and Reality*. New York: Grossman.

Reich, W. (1925), *The Impulsive Character*. New York: International Psychoanalytic Press.

Robbins, M. D. (1976), Borderline personality organization: The need for a new theory. *J. Amer. Psychoanal. Assn.*, 24:831–854.

Santostefano, S. (1978), *A Biodevelopmental Approach to Clinical Child Psychology*. New York: John Wiley.

Schmidt, V. (1924), *Psychoanalytische Erziehung in Sowjetrussland*. West Germany: Int. Psychoan. Verlag.

Selman, R. (1980), *The Growth of Interpersonal Understanding, Developmental and Clinical Analyses*. New York: Academic Press.

Tolpin, P. (1980), The borderline personality: Its makeup and analyzability. In: *Advances in Self Psychology*, ed. A. Goldberg. New York: International Universities Press.

Vaillant, G. (1977), *Adaptation to Life*. Boston: Little, Brown.

Wack, R., & Noam, G. (1979), Familientherapie und "Psychosoziales Holding Environment" bei Borderline Personlichkeitsstorungen in der Adoleszense. In: *Familientherapie und Gesellschaft*, ed. W. Dierking. Weinheim, West Germany: Beltz Verlag.

Weinberger, D. (1978), *The Nature and Genesis of the Borderline Adult: Some New Perspectives*. Unpublished manuscript.

Winnicott, D. (1958), *Collected Papers: Through Pediatrics to Psychoanalysis*. New York: Basic Books.

Wolf, E. S. (1976), Recent advances in the psychology of the self: An outline of basic concepts. *Comp. Psychiat.*, 17 (1):37–46.

Wolff, P. H. (1960), The Developmental Psychologies of Jean Piaget and Psychoanalysis. *Psychological Issues*, 2, Monographs, 1/2. New York: International Universities Press.

Zetzel, A. (1971), A developmental approach to the borderline patient. *Amer. J. Psychiat.*, 127 (7):867–871.

Zilboorg, G. (1941), Ambulatory schizophrenia. *Psychiat.*, 4:149–155.

Zulliger, H. (1957), Psychoanalyse und padagogik. In: *Freud in der Gegenwart*. Frankfurt: EVA.

Chapter 24

Psychoanalysis and Special Education: The Concept of Exceptionality in Physical Disability

GASTON E. BLOM, M.D.
KERSTIN EK, Ph.D.
MADHAV KULKARNI, Ph.D.

In 1975, landmark federal legislation was enacted to provide a free appropriate public education delivery system for all handicapped children. Actually, PL 94-142 (Education for All Handicapped Children Act) was the culmination of legislation dating from 1965 and a previous history of litigation on schooling for handicapped children.

An important earlier companion piece to PL 94-142 is section 504 of the Vocational Rehabilitation Act of 1973 (PL 93-112) which is a civil rights act for handicapped persons of all ages under all social public contexts.

The rights, entitlements, and opportunities for handicapped people accompanied similar developments for

This study was completed when the authors were faculty and research assistants at the University Center for International Rehabilitation, Michigan State University, East Lansing, Michigan.

other minority-status persons in the 1960s. Moreover, not only the handicapped minority was made visible but also the social practices which isolated, segregated, and institutionalized them in the world where able-bodied citizens were in the majority.

The implementation of these legislative acts through rules, regulations, and guidelines has fostered the development of social policies of deinstitutionalization, least restrictive environments, normalization, barrier removals, accessibility of facilities, due process rights, adaptive aids, independent living, and mainstreaming. Such policies challenge labeling, negative expectations, and deficit programming which have typified traditional forms of service to disabled people.

The practices of sexism, povertism, and ageism have also been challenged, stimulated by the social movement against racism. The court decisions and legislative acts of the 1960s promoted a change in values of the dominant social majority. While resistance against social change still exists, change has led to revisions in psychological concepts about femininity, ethnic status, poverty, and old age. In a similar fashion the psychologies of physical disability are undergoing critical scrutiny. Social change has fostered advocate, participatory, and advisory roles for disabled consumers and their families in relation to professionals.

The prevalence of physical disability in people of all ages, previously ignored and unknown, has been identified in various categorical groups. It has now been more accurately estimated to be 10 percent of the child population, nine to nineteen years of age, and 17 percent of the adult population sixteen to sixty-five years of age (Goldensohn, 1978). Based on surveys and reports, the Bureau for the Educationally Handicapped published estimated numbers of handicapped children from nine to nineteen years of age in the United States (*American Education Reprint,* 1976) as follows in Table 24.1.

The social emergence of children with physical disa-

TABLE 24.1
Estimated Number of Handicapped Children (0–19 years)
1975–1976

	Numbers	Percent Served	Percent Unserved
Speech Impaired	2,293,000	88	12
Mentally Retarded	1,507,000	90	10
Learning Disabilities	1,966,000	13	87
Crippled, Health Impaired	328,000	78	22
Deaf	49,000	92	8
Hard of Hearing	328,000	20	80
Visually Handicapped	66,000	65	35
Deaf-blind, Multi-handicapped	4,000	40	60
Total	6,577,000*		

*This does not include the severely emotionally disturbed, who total 1,310,000.

bilities within schools and other human service delivery systems provides the basis for an examination of the concept of exceptionality in psychoanalysis. Such an examination may suggest ways in which psychoanalytic perspectives can make contributions to the field of special education.

PSYCHOANALYTIC PERSPECTIVES ON PHYSICAL DISABILITY

FREUD'S INITIAL VIEW

One of the earliest references to a psychoanalytic psychology of physical disability can be found in Freud's paper "Some Character-types Met With in Psycho-analytic Work" (1916). In this presentation, Freud referred to a number of character traits found in patients who resisted the analytic investigative process. One group of patients was named "The Exceptions," who resisted appeals to renunciate some pleasurable satisfactions, to make a sacrifice, to accept some temporary suffering for the sake of a better end, or even to submit to a realistic frustration which applied to everyone. These patients said that they had renounced and suffered enough. They had a claim to be spared any further demands. They were not willing to accept a disagreeable necessity because they were exceptions and intended to remain so. Freud indicated that everyone would like to claim special privileges over others. Yet, when a person proclaimed himself as an exception as well as behaved like one, there had to be a special reason.

Freud believed the special reason could be commonly found in the early lives of these patients. They had been subjected to a painful experience or suffering in earliest childhood, for which they were not responsible and could look upon as an unjust disadvantage. They not only claimed privileges over others, but also rebelled against the injustice of their fate. Freud cited brief case examples of a woman with a painful organic disorder of congenital origin and a man who was the victim of an accidental infection in infancy.

Presumably, Freud obtained limited information from these cases because of their resistance to analysis and was therefore unable to clarify directly their behaviors. Instead, he offered a literary interpretation from Shakespeare's portrayal of King Richard III as an exception which was motivated by the king's alleged physical deformities. In the opening soliloquy of Shakespeare's play, Gloucester, who subsequently becomes king, passionately expresses his low self-esteem and bitterness about his deformity. Freud interprets the soliloquy to signify: "Nature has done me a grievous wrong in denying me the beauty of form which wins human love. Life owes me reparation for this, and I will see that I get it. I have a right to be an exception, to disregard the scruples by which others let themselves be held back. I may do wrong myself, since wrong has been done to me." According to Freud, Richard III refused to live by the same rules as other people. He made his own rules. He denied the reality principle in favor of the pleasure principle. Freud, like others, accepted the evil reputation of Richard III, promoted by Shakespeare, even though historical facts do not support this view entirely.

Freud also pointed to another group of exceptions, namely women, since he felt they claimed privileges and exemptions from many of the troublesome aspects of life. Based on his psychoanalytic work, Freud indicated "that women regard themselves as having been damaged in infancy"—and many remain reproachful to their mothers for "having brought them into the world as women instead of as men" (p. 315). Freud viewed the claims of the physically disabled and women as resting upon the same foundation of the castration complex and early narcissistic injury.

LATER PSYCHOANALYTIC STUDIES

This psychoanalytic view of physical disability as the negative exception became a prototypical concept that still remains in psychoanalytic and psychiatric literature. The concept consists of the following aspects: early narcissistic injury, a disturbance of the body ego, the denial of the reality principle, fixation on the pleasure principle, superego defects, and a destructive bitterness toward the world and able-bodied persons. A historical review of psychoanalytic literature on the exception from 1954 to 1976 further elaborates on Freud's initial view, with only some modifications.

Jacobson (1959) focuses on women as exceptions, both those of great beauty and those with physical disabilities. According to Jacobson, very few women of outstanding beauty have happy or peaceful lives. Referring to Helen of Troy, she indicates that beauty can have a devastating effect on women's lives and on those close to them; the human mind is inclined unconsciously to equate and confuse physical perfection with moral perfection and physical imperfection with moral imperfection. The narcissism of beautiful women is well known. It is a counterpart of negative self-consciousness characterizing "the deformed." "Belles love their own perfection; cripples hate their defect."

The cases of handicapped women presented by Jacobson are categorized into two groups of exceptions — rebellious and masochistic types. The psychology of the rebellious type consists of narcissistic-aggressive oedipal strivings with a resistance to accept oedipal laws in their relationships with men. There is a spiteful denial of their own conscience along with a triumph of their unconscious self-destructive trends. A cry for love that they never received from others dominates. The masochistic type is described in a case of residual paralysis after childhood poliomyelitis where the patient's feelings of being exceptional were expressed through the conviction of a special moral calling. This woman unconsciously identified herself with Christ and felt chosen to suffer for the crimes of mankind. Jacobson's conclusion is that all exceptions, physically disabled or body perfect, may claim exceptional rights or rights to be treated that way by the outside world; however, they pay a price for not submitting to ordinary rules of life and reality.

Narcissistic ego impairment has been reported in eight adult patients with minor congenital and early acquired anomalies or imperfections (Niederland, 1965). These include chest deformities, umbilical hernia, bony exostosis, cranial and thoracic deformity, imperfect left arm, and congenital torticollis. While some of these disabilities were visually inconspicuous, they were all associated with some functional impairment in childhood. However, psychological consequences far exceeded the minimal degree of disability. These patients had features of an adult narcissistic disorder: compensatory narcissistic self-inflation, fantasies of grandiosity and uniqueness, aggressive strivings for narcissistic supplies from the outside world, impairment of object relations and reality testing, and excessive psychological vulnerability. According to Neiderland, while psychic traumata in childhood are often resolved in the course of development, an early body defect tends to remain an area of unresolved conflict through its concreteness, permanence, cathetic significance, and relationship to mutilation and castration anxieties. The development of the body ego is affected from the start resulting in a faulty, sometimes bizarre and distorted body image. Narcissistic injury in these patients was expressed in self-aggrandizement, heightened aggressiveness, castrated defectiveness, and fantasies of revenge, rebirth, and immortality. In gifted persons fantasies become a source of creativity and artistry, but other fantasies contain revenge and suffering. Niederland concluded that patients with congenital or early acquired malformations are prone to suffer from a permanent disturbance of their self-image.

The emphasis on narcissistic impairments in persons with congenital disability is also stressed by Parker (1971) in a report of a girl with spina bifida. He indicates that a congential defect always creates a barrier in the path of normal personality development. Heightened aggression and resentment against the injustice of fate are reflected in various attitudes and behaviors. A grossly distorted body image, usually out of proportion to the actual severity of the body deformity, inevitably results in disturbed character formation and psychopathology. Special difficulty exists in those individuals who think that their defect makes them immune to laws governing normal people, and who do not internalize a stable and consistent system of values. Maintenance of firm limits in a framework of love and consistency on the part of both parents can mitigate against this development.

Mattson (1972) stresses the long-range influence that family attitudes and behaviors have on children with chronic physical disorders. In later childhood and adolescence, children with congenital deformities often become shy and lonely, harboring resentment toward ablebodied persons whom they see as owing them payment for their life sufferings. Usually, these negative exceptions are raised in a family that emphasized their defectiveness and isolated and concealed them from the world in an embarrassed fashion. As a result, they identified with their family's negative view of themselves and developed a self-image of a defective outsider. Two other behavior patterns associated with chromosomal and paranatal disorders are described by Mattson which he also relates to family reactions and to child rearing. One behavior pattern consists of fearful, inactive children lacking in outside interests and being overly dependent on their families who have overprotected and excessively worried about them. The other behavior pattern consists of adolescents who engage in risk-taking activities, deny their own reality and the danger, and are active, defiant, and rebellious; the families of these rebellious exceptions were also overly concerned and especially guilt ridden about their children's physical disabilities.

The influence of parent behavior toward a physically impaired child is also emphasized by Furman (1968) in the analysis of a three-and-one-half-year-old girl, born with a deformed and blind left eye. Although physically impaired, she suffered more from being treated by her parents as an exception who could do no wrong. The congenital deformity aroused neurotic reactions in the parents. For instance, they had never mentioned the eye deformity to the girl. They treated her like a little princess. The mother abdicated her maternal guiding role because of guilt feelings. Furman indicates that it is not unusual for parents to encounter turmoil within themselves in dealing with their child's deformity. He suggests that parents should be referred as early as possible for professional assistance in dealing with their child's emotional development. Parents often need help in dealing with their guilt, depression, and anxiety in order to facilitate discussions with their child regarding the physical defect. If this can be done, the parents may be able to help their child separate feelings about the impairment from normal developmental conflicts and support the child's self-esteem. Furman identifies an important parental task as helping the child understand that although different from others in body, he does not differ from them in the nature of his feelings.

Other psychoanalytic studies have emphasized distorted intrapsychic processes and development in congenital disabilities. Kaplan (1959) stresses that psychological reverberations within the person go far beyond the actual physical disability. She also ties the reactions to disability to the universal family romance fantasy. This fantasy of being the child of parents more beautiful, famous, and important than the parents one actually has is an attempt to regulate self-esteem after disillusionment with real parents. Kaplan (1974) indicates that persons born with exceptional genetic qualities such as physical deformity, unusual beauty, or special talent are especially prone to a more profound family romance fantasy. Such persons would have more difficulty internalizing a realistic superego; they would tend to be rebellious and spitefully deny their conscience.

This dynamic formulation for the exception is also postulated by Gediman (1974). She describes two young adults who regarded themselves as exceptions. One patient was a man with a noticeable birth defect and the other was a beautiful woman. Both denied their physical difference from others and expressed grandiose fantasies that fate and fortune would bestow grandeur upon them by providing contact with famous, beautiful parental figures.

Kris (1976) indicates that exceptions are no longer uncommon in clinical practice, but very nearly the rule. This is questioned by Leopold-Lowenthal (1976) who doubts if exceptions were so uncommon in clinical practice in 1916 when Freud published his original article. He further believes that many persons with disability probably did not need psychoanalytic treatment at that time.

However, Kris (1976) offers a somewhat different psychodynamic explanation for the exception. He emphasizes a particular aspect of libido theory, namely, the distinction between active and passive aims, and indicates that in his psychoanalytic experience exceptions have a block in the satisfaction of their passive libidinal wishes. They have difficulty in experiencing being taken care of, being loved, and being admired, and suffer from emotional starvation. This leads to a compensatory increase of active libidinal demands for love that also cannot be satisfied because of the block. Physical injury or disability need not make a person an exception, rather it may develop as the result of the rejection of passive libidinal wishes. Again the characteristics of exceptions described are similar to previous cited studies including demands, self-critical attitudes, self-pity and self-indulgence, envy, intolerance for being in error, and anxiety and guilt. Kris also states that exceptions suffer from narcissistic problems and sometimes have narcissistic personality disorders.

Lipton (1976) expresses uncertainty about the universal effects of congenital and early acquired physical "defects" on personality. He indicates that except for conditions as blindness and deafness, disabilities may not be pathogenic. A necessary condition for pathogenicity is "the attitude [to the defect and to the patient] of important figures in the environment, especially the mother"

(p. 113). Denial and distortions of anxious overprotection on the part of parents can result in psychological damage. Lipton reports that minor physical defects lend themselves to the formation of character disorders, especially with active-passive conflicts. Narcissistic overcompensation may be expressed through ambitious strivings in fantasy and/or in reality. A distorted or incomplete body image can exert an unfavorable influence on learning, thinking, and time-space orientation.

In a review of the psychoanalytic literature one of the authors (Ek) found only one instance where an indivdual was reported as positively adapted to his disability (Lussier, 1960). This was a boy who was born with malformed shoulders, extremely short arms, and hands with three fingers and no thumbs. Peter started analysis at age thirteen because of aggressive behavior difficulties. At that time, the measurement from his shoulders to fingertips was not quite eight inches.

In the analysis, Lussier found that Peter did not exhibit masochistic satisfaction, passivity, or self-pity. He did not want to be an object of pity. He wanted to prove, both consciously and unconsciously, that he could do things with his short arms. He actively strived to achieve his goals. Some of his daydreams were to be able to play the trumpet, ride a bike, and obtain a swimming certificate. He wanted to impress people by his performance and not derive gain from his disability. According to Lussier, his mother's shame about his disability initiated Peter's strivings. Lussier viewed the strivings as compensatory mechanisms based on strong denial of reality. Peter built a fantasy world where handicap did not exist. Reaction formations developed as defenses against deep-seated feelings of insecurity and inferiority. However, in the analysis, Peter appeared to have a more generous and realistic assessment of his potentialities than his parents and analyst. Peter used fantasy to master reality and to develop a stable ego identity. He dared to test his "dreams," many of which became realizable.

Lussier (1960) groups physically disabled people into two categories, "the active and the passive ones" or "the doers and the dreamers." He wonders if Peter's drive toward activity is characteristic for all individuals in the active group or if he is to be regarded as an exception. Lussier finds Peter's denial of reality by fantasy especially interesting and quotes Hartmann (1939): "what are the positive adaptive elements of fantasy? . . . There are avenues of reality-adaptations which, at first, certainly lead away from the real situation . . . there are fantasies which, while they remove man from external reality, open up for him his internal reality" (pp. 17–19).

A CRITIQUE OF "THE EXCEPTION"

Freud's original formulations about the exception in 1916 became the starting point for a psychoanalytic psychology of physical disabilities. Psychoanalytic publications since then have lent support to these formulations. However, a few authors have extended the concept of the exception to issues much broader than disability. For instance, denial of passive libidinal wishes in general may result in personality characteristics typical for the exception. One author, Kris (1976), has viewed the exception from a more universal perspective in the development of identity.

Starting with Freud and those contributors following him, the negative self-view, which is the nucleus of the exception character type, has been assumed to have a biological or physical basis from the disability itself. A cultural influence or determination from the experience of disability has not been considered. An actual inferior cultural status might very well be translated by a disabled person into internalized mental self-representations of castration and mutilation. In the culture of Freud and those of the modern world, being disabled is viewed as being inferior, distorted, and stigmatized. The disabled experience prejudice, rejection, and social isolation from society. Society may also influence parental attitudes unfavorably.

The concept of the exception has also focused almost entirely on a negative aspect. Only two psychoanalytic writers have mentioned the positive exception as a possibility. One describes an exception in positive terms but almost fails to recognize its existence (Lussier, 1960). He does acknowledge, however, that his patient had a more realistic assessment of his own capabilities and calls him an excellent example of an "active disabled" person.

The neglect of the positive exception and the invariable emphasis on maladaptive personality outcomes for a disabled person may be the consequences of a number of factors. One, such individuals may not come to the attention of psychoanalysts. Two, the pathological bias of a therapist may give an unbalanced view of the disabled person.

THE PATHOLOGY IMBALANCE

Human service professionals, particularly those with a medical orientation, have brought to the field of physical disability a chronic disease paradigm for assessment, remediation, and intervention. While a medical orientation of diagnosis, etiology, treatment, and prognosis may have initial relevance to physical disability, it quickly loses significance and importance over time. As physical characteristics become stable and/or enduring, what matters most is functional status in personal and social life and not chronic disease characteristics.

A pathology orientation influences language in referring to disability. Metaphors such as disorder, defect, affliction, impairment, deficiency, and deficit elicit negative images and have powerful psychosocial effects (DeLoach and Greer, 1981). Consumers with disability are concerned about the influence of labels and the consequences of their being viewed as patients, or clients, or having a disability identity or having no identity at all. Terminology in disability is in a process of change and modification. Professionals need to keep up to date on these changes. A distinction needs to be made between special words used by insiders and words used by professionals.

Persons with a disability also relate experiences where their behavioral achievements are viewed by the able bodied as exceptional, inspirational, and remarkable and also where their mistakes or errors are seen as evidence of deficit (Vash, 1981).

Social psychologists John Gliedman, Beatrice Wright, Constantina Safilios-Rothschild, Betty Galdiamond, Joseph Stubbins, and Gunnar Dybwad, among others, have studied the mechanisms involved in the pathology orientation to disability. The perception of disability as an incurable chronic disease can spread to social, psychological, educational, occupational, and economic realms. Wright (1960) long ago referred to the negative spread phenomenon whereby a person with a visible, functional limitation in one area is assumed without justification to have limitations in many other functional areas of life.

The insider-outsider perspective is another mechanism by which able-bodied persons assign negative attributes to people with disability (Hohmann, 1975; Wright, 1975). The insider perspective is the way the person with disability perceives himself and his own situation in constrast to the outsider perspective which is the appraisal of disability by an able-bodied person. The outsider frequently views disability or a disabled person in negative stereotyped terms such as tragic and depreciated. This does not usually correspond to how the insider views his situation.

Over the last ten years, disabled persons have reacted against derogatory public views of physical disability; they have insisted on changing reference terms such as *crippled* to *disabled* and *disabled* to *handicapped.* Even though some change in public view has occurred, the professional outsider may take the position that the insider must face and adjust to the reality of what he cannot do (Wright, 1975). The outsider thinks in normative and majority terms and does not identify with the uniqueness of the insider's perspectives. The insider may be able to perceive his disability as different, not bad (Hohmann, 1975). Disability may be seen as an inconvenience or a fact of life; DeLoach and Greer (1981) indicate that close to 60 percent of disabled people do so. While conflict and struggle exist in the lives of disabled persons, satisfactions and positive resources are also present but often ignored by professionals (Wright, 1980).

Gliedman and Roth (1980) point out that able-bodied developmental norms and average expectable environments do not fit the facts of disability. Disabled children may grow up with quite different time-tables for developmental events and different socialization experiences. Disabled children grow up with home and social contradictions, more exposure to television, less contact with peers outside of school, more exlusion from and repression of sexuality, greater utilization of fantasy, more time alone, and more opportunities to develop adult-child interpersonal skills. However, such differences do not have to be confused as maladjustment. There are also myths about disablement. DeLoach and Greer (1981) address some of them: body and mental fragility, deification of normality, omniscience of experts, and asexuality of the disabled.

Ideologies about disability emerge from the diseased and able-bodied perspectives. Goffman (1963) indicates how ideologies contribute to stigmatization. Wolfensberger (1972) refers to "human management professions" as being influenced by both conscious and unconscious ideologies which determine beliefs, attitudes, expectations, views of reality, values, and actions toward deviant individuals. Disabled persons are frequently perceived as deviant, a socially defined human difference that is negatively valued. Wolfensberger provides a review of labels assigned to mentally retarded persons during different historical periods which influenced social treatments. While some labels are less conscious today, they still remain a part of the historical unconscious. A mentally retarded child or adult may be perceived as subhuman, a menace, an object of dread, an object of pity, a holy innocent, a diseased organism, or an eternal child. Each of these perceptions has particular individual and social consequences. Similar labels are applied to persons with physical disabilities; in fact, views of retardation are the prototypes for all disabilities.

The clinical approach to psychopathology contains operational biases which in their universal application to persons with physical disability may function as negative expectations. These include the central role of internal conflict in behavior, a suspicion toward prosocial behaviors as defensive, an emphasis on autoplastic adaptation, and mistrust of alloplastic change. Criteria of treatability with dynamic psychotherapy which include high intelligence, body endowment intactness, and internal not external conflicts may unfortunately rule out this mode of treatment for mentally and physically disabled persons (Stubbins, 1982).

ADAPTIVE ASPECTS TO EXCEPTIONALITY

EMPIRICAL STUDIES

There is empirical evidence for coping, competence, resilience, and good quality of life in children with acquired and congenital physical disabilities. Examples can be found in newspaper, magazine, and television accounts of handicapped children where the emphasis is placed on the "remarkable," "astounding," "inspirational" responses in overcoming the consequences of disability.

Over the last three years a random selection of newspaper stories of children who cope with physical disabilities was obtained. The headlines of these accounts are listed in Table 24.2. In the parenthesis after the headline, the type of disability present is indicated.

TABLE 24.2
Headlines of Newspaper Stories About Children
Who Cope with Physical Disabilities

Disabled athlete competes in own league (double leg amputee)
A chair-car-elevator sets him free (thalidomide congenital limb deformities)
Special kind of gymnast overcomes (congenital malformed right arm)
He walks with help—and courage (double leg amputee, acquired)
Accident victim prepares to graduate (brain damage)
Ruling frees rolling teen for a life on the road (degenerative neurological disease)
Patty, a free spirit with spunk (cerebral palsy)
Short, spunky is her style (osteogenesis imperfecta)
Teen girl honored as most courageous athlete (brain damage)
A progressive handicapped achieves goals (cerebral palsy)
Electric "wheels" fail to hamper Arnie's life style (osteogenesis imperfecta)
He hates the word handicap (congenital glaucoma, blindness)
Plucky six-year-old amputee sparkles (double foot amputee, acquired)
Plucky paperboy (spina bifida)

A content analysis of these newspaper accounts reveals a number of common elements in the descriptions of these children. Particularly impressive is the presence of social skills, the successful use of adaptive devices, the view of disability as a hinderance and inconvenience, a high level of available emotional energy, risk taking, the absence of identification as a victim, and the encouragement of independence and positive expectations by parents and teachers. Such examples of positive adaptations are viewed as unique, rare, and exceptional rather than being in the realm of average expectable outcomes.

There is further empirical evidence of coping, competence, resilience, and quality of life in the present and future of children at risk because of unfavorable environments, endowments, and chance events. One source of evidence comes from outcomes of longitudinal developmental studies on "normative" populations (Block and Haan, 1971; Murphy and Moriarty, 1976; Murphy, 1981; Werner and Smith, 1982). Another area of information is the favorable outcome of many children at risk as a consequence of premature birth (Sameroff and Chandler, 1975); children of parents with chronic illness and depression (Anthony, 1975), or parents with schizophrenia (Bleuler, 1974; Mednick and Witkin-Lanoil, 1977; Garmezy, 1981); of disadvantaged urban environments (Neuchterlein, 1970; Rutter, 1979); and of hostile rejecting communities in school desegregation (Coles, 1964). A third source of information is from studies of children experiencing acute and chronic stress including community disasters (Blom, 1984).

CONCEPTUAL BACKGROUND

In addition to empirical studies, there is a conceptual basis for coping and competence. White (1959) views the motor practicing and exploratory activities from earliest infancy onward as independent of drive, affect, and conflict motivation. These activities are directed at the child's own body parts and at the inanimate and animate social world. They create effects and consequences on the body, things, and people from which their realistic properties are extracted. This leads to the development of reality relations. The ability of the child to create such effects is based on the effectance motive and the feelings associated with such consequences create a sense of efficacy. Accumulated experiences in childhood from multiple interactions and transactions during maturational development give rise to competencies and feelings of competency. Initiative, which creates interactions, and recognition of positive results of actions from the self and others, foster the building of competence (White, 1963). It is impeded if problems in initiative, recognition, or both are present (White, 1979).

White (1979) further elaborates on mastery, coping, and defense as strategies of adaptation in reality relations. In mastery, frustrations are overcome and adaptive efforts achieve successful resolution. Coping consists of reactions to internal and external problems as challenges, and of responses with behavior characteristics such as contending, striving, persisting, and being courageous and heroic. In comparison, defending is a response to danger and attack where anxiety is central. Defensive responses of information reduction, cognitive constriction, and emotional rigidity may be adaptive for a short time range but can cause difficulty if they are prolonged.

Haan (1977) makes a clear distinction between defending and coping ego processes in adapting to the environment and inner life. Defending is characterized by behavior styles which protect the person from threats and dangers of internal emotional states and/or of external environmental events. In contrast, coping consists of problem solving, mastering, or overcoming inner and/or outer events which are experienced as challenges. Murphy and Moriarty (1976) also refer to defenses as protecting and coping as mastering. They see development as proceeding from an interaction of individual vulnerabilities and strengths with environmental stress and support over time.

From a psychosocial perspective, Wright (1980) distinguishes coping processes from succumbing processes in adult responses to physical disability. Coping is associated with positive strivings and possibilities, efficient and effective body care procedures, self-understanding, and reduced negative expectancies. In contrast, succumbing contains self-pity, body and social fears, aversive experiences, disability strangeness, unsuccessful body care activities, and negative views of the self and the world. With disability playing a central role, succumbing focuses on difficulties rather than on challenges. Wright examines and critiques the biases and expectations of human service professionals and service delivery systems that tend to reinforce succumbing processes.

CLINICAL STUDIES OF COPING WITH PHYSICAL DISABILITIES

This empirical and theoretical background has led to preliminary psychological studies by the authors of children and adults with different physical disabilities who could be identified by others as adapting very well. The children were selected by school personnel and the adults nominated by peers with disabilities. A number of these adults had congenital disabilities or disabilities acquired in early childhood which made it possible to determine adult outcomes of childhood situations with disability.

CHILDREN WITH PHYSICAL DISABILITIES

Five children with physical disabilities have been studied to date. They are listed in Table 24.3 below.

TABLE 24.3
Children with Physical Disabilities—Age, Sex,
Characteristic

16-year-old girl with muscular dystrophy
15-year-old boy with mild mental retardation and speech disorder
14-year-old girl with congenital blindness
10-year-old boy with learning disability
8-year-old girl with progressive genetic blindness

The children were interviewed at school with a technique modified after Garmezy (personal communication, 1982) in which they were first asked to rank order eight topics according to their discussion preference. Then these topics were explored in their selected order. Interviews were rated on ten coping dimensions upon their completion. Stress scores, school information, home information, and standardized checklist data were obtained.

All five children were partly integrated in regular school classes. Stressful events were often present in their lives in addition to the stress associated with disability. Three children had parenting experiences that were optimal while two did not.

As a group, the five children had high prosocial behavior scale scores and high coping dimension ratings. They preferred to talk about school, friends, interests, and activities while worries and feelings were less often selected for discussion. Some of their psychological characteristics included adept peer and adult social relationships, enjoyment of school, inner locus of control, resistance to victim identification, avoidance of socially dysfunctional behaviors of other children, and autonomous thinking. These findings are consistent with those reported in stress resistant children.

CASE EXAMPLE 1

An illustrative example is Carol Ann, age fourteen years, who has been totally blind since birth. She attended a school for the blind full time until two years ago. She was then mainstreamed at a junior high school while still spending two hours every afternoon at the school for the blind where she uses the optacon and other aids. Carol Ann is an A and B student which requires spending many hours each day doing homework.

Carol Ann is the youngest of four children living alone

with her parents. Three older brothers are married and
live out of state. Her mother, age forty-nine, works out
of the home as a brush salesperson. Her father, age fifty,
is a school teacher who only works as a substitute because
of poor health. The family is religious and attends church
regularly.

Carol Ann's blindness was discovered shortly after
birth. Her parents have maintained professional help and
services since an early age and have encouraged her to
become involved in many activities.

Carol Ann is a pretty girl with long blond hair, blue
eyes, and of average height, weight, and physical maturity for her age. She does not look blind and displays
no "blindisms." However, when first seen, she had rapid
eye movements. As she became comfortable, they disappeared.

Carol Ann is a white-cane user and requires minimal
mobility assistance. She does not hesitate to ask those
around her for directions and orientation when necessary.
She travels to school in a special bus or a cab. When asked
how she felt riding the bus, she replied—"no big deal"
and added, "How else would I get there?" This matter of
fact, realistic response seemed quite characteristic of her.
When mobility training was discussed further, Carol
went along with the use of a cane but said she wanted
to have a guide dog. She expects to get one in about two
years. As she explained, "If I go out by myself and get
lost, I can't tell my cane to take me home but I can say
that to my dog."

Carol Ann easily discussed her blindness but never
belabored the issue. Again, it appears to be "no big deal."
She did not want to be thought of as blind. She was first
and foremost a person. "People with blindness are different just like all other people. If people expect me to choose
a blind person for my hero, I don't have one." She doesn't
feel sorry for herself except when it takes so long to do
homework and she would prefer to go out riding. She

needs a reader or uses a tape recorder to do homework. She is active and has many interests such as horseback riding, caring for a new colt, skiing in winter, taking judo, guitar, and piano lessons, and sculpting.

Carol Ann wishes for things which are attainable. She would like to go to college, but wants to progress in her hobbies. While having many acquaintances, she has a few special friends. She protests with some pleasure how her brothers are horrible because they hold her down and "tickle me to death."

Carol Ann thinks of herself as a person and views her disability as a secondary characteristic. At times it is an inconvenience, occasionally it has advantages. Carol Ann indicates that if she were not blind, then she probably would not have a horse. She is active, friendly, reality oriented, and thinks for herself. There is no evidence of bitterness and victim identification. Her parents have fostered independence, active living, and many interests.

ADULTS WITH PHYSICAL DISABILITIES FROM CHILDHOOD

In a separate study of adults who cope with physical disabilities (Blom, Ek, Irwin, Kulkarni, Miller, and Frey, 1982), a subgroup of four adults was identified as having congenital or acquired impairments from childhood. The adults in this larger study were nominated by adult peers with disabilities and interviewed in one or two sessions for a total time of four to six hours. Interviews followed a schedule designed to include those topics identified by disabled persons as important in their lives as well as by the literature on independent living. The interviews were tape recorded and written up shortly following their completion. After discussions by a research group, a summarized case study was prepared for each subject. In addition, two behavioral inventories were constructed on coping process behaviors and competence outcome behaviors. These inventories were then applied to the original interview data. Indices of independent living and productivity were also obtained following a method described by DeJong (1981).

The findings on the four adults with childhood physical disabilities are summarized in Table 24.4. As can be seen, three of the four adults were productive, independent, coping, competent, and satisfied members of their community. One adult was less productive on the independent living index since he was unemployed, yet he was active in the community and in leisure activities; his rating on coping was high and on competence moderately high.

CASE EXAMPLE 2

An illustrative example of this group of subjects is D. M. who is twenty-seven years old. She developed poliomyelitis as an infant around one year of age which necessitated hospitalization for six months.

The youngest of four children, D. M.'s earlier childhood identities were teacher's pet, being cute, poor kid, and wonder kid. During childhood and adolescence she had nine surgical orthopedic procedures for problems with physical mobility. This resulted in spending much time in hospitals where she more often than not was a model child patient. D. M. was always a good student within regular mainstream education, graduating from high school in the top 10 percent of her class.

At that time she left home to attend college, an important turning point for change in life-style, views, and values. She made positive and progressive changes in independence and self-confidence without the understanding of parents who had low expectations for her. This created a gap that was filled by a relationship with her oldest married brother's family. She obtained some financial assistance from the disability system which saw

TABLE 24.4

Adults With Physical Disabilities—Age, Sex, Characteristic, Ratings

Subject	Age	Sex	Characteristics	Congenital	Acquired	Independent Living	Productivity	Positive Coping Score	Positive Competence Score
BK	31	M	Cleft Palate, Blindness	X	X	*LR	Moderate	25/28 (High)	20/31 Moderate
DM	27	F	Poliomyelitis		X	LR	Most	26/28 (High)	27/31 High
GP	28	M	Dwarfism	X		LR	Most	26/28 (High)	30/31 High
LP	21	M	Cerebral Palsy	X		LR	Most	24/28 (High)	27/31 High

*LR = Least restrictive

her as too capable to merit further support. In the work world, she quickly moved into management and advising functions. Yet, she left a secure occupational position in order to develop further. In this and other situations she has taken risks and relinquished security in favor of fostering greater self-potential.

D. M. is of somewhat short stature, 4 feet 11 inches tall. Currently, she is limited in mobility and strength in both legs and uses crutches and a motorized wheelchair to get around. Recently she moved into an accessible first-floor apartment—her first experience in living alone. D.M. drives a car and works full time in rehabilitation-related work. She feels in control of her own health and medical decisions. She is very active as an advocate in handicapped affairs and has friends with and without disabilities. She leads an active life of full-time work, part-time education, advocacy, friendships, and active leisure. Her hobbies and interests are varied—music, reading, politics, gourmet cooking, traveling, and television comedy programs—more than time allows.

D. M. is likeable and personable with verbal fluency. She has leadership abilities and takes advantage of opportunities that have developed in her life. She learns from experience. She is a problem solver and doer, going after what is realizable. Her perceptions are accurate and rational. She can be courageous and tolerate unpleasant emotions. She has a sense of humor and maintains good self-esteem. D.M. feels ownership of her own body and sees herself as a person and not as a victim.

D. M. has considerable self-awareness and insight fostered from personal counseling, special group experiences, and a psychological belief system. She is aware of her psychological strengths and weaknesses. While not teased a great deal as a child, she has had personal experiences with prejudice, stereotype, and negative spread. One of her heroines is Margaret Mead who is seen as an innovator, maverick, risk taker, self-believer, and someone who was willing to do the socially unacceptable. D. M.'s advice to persons with disability includes being an autonomous thinker, reflective, and one's own decision maker.

On objective measures D. M. ranks high on indices of independent living with a least restrictive living arrangement and a most productive life style of full employment, part-time school, organizational memberships, home making, and active leisure. On the behavior inventories for coping, she has 26 positive ratings (out of 28 items) and for competence and quality of life, 27 positive ratings (out of 31 items). These findings are consistent with interview data.

There are limitations to these pilot studies of children with physical disabilities who cope and of adults who cope with congenital and acquired disabilities from childhood. They were a selected small group not studied in depth or followed developmentally over time. Yet, they support the existence of a coping group which is represented high on a continuum of adaptation. Further studies are in process. Psychological instruments will be developed which can be applied to larger populations of people with physical disabilities to further verify a subgroup of coping individuals.

NEEDED: A PSYCHOANALYTIC PSYCHOLOGY OF DIFFERENTNESS

It is universal within human experience to have anxieties about bodily injury, illness, disfigurement, change, and imperfections. Such anxieties are accentuated within cultures such as the United States which places a high value on beauty, youth, health, well-being, and functional perfection. One of the ways in which bodily anxiety may be handled is through denial, displacement, and projection. Such defense mechanisms can lead to negative personal attitudes toward those already disabled. They are also reinforced by societal values and attitudes. This means that a person with a disability can be responded to by another individual (outsider) with outward aversion, dread, and avoidance based on an inner experience of anxiety that is not tolerated.

Psychoanalytic developmental psychology has identified the emergence of different anxiety clusters in a series during the process of development. The earliest anxieties consist of innate archaic fears of unknown impressions followed by fears of strangers and separation. Fears of mutilation and injury follow and in middle childhood there are anxieties of punishment, social failure, disfigurement, and death. Finally, in adolescence, there are fears of bodily change, loss of emotional control and sexual expression. In adult life there are reactive anxieties of childhood and existential fears of life. Physical disability may activate these various forms of developmental anxiety in the outsider and the insider.

Accompanying the developmental anxieties of children are the anxieties of parents. They experience existential parental and other adult anxieties as well as the reactivation of anxieties from their own childhood. Parental anxieties may interfere in helping disabled children with their own anxiety. Adults of the extended family and nonfamily members such as teachers, therapists, doctors, and friends have an influential role in helping children with disability deal with anxiety more effectively.

A universal existential anxiety which most pregnant mothers and many fathers experience is that their child may be born with a handicap. This can be viewed as an adaptive mechanism to deal with that possible fate rather than being seen as a pathological fear based on unconscious factors. It is an anxiety with a realistic basis in that one child in forty suffers from a serious handicap (Keniston, 1977) and 10 percent of the child population from birth to nineteen years of age has congenital and acquired disabilities (*American Education Reprint*, 1975). Physical differentness is a fact of life and is present throughout the life span until death.

One concept which has been developed from consumers with physical disability is the reference term *temporary able bodied* for the majority group of able bodied. The authors are in agreement that this concept can foster a normative psychology of differentness. Temporary able bodied connotes the possibility that anyone may become disabled. Then a child or adult with a disability does not have such great social distance from a temporary able-bodied person. If disabilities are also considered physical and/or mental characteristics, then a negative psychological category label need not be attached to a person who is different. Words, their meanings, and created images have powerful attitude effects and deserve monitored attention by individuals and society.

In addition to the individual psychological level of response to disability, there are societal factors which strongly influence the psychological response. It is at this level that major social change has occurred to guarantee the civil rights, freedoms, and opportunities of disabled persons and their families. This creates the opportunity through social development in home, school, and community to reduce social distance between disabled and able-bodied persons. Policies have been created through legislation and government regulations for the appropriate integration of temporary able-bodied and disabled persons to their mutual benefit. However, common sense and psychological awareness recognize resistance to social change and to the acceptance of human differences. It is here that psychoanalytic insights can identify the individual and social mechanisms which foster resistance.

Psychoanalytic studies of children and adults who cope well with physical disabilities should be encouraged to counteract the transpositions from the study of pathology to normality. The psychoanalytic treatment of selected patients with disabilities who have symptoms, conflicts, and developmental arrests may create faulty psychological impressions and generalizations about physical disability. Particularly needed are findings from the study of individuals with disability who grow up normatively. Different developmental norms and social environments exist and need to be understood. Being physically different does not have to mean psychological abnormality or pathology. Some noteworthy efforts have been in process for a number of years with psychoanalytic developmental studies of blind and deaf infants and children and their parenting (Burlingham, 1972; Schlesinger and Meadow, 1972; Fraiberg, 1977; Galenson, Miller, Kaplan, and Rothstein, 1979).

SUMMARY

Starting with the civil rights movement for ethnic minorities in the 1960s, there has been a social emergence of children with physical disabilities. This has been highlighted by federal legislation in 1973 and in 1975, particularly through PL 94-142, the Education of All Handicapped Children' Act. These developments have led to a critical examination of current theories and practices of professionals regarding physical disabilities.

This presentation has reviewed psychoanalytic perspectives on physical disability starting with Freud's original view of the negative exception. This prototype has persisted in psychoanalytic publications up to the present time. "The exception" is critiqued as it neglects the role of social prejudice in fostering negative self and object representations.

Adaptive aspects of exceptionality are discussed from empirical and conceptual studies. Pilot clinical studies are presented of children with physical disabilities and of adults with congenital and acquired physical disabilities from childhood. These studies are based on subjects who were successful adapters.

Finally, the case is made for a psychoanalytic psychology of differentness that is normatively based. Attention is directed to the range of adaptation in persons with physical disability similar to psychoanalytic developmental studies of blind and deaf children.

REFERENCES

American Education Reprint (1976), Education of the handicapped today and a bill of rights for the handicapped. Washington, DC: U.S. Government Printing Office.

Anthony, E. J. (1975), Naturalistic studies of disturbed families. In: *Explorations in Child Psychiatry*, ed. E. J. Anthony. New York: Plenum Press.

Bleuler, M. (1974), The offspring of schizophrenics. *Schiz. Bull.*, 8: 93–107.

Block, J., & Haan, N. (1971), *Lives Through Time*. Berkeley, CA: Bancroft Books.

Blom, G. E. (1984), Children who cope: Some implications for intervention and prevention. In: *Child Nurturance*, Vol. 4, ed. R. P. Rogers, G. E. Blom, & L. E. Lezotte. New York: Plenum Press.

———— Ek, K., Irwin, S., Kulkarni, M., Miller, K., & Frey, W. (1982), Coping with handicaps: Implications for adults with physical disabilities. Paper presented to the National Rehabilitation Association Annual Meeting, September 20.

Burlingham, D. (1972), *Psychoanalytic Studies of the Sighted and the Blind*. New York: International Universities Press.

Coles, R. (1964), *Children of Crisis*. Boston: Little, Brown.

DeJong, G. (1981), *Environmental Accessibility and Independent Living Outcomes: Directions for Disability Policy and Research*. East Lansing, MI: University Center for International Rehabilitation, Michigan State University.

DeLoach, C., & Greer, B. G. (1981), *Adjustment to Severe Physical Disability: A Metamorphosis*. New York: McGraw-Hill.

Fraiberg, S. (1977), *Insights From the Blind*. New York: Basic Books.

Freud, S. (1916), Some character-types met with in psycho-analytic work. *Standard Edition*, 14:311–331. London: Hogarth Press, 1957.

Furman, R. (1968), Analysis of a child with a congenital defect. *Internat. J. Psycho-Anal.* 49:276–279.

Galenson, E., Miller, R., Kaplan, E., & Rothstein, A. (1979), Assessment of development in the deaf child. *J. Amer. Acad. Child Psychiat.*, 18:128–142.

Garmezy, N. (1981), Children under stress: Perspectives on antecedents and correlates of vulnerability and resistance to psychopathology. In: *Further Explorations in Personality*, ed. A. I.
Rabin, J. Aronoff, A. M. Barclay, & R. A. Tucker. New York:
John Wiley.

Gediman, H. K. (1974), Narcissistic trauma, object loss and the family
romance. *Psychoanal. Rev.*, 61:203–215.

Gliedman, J., & Roth, W. (1980), *The Unexpected Minority: Handicapped Children in America*. New York: Harcourt Brace Jovanovich.

Goffman, E. (1963), *Stigma: Notes on the Management of Spoiled
Identity*. Englewood Cliffs, NJ: Prentice-Hall.

Goldensohn, R. M., ed. (1978), *Disability and Rehabilitation Handbook*. New York: McGraw-Hill.

Haan, N. (1977), *Coping and Defending: Processes of Self-environment
Organization*. New York: Academic Press.

Hartmann, H. (1939), *Ego Psychology and the Problem of Adaptation*.
New York: International Universities Press, 1958.

Hohmann, G. W. (1975), The insider-outsider position and the maintenance of hope. *Rehab. Psychol.*, 22(2):1361–1364.

Jacobson, E. (1959), The "exceptions": An elaboration of Freud's character study. *The Psychoanalytic Study of the Child*, 14:135–154.
New York: International Universities Press.

Kaplan, E. (1959), The role of birth injury in a patient's character
development and his neuroses. *Bull. Phila. Assn. Psychoanal.*,
9:1–18.

Kaplan, L. J. (1974), The concept of the family romance. *Psychoanal.
Rev.*, 61:169–199.

Keniston, K. (1977), *All Our Children: The American Family Under
Pressure*. New York: Harcourt Brace Jovanovich.

Kris, A. O. (1976), On wanting too much: The "exceptions" revisited.
Internat. J. Psycho-Anal., 57:85–95.

Leopold-Lowenthal, H. (1976), A discussion of the paper by Anton O.
Kris "On wanting too much: The 'exceptions' revisited." *Internat.
J. Psycho-Anal.*, 57:97–99.

Lipton, E. L. (1976), Psychoanalytic child development research and
the practice of general psychiatry. *Internat. J. Psycho-Anal.*, 57:
113–116.

Lussier, A. (1960), Analysis of a boy with a congenital deformity. *The
Psychoanalytic Study of the Child*, 15:430–453. New York: International Universities Press.

Mattson, A. (1972), Long-term physical illness in childhood: A challenge of psychosocial adaptation. *Pediatrics*, 50:801–811.

Mednick, S. A., & Witkin-Lanoil, G. H. (1977), Intervention in chil-
dren at high risk for schizophrenia. In: *Primary Prevention of
Psychopathology: The Issues*, Vol. 1, ed. G. W. Albee & J. M.
Joffe. Hanover, NH: University Press of New England.

Murphy, L. B. (1981), Explorations in child personality. In: *Further*

Explorations in Personality, ed. A. I. Rabin, J. Aranoff, A. M. Barclay, & R. A. Tucker. New York: John Wiley.

———— Moriarty, A. E. (1976), *Vulnerability, Coping and Growth From Infancy to Adolescence.* New Haven, CT: Yale University Press.

Neuchterlein, K. H. (1970), *Competent Disadvantaged Children: A Review of Research.* Unpublished doctoral dissertation. University of Minnesota, Minneapolis.

Niederland, W. (1965), Narcissistic ego impairment in patients with early physical malformations. *The Psychoanalytic Study of the Child,* 20:518–534. New York: International Universities Press.

Parker, B. (1971), A case of congenital spina bifida: Imprint of the defect on psychic development. *Internat. J. Psycho-Anal.,* 52: 307–320.

Rutter, M. (1979), Proactive factors in children's responses to stress and disadvantage. In: *Primary Prevention of Psychopathology,* Vol. 3, ed. M. Kent & J. Rolf. Hanover, NH: University Press of New England.

Sameroff, A. J., & Chandler, M. J. (1975), Reproductive risk and the continuum of caretaking casualty. In: *Review of Child Development Research,* Vol. 4, ed. F. D. Horowitz. Chicago: University of Chicago Press.

Schlesinger, H., & Meadow, K. (1972), *Sound and Sign.* Berkeley: University of California Press.

Stubbins, J. (1982), *The Clinical Attitude in Rehabilitation: A Cross Cultural View.* New York: World Rehabilitation Fund.

Vash, C. L. (1981), *The Psychology of Disability.* New York: Springer.

Werner, E. E., & Smith, R. S. (1982), *Vulnerable but Invincible: A Study of Resilient Children.* New York: McGraw-Hill.

White, R. W. (1959), Motivation reconsidered: The concept of competence. *Psychol. Rev.,* 66:297–333.

———— (1963), Ego and Reality in Psychoanalytical Theory. *Psychological Issues,* Monograph II, 3/3. New York: International Universities Press.

———— (1979), Competence as an aspect of personal growth. In: *Primary Prevention of Psychopathology: Social Competence in Children,* Vol. 3, ed. M. W. Kent & J. E. Rolf. Hanover, NH: University Press of New England.

Wolfensberger, W. (1972), *The Principle of Normalization in Human Services.* Toronto: National Institute of Mental Retardation.

Wright, B. A. (1960), *Physical Disability: A Psychological Approach.* New York: Harper & Row.

———— (1975), Sensitizing outsiders to the position of the insider. *Rehab. Psychol.,* 22(2):129–135.

———— (1980), Developing constructive views of life with a disability. *Rehab. Lit.,* 41(11–12):274–279.

Part IV

Learning and the Teacher

Introduction: Part IV

> [M]any aspects of psychoanalytic human development may be conceptualized in learning theory terms. As a limited learning theory this differs dramatically from existing learning theories of academic psychology. Although many differences exist, the primary one is that it [learning] occurs within the context of intense object relationships and is not particularly related to such concepts as "reinforcement" or "gratification." It is a learning theory addressed to character development, not to academic content. The key modes of "learning" are the internalization processes.
>
> Seymour L. Lustman (1970)

What can the developmental theories of psychoanalysis tell us about normative and pathological patterns of learning in the educational situation?

What is the relationship of knowledge and skill to personality development and maturation?

Can psychodynamic understanding be of practical use to the beleagured classroom teacher, faced with the unremitting pressures and demands of disparate groups of children from many different family backgrounds, some of whom may be gifted, mentally retarded, learning disabled, physically/developmentally impaired, emotionally disturbed, socially alienated, neglected, abused, addicted, and so on.

What constitutes psychological literacy in pedagogy given the changing realities of schooling today?

These are some of the questions the contributors to this section of our volume address in the following chapters. When Lustman wrote the paper from which the above excerpt is taken, he was responding to an emerging problem in education, namely, the unprecedented numbers of impulse-ridden, developmentally impaired children from culturally and/or economically deprived families who were appearing in primary-school classrooms. He spoke then (1970) of the "clinical dimension in education" and argued that the critical question, "How to make maximal use of the teacher as a crucial object in the lives of children?" could best be answered through collaboration between education and psychoanalysis. Today, the problems Lustman addressed can no longer be confined to one sector of the school population, the culturally disadvantaged. The phenomenal growth of the special education movement in public education in the 1970s and 1980s testifies to the fact that the need to recognize the so-called "clinical dimension" in education is now a fact of life in most schools. More and more of the young children starting school have been subjected to severe developmental deprivation, damaging disruptions in their early relationships with parents and/or primary caretakers, and exposed to any number of traumatic life experiences (divorce, multiple caretakers, chronic illness, abuse, neglect, and so on) which have impeded or impaired their development. As a result, they are unprepared to cope with the tasks of school learning. Teachers, too, albeit for different reasons, are unprepared to understand, let alone cope with, the complex problems with learning and impulse control such children present. Thus, what has changed most in the last twenty-five years in the schools has less to do with subject matter and teaching methodology and more to do with the human variables in the educational situation.

An understanding of the human variables in education, the dynamic interactions of teachers and learners, in particular, is the missing dimension in educational discourse and practice. The challenge to psychoanalysis and education is to forge a partnership aimed at the scientific study of this missing dimension.

The chapters in this section of our volume are based on the proposition that psychoanalysis is a process or form of inquiry, grounded in a set of assumptions about human development and behavior, which have significant implications for research and practice in education and schooling. The generative possibilities of psychoanalytic propositions about the nature and development of human learning have been considerably enhanced in recent years by the confluence of two areas of inquiry: infant developmental studies and the explanatory theories of psychoanalysis. As Michael Basch sees it, "[W]e are faced with . . . the need to reexamine our basic [psychoanalytic] theories in an attempt to recast them in accordance with the best knowledge available today regarding the maturational process in infants and children" (1982, p. 735). This mutual need to realign theory and practice "in accordance with the best knowledge available today" calls for joint inquiry by psychoanalysts and educators. The chapters that follow are a response to this challenge.

Among the developmental theories relevant to education, psychoanalysis is unique in its elaboration of the significance of unconscious motivation in human relationships. It has studied the conditions that mediate the vulnerability of the individual to influence, as well as the nature and origins of obstacles to influence. Through the study of "transference" phenomena, psychoanalysis has elucidated the mechanisms underlying a wide range of human interactions in which inappropriate or discrepant behavior and/or perceptions seem to occur. With its traditional emphasis on the study of motive, meaning, and affect, psychoanalysis contributes an added dimension as well as a balancing perspective to the already well-established educational emphasis on cognitive modes and subject matter mastery in the teaching-learning process.

All of the contributors to this section are members of the faculty and staff of the Institute for Psychoanalysis in Chicago and are directly or indirectly involved in its Teacher Education Programs (TEP). Glorye Wool, Marilyn Silin, Linda Cozzarelli, Ner Littner, Miriam Elson, and Kay Field have all been actively involved in the development of the TEP and its several offshoots.[1] Michael Basch has contributed informally and formally to the Program's theoretical perspectives and has participated in a number of its community conferences. Thus, all the chapters in this section may be said to reflect aspects of the authors' experiences with teachers in the TEP. In this sense, the chapters are rooted in a common core of collaborative work with educators, namely, the attempt to incorporate psychoanalytic knowledge of personality development and relationship dynamics and of the process of change into psychologically enriched programs of teacher education.

The intent of the contributors to this section is not to offer psychoanalytic solutions or panaceas for all pedagogical problems or new instructional methods to replace those in use. The aim is a more modest one: it is hoped that the contributors will elucidate and demonstrate the organizing and sensitizing role of psychoanalytic theory in the development of teachers' understanding of their interactions with children and the consequences for learning and teaching. The lack of a comprehensive theory of human psychological development and behavior has driven teachers to a search for methods and tech-

---

[1] A program designed for the faculty of the Chicago City Colleges, and an advanced, three-year program for leadership training in Clinical School Services (i.e., psychology, social work, etc.) are among the TEP offshoots.

niques to manage surface behaviors. Out of a theoretic approach should come new ways for teachers to think about themselves and their relationships with others within the terms of a coherent theory.

It is further hoped that teachers will find a renewed sense of purpose and direction in their work and an enhanced professionalism. We recognize, of course, that the issues confronting American education are legion and infinitely complex. Multiple perspectives—philosophical, theoretical, epistemological, cultural, organizational, as well as psychological/developmental—are required if we are to understand fully and deal with the tasks and responsibilities of education in a changing society.

Each chapter builds upon the previous one. The first chapter by Glorye Wool, "Relational Aspects of Learning: The Learning Alliance," compares the psychoanalytic and the educational situations and finds significant congruence between developmental structure formation and structural change during the course of psychoanalysis, and the acquisition of knowledge in the educational situation. In both contexts, learning is viewed as a process of internalization. Citing recent developmental studies which document the remarkable inborn capacities infants have for learning and growing within a dynamic human context, she goes on to delineate how the adult learner, using his inner cognitive and affective capacities, connects with the facilitating environment, thereby creating new knowledge, and, in effect, a new part of himself.

Wool's chapter is an elaboration and extension of the concept of the learning alliance, originally promulgated by Joan Fleming. Examining the components of this special instrument of learning, she explores the roles played by affect regulation, idealization, and integration. Throughout her chapter, Wool emphasizes the transitional nature of learning in line with Fleming's view that learning based on Winnicott's concept of transitional phenomena is a transitional and therefore creative process.

In his chapter, "The Teacher, the Transference, and Development," Michael Basch elucidates the significance of psychoanalytic developmental theories and the findings of recent developmental research for understanding the interactive dynamics in teaching. Noting the widespread incidence of developmental pathology and learning deficiencies in primary grade children, he suggests that "like it or not, the teacher, if he or she is to be successful, must function as a psychotherapist, not in the formal sense of conducting therapy sessions . . . but in the practical sense of being alert and responsive to the psychological needs that students evince both by what they do and what they do not do." He bases this view of the teacher as psychotherapist on new knowledge about human learning coming to us from infant research. We now know that learning in the first two years of life is "the time of greatest learning," the time when a child's behavior patterns, expectations, and attitudes toward self and others are laid down (learned). The importance of teachers' understanding of transference phenomena derives from these findings. Basch argues that "teachers are in the best position to have an early corrective influence on the personalities of their charges."

Anticipating the charge that a psychotherapeutic function would add to the already heavy demands currently being imposed on educators, he points out that "psychotherapy, in the broad sense of the word, is not only something that any person capable of establishing an empathic relationship is able to perform. It is a function that most of us perform without realizing it"— in a variety of everyday situations, when we talk over problems with friends, when we calm a child, comfort the sick, and the like. Basch defines psychotherapy as "the art of helping people to examine themselves and their respective situations so that they will eventually be able to come to decisions that make sense, given their particular personalities and their circumstances. According to Basch's general definition of psychotherapy, then, teachers may be performing a therapeutic function insofar as they influence the decision to learn in their students.

The roots of human motivation for learning and their implications for teachers are examined in the remainder of the chapter. Basch first compares the explanations propounded in Freud's psychosexual theories (in terms of the oral, anal, and phallic stages) with those coming out of infant research. The Freudian theory, he avers, has little relevance for professionals "who are not engaged in the treatment of neurotic children and adults." Turning to infant research, he considers the finding of "the inherited propensity for mastery and extension of control over the environment" demonstrated in infancy as far more significant for teachers, "because it is in this developmental line that the groundwork is laid for many so-called learning problems of various degrees that teachers face daily in their classrooms."

Elaborating this point, Basch reminds us that White's concept of "effectance pleasure," that is, "pleasure through mastery" is the fundamental incentive for maturation. This formulation underscores the importance of affect in the learning process. The emotionally healthy child learns not for the sake of learning (not for mastery alone) but for the positive response of the adult caretaker. Without such a background of self-esteem in which a child finds himself effective through interaction with adults, other forms of rewards for learning in the classroom may be meaningless. Lacking this incentive for learning, Basch points out, a child falls back on the only source of transactional satisfaction familiar (and available) to him—attracting the interest of peers through outrageous behavior.

Because of the fundamental importance of fostering affective development during the formative years, Basch finds the current emphasis on early stimulation of cognitive development in infants and young children misplaced and potentially harmful. He attributes past failures in affective communication between parents and children to the problems children bring to teachers via transference. What can the teacher do, if anything, to influence "the self-destructive course on which such children have been set?" It is this question that ultimately defines the basic task of teachers as enablers and facilitators of the learning process. Inasmuch as more and more children in our schools today belong to this category of learners, Basch's idea of the psychotherapeutic role of teachers takes on new meaning. For it is the emotional or affective set of the child that has as much or more significance as his intellectual endowment. The challenge to the teacher is how to provide children with the sense of effectance pleasure, the sense of achievement, which is everyone's longing to become as Kohut put it "an independent center of initiative."

The theoretical issues raised in chapter 26 by Basch become the issues that frame the presentations in both chapters 27 and 28. Chapter 27, "The Learner as Teacher, the Teacher as Learner," by Miriam Elson describes her experiences as the instructor in a course for adult learners—teachers on the faculty of the Chicago City Colleges[2] Drawing upon her work with these teachers, Elson illustrates the dynamic complementarity in the teacher-student relationship, in particular, the parallel process in which the teacher learns as he teaches and the learner teaches as he learns. Elson locates the fate of both teaching and learning in this parallel process. Chapter 28, on transference distortions in the teaching-learning process, coauthored by Linda Cozzarelli and Marilyn Silin, describes the influence of transference distortions on pupil learning in an elementary school classroom. These two

---

[2] This course, "Stress, Change and Growth in the Human Life Cycle," was part of a multiple course offering in the Chicago College Teacher Education Program.

chapters illustrate different pedagogical aspects of the self psychological theoretical point of view in psychoanalysis elucidated in the chapter by Basch. Both chapters address the problems teachers encounter in work with students suffering from developmental deficits in self organization that impede or impair their ability to learn in school.

The college students described in Elson's paper and those mentioned by Basch come from the same segment of the population—from socioeconomically and culturally disadvantaged families. Trained to think in terms of a knowledge base rather than process, the frustration, discouragement, fatigue, and ebbing self-esteem the teachers suffered in their work with their students made for a severe morale problem and a loss of pleasure in their work. She is impressed by the high quality of the teachers' writing, their sensitivity, and their wit, noting that a red thread of despair and anger runs through all of it.

Elson found Kohut's evolving theories of self psychology most pertinent to the experience of the adult learner and provides an excellent brief summary of the concepts having most salience in the educational situation; for example, transference reawakening of students' infantile needs and expectations in the relationship with the teacher, the selfobject functions of the teacher, the process of transmuting internalization in facilitating growth in learning, empathy and change in self-image and aspirations. Her case material illustrates the pertinence and utility of these theoretical constructs for teachers.

Linda Cozzarelli and Marilyn Silin, in their chapter, "The Effects of Narcissistic Transference on the Teaching-Learning Process," offer specific classroom examples and further elaboration of the theoretical formulations elucidated and illustrated in the preceding chapters by Basch and Elson. In their discussion of transference-countertransference distortions, the authors highlight the adverse effects on both student and teacher of narcissistic issues engendered in their classroom interactions, noting, in particular, the mutual feelings of worthlessness and low self-esteem each one tends to mirror and reinforce in the other. Their case examples point up the dilemma faced by teachers as they try to distinguish between the educational and the psychological elements in problematic situations when they are themselves so inextricably involved in the very problems they are trying to resolve. This chapter is further testimony to the sensitizing and practical usefulness of a dynamic theoretic perspective that enables teachers to understand the geometry of the emotions in relation to the motives and meaning underlying student behavior and communications.

Ner Littner, in his chapter, "Reflections of Early Childhood Family Experiences in the Educational Situation," differentiates between "realistic" and unrealistic (i.e., [transference] emotional feelings toward and reactions to children experienced by teachers) and proceeds to explain how understanding the mental mechanisms involved in these emotional transactions applies to the tasks of learning and teaching and the purpose of education.

In the first part of his chapter, Littner focuses, in particular, on "those factors that influence a child's ability to form a positive relationship (e.g., learning alliance) with the teacher, and through this relationship, to learn how to learn." Acknowledging the differences in the mother-child and teacher-student relationships, Littner maintains that there are important similarities in what the child needs from both (e.g., "patience, consistency, appropriate discipline, nonpunitiveness, and conscious recognition of the teacher's own problems so that they do not interfere with his teaching abilities"). In addition, two other sets of factors need to be considered. Personality characteristics of the teacher may limit his sensitivity to the differential needs and communications of individual children and lead to inappropriate and/or negative responses and interventions; and situational factors within the school may interfere with or impair the teacher's capacity to function in an emotionally positive fashion with children. On the latter point, he emphasizes that "the teacher himself needs to be treated in the same way he should treat the child!"

Littner, like Basch, sees the relationship between teacher and child as rooted in and shaped by the child's earliest mothering experiences. After reviewing the conditions that make for good mothering (and fathering), he delineates the problems that mitigate against a positive parenting relationship and by extension, a positive teacher-student relationship.

The remainder of his chapter is devoted to discussion of the modern prototype of disturbance in the parent-child relationship—the situation of the student who is a victim of divorce and the harmful effects this event may have on his school functioning. The major factor, according to Littner, is that divorce may make the child particularly sensitive and vulnerable to loss and separation from meaningful adults in the educational situation. He then proceeds to examine, in detail, the different ways in which separation reactions may be triggered and manifested in school. He identifies and discusses three principal areas in which "interferences with the learning process may occur in the presence of strong separation reactions: in the development of the learning process; in the area of behavior; in physical symptoms; and in combinations of all of these." He then delineates the spectrum of psychological defense mechanisms children may employ to cope with loss and separation in each of the above areas.

Finally, Littner provides a number of helpful suggestions on "how the school can help the child of divorce." The importance of this chapter goes beyond this subject, however. For Littner simply uses it to expound on the

dynamic-developmental issues that determine whether
or not children will learn how to learn in their relationship with their teachers, or to use his words, develop "a
positive learning stance." In so doing, he provides a detailed overview of the potential effects, positive or negative, that the emotions may have on the teaching-
learning process, and the various mental mechanisms
(defenses) individuals employ when anxiety gets in the
way of learning.

This section concludes with a chapter by Kay Field,
"Some Reflections on the Teacher-Student Dialogue: A
Psychoanalytic Perspective." The purpose of her chapter
is to inquire into the crucial question of how teachers
themselves experience the learning process and how this
relates to and affects the parallel learning process of their
students. The classroom observations and reflections of
the faculty and director (the author) of a psychoanalytically informed educational program for Chicago-area,
practicing teachers, offered under the aegis of the Institute for Psychoanalysis in Chicago, provides the data
source. Specifically, the process notes of one instructor
form the basis of a narrative report detailing the phenomena and vicissitudes of the learning process as it un-
folded over a period of twenty-two weeks in a course
entitled "Teacher-Student Interactions in the Classroom." The report of the instructor's observations and
reflections is accompanied by the author's running commentary. Together they provide a rich picture of the subtleties, complexities, and unpredictability of the teaching-
learning alliance during the twenty-two-week duration
of the course. The developmental-dynamic concepts examined in the preceding chapters in this section are vividly etched in this illustrative "process portrait" of a
group of teachers learning about the psychological meaning that being taught has for their pupils through examining their own experiences as learners in this course.
The chronicle of their experiences gives practical here-

and-now meaning to the conceptual material introduced in the preceding chapters; for example, learning as a developmental process, transference and countertransference issues, the reciprocal, complementary nature of the learning-teaching process, the teaching-learning alliance, the role of the group, the significance of contextual variables on learning, the powerful influence of the emotions in motivation, and so on. The dramatic changes noted in these teachers' self attitudes and learning raise important questions about the process of change in teacher education and school reform.

In all the chapters in this volume the aim is to advance a conception of knowledge in education, not as content per se, nor as structure, but knowledge which is the product of a dynamic-developmental process, a contextually relative exercise of capacities for imaginatively ordering our experience. Teachers are viewed as persons in interaction with their milieu. In short, the uniqueness of psychoanalytic developmental theory lies in its elaboration of the meaning and significance of unconscious motivation in human learning. Research adopting a teacher-practitioner perspective should advance significantly the dialogue between educators and psychoanalysts. The issues to be examined include, but are not limited to, the nature of motivation, the quest for meaning, the development of the self "as a whole," and the role of affect in the learning process, to name a few.

REFERENCES

Basch, M. (1982), The significance of infant developmental studies. *Psychoanal. Inq.*, 1(4):731–738.

Johnson, M. (1985), Elbaz and Freema on *Teacher Thinking: A Study of Practical Knowledge. Curr. Inq.*, 14(4):465–468.

Lustman, S. (1970), Cultural deprivation: A clinical dimension of education. *The Psychoanalytic Study of the Child*, 25:499. New York: International Universities Press.

Chapter 25

Relational Aspects of Learning: The Learning Alliance

GLORYE WOOL, M.D.

INTRODUCTION

In 1912, Freud wrote, "Some years ago I gave as an answer to the question of how one can become an analyst: 'By analyzing one's own dreams'" (1912a, p. 116). He pointed to the merits of the Zurich school requirement that everyone who wishes to become an analyst shall first be analyzed by someone with expert knowledge.

> Anyone who takes up this work seriously should choose this course. . . . [T]he sacrifice involved in laying oneself open to another person . . . is amply rewarded. Not only is one's aim of learning to know what is hidden in one's own mind far more rapidly attained and with less expense of affect, but impressions and convictions will be gained in relation to oneself which will be sought in vain from studying books and attending lectures. . . . [W]e must not underestimate the advantage to be derived from the lasting mental contact that is as a rule established between the student and his guide [Freud, 1912a, pp. 116–117].

Freud was here, in effect, introducing the concept of

the learning alliance. Addressing an audience of those aspiring to be psychoanalysts, he pointed out what he had discovered through personal experience, the advantages of learning abetted by a supportive human relationship. His reference was to his having shared his self-analysis, largely through an exchange of letters, with his mentor and friend Wilhelm Fliess (Schur, 1979).

It was in his (1912b) paper, "The Dynamics of Transference," that Freud introduced the concept of the therapeutic alliance (Friedman, 1969). Perhaps even then the congruence between these two concepts—the learning alliance and the therapeutic alliance—was being suggested. That congruence was made explicit many years later by Joan Fleming (Fleming and Benedek, 1966; Fleming, 1972, 1979). Following a long tradition of converging interests in psychoanalysis and education, Fleming, during her many years on the faculty of the Institute for Psychoanalysis in Chicago, developed a special interest in psychoanalytic pedagogy. This led her to study the vicissitudes of the psychoanalytic supervisory process. Throughout her work, Fleming emphasized the experiential aspects of learning, making its dynamic context the focal consideration in understanding the process by which learning takes place.

Many of the chapters in this volume refer to the contextual nature of learning (see especially Litowitz, chapter 12), noting the importance of the relationship between the student and the teacher. Some authors emphasize the interpersonal point of view. This is the traditional point of departure of many developmental psychologists, whose work is based on direct observational studies of parent-child interaction. Some investigators (Mahler, Pine, and Bergman, 1975) draw inferences as to intrapsychic processes from their observational data. This intrapsychic point of view is traditionally the observational vantage point of psychoanalysts who do reconstructive studies of development through the analysis of transference phenomena. (See especially Kohut, 1971, and Wolf, chapter 15). In this chapter the process of learning will be considered from a third viewpoint, namely, that of "transitional" experience. This is that area bridging interpersonal and intrapsychic experience designated as transitional by Donald Winnicott (1951). The focus here on the transitional aspects of learning follows the lead of Fleming, who first applied Winnicott's concept of the transitional object to the field of education. She proposed that the teacher functions as a transitional object and that learning is mediated by a form of transitional experience.

Similarly, Fleming adapted the concept of the therapeutic alliance to education. Just as Freud appeared to have done in 1912, Fleming saw important parallels between the analytic situation and the educational situation, stressing the essential congruence between the analytic and learning alliances. She proposed that, just as the therapeutic alliance is the vehicle of analytic change, so is the alliance between teacher and learner itself the vehicle of learning.

This chapter is an attempt to elaborate on Fleming's concept of the learning alliance. Emphasis will be placed on two focal issues, the significance of a dynamic relational context for learning and the processes of internalization. Consideration will be given to the analogies between normal growth and development, change in the psychoanalytic context, and the acquisition of knowledge in the educational situation.

Investigators especially interested in self psychology would naturally see the learning alliance in the light of Kohut's concept of the selfobject (Kohut, 1971). The alliance could indeed be conceptualized in selfobject terms (see Muslin and Val, chapter 7; Wolf, chapter 15). Such a view is discussed later in reference to the Freud-Fliess relationship. In that context, Kohut's idea of that relationship as a special variant of a selfobject transference is noted. For present purposes, however, particular emphasis will be placed on the learning alliance as a transitional phenomenon. This approach is dictated by the wish to adhere to Fleming's adaptation of the concept of transitional experience as it applies to the educational process. In the discussion to follow, the learning alliance will be viewed as a variant of what Winnicott (1958) designated as "being alone in the presence of another." He proposed that the mature person's capacity to be alone came only through that individual's opportunity during early childhood of being alone in the presence of a "good enough" mother. Here he was describing how the human context, through a transitional process, contributes to inner growth, burgeoning independence, and the eventual capacity to function on one's own. Analogously, the learning alliance provides just such a transitional context for the acquisition of knowledge and the capacity, as the student matures, for individual scholarship.

THE NATURE OF THE TEACHER-STUDENT RELATIONSHIP

Psychoanalysts have long been interested in the educational process. Their primary focus has been on the psychopathology of learning, with emphasis on cognition and perception. Contributions have been made in delineating the areas of accord between cognitive theory and the psychoanalytic theory of therapy. For example, Michael Basch (1977), in his explication of the relevance of perceptual and cognitive psychology for psychoanalysis, demonstrated that "Freudian and Piagetian psychologies enhance and complement one another." Basch summarized: "[R]ecent studies in perceptual and cognitive development buttress the clinical findings of psychoanalysis regarding the significance of early experience . . . while offering an explanation for the 'mental apparatus' that unites learning theory with the psychoanalytic concepts of conflict and defense" (p. 262).

The emphasis here will be on the affective and relational aspects of learning. Joan Fleming articulated this approach as follows:

> A teacher uses himself as an instrument to stimulate active participation in a creative learning process. Whether this relationship is called a therapeutic alliance or a learning alliance actually makes little difference. The essential job is to serve as a catalyst for the preconscious and conscious experiential and cognitive processes that go on in the mind of a student or patient that help him grow and mature in knowledge, wisdom and skill [Fleming, 1979, pp. 28–29].

Analysts have always paid close attention to the nature of the relationship between analyst and patient. Freud believed that there was an epigenetic progression of object relatedness from the autoerotic, through the narcissistic, to that of object love and hate, and pointed to transference aspects of each of these developmental stages in the analytic relationship. Although recognizing the importance of preoedipal experiences for development and for analysis, Freud focused on issues of oedipal structural conflict and triadic object relatedness. Later investigators added to this focus by studying the diadic relationship activated as part of the analytic experience. Processes designated as the "therapeutic alliance," the "working alliance," the "diatrophic relationship," and/or the "holding environment" came to be considered integral to the analytic process. The therapeutic alliance was seen in the light of the developmental paradigm of the early mother-infant relationship. Maxwell Gitelson (1962) saw the establishment of the diatrophic relationship as essential to the beginning phase of analysis:

> The diatrophic attitude arises as a response to the patient's need for help even as the parent responds to the anaclitic situation of the child. . . . In its ego-controlled

form, that is, as a form of regression in the service of
the ego, it is the basis for analytic empathy. It con-
verges with the patient's need for ego-support and in
this context the analyst, like the mother, has the function of an auxiliary ego. This is the basis of a good
psychoanalytic situation [p. 198].

Ralph Greenson (1967) considered the working alliance "a full and equal partner to the transference neurosis in the patient-therapist relationship" (p. 191). He
stressed its essential function—to provide the capacity to
work purposefully in the analytic situation. "The actual
alliance is formed essentially between the patient's reasonable ego and the analyst's analyzing ego. The medium
which makes this possible is the patient's partial identification with the analyst's analytic approach" (pp.
192–193). Elizabeth Zetzel (1964) added an important
dimension in her discussion of the nature of the therapeutic alliance. She distinguished between the earliest
mother-child relationship in which ego boundaries are
not yet delineated and archaic omnipotence prevails,
from the later period during which the child gains awareness of his separate identity, achieves some measure of
reality testing, and establishes an underlying attitude of
trust which permits him to sustain an object relationship.
It is the successful mastery of the developmental tasks
of this later diadic period which permits the establishment of the therapeutic alliance. Zetzel's point, that partial resolution of the original symbiosis is a prerequisite
to the therapeutic alliance, is also important in understanding the nature of the learning alliance.

One can postulate a line of development that proceeds
through the partial resolution of the original infantile
symbiosis toward relative self and object constancy is re-
established as the "basic transference" in analysis, and
continues to serve throughout the analysis as the vehicle
for the therapeutic split and the working through process.

The specific content to be worked on would, of course, vary according to the phase of the analysis, but the essential functions of the therapeutic alliance persist throughout. Congruently, just as the therapeutic alliance may be seen as analogous to the early parent-child relationship, so may the teaching-learning alliance be viewed in the light of these developmental and therapeutic paradigms. It is the diadic relationship that allows the teacher to use himself as the instrument of learning in a way analogous to the analyst's use of himself as the instrument of analysis. The learning alliance may in this way be seen as a variant of the therapeutic alliance; although the aim and content may differ, they are identical in origin and mode of operation.

THE QUALITIES AND FUNCTIONS OF THE TEACHER

AFFECT REGULATION

The basic trust, confidence, and optimism inherent in the learning situation can only partially stem the tension associated with the effort to learn and the resistance to learning that naturally accompanies this tension. If, as is likely, the teacher is the recipient of preoedipal and oedipal transferences, unconscious parapractic struggles over infantile objects can only intensify the student's anxiety. Just as analytic progress requires regression, so does learning, and this temporary but necessary regression in itself may evoke further anxiety. The teacher must help the pupil regulate tension optimally, stem undue regression, and temper resistance. Provided with such a helpful matrix, the struggling pupil may delay gratification, risk making mistakes, and tolerate not knowing, while actively engaging in trial and error exploration. Within the supportive ambience provided by the teacher, the student may remain hopeful and confident that new solutions to problems will indeed be found.

Here is an example from Fleming (1979) of how she helped a group of novice supervisors overcome the anxiety that was impeding their competence as teachers:

> I entered upon this project with an interest (even an ambition) to give them a systematic course in the aims, content, and pedagogic methods useful in teaching a beginning supervisor how to teach a beginning resident how to communicate and work with a patient. . . . My disillusionment with myself came quickly and my goals and methods had to be revised. We were not on the same track. They were scared and I wanted to talk about theories of teaching. When I turned on my empathic radar . . . I made a diagnosis of transference distortion in their image of a supervisor. They saw a supervisor and a teacher as an exalted, omniscient, omnipotent authority. They were trying to see themselves as such and having realistic trouble. Their anxiety and sense of helpless inadequacy was interfering with their learning. . . . At that point I shifted my stance and, as a teacher who also knew something about anxiety, regression, and overidealization, I decided to tackle the distortion in the exalted image of a teacher with which they were now identified and then go on to their feelings of inadequacy [p. 12].

She responded to their request that she tell them what to do by explaining, "I can't. I have no magic formulas. But it might help if we talk about what being a supervisor means to you" (p. 12). She found that the students were afraid that they did not know enough to be teachers. Her implicit response was that it was all right not to know something, that no one was as omnipotent as they were expecting themselves to be. Their anxieties were relieved as they began to view their teaching task more realistically. Here, as a teacher of teachers, Fleming provided what was necessary for her students to understand, tolerate, and finally to regulate the anxiety that was impeding their learning.

IDEALIZATION

Mutual idealization seems an essential component of any teaching-learning situation. It is acknowledged that the most effective teacher is the one most admired. Idealization of the teacher invites the learner to extend himself in mastering the task, in the service of gaining the dual gratifications of commendation from the teacher and appreciation of one's own skills. From the teacher's point of view, appropriate idealization of the learner is of equal importance. A teacher cannot be effective if he is not hopeful that his students can and will learn. It is generally recognized that students progress or not in accordance with the expectations of their teachers (Elashoff, 1971). Mutual idealization provides a framework for the complex work of learning. Idealization in this sense is not experienced as a grossly unrealistic ascription of magical powers to either of the parties, but rather as the realistic appreciation of the individual's potential for growth. It refers to the healthily omnipotent force of the shared ego ideal which facilitates mastery. It does not refer to the kind of overvaluation of the teacher that inhibits learning. Fleming cautioned against what she called "learning by identification with an idealized teacher." This, she said, "strengthens affectivity at the cost of objectivity and cognitive thinking organized as secondary process and necessitates working through the regressive pull of hero worship" (1979, pp. 9–10). The example given above demonstrates not only Fleming's affect regulating function in her work with students, but her function as well in correcting the transference distortion of overvaluation. The degree of disillusionment was optimal. What was preserved was the mutual high regard she and her students had for each other's capacities, the appropriate, reality-based idealization which facilitates learning. This was the kind of idealization Freud had in mind when he wrote of the schoolboy's relationship to his teacher: "We studied their characters and on theirs we formed or misformed our own. . . . These men became our substitute fathers. . . . We transferred onto them the respect and expectations attaching to the omniscient father of our childhood, and we then began to treat them as we treated our fathers at home" (Freud, 1914, p. 244).

Herbert Schlesinger (1981) also noted the disadvantages of identification with an overidealized teacher, but went on to clarify the facilitating role of identification for learning.

> [P]art of the supervisor's task is to become aware of the nature, strength, and vicissitudes of the learning alliance . . . and to attune his teaching methods to the readiness of the candidate to learn in this context. . . . Referring to identification among resistances to analysis and to learning should not obscure the fact that this process is also one of the normal phenomena of development and often a useful, if temporary, phase in both the therapeutic and learning situations. . . . As trial identifications, these imitations can be useful ways for a candidate to try out something new to him. That they may also represent incipient resistances to learning will, of course, also be considered by the supervisor. . . . The supervisor must recognize that he serves the candidate as a model in terms of how he would handle the clinical episodes under discussion and also in terms of how he reacts and associates to, and reflects on, the material the candidate reports [p. 35].

INTEGRATION

In exercising his organizing, synthesizing, and integrating skills, the teacher makes a third major contribution to learning. Parents, as the first teachers, convey to the child concepts of time, of the connection between present and past, ideas of cause and effect, of actions having consequences, of certain affects being connected to given experiences, ideas of similarity and difference, continuity and discontinuity—the myriad of associations integral to all experience. So too does the teacher present models for such associational and organizational functions. Turning once again to the teaching of analytic technique as an example, a supervisor may share with his student the intricate associational activity that led to the formulation of a given interpretation. His associations, in addition to references to the patient's material, may also include references to clinical theory, his own countertransference position, his estimation of his student's countertransference reaction, references to literature and art and so on. In so communicating his own thinking processes, the analyst-teacher demonstrates his cognitive activity of connecting, ordering, patterning, and establishing meaning. Thus he provides not only content but a model for an analytic mode of empathic and cognitive integration.

In their studies of the parallel process in supervision and in treatment, Ekstein and Wallerstein (1958) cogently demonstrate the concordance between the learning and treatment situations. They show how the patient's problem in therapy may be used to express the therapist's problem in supervision or the other way around. The pedagogic task is to help the therapist notice and resolve such difficulties within himself. As an example, the authors present the supervisory work with Dr. R., who made much of his patient's passivity. He was totally unaware of his own passive stance in the treatment and in his behavior with the supervisor. He became quite uneasy when these trends were gently brought to his attention. The authors summarized: "The focus . . . with this beginning student had been on converting the completely externalized problem of 'handling the patient's passivity' into the very personal struggle of dealing with his own passive tendencies. . . . Only as this problem was coped with, was the student free to learn to deal in a technically more effective manner with the marked passivity in the patient" (p. 182). This was not a treatment effort involving interpretation or working through, but a teaching technique directed toward enhancing the student's therapeutic skill. It was mediated by the affect modulating influence of the learning alliance. Fleming and Benedek (1966) present further examples which differentiate teaching from therapeutic techniques; sometimes there is a fine line between the two. Often, in their examples, a teaching intervention stimulates the student to work on the problem in his own analysis.

LEARNING AS INTERNALIZATION

In *Mourning and Melancholia* (1917), Freud described a process by which loss leads to the replacement of an object cathexis by an identification with the lost object. He was beginning to construct a theory of superego formation. Later he described this process as follows: "A portion of the external world has, at least partially, been abandoned as an object and has instead, by identification, been taken into the ego and thus become an integral part of the internal world. This new psychical agency continues to carry on the functions which have hitherto been performed by people in the external world . . ." (Freud, 1938, p. 205). In *The Ego and the Id* (1923), Freud elaborated on this construct. He noted that the need to give up both positive and negative oedipal objects leads to identifications with both parents. These identifications are modifications of the ego, designated as the ego ideal or superego. Freud commented, "we have come to understand that this kind of substitution has a great share in determining the form taken by the ego and that it makes an essential contribution toward building what is called 'character' " (p. 28).

Extending Freud's paradigm of structure formation, other authors have added various dimensions to Freud's model of internalization. Sandler and Rosenblatt (1962) describe how the child enriches his inner life through various forms of identification. They define identification as a "modification of the self-representation on the basis of another (usually an object) representation as a model. . . . More enduring identifications would be manifested as organized changes in the self-representation" (p. 137). They go on to state that "the representation used as a model in identification may . . . be largely based on fantasy. . . . A child may also identify with an ideal self . . . based on parental example or precept" (p. 137).

Roy Schafer (1968) expanded the concept: "Internalization refers to all those processes by which the subject transforms real or imagined regulatory interactions with his environment, and real or imagined characteristics of his environment, into inner regulations and characteristics" (p. 9). In this view of internalization, Schafer emphasized the roles played by introjection and identification, defining introjection as the interiorization of an object relationship, and identification as the modification of the subjective self. He stressed the essential activity and, by inference, the creativity of the internalization process.

Heinz Kohut's concept of transmuting internalization (1971) enlarges Freud's paradigm to include the acquisition of functions formerly provided by the selfobject, particularly those modes of affect regulation necessary for self cohesiveness. Marian Tolpin (1971) proposed that the soothing functions of the transitional object become internalized as part of the self by a process of transmuting internalization. George Klein (1976) emphasized the structuralizing significance of identification. The identificatory process is motivated by the need to "reverse voice," that is, to make active what was formerly a passively experienced trauma. As such, identifications are modes of achieving competence; they are structural products signifying an extension of the self.

All of these theoretical models are attempts to delineate the complex processes by which experiences within a relationship become transformed into aspects of the individual's inner psychological world. Educators too, struggling with these same issues, have attempted to explicate the complex processes by which experience leads to the acquisition of knowledge. For example, George Pearson (1952), speaking of learning, emphasized the student's unconscious identification with the teacher as an ego ideal. "The successive incorporations of several admired and loved teachers gradually form a particular part of the ego, the ego ideal. . . . The individual begins to desire to learn for the sake of learning. No longer does he learn to please the teacher but now he learns in order to please and so be loved by his ego ideal" (p. 333). Zabarenko and Zabarenko (1974) address the issue of internalization in learning as follows: "For adult learners . . . learning induction can most usefully be seen as a continuum of developmental processes extending from the most archaic to the most advanced. The continuum includes incorporation, introjection, imitation, identification, synthesis, and creativity" (p. 326). They go on to say that in adult learners with established identities, identifications with teachers become less important as unconscious mechanisms of self-learning assume increasing importance. Roy Schafer (1968) emphasized the similarity between learning and internalization.

> Learning is so closely related to internalization that one finds it difficult to untangle the two concepts. . . . To learn is to modify behavior on the basis of previous behavior. Behavior is here understood to include thinking, feeling, and other subjective processes, as well as observable psychomotor acts. One might also speak of

learning's having occurred when it can be shown that previous experience has influenced present behavior. The more long-lasting the modification or the influence . . . the better the learning. . . . In general, learning during early childhood is closely tied to relations with parents and siblings. These are the very relations that are the fertile soil and rich sustenance for introjection and identification. It seems safe to assume that introjection and identification play a crucial part in the first major learning experiences [pp. 29–32].

LEARNING AS A CREATIVE PROCESS

In the discussions cited above, internalization is presented as a dynamic process leading to expanding autonomy via the taking from the external world functions and qualities which become imbedded in character structure. Beginning with Freud, many commentators emphasize the crucial role of frustration in stimulating structural elaboration. The felicitous experience of optimal frustration and/or of optimal disillusionment, in an ambience of optimal gratification, permits the establishment of abiding psychic structure. The effective teacher, like the effective parent or analyst, while providing a supportive environment, perceives when and how to frustrate the wishes for passive feeding, when to give, when to withhold, so that the tension fueling the internalization process is kept at optimal levels. Such an empathically attuned teacher knows when to lead, when to follow, how to oscillate between active and passive roles, when to accept idealization, and when to encourage appropriate deidealization. The learning process then, permitting numerous microidentifications and minute acquisitions of content, is similar to the working through process in analysis or to growth in normal development.

Donald Winnicott emphasized the creative nature of these processes. He proposed that the transitional object belongs to the area of illusion, that intermediate area to which subjective and objective experience both contribute. The infant, in effect, creates his own anxiety-relieving object. Because of the mother's special capacity to adapt to the infant's needs, the baby is allowed the illusion that what he creates actually exists. This intermediate area of experience, especially significant in infancy and early childhood, persists in some measure throughout life and is integral to all creative endeavors in the arts, in the sciences, and in religious life (Winnecott, 1951).

In his study of creativity, Paul Pruyser (1979) expands these concepts from Winnecott. The world of illusion, he says, lies between the autistic world and the realistic world. Each of these worlds is composed of unique sets of processes, observations, and objects. The autistic world is the idiosyncratic world of primary process thought, omnipotence, and hallucinatory experience—the world of dreams. The realistic world is the world of reality testing, facts, logical connections, adaptive resourcefulness—the world of working. The illusionary world is composed of adventurous thinking, orderly imagination, inspired connections, verbalized images, cultural needs, and symbols. This world of illusion, mediated by the transitional object, becomes the world of play and creativity. In play and introspection one sees a sphere sui generis, a mode of experience distinct from the autistic and realistic. Illusionistic processing is different from primary process and from realistic thought. Illusion lies beyond the ordinary division of what is subjective and objective. This can be seen in works of art, in myths, in theories, and in wit. "The illusionistic approach . . . gives to the human mind some power to operate by rendering the resistance of things manageable, thus enhancing possibilities for a creative advance" (p. 320). Pruyser goes on to show how illusions express wishes and, as such, engender ideals. "Without the idealism embedded in wishes there is no art, religion, science, or play—in a word, no creativity"

(p. 327). He describes a process by which, through partial identification with creative minds, one participates vicariously in creative acts. For example, "listening to Bach entails a bit of being Bach . . . reading Dostoevsky is identifying oneself with . . . Dostoevsky's psychological acumen" (p. 328). He goes on to say that the educational philosophy of Whitehead and the classical idea of the university are based on this principle of vicarious creativity.

These ideas about the creative value of illusionary processing remind one of Goethe's notion that if we treat people as if they were what they ought to be we can indeed help them become what they are capable of being. They are congruent as well with the findings of developmental psychologists who study the empathic alignments that parents make with their children's potential selves (Stern, 1983). Parents are not only attuned to the current affectual state of the child, but they are also empathically aligned with the child's potential state of being. This is what enables parents to encourage development. With the aid of illusionary thinking, they respond to the child as if he were the person he is about to become. For example, mothers facilitate language acquisition by speaking to their children at a level pitched several months ahead of the child's present verbal level, but no further ahead than that. The level so chosen is exactly suited to the optimal encouragement of language. This expectant empathic mode seems actually to provide the basis of all motivation. By empathizing with the child's potential, parents inspire striving for greater competence. They provide the "carrot before the horse" which induces learning and development.

With respect to the creative aspects of learning, the development of the capacity for scholarship or self-learning seems analogous to the development of the capacity for self-analysis. In their research on the course of the analytic process, Nathan Schlessinger and Fred Robbins

(1983) found that a significant outcome of a successful analysis was:

> [T]he development of a preconsciously active self-analytic function, in identification with the analyzing function of the analyst as a learned mode of coping with conflicts. As elements of the transference neurosis reappeared and were resolved, the components of self-analytic function were demonstrated in self-observation, reality processing, and the tolerance and mastery of frustration, anxiety, and depression. The resources gained in the analytic process persisted, and their vitality was evident in response to renewed stress [p. 9].

In studying the fate of the analytic alliance, these investigators found that former patients, when in conflict, would utilize a "benign presence," either a spouse or friend or the remembered analyst, to facilitate the working through of that problem. This creative use of a real or imagined analytic "partner" attests to the importance of the analytic alliance as a matrix for the analytic process and the development of the capacity for self-analysis. The therapeutic alliance, the instrument of analysis according to Fleming, has as its legacy the self-analytic function. The use of a benevolent other for self-analytic purposes is clearly a creative act much like the transitional or illusionary experiences discussed above; it is, in effect, the creation of a special self-analytic transference. Perhaps in an analogous way, the independent scholar creates self-learning transferences, utilizing a family member, colleague, or friend, or the remembered presence of a valued teacher to facilitate the task of his immediate learning.

SOME EXAMPLES OF LEARNING ALLIANCE

In studying the course of Freud's self-analysis, as disclosed in his letters to Fliess and *The Interpretation of*

Dreams (1900), Max Schur (1979) found evidence of an early phase characterized by the unfolding of transference phenomena directed toward Fliess. "Fliess was not only Freud's admired friend, his sounding board and therefore a substitute analyst; he was also the only one who not only believed in Freud's theories but also took the repeated changes of Freud's tentative formulations for granted, encouraging any new discovery, however revolutionary, and provided Freud's only 'audience' . . . his only protection from complete isolation" (p. 105). As long as Freud needed this supportive, exalted personage as mentor and facilitator of his analysis, he "created" him as such; only later could he allow the gradual dissolution of the transference relationship to Fliess. Heinz Kohut (1976) proposed that Freud established a special kind of transference relationship with Fliess, a transference in the narcissistic sphere, which sustained Freud through a period of intense creative activity. He designated this the "transference of creativity." Such a transference may be seen as having the qualities of illusion noted in the discussion above of transitional experience.

Much less is known of the relationship between Socrates and Plato, but some understanding of that relationship might illuminate the processes of teaching and learning. It is interesting that almost all of what is known about Socrates as a teacher comes from the writings of his pupil Plato; in these works, Plato actually ascribes words to his mentor, perhaps even quoting him, although that we cannot know. Socrates was said to have used the maieutic method of discourse, from the Greek word "maiutikos," meaning "of midwifery." His mother was a midwife, and he claimed to practice the same art.

> All that is true of the art of midwifery is true also of mine, but mine differs from theirs in being practised upon men, not women, and in tending their souls in labour, not their bodies. But the greatest thing about

my art is this, that it can test in every way whether
the mind of the young man is bringing forth a mere
image . . . or a real and genuine offspring. For I have
this in common with midwives: I am sterile in point of
wisdom . . . I question others but make no reply myself,
because I have no wisdom in me . . . and the reason of
it is this: The god compels me to act as midwife, but
has never allowed me to bring forth. I am, then, not at
all a wise person myself . . . but those who associate
with me . . . make wonderful progress . . . and it is
clear they do this, not because they have ever learned
anything from me, but because they have found in
themselves many fair things and have brought them
forth. But the delivery is due to the god and me [Plato,
Theatetus, 1921, pp. 35–37].

In Plato's dialogue Laches (Plato, 1924) a student tells
another what it is like to be a student of Socrates:

Whoever comes into close contact with Socrates and
has any talk with him face to face, is bound to be drawn
round and round by him . . . and cannot stop until he
is led into giving an account of himself . . . and of the
kind of life he has led hitherto. . . . Socrates will never
let him go until he has thoroughly . . . put all his ways
to the test. . . . I delight in conversing with the man,
and see no harm in our being reminded of any past or
present misdoing: Nay, one must needs take more careful thought for the rest of one's life, if one . . . is willing . . . and zealous to learn as long as one lives [p. 37].

As Ballard in his essay on Socratic ignorance (1965)
concluded, Socratic dialogue gave rise to abiding alterations in the characters of both participants.

In their essay on the philosophy of education, James
Dickoff and Patricia Jones (1970) explore the essentials
of Socratic dialogue. They show how the opposition of two
poles—the leader and the led—is essential to such a dialogue. Both poles are active: the leader (teacher) provokes

responses through the technique of Socratic irony, that is, through questioning, assesses the pupil's state of mind, guides the interaction to shape that state of mind, and sustains appropriate interest in the interaction. The pupil is active in giving relatively uncensored responses and in contributing his interest to the encounter. Each of the poles must be passive as well as active: the pupil must submit to scrutiny, accept the discomfort of exposure, allow himself to be led, at least temporarily; the teacher must yield to the pupil the opportunity for response, must then be led by that response, and must submit to the exposure, at least to himself, possibly evoked by the pupil's response. The question-answer pattern provides a framework for an elaborate intellectual endeavor, the process of articulating a problem, exploring possible solutions, provisionally selecting one resolution as the basis for action or for further exploration, and so on. This verbal exchange serves the ultimate aim of dialogue: to enlarge the pupil's capacity to raise appropriate questions and to eventually become himself an independent leader of dialogue.

The nature of Socratic teaching as depicted here corresponds strikingly with the nature of the learning experience depicted above. In both, a shared amalgam of affective and cognitive experience fosters the student's independence and enriches the inner lives of students and teachers alike.

Each of these two relationships—Freud/Fliess and Plato/Socrates—illustrates the operation of a learning alliance. In each example, the student, in interaction with the teacher, enlarges not only his body of knowledge, but his confident sense of himself as a scholar. In parallel fashion, the teacher is enhanced by the acquisition of knowledge and by the affirmation of his role as mentor. Fleming, in her studies of learning relationships such as these, explored the contextual nature of the educational process. It seems appropriate to speculate that her own

experiences with her friend and teacher, Thérèse Benedek, helped shape her scholarly interests in these matters. They originally worked together an analyst and
analysand, then mentor and pupil; they went on to become colleagues and collaborators in research and educational projects, and lifelong friends. Some day, perhaps,
biographical studies will permit us to trace the ways in
which mutual influences between these two psychoanalytic theoreticians came to fruition in their creative endeavors.

SUMMARY

This has been an elaboration and extension of the concept
of the learning alliance as promulgated by Joan Fleming.
In investigating the qualities of this special instrument
of learning, the roles of affect regulation, idealization,
and integration were explored. Areas of congruence were
found between developmental structure formation, structural change during the course of analysis, and the acquisition of knowledge in the educational setting. Learning,
then, was viewed as a process of internalization. An effort
was made to delineate how the learner, using his inborn
cognitive and affective equipment to connect with the
facilitating environment, creates new knowledge and, in
effect, a new part of himself. The transitional nature of
learning was emphasized throughout the chapter, in line
with Fleming's view that learning, à la Winnicott's transitional phenomena, is a transitional and therefore creative process.

REFERENCES

Ballard, E. (1965), *Socratic Ignorance, An Essay on Platonic Self
    Knowledge*. The Hague: Nijhoff.
Basch, M. F. (1977), Developmental psychology and explanatory the-
    ory in psychoanalysis. *The Annual of Psychoanalysis*, 5:229–263.
    New York: International Universities Press.

Dickoff, J., & Jones, P. (1970), Proceedings of the 26th Annual Meeting of the Philosophy of Education Society, ed. H. B. Dunkel. Normal, IL: Philosophy of Education Society, University of Illinois.

Ekstein, R., & Wallerstein, R. (1958), *The Teaching and Learning of Psychotherapy*. New York: Basic Books.

Elashoff, J. (1971) *Pygmalion Reconsidered: A Case Study in Statistical Inference: Reconsideration of the Rosenthal-Jacobson Data on Teacher Expectancy*. Worthington, OH: C. A. Jones.

Fleming, J. (1972), Early object deprivation and transference phenomena: The working alliance. *Psychoanal. Quart.*, 41(1):23–49.

———— (1979), The education of a supervisor. Paper presented at the Chicago Institute for Psychoanalysis, November.

———— Benedek, T. (1966), *Psychoanalytic Supervision: A Method of Clinical Teaching*. New York: Grune & Stratton.

Freud, S. (1900), The Interpretation of Dreams. *Standard Edition*, 5:339–723. London: Hogarth Press, 1953.

———— (1912a), Recommendations to physicians practicing psychoanalysis. *Standard Edition*, 12:109–121. London: Hogarth Press, 1958.

———— (1912b), The dynamics of transference. *Standard Edition*, 12:97–109. London: Hogarth Press, 1958.

———— (1914), Some reflections on schoolboy psychology. *Standard Edition*, 13:241–245. London: Hogarth Press, 1955.

———— (1917), Mourning and melancholia. *Standard Edition*, 14:243–259. London: Hogarth Press, 1957.

———— (1923), The ego and the id. *Standard Edition*, 19:19–28. London: Hogarth Press, 1961.

———— (1938), An outline of psychoanalysis. *Standard Edition*, 23:141–207. London: Hogarth Press, 1964.

Friedman, L. (1969), The therapeutic alliance. *Internat. J. Psycho-Anal.*, 50:139–153.

Gitelson, M. (1962), The curative factors in psychoanalysis. *Internat. J. Psycho-Anal.*, 43:194–205.

Greenson, R. (1967), *The Technique and Practice of Psychoanalysis*. New York: International Universities Press.

Klein, G. (1976), *Psychoanalytic Theory: An Exploration of Essentials*. New York: International Universities Press.

Kohut, H. (1971), *The Analysis of the Self*. New York: International Universities Press.

———— (1976), Creativeness, charisma, group psychology. Reflections on the self-analysis of Freud. *Psychological Issues*, Monograph 34/35, 2 & 3/9, ed. J. E. Gedo & G. H. Pollock. New York: International Universities Press.

Mahler, M., Pine, G., & Bergman, A. (1975), *The Psychological Birth of the Human Infant*. New York: Basic Books.

Pearson, G. (1952), A survey of learning difficulties in children. *The Psychoanalytic Study of the Child*, 7:322–386. New York: International Universities Press.

Plato (1921), VII, Theatetus Sophist, ed. G. P. Goold. London: William
     Heinemann.
——— (1924), II, Laches, Protagoras, Meno, Euthydemus, ed. G. P.
     Goold. London: William Heinemann.
Pruyser, P. (1979), An essay on creativity. Bull. Menn. Clin., 43:294–353.
Sandler, J., & Rosenblatt, B. (1962), The concept of the representa-
     tional world. The Psychoanalytic Study of the Child, 17:128–145.
     New York: International Universities Press.
Schafer, R. (1968), Aspects of Internalization. New York: International
     Universities Press.
Schlesinger, H. (1981), General principles of psychoanalytic super-
     vision. In: Becoming a Psychoanalyst: A Study of Psychoanalytic
     Supervision, ed. R. S. Wallerstein. New York: International
     Universities Press.
Schlessinger, N., & Robbins, F. P. (1983), A Developmental View of
     the Psychoanalytic Process. Emotions and Behavior, Monograph
     No. 1. New York: International Universities Press.
Schur, M. (1979), Some additional "day residues" of "The specimen
     dream of psychoanalysis." In: Freud and His Self-Analysis, ed.
     M. Kanzer & J. Glenn. New York: Jason Aronson.
Stern, D. (1983), Implications of infancy research for psychoanalytic
     theory and practice. Psychiatry Update, Vol. 2. APA Annual
     Review, ed., L. Grinspoon. Washington DC: American Psychi-
     atric Press.
Tolpin, M. (1971), On the beginnings of a cohesive self. The Psychoan-
     alytic Study of the Child, 26:316–352. New Haven, CT: Yale
     University Press.
Winnicott, D. (1951), Transitional objects and transitional phenom-
     ena. In: Collected Papers: Through Pediatrics to Psychoanalysis.
     New York: Basic Books.
——— (1958), The capacity to be alone. Internat. J. Psycho-Anal.,
     39:416–420. Folkestone: Dawson.
Zabarenko, L., & Zabarenko, R. (1974), Psychoanalytic contributions
     for a theory of instruction. The Annual of Psychoanalysis,
     2:323–345. New York: International Universities Press.
Zetzel, E. (1964), The therapeutic alliance in the psychoanalysis of
     hysterical syndromes. Unpublished paper referred to in: The
     theory of psychoanalytic therapy: A panel report. J. Amer. Psy-
     choanal. Assn., 12:620–631.

Chapter 26

The Teacher, the Transference, and Development

MICHAEL FRANZ BASCH, M.D.

Second only to parents, teachers are the most important figures in a child's development. Unlike other animals, we are not born with our adaptive patterns already set, and we depend on others to show us not only how to get along in the world, but, literally, what it means to be human. There are unfortunate infants who are raised in isolation, often by psychotic parents, who are not spoken to or otherwise stimulated, and these babies, if they survive, neither speak nor otherwise relate in a meaningful way to other human beings. More important, when found and rescued, after spending their early years in such a situation they no longer can learn no matter how kind, well meaning, and skilled their new caretakers may be. This shows both how dependent the actualization of our potential is on the appropriate intervention of the adults around us at the beginning of life, and that, though extremely flexible and with a large margin of safety for error, there are limits to our capacity for mental growth.

Fortunately such tragedies are few and far between. Yet, there are many children who enter the primary grades significantly deprived of those early experiences that would enable them to make the most of the new learning situation to which they are now exposed. This is most evident in those children who come from socio-economically deprived homes and whose inability to adapt to the relationships of the classroom clearly signals that much more needs to be done for them than simply to expose them to the opportunity to learn. However, there are many children who show no such outward difficulty; children who have learned how to behave and conduct themselves quite appropriately, yet who carry scars that prevent them from making the most of what is offered to them in this new situation. So, like it or not, the teacher, if he or she is to be successful, must function as a psychotherapist, not in the formal sense of conducting therapy sessions with students, but in the practical sense of being alert and responsive to the psychological needs that students evince both by what they do and what they do not do.

Teachers and psychoanalysts alike can benefit a great deal from research conducted in early development (Stern, 1985). Infant research is a relatively new field. In years past we assumed that since infants could not speak they had nothing to say, and that babies were born tabula rasa, and spent the first couple of years of life marking time and developing their muscular and nervous systems until they could begin to participate, at about age two, in everyday social life, an existence governed by adaptation primarily through speech.

We now know that this is not so. Infants are alert and responsive to stimulation even before they are born, and everything that happens to them and that they do is registered and has an effect on their future personality and behavior. Indeed, the first two years of life are probably the time of greatest learning: most important, the attitudes that the older child and eventually the adult have toward other people are laid down in those early years. By the time they go to grammar school, children have formed concepts about who they are and what they may expect from the world. The teacher is not then a new person whom the child encounters on the first day of school, but someone toward whom the child directs hopes, fears, and wishes that were developed in earlier contacts with parents and other significant people. Often the attitudes that are brought to the classroom are inappropriate and counterproductive, preventing the child from benefiting from the new situation and losing the opportunity held out to him to make up for what he has previously missed. It is this display of behavior patterns that do not seem to be directly related to what is going on here and now, but are preconceptions based on earlier experiences and one's reactions to them that, of course, constitute the transference (Basch, 1980). It is the management of the transferences that people have toward us as authorities and/or helpers that determines how successful both teachers and psychoanalysts will ultimately be in carrying out their respective tasks.

Just as war is too important to be left to the generals, so psychotherapy should not simply be left in the hands of psychotherapists. By the time people become patients it is in a sense too late; their presence in therapists' offices is an indicator that what might or could have been done earlier in their life was not done, that the opportunity for reasonably healthy growth was missed. Teachers are in the best position to have an early, corrective influence on the personalities of their charges. Indeed, looking at the other end of the spectrum, I cannot think of any successful person who, when giving biographical information, has not credited a teacher's influence for contributing significantly to his or her accomplishments. What is singled out is not usually the knowledge that that teacher imparted, but rather the impact of his or her personality that permanently altered the student's outlook. It is the vistas that are opened by a good teacher for which a student is grateful in later years. What makes the difference is that as a result of their relationship the student's view of himself is permanently altered. Might the converse be true, namely, that many who do not live up to their potential have failed, relative to what they might have done, because they were not fortunate enough to have such an experience?

That they function as psychotherapists may seem to be one more unfair demand being made on our educators. After all, is psychotherapy not a highly specialized field for which extensive training is necessary? In one sense, yes, there is a group of people whose psychological problems are such that only a specially skilled individual can hope to help them, and we certainly should not expect that the teacher be held responsible for carrying out that job. However, psychotherapy in the broad sense of the word is not only something that any person capable of establishing an empathic relationship is able to perform, it is a function that most of us do perform without realizing it. After all, have we not given a willing ear to a friend and, based on our knowledge of his personality and the situation in question, talked things over with him to good effect; calmed down a child by putting some upset into perspective; comforted a sick person by our presence? But then, should one dignify such attempts to be helpful with such a fancy label as "psychotherapy"?

Literally, the term *psychotherapy* refers to the healing of the mind or spirit, and it is the elusiveness of that noun *mind* that frightens people and makes them think that only special initiates can deal with such a mysterious and mystical entity. This misconception harks back to ancient times when it was believed that the body was inhabited by a spirit, a direct link to the gods who communicated with and controlled the individual through that agency, and that only the priests, a select, anointed group, could deal with its disturbances. That gradually the physician took over the care of the mentally sick did not change the basic attitude of the population at large toward the workings of the mind, especially when something went wrong with that invisible whatever-it-was. Even today psychiatrists are regarded with fear, called witch doctors or head shrinkers, as if they were engaged in a mysterious craft beyond the pale of ordinary mortals. Therefore, it is not surprising that psychotherapy is regarded as both arcane and esoteric. However, if for the moment we disregard the philosophers' failed attempts to define *mind* in a satisfactory way, and focus instead on how the term is used in everyday life, we may get a different perspective. When someone says: "I can't make up my mind," that simply means that he cannot come to a decision about some matter. If you examine other situations in which the term *mind* is referred to, you will always see that it is a synonym for the process of coming to a decision. To say someone's mind is weak, confused, disturbed, or troubled indicates that, for various reasons, such persons are not able temporarily or permanently to engage in the decision-making process that makes for healthy adaptation. Psychotherapy, then, is the art of helping people to examine themselves and their respective situations so that they will eventually be able to come to decisions that make sense given their particular personalities and their circumstances. Difficult as that task can sometimes prove to be, thinking of "mind" as the decision-making process carried out by the brain is a lot less mysterious than continuing to believe that we harbor some strange homunculus within our brain that guides our destiny.

Looked at this way the task of the teacher as psychotherapist becomes clearer. None of us can erase the past or guarantee the future. As therapists we deal with the decision-making process in the here and now and try to help people do the best with what they have or can develop. You may well ask, If psychotherapists are focused on the present, why do we always read of psychoanalysts encouraging their patients to rummage in their past lives? Some individuals, as Freud discovered, need to understand their past because, unbeknownst to them, their present decision-making process is so encumbered by past events, real or imaginary, and the feeling of guilt and shame associated with those occasions, that only if that first becomes the focus for therapy can the person eventually become free to deal with the present effectively. As analysts we look at the past for the sake of the present, but the patients who are in need of our specialized help are only a small minority of the many individuals who could use some help in reshaping and giving direction to their lives.

As professionals we have certain basic convictions, spoken or unspoken, that guide our working lives. As a psychoanalyst I operate on the belief that understanding oneself is helpful and worthwhile, and that is the only thing that I have to "sell," so to speak. Educators, on the other hand, operate on the premise that to develop one's general ability to think clearly makes for a better life, and they are prepared to impart to their pupils the skills necessary to achieve that capacity. How my patients and teachers' students then use whatever they have gained from our respective efforts is out of our hands. We hope, of course, that they will use it to good advantage, for themselves and for those around them, but whether they do or do not cannot be our concern, for we have no control over that. I emphasize this point in the interest of clarifying that at best our capacities are limited while our responsibilities are heavy enough without setting goals for ourselves that are bound to be disappointed and leave us discouraged and less able to do what we may really be expected to accomplish. Teachers want their students to make a decision to learn, and to accomplish that the teacher has to be prepared to function as a psychotherapist with many students—a great deal with some, a little with others—but probably there is no child that does not implicitly look to his teacher for that assistance at one time or another. As we will discuss, to function as a psychotherapist means, first of all, to be empathic; that is, to be alert to signals that the child is sending that something about his emotional life needs to be understood and, second, to address that need appropriately. Why should that be necessary in the classroom? Should it not be obvious to a child by the time he or she is of school age that the more one knows the better it is? After all, children are continually confronted by situations in which superior knowledge gives adults control and power, why would they not eagerly seize the opportunity to avail themselves of that knowledge when it is offered to them? The fact is that learning for learning's sake is a very late development; when children study they study either in order to get the approval of the teacher, or, unfortunately only too often, to avoid the punishment that not studying entails. Again one may ask, Why then do some children not study even though the teacher is ready and willing to give approval and praise for a job well done? Here is where a knowledge of the developmental process and its recapitulation in the transference becomes so important.

Sigmund Freud was the first scientist to demonstrate systematically that human behavior, no matter how bizarre, was purposeful and that its meaning could be deciphered if one had the opportunity to examine its symbolic significance in detail. And, of course, psychoanalysis is the method for getting that close look. Freud made a significant contribution to pedagogy through his retrospective demonstration in the psychoanalysis of adults that children have a psychological life and that their experiences have a great deal to do with shaping the adult personality. Unfortunately, Freud constructed a theory of development based on his studies of the character formation of one particular group of patients, namely, those suffering from psychoneuroses. Central for the development of these patients and for their adult problem is the Oedipus complex. In the cases Freud studied, the patient's neurotic symptoms were based on an inability to go beyond this early stage of sexuality and the subsequent forbidden, incestuous significance that adult sexual impulses had for them. The problem for us is that Freud assumed that the sexual instinct and the Oedipus complex were focal for all development and that basically no matter what a person's difficulties might be he or she was always in one way or another engaged in trying to resolve problems in the area of childhood sexuality. Not only do undergraduate and graduate courses in psychology teach students to think of development in terms of the oral, anal, and phallic stages of psychosexual development, but the popular literature is loaded with explanations based on that frame of reference. Both work with psychoanalytic patients with other than neurotic problems, as well as direct observation and experimentation with infants, has shown that other factors need to be considered if we are to get an accurate picture of development. As a matter of fact, psychosexual development and the Oedipus complex are the last things that professionals for whom early development is important but who are not engaged in the treatment of neurotic children or adults need to worry about. Much more significant is the inherited propensity for mastery and the extension of control over the environment that every infant demonstrates. It is the vicissitudes of this developmental line that lay the groundwork not only for much of the pathology with which the psychotherapist has to deal, but also for many of the so-called learning problems of varying degrees that teachers face daily in their classrooms.

Infants are born with a readiness and a propensity for ordering stimulation, prefer the unfamiliar, and are selectively attuned to what the environment has to offer, giving precedence to human stimulation above all else. Infants learn quickly. When only a few days old they can be taught, using the sight of a brightly colored object as a reward, first to turn their head to the left when they hear a bell and to the right when they hear a buzzer, and then to reverse those connections (Basch, 1977). Above all, infants, like older children and adults, get gratification from being a cause, from making things happen; this leads to what White (1959) has called "effectance pleasure." One fascinating experiment exposes an infant to a show of brightly colored lights. The baby follows this novel stimulus with great interest. After a number of repetitions the stimulus has become familiar and the baby loses interest, until he finds out quite by accident that by turning his head 30 degrees to the right he can turn the lights on. Then there is no stopping him—after a while he does not even look at the lights he has brought into being, it is enough that he is able to make them appear (Papousek, 1969).

It is the search for competence; pleasure through mastery, not the gratification of bodily stimulation or organ pleasure that Freud linked to sexual development, that provides the incentive for maturation (Broucek, 1979). It is when there is a failure of mastery, the frustration of being persistently ineffective, that the infant, just as happens in later years also, turns to autoerotic activity for the compensatory gratification or organ pleasure. Then, so to speak, the infant can at least be effective by stimulating himself and getting some reward through that route when all else fails.

How is it then that, when all is said and done, most of us do achieve functional maturity and do not spend our lives arrested in self-stimulating frenzies? After all, it is one thing to arrange an experiment that permits an infant to experience a high degree of effectiveness, but ordinary life is filled with frustrations for a little creature who has neither muscular skills nor logical reflection available to make things happen. Being hungry he cannot feed himself, much less set about obtaining food; though eager for novel stimulation, the infant has no way of changing his locale, and so on. Obviously here is where parents enter the picture. For many years a baby depends for physiological support and psychological input on the good offices of concerned care givers. Although quite immature in many functions, in order to assure as much as possible that he will get what he needs from the adults around him he is born with a fully developed, highly effective system for communication.

We adults are so focused on speech that we forget that what is really important in communication is affect, the feelings conveyed between speaker and listener. It is not what is said, but how it is said that is important. Depending on the emotion conveyed, "Yes" can mean "No," and "No," "Yes." We take that so much for granted that we pay no attention to this complex signaling that we do day in and day out, and to which we are constantly alert. The amazing thing is that we are born with the facial expressions for the basic affects in place. For example, an angry baby looks exactly like an angry adult; and, furthermore, the picture of a happy Chinese baby is readily identified as being happy by an African tribesman who has never seen a person of Asian birth. In other words, affect is the universal language, one that we all "speak" from birth on (Basch, 1976).

To return to the question of pleasure through mastery. Infants continuously need the helpful intervention of their parents in order to meet their needs, and they send, through typical facial expressions, bodily movements, and sounds, messages indicating surprise, interest, joy, anger, distress, fear, shame, or disgust, as well as combinations of these basic affects. The empathic parent, the parent who is free to receive her child's signals and respond to them appropriately, creates a climate in which the infant has more than enough opportunity to lay down memory traces of age-appropriate successful achievement and as a result may be expected when a concept of self develops, around eighteen to twenty-four months of age, to have a reasonable belief in his effectiveness and the ability to control, or master with satisfaction, the tasks that lie ahead of him. Above all, the most important aspect of mastery is his ability to engage his parent's response with his messages, leading to the confident expectation that he can make himself understood, if not immediately, then eventually, and that his expressed needs will be given consideration and are of potential significance, even though they may not always carry the day.

A system for maturation as flexible as ours leaves room for error; there is no guarantee that a parent or other adult will respond in a meaningful way to the infant's signals. Infantile or early effective development, which can be looked at initially as a response to the strength and duration of stimulation, undergoes a series of maturational steps. Once self-awareness becomes a possibility, around the age of eighteen to twenty-four months, affective reactions are experienced as feelings; that is, affective reactions related to the self. With further cognitive maturation, feeling states become associated with increasingly sophisticated judgments about experience, then we speak of "emotions." Eventually it becomes possible to decenter, as Piaget calls it, and recognize others' affective states as independent of ours, yet worthy of consideration and understanding; this is the basis of empathy, the ability to put oneself in another's shoes (Basch, 1983). This developmental line of affective development is not an automatic progression; it depends on age-appropriate stimulation, especially in the early years of life.

We now hear a great deal of argument about how quickly and to what degree the cognitive development of infants and young children should be stimulated. In my judgment, the emphasis on such skills as reading is misplaced. It is the affective development of infants and toddlers that should be our concern. Without appropriate transactions between mother and child, and father and child, the range of affective responsiveness and receptivity remains undeveloped or shallow. The capacity to respond to a wide range of nonverbal, or not necessarily verbal, communicative signals will not develop if the infant has no experience in that area. When parents "talk" to their babies they are not conveying verbal signals as such, the verbal content of what they are saying is obviously lost on the baby, but, rather, by the variance of pitch and intonation of the voice, as well as by the facial expression and bodily tension they exhibit, the parents stimulate the affective responsiveness of the infant. This process is readily observable in the newborn nursery of any hospital. One child, being in pain from some somatic disturbance, begins to cry, and soon all the other babies, although not themselves in any pain, are wailing also. This is not because they are able to reflect on the state of the distressed one and feel sorry for him (infants are not capable of such a sophisticated response), but because the intensity of the crying causes them automatically, that is, through the stimulation of the vegetative, nonvoluntary, autonomic nervous system, to respond in the same way. This is similar to what happens in the animal world where it has been said correctly that animals "infect" each other with their affective states. The evolutionary advantage of such automatic communication is obvious. A cry of danger by one animal in a pack leads all his companions to take it up, bringing the entire group into the required state of alertness. Human beings differ from other animals in that neither our behavioral nor our communicative programs are rigidly determined by heredity; they are not, to use computer language, "hard wired." Other animals are born "knowing" what friend and foe look like and how they are to respond to one or the other. Human beings have much greater flexibility and depend for the activation of the communicative system and the development of adaptive behavioral "scripts" on those who raise them. Therefore, a mother who is psychologically depressed is likely to send signals of despair and distress to her infant who responds in kind, wailing, fussing, and displaying generally irritable, unfocused behavior which only increases the mother's frustration and deepens her sense of depression and inadequacy. This vicious cycle once set up perpetuates itself, the child experiencing only a minimum of pleasure, protecting itself against the incessant distress signals sent out by the mother by withdrawing into sleep, or else trying to get as much soothing out of food and/or auto-erotic stimulation as it can get. If there are no other adults or older children who expose the child to other affective experiences, it is not surprising that in extreme cases such a child might well grow up to be passive, obese, sullen, and withdrawn. Perhaps with his peers such a child may achieve some modicum of stimulation and satisfaction, but his past experience with tension regulation having been unsatisfactory, he is likely to overreact. Such children, in an attempt to hold attention, may well become the clowns or the delinquents in the group. Once in the presence of adults their uncommunicative stance is resumed or "transferred," their past experience having ingrained in them that withdrawal is the least painful alternative in such situations. Not surprisingly such a child, when it enters the classroom, may well present as a behavior and learning problem.

Reasonably emotionally healthy children learn, not for learning's sake, but for the positive response of the adult. If there has been no background in which self-esteem has been enhanced (i.e., in which children have found themselves to be effective, through interaction with adults), the emotional rewards of the classroom are literally meaningless. Instead, such a child may well fall back on the only source of transactional satisfaction familiar to him or her, namely, attracting the interest and admiration of his peers through outrageous behavior.

What has happened in such a case is that the child has "transferred" his past expectations and behavior patterns onto the new situation. The question now is whether or not the teacher can do anything to alter the self-destructive course on which such children have been set.

It should be clear that the example I have given, though not uncommon, is not exclusive. There are many reasons for failure of empathic fit, the lack of effective understanding and responsiveness, between parent and infant. A parent's depressive problem is only one not uncommon example of how the communicative system of infants comes to be understimulated. By the same token, overstimulation, an exaggerated need of the parent for the child's response, can also lead to withdrawal and fear of interaction. Furthermore, my example as presented is, of necessity, simplistic. Usually there is no such direct one-to-one correlation between what happens in infancy and what transpires later. The wide margin of safety in which our growth takes place leaves ample opportunity for benefiting positively from the sometimes seemingly minimal and transient but positive transactions that the infant and child have with the environment. Here also what Freud called the "complemental series" must be considered. Heredity, accidental circumstances, intercurrent physical illnesses, and many other factors over and above child-parent transactions come into play as the personality of the youngster is developed. It seems that some children can do a great deal with very little; others, no matter how much has happened that is positive, are so fragile that it is the negative aspects of their upbringing that carry the day. Furthermore, life is not so cut and dried; there are degrees of severity when it comes to psychological problems, and there are often areas open to development while others are closed off. Be that as it may, the child who is unresponsive to the atmosphere of the classroom and the teacher's effort is only too familiar, and my point is only that the emotional or affective set of the child is of as much or more significance as his intellectual wherewithal, and it is with problems in the former sphere, as exhibited in the transference to the teacher, that the psychoanalyst can potentially be of some help to the educator.

Perhaps the most important thing that we teach our students when we function as supervisors of the work of candidates for psychoanalytic training is that they permit themselves to become aware of the feelings and emotions aroused in them by the behavior of their patients; but then, rather than simply reacting, to put themselves as best they can in the place of that patient and figure out what the purpose of that behavior might be. What the therapist does with his patient is then based on that tentative understanding. For example, if a patient becomes insulting it is important to experience one's reaction, perhaps a wish to reject the patient in turn, but then, rather than withdrawing from the patient as one might well want to do, perhaps confront the patient with what he has done, not angrily but with curiosity, and help him to come to some understanding as to why he would behave that way with the very person he counts upon for help. Eventually one is usually able to trace the origin of such self-defeating behavior to situations in which the patient's self-esteem was seriously hurt causing him to retaliate. Once people understand why they behave the way they do they are often relieved of the necessity of blindly repeating such patterns and are able to respond more selectively and productively to the present. As I have said before, it would be an unwarranted confusion of roles for the teacher to act as if he were a psychotherapist in the formal sense; however, the attitude of a therapist to a patient can profitably be carried over to the classroom when it comes to evaluating and responding to the seemingly negativistic, disinterested, and nonproductive attitudes of the difficult student. Rather than taking such a student's behavior, whether passive or active, as a reflection on one's own person, skills, or abilities, it makes more sense to think of it as a transferred pattern, a way of dealing with the adult world that, inappropriate as it may be, made sense at one time and is now beyond the child's ability to control.

Tolerance and kindness are usually not enough to make for a change. What one has to figure out is how to give such a child at least a taste of pleasure through mastery, a sense of achievement. This cannot be artificial; children know when they have succeeded in a meaningful way and only real success will make inroads on their insecurity. How to accomplish this is, of course, the purview of the teacher. All that we as therapists can hope to convey is some insight into the developmental vicissitudes that, when understood, leave the educator in a better position to deal with the emotional obstacles that children unconsciously bring to the learning experience. The teacher cannot undo a child's past, but what can be done is to go beyond the admittedly often difficult surface manifestations of behavior so as to tap the longing within every human being to exercise effective control over his environment; to become, as Kohut (1971) put it, a center of initiative.

REFERENCES

Basch, M. F. (1976), The concept of affect: A re-examination. *J. Amer. Psychoanal. Assn.*, 24:759–777.

———— (1977), Developmental psychology and explanatory theory in psychoanalysis. *The Annual of Psychoanalysis*, 5:229–263. New York: International Universities Press.

———— (1980), *Doing Psychotherapy*. New York: Basic Books.

———— (1983), Empathic understanding: A review of the concept and some theoretical considerations. *J. Amer. Psychoanal. Assn.*, 31:101–126.

Broucek, F. (1979), Efficacy in infancy: A review of some experimental studies and their possible implications for clinical theory. *Internat. J. Psycho-Anal.*, 60:311–326.

Kohut, H. (1971), *The Analysis of the Self*. New York: International Universities Press.

Papousek, H. (1969), Individual variability in learned responses in human infants. In: *Brain and Early Behavior*, ed. R. J. Robinson. London: Academic Press, pp. 251–266.

Stern, D. N. (1985), *The Interpersonal World of the Infant*. New York: Basic Books.

White, R. W. (1959), Motivation reconsidered: The concept of competence. *Psychol. Rev.*, 66:297–333.

Chapter 27

The Teacher as Learner, the Learner as Teacher

MIRIAM ELSON, M.A.

The urge to understand human behavior, one's own as well as that of others, profoundly motivates us as teachers. Our hope is that as we understand the complexities of human behavior, we can govern ourselves more effectively and with greater enrichment in our professional and personal lives. Though we meet our students in the context of assisting them in the mastery of a specific field or skill in which we have been designated as competent, inevitably a special relationship arises. It is this relationship, this special dimension of teaching, which I seek to describe. For in this experience the teacher learns as he teaches, and the learner teaches as he learns. It is here that an understanding of the complexities of human behavior may facilitate this parallel process and free it from constrictions which impede teaching and learning.

Since our earliest learning arises in the intimate relationship of parent and child, each new course reawakens in students the need to have a target of idealization and to have their efforts admired. Though age may dim its intensity, the capacity to be so aroused and the teacher's ability to quicken and mobilize this capacity for the pursuit of learning is the essence of teaching.

This is true for all levels of education but has particular relevance for the community and city colleges which
face, by reason of the admission of previously excluded
populations, a broad range of students with learning difficulties and deficits not previously seen in the college
system. As faculty and administrators seek to assist their
matriculants in finding meaningful levels of competence,
they are at the forefront of the attempt to redress past
failures of society.

The faculty of Chicago's Community Colleges prepared for teaching in an era in which students attracted
to these colleges looked forward to completing their education in four-year colleges, and many went on to graduate training for the professions. Standards were high;
the faculty experienced a sense of fulfillment and self-
esteem in their ability to help these students work toward
life goals.

With the increasing demand by broad groups of learn-
ing-handicapped populations for access to higher education, the colleges opened their doors to large numbers of
students for whom the associate of arts degree was the
final degree, and for many, a never-attained goal. The
need for remedial work was extensive. Although remedial
work has always been a need, in high prestige institutions
as well as community and city colleges, and some provision for this had always been made, the sheer numbers
of students with such needs overwhelmed the services.
Administrators and faculty had been given little preparation for absorbing such students into traditional classes.
Thus, the burden of responding to their needs while maintaining responsiveness to the general class enrollment
posed enormous difficulties.

There were many efforts undertaken to overcome
these rapidly burgeoning problems. One, for example,
was the Loop College Individual Needs Program. Designed to be a total support service and academic program
for high risk and other nontraditional students during

their first semesters at Loop College, the program attempted to address and solve the specific problem of high dropout rates among freshmen, poor academic preparation for traditional and vocational-technical curricula, poor study habits and communication skills, weak student self-concept, such as the belief that they would not succeed as college students, and unrealistic academic/career expectations.

A report of this program (Barshis, 1980) and the results of a three-year study are impressive in that there was a 91 percent retention rate for these high-risk students, 90 percent of whom were free from academic probation. Of first-semester high-risk freshmen, 80 percent committed themselves to specific career and academic programs with a specific major. Notable was the built-in feature of spotting and tracking, not in a policing sense but in close supervision of attendance, performance, and ready intervention with helping techniques when these were necessary. The success of the program was based on concern of the instructors for their students, and their enthusiasm for what they were doing as well as a readiness to learn additional ways of reaching their students to make their help more effective.

This is not to suggest that such attitudes, basic to successful teaching, are not found generally in the faculty, but that with nontraditional students they made the crucial difference.

Many other modes of intervention were undertaken, as in the widespread adoption of mastery learning programs (Bloom, 1981). Originally designed for the primary grades and for those high school subjects which lent themselves to small divisions of subject matter, its use was adapted to college-level classes. By subdividing relatively complex materials into smaller tasks, these could be presented in stepwise manner from the simplest to the more complex forms. The adaptation of this method for college teaching added to the tasks of an already overburdened faculty, and so assistants were brought in to handle the additional tutoring and grading of mastery learning tasks.

Underlying such approaches was the pressing need in all departments and subject areas to relate program structure and content to the changing nature of the student body. In the field of human services, for example, the question posed was what the most effective mix of academic and competency-based training for child care might be (Swift, 1974). Swift emphasized that training programs must provide options that allow the student to enter training at whatever level of skill and knowledge they have achieved and to continue upward without arbitrary repetition of matter at a level already mastered. Such a model Swift visualized as a spiral curriculum in which the concepts to be learned are visited and revisited in increasingly complex and differentiated fashion. Basic to her discussion is the manner in which a learning alliance is established which facilitates the evolution of a parallel process between teacher and student, each learning from the other. More than a role model, which conveys the sense of unlikeness between the two, the teacher absorbs and defines the student's anxiety, and, through her own self-understanding, makes it possible for the student to tolerate the insecurities and ambivalence of the learning environment.

The previously excluded segments of our society to which these programs were addressed included large numbers drawn from an older population, educationally unprepared for college-level work, many employed and with families to support, economically marginal, and often bearing the trauma of untreated emotional and physical illness. Frequent absences and dropping out of courses affected the morale of faculty and of administration who were held accountable for the numbers completing courses for which students had enrolled. Financial support to the colleges was also based on numbers without regard to the grave complexity of ministering to their educational needs. Given these circumstances, even the most dedicated and gifted teachers experienced fatigue, a loss of pleasure in their goals, and ebbing self-esteem.

Stressing the psychodynamics of education, Don Barshis, Dean of the Faculty, Staff Center of the Chicago Citywide College, and Kay Field, Director of the Teacher Education Programs of the Chicago Institute for Psychoanalysis, designed a unique series of continuing education courses for the college educator. Specifically focusing on the experience of college teachers in the classroom and in their advisory function, these courses were planned to broaden understanding of psychological health and impairment.

In presenting one of the courses, "Stress, Change and Growth in the Human Life Cycle," I had occasion to work with a broad range of faculty members representing each of the city colleges and the gamut of educational fields. The purpose of the course was to examine the continuous unfolding of developmental and interpersonal experience from late adolescence through young, middle, and late adulthood. Through study of theoretical, clinical, and research-oriented literature, our focus was on defining and understanding concepts of psychological health and impairment. Each class member kept a weekly log and prepared vignettes reflecting typical problems encountered with student, peer, or authority figures. Through shared experience and insight, they uncovered a wider array of available resolutions based on a deepening awareness of the interplay of emotion and learning. A broadened recognition of personality development as a *process*, with a range of adaptive or maladaptive behaviors from normality to pathology, led to observation and understanding rather than judging and labeling.

Many of the vignettes so prepared are worthy of publication not only for the strength, sensitivity, and wisdom of their teaching interventions, but for the wit and verve with which they were written. Still, there is a despairing quality, a sense of frustration and anger which reflects the difficulty of the tasks they face and their own very high expectations of themselves and their skills. This exceptional faculty provided a learning experience for me as indeed they had for their students, and thus illuminated in broad relief the twin process of teacher as learner and learner as teacher.

As we considered the various explanatory systems of human behavior which might assist us in our teaching and learning tasks (Freud, 1914; Hartmann, 1939; Erikson, 1956; A. Freud, 1965; Piaget and Inhelde, 1971; Mahler, Pine, and Bergman, 1975; Kohut, 1977) it was Kohut's evolving theories of self psychology which to me seemed most pertinent. The view of human development based on the taming of the drives, each of which must be neutralized and sublimated as they achieve ascendancy, the view of the human infant as a bundle of such drives which must come under the civilizing influence of caretakers, does not do justice to our current knowledge of neonates and the course of childhood. The newborn today is seen as an assertive, seeking, responsive being, capable of cueing his parents to his needs and wishes by an array of signals and signs with which he is endowed (Tolpin, 1971, 1980; Basch, 1980). In a process of mutual engagement, and in tune with the infant's capacity to accept mild frustration, parents perform a mirroring, confirming, guiding function, and they are the target of idealization. Those who perform various functions for the child, in tune with his changing needs, are selfobjects, initially undistinguishable from the child's forming self. Through such myriad interactions, the child transmutes the caretaking functions of his parents, selfobjects, into a self and its functions. The selfobjects and their functions, precursors of psychic structure, are uniquely altered by the special endowment of the child. They are transmuted and internalized and they become the psychic structure: the self and its functions.

Kohut views this self as bipolar. The child who is joyously received and mirrored lays down the rudiments of his ambitions in one pole which is imbued with grandiosity and perfection. As he is permitted to merge with the idealized perfection and power of those who carry him and minister to his needs, he acquires the rudiments of his ideals and goals in a second pole. It is the relationship between these poles, the strength and harmony of their interaction, and the skills and talents which are elaborated through nature and nurture which define the cohesive nuclear self, continuous in time and space (Kohut and Wolf, 1978).

This self has been defined operationally by Basch (1980) as "the uniqueness that separates the experiences of one person from those of all others while conferring a sense of cohesion and continuity on the disparate experiences of that individual throughout his life. The self is the symbolic transformation of experience into an overall goal-oriented construct" (p. 10). Parents who are able to function in empathic merger with the forming self of the child allow him to use their psychic organization as his own, and, at the same time, phase specifically in tune with his changing needs, accept his separateness as a center of his own perception and initiative.

The cohesiveness of this nuclear self may, under stress, be subject to fragmentation, to disintegration. The capacity to restore cohesiveness, to regulate stress by undertaking remedial steps, drawing upon one's own resources and that of one's selfobjects—family, friends, teachers—is acquired in the early phases of the forming self of the child. Myriad experiences of having been soothed and comforted, functions performed by selfobjects, are transmuted into psychic structure—a self and its functions. And this psychic structure, laid down in the earliest years, includes the capacity to monitor one's anxiety and to take those steps which will resolve stress. This capacity will determine whether stress becomes a potential for change and growth or whether, because of the absence or failure of appropriately soothing selfobjects, deficits will occur which inhibit growth and leave only regressive modes of dealing with stress.

The emotional experiences of one's earliest years are carried forward throughout life; they reverberate whenever one finds oneself in a position of dependency on another (Basch, 1980). Stress will bring to light deficits or difficulties in one's self-esteem, doubts about one's goals. To undertake new learning exposes individuals to anxiety that they may not succeed, that failure and shame may be the outcome.

The adult learner experiences the arousal of feelings of earliest pleasurable expectation but also of helplessness, of the need to have a meaningful image of himself mirrored, confirmed, and guided, of the need to merge with the strength and wisdom of an idealized selfobject. Although this is true generally for anyone in a new learning situation, what is particularly hard for those who are new to the demands of higher education is the shame of not knowing at an age when one should know. Many have had earlier experiences of being ridiculed or shamed, of reaching out and being rebuffed by parents or teachers who have major self deficits, who themselves have experienced earlier deprivations and are overwhelmed by numerous burdens. They may have had earlier experiences in which the level of performance expected of them was beyond their ability. Their efforts may have been demeaned, leaving a sense of helplessness and shame in their wake.

It is not that teachers now undo the past and enact the role of more benevolent parents. It is that in this new relationship, the old need to be mirrored, confirmed, and guided is reawakened. The teacher becomes a new selfobject whose competence and strength can be idealized and merged with. In an empathic relationship, the disappointments and failures of the past can be newly understood; these are not handled impatiently or punitively but with a recognition of the deficits and needs which can now be responded to in a realistic manner. As we have said, we cannot change the past for these students but to have one's feelings and efforts understood in the present may help greatly. Although discussing this in the field of psychotherapy, Basch (1980) illuminated how focused empathic response to problems currently experienced may bring about healing. Such focused response in the present may perform a soothing and guiding function enabling the student to fill in a minute bit of psychic structure, thus enabling him to pursue educational paths which may lead him to realistic goals.

Until the late 1960s, preparation for college education more typically included a traditional high school diploma. The college population more typically included students in the age range of late adolescence and young adulthood. And these college years were viewed as a period during which problems of ego identity were to be resolved. It is now thirty years since Erikson (1956) first published a set of observations about college youth which he described as an identity crisis. The tasks of the college years included separation and individuation from the family, finding a vocation in which one could feel useful and wanted, establishing a set of standards and values which now more clearly emanated from a student's self as a center of his own perception and initiative. This was also a period during which the capacity for sexual intimacy led toward the choice of an enduring partnership.

The sweep of social change has made this more difficult for all adolescents, but, in greater measure, the students we are describing have not had, and do not have, a secure threshold from which these tasks can be assumed in a more measured way. Many have experienced severe loss and deprivation through death, illness, desertion, or

divorce of parents. Some have plunged into parenthood
long before their own parenting needs have been adequately met. Economically marginal, they have had to
accept any vocation which would provide subsistence.
Many have known unemployment; they have known the
corrosive experience of poverty and untreated illness.
Undertaking new steps in learning, then, can arouse at
times unmanageable anxiety and fear expressed in dropping out or not taking advantage of the aids that are
provided for them as learners.

The impact of such lives upon the educator can arouse
feelings of despair and hopelessness, for the learning
tasks which are necessarily assigned to assist students
in acquiring competence in a given field appear meaningless in the face of seemingly insurmountable burdens
of reality. And yet, as one teacher described her experience: "I see my students at their most human, most brave,
most endearing. . . . They teach me courage and honesty. . . . They make me more aware of my own fears and
anxieties. . . . Now why am I crying. . . . I'm not crying. . . .
And I'm not afraid. . . . I am the teacher."

It is a bitter tangle of unsolvable problems which some
students present as they struggle to extricate themselves
from one predicament and find themselves plunged into
another. The only order in some lives is the order they
find in school. And this may be true for some teachers as
well. As one faculty/student noted, "teaching gives order,
structure and identity to our lives. . . . Some students are
ghettoized, made to believe they cannot learn and deserve
their illiteracy, and we can help them surmount this barrier to learning." In so doing, the teacher has a sense of
power and goodness, and this competence in turn may be
idealized by the student who is permitted a sense of
merger with the strength and competence of the teacher.
The functions which the teacher performs for the student
are now transmuted bit by bit into those functions which
he can perform.

Perhaps more starkly than in any other course, initial English courses provide illustrative experiences which dramatize the teaching and learning process. One device employed to facilitate writing is the use of a daily journal in which students are invited to set down their experiences. Their capacity to express themselves in writing evolves from a mundane recital of daily events—"I woke up. The day was rainy. I got ready for school"—to a most beautiful description of a student's feelings for her dying mother. Others write of the disorder of their brutalized lives, the cruelties they have endured, and the losses. The task of writing up an experience for reading aloud to the class by the teacher seems a mickeymouse activity in the light of the stark reality with which they grapple. As one teacher wrote in her own class log (a task required for the Institute courses), "What students write of their own grief ignites ours; their fears ignite our fears." Torn between the wish to maintain distance from such suffering and the wish to find some comforting word, this teacher asks, "Who am I comforting?"

And yet, the teaching of spelling, punctuation, paragraphing, the logical expression of ideas is basic to the pursuit of higher education. To teach these processes to students who are at the level of illiteracy or barely above it poses new teaching tasks; often the use of a dictionary must be assisted by a second phonetic dictionary so that they may find the spelling which will guide them and unlock meaning.

Let me quote from a paper written for a basic English class in which a student describes a wish to be closer to people, to find out whom she can trust because "I have a great need to express my inner feelings and in my heart and mind I know that if these feelings doesn't come out soon I'd bust wide open with all my emotions pouring out like rain creating one big flood representing all my stored tears contained in my eyes bursting to get to the surface to show me just how great my need really is to be open

with people." Her instructor is a rather reserved young
man, somewhat overwhelmed by her response to his efforts to help her learn to punctuate, to paragraph, and
structure her thoughts. He expressed a feeling of profound disappointment at the glaring lack of her ability
to master sentence structure, and he is concerned about
his effectiveness. It is true that this student is learning
very slowly, but what has been reactivated is a longing
for merger with one in whose strength, calmness, and
competence she can bask, through whom she can achieve
a meaningful image of herself, and, in the process, acquire
a bit of the structure of self-esteem regulation. Even a bit
of such structure, newly acquired, can carry her along to
further cohesiveness, can help her tolerate the anxiety
of learning, and can facilitate the mastery of technical
skills.

The examples I have used are relatively clear in meaning and spelling, but many students are only protoliter-
ate. It requires the most thorough, diligent reading, and
some knowledge of the student's typical speech, to yield
an understanding of the thought which the student
strives to express. In a course devoted to understanding
the physical and social development of the toddler, students are required to write up observations of behavior.
From virtually illegible writing one teacher deciphered
a student's paper:

> [T]he parent some of the time is not in control but when
> the right amount of prsure on the child he or she will
> to what there are told to. Sometime the parent are in
> control of the situation. But when you get a parent
> have a child like to do what he or she like to do the
> child have control of the situation. . . . I were in the
> Jewel where I picking up cake for daughter who have
> just became 16. When a lady who have a baby with her
> and the child kept takeing candy off the shafe. When
> the lady will take if from the child. He just go back and
> take of agian and agian. Tell she had to use force on

the child. He just go back and take off agian. But the more force she use the more the child did it. But when the father can up the child stop. I guss I will have saide the child care in control of the situation until the father can in the picter. Then and only then the parent wate in control.

There is no question that this student described the question of who is in control. The problem lies in assisting her to express her thoughts in written form so that she can become employable in the field she has chosen, and this is a long, slow process.

Whether the course is biology, mathematics, sociology, or child care, the teacher provides a holding environment (Winnicott, 1965; Modell, 1976). This holding environment is one in which the empathic understanding of the teacher creates the conditions which allow the student to reveal what he does not know. Seeing the student at his least effectual, and yet not breaking off contact or shaming him because of his limitations, becomes in itself a novel, healing experience for the student. The feelings of shame that are aroused by not knowing when one feels one should know, if they are absorbed and understood by the teacher, may further reduce barriers to learning. A number of teachers refer to the fact that after a particular intervention which has been helpful to a student, he will confide shyly, "You remind me of my first grade teacher."

This reaction can be misunderstood as regression but it can be better understood as the reawakening of that early need to be mirrored, confirmed, guided, to merge with the power and goodness of an idealized figure from which new learning can emerge.

Just as in our earliest lives we needed the soothing, calming functions of parental selfobjects to help us acquire the ability (self functions) of soothing and calming ourselves in the face of stress engendered by unfamiliar tasks, so now the teacher is a needed new selfobject en-

abling the student to absorb the stress of learning. When
understood in the light of the process which has been set
in motion by becoming a student, manipulative, demanding, or clinging behavior aroused in some students
takes on new meaning. Such behavior may reflect the
reactivation of enormous deficits. We tend to draw back
and place as much distance as possible between ourselves
and those who have been the victims of genetic deficit,
family or social neglect, or who suffer the scars of marginal living produced by untreated emotional illness and
poverty. A student's expectation that he will be ridiculed
because of ignorance, or clumsy expression, or slowness,
may release demanding behavior which drives others further from him. And yet, his noisy demands actually reveal
underlying needs which he cannot adequately identify.
The capacity to recognize such needs *does not mean that
the teacher now becomes the student's mother, or that he
is teaching by means of an arm around the shoulder.*
Rather, it is a mark of skilled pedagogy to be able to
identify and absorb a student's stress. The teacher uses
himself in a way which now lends structure to the distressed student. Recognition that the student may have
limitations does not mean scorn—neither does the teacher
offer false reassurance. By sharing a student's disappointments, and helping him to identify the skills he needs to
master, the teacher is offering himself temporarily as
structure for the student. Such interest allows the student
to acquire, although perhaps minimally, the skill to examine the elements of a task, to attempt to master them.
When he meets disappointment and a sense of his limitations, experiences which even the wisest among us
undergo, he may absorb those self-soothing, calming
functions, which initially the teacher has performed for
him, as a bit of psychic structure which becomes his own.
He learns to identify the smaller tasks and to seek out
and use the many teaching aids available to him.

There are myriad interchanges through which the

teacher communicates and performs these functions. Even a smile, a comment on a paper, a reference to previous work, can act as powerful reinforcers within the context of a meaningful relationship. The narcissistic vulnerability of new learners, or old learners who are once more attempting to enter the educational arena, is often startling. Praise of another student may arouse old envy, or a sense of incompetence, not because an individual is unable to admire the work of others, but that too often in his own past such performance has been used to downgrade or demean his own. He may simply not return to class. To be able to respond to the needs of such students in the context of specific tasks which have been assigned, releasing a surge of energy to tackle a problem once more, may be enormously powerful in repairing self-esteem. For "dashed hopes" may then be restored in "redirected ambitions" (Goldberg, 1973).

In the Institute classes, highly competent city college faculty who were our students taught us much about the manner in which they sought to discharge their tasks to these students while meeting their responsibilities to the majority of those whose limitations were less glaring. Sensitivity to the needs of these students has in the past been regarded as a pejorative term signifying softness and sentimentality, and less than rigorous attention to academic demands. Yet the basic task of teachers is to assist students in achieving synchrony between academic and personal development (Bruner, 1966). It is here that the discrepancy between aspiration and reality impinges most painfully on the conscientious instructor.

As one teacher wrote,

> Teaching these students is a traumatic event; teaching in the city is a traumatic event . . . teaching in this system is a traumatic event. It all hits on us every day, chips away at us every day . . . and we cope . . . or don't cope . . . with the trauma and anxiety every day . . . but

when the fragile wall between us and them breaks
down, I do not know if you can put the teacher back
together again.

Recognizing the self in the other can be immobilizing,
but it can also, through an increased understanding of
human behavior, release fresh energy to cope with seemingly intractable problems. Confronting a student's limitations stimulates awareness of one's own limitations
and of those of society in a poignantly intimate manner.
Yet learning what one is not can be helpful in learning
more about what one is. One remembers one's own aspirations and disappointments, one may relive the pain-
fulness of one's own failures, events from which no human
being is free, however fortunate his life may seem.

Prominent among faculty members who were our students was the high degree of conscientiousness in their
teaching. From the sessions devoted to group examination of cases prepared by individual teachers, they
learned much from each other of possible new areas of
intervention. They learned also about their differences.
They could vent anger at the insurmountable difficulties
presented by given students for whose inclusion in a given
course there had been no preparation. From our shared
understanding of these difficulties and the professional
manner in which they attempted to resolve them, teachers could take new pride in being at the forefront, the
cutting edge of society's efforts to bring into the mainstream of higher education previously neglected populations. They studied a broad array of maladaptive
behavior which could be identified as defensive or strategic—inept attempts to cope with reality in defense
against anxiety—and methods of helping students achieve
more adaptive resolutions. And they examined the categories of serious emotional disturbance for which other
than teaching interventions were necessary. They sought
ways of overcoming the lack or insufficiency of a referral

service through which students with serious emotional difficulties could be guided to possible sources of help. And they struggled with the enormous incursion of time occasioned by having to provide a holding environment for these students. Our purpose was not to make therapists of teachers. Rather we worked together toward understanding the barriers to learning, the unexpected hostility, so difficult to withstand, by which students covered over the shame of not knowing and the fear of failure. The basic striving to grow is universal and is laid down in the genes, but the learning disabled are disabled because of deficits in nurturant learning experiences. As the instructor provides acceptance, what is communicated is that the student is an acceptable human being whose learning difficulties can be examined and understood. This in turn releases energy for progression in cognitive development rather than regression.

To be able to understand that students make teachers into what they want them to be by transference (an expectational set derived from past experiences with earlier depriving, thwarting, or punitive figures) enables the faculty to feel less threatened. Learned responses to the act of learning can be exposed and examined. By helping a student to understand how one lives with mistakes as a phase in learning, by increasing his capacity for self-evaluation and reaching out appropriately for assistance, a teacher thus temporarily offers himself as self structure. Such an experience may take a student only a small distance but even a small bit may make a vast difference.

One problem not uncommonly encountered was that success in mastering given course material could unduly stimulate a student to make plans for inappropriate goals. Teachers would express a sense of fear and guilt at the likelihood of the student's failure and their part in stimulating such fantasies. They came to recognize that equally important in being able to mirror a student's dreams is the task of guiding a student into more appropriate goals, to share pleasure in his capacity to dream, and, while not subjecting his dream to scorn, helping him to tailor his aspirations.

Lending oneself as structure to such a student enables him to acquire and transmute certain missing functions which the teacher initially performs: examining the reality of one's abilities and capacities, dealing with the anxiety aroused by attempting to master new and difficult tasks, and defining goals which are reachable.

This brief opportunity to merge with an idealized, competent figure obviously will not heal enormous deficits but will permit a student to transmute a bit of the function performed by the teacher into a function which he now initiates and performs for himself. It is a bit of psychic structure which he acquires enabling him to express his ambitions through such talents as he may be able to elaborate into skills directed toward a reachable goal. As one faculty/student commented, "I am more detached, yet I think I am more observant and responsive. I am more aware and more able to meet [my students'] needs, less guilty when I cannot, and I have much more respect for my very real teaching ability, for what I do manage to do for these students."

The teacher as learner experiences intense anxiety in bringing into the open anger at the lack of adequate recognition for one's efforts, fears of incompetence, disillusionment with one's level of progress, disaffection for one's profession. These are the stresses of mature adulthood. I, too, confronted these anxieties within myself as I sought to understand these stresses, the nature of the educational system and the faculty. Whether such stress can lead to growth and change in the direction of greater competence, or whether it will result in stagnation and regression depends on the opportunity to examine these stresses in an empathic milieu.

And such a milieu was what we attempted to provide in our courses. We found ourselves working to strengthen the capacity to accept and tolerate conflict and ambivalence. As Jaques (1980) wrote: "The successful outcome of mature creative work lies in . . . constructive resignation both to the imperfection of men and to shortcomings in one's own work. It is this constructive resignation that then imparts serenity to life and work. . . . Inevitably, imperfection is no longer felt as bitter, persecutory failure" (p. 9).

Thus the teacher as learner and the learner as teacher, in a parallel process, inform and strengthen each other's work. In the face of intractable problems, one does not give way to despair, though one may experience anger and sadness; rather one finds renewed energy to lend those skills we do possess to bring about needed change.

REFERENCES

Barshis, D. (1980), *Report of the Individual Needs Program.* Unpublished report to the faculty and administration of the Chicago City Colleges.

Basch, M. F. (1980), *Doing Psychotherapy.* New York: Basic Books.

Bloom, B. S. (1981), *Evaluation to Improve Learning.* New York: McGraw-Hill.

Bruner, J. (1966), *The Process of Education: Toward a Theory of Instruction.* Cambridge, MA: Harvard University Press.

Erikson, E. (1956), The problem of ego identity. *J. Amer. Psychoanal. Assn.*, 4:56–121.

Freud, A. (1965), *Normality and Pathology in Childhood.* New York: International Universities Press.

Freud, S. (1914), On narcissism. *Standard Edition*, 14:69–102. London: Hogarth Press, 1957.

Goldberg, A. (1973), Psychotherapy of narcissistic injury. *Arch. Gen. Psychiat.*, 28:722–726.

Hartmann, H. (1939), *Ego Psychology and the Problem of Adaptation.* New York: International Universities Press, 1958.

Jaques, E. (1980), Midlife crisis. In: *The Course of Life: Psychoanalytic Contribution Toward Understanding Personality Development.* Vol. 3, *Adulthood and the Aging Process*, ed. S. Greenspan & G. Pollock. Washington, DC: National Institute of Mental Health, pp. 1–23.

Kohut, H. (1977), *The Restoration of the Self.* New York: International Universities Press.

———— Wolf, E. S. (1978), Disorders of the self and their treatment: An outline. *Internat. J. Psycho-Anal.*, 59:413–424.

Mahler, M. M., Pine, F., & Bergman, A. (1975), *The Psychological Birth of the Human Infant*. New York: Basic Books.

Modell, A. (1976), The holiday environment and the therapeutic action of psychoanalysis. *J. Amer. Psychoanal. Assn.*, 24:285–308.

Piaget, J., & Inhelder, B. (1971), *The Psychology of the Child*. New York: Basic Books.

Swift, J. (1974), Issues in program structure and content. Paper presented at the Conference on Child Care Training for a Changing World, Pittsburgh, Pennsylvania.

Tolpin, M. (1971), On the beginnings of a cohesive self. *The Psychoanalytic Study of the Child*, 26:316–354. New Haven, CT: Yale University Press.

———— (1980), Discussion of psychoanalytic developmental theories of the self: An integration by Morton and Estelle Shane. In: *Advances in Self Psychology*, ed. A. Goldberg. New York: International Universities Press, pp. 47–48.

Winnicott, D. W. (1965), *The Maturational Processes and the Facilitating Environment*. New York: International Universities Press.

Chapter 28

The Effects of Narcissistic Transferences on the Teaching-Learning Process

LINDA A. COZZARELLI, M.A.
MARILYN SILIN, M.A.

I. DISRUPTIONS IN THE LEARNING PROCESS

Oftentimes teachers are confronted with students' behaviors which evoke anxiety and elicit a range of feelings and reactions that may lead to a disruption of the teaching-learning process. While some of the students' behaviors may arise out of their developmental needs or life stresses, a student's specific response may also be precipitated unwittingly by the teacher's behavior. The teacher must be able to assess the dynamic interaction between herself and the student, to ask how residues from the student's previous relationships might have become transferred to his relationship with her. She must also be aware of her own needs, her reactions to these transferences, and acknowledge the unique meaning of her relationship to her students in terms of herself as well as a transference figure. Thus, in trying to understand disruptions in the teaching-learning process, the teacher must not only look to the student and his environment but to herself as well. The awareness of these dynamics and their subsequent understanding enables teachers to consider a range of alternatives in handling difficult situations.

Under the impact of psychological forces and limitations imposed by reality, teachers may feel a bind between wanting to meet the student's expectations beyond the appropriateness of a classroom and wishing to withdraw, and feeling as if there were little they could do to help. When the teaching-learning process is disrupted, it may be difficult for a teacher to distinguish between problems which are educational and those which go beyond the educational sphere. These dynamics are illustrated in the following vignette.

CASE EXAMPLE 1

Mrs. A. is a very talented high school biology teacher who is popular with students. Her class is for gifted students capable of independent study who design and execute a science project over a two-year period. Instruction is individualized, and Mrs. A. has spent long hours with her students outside of regular class time. While Mrs. A. acknowledges that she is a good teacher, she often minimizes her importance to her students. She has stated that she provides little more than a place to work and supplies and that her students could go on without her because they are so gifted. In fact, she provides support, nurturance, and an optimal environment for learning and the expression of creativity.

During a summer between a two-year project, Mrs. A. had a baby. She returned to teaching as scheduled and felt that there had been no disruption for her students. Most of her students' work continued to progress, however, one of them, David, seemed increasingly to need more attention from her which was requested as a need for more supervision. David was a bright and talented student who, until Mrs. A.'s class, was considered to be an underachiever with little enthusiasm for work. In Mrs. A.'s class, with her considerable support and attention, David had begun to be more productive and his talent emerged. Mrs. A. attributed this to David's finally having discovered an interest. Now David's demands caused Mrs. A. to feel angry at him. Because she liked David, and also because she could not accept that her needs and her investment in her students had changed, she could neither acknowledge his need nor her feelings. Mrs. A. began avoiding David, but stated that she was purposely not as available to give as much supervision because David needed to be more independent. His work began to slide. As the school year progressed, other students' projects were inexplicably not working. The classroom atmosphere became tense and suspicious. Mrs. A. was perplexed. Eventually, some of the students discovered David sabotaging their work, and he was suspended. In a discussion of the incident, Mrs. A. tearfully stated, "I'm not his mother. He wanted too much."

Mrs. A. was caught in her wish to give versus the reality of the demands of her own life. She could neither acknowledge to herself nor to David that she was not as available as she had been before the birth of her child. In addition, she was unaware of her importance to David, either as a transference figure or for herself in her own right. It also was difficult for her to consider the nature of David's need for her and the developmental issues which his need reflected. The shift in Mrs. A.'s investment due to her own changing needs and life situation was experienced by David not only as a loss of Mrs. A., but also as a loss of the supportive, nurturing, admiring functions which were so meaningful and had enhanced his sense of self-worth. Her unsuspecting withdrawal of them touched a previously existing area of psychological vulnerability, and threatened David's self-integrity. David, enraged by both the loss and the assault he experienced, sought revenge.

This example illustrates the impact and the interplay of a multiplicity of situational factors, psychological issues, and transference-countertransference phenomena on the teaching-learning alliance. The psychological factors regarding David's self-esteem and self-integrity and the special meaning Mrs. A. had for him are most clearly illuminated when viewed in terms of self psychology as delineated in the work of Heinz Kohut (1971). Self psychology provides a useful framework for understanding some dynamics of the teaching-learning process and the transference-countertransference phenomena which can enhance or inhibit teaching and learning.

II. IMPORTANCE OF THE TEACHER

Much like parents, teachers nurture capabilities and encourage growth and mastery. They temper the student's grandiosity by empathic responses which help the student maintain his self-esteem and develop a sense of what is realistically possible. Like parents, teachers also represent idealized figures who are seen as people who know all and can do everything. At the stage when children are deidealizing their parents, teachers may become their new heroes. Teachers provide further opportunities for children to gain feelings of self-worth, competence, enjoyment in achievements, and to experience meaningful relationships from which alternate values, goals, and ideals spring. Given these functions which teachers fulfill, they then become possible targets for a reactivation of archaic narcissistic needs and transferences, as well as for an appropriate expression of the child's normal narcissistic needs. Even a normal narcissistic equilibrium can be thrown off balance when a child goes into a new classroom, begins with a new teacher, or learns new skills. For example, the typical outgoing, talkative, social six-year-old entering first grade often becomes shy, unenthusiastic, and more clingy at home, until the first grade teacher is established in the child's eyes as a dependable, giving parental figure who praises the child appropriately for his good behavior and accomplishments. Another example is the nine-year-old who either becomes tense and anxious or is arrogant and aloof when he is faced with having to learn a musical instrument at school because he is fearful of making mistakes and looking foolish. His feelings subside and he relaxes when his teacher is supportive, helpful, and appreciative of his efforts. New beginnings recapitulate, no matter how fleetingly, the initial learning experience between parent and child, reactivating the fluctuations of the child's earlier sense of self-esteem and the defenses the child has developed to bolster it.

The understanding that children's narcissistic needs may be transferred or imposed upon the teaching-learning process offers useful insight for the teacher faced with the dilemma of understanding children's behavior. Students who experience difficulties in learning and social relationships may develop defensive patterns against feelings of inferiority brought on by fears of failure. The effect of low self-confidence and painful feelings of worthlessness can elicit self-protective behavior patterns. For example, teachers are acquainted with children who are arrogant, apathetic, or lacking in vitality. They are familiar with children who are bored or boring and lack energy to be involved in relationships or tasks. There are other students who are compelled to perform and be the center of attention. Teachers also observe children who are easily influenced by others, who seek out leaders to follow, or who are so needful that they act as if they were satellites to the teacher or to other students. These are children who may well be dealing with feelings which refer to how they feel about themselves. Their behavior in class may reflect low self-esteem or a poorly integrated sense of who they are.

In a busy classroom, it is difficult for a teacher to readily determine whether a child's behavior pattern is a defense against feelings of emptiness and low self-esteem or a defense against anxieties arising from intrapsychic conflicts. The teacher's observation of the student, the awareness of her own feelings and reactions toward him, and her empathic understanding of his total personality provide diagnostic clues. She might assess the child as follows: Does the child show enthusiasm for age-appropriate activities and learning, risking failure, and enjoying success? How does he respond to not knowing or criticism? Does he have a realistic appreciation of his abilities? Does he respond to others as separate, autonomous individuals with needs of their own or are other people viewed only as handmaidens to his needs? Does he use others' feelings about him as guideposts to his own feelings about himself? Does he need to impress his teachers and peers, and without their admiration becomes frantic or depleted, marginally operating in the classroom?

Of significant importance is what the child seeks in his relationships to fulfill his narcissistic needs. Is he searching for admiration or affirmation of his totality as a person? Is he searching for someone to idealize, in whose glory he might bask? Is his behavior defensive against those needs as an attempt to protect himself from further disappointment? Does his behavior seek to fill a deficit, allowing him to feel whole for a while? Children respond to the total personality of the teacher, and, in a reciprocal fashion, to the respect, appreciation, and enthusiasm the teacher communicates to the child about himself.

The teacher as a unique person, her personality, values, ideals, and behavioral patterns, are real facets of the teaching-learning process to which the child must adapt. However, the teacher may unwittingly become a transference figure based on the child's past and/or present experiences in his developing sense of self. These transferences may stimulate positive reactions which may facilitate the teaching-learning process, or conflictual ones which may obscure the educational goals if she finds her own self-esteem shaken. When this occurs, and it does at times with every teacher, she has the added task of trying to become aware of her own narcissistic issues. These may include how she responds to idealization or the lack of it, to confrontation with a child's grandiosity, to the drain on her by a child's need for admiration, or the burden created by the necessity of her ongoing physical and psychological presence for a child to function in class.

For example, a teacher may feel insulted and angry when a bright but troublesome third grader interrupts and finds flaws with her logic, or criticizes her classroom presentation by asking questions which point out her shortcomings. His comments punctuate her sentences as he states, "That's not true." "That's not what you said before." "I think it should be――――." The pupil's criticisms of the teacher and the inappropriate display of his knowledge is experienced by the teacher as an assault on her competence. Her anger in response to the humiliation she feels causes her to withdraw from the provocative child. Unknowingly, he has caused her to experience how he feels and to repeat the pattern of withdrawal to protect herself.

III. NATURE OF NARCISSISTIC TRANSFERENCES

In describing transference, Anna Freud delineated types of transference reactions: transference of habitual ways of relating, transferences of current relationships, and transferences of past experiences (Sandler, Kennedy, and Tyson, 1980). The differentiation of these types of reactions provides a useful framework for understanding the student in his relationship with the teacher. By looking at the chronicity of a given reaction, when it began, what precipitated it, and what the pattern is, the teacher may be able to determine whether the reaction is a characterological one or a temporary one related to a transient stress, or whether an internal or external strain has caused the child to regress to earlier modes of functioning.

In transferences involving habitual modes of relating, residues of the child's earlier relationship with his parents are transferred to significant adults in the child's environment. These residues are ingrained in the child's character. Thus, the child relates to his parents, teachers, doctors, baby-sitters, and others in patterns characteristic of earlier phases of development. He may not distinguish among them as individuals or distinguish present relationships from those of the past. An example of such a transference is the latency child who is habitually shy, anxious, or suspicious of adults (Sandler et al., 1980).

The transference of current relationships involves the re-creation of concerns from other areas of a child's life in his relationship with his teacher. These concerns are either the result of the child's present phase of development, the concomitant psychological issues regarding his feelings about himself and his relationship with others, or the impact of a current reality situation. Examples of transferences involving such dynamics would include an angry interchange between parent and child which might cause the child to display feelings of anger toward the teacher, or a five- or six-year-old child's phase appropriate feelings of competition toward a teacher of the same sex, or the stress of a divorce which may precipitate needy, regressive behavior in the child. In transferences involving current relationships, the child's current relationship with his parents is displaced onto his teacher or continued with her as an extension of his parents (Sandler et al., 1980).

In transferences of past experiences, a child alters his usual mode of relating and regresses to an earlier mode because of stress felt at school or at home. The child can transfer his feelings, fantasies, wishes, and fears onto his teacher. The example of David and Mrs. A. is illustrative of this (Sandler et al., 1980).

The nature of narcissistic transferences can be understood by using these distinctions. More importantly, however, the narcissistic transferences fall into two categories: the mirror transference, related to the grandiose self, and the idealizing transference, related to the idealized parent image. A mirror transference involves a child's intense need for the admiring, confirming responses to his exhibitionistic self. These responses help a child feel worthwhile and maintain his self-esteem. An idealizing transference involves attributions of omniscience and omnipotence and moral perfection to a meaningful person. By merging with the person who holds these qualities, the child feels protected. While these two types of narcissistic transferences are distinct entities, they have a common denominator. The child is interested only in the functions the significant adult fulfills for him. He is not concerned with the adult as a separate, autonomous individual (Palombo, 1976).

Understanding this concept, we can see that in the classroom when narcissistic transferences occur, the student is not interested in the teacher as an individual with wishes and feelings of her own, rather as someone who, as in the early parent-child relationship, can be a psychological part of him. The teacher is seen in large part as one who provides functions which the student may lack, which may have developed unevenly, or which may be in temporary deficit because the student is in a transitional state. Examples of the latter would be entering a new class or the transitional periods from early childhood to latency and puberty to adolescence, in which the student is phase appropriately reorganizing his psychological and physical sense of self (Kohut, 1972).

The pattern in which a teacher is seen as a servant

contrasts to the pattern where a student is intensely interested in the teacher as a person and may go to all
lengths to be liked by her. Relationships which have
strong narcissistic elements look as if they have interpersonal qualities, but, in fact, the child experiences the
teacher as if she were fulfilling some need which, in turn,
enables the child to feel complete. This can be disturbing
to a teacher because she then begins to view herself as
being exploited. Her importance is only in what she provides. This can cause the teacher to feel a range of reactions which may include feeling that the child expects
too much, feeling irritation at the child, feeling dislike
for the child, and feeling a failure as a teacher.

The two following vignettes are examples of narcissistic issues and transferences in the teaching-learning
process.

CASE EXAMPLE 2

Jack was a ten-year-old in fifth grade. His academic work
was satisfactory, but he was an ungratifying youngster
to have in class. He was arrogant and seemed to carry a
chip on his shoulder. The teacher felt as if she had no
effect on him. He didn't enjoy the class. He begrudgingly
handed in his work, but even a good grade did not make
him happy. He seemed disdainful of the other children
and their activities. Most of the time he did nothing obviously wrong in terms of classroom rules, but one day
he returned from recess very late. When the teacher
asked him to explain, he shrugged and refused to answer.
The teacher felt so angry at his insolence and at her
powerlessness that she sent him to the principal's office,
a measure to which she rarely resorted. Jack seemed to
respond to her request with indifference. As he walked
to the office the teacher watched him and found herself
in a silent rage.

The principal had no better luck in getting Jack to account for the twenty-minute tardiness. In face, the principal felt so frustrated that he told Jack to sit on the bench in the office for twenty minutes, and to write one page on the necessity of returning from recess on time. To the principal's surprise and consternation, Jack walked away from the bench after ten minutes, without attempting to write the assignment. The secretary told the principal that Jack just shrugged his shoulders and walked off, as if no authority in the world held any meaning for him.

In this vignette, we encounter a boy for whom adults seemed to have little significance. Most fifth graders admire their teachers and, in turn, want to be admired by them. Most ten-year-olds are motivated to get good grades to the point of becoming unduly distressed by small imperfections in their productions. Finally, most latency age children idealize the school principal and identify with the values for which he stands; they would have been embarrassed to be sent to the office, and felt guilty about the punishment. The teacher knew all of this intuitively, and therefore Jack's lack of responsiveness stood out as completely uncharacteristic and distressing. We can feel how this boy might represent a chronic source of discomfort to any teacher. His lack of enthusiasm for learning and his lack of respect for all adults in authority might propel a teacher to question her own competence, or to look for reasons within herself for her failure to reach this child. Finding no specific reason to fault herself or her techniques, the teacher might then blame the student (or his parents) and give up trying to reach this child, feeling there was little that could be done.

Using self psychology as our frame of reference, we might say that Jack covered feelings of emptiness and worthlessness with a cold, disdainful facade. His behavior seemed to communicate that he was "everything" and his teacher "nothing." A teacher would have to be an unusual person if she did not respond by feeling as if she were, indeed, "nothing," and to seek the source of her pupil's failure in her own inadequacies. However, understanding the parallel process sometimes helps us gain insight into the child's feelings. Jack did to the teacher, in the transference, what other significant people had done to him. As a result of his parents' self-absorption, their inattentiveness, and their dissatisfaction with him, Jack felt neither valued nor appreciated by them. If the teacher had been able to accept her feelings and use them in understanding Jack as a boy whose arrogance was a defense against feelings of low self-esteem, her feelings of insignificance might not have been disruptive. The realization that her feelings were a reflection of Jack's might have modulated her anger toward him and allowed her to reestablish her self-esteem. She might then have been able to look for other ways to enhance Jack's self-worth. Understanding Jack also could help a teacher feel empathy for him. Could a teacher find some way to appreciate Jack for some small aspect of his self? Could a teacher discover in herself some spark of interest in anything important to Jack whether it is sports, clothes, a television show, or even a bit of schoolwork for which Jack expressed the tiniest bit of enthusiasm? Would it be possible for a teacher to create a special interest area with Jack in which she feels and exudes enthusiasm, and to which Jack would respond? A small, but meaningful interaction might give Jack a feeling that not all of him is perceived as worthless and the part which becomes interesting to the teacher, could, in turn, grow in positive significance to Jack. In this fashion, a circular, gratifying, growth-producing cycle might be initiated.

For a teacher to find the resources within her, to reach out to such an unrewarding child, it is helpful to be able to identify her own narcissistic needs, then to try to put herself in the child's shoes, and to attempt experientially to reach out to him at whatever level, in whatever sphere, he can accept her. If, by chance, this does produce a need-satisfying experience for the child, it will raise the self-esteem of the teacher and give her energy to meet the demanding situation once again.

CASE EXAMPLE 3

Owen was a four-year-old in day care. When it was his turn to show something in show and tell he was charming, winsome, and verbal. When a teacher asked for volunteers, Owen was the first to raise his hand. However, his attention span was short and when the three teachers were busy with others, Owen would often get into trouble by hitting anyone who was passing by, by knocking over someone's block tower, or by making a lot of noise. The teachers described him as an overstimulated child, more aggressive than the others, and on some days he seemed hyperactive. They thought he should have more structure during the day, less free time to get into trouble, and because he was bright, they thought he would respond well to challenging projects.

These measures did not calm him down. It became apparent that only when Owen had the complete attention of any teacher, or when he was in the limelight of the whole group, did he quiet down. Without either of these, Owen became wild, as if the physical activity itself were a compelling force. The teachers became more frustrated as the semester continued. He did not seem to discriminate among them, but upon very close observation, it looked as if the head teacher had more of an effect upon him than the others. She could go over to him, if he was screaming or fighting, and by her mere presence, he would begin to quiet down.

In light of our understanding of the growth of self integrity and self-esteem, we might hypothesize that Owen felt empty and panicky without the admiration of an audience, or without the attention of a teacher who could soothe him. Hitting, yelling, knocking over blocks, or running gave him body sensations which stimulated his physical senses so that he felt a body-self. "I am nothing, unless I feel myself," his behavior seemed to communicate. He had not developed the inner sense of "me" which is so easily observable in toddlers who are in love with the world, whose body sense and mastery of behavior exudes confidence and enthusiasm. Closer observation of Owen showed that between bouts of fighting, screaming, or limelight attention, he appeared depressed and deflated. His wish for recognition was so overpowering that out of desperation, he resorted to negative behavior which not only allowed him to experience himself, but evoked the attention he so needed.

When the teachers began to observe the depression and deflation, they realized that Owen's aggressive hyperactivity might be a defense against his feelings of nothingness and a cry for attention, rather than attacks against them, or against the other children. They decided to try to build on the beginning meaningful relationship between Owen and the head teacher, to enhance the positive feelings that already had started to grow. They realized that to give Owen projects was not enough. He needed an important adult who enjoyed and respected him, who responded to him affectively, and thus gave emotional significance to the activity. The staff then decided to try to provide a total environment of caring and concern, with the hope that by offering themselves as sources of good feelings for him, Owen would internalize these and take them as his own.

In summary, the teaching-learning process at any given time is affected by the interplay of the previously mentioned factors: the child's developmental phase, life stresses, the teacher's uniqueness, and the transference-countertransference phenomena which arise between them. While acknowledging the multiplicity of psychological issues which can affect this process, this chapter has focused on the effects of narcissistic issues and transferences. The interplay of the narcissistic needs of teachers and students profoundly affect how the teacher teaches and how the student learns. The vicissitudes of self-esteem of both teacher and student influence one another. Awareness of this process provides an additional and significant dimension to understanding and enhancing the teaching-learning process.

REFERENCES

Kohut, H. (1971), *The Analysis of the Self.* New York: International Universities Press.

———— (1972), Thoughts on narcissism and narcissistic rage. *The Psychoanalytic Study of the Child*, 27:360-400. New Haven, CT: Yale University Press.

Palombo, J. (1976), Theories of narcissism and the practice of clinical social work. *Clin. Soc. Work J.*, 4(3):147–161.

Sandler, J., Kennedy, H., & Tyson, R. (1980), *The Technique of Child Psychoanalysis: Discussions with Anna Freud.* Cambridge, MA: Harvard University Press.

Chapter 29

Reflections of Early Childhood Family Experiences in the Educational Situation

NER LITTNER, M.D.

INTRODUCTION

As a practicing child psychiatrist, I have discussed with many teachers the problems that some of their students are having in school. I have always been intrigued by the fact that the teacher and I frequently shared identical attitudes toward the child and often toward his parents.

The child psychiatrist is trained to be aware of his own feelings about the child. In therapy sessions it quickly became apparent to me that the one emotion that I rarely felt toward the child was that of pure, benevolent, helpful interest. More often I found myself experiencing feelings that sometimes were quite intense. As I studied my personal reactions to different child patients, I realized that I was experiencing a wide range of emotions. Sometimes I would find myself proud of the child's accomplishments, at other times I would be disgusted by

Acknowledgment. This chapter was first presented to the annual Meeting of the Independent School Association of Greater Chicago, March 3, 1983.

his failures. Sometimes I would worry about him and the possibility that he would get into trouble. I would get angry at the child's provocativeness, his coming late, his missing appointments. I would feel rejected by his depreciation of my help, his loud protestations of the more enjoyable times he could be having elsewhere or his complaints about how much more help he could be getting from someone else. Sometimes I would find myself bored or disinterested by the monotony of his sleep-inspiring productions. Sometimes I would feel afraid of being hurt by my adolescent patient who was, in fact, bigger or stronger than me and who seemed quite intimidating with his stories of brutal beatings or his actual brandishing of a switchblade knife under my nose. Sometimes I found myself feeling protective of the child, wanting to do all sorts of things for him and expecting very little responsibility on his part. Sometimes I would be aware of feeling utterly helpless as I watched the child's determined march into self-destructive behavior. Sometimes I felt extremely guilty over how angry I would get at the child; and sometimes quite ashamed at finding myself sexually stimulated by a provocative, adolescent girl patient.

In addition, I also became aware of a variety of intense emotions toward the people mentioned by the child, whether they were parents, brothers and sisters, teachers, or indeed other therapists. I found myself liking or disliking them, being angry or depreciating of them, or even feeling competitive with them.

As I examined my own feelings, thoughts, and behavior objectively, I realized that on occasion my reaction or a part of it was quite realistic in terms of the specific child; at other times it was quite apparent that the way I was feeling and reacting was quite unrealistic and was being provoked in some manner by the child himself.

As I discussed problem children with their teachers it was clear that the teachers were occasionally experiencing much the same emotional reactions to the child and his parents as I was.

An example of this is the child toward whom one feels intense dislike. If one examines the matter carefully, it becomes apparent that children can be dislikeable for many reasons:

1. Some of the reasons relate not primarily to the child but rather to us. For example, something about the child may bother us because of some prejudice within us; the child's appearance, sex, age, size, color, race, and so on, may provoke an irrational action in us because of problems of our own.
2. A second group of reasons are child related but not child provoked. For example, the child may be really dislikeable but not consciously or unconsciously attempting to be so. Toward these kinds of children, almost any observer would react in a negative way.
3. A third group of reasons are child related and child provoked. In such cases the child, unconsciously, is attempting to make us not like him. He acts in such a way as to turn us off, to have us be angry with him or become disgusted with him so that we end up unable to like him no matter how hard we try.

This type of child is using a mental defense mechanism; that is, he is employing the relationship between himself and others, not for realistic reasons but for irrational purposes that enable him to deal with inner conflicts of his own. This mechanism is called projective identification. In effect the child grows up exposed to certain attitudes in his family which he then internalizes. He now unconsciously expects these attitudes to be expressed by others. He deals with this expectation by learning to provoke these specific attitudes, or related attitudes, from others. The successful provoking of such attitudes and behavior from others then becomes used as a defense mechanism for dealing with an innumerable variety of emotional problems.

How is this mental mechanism relevant to the educational situation? How does the knowledge that, as a result of traumatic early childhood experiences, a child unconsciously may try to manipulate our feelings in order to elicit from us a specific emotional reaction and behavior help us help a child to learn? To answer this question, let us look at learning, teaching, and the purpose of education.

THE EDUCATIONAL GOAL

What is the major goal of the educational system? Is it to teach the child specific material that he is expected to learn? I believe that most of us would agree that the sheer memorization of content, while certainly necessary to some degree, is not the major educational goal. A six-month-old baby can be toilet trained; but such toilet training is not basically "learned" by the infant. It is rather a conditioned-reflex response, a programming of the young child. It readily breaks down under stress. Similarly, in the educational situation the sheer memorization of content does not mean that the child or the student is able to use the material freely in appropriate situations. What we wish to accomplish through education is to teach the child how to learn, to help the child develop a learning stance.

In order for the child to develop this learning stance four factors must come together: (1) an emotional, intellectual, and physical ability to learn; (2) a conscious desire and motivation to learn; (3) the ability to develop a positive relationship with the teacher; (4) a teacher whose teaching stance enables the child to develop this positive relationship. I will focus particularly on those factors that influence a child's ability to form a positive relationship with the teacher, and, through this positive relationship, to learn how to learn.

THE SOURCE OF THE CHILD'S ABILITY TO DEVELOP A POSITIVE RELATIONSHIP WITH THE TEACHER

How and where does the child learn to develop a positive relationship with the teacher? Research has shown that this results from the child's earliest relationship with his mother.

The ability to relate to and trust another person depends on the nature of the child's earliest mothering experiences. If the mother is able to understand and meet the baby's needs, then the child will learn to relate to and trust her. From this comes the child's later ability to form intimate one-to-one relationships with others, and to allow himself to be close to others. The mother-baby relationship is the model for *all* future relationships.

If the child trusts the mother and has a good relationship with her, it will be easier for him to relate to the father. If he has a poor relationship with the mother (for example, she may have a postpartum depression), then it will be much harder for him to learn to relate to the father. However, if the father is able to be close to the baby, the child may gradually form a close relationship to the father which will then serve as a model for future relationships. But the details of the first relationship with his mother will always influence his later relationships in terms of an initial trust or distrust of others, particularly of women.

When I use the word *mother* I am referring to the so-called *psychological mother*; that is, the one whom the child regards as his mother.

The psychological mother is the person with whom the child has the actual mothering experiences, partic-

ularly in the crucial first year of life when he develops
the so-called bonding relationship. Usually, the psychological mother is also the biological mother. She has the
care of the child and the major twenty-four-hour responsibility for mothering him. She may be home all the time
looking after the growing child; or she may be working
and have assistance from grandparents, a husband, a
nurse, a housekeeper, a neighbor, older children, or teachers in a day-care center, a nursery school, or a regular
school.

In most cases the biological mother is also the psychological mother. However, this is not, of course, always
the case. Occasionally, it is the father who has the major
care of the baby in the first year of life. When this happens, the bonding will occur between the father and the
baby.

When the child is fortunate enough to have a mother
who is able to care for him on a consistent basis during
the first few years of his life and to be empathic with and
responsive to his needs, he will have made a good beginning in his ability to develop positive relationships with
others, and particularly with his teachers when he goes
to school.

In addition, during his second year of life, the child
starts to develop what is called "object constancy"; that
is, he is able to develop and fix within his mind a comforting picture of his mother and her care of him. These
so-called mental representations allow him to separate
from her, to be on his own, and to function in an appropriate, independent manner.

When we examine the nature of the mothering care
that allows the child to develop an ability to form a strong
positive relationship with others, certain factors stand
out. (Although I am focusing on the earliest relationship
the child forges with his mother, the following details
will apply, of course, to the relationship that he develops
with his father as well.)

The ideal mothering that serves as the model for all future relationships basically includes the ability to be empathic with and responsive to the child's developing physical and emotional needs. This presumes the mother's capacity to compartmentalize her own needs and problems so that they do not interfere with her mothering capacities.

This ideal mothering includes such qualities as: (1) being able to individualize the child and to recognize him as being different from other children; (2) treating the child fairly and showing no favoritism; (3) not exploiting or utilizing the child excessively for fulfilling the mother's own needs; (4) giving the child appropriate opportunities to express his own feelings verbally without fear of punishment or retaliation; (5) being patient with him; (6) being available to the child when needed; (7) exhibiting relative consistency and predictability; (8) providing realistic discipline; (9) helping the child cope appropriately with the tasks of growing up (this includes helping the child avoid overwhelming stresses before he is prepared to deal with them adequately); (10) avoiding the use of punishment or fear as a means of motivating the child; (11) teaching the child, through her behavior, that she means what she says. Ideal mothering, of course, includes an interest in and motivation for learning that will inspire similar interest and motivation for learning on the part of the child.

PROBLEMS THAT INTERFERE WITH THE CHILD'S ABILITY TO FORM A POSITIVE RELATIONSHIP

When it is not possible for the child's mother to maintain this consistent and empathic care of him in his earliest years; when a series of baby-sitters come and go and they have the major responsibility for his care; or when the major responsibility for his early care is split between a series of day-care center personnel, or the television set, or a catch-as-catch-can variety of people, then the child may have great difficulty in trusting others, in learning to develop positive relationships with others, and in developing true object constancy.

Such children may develop a variety of problems that emerge in later years. These difficulties include problems in relationships with others and oversensitivity to change and separations, particularly to separations from people with whom the child is involved. In addition, the child may have concerns about growing up and may find it easier to remain a child emotionally.

This lack of consistent and empathic early mothering is only one example of a type of early childhood traumatic experience which may cause the child problems in forming a positive relationship and later difficulty in learning how to learn in the educational situation. It is important to recognize that not all children who have been exposed to such inconsistent, nonempathic, early mothering care develop later emotional difficulties. Some children, because of either a strong heredity or later positive and corrective living experiences, recover from the traumatic effects of the early inconsistent care and grow up with no apparent problems. However, many children do not, and it is these children who concern us in the educational situation.

OTHER TYPES OF TRAUMATIC FAMILY EXPERIENCES THAT INTERFERE WITH THE DEVELOPMENT OF A LEARNING STANCE

In addition to inconsistent, unempathic mothering there are many other kinds of stressful and traumatic family experiences which may scar the child emotionally and later interfere with his ability to learn how to learn. Children who are adopted, children who experience the early loss of a parent through severe sickness, hospitalization, or death, children who are exposed to divorce and to repeated separations from a noncustodial parent are frequently encountered in our school systems. Many of them, of course, have made peace with the problems involved and are able to learn without difficulty. But many of them do not make peace with these emotional pressures and bring their consequences into the educational situation.

Such traumatic situations for children have one factor in common. They tend to sensitize the child to situations of change and loss. The child who is adopted tends to feel that there is something wrong with him and that there is always the possibility that he will be rejected by anyone to whom he gets close. The child who has lost a parent through death or divorce also tends to feel that there is something wrong with him and that he is in danger of being abandoned by anyone with whom he becomes emotionally involved.

Therefore children who have not recovered from early inconsistent mothering, or from the psychological impact of adoption or loss of a parent through death or divorce, tend to be hypersensitive in the educational situation to changes, losses, and to separation experiences.

Let us see how divorce, for example, may affect the child's functioning in the educational situation in terms of his ability to form a positive relationship with his teacher and his unconscious need to use the relationship with his teacher to provoke harmful changes in the teacher's teaching stance.

THE TEACHER'S CONTRIBUTION TO THE CHILD'S DEVELOPMENT OF A POSITIVE RELATIONSHIP WITH HIM

The teacher's goal is to help the child develop an ability to learn how to learn—that is a suitable learning stance. The teacher, of course, is not the child's mother, father, bodyguard, policeman, or older brother or sister. Nevertheless, the qualities that the mother employs in helping

the child develop a positive relationship with her are
similar to those that will later help the teacher in helping
the child develop a positive relationship with him or her,
and, through it, an appropriate learning stance: patience,
consistency, encouragement, fairness, unwillingness to
play favorites, empathy, consistent and appropriate discipline, nonpunitiveness, and compartmentalizing his
own problems so that they do not interfere with his teaching abilities.

Similarly, personality characteristics of the teacher
that will interfere with the child's ability to develop the
positive relationship with the teacher that can facilitate
a proper learning stance include the following: treating
the children all alike and not individualizing their needs;
playing favorites; making no attempts to understand
what is on the child's mind and what is bothering him;
impatience and inconsistency; discipline that is unrealistic and either too rigid or too lax; the use of fear, intim-
idation, anxiety, excessive criticism, punishment, or
shaming of the child; threatening the child with loss of
the teacher's love or interest as a means of motivating
him; allowing or stimulating excessive competition among
the children; and excessive expectations that put more
pressure on the child than he is able to manage. If the
child experiences repeated failures at school, repeated
criticism over lack of accomplishments, or repeated prohibitions that are unnecessary, his ability to form a positive relationship with the teacher will be impaired.

Positive contributions to a healthy relationship with
the child cannot be made in an emotional vacuum. In
essence the teacher himself needs to be treated in the
same way that he should treat the child. A good teaching
environment requires good working conditions, a realistic
salary, and proper emotional support. When the teacher
is treated fairly, consistently, patiently, and with respect,
when he has the opportunity to express his feelings without fear of retaliation, and when he feels that he is not

being criticized unjustly or excessively, and is not being exposed to excessive favoritism or competition, his morale will be good.

A teacher who is treated by the administration of his school appropriately and empathically will be able to be the best teacher he is capable of being; will be able to create a teaching environment in which the child can be the best student that he is capable of being; and will be able to develop a positive relationship with the child that will allow the child to learn how to achieve his maximum learning potential.

THE STUDENT WHO IS A CHILD OF DIVORCE

When the child of divorce is harmed by the divorce (and this includes the damage from any family problems before, during, and after the divorce), his life within the school setting may be affected in the following ways:

1. The child may experience ongoing pressures from his parents because they are not psychologically divorced, even though they may be legally divorced. As a result, the parents may cling to each other indirectly by quarreling over every single detail of the child's life, including his functioning at school. The school may thus be caught in the parents' battling, just as the child is caught between them at home.

2. The child of divorce is particularly sensitive and vulnerable to loss of or separation from meaningful adults. This is a result of two factors: (a) his painful feelings of abandonment by the noncustodial parent, and (b) his great concern that he might be deserted by the custodial parent. This Achilles heel about separation may show itself in many ways. At home, if his mother remarries, he may try to force his stepfather to reject him, in the same way in which he felt he was rejected by his own father.

Along with this tendency to provoke others to reject

him, the child as he grows up will tend to seek out relationships in which he is likely to be rejected. Investigation of these relationships may show that the nature
of the other person is such that rejection is inevitable.
The important fact is that the child will have unconsciously controlled the situation by seeking out this particular type of person. The child in these circumstances
develops an uncanny ability to find people who come
equipped with a great potential for rejecting him.

In school, he may show a general overreaction to any
event or trigger that suggests separation or loss from the
school, from his class, or from a teacher who is important
to him.

There are a wide range of school situations that may
trigger the child's oversensitivity to change and separation. At one extreme are the normal separation reactions
that occur in May and June as children prepare to leave
grammar or high school. That they are not expected to
learn much at that point, being too busy dealing with the
normal problems of separation and graduation, is an accepted fact. Usually, not much schoolwork is assigned
during this period. There are instead a variety of scheduled activities and graduation rituals all of which help
the children cope with the tensions of separation and
graduation.

A more pathological separation reaction is seen in those
students who have great difficulty in learning on Fridays.
They are so preoccupied with the problems of an impending weekend separation from school that their ability to learn may be seriously interfered with on the last
schoolday of the week. If such a vulnerable child is fortunate in having a sensitive, understanding teacher, his
learning responsibilities may be shifted to other days of
the week.

Any of the divorced child's basic steps toward independence may act as a trigger because they imply a traumatic separation experience from parents or home. Thus,

going to nursery or to grammar school, going off to high school, leaving high school and going to college, or graduating from college are moves that may act as a trigger because of the psychological meanings of loss and separation of that particular step.

Another group of triggers are the separations that the vulnerable student may experience from the teacher, or from some aspect of the school or the school system. These may include major separations such as promotions or graduations and the consequent need to leave a loved teacher; or minor separation triggers such as passing from one teacher to another; absences from a favorite teacher when either the child or the teacher is sick; or the change from having a single teacher to having a variety of teachers. For the particularly vulnerable student, there are hundreds of circumstances in the school system that may hit him in his Achilles' heel of separation and change.

Complicating the problem is the fact that similar reactions may be taking place in one or more of the student's teachers. For the teacher who himself is particularly vulnerable to separation experiences, there is also no shortage of triggers in the educational system. At the beginning these may include the symbolic meaning of becoming a teacher, which is part of becoming independent and growing up. The end of the school year also involves the teacher's separation from the students, from the school, and from the principal. As a result, the vulnerable child may find the problem doubled and compounded by the fact that his teacher is suffering from the same difficulty.

FACTORS DETERMINING A STUDENT'S VULNERABILITY TO SEPARATION AND CHANGE

A variety of factors determine how readily a separation trigger will touch off reactions in a student:

    1. The degree of vulnerability of the student to the

separation trigger is a result of the original separation conflicts and the degree to which the child's
later life experiences have preserved these conflicts.

2. The strength of the trigger stimulus may vary.
Thus the unexpected death of a teacher to whom
a student is very close is a strong stimulus; the end
of the school year is a minor stimulus.

3. Other stresses that the student is experiencing at
the time of exposure to the separation trigger will
also increase the degree of vulnerability. A student
suffering from external pressures such as poverty,
prejudice, or physical illness will also be more vulnerable.

HOW SEPARATION REACTIONS SHOW THEMSELVES IN SCHOOL

When separation conflicts are triggered by a stress situation, a student may manifest separation reactions in
a variety of areas. These may occur (1) in the area of
learning; (2) in the area of behavior; (3) in physical symptoms; and (4) in a variety of other symptoms. Frequently,
in fact, these symptoms are not limited to one area.

IN THE AREA OF LEARNING

Various kinds of interference with the learning process,
either chronic or acute, may occur in the presence of
strong separation reactions.

1. There may be interference with the development
of the learning process itself. For learning to occur, as we
have seen, the carrier wave of a positive emotional relationship between the student and the teacher is necessary. Therefore, if the student has difficulty in forming

relationships, he will have difficulty in learning how to learn. For example, before the child shows the development of object constancy, the actual presence of the teacher will be required for learning to occur. Therefore, at that stage a one-to-one relationship is necessary for learning to take place, and learning will be threatened by every separation experience. If the child has achieved object constancy, but has not become comfortable with simultaneous multiple relationships, he will have difficulty learning from more than one teacher.

2. Acute separation reactions may temporarily disrupt a learning process that is already formed because they disrupt the relationship in vulnerable students. For example, a vulnerable student may be unable to learn from a substitute teacher because he is reacting to the loss of the regular teacher.

There are specific periods preceding and following separations when the vulnerable student may show temporary cessations of learning. The first two weeks after the opening of school may be difficult for the vulnerable student, who has to establish a relationship with the teacher before learning can begin. The period from Thanksgiving through the first two weeks in January may also reflect, in the vulnerable student, difficulty with or a cessation of learning because of the interruptions of the relationships taking place at that time. The Easter, Passover, or Yom Kippur period may show a similar disruption. The last two weeks of school, for the vulnerable student, may also show disruption because the student is dealing with the ending of relationships with the teachers.

3. The intellectual faculties sometimes get caught up in defensive dealing with reactivated separation conflicts. As a result, less intellectual energy may be available for learning. Specific learning problems may also be manifested, depending on the specific mental defenses employed.

IN THE AREA OF BEHAVIOR

This is the area in which the child's unconscious attempts to provoke rejecting behavior from the teacher will become evident.

The divorced child's concern about loss of or rejection by the teacher may also show itself in more subtle ways. For example, in the "sour-grapes defense" the student says, in effect, to the teacher, "You're no good and you have nothing to offer that I could possibly want and, therefore, I don't have to worry or be concerned about losing you." With this defense there tends to be chronic depreciation and criticism of the teacher when a chronic separation problem is being dealt with. Sometimes "the sour-grapes defense" occurs acutely at the time of and preceding an impending separation.

There is also "the withholding defense." The student says, in effect, to the teacher, "I'll withhold whatever you want from me so that you will then angrily demand it, and this will reassure me that you are still interested even though you plan to leave me." The student withholds whatever the teacher may want—whether it is knowledge, insight, homework, essays, and so on. The student either does not do his assignments or else does them but "forgets" to turn them in.

Another defense involves truancy, running away, and dropping out. This is a way of dealing with the triggered conflicts through action. A frequent element in this defense is the "rejection first" reaction.

In using the "I'll reject you first" defense, the student says, in effect, "I'll reject you before you have the chance to abandon me." The student may not show up for school or may in some way turn away from the relationship with the teacher.

There are many other behavioral defenses, and one must study a specific student to know which particular response has been reactivated.

IN PHYSICAL SYMPTOMS

Excessive concerns about rejection or separation are also frequently accompanied by physical reactions. The "hallmarks" of separation anxiety are upper-respiratory infections such as colds and sore throats and earaches. Sometimes headaches and stomach aches occur. These are typical in the student who is suffering from a school phobia.

IN A VARIETY OF OTHER SYMPTOMS

1. Although such symptoms are not confined to children who have gone through a divorce or have lost a parent, the conflictual feelings related to the loss often result in a chronic pattern of lack of confidence and self-defeating behavior. In later years the child may show great difficulty in living up to his potential, whether in terms of relationships, intellectual, emotional, or physical functioning, or behavior. He may be unable to allow himself to enjoy the full happiness that he might have experienced had he not undergone the trauma of the divorce and loss. In school he may actually assume the role of a scapegoat.

2. When his parents become manipulators and each tries to turn the child against the other, this technique may rub off on the child. He may himself become a manipulator and try to play the parents and the school off against each other, or one teacher off against another, or he may try to manipulate the other children.

3. The child may show behavior or disciplinary problems, either with the teachers or with other children.

4. The preadolescent or adolescent student is normally dealing with issues of growing independence, sexual interests, and sexual identifications. The shock of the divorce and the loss of the noncustodial parent may make growing up and greater independence very threatening

to him. He may feel it is safer to remain a child emotionally. Sometimes the opposite happens and he decides
to start growing up as fast as possible. He then will show
traits of pseudomaturity and pseudoprecocity.

Sometimes his sexual development becomes frozen
and his latency characteristics seem to be perpetuated.
Or he may go to the other extreme—particularly if one
or both parents indulge in sexual promiscuity—and develop a precocious sexuality.

5. The child's sensitivity to loss may also cause him
to cling increasingly to the custodial parent and become
excessively dependent upon him. Sometimes this shows
itself in a school phobia, or in difficulty in leaving home
to go to school.

6. The need for excessive dependency upon the custodial parent may transfer itself to school. The child may
attach himself to one of the teachers in a highly over-
dependent manner.

HOW CAN THE SCHOOL HELP THE CHILD OF DIVORCE?

There are many ways in which the school can help students who are exhibiting, in the school setting, the impact
of the divorce of their parents:

1. By showing an awareness of and sensitivity to the
fact that many children of divorce display behavioral and
learning problems that are not caused by the school or
the teacher.

2. By making special efforts to work with the child's
parents.

a. The school must avoid being drawn into the fighting between the parents, being manipulated by one parent against the other, or being manipulated by the child
against the parents. The school and the teacher must
maintain a teaching stance, no matter how great the
provocation.

b. At the same time, the school must be aware that both parents, as well as the child, are under a great deal of pressure and need as much emotional support as is feasible.

c. It is crucial that the child maintain his contacts with the noncustodial parent. As far as possible, the school should help the noncustodial parent remain in the picture and maintain his interest in the child's functioning in school. While such an effort may pose delicate problems in the school's relationship with the custodial parent, it will be helpful to the child if the school does its utmost to keep the noncustodial parent informed and involved. This includes, when appropriate, keeping him informed of all matters concerning the child, his functioning at school, and the various school activities that involve him.

d. In the school's contacts with the custodial parent, the school should be aware that many custodial parents wish to freeze the noncustodial parent out of the picture. The school can help combat this situation by making clear its attitude that it is helpful to the child for the noncustodial parent to be kept in the picture.

e. The school must recognize that both parents, though legally divorced, may still not be psychologically divorced and may be keeping contact with each other through fighting over the child. The school should try to maintain an objective, evenhanded attitude toward both parents while avoiding any manipulative attempt by either parent to put the school in the middle of the parental battles.

3. In its educational efforts with the child, the school must face a variety of issues:

a. The child of divorce may be under a great deal of pressure that may carry over into the school area. An awareness of this makes it easier for the school to be more patient with the child.

b. Visits with the noncustodial parent may arouse

a great deal of tension in the child. This may result in a temporary regression in academic or behavioral functioning for a few days following each visit, particularly if the visit lasts more than several days. Knowledge of the visiting arrangements may therefore help the school to understand and be prepared for sudden changes in the child.

c. Divorced parents sometimes work out the most amazing visitation arrangements. Should the school be asked for its advice in regard to visitation, weekday or weekend visits that allow the child to be home in adequate time to unwind and get ready for bed should be suggested. I think it is better for most children to sleep in their own home the night before school; therefore I usually advise *against* the child sleeping at the home of the noncustodial parent the night before he is going to school.

d. Because divorce is a major stress in the child's life, children of divorce have a higher rate of emotional illness and a greater need for psychological therapy than children of intact families. For many reasons, a child's parents may be unaware of or may ignore the signs suggesting the need for psychotherapy. It is important therefore that the school be alert to evidence of deterioration in the child's academic functioning, behavior control, or relationships with the teachers or his peers. When such deterioration is present, the school needs to consider the possibility of alerting both parents to the child's problem functioning at school and the need for a psychiatric evaluation.

e. Because of the increasing frequency of divorce, some schools have instituted classes that include all children dealing with the problems faced by the parents and children of divorce. Other schools have been quite successful with group sessions specifically designed for children of divorce. The possibility of offering group sessions for parents of divorce might also be considered.

f. All children develop best when cared for by a mother and a father. In divorce the child's contacts with the noncustodial parent are diluted. If the custodial parent remarries, then the child again has the opportunity to be brought up on a daily basis by parents of both sexes. If the custodial parent has not remarried, then it would be in the child's best interests if one or more teachers were of the same sex as the absent parent.

g. It is crucial for teachers to learn how to deal appropriately with the manipulative defenses that are so typical of the divorced child. The following issues should be kept in mind by the school:

Helping Vulnerable Students Prepare for Changes

This kind of preparation allows the child to take changes slowly, one step at a time. It means breaking down a task into its components, so that each can be dealt with at a rate appropriate for the student. For example, for some children, starting a new school requires a familiarization process in which they can get to know the physical geography of the school and perhaps meet the teachers or see the classroom before actually starting. It is important not to put too much pressure on the vulnerable child until he gets used to the new teacher and the new situation.

Remaining Aware of Vulnerable Students

There must be conscious recognition by the teacher of those students liable to irrational separation reactions. Although teacher changes should be kept to a minimum to reduce pressures on all students, this is particularly important for vulnerable students. Not much can be expected of vulnerable students at periods of change. There must be awareness of when specific students are ready for teacher specialization and are ready to learn from more than one teacher at a time.

Preparing for Endings and Separations

This means openly recognizing with the student that there may be problems in the beginning and ending of a relationship. Sometimes it is important to discuss the evidence of the separation reactions in the student. The last session should be set up without formality or ritual, and with little pressure. Parties or the serving of food to celebrate the ending of a class or relationship are probably helpful, particularly for the more vulnerable student.

Fostering Understanding on the Part of the Teacher

It is important in preventing or dealing with separation that the teacher be intellectually and emotionally aware that reactions may be occurring with some or all of the students. The teacher should also be aware that he himself may be experiencing a separation reaction. Of crucial importance is the recognition of unrealistic reactions, because these tend to be blocked out and not dealt with by either student or teacher.

It is important that the teacher recognize and resist provocative attempts by the vulnerable child to divert him from his teaching stance. Attempts to make him angry at the child and punish him, to be made guilty, frustrated, or distant, must be particularly recognized and resisted.

The teacher who fails to recognize that the student is having a separation reaction (for example, to the teacher's being sick) may cause unnecessary difficulties for both the teacher and the student.

1. The teacher may take seriously and at face value the student's "sour-grapes" depreciations, be upset by them, get angry at the student, argue with or reject him, or retaliate in other ways, thus giving

both the teacher and the student a more difficult time than necessary. The teacher may even angrily dump the student on some special resource person.

2. The student's learning may be temporarily interfered with because of the rejection and counterrejection process going on.

3. The other students may recognize the real situation and may realize the teacher's lack of understanding of what is bothering the vulnerable student. This may interfere with their relationship with the teacher, with their own learning, and with their ability to help the vulnerable student.

On the other hand, when the teacher does recognize that the student is having a separation reaction, particularly an irrational one, many benefits may accrue.

1. The teacher becomes less defensive about the child's reactions and therefore is able to deal with them more readily.

2. The teacher understands the student better and can use his normal empathy and common sense to help the student.

3. The teacher is more understanding of the student's behavior defenses (for example, "the sour-grapes" or "I'll reject you first" defenses), and therefore less threatened by them. The teacher is less tempted to get angry at the student and to retaliate or withdraw. This tends to deactivate the student's provocative defenses and helps the youngster deal more maturely with irrational separation feelings.

4. Children of divorce usually have been exposed to, and damaged by, many scenes of bitter quarreling between adults. To demonstrate to the child that adults *can* get along with each other, it is helpful

if the school presents a role model where teachers get along well with each other, where the teachers try to get along with the child's parents, and where disagreements can be resolved by attempts at reasonable discussion and compromise.

CONCLUSIONS

1. A major goal of every educational institution is to provide an environment in which a child can learn how to learn.
2. The educational institution must also provide a working situation that will allow the teacher to be the best possible teacher that he is capable of being.
3. The teacher then needs to provide the student with circumstances that will allow the child to form the most positive relationship that he is capable of forming. This in turn will give the child the opportunity to develop an appropriate learning stance.
4. The teacher is aware that the child, because of his unresolved prior traumatic family experiences, enters the school overly sensitized to certain specific situations.
5. The teacher is aware that, as a result of these emotional problems and oversensitivities, the child may have difficulties either in forming a positive relationship with the teacher or in using the relationship to develop an appropriate learning stance.
6. The teacher also is aware that because of these oversensitivities the child unconsciously may attempt to manipulate the teacher into experiencing feelings and exhibiting behavior that will interfere with his usual teaching stance.
7. The teacher must do everything that he can to recognize and avoid this manipulation of his feelings, attitudes, and behavior so that he is able to maintain an appropriate teaching stance.

8. The teacher, aware of the child's oversensitivities, also attempts to arrange the teaching situation to work around or minimize those circumstances that trigger the child's oversensitivities.

Chapter 30

Some Reflections on the Teacher-Student Dialogue: A Psychoanalytic Perspective

KAY FIELD, M.A.

> Human beings at any age are drawn into a voracious effort after meaning.
> Sir Frederick Bartless

> ... teaching is a form of dialogue, an extension of dialogue.
> J. Bruner

> The psychoanalytic dialogue is a process that goes "beyond" and "behind" the manifest contents of mental life.
> Barnaby Barrett

PROLOGUE: THE CLASSROOM REVISITED

The world of the classroom and school—the world that teachers and students inhabit—is something which, in large part, they themselves help to create through their interactions with one another. It is a constantly changing

Acknowledgments: I am particularly indebted to the late Joan Fleming for her unflagging interest in our work with educators, her penetrating insights, steady support, and inspirational guidance during the formative years of the Program. To me, personally, she was mentor, colleague, and friend. I also wish to express my appreciation to Ner Littner, Harold Balikov, Bertram Cohler, and George H. Pollock for their important, ongoing contributions to and investment in the development of the Teacher Education Program. The Program world, just as the persons in it are changing and growing. The disparate images and deeply personal expectations they bring to their encounters with each other are rarely if ever recognized or acknowledged as such either by the parties involved or by classroom observers; yet, their potential for influencing teacher-student transactions and the process of change through learning can be profound.

To be a teacher is to have a thousand selves, for the image of every teacher is, in part, the creation of the learner: "She [my mother] was so embedded in my consciousness that for the first year of school I seemed to believe that each of my teachers was my mother in disguise" (Updike, 1984). "Half human, half divine," was the way Ernest Boyer remembered his first grade teacher (1985).

By the same token, the "real" self of the student is subject to the projections of his teachers. For teachers, too, "create" their students out of perceptions shaped by their current needs and past experiences. We see an illustration of this process in the following vignette, recounted by a seventh grade teacher.

> J. came to my classroom with a long history of academic failures and intractable behavior problems. With each passing year his reputation grew steadily worse, so when he arrived in my room I had been duly warned what to expect. The first few days in my room he was, as predicted, a disruptive influence in the group. He was reckless, impulsive, disorganized and utterly unpredictable, constantly in and out of his seat, roaming the room at will, pushing, poking, teasing the other

---

faculty as well as the many students who have attended his classes have benefited enormously from Richard Herbig's teaching and his understanding of group process issues in the educational situation. Finally, I wish to thank the students who participated in the seminar described in this chapter. We learned as much from them as we taught. In this sense, they were better teachers than they realized.

I am deeply indebted to Glorye Wool for her penetrating insights and unstinting assistance in the preparation of the commentary.

children, and seemingly oblivious to my admonitions. Despite all this, I found myself drawn to J. and resolved that I would find a way to help him. Well, I did just that during the course of the year that he was in my room. It wasn't easy but it was worth it. But now, none of the teachers believe me when I describe how he's improved. What will happen to him when he leaves my room and moves on to the classroom of one of my skeptical colleagues? Will he be able to hold on to the gains he made with me?

The curriculum, too, is, in part, the invention of both teacher and students. Each one projects distillates of his own inner perceptions and experiences, past and present, onto the subject under study, be it mathematics, reading, history, or literature. Stringer (1973) describes the teacher's unique personal contribution to this process:

> The teacher gives not only of her knowledge but also of her value system, her perceptions and behavior, and her conscious and unconscious feelings about herself and her pupils. . . . [Therefore] the quality and quantity of that communication depend on forces operating within her or upon her and to a considerable degree determine how much of the prescribed curriculum pupils learn [p. 429].

I tell these "tales" to illustrate that "reality" like beauty is often in the eye of the beholder. The personal meanings and powerful affects that teachers and students, at all levels of the educational system, invest in and project on each other creates a situation in the classroom that makes each vulnerable to the other's intentions. How do these covert, conscious, and unconscious processes affect learning? In the tales of the two first graders we see that the school patterns of young lives do not arise de novo, but carry the imprint of a nursery prehistory which predated schooling. As Basch (chapter 26) notes, "the teacher is not a new person whom the child encounters on the first day of school, but someone toward whom the child directs hopes, fears and wishes that were developed in early contacts with parents and other significant people." Each boy perceived his teacher not as the person she believed herself to be but as the person they needed her to be—a protecting, omnipotent, mother figure.

The story of J., on the other hand, reveals that the same psychic mechanism (transference) applies to teachers no less than children. The reporting teacher's response to J. is in striking contrast to that of his previous teachers. The boy they saw was an impossible failure and troublemaker; not so for his teacher (e.g., "I found myself drawn to J. and resolved that I would find a way to help him"). We do not need to go into the personal psychological reasons for the contrasting perceptions and responses of the former teachers to the same boy to make the point that this teacher's contrary response set in motion a new interactive dynamic which made it possible for J. to learn. However, from the standpoint of the relationship between J.'s teacher and her colleagues, his gain became her loss. For her "success" with him appears to have been at the expense of her becoming an "outsider" in the group of her colleagues. It was as if she had deserted them and gone over to the side of their "enemy" when she allied herself with J.

The above vignettes open up the largely invisible psychological landscapes of classroom life. They give a glimpse of the interpersonal tensions, multiple realities, and complex dynamics that give meaning and direction to the day-to-day activities of teachers and pupils. In a classroom, in a school, a field of forces is at work. No single aspect can be fully understood apart from the total context. When educators view the participants in the learning process in isolation, asking one set of questions about the teacher and another about the student, another about the curriculum, the teacher's experience is likely to be seen as anomalous. Teaching is obviously an interactive affair, fraught with strong feelings. To ignore these phenomena and processes is to trivialize the day-to-day events and pressures on teacher and taught, and so distort their meaning. The predicament of teacher education is rooted in this hiatus.

To illustrate the salience and utility of a psychodynamic perspective in teacher education an account of the learning experiences of a group of teachers in a psychoanalytically oriented program of teacher education will be presented. The teacher-student relationship is conceived here as a special form of communication between the generations; their "dialogue" in the classroom context is considered both the vehicle and the subject of study. I am using the word *dialogue* here in much the same sense it was first introduced by Spitz and more recently by others in psychoanalytic developmental research, meaning the multiple and diverse ways, consciously and unconsciously, that teachers and students use to communicate and thus influence the way they are responded to.

BACKGROUND

In the next chapter of this work I trace the evolution of the Teacher Education Program of the Institute for Psychoanalysis from its inception in 1965, as it was conceived and experienced by its faculty. The fact that the program operates at the interface of education and psychoanalysis, a largely uncharted and unstudied realm, creates many new tasks and challenges for its faculty, not the least of which is learning how to teach psychodynamic concepts to teachers, and learning about learning, their own and their students', in the process. The struggles of the faculty, their efforts to forge a new professional identity for themselves as psychoanalytic educators of teachers are recounted in my next chapter. Of particular interest was our discovery that certain aspects of a teacher's case presentations in the Program seminars paralleled some of the very problems she was experiencing with that child in her school classroom. Nor did the parallels stop there; they reappeared in our faculty meetings during which we examined our own teaching experiences in the Institute classes. The decision to investigate these phenomena further ushered in a more intensive effort to examine process issues.

The impetus for writing this chapter came out of the realization that discussing issues out of context raised more questions than answers. To fully understand each other's experiences and formulations we would have to follow the unfolding process of teaching and learning in our respective classes. We were fortunate to have on our faculty one member who had the courage and the curiosity to take up this difficult challenge. His narrative account of his work with a group of teachers in the program over a period of two quarters, or twenty-two weeks, became the focus of our study and is the subject of this chapter.

Generally speaking, there are two perspectives from which to view the teaching-learning process. One tells us how the world looks to a fixed focus camera; the other how it looks to the mind of particular individuals at a particular time and place. Cronbach and Snow (1977) conceptualized the latter perspective as follows:

> To come to understand interactions, it will be necessary ultimately to study events as they unfold in time. There is, first, the set of entering characteristics of the learner (ability, trait, anxiety and stereotypes of teachers, for example). There is, second, the objectively observable treatment. This refers not to the "treatment variable" in the experimenter's mind but to the signals actually delivered to Ss. . . . Third, there is the learner's perception (of the teacher, of his likelihood of succeeding, of the rewards and penalties in prospect, etc.) and his concomitant emotional states. Fourth come the acts of

the learner as he engages with his task, *some of them* directly observable and some internal events that can at best be *inferred*. The final set of events is represented in the "dependent variables" of the experiment. Research to date has not tried to depict this panorama [p. 412; emphasis added].

This report, then, is an attempt to understand "this panorama."

In this chapter we hope to demonstrate the organizing and sensitizing role of psychoanalytic theory in the development of teachers' understanding of their professional role. In our focus on the instructor and his sense of the week-by-week interactions with his class, his frustrations and feelings about his work, we are reversing the traditional figure-ground Gestalt that we are so accustomed to in professional and public discourse on education.[1] In the latter case it is what the teacher transmits (the "objective" course of study), how much of it the child can retain and reproduce (the measurable products or outcomes of instruction), that are focal; whereas our interest here is on the overt and covert processes and interactions that help or hinder teaching and learning.

The report to follow is entitled "Process Portrait: A Partial Examination of the Process in a Seminar Group of Teachers as Experienced by the Class Instructor." It is an experiential account of one instructor's encounter with the mixed hopes and fears of a group of adult learners, teachers, and his coping with the manifest resistances to learning, his struggle to form an alliance, and his own ups and downs in the process. The instructor is a psychoanalytically trained educator, social worker, and psychotherapist with wide experience in school consultation and clinical supervision. The instructor's process

---

[1] In the interest of confidentiality neither the instructor, the students, nor their respective schools are mentioned here by name.

notes include his observations and interpretations of the ongoing process.

Before turning to the instructor's report, termed by him a *process portrait*, I should comment briefly on (1) the philosophy of the program; (2) the two courses; (3) the students (teachers) in the seminar; and (4) the teaching methodology.

PHILOSOPHY

Two distinct principles of the psychodynamic approach to the learning process are demonstrated in this report. The first concerns the educational objective of self-awareness and self-knowledge. It is based on the assumption that if a teacher is in touch with his own feelings and understands himself better, he will be in a better position to understand his students, and, therefore, better able to facilitate learning.

The second principle concerns the method of achieving such understanding. It stresses the reciprocal nature of the teaching process and the concept that the interactions between teachers and students are a crucial determinant of the course of learning and its eventual outcome. It follows, then, that the critical factor in the process lies in the teacher's ability to establish a process of communication (dialogue) which involves the students as active partners in the learning process. The teacher acts basically as a catalyst and a facilitator in the learning process, and helps the student realize that part of his problem with learning is within himself rather than in the external environment (the teacher, the classmates, the subject matter, the rules and materials of instruction, and so on) though these also may be involved. The most important lesson that the teacher seeks to teach his students is that they cannot learn passively but must actively work at their own learning.

While the teacher's goal and methods are educational,

the teaching task is not unlike that of a therapist in that both seek to involve the student-patient as active partners in the process. To assist in this effort, both teacher and therapist employ the skills of human relationship that provide emotional support, evoke the courage to face the inevitable tensions and anxieties inherent in true learning, and develop the initiative and strength needed to find new ways to cope with problems. He seeks to activate the students' potentials for learning and strives to help them tolerate the inevitable frustrations and tensions that arise, knowing that self-knowledge and personal meaning are the real motivation for learning.

We regard these shared tasks of teacher and students as fundamental and basic to the accomplishment of positive teaching goals, regardless of the subject matter and the techniques employed. To elicit in the student the desire (e.g., motivation) to learn may be the first step in the process and may require techniques which make tangible, measurable outcomes slow to appear. To further enlist the active cooperation of the students in a learning alliance akin to the basic trust of a child with his mother may be all any teacher can do with certain students (be they children or adults), a process that takes time.

Thus the element of time becomes an important consideration in an educational program that conceives the learning-teaching process in this way. The report to follow chronicles the students' involvement in this process during the first two quarters (twenty-two weeks) in a two-year course of study. This account demonstrates how one instructor attempted to incorporate the above principles in his work with a group of teachers.

THE COURSE OF STUDY

The two seminars are part of a curriculum sequence in the program which focuses on the dynamics of interpersonal relations in the educational situation. In the first quarter (eleven weekly class meetings) "The Dynamics of Teacher-Student Transactions in the Classroom" was the subject of study; the second quarter extended the scope of focus to include "Interactions with Colleagues, Parents, School Administration, and Allied Professions." Concurrently, students also take a course on the dynamics of personality development across the life span with another instructor. In this latter course attention is given to the intrapsychic and interpersonal dimensions of development and mental functioning.

THE STUDENTS

A heterogeneous group of twelve employed teachers, they differed from each other along a number of dimensions: range of ages, from twenty-three to fifty-five years, ethnicity, training backgrounds, school roles, and experience. What they all shared was a growing sense of uncertainty about their professional role and identity, profound frustration over their relationships with students, with other staff, worry about their professional competence, pervasive feelings of powerlessness, and, most pernicious of all, deeply eroded self-esteem. Most expressed a wish for opportunities for honest "shop" talk with other teachers. While they all struggled with pent-up feelings of anger, they feared exposing themselves and their "failings" before colleagues, as well as superiors. The need for clarification, support, and affirmation, for help in making or reconsidering unsatisfactory decisions pervaded the group and were experienced by new and old teachers alike. Of course, for sheer survival, these needs were handled through a variety of defense mechanisms (e.g., overcompulsivity and obsessiveness, rigidity or timidity, inhibition or acting out behavior, and so on). We do not believe that these are necessarily inherent aspects of the teacher's professional personality but products of a school culture that tends to value "products" over persons.

METHODS

Teaching methods must be related to both training goals and program philosophy. If the transmission of information is the foremost goal, as it is in most programs of professional education and schooling, the most effective teaching method is probably simple didactism. The form of knowledge we sought to transmit, however, was of a different kind; more elusive, subtle, and complex. We wanted to teach in a way that reached the head and the heart. We sought to make certain that experiential as well as conceptual knowledge would be as well assimilated and usable as possible by students. This required that our teaching methods provide them with ample opportunities for testing so they could integrate their new knowledge in contexts and conditions approximating those of their classroom. Nomological knowledge (e.g., facts, laws, theories, techniques), therefore, was not our primary focus, even though we considered such knowledge an important part of our course of study. The use of case presentations drawn from the classroom and seminar discussions of this material seemed well suited to our purpose. Along with this, we hoped to foster the teachers' capacities for self-awareness, introspection, and empathic observation. Toward this end we sought to initiate a developmental process and a way of thinking about their own learning and their professional experiences that would embody these goals, knowing that the process would need to continue after they completed their two years in the program.

Recognizing that teachers work in a group situation, the instructor taught *through* the group rather than *to* the group, as is usually the case. In the former approach, students, through their presentations of themselves and their case material, helped create the curriculum, and, as a result, learned as much from each other as they did from the instructor. Because the opportunities for such collegial learning is rare in most schools, all our students have placed high value on this feature of the program. We have found that teaching through the group makes for more integrated learning and creative thinking. The professional attachments students make in the process often outlast by many years their participation in the program. Many of these groups go on meeting after graduation, thereby continuing the collegial process on their own terms.

The instructor in this group defined his role as that of a "special participant" in the learning process. Geoffrey Wicker's (1978) term for this role, *agent-experient*, that is, one who must try to become aware of his own influences on the phenomena he is trying to at the same time understand, best conveys what the instructor intended. In this sense, the teacher is at once the subject and object of influence: his own influence on students and his students' influence on him. Throughout the narrative, the teaching model the instructor presented exemplified the very qualities he sought to develop in his students, namely a self-observing, introspective teaching stance attuned and responsive to the group, as well as to its individual members. Calling this phenomenon "deutero-learning," Bateson offered the following formulation: "In any given learning situation one learns not only what one is supposed to learn, but also something about the process of learning itself" (1942). The teacher, in the process of teaching, becomes aware not only of the subject matter he is supposed to be teaching, but also of the process of teaching itself.

On this note, we turn to the instructor's own words.

I would like us first to look at the process that the group and I went through during the course of the twenty-two weeks (two terms); second, to consider how process issues and content were interwoven in the service of the ultimate goal of the program, that is, to foster the professional growth of teachers so as to enable them to be more empathic and skilled teachers of their students; third, to consider how we might better conceptualize and refine this process so as to better adapt and apply it to our educational goals. I agreed to undertake this assignment because of some of the questions, concerns, and anxieties that I experienced during the course of my work with this group of teachers. I found the process that was unfolding fascinating and making more sense to me. At the same time I began to be aware, sometimes painfully so, of the inherent subtleties and complexities in the process, and realized that there was far more to be learned from this experience. At times, because of its powerful emotional impact, and some of the defenses and resistances in which I was inadvertently caught up, I questioned whether I had captured the focal concerns of the group. I also wondered at times how effective this approach was in meeting our training goals, namely to increase teachers' awareness of the experiential and subjective side of the learning process by self-observation and empathic introspection. (I am thinking of our combined experiential and cognitive approach in contrast to a more didactic approach.) Can we put together and better conceptualize what seemed to be happening in this different type of learning experience?

There are several vantage points from which one might examine the shifts and alterations that transpired over the twenty-two-week period. For example, we might consider how the group shifted in its relationship to the teacher (myself), that is, the vicissitudes of the teaching-learning alliance; some of the shifts in my subjective reactions; the shifts occurring among the group members themselves in relation to one another. . . . I decided to focus on the overall process that the group seemed to be going through in its struggle with its own learning and this type of learning expe-

rience . . . to help the reader determine what was tran-
spiring in the class and to what degree the content and
the process were interactive. I have summarized briefly
the content under discussion in each quarter. I do not
wish to leave the impression that I overlook or minimize the importance of content per se, only that I am
highlighting process issues in this report.

In a way, the instructor's vivid and detailed narrative
description of events during the twenty-two weeks speaks
for itself. His purpose in writing it, however, was to stimulate a dialogue with the faculty of the program. His
presentation sparked a lively, spirited exchange among
the members of the faculty and raised a number of issues
which have been the subject of discussion and analysis
ever since. The following excerpt, taken from the ensuing
faculty discussion, conveys the issues and concerns that
invariably surface in such interdisciplinary ventures:

> [O]ne of the things that struck me about this . . . is
> that implicitly, or perhaps explicitly, you're using a
> therapeutic paradigm . . . you're dealing with conflict,
> anxiety, and defense, you're involved with working
> through; you encounter resistance and response, you
> confront regressive processes, . . . all kinds of nonspe-
> cific transferences, and possibly even specific transfer-
> ences. . . . I don't mean that you're *following* a
> therapeutic paradigm, only that *you make your obser-
> vations of the process from that frame of reference*, then
> use them as the raw data for studying the
> material . . . [emphasis added].

Not surprisingly, this suggestion touched off the age-
old controversy over the teach versus treat issue to which
Fleming (personal communication, 1965) had earlier responded, as follows:

> Is it a question of "territoriality" or what? Only teach-
> ers teach and only therapists treat? If so, what do par-

ents do? No teaching and no treating? "Roles" and "titles" are so often confused as if they had equivalent meaning. I gave a certain woman in my life the title of mother, but she functioned in many roles according to my needs and her capacities. Others called teachers functioned in multiple roles, too. We get caught up in terms which take on exclusive and special meaning when we want them to. By doing that we build fences around our private claims.

The instructor's use of himself in the seminar demonstrates the validity of Fleming's statement.

Two comments toward the close of our meeting suggest how the faculty ultimately resolved this issue: "The therapeutic paradigm really is *the paradigm of every human experience. . . .*" and "Teachers have a double job—to teach a subject and to be therapeutic in terms of *understanding* what's going on, *not necessarily making therapeutic interpretations.*"

The instructor's narrative is accompanied by a commentary written by the author. It echoes many of the ideas that came out of the faculty discussions stimulated by this report. However, I take full responsibility for the formulations and inferences drawn from the material. It is entirely possible that the instructor may disagree in places with my construction of the dynamics. My comments reflect the difference in our vantage points and thus are a continuation of the dialogue at another level. The instructor's narrative dates back several years to the early history of the program, yet it sheds light on issues which are very much alive today both in the TEP faculty and for teacher education generally. Thus the intent of my commentary is to provide a perspective that encompasses the past and the present, and to do so from my position as director of the program. It has been said that "a person living on the border of a province is better able to decide which peaks inside of it are the highest than an observer standing amidst the mountains themselves"

(Tegner, 1900). I am the "person living on the border."
My hope is that the commentary will convey a sense of
the generative possibilities of a psychodynamic-devel-
opmental frame of reference in teacher education.

However, the instructor will have the last word. Having written this report several years ago, he will want to
reflect on the changes in his thinking and his teaching
which have occurred in the interim. His retrospective
comments follow his report.

Neither the instructor nor I make any claim to "objectivity" in our reports since what we sought was to
record subjective phenomena and intersubjective communication. It is the dearth of such data on classrooms
that was the impetus for writing this chapter. Neugarten
and Datan (1973), commenting on the need for such data
in social science research, said: "Psychologists (educators
also) would do well to make greater use of the person
himself as the reporting and predicting agent, by gathering systematic and repeated self reports along with
other types of data, to combine the phenomenological and
the "objective perspectives" (p. 15). Our report is presented in this spirit.

THE PROCESS OF A TEP SEMINAR GROUP AS EXPERIENCED AND REPORTED BY THE INSTRUCTOR "A PROCESS PORTRAIT"

> First we see the hills in the painting,
> then we see the painting in the hills.
> Li Li Weng

REPORT

Session 1

Very early in the first meeting I briefly explained the
purposes and procedures of the course, emphasizing my

expectations of students' involvement and shared responsibility for the learning. I asked that they consider what it feels like to be beginning this course. This mobilized the usual anxieties, fears, uncertainties, and defensive operations. At this point and throughout the course, I tried to demonstrate the connection between some of their own here-and-now experiences with similar reactions experienced by their pupils. The teachers responded to my explanations with a host of anxious questions. "Yes—just what *are* we here for?" "How *are* we going to go about this whole business?" "Is this to be a form of group therapy?" Underlying these questions were their fears, doubts, and discomforts as they struggled with the meaning of being a member of such a group. During this first evening, in response to talking about "Just how *are* we going to do this?" I introduced the case presentation method. While this technique promised practical help it also mobilized their fears of exposing professional inadequacies to peers and instructor (I). The evening concluded with mixed feelings of hopefulness and anxiety: "Well, let's get on with it anyway."

COMMENTARY

Session 1

Notice how the instructor's (I's) invitation to talk about their "feelings about beginning" strikes a discrepant note in the group (G) and anxiety is mobilized. Their anxious questions suggest that they felt they were being asked to reveal their innermost thoughts and concerns. In school such private feelings are ordinarily kept private. After all, expression of affect is contrary to accepted practice in educational settings.

Sensitive to the rising tension and anxiety in the G, the I attempts to move closer to the experiential world

of teachers, calling attention to the parallels in their encounters with pupils in their classrooms. This seemed to
offer a ray of hope even though it did not fully allay the
G's anxiety.

REPORT

Session 2

By the second meeting, I became aware of heavy resistance. It took various forms, such as "misunderstanding"
what I said, informing me how the group ought to be
organized, what my position as instructor ought to be,
and so on. In short, they seemed to be reversing our
roles—teaching me how to teach according to their rules.
I asked them to take a look at what they were experiencing. This helped them recognize how they were resisting getting started. We began examining the various
ways we avoid, resist, and otherwise defend against moving into our work. One student summed it up for the
group, noting that the fear and anxieties that we had
been talking about in regard to the childrens' "problems,"
paralleled our own concerns about presenting cases. With
sudden insight she laughingly remarked that "it might
turn out that the teacher was really the problem not the
student." With this insightful remark, there was a low-
ering of tension and a feeling of relief, manifested verbally and behaviorally in the whole group.

COMMENTARY

Session 2

Anxiety continues to mount, hence the "heavy resistance."
In defense against their anxiety, the students resist get-

ting started on their work, by reversing roles with the I, "teaching him how to teach." By calling attention to their defensive maneuvers, the I helped them see how their efforts to handle their anxiety were paradoxically interfering with their learning. The I's tactful presentation of the idea of a parallel between their experiences in the seminar and in their own classrooms set the stage for the student's cogent statement of that parallel! In the shared group experience this new perspective allowed the students to be somewhat more tolerant of their current anxiety.

REPORT

Session 3

In the third session, I began to attach names to some of the feeling states that they had experienced the previous week. My purpose was to help them connect and conceptualize those states (to get a handle on them, so to speak) as well as to remind them where we were the last session. This session was marked by an expression of warm, friendly feelings. These were verbalized as well as demonstrated in group behavior. There was talk about the relief they felt in knowing about these shifts and turns in teacher-student relating. As I listened, I thought that along with the genuine relief there was also a quality of "whistling in the dark." As if to say, "You really *aren't* going to take a poke at me or ridicule me if I say such and such, are you?" The students began talking to each other about feeling more comfortable in discussing each other's work. For my part, I had a feeling of being shut out, as if they were banding together to exclude me. I imagined that they were thinking, "You're not giving us anything" (e.g., to take notes on); "You should be giving us more." At the same time, I noted genuine attempts by the group as a whole to get into and on with the case material, and to connect it to their own experiences in their classrooms. There was also a more modulated affect tone in the room; there were neither the highs nor the lows that seemed typical of the previous two sessions.

COMMENTARY

Session 3

This was an exciting, if puzzling, session. Typically, teachers have difficulty with affect, their own and their students'. They turn to cognitive action to rationalize, avoid, escape, deny, or disavow the affective aspects of their transactions with students. Here the I was providing them with an opportunity to recognize feelings and put them at the service of intellect. By naming the affects evoked in their previous interchange the I was, in effect, telling the group that their feelings were a legitimate object of study. The response of the group—the "relief" the "warm, friendly feelings," and the task orientation —appears to have confirmed the validity of the I's approach.

However, his own reaction, his sense that their response was defensive, is puzzling. He observes that the group is becoming more cohesive, purposeful, and task oriented than before but he wonders whether this is in the service of shutting him out. How can we understand the disparity between his observations of the group and his subjective reactions? Could it be that the I felt less needed *because* rather than *in spite of* what had been accomplished thus far? Because the students feel more comfortable, more trusting, more protected in their relationship with the I, they now are ready to move toward learning about each other. Looking at the learning process developmentally, it would seem that the I is in a position parallel to that of a parent whose child, by virtue of maturation and good parenting, begins to move outside the parental orbit and reaches out to others in his environment. The child takes this step not out of rejection and hostility but rather because he is no longer as dependent on an omnipotent parent. Just as parents may feel unneeded, hurt, and rejected when their children begin showing more interest in others (e.g., peers, teachers, and so on), so it may be for the I as the group moves into a similar developmental transition.

REPORT

Session 4

In the fourth meeting there was a continuation of the same friendly tone in the class but this time with an additional "glad handing" quality. This quality became more apparent when a member of the group announced that one of their number had become ill and would be withdrawing. This statement elicited expressions of deep personal sadness and serious concern. This was a disproportionate show of feeling, since they really didn't know this person. I began to wonder if there were some feelings toward me which they were struggling with. It turned out that I had somehow "overlooked" what triggered the exaggerated reaction to the loss of the group member. At the beginning of this session I had announced some additional, taxing course requirements. Out of my own mixed feelings and discomfort in giving this assignment I had not "heard" their frustrated angry reactions. Later, it dawned on me that indeed they were angry with me. I now recalled having heard their mumbling and grumbling in the background. It now appeared that it was their reaction to this assignment that triggered the overreaction to the loss of the group member; then a process of denial, displacement, and reaction formation took place.

I did feel that, in spite of this, they were really into the case presentation in a way that they had not been up until this point. Then something interesting happened. They went through a very intense analysis of one teacher's case, taking it apart, trying to put it together differently, making new connections, and so on. When I attempted to help them with this, they rejected everything! They would have nothing to do with any of my suggestions, and fell back to talking about gimmicks and techniques that would solve the teacher's problems, all the while fiercely resisting any further consideration of the dynamics. Perhaps they felt I had burdened them enough that day.

COMMENTARY

Session 4

Note that the I persisted in suspecting that what seemed like a friendly tone in the class concealed hostility. He speculated that the group's disproportionate reaction to the loss of the group member was, in fact, a displacement. Looking at their interchange from a transference perspective, the I realized that it had been he who had triggered the group's sadness and concern by assigning more work. The I acknowledged that he had failed to register the group's angry grumbling because of his preoccupation with his conflicted feelings. From the group's perspective, it felt as if the I was emotionally unavailable ("lost" to them). It was safer and easier for them to speak about their loss of the classmate than the loss of the instructor. There was another issue at work here that escaped the I's attention. Why had he chosen to make the burdensome assignment at that particular time? Could it be that, having felt excluded and rejected by the group in the previous session, he sought a way to regain entry to the G? To give an assignment is a natural way to accomplish this, but in this case it had unintended repercussions, namely, derailment of learning.

At first, the G's discussion of the case material integrated the I's dynamic approach. But now, in their disappointment with the I over the new assignment, they rejected his ideas and shut him out again, but this time in anger.

Such disruptions in the student-teacher relationship are inevitable, regardless of the skill and empathy of the I.

REPORT

Session 5

By the fifth session, I felt I had made some sense out of the turn of events in the previous session. I began this session by recapitulating what I thought had transpired between us. I acknowledged that I had failed to register their signals of displeasure when I had made the additional assignment. Their response was immediate: lively discussion about what had really occurred and where they were now. But there was increasing awareness of "how difficult all this was." As the class ended, one of the students remarked, "This isn't going to be exactly the way we had hoped it would be; it is more upsetting than we anticipated."

As I thought about their sober acceptance of the difficulties of learning in this way, it came home to me that there had been a significant shift in the G's affective position. In contrast to the angry, almost defiant, interpersonal struggle with me of last time, there emerged the beginning of tenuous awareness of the intrapersonal struggle that learning entailed.

COMMENTARY

Session 5

In contrast to the traditional didactive situation, here we have an opportunity to see an active engagement of the I and student in the struggle to learn and to teach. Neither blaming the group nor apologizing, the I shared with them his discovery—he had failed to perceive their distress with the new assignment. Perhaps the lively discussion in response to his acknowledgment signaled that he understood their feelings. However, as they discussed the issues more fully, perhaps there came the realization that their part in this would have to be greater than they had anticipated.

His willingness to acknowledge his fallibility led students to feel listened to, respected, and understood. Their trust in him had been further strengthened. Wouldn't this be a way to account for this dramatic shift away from their defensive adversarial stance to joining with each other and with the I in coping with the internal struggles inherent in learning?

REPORT

Session 6

In the sixth session, I sensed an air of disappointment, fatigue, and uncertainty in the group. It was palpable, yet unspoken. The group attitude, as I saw it, might be described as resentful and demanding, best summed up in the question: "Now what?" "Just what *will* you give us?" Marked ambivalence toward me and my role was manifest. Concerns about the proper relationship between teacher and students surfaced (dependency issues, passive vs. active, and so on). Under all of this I sensed a wish that I teach more didactically, more directively. Mostly, however, they came across as uncertain, inhibited. There seemed to be a shared decision in the group to sit back, and wait passively for me to "instruct" in the traditional way. Put another way, I felt that they were at a point where they were trying to redefine the teacher-student relationship. As part of this, they also were tussling with the related issue of what the structure and the purpose of their particular group ought to be. I felt they were in the process of reworking certain issues previously touched on in their first and second class meetings.

The case presented involved an adolescent girl who clearly wanted and had captured the teacher's involvement with her and her problem. What was more focal in the material was the girl's limit testing, provocation, and, at times, punishment-inviting behavior. As the class began to look behind some of this behavior they picked up on many of the issues mentioned above, particularly noticing the girl's reference to her "badness" as she signaled her need for external controls and limits, while seeking "deserved" punishment from others (parents, teachers, and so on). My pointing out the significance of sexuality at this stage of the girl's development was helpful. It seemed to liberate their thinking, and new, important, and previously omitted material was introduced and new dynamic connections discovered.

During the case presentation and discussion that followed it, their comments and associations focused on questions of limits, boundaries, what is permissible behavior, and legitimate emotions in the classroom. I continued to work on identifying their emerging resistance. In retrospect, I think I should have done more of this, and more actively than I did, throughout the course.

COMMENTARY

Session 6

Group is at a transitional stage in learning. The disappointment, fatigue, and uncertainty the group brought to this session are the experiential consequences of the preceding one. It is as if they were being asked to discard a familiar approach to teaching and learning before they had a new one to take its place. Small wonder that they feel uncertain and confused. Unlike the smooth, linear, incremental process of learning they expected, they found they were caught up in an arduous, self-involving, back and forth struggle which was at times frustrating and discordant, and, at other times, gratifying and confirming.

The problems presented by the adolescent girl in the case example neatly parallels and echoes many of the issues the students were currently grappling with in the seminar. Clearly, the case served as a vehicle which enabled the students to work, albeit indirectly, on some of the very same issues which were currently operating in the seminar. The girl's dilemma stemmed in part from the adolescent developmental experience of change and transition. Like the girl, the G worried about issues related to limits, boundaries, and controls, wanting change and fearing it simultaneously.

REPORT

Session 7

In the seventh session, the group began by expressing concerns similar to those noted in the previous meeting. While many of their concerns were due to feelings sparked in the previous meeting, I also saw them as related to the case under discussion. It concerned a thirteen-year-old (very disturbed) impulse-ridden girl whose behavior was often quite primitive. There was the constant worry that she would lose control and become unmanageable. At times, her impulsivity made her dangerous to herself and others. The class gradually came to realize that the problem was not only concern about the girl's behavior but concern about the feelings she aroused in us! Thus, through the case and their experiences as students in our group, parallel situations, the issue of anxiety, and how a teacher copes with it became very much alive. Our discussion of the idea of dealing with anxiety through action versus verbalization took on new meaning for them. At this point, we seemed to be moving into a higher level of group involvement in the presentation of case material and in the learning experience of the group as a whole. They were becoming more reflective and introspective about their teaching experiences. They were also turning to each other more than they did earlier, to inquire: "How did you feel?" or "Exactly what did you mean when you said what you did?" Now they gave me more direct feedback about what they were finding most helpful in my approach and expectations. For example, they felt that when I pulled together the case discussion for them at the end of the previous hour this had been very helpful. While I believed they meant what they said I nonetheless wondered to what extent this was compliance in the service of resistance?

COMMENTARY

Session 7

In this session the balance of tension in the G appears to have undergone a marked shift. Up until recently, the students were mainly preoccupied with managing their feelings in relation to learning in the seminar. Now, we see the focus of their interest shifting to the case material—the problems presented by the students in their classrooms occupied center stage. In other words, the G had become more task oriented. The cases are vehicles which allow them to work simultaneously on their problems with learning in the G and with those their students present in their classroom. It would seem that they were sensing the dynamic interrelationships between their own and their students' issues. This was a significant integrative achievement. The tenor and content of this session suggests that the students have become more emotionally involved in the learning process and have begun revising their image of themselves as teachers and learners. But notice that the I was not so sure that all resistance had been overcome.

REPORT

Session 8

At the beginning of the eighth meeting I clearly felt the group's reluctance to begin, although they denied it. The discussion revolved around the theme that growth is a slow and sometimes painful process. They were saying in effect, let's not attend to the meaning of our feelings, just tell us what to do with them. They appeared to be overwhelmed and hopeless about the impact of learning in this way. We continued our discussion of the case started last time. It became apparent that the case material had had more to do with the tone of the group than I had realized. Unlike the last case, this one concerned a psychotic child. The teachers were struggling with profound feelings of responsibility and frustration in coping with seemingly impossible situations. Their helplessness was compounded by a total lack of support and empathy from school colleagues. They were troubled by the guilt and anxiety evoked by the discussion of the psychotic child, feelings of anger and wishes to be rid of her were evoked, leading to tremendous guilt and anxiety. This case was so extreme that I later spoke with the teacher and urged her, for everyone's sake, to insist that the girl be removed from the classroom and get immediate psychiatric attention. Given this disturbing case material, the group seemed to erupt, and many kinds of thoughts and feelings broke through. They spoke of feeling overwhelmed, of being able to do so little to help, of pervasive feelings of hopelessness and helplessness. Eventually after a good deal of ventilation we moved into taking a look at what could be done realistically for this severely disturbed child and for the painful and disturbing feelings she evoked in us. We talked about such things as coming to terms with painful reality, recognizing and accepting the limitations of one's role, setting less ambitious, less perfectionistic goals, and partializing tasks. We also recognized that feelings of "hopelessness" might serve as a rationalization for doing nothing.

COMMENTARY

Session 8

It would appear that the G's resistance to learning in this session stems from feelings evoked by the case. In this session, the I senses a "reluctance to begin," which the G denies. The students are reverberating to the overwhelming intensity of affect and the primitive nature of this psychotic child's situation. Here the learning alliance, the working partnership, made it possible for the students to risk expressing the problematic feelings they had been trying to suppress. They had learned they could count on the I to listen empathically and to support them in their effort to understand and manage their anxiety. After looking at the data of their own subjective experiencing they could better identify the nature of the child's problem and plan appropriate classroom interventions. While sensitive and intuitive teachers have always drawn upon their subjective experiences in responding to problem situations, they lacked a theoretical frame of reference that could explain why their interventions were indeed helpful. One of the I's tasks was to provide and demonstrate such a theoretical framework.

REPORT

Session 9

Again, they and I became aware that something was getting in the way of our work. They attributed it to a holiday reaction (which I had not been aware of because I had not had a holiday!), saying, "It's really hell getting back and getting started again." They talked about not wanting to resume work at all and what getting started meant to them. Some noted that we were approaching the end of the quarter. The case presentation dealt with a parallel issue. The entire class vigorously denied the importance of the teacher for the child in the case. Of all the cases presented, this was one in which it was obvious from the boy's response that this teacher had touched the life of this boy very deeply. When I commented on this striking misperception in their discussion of the case, they simply acknowledged my statement and went on.

COMMENTARY

Session 9

Beginning with this session separation issues were dominant. Separation themes pervaded the session, beginning with the students' complaints about reentry after a recent school vacation, going on to anticipate the ending of the quarter.

The case presentation, once again, became the vehicle for airing the G's immediate concerns and conflicts. Perhaps their vigorous denial of the importance of the teacher for the child suggested that they, in kind, would have preferred that the I be less important to them; this would have been a way to prepare for the separation at the end of the quarter.

REPORT

Session 10

A striking transformation had occurred! It was best expressed in the words of a student, "Let's stop all this intellectualization and face up to the fact that we are using the case to bring in some of our own concerns." This remark evoked general agreement. Almost immediately, a refocusing took place. One student picked up on this shift thus: "Let's get right into the case and find out what this teacher is worried about and wants help with." It involved a twelve-year-old male, in the sixth grade, who had never been able to read. While this was the overt problem, the presenting teacher and group noted manifestations of narcissistic pathology. Unlike previous case presentations, this one was rather "low key." This may have resulted from the material itself—rather technical; the group's reactions to the presenter—more ambivalent; or the presenter's motivation—seeking approval and/or admiration.

The G noted that they had been taking a more active role in their learning and indicated that they wanted some recognition of their progress in this area. They did recognize, however, that they had only just begun to work in this way. They went on to reflect on the emotional experience of being an educator and their feelings about themselves as teachers and persons. I wondered whether this discussion was stimulated, at least in part, by the two case presentations in previous classes which had had to do with children who had suffered severe narcissistic injuries. They spoke about the way one part of the self perceives, relates to, and handles the other part. The issues of the divided self of the teacher and their sense of personal inadequacy dominated the discussion.

COMMENTARY

Session 10

Initially, the I observed a "striking transformation" in the G. In contrast to the previous session, the G seemed energized and eager to get down to the business of learning. The insightful comment by a student succinctly got to the crux of the situation, and, judging by the G's response, apparently expressed their thinking as well ("face up to the fact that we are using the case to bring in some of our own concerns"). A refocusing occurred which further defined and elaborated the kind of help the presenting teacher and, by extension, the members of the G hoped to get from the case discussion.

While the manifest problem concerned a twelve-year-old boy who was a nonreader, further exploration revealed the presence of a number of narcissistic character problems as well. It is no coincidence that this case led the G into a kind of personal stocktaking or evaluation of themselves as teachers and as learners. Not surprisingly, issues of self and self-esteem were dominant ("the issue of the divided self of the teacher and the sense of personal inadequacy").

REPORT

Session 11

Student reactions were mixed. Some arrived late, some were "giddy," some overtly angry. They opposed whatever I did or said. The discussion emphasized external problems in the school system, the family, and so on. The case for the evening involved an angry, depressed, but very bright seventh grade boy. He was suspicious and quick to project his negative, hostile feelings onto others in the school. The presenter was caught up in her own feelings of anger, exasperation, sympathy, and identification with the boy. In her presentation, the teacher's negative feelings about the "system" and its degrading effect on teachers erupted and became the focus of discussion. They spoke about their dissatisfaction with their work lives, and eventually got into the dissatisfaction they were feeling with me. They spoke vaguely about wanting "something" which I hadn't provided. But they weren't able to articulate what this something was except in general terms. It seemed to me that their message was: "You're to blame for not providing something we need, but then again, we're not sure we want you to know what it is." I now believe they were reacting, at least in part, to my failure to tune in on their concerns. I had allowed my own need to complete the case reports to take precedence over the separation issues with which the students were grappling. They reluctantly went along.

Near the end, I reminded them that this was our last class meeting for the quarter. This had come up in the beginning of the session but somehow had been tabled. They dealt with the "ending" individually, as they left the classroom, some expressing positive feelings—a pleasant wish, a "thank you" for a comment I had made on a paper, and the like.

COMMENTARY

Session 11

Here was the last session of the first quarter, yet somehow the separation issue got lost in the shuffle. General regression was signaled by diminished group cohesion, giddiness, and negativism. The I, too, was affected: "my failure to tune in on their concerns." Perhaps the I felt threatened by the intensity of the G's emotional barrage and sought to temper it by steering them away from separation issues.

As in previous case discussions, this one, too, paralleled the G affect state that emerged. The seventh grade boy under study was described as "angry, depressed, deprived." They, too, like the boy, felt *angry* at the I for "tuning them out," *depressed* over separation from him and each other, and *deprived*, wanting something he hadn't provided. Although there had been some shaky moments in the learning alliance during this session, it was clear at the end that the G was committed to continuing their work the next quarter.

A PARTIAL EXAMINATION OF THE PROCESS OF A TEP SEMINAR GROUP AS EXPERIENCED AND REPORTED BY THE CLASS INSTRUCTOR—SECOND QUARTER

> It takes great wisdom to be able to follow a learning pupil sensitively enough to know what the next step is for him, and you don't press the next step. You watch it happen. If it sticks, you help it a bit, but it's not a transmission or an imposition or a filling of a vessel or any of these things. Those are all bad images of the real teaching function: the real one is this penetration of the intelligence of one intelligence into another.
>
> Scott Buchanan

REPORT

Session 1

The second quarter started after a two-week break. Some of the typical reunion reactions (e.g., what it felt like to be getting back) characterized the opening session. But in contrast to the preceding term, rather than my having to elicit such feelings, the students clearly were more aware of their feelings and more able to verbalize them spontaneously. They approached the second term with eagerness and renewed energy.

They immediately questioned what the nature of the course would be and how it would differ from the last one. I indicated that we would be broadening our scope beyond the classroom context, focusing on areas of interpersonal experience, namely, teachers' relations with parents, colleagues, and administrators. Following this overview, anxiety emerged, taking the form of demands for clarification, objections, alternative goals, and so on.

As the discussion continued, it became apparent to all that the group was regressing, demanding that I tell them exactly what I expected of them. At the same time, they were resisting consideration of their own concerns about the subject matter. Suddenly, we recognized that it was the specific issue of looking at their relations with parents and colleagues that was worrying them. They acknowledged that these were highly conflictual and troubling areas of their work. They soon became aware of how they were resisting getting started—either by "drawing a blank" or jumping headlong into highly charged problem areas with administration and parents, or by clinging to the familiar case format of the first quarter.

Several noteworthy discoveries emerged from this first meeting. For example, we found that some of the same issues, for example, trust and confidentiality, raised in the beginning session last term surfaced again. However, unlike the first time, now the students initiated the effort, recognized the problems they were having, and ultimately resolved them in a less anxious, more matter-of-fact fashion. It became clear to me, and to the group itself, albeit somewhat later, that this time around they were taking more initiative about identifying the topics that were most valid and relevant for them, both in the context of the course objectives and in their professional situations. A lively exchange of ideas and questions followed, as they proposed the specific issues they wished to explore. However, even though they felt freer to disagree with each other, they nonetheless focused on external sources of concern (sociological, organizational, situational). They were not yet ready to tackle their inner concerns.

COMMENTARY

Session 1

In the final session before the two-week interruption, the learning alliance appears threatened, but as the G reconvenes for the new quarter, the affective climate in the G is positive. A reversal in this affective quality occurs immediately after the I outlines the new coursework for the quarter. No sooner does the I announce that they would be studying the dynamics of authority relations, a subject area highly charged with psychological meaning, than the G appears to reenact with the I just such a conflictual relationship. In effect, the G manifests what Ekstein and Wallerstein termed "a problem about learning" in contrast to "a learning problem," the former being due specifically to anxiety mobilized by the subject matter under study. As the I observes, "they were resisting con-

sideration of their own concerns (anxiety) about the subject matter, reenacting rather than verbalizing their
anxiety-laden fantasies."

It is interesting to contrast this session with session
11. In the latter, the tense interchange between I and G
had touched on the I's vulnerabilities and stimulated anxiety that had temporarily blocked communication between them. In this session, even though the I is again
the target of discontent, he intervenes empathically and
helps them recognize how they are abdicating responsibility for their own learning. The I's intervention has a
catalyzing effect and frees the G to move ahead. The reemergence of the same issues raised in the beginning suggests that a process of remembering, connecting, and
reworking of past issues is under way as they approached
a new level of learning. We see this in the vitality, initiative, and involvement of their discussion. The G heard
the announcement that one of their colleagues was leaving teaching in the context of their own changing professional identities. No wonder they reacted with shock. His
departure from the G, now a cohesive psychological structure in which they had found support, affirmation, and
stimulation, undoubtedly is an even more immediate and
personal blow. Their angry attack on the student suggests
that his leaving the G is experienced as his rejection of
them.

COMMENTARY

Session 1

Suddenly, one of the students, who clearly appeared more
ill at ease than usual, announced that over the semester
break he had decided to leave teaching! This proved to
be a shocker. Initially, the G manifested a need to dismiss,

minimize, or deny its emotional effect on them. Instead
they resorted to externalization and intellectualization,
denouncing and attacking the institutional structure and
the constraints of the school establishment. Eventually,
they came around to addressing the teacher himself, putting him on the defensive. After several such exchanges,
the I suggested that they take a look at what was happening. Clearly, his announcement had been threatening
to some teachers in the group. They, in turn, had subtly
and at times not so subtly, attacked him, albeit under the
guise of asking questions. Both the teacher and those
attacking him were becoming more guilty and with this
the level of tension and anxiety in the group rose. The
class ended on a rather anxious, uneasy, disquieted note.

REPORT

Session 2

The class was still reverberating to their classmate's announcement of the previous session. After making some
unsuccessful attempts to move into the course material,
the class as a whole recognized that something was getting in their way. It became apparent to all that their
feelings about the previous week's announcement were
still very much alive. When I suggested that the announcement seemed to have triggered something inside
of them (referring to the pervasive "shock" reaction) they
expressed feelings of being overwhelmed, frustrated, angry, "fed up." It seemed to me that these were in the
nature of associations to feelings about their own teaching experiences. There were some efforts to differentiate
their situation, their feelings, their goals, their ways of
coping from those of the teacher in question. After working through their reactions and perceptions of the "shock"
announcement the teachers were able to return to the

business at hand, which, as I saw it, involved a wish for clarification of the scope and goals of the course, and their unconscious resistance to opening up such highly charged material. They continued to struggle with questions about what they would be studying until they were clarified and resolved to their satisfaction. They then moved to the next step, namely, to focus more directly on the individual case presentation.

The youngster being presented had suffered several serious physical handicaps from a very early age, with obvious impairment and constriction in his personality organization and school functioning. The group first considered the boy's strengths and then the deficiencies associated with his physical limitations. I was impressed by their ability to deemphasize the pathology and to focus instead on the process of his development, noting to what level and in what areas he had advanced. I believe the class ended with a better grasp of the boy's current difficulties and his potential for learning, and with a more hopeful attitude about what a teacher could accomplish with such a seriously handicapped youngster.

As the session drew to its close, I privately noted several things. I was struck by the way they were able to work through their shock reaction and focus on the material at hand. I also noted that a number of the participants were evincing a willingness and a readiness to take over some of the regulating and protective functions that I had been performing.

COMMENTARY

Session 2

The group has remained cohesive and the learning alliance stable and even strengthened. We see no indication of defensive avoidance or denial of the intense affects mobilized in last week's session. Instead they have continued to reflect on their reactions to the event, partly to bolster their professional self-esteem and partly to affirm their professional commitment. We see evidence of greater capacity for introspection and self-scrutiny. Their discussion of the case vignette appears to bear this out. The child, seriously handicapped, had struggled against heavy odds and narcissistic injuries. He posed a difficult challenge for those who would help him. In the discussion the G found that there were many ways teachers might assist such a child if they recognized his strengths. It is almost as if, in their concentration on developmental issues rather than on pathology, they were simultaneously discovering not only the youngster's potentials for growth but their own as well. At this point, it appears that the students, in working through the loss of their colleague, had taken a step forward in their own development.

REPORT

Session 3

The teachers began to consider how best to pursue the course goals as their first order of business. They decided that they wanted my help in "talking with kids," "talking with parents." Whereupon, three or four class members immediately volunteered, offering vignettes highlighting the troubling aspects of such interpersonal communications.

Most gratifying to me at this point and throughout this second term was the marked continuity in the sessions. They would remind each other about what they had planned to consider the previous session and were able to get to it with little or no prompting from me. After several vignettes were presented everyone recognized the need for an anchoring frame of reference to help them explain some of the inferences I was deriving from their observations. I thought they needed to know how I had been able to arrive at my interpretations. In short, they needed to learn how I thought about the encounters with students that to them were so puzzling. So we "stepped back," so to speak, using ourselves and our experiences in this group as our data of observation. We began to think about what to observe and listen for and listed five or six areas, such as "observed behavior, speech patterns, affective communications, content, anxiety triggers, sequences, and so on." During this discussion I was becoming aware of several new developments in the group. These included a growing capacity for empathy, more awareness of the repetitious quality in the patterns of their interactions with children, a questioning of certain of their assumptions and attitudes, and a greater readiness to recognize, articulate, and use their feelings as tools in understanding and responding to problematic situations. At the same time, they seemed to be more comfortable about waiting to respond, less compelled to "do something," before they really knew what was going on. I also noticed a significant shift within the group itself. There was a more sustained focus on the case material and readings, in contrast to the digressions, resistances, and preoccupation with interpersonal issues that were such frequent occurrences in the first term. I sensed the emergence of a new freedom, a diminished anxiety about self and others in the group. As a result, attention to the task at hand had become more concentrated and sustained.

COMMENTARY

Session 3

It appears that the learning alliance is now strong and stable. The defensive intellectuality and resistance to

new learning noted in the first quarter is replaced by a
spirit of inquiry and openness to learning. The members
of the group are no longer passive and dependent on the
I, but join with him as active partners. They participate
in setting the learning agenda, and identify the issues
they want him to address. It is clear that they now feel
safer, more connected to each other and to the instructor.
They manifest more self-awareness and less narcissistic
vulnerability. Therefore, they are more willing to risk
moving into new areas of study. Their recognition of a
need for an explanatory theoretical framework represents
a significant integrative step in affective-cognitive functioning. They have moved from a more or less technical,
how-to-do-it, instrumental approach to problem situations, to a more empathic, inquiring, humanistic approach, a mode enriched by subjective experience.

That the G is beginning to identify with the I's way
of looking at and thinking about problem situations is
reflected in the I's observations: "they seemed to be more
comfortable about waiting to respond, less compelled to
do something before they really knew what was going
on." Their growing capacity for empathy goes hand-in-
hand with their increased capacity for self-observation.

REPORT

Session 4

This meeting testified further to the emerging spirit of
initiative and autonomy in the group. They presented me
with a "new form of report card" which they had devised
for their students. They wondered whether their new report card reflected what they had been learning here. The
report card became a springboard for identifying and examining valuable issues in their own learning. They expressed appreciation of the role the group played in

facilitating their learning (e.g., how they had been using each other to ventilate feelings and to grapple with problems). They began to wonder about the possibility that they had a part in their own powerlessness. They reminded each other of the difficulty they had had in expressing negative feelings—dissatisfaction, irritation, criticisms—even in a group like this in which dissent and difference were accepted and respected. With a flash of insight they saw how they tended to externalize problems, to blame parents, the "system," the principal, rather than face their own feelings; and they began to wonder whether, without realizing it, they sometimes chose the role of victim. Was it possible, they asked, that they were colluding in their powerlessness by their resentful compliance, their defensive silence, and their general passivity? Was this the way they hid from their own anger and anxiety? This eventually led to their considering alternative ways of coping with such problematic feelings. They now began asking questions of themselves: "Just what are we doing?" "Are we kidding ourselves, or might there be other, less self-punishing ways to survive in the system?"

COMMENTARY

Session 4

The group members themselves are becoming aware that they are changing and that it was this change itself that they wished to have evaluated via discussion of the report card. But how does one evaluate subjectively experienced change? How can such changes be translated into their classroom interactions with students? They are puzzled by the discrepancies in their experiences in the seminar and in their classrooms. They appear to be considering what they've accomplished in the course thus far. Their reflections are indirect questions for the instructor. Was he pleased with their progress? Were they measuring up to his expectations? How does he evaluate them? Were they changing, growing? Did he recognize and appreciate the extent of their efforts? What is most impressive in this session is the degree of introspective thinking implicit in their questions. It is as if they are now rethinking and reexamining some of their ideas and assumptions about teaching and learning.

REPORT

Session 5

I had the feeling that the group had been undergoing some kind of transition. While they continued to work and rework issues from previous sessions, I sensed a different quality in the group. For one thing, they seemed more and more to be looking for parallels between their problematic encounters with students in their classrooms and their relations with me. In this session, problems with authority and issues of control dominated the class discussion. Quite spontaneously, several individuals recalled their reactions to incidents that had occurred in their class with me this quarter and last. They joked about the times they had asked endless questions, "forgot" assignments, "misunderstood my statements," rather than get into the work at hand, just as their students had done with them in their classrooms. Then several students talked about their constant worry about losing control of their classes, especially when they had to contend with the provocations of certain belligerent and defiant kids who instigated misbehavior in others. In the course of this exchange in which most members of the group actively participated, someone raised a question about the case presentations. Did they have to follow the guidelines I had given them? Couldn't they dispense with the guidelines in writing up their cases? They felt the guidelines were too constricting. After a spirited discussion of the pros and cons, they agreed to my suggestion that we think about this question and its implications between now and our next meeting. The theme and sequence of the class discussion centered on problems with authority and control in their schools, in their classrooms, and now with me. Could the issue of the case guidelines be a challenge to my authority, a test of my control? Or were they in fact looking to me as a model to demonstrate for them how best to deal with challenges to authority?

In retrospect, I now see the remarkable continuity of theme and process in the third, fourth, and fifth sessions. In all three sessions the group had been moving toward assuming more initiative and control over the focus and direction of our work.

COMMENTARY

Session 5

One senses an undercurrent of anxiety in the G. Without knowing it, they are challenging the authority of the I through questioning the value of the case guidelines. With consummate sensitivity and skill, the I encourages further thought on this highly charged issue. Of all the problems teachers face in their work, the developmental tasks and conflicts around authority and control versus initiative and autonomy are among the most critical and pressing.

REPORT

Session 6

We spontaneously decided to pull together and summarize the questions that had been raised and the issues we had been examining. In this connection a lengthy discussion ensued about what happens when a teacher takes a different approach to children's learning and begins using new criteria in evaluating children's performance. The uncertainty, the anxiety, the self-doubts, and the guilt that accompany such changes were aired. One might see this as an expression of the students' effort to come to terms with the disparities in the values, methods, and priorities existing in their schools and those they were encountering in their institute classes. As a part of this, they were also involved at some level in comparing and possibly emulating my teaching approach. I think, too, that many were beginning to realize that change involved far more than changing one's overt style, and, from their own experience in this group, recognized the internal repercussions of change, the affects and resistances mobilized, and so on. In an interesting exchange, the group members compared and contrasted their experiences in this group and those occurring in their classrooms. They spoke about the reactions of their students and colleagues when they altered their approach to teaching in accordance with their new convictions and beliefs.

Several of the students summarized the main points of our discussion as follows: everyone talks about the need for change and mostly they see change as a simple act of will and rationality, forgetting its internal ramifications. One must always take into account the particular conditions and constraints in one's own situation and come to terms with the fact it may be impossible to change certain things even if one wants to. The trick is in knowing what can or can't be changed. There are no two situations alike, just as no two people are alike, so finding a solution to fit one's own situation cannot be generalized and passed on to others. Finally, the hardest task of all is to distinguish between external demands, and internal wishes and needs. Here I quote from the written comments of a student after this session:

I found this class very satisfying. I think we're beginning to focus on the areas most of us are most interested
in: the teacher himself, his responses, feelings, frustrations, etc. The fact that some of us students actually
initiated this change of focus is also important, as is
the fact that the I so readily accepted this tentative
redirection. I am anxiously anticipating the remaining
classes.

COMMENTARY

Session 6

What happened to the anxiety that emerged in the last
session about control issues? Isn't it interesting that no
one brought up the unresolved question of the case guidelines (the challenge to the instructor's authority)? Perhaps the I's calm acceptance of the validity of their
challenge was enough to defuse the issue and permit the
G to assume greater initiative. In an ambience of positive
feeling they seem eager to review what they had been
learning and what it means to change.

The quoted comments of the student at the end of the
session neatly summarize the issues that have been
worked through thus far. They catch the very essence of
their learning experience in the course and perhaps signal an awareness that the end phase is
approaching—"*anxiously* anticipating the remaining
classes."

REPORT

Session 7

This session had important threads from the previous
one. (I was more able to see the continuity than I had

been in the first quarter.) There were several things that impressed me in this meeting. The group members had taken much more responsibility for presenting their vignettes themselves, were more open and candid with each other in expressing their feelings. One particularly sensitive area involved losing control of their students and the feelings of shame and anger associated with this. The degree to which they were able to use each other for clarification, insight, support, and so on without at the same time needing to exclude me, was most striking and gratifying. The other side of this was that I, too, was changing, as I began to see my role in the group differently, and gradually accommodate to it more comfortably. I conceptualized my role at this stage as "special participant." Also evident was a lessening of their need to always know what I thought about issues or to explicitly or implicitly press for my approval of their ideas.

In the discussion of the case material the central issue revolved around fears of losing control of classes and the realization that this is a two-tier process—dealing with one's own anxiety over losing control over oneself and dealing with the disorder or incipient disorder in one's classroom. What were the priorities, they wondered, for the teacher. All seemed in agreement that one must have basic order within oneself before one could hope to achieve order in one's classroom. They felt this was a precondition in all learning, but always a delicate balance.

As the class was drawing closer to its end, a student raised a question about the required comprehensive case study. When I turned this question back to them, they made it very clear that at this stage in their learning, they felt that presenting a short vignette would be preferable and more in line with their current needs. In listening to them, I, too, began to feel, albeit with growing anxiety, that they were probably correct. Earlier in the year, I might have seen this as a resistance-avoidance maneuver. Now I recognized, and later shared with them, what I thought was going on, based on my feelings and reactions to their discussion. I told them that while I was in substantial agreement with them about the greater usefulness of vignettes, still I felt uneasy. I wondered why I was feeling so uncomfortable? Was it because I took their request to mean that by going along with them I'd be losing control of my role as group leader? Related to this was my anxiety about going contrary to my own administration on this matter. Earlier in the evening we had talked a bit about the disparity, and often the conflict, between one's own views about learning and the methods for implementing them, versus those of one's "administration." In other words, how free are we to "practice what we preach?" Here again, we confronted a reverse parallelism, namely, authority conflicts in the instructor. I shared with them some of the reasons for my uneasiness and anxiety about going contrary to my administration on this issue, acknowledging that I felt this way despite the fact that I knew full well that my director would respect my judgment on this matter. I felt that the question at issue in the group was a challenge for them and for me. It turned out that I had been pretty much on target in identifying the focal issues. One group member responded to what she saw as my "openness and honesty." Someone observed that after tonight's meeting there would be only three more class sessions. The discussion took on a tone of mild self-reproach, reflected in the comment, "It took us so long to get to this point!" I, on the contrary, felt they were really seizing the initiative and defining their new role as active participants in the learning process. They did note that they now were beginning to use each other in their learning more appropriately.

Under the stimulus of the approaching end of the course they began reflecting on how they had started, appreciating the struggles they had gone through to reach their present position, and contemplating with apparent regret the "not-too-distant" ending. They reminded each other that, unfortunately, all good things have to end.

COMMENTARY

Session 7

An extraordinary shift has taken place. The I now defines his role as a special participant. This is in response to the emergence of a new level of collegiality and mutuality between himself and the G. This shift in the relational structure within the G rests on a dynamic interplay of forces simultaneously experienced by both teacher and students. The I refers first to his pleasure and gratification over the growth he now sees in the G. His students' progress in learning validates and confirms him as a teacher.

This shift toward mutality permitted the instructor to trust the students' judgment that the vignettes would be more valuable than the prescribed case study. But with this he was thrown in conflict with the administration, even knowing full well that his director would trust his judgment as he trusted his students. Here was an early "authority transference" at play. It turned out that indeed it was decided that they would do vignettes, attesting to the students' autonomy and the I's freedom from transference distortion.

Doesn't it appear that everyone was ready to enter the termination phase?

REPORT

Session 8

As the session got under way, a puzzling change in the tone of the group was immediately apparent. I had a vague sense of resistance but was unable to explain it. Nonetheless, the two or three people who had offered to present vignettes that evening were, again, well prepared, very involved, and elicited a satisfactory level of group interchange. The resistance I sensed became clearer in the case presentations. Interestingly enough, these revolved around student behaviors which, at first, seemed appropriate but, which in reality, masked powerful resistances to learning (e.g., a child's constantly getting the teacher caught up in irrelevant questions, when his real problem was getting into the learning task itself).

I began to understand the group's resistance as they began insisting once again on my telling them the "right answers." One individual made an intense effort to push me into taking a more directive role in the group. This helped draw the attention of the others to what was happening. Once again they were deferring to my "authority," more likely my omnipotence, despite the work we had done earlier on this very issue. With a flash of insight, several people recalled that an earlier case presentation had made us aware of how much a part of us is like a small child who needs to maintain the image of the omnipotent parent.

As some members of the group were visibly struggling with these observations, others became more actively involved in the discussion. They noted how in this quarter they had made many attempts to set me up as the "all-knowing" teacher, to get me to tell them the answers. If I couldn't and/or wouldn't comply, they felt angry and/or disappointed, as if I had been withholding or depriving. On the other hand, if I complied with their attempts, they were also resentful, as if I were infantilizing or patronizing.

As the class drew to a close, the majority was struggling with this issue, except for one member of the group who seemed to be "stuck" on getting my admiration and approval, desperately pushing for a closer, more exclusive one-to-one relationship with me. Still another student seemed intent on wanting me to supply her with the motivation, the "answers," the direction needed for learning.

COMMENTARY

Session 8

Here again we see how students make their teachers into what they want them to be. The last session was marked by a spirit of mature mutuality in the teacher-student relationship. Reciprocal feelings of trust, gratification, self-affirmation, and aspiration had reached a high point. Most likely, the regressive shift in this session was precipitated by the reminder that only three weeks remained before the end of the quarter. None of the regressive shifts in response to separation was as dramatic as this.

The instructor admittedly experienced the shift as disconcerting and disappointing. But he helped the G discern the resistances first in the children described in the case vignettes and eventually in themselves. All but two of the students were enabled to reverse the regression. The instructor's empathic response to the G's resistance actually strengthened motivation, furthered learning, and brought about deeper insight into their relationship with him.

REPORT

Session 9

Several of the vignettes presented in this session centered on interactions with aggressive, violent children in the classroom. Initially, their questions focused on how best to handle such children. Soon several teachers began recalling their feelings and reactions to such behavior. We began to look more closely at the gamut of emotions these situations evoked: fear, rage, helplessness, counter-aggression, and so on. They observed that these kinds of feelings were not necessarily confined to the disturbing kids, but often arose in connection with other, so-called normal kids, and with school administrators as well. Because of the open, free flow of communication with me and with each other, I felt no need to call their attention to the issue of parallel process and its implications. We did take note of how one could use one's angry responses to another person as a means of understanding that individual's emotional situation. This proved to be an exciting and useful insight.

Somewhere near the end of this session, the issue of the "class scapegoat" came up. This was a poignant, and, for me, somewhat troublesome issue. I was aware, as I think were several of the group members, that although they were speaking generally about classroom situations, they were also referring to a specific person in our group, who, for some time now, had seemed determined to gain an exclusive relationship with me. I think we all realized that our annoyance with her had been mounting as her efforts became more overtly inappropriate. Prior to this session, I had been asking myself how best to deal with this student within rather than outside the group, but I had decided to do nothing or say nothing, with the full awareness that it would take careful monitoring lest I inadvertently let my irritation with her collude with the group in making her the "class scapegoat." If this happened I would be creating the very exclusive special relationship (albeit negative) she seemed bent on getting. Instead, I turned her repeated inquiries away from myself and directed them to the group. I felt that I should not assume full responsibility for this individual, because doing so would deprive the group of its responsibility for coming to terms with and dealing with her. While I don't believe that much got resolved, I do think that it gave the class members a valuable opportunity to learn, first-hand, something about the dynamics of scapegoating, the feelings it evokes, and how such feelings affect everyone in the group, the teacher as well as the other group members.

COMMENTARY

Session 9

Over and over again students use the case vignettes as the vehicle for dealing with emerging problems in their own learning. In this session the issue carried over from the previous session centers on the problem of hostility, their own and that of their pupils'.

It will be recalled that a few students at the end of the last session were conspicuous for their demanding-ness toward the I. Unwittingly continuing this theme, the G focuses now on angry, demanding, disruptive children. While they initially raise "how-to" questions they quickly turn to the "gamut of emotions these situations evoked." Broadening their focus they began to consider the feelings evoked in other difficult professional en-counters. It would appear that the G's aim in both is to work through the problematic feelings evoked in such situations, but now in the transference relationship with the I it is as if they are looking to him to demonstrate how he copes with such situations.

Scapegoating is a common group phenomenon, and is always a problem for teachers. While it becomes focal in this session, the I notes that "actually it had been going on from the beginning." Often the student so singled out invites the scapegoating. This seems to be the case here. What is happening is essentially a specific, idiosyncratic response, presumably transference based, of an individual student to the instructor. Using his understanding of the phenomena of transference, the I deflected the scapegoating process and forestalled the threatened exclusion of the student from the G.

It is interesting that the scapegoating issue erupts at this particular juncture. Perhaps the stress of the impending termination is making everyone more vulnerable.

REPORT

Session 10

The main themes and affect tone of the previous session continued in this one. Initially, a few students, via their vignettes, voiced their frustrations over changes in the family and in society, and how these impede their work with children. But, along with this, they also were in touch with the subjective implications of what they were saying. This was done in terms of sharing with each other their painful doubts about the value of being a teacher, about the limits of what they can really accomplish, and whether teaching is for them. They questioned their expectations of themselves, their ambitions, and their ideals. Among the questions raised were: How does one cope with the inevitable discouragement over not living up to one's ideals, how realistic they really are, and how one's goals might be modified to fit the circumstances. This brought them back to the subject of work models, the kinds of relationships one introjects, how one utilizes other models and finds better ways of coping, and so on.

Emerging from the discussion was the realization of the changing nature of their self-image, their ideals and goals, along with a reassessment of the possibilities and limits in their current work. A note of ambivalence per-

vaded the discussion. On the one hand, they seemed relieved to be able to share with each other their changing
image of themselves and their professional identity, and
on the other, they seemed uncertain and anxious about
what this might mean for them in their work. What also
began to emerge was their attempt to rethink and consolidate concepts we had worked on. Throughout their
discussion there was an unmistakable note of sadness
about the approaching end of the course. As I briefly
remarked on this, their sadness became more overt. Behind this was a certain anxiety over whether they could
manage to "get all the pieces together" prior to our ending. I reminded them of some of our previous discussions
affirming their oft-reiterated convictions that life itself
is an unending learning process. Again, I felt that one of
the students captured it best in her write-up about this
session. She pointed out: "I feel definitely all the bits and
pieces of insight falling into a pattern which is proving
helpful to me in the classroom. I am now aware that there
has been a very positive dynamic or process in every
session of Transactions and the Urban Teacher."

COMMENTARY

Session 10

The G moves quickly from "the frustrations over change"
vis-à-vis society, families, and the children in their classrooms to their own frustrations over change vis-à-vis the
seminar. They consider the effects of these changes on
their own reading experience, their professional identity,
their teaching function, and their self-esteem. What is
noteworthy here is their willingness to examine and
share their feelings with one another—their anxieties,
self-doubts, discouragement, and uncertainties. The impetus to reexamine their self-image and expectations,

their ambitions, and their ideals runs through their discussion like a red thread. They talk about alternative "work models," "introjects," and wonder whether they might "find better ways of coping," all of which suggests that they are thinking about their relationship with the I and comparing it to the relationships they now establish with their students. Concomitant with the students' idealization of the I is seen their strengthened sense of self and their growing capacity for self-scrutiny.

There is little doubt that they have reached a developmental transition in their learning. For the I and students alike the problems now emerging derive from the affects, conflicts, and anxiety mobilized in this termination phase. As the I picks up on the note of sadness in the G, he demonstrates once again the efficacy of the empathic identification of a feeling state. His articulation of the affect helped to move the process forward. The G's sadness with the ending of the course could now be acknowledged and expressed.

REPORT

Session 11

This was our final class meeting. Some individuals used the first part, even before class, to complain about the instructor in the other class and to voice their worries about the new instructor they would be getting next term. I understood their wish to elicit my concern and appreciation for the pressure they were under and their wish to assure my continued involvement with them.

During the remainder of the session, they continued to work on the concepts of ego ideal and self-realization. They related these concepts to themselves in ever more direct and practical ways.

In the main, however, the focal theme of this session

related to the meaning of the ending of the term. Again, one of the students captured the affect in the comments he recorded after the session:

> [T]he discussion involving one's feelings when something ends (i.e., school, class, etc.) was revealing. There is a separation which the individual must deal with. Often one can't do this at the moment of separation, but can do it after the separation has occurred. . . . The discussion, at this time, made me aware of some very strong internal feelings. During most of the session, I was thinking that this was our last class, and I was surprised at how disturbed I felt. This has been a difficult session for me to sit through, because it is the last one. Even the delicious Chinese dinner we had couldn't change my feelings. I enjoyed this course and the professor very much. I am sorry to see it end.

COMMENTARY

Session 11

The dominant affective theme throughout this final session relates to the ending of the term. The G expresses it initially in a litany of complaints, worries, and veiled accusations. They feel overburdened and pressured by course requirements; they are *worried* about the new instructor; they are *angry* at the instructor in their other class; and, they *complain* about all of this to the present I. In short the students are overwhelmed, confused, anxious, suffering the press of very powerful internal feelings and conflicts mobilized around ending their work with this instructor. As the student quoted put it, "I was thinking that this was our last class, and I was surprised at how disturbed I felt."

The conceptual material, "concepts of ego ideal and self-realization," reflect another aspect of the G's separation experience. According to the I, they had been preoccupied for some time with these concepts, suggesting that they have been actively engaged in reexamining and reevaluating their own professional and personal values, goals, and aspirations. The fact that they are relating "these concepts to themselves in ever more direct and practical ways" testifies to the constant and simultaneous interweaving of conceptual and experiential modes that has characterized their learning in this course.

REPORT

I would like to add some observations of my own as to how I saw and experienced this term differently from the first. To begin with, I went into this term with a clearer idea of my role and function in the group. I conceptualized my role as a "special participant," responsible for providing whatever part of the "group ego" that seemed to be missing and needed at the moment. In actuality, I was even more inactive, generally speaking, during their discussions this term than I had been the first. I truly felt myself to be more like a special group member or collaborator rather than being excluded, or "teacher," in the traditional sense as imparter of knowledge.

Between the first and second terms, I became more aware of a certain distancing, defensive posture that I had taken in the first term. I became more comfortable being more involved in the group, under the guidelines spelled out above, and sharing some of my objective-subjective reactions to facilitate further group learning and progress. This quarter there was a noticeable decrease in our focus on the group and the group interaction per se. When this did occur, it was more likely for the purpose of illustrating what goes on in people in such circumstances, rather than needing to examine and deal with it directly as their resistance to learning. Putting it another way, there was more, at times almost exclusive, focus on the issues and concerns being raised in the learning situation. I think, overall, the tone of the group was happier, freer, more buoyant, and purposive than it was during the first quarter. There also was more of a feeling of partnership, again with less need to call attention to this fact, than during the first term. As I mentioned before, there clearly was more overt evidence of their coming to terms with the continuity and frustrations in their learning and in the learning process generally.

In addition to the constant reworking of old themes (e.g., freedom versus control, feeling versus action), it was apparent to me that these themes were now being considered more from the standpoint of the self of the teacher as center, and in terms of the teacher's own affective life in the classroom. All of us were aware of undergoing a continuing freeing up process, and its consequences, some of which, inevitably, proved to be disquieting. For the most part, I would say that the intensity of affect expression in the group seemed more modulated than it had been the first quarter, as well as being more joyful. Certainly, the tendency toward displacement and projection was far less. The members of the group were more actively involved in the group process and in applying new concepts and insights to their work situation.

ADDENDUM: IN RETROSPECT—THE INSTRUCTOR'S REACTION

It was with mixed feelings and the encouraging support of the author that I agreed to reexamine this material after some thirteen years.

This group was one of the first that I had taught in the Teacher Education Program. Never before in my limited teaching experience had I taken this approach, although I myself had had learning experiences of a similar nature. When the faculty asked me to assemble and present this material back then, I agreed for several reasons. First, because I welcomed the assistance of several members of the faculty, whose experience and insights I trusted and valued. Second, I sensed, even then, that my unorthodox approach to teaching had stimulated highly mixed reactions from some students and some members of the faculty. Anxious as I was, I wanted to confront their questions. I suppose I had hoped that such discussion and scrutiny would yield more insight into what I was doing, and enable me to better conceptualize it. Not the least of all this was my need for the support and validation of those members of the faculty I most respected and valued.

A word about my sources of information about the learning needs and problems of students in the group. Some sources are obvious from the text, namely the actual content of the class session, as manifested in the communications and behavior of the students. Equally important was what I subjectively experienced in the classroom interchange. This experiential data, subject, of course, to testing and feedback, provided a clue to the nonarticulated, inner dimensions of the teachers' experience and served as an additional mode of "knowing." Another source of information came from the "logs" students regularly submit to the instructor. These are brief, written comments by students on their experiences and reactions to each class meeting.

Upon reviewing this material I found myself reexperiencing some of the anxiety and insecurity I felt when I taught this group. I brought to this class some strong convictions about what the instructor's role should be in a course of this nature. I believed that it should convey and demonstrate the essential qualities of a teacher-student relationship, which involved the full use of the self of the teacher and the students engaged in a process of mutual and reciprocal interaction. This meant that there could be no place for the usual omniscient instructor, one who presumed to know, in advance, what the students ought to learn; that is, a preconceived curriculum. A course focusing on people and relationships should be structured to elicit the actual, immediate concerns of the teachers, in order to fully engage them in the learning process. To make such learning come alive, it seemed to me that we would have to demonstrate the parallels in their learning experiences in the program seminar and in their teaching experiences in their own classrooms.

Reviewing this material brought back not only the anxiety I experienced then, but more to the point, a sense of myself as a beginning teacher, literally a neophyte, going forth with a special courage borne of my idealistic quest for new ways of engaging teachers in a vital and personally meaningful educational experience. While I cringed a bit when I recalled some of my experiences with this class, I also felt a sense of appreciation for the integrity of the effort, which is to say that I really tried to "practice what I preached." Some of the distancing and standoffishness in some of my reactions to students I now could see were motivated by my insecurity and anxiety. Today, while I am more secure and experienced as a teacher, what I strive for in my teaching remains basically unchanged. Then, and now, I believed that my effectiveness as a teacher depended on two corollary achievements: my capacity to tune in on my own feelings as a means for increasing my sensitivity to the feelings and concerns affectively communicated by students, and second on my ability to integrate and facilitate cognitive-affective and experiential modes of learning.

This kind of learning takes time, particularly in the education of teachers, because they are relatively unprepared in the use of affect and inner experience. In fact, teachers generally are uncomfortable about affect expression, whether by students or themselves. A basic knowledge of human behavior and development, and, in particular, of the interpersonal and transactional issues inherent in classroom life, is a missing ingredient in their professional training.

The author and I realize that because this approach to teaching runs counter to traditional school practice, it is likely to raise questions, even some skepticism. It did so even within the Program faculty. We hope that it continues to do so, because we believe that dialogue, be it in the classroom or in other contexts, is the vehicle, par excellence, for generating new ideas and fresh insights. On the other hand, we recognize that attention to the concrete experiences and needs of classroom teachers, an essential ingredient of a psychodynamic approach, has been sorely lacking in education. As W. McKeachie noted, the "informative feedback" requires some qualification. "I may know that my performance could be better. I may be motivated to improve, but if I don't know what to do differently, then I'm not likely to get better" (1976, p. 825).

I think that a perceptive visitor to my classroom then, some thirteen years ago, and now, would note this as an area of change in my emphasis. I now know that insight alone is not enough to produce change in behavior. So today an observer of my classroom would observe a more consistent effort on my part to pay more attention to connecting and converting insight into some form of action; to translate what we know into some kind of concrete action—"effective responding." As McKeachie put it: "Feedback with motivational support and suggestion for improvement produces more change than . . . feedback alone" (p. 825).

Perhaps I should be more concrete about how my teaching technique has changed. Should one of the teachers in that group return to one of my classes today, he would likely find me "more mellow," referring to such attributes as:

1. A relatively less confrontational approach, especially early in the learning process.

2. A more empathic response to phenomena I formerly saw as resistance to learning, and now attribute to individual feelings of personal vulnerability and tension associated with the inevitable shifts and changes occuring in the teaching-learning alliance. Here my thinking is most influenced by the contributions of psychoanalytic self psychology.
3. I am less prone to "read" transference implications in group phenomena.
4. I tend to be more comfortable with and more flexible in responding to personally directed student criticisms of me and/or my pedagogic style.

Essentially, what I am saying is that after many years of relative success with this model of teaching I have learned from my students and grown along many dimensions, so that I tend to be more trusting of my pedagogical abilities and more aware of my limitations. In any case, I have far less need to project my self-doubts about my teaching onto my students (see, Session 7).

I continue to believe that it helps to have conceptualized a model of one's role (e.g., as "special participant") to maintain a sense of direction, particularly at those times when tensions rise and the intensity of affect threatens to derail learning and pull one off-course. Today, I make more of an effort to integrate affect and cognition in the hope that teachers will become more proficient in using both dimensions of knowing and communicating.

Unchanged, except for somewhat increased teaching skills and sensitivity, is my persistent effort to make use of parallel process phenomena (see chapter 28). This refers to the recognition that manifestations of teachers' problems with learning in my class may be indicative of that teacher's problems with teaching in her own classrooms, thus making this dimension a vital part of the living curriculum of the course.

Formerly, my teaching, my professional training, and my clinical experience were more oriented to "pathology" (see chapter 31). I have come to appreciate the importance of a more normative approach just as I have discovered the gratification of working with relatively healthy, better functioning groups of students in my classes—another parallel process.

Although today it appears that I am more assertive and directive in my role as group leader, the shift is a subtle one. It appears as more self-confidence and assurance in contrast to some of the tentativeness I felt then. I have a firmer grasp and clearer sense of my goals and direction, and am less apt to be deflected and moved off-course. However, as anyone who works with groups knows, each group is different and influences the instructor and the learning process in accordance with its unique needs and strengths. In other words, I no longer suffer from the delusion that influence flows in one direction, from instructor to students. Instead, I know it to be a process that involves a mutual and reciprocal influence in both directions.

One of my goals as I begin with a group, is "to get a sense of process started" which can grow and develop over time for the duration of the course. This concept is predicated on the principle that learning how to learn is an experiential developmental process that takes time and involves the use of the total self of both learner and teacher. Unlike the view that sees the acquisition of knowledge and information as an end in itself, this kind of learning emphasizes the use and integration of knowledge. I do not minimize, however, the importance of teachers acquiring a comprehensive knowledge base. It is not a dichotomy but an integration between content and process, between inner and outer experiences, between cognition and affect that I am proposing here. My hope is that this approach will encourage a more reflective teaching stance and result in more creative and flexible modes of coping with the ever changing demands of teaching, and, no less important, in the continuing growth of the total self of the teacher.

We do not wish to imply here that our approach to teaching should replace existing programs of teacher education. That would be a gross oversimplification of the broad range and diversity of theoretical and technical knowledge that should be included in the professional education of teachers. Rather, we are saying that the issues elucidated in this chapter are essential components in all teacher education, preservice and in-service. Neglecting them truncates the development and creativity of teachers just as it devitalizes and stunts the teaching-learning process. An exclusive focus on the technical, rational aspects of teaching deprives children of the emotional nutrients needed for healthy development and success in learning, and blunts teachers' sensitivity to student communications.

Both the author's and my own contribution here represent an effort to demonstrate how we struggle with this dual goal of helping teachers grow in their own learning so that they can better help their students do likewise.

SUMMARY

We have seen how a group of teachers participated in an extensive and intensive learning experience over a period of twenty-two weekly sessions. The issues they raised throughout touched on concerns felt by most teachers in schools everywhere in the last two decades: increasing numbers of dysfunctional and maladapting children in their classrooms; higher expectations of curriculum planners and parents; tremendous pressures and criticism from society; lack of needed supportive and consultative staff; little opportunity for collegial interchange with fellow teachers.

The spirit, attitudes, and affect characterizing the

group at the beginning were in striking contrast to those seen toward the end of the twenty-two weeks. The group initially presented as passive, disgruntled, and distrustful, noticeably defensive, and resistant to learning. Pent-up feelings of personal anger and resentment, combined with inhibition of personal assertiveness and aggression, were manifested in an overconcern with rules and structure, fairness and objectivity. This tendency to distrust and inhibit feelings, particularly of the negative variety, was not limited to this group, by any means. Problems with affect expression are frequently encountered among teachers with whom we have worked. Since it is so widespread in the profession, we are inclined to attribute this more to the effects of training and strongly entrenched attitudes in the culture of our schools than to teachers' personality. It is this dynamic, we believe, that is at the root of most teacher self-esteem problems.

Teachers in the group often expressed doubts about their professional identity, and voiced deep feelings of frustration and tension in talking about their work. They seemed to feel overburdened and discouraged about the possibility for substantive change in their work or in themselves. All in all, they projected a sense of futility, meaninglessness, and worthlessness about their professional lives that was profoundly troubling to all of us on the faculty, and to the instructor in particular. However, there was another side to the picture that we also recognized. The teachers came to the TEP because they cared deeply about the children in their classrooms and worked hard and valiantly to make a difference in their lives. It was this desire and this hope that made for whatever sense of professional mission and commitment they felt.

As the group learned to trust the instructor and one another more, it became a more cohesive entity, which, in turn, helped the individual members feel less vulnerable, more willing to take risks, more tolerant of ambiguity about not finding immediate answers or solutions to problems. The teachers were beginning to have what Balint (unpublished manuscript) has called "the courage of one's ignorance." As teachers began to feel more secure in the group they evinced a greater capacity for intuitive modes of thinking about professional problems, as if they were more comfortable about trusting their hunches and feelings and, therefore, more open to insight.

While the development of a teaching-learning alliance was a crucial achievement for the group and made learning possible, there were times when the alliance was disrupted by a variety of events; for example, interruptions due to transitions, vacations, illness, loss of a group member; anxiety mobilized in connection with certain case presentations and curricular topics and themes (e.g., authority issues), and/or school-related crises. As the group gained confidence from finding themselves increasingly able to make sense of their experiences and to cope with difficult situations, they opened up deeper areas of feeling and ultimately became more motivated to absorb and integrate conceptual knowledge and theory.

While integrating knowledge and affectivity is a process that would need to go on for a much longer time than the twenty-two weeks of this course, longer even than the two-year duration of the Program, there already were indications of growth in the teachers' capacity for reflectivity and empathic observation of others. The teachers had started asking different kinds of questions about children and classroom situations (e.g., why, rather than how-to-do-it, kinds of questions); more and more, they showed curiosity about motives of behavior they once thought inexplicable or too "weird" to figure out; they began thinking more about patterns in behavior than about isolated actions; and, most important, from our point of view, they were becoming cognizant of the fact that they couldn't exclude their own role in students' behavior any more than the effect the student was having on them. Their view of causality as flowing in one direction from teacher to student appeared to be shifting to one that went both ways.

That the teachers were beginning to look more closely at their expectations for themselves and their students could be seen in the questions they were raising toward the latter part of the second quarter about their assumptions, expectations, and the responsibilities and limits of their professional role. One cannot escape the impression that, despite the separation anxiety mobilized in the transition to another instructor and beginning a new course, this group of teachers was already showing signs of growth in learning and professional competence. As a part of this process the teachers seemed to be deriving more satisfaction and a sense of empowerment that was conspicuously lacking when they started this class. One might even say that they had undergone what amounts to an emancipatory growth experience.

Lest this statement be taken to mean that no problems remained and that there would be steady progression toward desired outcome, let me hasten to dispel such a notion. The myriad problems facing teachers are much too complex to yield to a single course, or, for that matter, to all the courses in the two-year program combined. The predicament of teachers is not susceptible to amelioration through the simple agency of educational interventions alone. Their problems are embedded in the contextual matrix of the system as well as in themselves as persons. Nonetheless, learning is the business of teachers; learning about how they experience and approach their own learning as well as about that of their students is an essential achievement, a prerequisite accomplishment for coping with their manifold responsibilities and tasks.

In 1962, Sarason, Davidson, and Blatt described the problem teachers have with learning and change.

[E]ducational psychology (as the psychology of learning) is viewed as something which has to do with how children learn and not with how teachers learn. The student in the process of becoming a teacher is not made acutely aware of how he is learning, that is, to use himself as a source of understanding of the nature of the learning process. . . . [O]ne of the major reasons so many teachers are dissatisfied with themselves in their work is that their training did not illuminate the nature of their learning processes and how this relates to and affects the learning process of their pupils. They teach, but in the process they tend neither to give expression to their own experiences as a learner or to perceive the identity between themselves and their pupils. As a result, the teacher tends to function as a technician who applies rules which are contradicted both by her own learning experiences and her pupils' unproductive learning [p. 118].

This experience is only the beginning of their educational journey. It will take time for assimilation and integrated learning to occur. Will it be "smooth sailing," so to speak, for the teachers in this group for the remainder of the time they're in the program? On the contrary, they will constantly work and rework the issues they confronted in the twenty-two weeks. Setbacks, tensions, frustrations, and anxiety are not only inevitable, they are necessary—provided they are not excessive—if growth and learning are to occur. These provide the impetus for and are an integral part of all developmental learning. Evidence of destabilization in the group began emerging as they prepared for the transition to a new class and a new instructor.

What stands out clearly in the evolution of this group is the phenomenon of process, the shifting balance of tensions, the forward and backward movements, the reciprocating sequences that accompanied their efforts to resolve problems. In the crucible of this class we have seen manifestations of the intrapsychic processes of transference-countertransference (see chapter 26), anxiety and defense, regression and progression, and the full gamut of conscious and unconscious affect and fantasy that accompanies all of these.

Barzun (1954) used the term *the phosphorence of learning* to describe the vitality and excitement generated when teaching succeeds in engaging the whole person, mind and heart. To my mind, this is a fitting description of what happened in this group. The dialogic process between the instructor and the group over the twenty-two weeks appeared to facilitate mastery of the psychological issues addressed.

CONCLUSIONS AND IMPLICATIONS

This report suggests that teacher education programs which incorporate and utilize inner motivational forces and subjective experience, and which focus on the developmental-interactive aspects of the learning process, will be likely to have a significant and highly positive effect on teachers' attitudes (toward pupils, self, and work) and on their openness to new knowledge. The "process portrait" reveals in vivid detail the psychological complexities, contradictions, ambiguities, tensions, and challenges that are inherent in the everyday work of teachers. It also opens up many new questions and modes of inquiry regarding the professional development of teachers and the process of change in education.

We can only speculate as to the generalizability of a program such as this. It seems reasonable to assume, however, that the following characteristics of the program have played a significant part in its effectiveness with this group of students, in particular, as well as with the many other groups since which have continued to participate in the program.

The curriculum was, in part, the creation of the students, in the sense that they brought in issues and problems from practice that were of current concern to them,

and processed them in the group and in their relationship
with the instructor. The preformed or official here-and-
now course of study was always related to process issues
so that content and process were interwoven and inter-
dependent. The balance between the didactic, the pragmatic, and the technical elements in the curriculum
allowed abundant opportunity for discussion, testing, and
integration. The formal curriculum provides a *knowledge
base* that gives teachers a coherent, theoretic frame of
reference which illuminates inner motivation in human
behavior and mental functioning across development. A
theoretically coherent frame of reference allows teachers
to make sense of the multiplicity of phenomena they encounter and relate what they know to themselves and to
the exigencies of their role.

The methodology incorporates the principles of reflectivity and empathy. All teachers know more than they
think they know, more than they can put into words.
They operate from a repertoire of unarticulated, largely
unexamined thoughts, ideas, intuitions, habits, attitudes.
A reflective approach to practice allows teachers to discover what they "know" (intellectually and experientially) and gives them an opportunity to reexamine and
reorder the aforementioned repertoire. A coherent theoretic frame of reference together with a reflective approach fosters motivation, professional curiosity and
commitment, personal vitality, and, ultimately, a creative professionalism.   The teachers learned to appreciate the developmental nature of the learning process;
the inevitable ups and downs in learning, in motivation,
mood and morale, the changing themes over time, the
vicissitudes of the learning-teaching alliance, and the
reciprocal mutuality of the teaching-learning
process—teacher and students both teaching and learning from each other during the process. Teachers do not
learn about children or about the learning process by

reading about them but by active involvement in a process.

The group as a whole had an important function in facilitating individual learning. The opportunity for group continuity (students were together for the entire two-year duration of the program) was a crucial factor in the development of a cohesive group entity which served both as context and as instrument of the teaching-learning process. On the one hand, the group provided a safe, supportive, and confirming matrix in which to exchange ideas and experiences and to acknowledge self-doubts, worries, and mistakes. On the other hand, the group served both as a selfobject (see chapter 15) and a transitional object (see chapter 25) in the sense that it served motivating, tension absorbing, regulating, and self-validating functions for the individual members. Students placed high value on the group experience and acknowledged its importance in their learning. From the standpoint of the instructor also, the group played a strategic role in the establishment and maintenance of the teaching-learning alliance.

The fact that the classes were held at the Institute, away from the distractions, pressures, and conflicts associated with their daily school lives, was both positive and negative. It was positive in the sense of the anonymity, safety, and freedom it conferred, since most of the teachers in the group came from different schools. This is not to say that it obviated teachers' fears of self-disclosure, since these were mainly borne of internal expectations, self attitudes, feelings acquired in the school culture and in their own past educational experiences. But it, nonetheless, afforded teachers a sense of safety in relation to external concerns. The negative side derived from the fact that it was the Institute for Psychoanalysis, which, for many teachers, was a place of mystery and arcane practices. Thus the fantasies, apprehension, and uncertainties that new groups of teachers bring to the program constitute an important part of the beginning stage in their learning. The most powerful aspect of the setting is a function of both sides, the positive and the negative, because in the process of working through these issues, the students discover that feelings of all kinds may be openly acknowledged, are indeed invited. The experience of being respected, listened to, and understood builds intrinsic motivation, confidence, and courage for learning.

The instructor conceived his role as that of "special participant" in the group—catalyzing, enabling, facilitating, and regulating students' learning, and he was an active partner in a shared, self-involving experience. His method and style of teaching is rooted in a real belief in people and a conviction that the true subject of education is human beings. He does not present himself as the expert who has all the answers. From the outset, and consistently throughout the two terms, his teaching stance invited partnership and working together on problems. He used himself as a resonating instrument, tuning in on and responding to the behavior, affect states, and communications of students, thus modeling the qualities he was attempting to foster in the teachers.

Evaluation as a formative process was an integral part of the teaching method. As such, the students assumed responsibility for providing evidence of their learning through their participation in discussions, preparation of case material, response to readings, and their functioning as group members. However, the positive results of this approach to teaching and learning do not "lend themselves to statistical treatment, [but are] subtle and important effects upon such variables as spontaneity, creativeness, imaginativeness, solidarity and cohesion" (Bovard, 1985).

We realize that the work we are doing in this program represents but a small step toward the kind of interdisciplinary collaboration we believe is a practice imperative facing all the helping professions. Our program is an attempt to demonstrate a direction such collaboration might take in the education of teachers. It is not intended to replace educational theory or to suggest that it is time for a synthesis of data from these two fields of study. That would only subvert the intent of the undertaking, which, as we see it, will require a systematic effort by researchers and practitioners in education, psychoanalysis, and the mental health fields to begin pooling and contrasting their knowledge and findings with respect to the issues highlighted in this chapter. The inquiry we seek is one that focuses on the human contexts of the educational situation. Leon Kass (1984) poses the central question for psychoanalysis, for education, indeed for all scientific endeavors: "Is there not something finally defective about objective thinking if it is in principle blind to the mind of the thinker who thinks?" (p. 30). Knowledge of "our inward experience of ourselves as passionate, purposeful and thoughtful human beings" is, in the final analysis, the source of all motivation for learning.

REFERENCES

Balint, M. (1976), Learning, training and freedom to feel. In: *Experience of Balint Counseling in Small Groups*, ed. B. Barnett.

Barrett, B. (1982), unpublished manuscript.

Barzun, J. (1954), *The Teacher in America*. New York: Doubleday/Anchor Books.

Basch, M. F. (1982), Infant research: The dawn of awareness. *Psychoanal. Inq.*, 1(4):731–737.

Bateson, G. (1942), Social planning and the concept of "deutero learning." In: *Psychoanalytic Supervision*, ed. J. Fleming & T. Benedek. New York: Grune & Stratton, 1966, p. 80.

Bovard, E. W., Jr. (1985), The psychology of classroom interaction. *J. Ed. Res.*, 45:215–225.

Boyer, E. (1985), *ASCD Update*, 27(3):1, 5/85.

Bruner, J. (1983), *In Search of Mind*. New York: Harper & Row, p. 191.

Cronbach, L. K., & Snow, L. E. (1977), *Aptitudes and Instructional Methods, A Handbook for Research on Interactions*. New York: Irvington Publications, p. 412.

Ekstein, R., & Wallerstein, R. S. (1958), *The Teaching and Learning of Psychotherapy*. New York: Basic Books.

Kass, L. (1984), Modern science & ethics: Time for a re-examination. *University of Chicago Magazine* (Summer 1984) p. 30.

McKeachie, W. (1976), Psychology in America's Bi-Centennial year. *Amer. Psychol.*, 31(12):819–833.

Neugarten, B., & Datan, N. (1973), Sociological perspectives on the life cycle. In: *Life-Span Development and Psychology—Personality and Socialization*, ed. P. B. Baltes & K. W. Schaie. New York: Academic Press.

Sarason, S., Davidson, K., & Blatt, B. (1962), *The Preparation of Teachers*. New York: John Wiley.

Stringer, L. (1973), *The Sense of Self*. Philadelphia: Temple University Press.

Updike, J. (1984), Men and their mothers. *Vogue*, November: 441.

Wicker, G. (1978), Unpublished memorandum, M.I.T. In: *The Reflective Practitioner*, ed. D. Schön. New York: Harper Colophon Books, 1983, p. 322.

Chapter 31

A Psychoanalytic Contribution to Education: The Teacher Education Program of the Institute for Psychoanalysis in Chicago, 1965–1977

KAY FIELD, M.A.

In his (1925) preface to Aichhorn's *Wayward Youth*, Freud wrote that "none of the applications of psychoanalysis has excited so much interest and aroused so many hopes, and none consequently has attracted so many capable workers as its use in the theory and practice of education" (p. v). In spite of Freud's enthusiasm, and that of many other child analysts in those early years, there has been relatively little systematic study of the relationship between psychoanalysis and education. Aside from the important contributions of the Riess-Davis Clinic, the relations between psychoanalysis and education have consisted of little more than random and sporadic efforts, the major exception being in the area of the treatment of children and in psychiatric consultation.

This chapter was first published in the *Journal of the Philadelphia Association for Psychoanalysis* (1971), 4(1):21–43.

Nor has education consistently availed itself of the resources and potential of psychoanalysis. The fervent hopes for a psychoanalytic pedagogy voiced in the heyday of "progressive" education in the 1930s and 1940s were dashed with the emergence of the Sputnik era in education and revived, albeit to a lesser degree, with the coming of the alternative education movement and the early childhood education push in the 1960s. However, organized institutional initiatives for the application of psychoanalytic knowledge to teacher preparation were few in number and limited in scope.

When the Chicago Psychoanalytic Institute and the Chicago public schools began their pioneering collaborative venture in the early 1960s, the times were propitious for both fields. Both were in ferment; both were subject to public disfavor and criticism, and new community sources for help had to be found for the increasing numbers of "problem" children (those at risk) in the schools.

As the schools, particularly those of the inner city, became inundated with children whose emotional immaturity or psychopathology made it virtually impossible to go about "teaching as usual," educators inevitably found themselves asking different kinds of questions about their role. How to expand the traditional emphasis on cognitive development to include emotional maturation as well was the underlying theme of questions being asked by educators and mental health practitioners. On every side came the injunction to "do something" about the restless, belligerent, often violently disruptive, uncontainable children in the classroom and the school: those who defied authority, who failed or refused to learn yet were not mentally retarded; the dropouts, the drug addicted, and the multiply handicapped.

The relevance and potential contribution of psychoanalytic concepts to such problems as these are brilliantly demonstrated in Lustman's (1970) article on culturally

deprived children, in which he pointed out the significance of emotional immaturity for cognitive learning. His
delineation of this "clinical dimension" is an excellent
example of the practical application of psychoanalytic
knowledge to school practice. A model of education which
includes the concept of optimal individual functioning is
highly congruent with psychoanalytic developmental
theory. Dewey's dictum "teach the whole child," long a
part of educational rhetoric, if not of practice, was once
again becoming an educational imperative.

At the same time the concept of primary prevention
was gaining adherents, as was the role of cognitive emotional development in the early years of life. Noting the
critical position of the teacher in community mental
health, Menninger, Greenwood, Ack, and Trussell (1968)
caught the measure of the challenge in this eloquent reminder: "More than any other professional group, teachers bear an awesome responsibility for determining the
quality of our humanness. Every person who will ever
occupy a bed in a mental hospital, every parent, every
professional man, every criminal, every priest, everyone
in our society has known a teacher who might have influenced him . . ." (p. 5). Theoretical and clinical studies
dealing with developmental issues were appearing in increasing numbers in the literature, thus expanding the
focus and range of psychoanalytic thought and practice.
The downward extension of early formal education for
the young, motivated in part by the special problems of
children in the impoverished slum areas of our cities, was
a powerful incentive for educational interest in psychological studies of early child development.

Finally, the increasing focus on the effects of environmental factors on mental disorders was being reflected
in many lines of investigation. Studies of risk and vulnerability, parent-child interaction, and influence of family and life circumstances on mental functioning inevitably
brought the educational process into focus.

By virtue of its history, philosophy, and leadership, the Chicago Institute became the logical setting for a new venture in community mental health. For many years, beginning with the work of Franz Alexander, the Institute has taken a pioneering role in developing programs aimed at the applications of psychoanalysis to the related professions. The immediate forerunners of the Program for teachers to be described here were the Institute's interdisciplinary Psychoanalytic Child Care Program (1951–1961) and the program that replaced it, the present Child Therapy Program.

The link to the schools and the prime mover of the Teacher Education Program was Mrs. Sadie Nesbitt, a master teacher in a ghetto school, herself a graduate of the Child Care Program. A highly charismatic and gifted teacher, widely known and respected in the black community, Mrs. Nesbitt led a group of teachers and principals from three inner-city schools which urged the development of an Institute project to increase teachers' understanding of some of the difficult children in their classrooms. The enthusiasm Mrs. Nesbitt felt for her own Institute training ("the most meaningful experience of my entire professional career") sparked interest and kindled new hope in her colleagues. From this founding group of teachers, we obtained direct knowledge of the psychological realities of classroom life and came to know more about the specific tasks of the teacher. The information gathered in our meetings with this first group of teachers and others that followed helped to determine the purpose, content, and methods of the new program.

Unlike most teacher education where the emphasis is on educational didacticism, this new program focused on the key variable in the educational process: the person of the teacher, his perceptions, feelings, and interactions with pupils and adults in school. For this area, the psychological and emotional aspects of teaching, the contribution of psychoanalysis has proved to be of the highest relevance. The failure to study the importance of the psychological meaning and function of teachers in the educational process by both the schools and the teacher training institutions may explain why so many promising educational innovations have foundered and why basic change in practice has been so slow. The fact of the matter is that the meaning, the scope, and complexities of the teacher's role have been among the most neglected aspects of professional education. Newman's (1965) study of teachers' unmet psychological and emotional needs confirms our own findings that this is indeed the area in which professional training often fails teachers, and which many schools sweep under the rug. Most teacher training is based on the assumption that "verbalized knowledge is a sufficient condition for effective teaching behavior and that curriculum and method can be generated on logical grounds alone . . ." (Sarason, Davidson, and Blatt, 1962, p. viii).

The assumptions which support and shape our program derive instead from two interrelated questions: What are the essential psychological determinants of an effective pedagogy; and for which of these does psychoanalysis have the most relevance? Implicit in these questions is a methodological question: How is such learning best facilitated?

That one cannot acquire understanding of self and others by teaching a body of theory as if it were a discrete subject in a curriculum is a truism to all clinicians. Our task, therefore, was to find a format suited for infusion of our principles and goals into an educative process. That is to say, we sought to develop a training model consistent with psychoanalytic knowledge and insights, and one that met the psychological needs of teachers. Lacking either a psychoanalytic theory of instruction or a metapsychology of learning to guide our efforts, we were forced to proceed empirically, using the knowledge we have about the influence of unconscious emotional and transference factors on the teaching-learning process.

It is important to emphasize the gradual development of the Program, which from the beginning faced great complexities. The lack of relevant literature, the terminological barriers, the differences in educational philosophy as well as the disparities in role models are obstacles not easily surmounted, but they are also part of the challenge. The most profound challenge we faced, however, lay in ourselves, in recognizing and coming to grips with the narcissistic motivations, transferences and countertransferences, the buried feelings, perceptions, and attitudes toward teachers and schools within ourselves. The story of the Teacher Education Program is at bottom an account of the vicissitudes of these efforts.

In his analysis of the nature of the relationship between psychoanalysis and education, Kris (1948) recognized the difficulties and set forth some guiding principles, the validity of which has been repeatedly confirmed in our work with teachers:

> In any relationship between a more general set of propositions and a field of application outside the area of experience from which these propositions were derived, a number of factors must be taken into account. The more general propositions, in this instance those of psychoanalysis, must be formulated in a way that permits their operation in the field, here that of education. The process of application is likely to act as a test of validity of the propositions or of the usefulness of their formulation. Hence we are dealing not merely with a process of diffusion of knowledge from a "higher" to a "lower" level, from the more general to the "applied" field, but with a process of communication between experts trained in different skills in which cross-fertilization of approaches is likely to occur [p. 622].

The history of the Teacher Education Program demonstrates how we tried to deal with the four interdisciplinary challenges suggested by Kris: (1) the conceptual (from the general to the applied); (2) the attitudinal ("higher to lower"); (3) the methodological (communication); and (4) the integrative and creative (cross-fertilization).

HISTORICAL OVERVIEW: 1965–1977

The Teacher Education Program faculty were all highly motivated, skilled clinicians whose educational and didactic principles were identified with psychodynamic theory and technique as applied in the diadic-therapeutic and/or supervisory models of training in which the emphasis is on the affective-experiential mode. Their perceptions and attitudes regarding schools and teachers were derived from their personal and professional encounters within the traditional academic mode; that is, cognitive-expository. Thus the faculty's perception of the function of a clinical-educator was rooted in a dichotomy that conceived treating and teaching as polar opposites.

The teacher-students in the Program were no less caught up in a similar dichotomy. Despite their open disillusionment and frustrations with the academic model, and their avowed interest in the affective mode, their self-perceptions and identifications were derived from the academic model, namely, the rational-verbal, superego-oriented modes of learning. Thus, the faculty from the outset were confronted by a syncretistic dilemma running like a red thread through the history of the Program.

As I look back over the twelve-year history of the Program, three more or less distinct phases can be discerned, each marked by changes in the title, aims, curriculum, and methods of the Program.

During the first three years (1965–1968) the project went by the somewhat ambiguous title of "Mental Health in the Classroom." The ambiguity and openendedness of

the title reflected our lack of clarity about our goals and
methods of procedure. We started with eighteen teachers
from three elementary schools located in the Lawndale
ghetto of Chicago. This first phase was essentially a process of trying to grapple with the emotional problems and
conflicts of faculty and students, each of whom was struggling to escape from the constraints of the exclusively
cognitive orientation of the educational situation. The
initial task as we saw it was twofold: to identify the areas
of need that motivated the teachers to apply to the Institute and to find a suitable format. The teachers presented us with the following questions:

> How may the acting out child be maintained in a
> classroom situation? What kind of child simply can-
> not be maintained? How can a teacher manage such
> behavior with thirty to thirty-five children in class?

> What can be done for the quiet child who literally
> never speaks? When is this considered autistic be-
> havior? What should a teacher do if it is? Where
> can one get a diagnosis, if not treatment?

> How can teachers help parents to help their chil-
> dren? What are the dynamics involved in an inter-
> view with a parent?

> How can teachers have a clearer understanding of
> themselves and assess their own mental health and
> their ability to cope with certain types of problems?

> How does one bridge the gap of two cultures as one
> observes the southern white child coming to school
> to a black teacher or the southern black child com-
> ing to a white teacher, or the rural child coming to
> the city?

How can we be both mothers and teachers to these children and should we even try?

Rereading their questions reveals three basic concerns: (1) how to deal with the emotional impact of disturbed and disturbing children; (2) how to find resources which will enable them to remove such children; (3) how to cope with their subjective feelings and reactions—their own "mental health." Many investigators confirm that these are indeed the basic areas of need among most teachers, not just those enunciated by teachers in ghetto schools. Based on a number of empirical studies of the concerns and problems of several thousand teachers, students, and colleagues, Jersild (1955) observed:

> An essential function of good education is to help the growing child to know himself and to grow in healthy attitudes of self-acceptance.
> A teacher cannot make such headway in understanding others or in helping others to understand themselves unless he is endeavoring to understand himself. If he is not engaged in this endeavor, he will continue to see those whom he teaches through the bias and distortions of his own unrecognized needs, fears, desires, anxieties, hostile impulses, and so on [p. 13].

Given these needs the Institute was a logical place to which to turn; but by what method and in what format can such needs be met? Providing textbook information and didactic instruction, the standard academic formula, was ruled out immediately by both the teachers and ourselves. A case-seminar format utilizing material drawn from the daily classroom experiences of the teachers suited the needs of the faculty and the students. For the teachers the seminars at the Institute provided opportunity for ventilation, abreaction, and discharge of pent-up feelings in the company of understanding colleagues, supported by an empathic, nonjudgmental clinical leader;

for the faculty the format and the case material offered
no unusual challenges to their professional sense of themselves and their function. Thus the project started on the
clinician's turf, both as to the Institute setting, the format, and the clinical orientation. In electing a clinical
rather than an educational setting the teachers were in
flight from a burdensome school reality. In effect, they
were abrogating a part of their professional identity out
of their need for escape, support, and narcissistic repair.
Through the severely disturbed children whose cases they
presented in the seminars they indirectly sought understanding and help for themselves. And support and understanding were what the faculty was best prepared to
offer.

With the focus on the distal relationship with the child
and related others in the school, rather than on the proximal interactions of faculty and teachers in the seminars,
territorial lines and functions went unchallenged. The
clinical rather than the pedagogic skills of the faculty
(e.g., skills in listening, observing, communicating, and
empathizing) accounted for the air of excitement, pleasure, and challenge pervading the groups. It seemed that
teachers were discovering in the seminars "the fifth freedom, the right to know what one feels" (Kubie, 1960, p.
viii), a right largely denied or actively suppressed at all
levels of education, including the professional.

Despite all this the faculty began to have misgivings
which were difficult to identify. The teachers' lack of exposure to psychoanalytic ideas, their authoritarian posture, their need for quick results, and their moralistic
attitudes were a source of increasing frustration. Analytic ideas introduced in a setting that permits expression
of strong feelings and conflicting opinions can be seductive as well as anxiety provoking. The setting of the Institute combined with the unconscious pressures by the
teachers for a therapeutic experience created a pull that
could not be ignored. The fact that the teachers tended

to select only the most grossly damaged and intractable children to present could not be explained solely on the grounds that there were more of such children or that they were the major source of concern. We began to wonder whether this compliance with what the teachers perceived to be the clinician's affinity for psychopathology might not be a manifestation of a learning problem. For were these not the very children that teachers customarily refer to clinical personnel in the schools out of a secret wish to have them excluded from their classrooms? If so, it appeared that we were all involved in a process that could interfere with their learning and our teaching. In trying to teach dynamic concepts from the case, one instructor said:

> I found difficulty in getting students to assimilate too many new ideas if these were too radically different from more commonly held concepts. For example, one case often gave rise to several ideas. I suggested allowing dependence rather than pushing for independence in a little girl who had been forced to be overly independent after the death of her mother. This child, though she did the laundry and prepared meals at age nine, came to school dirty and unkempt. The group saw the problem as there being no one to teach her. I introduced the idea of a dirty facade being defensive, perhaps a protest against having to take care of herself, even testing out unconditional acceptance of herself. I advised not trying so hard to clean her up. They found this hard to understand. Helping teachers accept their anger and frustration toward a child and moving them to see some positives in a needy, dependent child proved difficult.

The faculty was troubled also by the problem of *drawing the line* between "treating" and "teaching." As one member of the faculty put it:

> I'm concerned about the danger of our unwittingly

making therapists out of the teachers. Even though we
want to use our psychoanalytic knowledge to clarify
the understanding of a child's behavior, should we not
be constantly alert to focus our thinking on the classroom situation? Shouldn't we try to be alert to the environmental factors to offset the dangers of our
knowledge of dynamics taking over? And then, I'm
wondering if we shouldn't be trying to learn more about
group dynamics—not group therapy—for the benefit of
our sessions with the teachers and for the carry-over
to the classroom?

The resistances to learning that we were feeling lay
within ourselves as much as within the teachers. They
were partly the result of a lack of clarity on the part of
both regarding manifest and latent goals. Lacking a clear
and mutually understood focus and goal (e.g., to teach or
treat), in a setting that encouraged release of strong feelings, mobilized a level of anxiety and resistance that interfered with both learning and teaching. As long as the
faculty saw themselves as clinicians first and teachers
incidentally, their capacity to understand and empathize
with a teacher's subjective reality was minimal. Nor
could the teachers on their part become aware of their
affective experiences as learners. Considerations such as
these made it necessary to seek a more suitable format
and method. To provide more structure and content we
organized the seminars around specific functional areas:
The Psychodynamics of the Classroom; Child Growth and
Development; and Classroom Applications of Developmental Psychology. Case material remained the primary
vehicle, only with a somewhat different emphasis in the
courses.

But these courses lacked two important ingredients:
first, a knowledge base to support the different mental
health tasks and professional competencies essential for
effective teaching; and second, a method by which cognitive and affective modes could be integrated in the

teaching-learning process. After a careful study and evaluation of the Program in 1967, Dr. Ner Littner suggested a conceptual ground plan. This set the stage for the next major step in the Program, the development of a sequential, integrated curriculum. His recommendations also helped us to conceptualize aspects of our own emotional experiences as teachers which until then we knew only preconsciously.

By 1969, with the decision to design a "core curriculum," the Program entered an important transitional era in its development. Training came into focus as the central objective, hence the change in title to "Teacher Training Program." Moving from a loosely knit series of informal case seminars to a unified, internally coherent training entity represented a major shift in our conception of the Program and, ultimately, in our view of ourselves as educators.

Faculty had increased in size and diversity along with similar changes in the student body. Teachers coming into the Program were facing a redefinition of their roles as the range and depth of psychopathology in the school populations grew. Many more teachers in the student body were now working with children individually or in small groups, their functions changing but in an ambiguous and ill-defined way. Their interest in diagnosis and technique pushed hard on the boundaries of the clinical situation. Faculty preoccupation with the common task of formulating a curriculum made for fluctuation and withdrawal in our engagement with the task of defining ourselves as "trainers of teachers." In faculty meetings, we freely shared our observations and feelings about what the teachers needed to know, what their problems and concerns seemed to be, and what new knowledge we should provide. We were using our meetings with each other much as the teachers had used their seminar meetings with us and with the same effect. This relieved us of having to look for change within our own disciplines and within ourselves.

At this stage of our deliberations we were unable to reach agreement about whether our educational objectives should be defined in content terms and cognitive outcomes (what students know), or in process and functional terms (how they experience and transform their learning in practice).

Inevitably, the effort to translate and apply intellectual understanding to the educational situation confronted faculty with new methodological and integrative challenges. Clearly, the key question was how to bring students to a deeper awareness of the emotional struggles and anxiety associated with their learning so as to increase their sensitivity to and empathy for those which children must also undergo. Let me cite excerpts from a few courses to illustrate how we sought to achieve this objective through the curriculum.

An instructor in the course on Personality Development, Dr. Harold Balikov, describes a student assignment as follows (personal communication, 1975):

> The aim is to create an experience within the context of the learning experience itself to demonstrate the components of the learning process and how they can be utilized for understanding of the unconscious learning process and the relatedness necessary for the teaching process. The aim of the experiment is to make students aware of their affective experiences that are unconsciously operating at all times, with special stress on the integrative ego component. The assignment I make consists of asking students to conduct a series of informal interviews with young children at different stages of development. The purpose of these interviews is to direct the students' attention to the emotional effects of and the ego solutions derived from being in a position involving polar opposites—between action and passivity, teaching-learning, etc.

For the course in psychocultural issues the instructor, Dr. Mark J. Gehrie, in a personal communication (1976), describing his goal, states:

> One of my requirements was for the students to subject themselves to an anxiety-provoking experience in a field or area in which they had no professional or personal expertise or familiarity. The point was for these students to put themselves in a situation where their anxiety about its newness and differentness became very evident to them by its intensity. Subsequently, the analysis of the project took the form of understanding the relationship between the experience of that anxiety and inability to function in a reality-related way in the situation. The point of choosing an unfamiliar circumstance was based on the effort to avoid the usual professional defensive postures that each of us has ready at hand to use in certain situations.

The structuralization, differentiation, and curriculum development that were the major tasks of the preceding period did indeed improve the quality of instruction but new problems began to emerge. The professional training of teachers and the culture of the traditional school have prepared them to take a directive, controlling posture toward children. The predominant view is that teaching is active, learning inactive, passive; in Fleming's words, "The jug-to-mug" mode of learning and teaching. The teachers' input and outcomes, cause-and-effect orientation ran counter to psychodynamic concepts. In essence, our training required considerable unlearning of ingrained attitudes, expectations, and modes of knowledge as well as the acquisition of a new body of knowledge and theory.

Knowing what to observe and how to observe is basic to all teaching. Related to this is the recognition that a child's overt behavior and verbalizations cannot be viewed as isolated acts or traits that need "correction" or change, but must instead be understood and responded to in the context of the total person. The emphasis we place on using observations to discover patterns and connections in children's functioning is very difficult for teachers accustomed to "on-the-spot" reactions to bits and pieces of behavior. That communication encompasses more than the verbal, conscious, rational elements in behavior, including a wide array of unconscious, affective, motoric elements as well, was not merely new but even a bit fanciful to many teachers. More important, it tended to be resisted because such knowledge threatens the very character defenses that led many teachers to their career choice. We began to see striking parallels between the cases teachers presented and the specific interactional dynamics they set up with their colleagues and instructor in the group. For example, in a course on normal learning one student's inability to recognize that the rebellion and anger implicit in his relationship with an acting-out adolescent in his classroom and his provocative encounters with his school principal paralleled his interactions in the Institute group in which his constant running chatter with his neighbors was a similar rebellion against the seminar structure and the authority of the instructor.

It was apparent that the shift to conceptual issues was having important emotional repercussions on the faculty as well as the students. For one thing it had the effect of placing faculty more directly in the experiential position of its teacher-students who also operate in a group situation subject to the myriad group and individual pressures, internal and external, that are an inherent part of the teacher's affective experience. The faculty now faced a learning task parallel to that of the teachers in the Program. True learning, as Ekstein and Wallerstein (1958) view the process, involves a shift in the ego state or internal self-organization of the individual as he moves from an established homeostatic position to a new and as yet unknown one. The transition generates tension and anxiety within the individual and is manifested through resistance to learning. Dealing with these resistances then in ourselves and in our students became and continues to be the major focus of the third and present phase of Program development. Thus, as the faculty worked within the more structured curricular format it became increasingly clear to us that the quality of the relationship between students and instructor had an effect on the outcome of the students' learning that was largely independent of the nature of the subject matter or the expertise of the individual instructor. This insight led us to examine further the manifest and latent interpersonal communications within the groups. We found ourselves using our observational and introspective skills to better understand the feelings and reactions evoked in us in connection with our role as teachers of teachers. From learning about the "teachers out there," the students, to learning about the teacher inside ourselves, brought us to a new level of insight about our function and a new appreciation of what it means to teach. Not only did this shift open up new teaching dimensions, it also helped to enhance and deepen the learning experiences of our students. The process began shifting to "becoming a teacher" (Fleming, 1969) instead of merely "being" a teacher, to the learning as well as the teaching aspects of the teacher's function. As we have become more consciously aware of and more comfortable with our dual identity as educators and clinicians we have found more points of convergence between "teaching" and "treating." The concept of a continuum rather than a dichotomy has freed us to use our clinical skills in our teaching and opened up new educational dimensions.

We are especially indebted to Drs. Ner Littner, Joan Fleming, Harold Balikov, and George Pollock, all of whom helped us to "see" and conceptualize the common denominators in teaching and therapy. Fleming (1969) pointed out that:

> A teacher uses himself as an instrument to stimulate
> active participation in a creative learning process.
> Whether this relationship is called a therapeutic alli-
> ance or a learning alliance actually makes little dif-
> ference. The essential job is to serve as a catalyst for
> the preconscious and conscious experiential and cog-
> nitive processes that go on in the mind of a student or
> a patient that help him to grow and mature in knowl-
> edge, wisdom and skill [p. 4].

Balikov (personal communitaion, 1975) emphasized
the principle that teaching and learning are a unity that,
like child rearing, requires two individuals. "Motivation
to learn," he said, "comes out of a personal experience
and a need to work out solutions to the conflicts, affects
and problems perceived." As instructors aware of our
"conflicts, affects and problems" with our students, this
statement held great cogency.

In our efforts to conceptualize and integrate these new
insights, Dr. Pollock clarified the applicability of the therapeutic paradigm in the educational and clinical situations. To the extent that we encouraged affective expression
and recognized it as intrinsic to the educative process we
could not avoid encountering the many drive-determined
aspects of learning; for example, conflict, anxiety, defense, repetition, regression, specific and nonspecific
transferences and countertransferences, and the like.
While we could not afford to ignore these manifestations
in our data of observation, neither could we ignore their
implications for the teaching-learning alliance. Not that
we contemplated turning teaching into therapy nor that
the faculty conceived its function as therapists rather
than teachers. On the contrary, this dawning recognition
of the commonalities in the two functions has furthered
our understanding of the differentials and, at the same
time, helped promote more integration of cognitive and
affective modes in learning and teaching.

In the last analysis any educational program rests on

the faculty's ability to perceive correctly and to differentiate the ever changing, objective, and subjective elements in the teaching situation. For the teachers, the special ambience of the Institute, its humanism and respect for the individual, contrasted sharply with the dehumanizing atmosphere of most schools and collegiate education. This contrast was an important factor in many ways, but most of all it significantly changed "the existing behavioral regularities" (Sarason, Davidson, and Blatt, 1962, p. 63) of the teachers' school experience and thus offered them a fresh perspective on themselves and their work. As one teacher put it: "I've never taken any educational program where I felt so personally involved, and where my feelings and ideas were so welcome and respected." Through the Institute, faculty and students have had access to a rare combination of human and intellectual resources which stimulate growth and provide glimpses of new frontiers.

Before describing the Program, I need to make clear what it does not attempt to do. An educational program for teachers offered by a psychoanalytic institute tends to evoke a number of questions and stereotyped attitudes held by both professions.

In the first place, the Program is not designed to turn teachers into therapists, nor do we intend to provide therapy of any kind, individual or group, for the teachers. What we do seek is to facilitate some small increments of change in the professional work ego of the teacher. In this respect, and also on the principle that there are therapeutic ingredients in the learning process (Kubie, 1968), we recognize a therapeutic effect on the students in the Program. We conceive of learning and therapy as a continuum. Viewing them as polar opposites creates a false dichotomy that only perpetuates the very notions about education that have for so long interfered with effective interdisciplinary efforts.

Second, I want to emphasize that we do not teach

theoretical or applied psychoanalysis to teachers per se. Rather the attempt is to bring a psychoanalytic perspective to the teaching-learning process. That there are clinical aspects to the educational experience just as there are educational aspects in the clinical experience is implicit in our premise. Teaching inevitably involves both aspects, and it is a recognition of the inseparable nature of the two functions that we hope to impart to teachers and to utilize in our educational efforts.

Third, the translation of psychoanalytic concepts for the educational situation does not constitute theoretical dilution or reductionism. We do, however, make an effort to eschew jargon, attempting to cast technical terminology into a language more suited to the diverse ideological backgrounds of teachers. Failure to do this, at least at first, tends to feed into the intellectual defenses so readily available to teachers in an affect-laden educational experience such as this.

Fourth, the aim of the Program has not been the development of a psychoanalytic pedagogy (defined as "a theory and practice of education which incorporates the findings of psychoanalysis" [Spranger, 1952, p. 60]) as it was originally conceived by Freud. Such a task is far beyond our capacity, and is both more utopian and less pragmatic than our goals. For example, the prospect of recruiting teachers in today's school climate who would be willing or able to undertake a personal analysis seems remote indeed.

Fifth, the title "Teacher Education Program" may be somewhat of a misnomer, implying that the Program covers all the professional educational needs of teachers. This is not the case. We have adopted the word *education* in contradistinction to *training* mainly to emphasize an epistemological distinction in our view of the body of knowledge we hope teachers will acquire and use. That teachers need to acquire skills in their training is indisputable, but we wish to take a position that posits skills based on a particular view of human behavior and mental functioning, not as discrete techniques to be used without regard to a basic psychological theory. The educational needs of teachers that this Program is concerned with are those mostly ignored or suppressed in the educational situation, from the earliest levels up through the professional. The needs we refer to here are the most complex and hardest to identify but nonetheless critical determinants of teaching and learning—the many unconscious, preconscious, unverbalized, covert inner needs and feelings that diminish the effectiveness of teaching and learning and detract from or impede the learning process for both child and teacher.

The basic assumptions of the Program are:

1. The psychological realities of the educational situation require the teacher to be simultaneously an educator in the pedagogic sense and a mental health agent in the clinical sense, a "psychological tactician" of the learning process (Sarason et al., 1962). Teaching and learning are deemed to be inherently affect laden, with important consequences for both teacher and pupil. Every teacher is subject to many pressures, both internal and external, to which she responds with many feelings. Her teaching effectiveness will be significantly enhanced if she can understand her own feeling reactions to her pupils, colleagues, parents, and/or superiors (Fleming, 1969).

2. Teaching requires an understanding of children's needs as well as the inner laws that govern mental functioning, and a recognition that the teacher's role is determined by both of these.

3. Teachers will be better prepared to cope with the exigencies of the classroom and better able to carry out their professional goals as they grow in self-

understanding and acquire the skills of introspection and the capacity for empathy.

The translation and implementation of these assumptions into a viable educational program for teachers has been the subject of ongoing study by our Program's faculty and administration.

Since 1965 we have worked with more than 3,000 teachers and related school personnel in the basic two-year Program and in its numerous offshoots.

The Program is designed to further the professional development and effectiveness of school personnel by (1) providing practical postgraduate study of the developmental and psychodynamic aspects of the educative process; (2) developing a basic understanding of the learning process that embodies these concepts; (3) developing an interdisciplinary model of training which promotes co-operation and collaboration between educators and members of the mental health professions; (4) preparing teachers to work effectively with a greater range of child behavior from the normal to the atypical, in the regular classroom, in special classrooms, and with individual students. In recent years, the Program has added new goals in response to changing student needs and concerns; (5) training for specialized roles, such as teaching maladjusted, disturbed, and learning-impaired children; (6) providing continuing education for special categories of school personnel, such as Head Start consultants and parent coordinators, school social workers, team leaders, supervisors, and administrators; (7) providing consultation services to school administrators and special services personnel.

The curriculum encompasses core knowledge and skills from two major content areas: the psychological sciences and the social and behavioral sciences.

During the first year the aim is to enhance the teacher's sense of professional identity and develop the introspective and interpersonal skills necessary for competent professional functioning by providing information on the biological, psychological, intellectual, and sociocultural aspects of normal development from birth through young adulthood, and by developing the necessary clinical skills to apply this knowledge prescriptively in the group situation and with individual children.

During the second year of study, the major goal is further pursued by focusing on the complex conditions and problems associated with atypical patterns of development in children. The theory and techniques necessary for work with the broad spectrum of atypical children—the gifted, retarded, learning impaired, the emotionally disturbed, social maladjusted, culturally deprived, and so on—constitute the main areas of study.

The objectives of the second year extend those of the first, but with particular attention to the specialized knowledge base and modfications in teaching techniques and skills required for work with psychopathological conditions. The linking concept is that of the teacher as a collaborating member of the school team, bridging the gulf between classroom and clinic.

The student body has become steadily more heterogeneous along several dimensions. In terms of demographic distribution the trend has been away from the predominantly inner-city student body, many of them black, that characterized the early period, to a more diversified group from all parts of the city and suburbs. A typical entering class of thirty-five to forty students will vary in: age (twenty-two to fifty-five years); experience (one year to thirty-five years); training backgrounds (B.A., M.A., to Ph.D., and an occasional M.D.); level of teaching (classroom—nursery school through secondary to college levels); teaching category: special education, learning-disabilities teachers, guidance counselors; school nurses; principals, librarians, school social workers, reading specialists, curriculum directors, and so on; and, of course, they vary in motivations, aspirations, maturity, and personality. These self-selected students tend to be more open to learning, more sensitive to children, and more highly motivated professionally. But for a small minority, personal psychopathology undoubtedly is a factor in motivation.

Student motivations, conscious and unconscious, are bound to be complex and varied in any program offered by a psychoanalytic institute. We considered it inappropriate and unnecessary to probe for unconscious material in the selection process. Undoubtedly, unconscious fantasies and wishes for personal therapy motivated many students. While the question of personal therapy is usually raised in the course of the admission procedure, it is with the intent of assessing expectations and motivation and not as a condition for admission. Although cogent for training in psychotherapy, the issue of analysis or psychotherapy is not seen as relevant to the training goals of this program.

It is, of course, unwise to generalize about the highly multidetermined motivations of so diverse a group of professionals, based on the rather superficial selection procedures we use (a detailed application form, autobiography, and a personal interview with a member of the faculty), but an impressionistic report by the faculty selection committee shows that the students fall roughly into three groups: the first, younger teachers, men and women, ranging in age from twenty-two to thirty years, introspective, uncertain, and troubled about their career choice and direction; the second, mainly women in their thirties or over, bright, competent, secure, firm in their professional identity, seeking more in-depth understanding of themselves and their students; the third falls into no one age bracket but is alike only in the sense that most are troubled individuals manifesting varying degrees of character pathology.

Lacking reliable empirical evidence of specific positive

or negative correlation between teaching competence and teacher personality, we have had to rely on our own experience with questionable applicants in making an assessment of suitability. We have found that an applicant's ability to handle the anxiety mobilized in the admission interview as he responds to queries about his background, motivations, concerns, problems, and so on, seems to be paradigmatic of his reaction to and ability to cope with the stresses and anxiety mobilized in the Program.

Evaluation of the Teacher Education Program has always been viewed as an integral part of program development, although on an informal basis. The basic goals of the Program are derived from the ever-changing professional needs, interests, and concerns of school personnel as these are perceived and articulated by those who have participated in the Program and/or its auxiliary projects.

We have not undertaken, as yet, formal evaluative studies of the Program, partly because of the well-known complexity of the data and the lack of suitable methodologies to measure growth and change in such subtle and elusive areas as "psychological mindedness" and "accessibility" to learning, and partly for economic reasons. Nonetheless we have used a variety of informal approaches to evaluation to guide program development and to evaluate our teaching effectiveness. Among the sources and methods of evaluation we have used are the following: (1) questionnaires distributed to students and to alumni during and after completion of the Program, seeking their individual reactions to the value and practicability of their experience; (2) reports on the school performance of students and alumni from principals, school social workders, and colleagues; (3) alumni inquiries regarding career changes and advancements; (4) observations and evaluation by Program faculty. The generally positive nature of most of the above (i.e., "more sensitivity to children," "fewer discipline problems," "appropriate referrals," and so on) is reinforced by other students, past and present, or referrals, and by the fact that the majority of our students have been either recruited by other students, past and present, or referred by special service personnel and school administrators.

An important component of this program is dissemination of relevant psychoanalytic knowledge and insights related to education. For instance, audiotapes have been prepared and distributed free to the Chicago public schools and are available for rental by other groups. The tapes cover such topics as The Disruptive Child, Cognitive Development, The Child at Risk, and so on, by such distinguished experts as Drs. Fritz Redl, Jerome Kagan, E. James Anthony, and Albert Solnit. There is a dearth of published material for school practitioners that bridges the gap between clinic and classroom, and it is the hope of the Program to prepare and distribute more such information.

The results of the Program thus far point to two significant conclusions: (1) the Teacher Education Program appears to be answering an important need in a neglected area of teacher training, one which directly affects teacher competence, the success or failure of the teaching-learning enterprise, and interrelated problems involving the mental health of children and staff; (2) the model of training evolved goes beyond the pedagogical and mental health functions of teachers, and also appears to have applicability to the training of school principals, supervisors, and trainers of teachers, and ancillary professions of school social work, psychology, guidance, and personnel work.

The increasing recognition of and interest in the Teacher Education Program in the Chicago area and other areas of the country among educators and school-related professionals, and the proliferating number of Program offshoots, attest to its vital role in the schools and in the community.

SUMMARY AND CONCLUSIONS

This chapter has described a psychoanalytically oriented program for educators and has highlighted some of its developmental vicissitudes. Mindful of the dangers of imposing psychoanalysis on the field of education in an effort to "psychologize" teachers we have tried instead to think psychoanalytically about the meaning and functions of teaching using our experiences as clinical educators to understand and assist the teacher-students in the Program. Our intent was to study the psychological position of teachers who work individually and collectively with many different persons, children and adults, in a variety of educational settings, with particular emphasis on the emotional effects of these diverse interactions on the self of the teacher. The hope is that such emotional awareness can be used by the teachers in the service of their professional task.

The problems we encountered were both general and specific. The general problems derive from the familiar communicational, epistemological, and hierarchical issues characteristic of interdisciplinary endeavors. The specific problems derive from the syncretistic dilemma posed by the task of integrating the dual function of clinician and educator in a program explicitly designed to implement the affective-experiential dimensions in teaching and learning.

Our delineation of the three phases of program development reveals the interplay between changes in the goals and structure of the Program and the changes in faculty perception and response to its dual clinical and educational function. Newly acquired insights were both the cause and the effect of its progressive development. The initial phase might be termed the *naive period*, characterized by the high motivation of the student body and the clinical zeal of the faculty. Lack of clarity regarding our educational goals and functions produced a variety of emotional repercussions and resistances that dictated a shift in emphasis during the second, or transitional period, when the faculty sought a solution to the teach-treat dilemma by focusing primarily on conceptual issues of curriculum. In the past four years, the third period, faculty attention has been directed to both process and content issues; that is, the interactional dynamics shaping the teaching-learning equation, and the facilitation of the teaching-learning alliance. Out of this effort a psychoanalytically oriented model of educating school personnel appears to be emerging. The aim is to integrate further and to adapt the affective-experiential and the cognitive modes of learning, employed so effectively in the clinical situation, to the educational situation. Our work in this complex and relatively unexplored terrain has only just begun, but it is the most exciting challenge we have faced so far, and one in which psychoanalytic knowledge and insights are most cogent.

The deeper we have looked at ourselves in our role as educators the more we have become convinced that our attitudes toward teachers and teaching were shaped to a considerable degree by the memories and perceptions of our childhood selves in our past school experiences. The bond that we shared with our teacher-students was based on the fact that each of us brought to the teaching-learning relationship what we had learned with the teachers in our educational past. It became the task of the faculty to undergo considerable self-scrutiny and un-learning to shed some of our past distortions and mis-perceptions about teachers, to recognize our own transference resistances to learning and change in the course of learning how to educate teachers in the here and now. Based on our experience, psychoanalytically trained professional educators are uniquely suited to this task of learning by discovery, insight, introspection, and empathy.

Our conclusions regarding the relevance of psychoanalytic psychology in the education of teachers are predicated on a program characterized by the following conditions: (1) a sequential, internally coherent, interdigitated course of study; (2) involving a minimum of two years of continuous study; (3) implemented by a cohesive, interdisciplinary faculty committed to a psychoanalytic frame of reference; (4) operating within the context of a psychoanalytic institute. This is not to suggest that adaptations and variations on the Institute's Teacher Education Program model would not be worthwhile, only that these are the criteria for evaluating our results.

From its inception the Teacher Education Program has endeavored to bridge the gap between learning in the classroom and in the treatment situation. What are the commonalities and differences? How do teachers make sense of classroom interactions and events? What impels or impedes learning for teachers no less than for their students? Questions like these have been occupying the TEP faculty and will continue to be the central focus of inquiry in coming years. In a program such as this the basic challenge is to develop a methodology based on the more general principles of psychoanalysis which effectively integrates the cognitive and affective determinants of learning within the range of educational contexts represented by its students. The reflective frame of mind expressed in the following student comment is one shared by the faculty as well. "I've been in the field for ten years and I'm afraid I'm getting stale. I need this opportunity to sit back and examine myself and what I'm doing for my students. I keep feeling that I could be more effective in my work."

We acknowledge that we have more questions than answers, as yet. But in this lies the impetus for the development of the Program. The work of the teachers in the Program offers persuasive testimony to the fact that we have broken new ground at a largely uncharted interface in multidisciplinary collaboration, namely, the exploration of the relational, subjective, and experiential worlds of teaching and learning. From teachers' accounts of their multiplex, emotionally charged encounters and interactions with students, their parents and their school colleagues, "one comes away . . . with a sense of humility about the complexity, subtlety and depth of human relationships" (Doehrman and Gross, 1976, p. 82) in the educational situation. It is this largely forgotten province in studies of teacher education and school practice that will continue to shape the agenda of the TEP in the future.

The fact that the Program emphasizes issues of motive and meaning in the teaching and learning process accounts for its appeal to teachers and its uniqueness in professional education. Analysis of the clinical material available in the educational situation not only tests and challenges pedagogical practices but psychoanalytic formulations on learning and change as well. Out of this joint inquiry by professionals in both disciplines, new questions and conceptualizations may one day emerge. Thus, while a program for teachers may not be vital to the pulse of a psychoanalytic institute, we firmly believe that it offers an unparalleled opportunity to extend the scope and applications of psychoanalytic thought and values. In closing, we wish to emphasize what Otto Spranger wrote in 1952: "the impact of Freud's discoveries on pedagogical theory and practice is so momentous that its integration into our educational system has barely started" (p. 60).

APPENDIX A: TEACHER EDUCATION PROGRAM

The curriculum is designed to develop in the trainees:

1. A capacity for self-awareness and understanding which yields insight and empathy for the motivations, feelings, and behavior of others which we

maintain is a prerequisite for relationships with both children and adults.

2. The competence to identify and diagnose the various emotional, social, and learning problems of students, to permit the early detection and prevention of potentially serious disturbances leading to school failure, truancy, school dropouts, delinquency, and other pathological conditions.

3. The skills to plan prescriptively for the educational needs of all schoolchildren within the broad spectrum of ethnic backgrounds, intellectual capacities, personality syndromes, and school settings, and to apply in practice such prescriptive planning on both an individual and a group basis.

4. The background and skills to communicate and obtain the active cooperation of parents in support of their children's education.

5. The capacity to communicate and collaborate with other professional disciplines (psychology, psychiatry, social work, pediatrics) and agencies outside the school, and the ability to coordinate and synthesize the relevant data (social, educational, psychological, medical) required for a prescriptive educational plan.

6. A comprehensive understanding of childhood psychodynamics and development, covering a wide range of normative and atypical behavior, and learning styles found in elementary- and secondary-school children and adults.

7. A methodology and repertoire of techniques for working with both normative and deviant children.

8. The interpersonal insights, skills, and attitudes to establish effective working relationships with parents, fellow teachers, and school administrators.

The curriculum encompasses the following areas of knowledge:

1. *The Spectrum of Personality Development.* Normative and pathological, from the earliest stages through adulthood. Six courses comprise this sequence: Dynamics of Personality Development I, II, III (3 quarters); A Survey of the Deviations and Disturbances of Personality Development: Psychopathology (1 quarter); Learning and Growth (1 quarter); Survey of Learning Difficulties (1 quarter).

2. *Human Communication and Interpersonal Relations.* Six courses comprise this sequence: Transactions in the Classroom: Teachers and Children (1 quarter); Beyond the Classroom: Transactions with Colleagues, Administration, Parents, and Community (1 quarter); The Impact of Anxiety on Learning (2 quarters); and Integration Seminar (1 quarter).

Courses meet weekly in two-hour sessions for eleven weeks (one quarter).

Case material based on teachers' first-hand experience with children, parents, and others in the school milieu is integrated with conceptual material in every course.

UNIVERSITY AFFILIATION AND ACCREDITATION

The Chicago Board of Education and many suburban school districts award two promotional (lane) credits for successful completion of each two-hour course in the Program. Effective January 1, 1973, the Teacher Education Program and the Foster McGaw Graduate School of the National College of Education entered into a cooperative relationship which offers Teacher Education Program students the option of taking certain courses for academic credit. A second affiliation, since 1980, is Northeastern University. The National College of Education accepts for Master's Degree credit a maximum of seven courses (fourteen credit hours) earned in the Program.

REQUIREMENTS FOR CERTIFICATION

In order to graduate and receive a certificate from the Teacher Education Program, a student must have satisfactorily completed all twelve courses in the two-year curriculum, submitted all required case studies (diagnostic and follow-up studies), special papers and reports, and demonstrated a knowledge of the basic literature in the areas covered in the curriculum.

REFERENCES

Doehrman, M., & Gross, J. (1976), Parallel processes in supervision and psychotherapy. *Bull. Menn. Clin.*, 40:3–104.

Ekstein, R., & Wallerstein, R. S. (1958), *The Teaching and Learning of Psychotherapy*. New York: Basic Books.

Fleming, J. (1969), Planned teaching in supervision. Mimeographed paper presented to Fourth Symposium on Psychotherapy, Boston, MA.

Freud, S. (1925), Forward to August Aichorn's *Wayward Youth. Standard Edition*, 19:273–275. London: Hogarth Press, 1967.

Jersild, A. T. (1955), *When Teachers Face Themselves*. New York: Columbia University Teachers College Press.

Kris, E. (1948), On psychoanalysis and education. *Amer. J. Orthopsychiat.*, 18:622–635.

Kubie, L. (1960), Introduction. In: *An Application of Psychoanalysis to Education*, by R. Jones. Springfield, IL: Charles C Thomas.

——— (1968), The psychotherapeutic ingredient in the learning process. In: *The Role of Learning in Psychotherapy*, ed. R. Porter. London: J. & A. Churchill.

Lustman, S. L. (1970), Cultural deprivation: A clinical dimension of education. *The Psychoanalytic Study of the Child*, 25:483–502. New York: International Universities Press.

Menninger, R. W., Fuller, F. F., Down, O. H., & Peck, R. F. (1967), Creating climates for growth. The Hogg Foundation for Mental Health, the University of Texas, Austin.

——— Greenwood, E., Ack, M., & Trussell, W. (1968), Education: The depressed profession. Mimeographed paper presented at the American Orthopsychiatric meeting, Chicago, IL.

Newman, R. G. (1965), Where we fail our teachers. Mimeographed paper presented at the American Orthopsychiatric meeting, New York, NY.

Sarason, S. B., Davidson, K., & Blatt, B. (1962), *The Preparation of Teachers*. New York: John Wiley.

Spranger, O. (1952), Psychoanalytic pedagogy. *Psychoanal.*, 1:59–70.

Afterword

KAY FIELD, M.A.

But there is one topic which I cannot pass over so easily—not because I understand particularly much about it or have contributed very much to it. Quite the contrary: I have scarcely concerned myself with it at all. I must mention it because it is so exceedingly important, so rich in hopes for the future, perhaps the most important of all the activities of psychoanalysis. What I am thinking of is the application of psychoanalysis to education, to the upbringing of the next generation.

Sigmund Freud

Nature came first: among the many is the one, things connect. . . . The scholar learns to tie things together, diminishing anomalies, discovering roots running underground, whereby contrary and remote things cohere, and flower from one stem.

Ralph Waldo Emerson

Nearly seventy years ago, Freud's concept of the fundamental linkage between psychoanalysis and education
(based on their mutual interest in "the upbringing of the
next generation") stimulated a richly creative dialogue
among a dedicated group of psychoanalytic pioneers—child
analysts initially trained as educators. In resurrecting
the linkage concept at this time, we have sought to renew
interest in re-entering that dialogue. It was not, however,
to simply reaffirm and pass on the developmental concepts formulated by Freud and his followers, but to review them within the emerging perspectives of contemporary psychoanalysis and infant research. Adrienne
Rich (quoted in Boone, 1987) pinpointed the difference
inherent in such acts of revision in a statement as relevant to the present position of psychoanalysis as it was
to literature fifteen years ago: "Re-vision—the act of looking back, of seeing with fresh eyes, of entering an old text
from a new critical direction is more than a chapter in
cultural [or scientific] history; it is an act of survival—we
need to know the writing of the past and know it differently than we have ever known it." The mandate of rapid
social change demands such acts of re-vision and re-ap-
praisal.

It was in this spirit and with this intent that the present volume was conceived and organized. The foregoing
chapters attest to the expansive vision and state of intellectual ferment within modern psychoanalysis: its
ability to encompass difference, to allow for a diversity
of viewpoints, and to accept challenges from within and
without its disciplinary borders. They provide a varie-
gated picture of the theoretical models of development
that have been evolving in the past two decades, from
drive theory, ego psychology, object relations, and self
psychology, each, apparently, bearing a complex and
somewhat ambiguous relation to the other; all, however,
embrace a dynamic view of the learning process, recognizing that the lives of us all are determined by the com-

plex interplay of multiple motivational forces, conscious and unconscious, which may operate in concordance or in conflict with each other. All are concerned with the study of subjective experience and the role of affect on learning; all are concerned with a common issue: how to account for the critical importance in all learning of relations with other persons.

By contrast, the dominant view of learning in education focuses almost exclusively on the cognitive, rational aspects of learning, and conceptualizes teaching and learning as a linear, unidirectional process aimed at the transfer by the teacher to the student of cognitive skills and discrete units of "objective" information about the external world of persons and things: whereas from a psychoanalytic perspective, learning is understood as a purposive search for some kind of sense, some kind of meaning. It is governed by a complex dynamic of interlocking cognitive, affective, and social forces. The central focus of this volume is on that dynamic and the manner in which it may support or impede learning, be it in the context of the family, the classroom, or the treatment situation. Learning, as defined here emphasizes developmental change in the inner psychic structures and experiences of the individual: such learning is powerfully motivated by one's personal strivings for wholeness and personal meaning. Knowledge of the external world is construed as a tool and the means one employs to achieve these ends rather than as an end in itself. The interaction between teacher and students is understood as a complementary, reciprocal process with each side acting upon and reacting to the other. What is learned then depends not only on how much knowledge the teacher possesses and seeks to transmit, nor even on what one confronts in a particular field of knowledge, important as these factors are; it also depends on what experiences and attitudes students and teachers (parent and child, analyst and patient) bring to their encounters with a particular subject and with each other and the feelings aroused in the process. Psychoanalytic perspectives emphasize the relational contexts of learning and provide the conceptual and technical tools for understanding the latent meanings and intents behind overt behavior.

The view of education represented in this collected work was best expressed by Zimiles (1987):

> [E]ducation represents a form of profound, multifaceted intervention in the lives of children. . . . [I]t represents a major theater of human development on whose broad stage the full drama of human psychological development is enacted . . . ; it plunges the psychologist into a level of complexity and compelling reality that is at first staggering. It is a complexity that can only begin to be ordered and understood . . . by viewing it through the lens of dynamic psychology.

Indeed, we extend this definition of education even further. It begins in the home under the tutelage of parents [or other primary caregivers], continues in ever-widening circles in our educational institutions, in the community, the workplace, and the treatment situation. Like learning, education today is conceptualized as a life-long process that can only be understood in relation to contextual factors and issues of personal history.

The foregoing chapters can be most readily understood in the context of the four principal objectives that guided the conceptual organization and focus of this volume. The aim in Part One of this four-part collection is to place the long-standing, complex, often ambivalent relationship between psychoanalysis and education in historical and theoretical perspective. The chapters in this section seek to show how the social and scientific forces operating within psychoanalysis and within society have influenced theory formation and the focus of psychoanalytic inquiry, and how theory changes, in turn, have influenced this dialectic. Recalling Bernfeld's concept of education as the response of society to the facts of development, the thrust of this section is on the implications for education of contemporary psychoanalytic developmental perspectives. Several chapters in this section are illustrative of a number of important way stations in the evolution of psychoanalytic formulations on learning in relation to education. Ways in which a more effective alliance might be realized based on significant changes within psychoanalysis itself are proposed.

In the next part, the developmental determinants of the learning process are considered in light of the emerging conceptualizations and guiding orientations of contemporary psychoanalytic inquiry and developmental research. The chapters reflect a diversity of theoretical positions regarding both the significance of preoedipal and oedipal determinants of later learning problems. They consider, as well, the value of traditional and more recent perspectives on gender differences as related to the manner of learning in childhood and adolescence. Two chapters examine the implications of the developmental course in girls and boys for differences in learning and in subsequent sense of competence as a student. Several chapters emphasize developmental factors based on normative rather than clinical perspectives on learning, and emphasize the significance of learning as a process facilitating increased adaptation as a consequence of the development of psychological structure. Cognitive and emotional development are understood throughout as intrinsically and directly interrelated in the study of learning, and problems in learning and development.

A number of contributors have suggested that problems in learning may derive from other sectors of development in addition to that portrayed by the nuclear neurosis, such as problems related to fundamental issues of self-esteem, tension regulation, and consolidation of a sense of self, all essential for achieving completion of psychological development. All are in general agreement,

despite theoretical differences, that the child's experience
of caretaking during the first years of life, prior to the
oedipal conflict, may be of at least as much importance
as the resolution of the nuclear neurosis in determining
later pathology in learning. Reformulations of the learning process in terms of self psychology implicitly include
consideration of emotional factors in the earliest years
of life as determinants of learning as well as the major
source of later learning problems. This point of view encompasses both the teacher's psychological contributions
to the learning process based on her past experiences as
well as those of her student. Psychotherapy, from this
point of view (see Rocah, Chapter 16) may be considered
as a kind of teaching-learning experience in which factors
leading to one's problems in psychological learning may
originate not only in conflicts related to the nuclear neurosis but also the child's early experience of caretaking.

The thrust of the final two parts of this work is on the
translations and applications of psychoanalytic developmental formulations in a broad range of clinical and educational contexts. In Part Three, the authors consider
a diversity of issues and problems with learning which
arise in the clinical situation, some focusing on the implications of emotional disorders for learning, some noting the implications of learning disorders for the treatment
of troubled children. The result is a wide-ranging exploration of the multifaceted interface of education and psychotherapy. Areas of similarity and difference between
the two with reference to issues of purpose, theoretical
perspective, specific techniques of intervention, and expected outcome are examined and discussed. Although
the chapters in this section reflect differences both in the
domains of learning to which they are targeted, and in
the substance of their theoretical viewpoints, they encompass a spectrum of possibilities which may have heuristic as well as practical value for clinicians and educators
alike. They highlight the essential unity of cognitive and

emotional development and emphasize the efficacy of a shared developmental theoretical framework in the treating and teaching of emotionally and learning-disordered children and adolescents.

In the final section, the aim is to explore the range of theoretical, clinical, and educational issues that confront the psychoanalytically informed educator. It is important to note that the contributors to this section—psychoanalysts, social workers, educators—are all members of the faculty and staff of the Institute for Psychoanalysis in Chicago and have been directly or indirectly involved in the work of its teacher education program, now in its twenty-fifth year. Thus, all the chapters in this section may be said to reflect aspects of the authors' experiences with educators, and, as such, are rooted in a common core of collaborative activity which, in turn, became a focus of joint inquiry. Among the many questions addressed by the authors, the pivotal question of concern to all of them was that first posed by Lustman nearly twenty years ago, "how to make maximal use of the teacher in the lives of children." From the expanded life course perspective of contemporary psychoanalysis that question becomes how to contribute to the optimal development of the teacher as well as the student, at all levels of the educative process from preschool through elementary and secondary school to college, graduate and professional education. The aim of this section is to demonstrate that psychoanalysis, with its traditional emphasis on the role of motive, meaning, and affect on the learning process contributes an added dimension as well as a balancing perspective to the deeply entrenched educational emphasis on cognitive functioning and subject matter mastery in the teaching-learning process. The intent of the authors was not to offer psychoanalytic solutions or panaceas for all problems of pedagogy or new instructional methods. Multiple perspectives—philosophical, theoretical, epistemological, cultural, political, as well as psychological—are required to fully understand and deal with the tasks and responsibilities of education in our rapidly changing society. What this section seeks to demonstrate is the bridging capability and integrative potential of contemporary psychoanalytic conceptualizations in such collaborative endeavors.

Viewed against this backdrop, there may now be some merit in trying to get away from specific chapter contributions so as to crystallize some implications of this multi-authored collection with respect to four key areas in education: research, teacher-student relations, curriculum, and group processes.

RESEARCH

Research in both education and in psychoanalysis has been strongly influenced by the technological ethos of science. Such research is conceptualized largely in accordance with a linear, ends-means, instrumentalist rationality in the quantitative tradition of science. It stresses objectivity and effectively distances or detaches the person from the subject being studied. The effect of this orientation is not limited to research. It is pervasive in our culture and a dominant influence in our educational institutions. It makes teachers and, ultimately, their students believe that objectivity and rationality represent the only legitimate concerns of the educated individual.

The infant research studies of the last two decades represent an alternative paradigm for the study of human learning in both its subjective and objective dimensions. They have ushered in a new era in psychoanalytic inquiry, one that combines the hermeneutic approach of clinical psychoanalysis with the empiricist, phenomenological approach of the natural sciences. Such a research model lends itself to the central concerns and subject matter of psychoanalytic inquiry—the study of wishes and intents, the force of human strivings for wholeness and personal meaning, the need for interpersonal relatedness and the nature of subjective experience and intersubjectivity. Nor is this emerging research model limited to the social sciences and psychoanalytic inquiry. It is being generally acknowledged within the natural sciences that the questions we ask in every realm of human knowledge are determined in some degree by subjective factors—by social and individual psychology as well as by logical, objective principles and evidence. As Cohler reminds us (Chapter 1) "the emerging interpretive or hermeneutic model of social science inquiry lends itself more readily to the approach of psychoanalysis as a human science than do the empirical approaches of the natural sciences, which cannot accommodate the validity of empathy and disciplined subjectivity as methods of study." Teaching, therapy, and research are essentially modes of learning. All three seek to describe the world as seen and interpreted by the learner, the patient, the research subject. "What a patient learns about himself in the therapeutic situation through interpretation and insight lies in the extent to which it fits and illuminates his experience" (see Rocah, Chapter 16). The researcher, too, seeks to describe the world as seen and interpreted by the person he is studying. The teacher's effectiveness depends upon her capacity to tune in on her student's perceptions and interpretations of the learning task and his experiences in the classroom. Understanding of human behavior and development is no less important for the teacher than it is for the clinician and the researcher. Each one needs to understand the empirical reality experienced and reacted to by the persons under study. Each one needs to recognize and understand subjective experience, the dynamics of human interactions, and the issues of motive and meaning in learning. Barbara McClintock (quoted in Keller, 1983), the geneticist referring to the changing orientation to research currently within the sciences, observed: "We are in the midst of a revolution which will reorganize the way we look at things and the way we do research" (p. 707). What she refers to as "having a feeling for the organism" corresponds to the holistic orientation of contemporary psychoanalytic inquiry, its emphasis on understanding the total or core self of the individual as the center of initiative. As Stern (1985) puts it, "The sense of self stands as an important subjective reality, a reliable, evident phenomenon that the sciences cannot dismiss" (p. 6).

TEACHER-STUDENT INTERACTIONS

Infant research has brought increased appreciation of the importance and feasibility of studying the patterns of interaction and mutual influence that exist between infant and care giver. Early learning requires not only individual effort on the part of the infant, as traditionally assumed; it is also contingent upon his interactions with caretakers in a reciprocal process of regulation, negotiation, and exchange. From infancy on, parent and child, and by extension, teacher and student, are held together in a shifting web of mutual dependency and interdependence. Elson, in Chapter 27 of this work, aptly captured this concept in the phrase "the teacher learns as she teaches, and teaches as she learns." The classroom is an interpersonal situation, by definition, one in which the teacher, like all the students in her class are present in the fullness of their subjectivity. This is a fact that calls for multiple perspectives—those of the teacher and her students, each reacting to and being influenced by the reactions that others have to them. Understanding of the deeply subjective nature of the teaching-learning process and the significance of the relational context in which it occurs requires of the teacher a capacity for empathic observation and communication as well as cognitive knowing. Without it, the teacher is prey to the powerful hidden forces operating both within herself, between herself and students, and within and between students and other students. "All of what we look at, whether or not we choose to look at it, and what interpretation we give to what we look at, is necessarily based on a complex, interactional system of which we, ourselves are a part" (Schlachet, 1984, p. 12). In the final chapters of this work, Field provides a "process portrait" of the teaching-learning process which highlights the experiential exchange, the shifting tensions, emerging conflicts, affective communications, the ups and downs of the learning alliance that inhere in teacher-student classroom encounters and shows how an empathic teacher struggled with all of this and was able to put it to effective, educational use.

This psychodynamic vision of the teaching-learning interaction is contrary to the implicit assumption in education that the student's response to the teacher, as expressed in his overt behavior, academic performance, and manifest attitudes, constitutes the major focus of educational concern. What is overlooked is the equally present, however repressed, dynamic of the teacher's response to a particular student group or class as a whole. It is clear that each person, teacher and student, is mutually caught up in a highly affect-laden process in which each one is highly vulnerable to the intentions of the other; each one guessing, assuming, inferring, believing, trusting, or suspecting; each generally satisfied or unsatisfied. The much-vaunted shield of teacher objectivity and neutrality falls away once we recognize the force of these subjective processes, and realize that there can be no objectivity without subjectivity. It is not the teacher's ability to function as an impartial, objective observer that makes for effective teaching, rather it is her capacity to tune in on the subjective experiences of students, to reflect on her own subjective reactions to individual stu-

dents and the group as a whole that confers the badge of
true professionalism and guides her interventive efforts.

Mention of the study of subjectivity, empathic understanding, and the use of the empathic mode by teachers
invariably evokes some oft-raised questions about the
distinction between teaching and therapy, and the danger
of overburdening teachers by introducing unwanted and
unnecessary complexity in their role. The answers to
questions like these, given thirty-five years ago by Marie
Rasey, teacher, and Karen Horney, psychoanalyst (1953),
are no less relevant today than they were then. To Rasey,
"any good piece of teaching will make the learner more
adequate, more courageous, more cooperative and more
understanding of himself and other people; and as a fruit
of such experience one dare expect an increased or stabilized basic confidence" (p. 176). To Horney, "every good
piece of analytical work well done . . . makes a person
less helpless, less fearful, less hostile and less alienated
from himself and others" (p. 176). When we concern ourselves with the inner world of students and teachers we
cannot avoid talking about the outer. Learning for the
teacher and the student is always about both.

GROUP RELATIONS

Winnicott's concept of the "holding environment" and the
formulations of modern clinical psychoanalysis, particularly self psychology, have shed new light on group phenomena and processes relating to group formation, group
cohesion, and fragmentation, all of which have direct relevance to the classroom situation. This is not to say that
these concepts refute earlier psychoanalytic formulations
based on drive theory, only that they expand our field of
observation and understanding and bring to the fore phenomena which had previously received scant attention
within psychoanalysis.

The "holding environment" furnished by the classroom group may function as a "container" of anxiety generated in the learning process, and as a structure and support system that fosters students' sense of increasing safety, trust, and well-being, and, in so doing, help to counteract feelings of vulnerability and isolation by enhancing their sense of connectedness to each other and to the teacher.

Feelings of risk, concern over self-exposure, humiliation, and failure, so prevalent in the beginning phase of group life, are "held" in common, so to speak, the group as a whole performing part of the function of managing and regulating the anxiety of its individual members.

In self psychological terms, the cohesive *group self*, to use Kohut's term (1978) functions as a selfobject for each member, "containing" and mediating the tensions and anxiety engendered in the learning process. The sense of being enfolded in the support and understanding of the "group self" emboldens the individual member to sustain the tensions of not-knowing and thus helps him risk failure in taking initiative and trying out new ideas, all of which are the very essence of the learning process. When the group fails to provide such validation and protection, when the student's search for confirmation and guidance (mirroring) meets with disappointment, but not disappointment so intense as to be overwhelming, he has an opportunity, through optimal frustration, to build the self structure needed for learning. On the other hand, when the group experience results in what Kohut (1978) terms "wounded self esteem, deflated fantasies of importance . . . it leads to the most dangerous forms of group tension . . . readiness for aggressive action and rage" (pp. 530–531).

In many cases, when the group selects an individual member for the role of scapegoat, it may be the result of hidden tensions in the group to which he may be particularly vulnerable. The important point to be made here is that foreground and background are parts of a whole system within a group which are in continuous interaction. Selecting one person to carry the tensions in the system—often by excluding or removing him from the classroom group—is a simplistic and futile response to a complex, dynamically interacting system. In Chapter 30 of this work (Field) we have an opportunity to see in operation the dynamic forces making for group cohesion and/or fragmentation and their effects on the learning-teaching process.

THE "HIDDEN" OR SUBJECTIVE CURRICULUM

Because educators deal largely with the learning of subject matter, the curriculum occupies a central place in educational discourse. By contrast, the human functions and subjective meanings of knowledge and knowing are central in psychoanalytic conceptualizations of the curriculum. Knowledge and skill are viewed in their functional relationship to personality development as tools for the individual to use in his own learning and quest for meaning rather than as ends in themselves.

The notion that the knowledge we seek to acquire exists in the outside world, independent of the wishes, beliefs, and intents of the knower, has been endemic in education. The attempt to draw a line between cognitive-factual knowledge and subjective, so-called "merely personal," knowledge is not only artificial but it also ends up distorting the realities of teaching and learning.

From a psychoanalytic perspective, the curriculum is a product of the dynamic interplay between teacher and students; it is shaped by their respective intents, interpretations, and subjective experiences. Because teachers and students are a heterogeneous group of individuals with different biographies and personalities, different racial, ethnic, class, and gender identities, they bring to the curriculum different perceptions, expectations, and associations, which, in themselves, are necessarily context-specific in both relational and situational terms. The shifting human contexts of learning and teaching preclude a fixed, standardized view of the curriculum. As Dewey once remarked, "Perhaps the greatest of all pedagogical fallacies is the notion that a person learns only the particular thing he is studying at the time."

While early psychoanalytic formulations focused mainly on the symbolic meanings of curriculum subjects, contemporary interest comes out of a systems theory orientation, which looks to the ways students experience the teaching-learning process, and to the influence of meaning and intents on student perceptions of and response to the materials of instruction. This orientation has led to increased appreciation for the effects of the subjective or "hidden" curriculum on student learning. In Cohler's view (Chapter 1) "renewed interest in the self has led to increased concern with the meaning of learning for students and increased appreciation of the role of the subjective curriculum." Greene (1977), recognizing the multiple realities in human learning, offers this view of the curriculum: "the curriculum may be regarded as a number of provinces of meaning, each associated with the kinds of experiences available to young people of different ages, with different biographies. . . . Our concern in teaching is to enable students to interpret these experiences, to acquaint them with and free them to reflect on the range of cognitive styles" (pp. 73–74). Clearly, knowledge does not reside between the covers of a textbook, or inside the minds of teachers; nor is it finite or unchanging. Instead, it is partly the product of student perceptions, needs, concerns, and aspirations and teachers' interpretations of them. As every teacher knows, to engage students in learning a particular subject requires recognition and understanding of their construction of the curriculum, how it relates to and gives meaning to their current life experiences, whether it engenders feelings of mastery, "effectance," confidence, self worth, and hope for the future.

What this very brief and, admittedly, incomplete discussion of four such critical and complex areas in education was meant to accomplish was two-fold: to highlight the more or less hidden landscapes of learning in education which come into view when observed through a psychoanalytic lens and to call attention to the new directions in psychoanalytic inquiry which invite cross-disciplinary dialogue and collaboration. The direction and focus of modern psychological thought requires no less. "An implicit assumption of modern psychological thought," according to Stern (1985), "is that the individual is constantly in transaction with his environment and that both are subject to change as a result of those transactions. The setting is at least as important as the actor, and both must be analyzed together as a single functional system if the act itself is to be made intelligible" (p. vii).

This work, then, is a testament not only to the contemporary relevance of Freud's concept of linkage but to the fundamental significance of this concept in the "upbringing of the next generation" (p. 610). Within Freud's vision there was then and is today a remarkable prescience. The words he wrote in 1921, far from being invalidated by the passage of time, have continued to offer enlightenment today in a world he never knew and could not imagine. As with every healthy science, psychoanalysis has been open to new ideas and responsive to the universal yearnings of women and men for a more humane scholarship, concerned with their unending search for personal meaning and integrity. A work of this kind offers no easy answers or panaceas; it raises many questions and leaves them unanswered. Certainly much more elaboration of the issues raised is needed. What the preceding chapters make clear, however, is that human learning, far from being a unitary concept, is highly variable and complex, so much so that neither psychoanalysis nor education, separately or collectively, can possibly lay claim to being the sole arbiters of truth and wisdom on the subject. What psychoanalysis offers the educator is, after all, *a* truth but not *the* truth about human learning. It is, however, a truth without which the work of the educator is vulnerable to being undermined by powerful forces operating within and between persons.

We have brought together in this work, psychoanalysts, psychoanalytically informed clinicians, social scientists, and educators, representing disparate theoretical and disciplinary perspectives, hoping thereby to demonstrate the unique bridging capability and integrative potential of contemporary psychoanalytic formulations. Inherent in the conceptual organization of this work is the conviction that concern with human learning, in its normative and pathological constellations, cannot and should not be the exclusive responsibility of any discipline or subgroup. Human beings are too complex to be fully understood by any one discipline. However, what a psychoanalytic perspective does do is deepen understanding of the learning process and broaden the base upon which further study can be based. Our hope is that this collected work brings us a step closer to the establishment of such a broadened base as well as contributes to its legitimation.

It is difficult to predict the future of either psychoanalysis or education, let alone their relation to one another. Both fields are in the throes of transition as are all the human sciences. The challenges they face are now all but overwhelming and there are no signs that the future will be any less so. There can be no doubt, however, that the best preparation for what is to be is to build bridges, to connect, to enter into dialogue. While we have tried to highlight the kinship between psychoanalysis and education, the fact is that the ties between them at the present time are far from strong. But as Sarason (1985) reminds us, "It is perhaps not happenstance that, in the modern world . . . the forces that have weakened the bonds that keep people together . . . that make them feel socially connected . . . are the forces that further weaken the always fragile connections among different fields of knowledge and inquiry. Labels are not the cause of this weakening, but once labels take hold, they become an almost insuperable obstacle to the perception of commonalities" (p. 201).

REFERENCES

Boone, J. A. (1987), How feminist criticism changes the study of literature. *Chron. Higher Ed.*, July 8, p. 76.
Freud, S. (1921), *New Introductory Lectures*, 11:600–621. New York: W. W. Norton, 1966.
Greene, M. (1977), Four curriculum theories: A critique in light of Martin Buber's philosophy of education. *J. Curric. Theorizing*, 6(1):5–151.
Horney, K., & Rasey, M. (1953), *It Takes Time*. New York: Harper & Brothers, p. 176.
Kass, L. (1984), Modern science and ethics. *University of Chicago Magazine* (Summer 1984), p. 30.
Keller, E. F. ed., (1983), *A Feeling for the Organism*. New York: W. H. Freeman.
Kohut, H. (1978), Creativeness, charisma, group psychology: Reflections on the self-analysis of Freud. In: *The Search for the Self*, Vol. 2, ed. P. Ornstein. New York: International Universities Press, pp. 793–843.
Lustman, S. L. (1970), Cultural deprivation: A clinical dimension of education. *The Psychoanalytic Study of the Child*, 25:483–502. New York: International Universities Press.
Sarason, S. (1985), *Caring and Compassion in Clinical Practice*. New York: Jossey-Bass.
Schlachet, B. (1984), *Relativism Revisited, The Impact of Life on Psychoanalytic Theory*.
Stern, D. (1985), *The Interpersonal World of the Infant*. New York: Basic Books.
Whicker, S., & Stiller, R. eds., (1960–1972), *Early Lectures of Ralph Waldo Emerson*, 3:65. Riverside Edition. Cambridge, MA: Harvard University Press.
Zimiles, H. (1987), Progressive education: On the limits of evaluation and the development of empowerment. *Harvard Ed. Rev.*, 89(2):203.

NAME INDEX

Abraham, K., 18, 41, 66, 195
Abrams, S., 31, 66
Ack, M., 929, 959
Adelson, J., 66
Adler, G., 641, 693
Aichorn, A., 11, 66, 638, 693
Aiken, W., 136
Ainsworth, M., 227, 240
Alber, J., 253, 264
Alexander, F., 388, 393
Alexander, J., 67
Anthony, E. J., xi, 23, 25, 30, 31,
    67, 99–125, 693, 714, 727
Applegarth, A., 31, 67, 487, 509
Arlow, J. A., 161, 178, 622, 634
Aronson, G., 22, 67
Axelrad, S., 225–226, 240

Bagley, W. C., 134, 142
Baillargeon, R., 27, 72
Baker, C. T., 481, 510
Bakhtin, M., 315, 327
Baldwin, J. M., 653, 693
Balikov, H., 940, 944, 959
Balint, M., 663–664, 693, 918,
    925
Ballard, E., 766, 768
Barbizet, J., 248, 264
Barnett, R., 262, 266
Barrett, B., 851, 925
Barshis, D., 791, 807
Barzun, J., 921, 925
Basch, M., xi, 6, 8, 20, 25, 28, 33,
    39, 42, 44, 45, 67, 324,
    349, 352, 397, 398, 399,

407, 429, 445, 447, 621,
    622, 634, 693, 735,
    738–740, 745, 750, 768,
    771–787, 794, 795, 796,
    797, 807, 925
Bates, E., 319, 324
Bateson, G., 340, 352, 862, 925
Beers, J. W., 335, 352
Bell, S. M., 227, 240
Bellak, L., 693
Beller, E., 471, 476, 489, 509
Benedek, T., 160, 161, 163, 178,
    748, 758, 769
Bennett, S. L., 460, 476
Beres, D., 622, 634
Berger, M., 524, 529
Berger, P., 30, 67
Bergman, A., 42, 77, 323, 326,
    403, 423, 449, 463, 477,
    485, 510, 523, 536, 644,
    649–650, 695, 748, 769,
    794, 808
Berlyne, D. E., 247, 250, 264
Bernfeld, S., 4, 7, 8, 11, 17, 22, 30,
    67, 96, 97, 638, 693
Berns, P., 456, 478
Bernstein, H. E., xi, 6, 49, 143–157
Bettelheim, B., 8, 22, 38, 68,
    544–545, 596
Biber, B., 524, 525, 536, 537
Bilikov, H., xvi
Binet, A., 117, 124
Bing, E., 489, 509
Bion, W. R., 615
Birch, H., 223, 242

SUBJECT INDEX